Advertising principles and problems

To Rita and Julia

ADVERTISING PRINCIPLES AND PROBLEMS

CHARLES J. DIRKSEN
Professor and Dean
Graduate School of Business
University of Santa Clara

ARTHUR KROEGER
Professor of Marketing
Graduate School of Business
Stanford University

1973

FOURTH EDITION
Richard D. Irwin, Inc., Homewood, Illinois 60430
IRWIN-DORSEY INTERNATIONAL, Arundel, Sussex BN18 9AB
IRWIN-DORSEY LIMITED, Georgetown, Ontario L7G 4B3

Fourth Edition

First Printing, January 1973

Second Printing, December 1973

Third Printing, May 1974

Fourth Printing, July 1975

Fifth Printing, September 1975

Sixth Printing, March 1976

ISBN 0–256–01402–7

Library of Congress Catalog Card No. 72–86624

Printed in the United States of America

PREFACE

In preparing the fourth edition of *Advertising Principles and Problems* the authors decided to continue to treat advertising as an accepted part of the marketing mix and to assume that management and the public recognize the place of advertising in modern society. They also reorganized the book to provide a more logical development of the subject from the teaching viewpoint and to emphasize what advertising is, how it functions, and its advantages and disadvantages.

Strategy is stressed rather than mechanics. However, a student will find ample information on the mechanics of advertising, as well as stimulating business cases that dramatize the way advertising fits into the total marketing program.

This edition has been arranged in seven major divisions: *Advertising Concepts; Advertising Strategy; Preparation of the Advertisement; Media Mix; Advertising Research; Integrating the Advertising;* and *Legal and Public Policy.* More emphasis is also placed on *Consumerism, Social and Economic Aspects, Demand Strategy, Media Selection,* and *Campaign Planning.*

The fourth edition includes 82 cases. Of these, 44 are new cases. The authors also used the corporate name of the company in 34 of these cases. A number of the 38 cases which were used in prior editions have been revised to improve them from the teaching standpoint. All of the cases are based on actual business situations—problems that have actually faced advertising executives. They are, however, problems that are succinct enough in nature to be analyzed without an extensive amount of additional information.

The cases make up 40 percent of the total book, and, while the cases do convey information, it is important to use these primarily as the basis for discussion. It is the decision-making process which can be developed through class discussions which should be one of the major objectives of the use of cases. The authors believe that there is merit in having the students develop generalizations (principles) from the discussions. A few examples of such generalizations are:

1. The market for a product is limited to those to whom it offers utility.
2. Cooperative advertising is adapted to products for which primary demand can be stimulated.
3. For a product of a highly individualized nature and for which strong buying motives can be stimulated, advertising may often be used as the sole method of sales promotion.
4. When a product enjoys brand dominance, the stimulation of primary demand may take the place of the stimulation of selective demand.

It is the opinion of the authors that the book is arranged in such a manner that instructors who do not use the case method will find there is adequate text material which can be used very effectively with the probing questions at the end of each of the 20 chapters.

The authors are indebted to their late colleague, Dr. Lawrence C. Lockley for his recommendations. They also wish to express their appreciation to John A. Dirksen and to their graduate students who assisted them in collecting the data for the cases. In addition, they wish to thank the American Association of Advertising Agencies, Inc., the Association of National Advertisers, Inc., many advertising agencies, and other companies for granting permission to use their materials and exhibits.

They are particularly indebted to Roy W. Brockman, Sr. and the late C. A. Holcomb for the use of special material. Finally, they would like to express their appreciation to Professors G. Dean Palmer, Virginia Polytechnic Institute and State University; Gordon G. Barnewall, University of Colorado at Boulder; and Sami M. Abdella, Rider College; as well as to their colleagues at other universities, for pertinent recommendations and testing of the material and cases during the preparation of this fourth edition.

December 1972

CHARLES J. DIRKSEN
ARTHUR KROEGER

CONTENTS

vii

PART II. ADVERTISING STRATEGY

4. Basic demand strategy   95

Selection of appeals. Appealing to persons influencing decision to buy. Contributions from the social sciences. Primary and selective demand: *Primary demand. Selective demand. Combining primary and selective appeals.* Primary demand advertising as a continuous process. The stimulation of primary demand: *Conditions relating to demand. Conditions relating to the product. Conditions relating to the market.* The stimulation of selective demand: *Conditions relating to demand. Conditions relating to the product. Conditions relating to the market.* Responsibility for stimulation of demand. Factors influencing need for advertising: *Stage of market development. Type of product as a factor.*

5. Copy strategy   130

Wants and needs. Nature of habits: *Dynamic qualities. Inherent drives and impulses.* The consumer: *Importance.* Buying motives: *Definition. Classification of motives. General limitations.*

6. Identification methods   158

Some basic definitions. Trademark registration. State registration. Nonregistrable marks. Trademark in conflict. Requirements for a good trademark. Classifications of trademarks. Loss of trademark. What steps to take in protecting a trademark.

PART III.   PREPARATION OF THE ADVERTISEMENT

PART V. ADVERTISING RESEARCH

PART VI. INTEGRATING THE ADVERTISING PROGRAMS

18. Campaign execution   526

Kinds of campaigns: *Local campaigns. The zone or regional campaign. The national campaign. Campaign execution. Other aspects of coordination. Putting campaign to work. Conclusion.* Cases:

19. Organization for control   565

Location of advertising department within the company. Organization of the advertising department. Size of the advertising department. Why advertisers use agencies: *Selection of the agency. Working with the agency. Evaluation of agency performance.* The retail advertiser: *Retail advertising organization. Why retailers normally do not use agencies.* The advertising agency: *Definition. Agency organization. Types of agency organization. Elements of agency service. Additional agency services. Sources of agency compensation. Agency recognition. The commission system. The agency industry.*

PART VII.   LEGAL ASPECTS

20. Legal and public policy   597

Power of government. Government regulation. Documentation of advertising claims: Regulation of competition. Ecology emphasis. Free encyclopedias. Control of advertising. *Federal Trade Commission analysis.* Unfair trade practices. Business ethics. Ethics of advertising: *Waste in advertising. General criticisms.* Summary. Cases: 1. Health Care, Inc.

SUPPLEMENTARY INFORMATION

PART I

Advertising concepts

chapter 1

NATURE OF ADVERTISING

I<small>T HAS BECOME</small> evident as we project our goals for the next quarter century that mankind faces tremendous problems that threaten his survival. We are confronted by a nuclear arms race that threatens to destroy us. Problems of world hunger, of population growth, of economic developments, and of environmental deterioration are threatening the future development of civilization and its very existence.

These are difficult and critical problems that cannot easily be solved. Certain practical breakthroughs are needed, and the requisite technology must be developed; however, the solutions will take a long time.

Although the potential for the improvement of society is extensive, we must also assess the goals of our activities in order to use our knowledge for the benefit of mankind.

Probably never before in the history of the world has there been such incessant discussion and analysis of political, social and economic problems as has taken place in the last ten years.

The effect of all this discussion has been profoundly unsettling, psychologically and physically. We have begun to agitate louder than ever for justice and economic security and to question some of our basic concepts about markets and the competitive efforts of businessmen to exploit them. And, yet, to have a competitive economic system, one of the essential functions is demand creation. Sound business practice requires that a manufacturer produce products the potential consumers want. The manufacturer must also see to it that prospective buyers are informed about the products.

As a result, a primary purpose of demand creation, from the economic and social standpoints, is to educate and inform buyers. At the same time by making the potential buyers aware of and stimulating their desires for more and better goods and services, it tends to promote a higher standard of living. Insofar as advertising activities involved in demand creation serve this purpose, the processes may be judged to be socially healthful. By expanding markets and making it possible for industry to secure mass production savings, it may permit lower costs of manufacture, resulting in lower prices, which will make additional products available to people with low purchasing power.

While there has been misuse of demand creation devices, nevertheless, they have played a significant part in the improvement of living conditions.

Definition

Demand creation takes three major forms: personal selling, advertising, and sales promotion. They differ only in the techniques used in applying them and in their points of incidence. They should be regarded as aids to each other rather than as mutually exclusive.

Personal selling is the most important and widely used means of demand creation. There are many types and include the personal selling behind the counter as well as the kinds of situations where the salesman personally seeks out his prospect and gets his attention.

Advertising is any paid form of nonpersonal presentation and promotion of goods or services by an identified sponsor. It is a form of selling and it urges people to buy goods or services, or to accept a point of view. Its most important characteristic as a marketing tool is that by its use an identical message can be conveyed to large numbers of persons simultaneously. It seeks to make people aware of things they need and to make them want these things. It introduces new products and describes new uses and improved features of familiar ones.

Advertising is seldom used to do the whole job of demand creation. Its principal function is to arouse the prospect's interest in the product, thus simplifying the salesman's job. As a result, advertising works with and for the salesman. It goes ahead of the salesman to tell the prospects about the products. It is designed for such purposes as to add to the number of people consuming a product; to induce present buyers to increase their consumption; to lengthen the buying season; to reach the individual who will influence the person who actually does the buying; to dispel existing prejudices or to correct mistaken impressions; or, to help shape the tastes, habits and customs of the prospects.

Finally, sales promotion might be defined as other auxiliary methods for building and maintaining demand for products. These include such activities as putting up displays, arranging point-of- purchase advertising, employing demonstrators, distributing samples, and correlating the personal selling and advertising programs.

Market dynamics

Fashion cycles, new ideas, and changing habits are three of the forces which make a market dynamic. However, what makes those forces formidable is the speed with which they spread and the unanimity with which they are adopted. Advertising is responsible in part for both the speed and unanimity. It has developed a public, almost coextensive with the population, that reveals an amazing willingness to conform. This public wants to have, to do, and to be what is popular at the moment.

A manufacturer, whatever he may make, however basic and staple the product, or however well entrenched it may be in the market, can no longer settle down and let things take their course. He must hold himself ready to act, and to act quickly, interpret the signs, anticipate the attitude of the public, and analyze each new invention for its effect on his business. As an example, even companies like United States Steel and International Business Machines continue to experiment, hoping that they will be able to anticipate each new invention.

Advertising costs

Many people believe that advertising increases the prices of the articles they buy. Whether or not this is correct is not easily answered because the contributions of advertising to the efficiency of marketing will depend on the conditions of demand and supply in a particular situation and on the skill with which advertising is used.

It is important to recognize that the costs of marketing may be reduced by greater efficiency in selling, in the selection of channels of distribution, in the use of advertising, and in improvements in packaging and shipping. On the other hand, these costs may be increased at least as much by increasing consumer services. More attractive packaging, the offering of a greater range of sizes, the offering of delivery service, the availability of return privileges, sales under credit terms—these and other services may increase the cost of selling.

The woman who buys a package of breakfast food pays not only for the contents of the package but also for the box; the airtight wrapper; a part of the rent, labor, light, heat, and power of the retailer; the cost of delivery; the carton in which the packages are shipped; and even a part of the wages of the lumberjack who cut the tree and of the costs of the mill operator who converted it into pulp out of which the carton was made. The price the consumer pays is a complex of a thousand prices. There is room for many economies between the point of origin and the point of consumption.

It is, therefore, not realistic to pick out advertising from the many factors which influence cost as a major determinant of price. As will be seen later, when advertising does not contribute more than its cost to marketing, it is advisable to use some other demand creation method.

Classification of advertising

In order to understand advertising, it is important not only to know what it is and what its function is in our economy but also to know something about the way advertising is classified. Advertising may be, and is, classified in many different ways by the people engaged in the field, and it is probably advisable to introduce some of the most commonly used terms at this point. A brief explanation of some of the major classifications used will be included in the following paragraphs. The sequence used in discussing the various classifications has no particular significance from an advertising standpoint but is based primarily on the probable familiarity of the reader with the terminology and concepts involved.

National, regional, and local advertising

Advertising reaches people through mediums, or media. Media are classified as national, regional, or local. The term "national advertising" usually is used to designate the type of advertising which is done by a manufacturer on a nationwide scale to stimulate the demand for his product among ultimate consumers. The advertising for automobiles, soft drinks, and food products appearing in such magazines as *Life*, and *Reader's Digest*, and the advertising for electric razors and cosmetics appearing on the nationwide television networks is national advertising. (See Figure 1–1. Ace Bowling Balls.)

If such advertising is confined to one region of the country, it is referred to as regional advertising. Whereas virtually all national advertising is done by the manufacturer, regional advertising may be conducted by the manufacturer, the wholesaler, or the retailer. A manufacturer of swimming pools, who operated only in the Pacific Coast states, might advertise his product in *Sunset* magazine (a regional magazine serving the Pacific Coast states) or on a network of television stations in the major Pacific Coast cities. Such advertising would be called regional advertising.

Local advertising is confined to one trading area or city, and usually is considered to be synonymous with the term "retail advertising." The advertising, familiar to all Americans, done by the department store in the city daily newspaper or on the local radio station is local advertising. The advertising may in fact be promoting the sale of nationally advertised brands of merchandise, but the stress is on the concept that the reader is to come and buy that brand in the advertiser's store rather than in some competitive store. Or the retailer may be attempting to induce the consumer to patronize his particular store and may not advertise any

FIGURE 1–1

How did "Mad Dog" Mulligan learn to control himself?

With a 16-lb. tranquilizer called the Ace Limited.

Mulligan, you see, used to be a fiery chap who suffered all the trials and tribulations of bowling. In fact, he was afflicted with just about every kind of alley ailment you can think of.

"You might say I stunk," Mulligan says.

But, alas, when Mulligan discovered the Ace Limited, wondrous things began to happen. For one thing, his game improved . . . almost as much as his disposition.

Here's why:

First of all, Mulligan is now able to hold a tight line. And he attributes this to the Limited's scientifically balanced

hard outer shell that doesn't overgrip the alley.

And when it comes to 1-3 pocket power, Mulligan digs the Limited's exclusive Action Center — that tiny inner core of bouncy, high-rebound muscle that delivers an extra kick that's good for extra pins.

Then, of course, there's the unique Ace-ite core — bright red for quick identification, and tough-textured for a more controlled release. And the distinctive "Limited" medallion which acts as a perfect tracking device.

"It's just one helluva ball," is the way Mulligan sums it up.

And it's part of a beautiful line, too. The Ace Limited Line. Featuring the Midnight Black and Turquoise & Black (both 12-16 lbs.) Hard Rubber balls for men and women. And, for those who prefer plastic, there's the Jet Black (15-16 lbs.) model with gold accents for men as well as the Honey Gold (12, 13 and 14 lbs.) ball for women.

To find out more about the Ace Limited, our lifetime guarantees and our great dealer profit margins, just ask your Ace Salesman. **ACE® BOWLING**

BUTLER, NEW JERSEY   AMERACE·ESNA CORPORATION

manufacturer's brands of merchandise. (See Neiman-Marcus advertising in Figure 1–2.)

Classifications based on audience to which directed

From the standpoint of the group, either the consumer group or the group that strongly influences the consumers, which the advertising is

FIGURE 1–2

designed to influence, the following four classifications of advertising often are used.

Consumer advertising usually is restricted to that type of advertising, whether done by the manufacturer or a dealer handling the product, which is directed at the ultimate consumer—the individual who buys the product for himself or for use in his household. An advertisement for toothpaste appearing in *Parents' Magazine* and *Better Family Living* would be an example of consumer advertising.

Industrial advertising is that advertising done by the manufacturers or distributors of industrial goods, designed to stimulate demand among the industrial buyers of such goods. The industrial goods might be raw materials, machinery, equipment, supplies, or fabricated parts. An advertisement for an electronic counter appearing in *Electronics* would be an example of industrial advertising. (See Figure 1–3.)

Trade advertising is that done by manufacturers to stimulate wholesalers and retailers to stock and sell the goods of the manufacturer. It is designed to obtain the aggressive promotion and sale of the manufacturer's line of products by the dealers who are logical outlets for such products. An advertisement appearing in *Chain Store Age* telling the grocer how much money he could make by stocking four new Gourmet Mixes would be an example of trade advertising.

Professional advertising is done by producers and distributors of products who are dependent on professional people to recommend, specify, or prescribe their products to the ultimate buyers or users. Manufacturers of pharmaceutical products and building materials advertise to doctors and architects, respectively, not with the expectation that they personally will consume the products, but with the expectation that they will prescribe, recommend, or specify them to those individuals or builders who will buy the products on the basis of professional recommendations.

Primary and selective demand advertising

Primary demand advertising is designed to increase the demand for a type or class of product, such as coffee, steel, cigars, or milk. It is usually done by trade associations or other cooperating industry groups; although, when a new type of product is introduced by one or several companies at approximately the same time, the individual firms will often use primary demand advertising to obtain initial demand for the product and get it established on the market. An example of this would be the initial advertising devoted to the promotion of color television sets, carried on for some years almost entirely by one firm (RCA); but later, when demand began to increase, carried on by a number of firms in the field. In contrast, selective demand advertising is designed to stimulate

FIGURE 1–3. Example of an industrial advertisement

The only expense HP spared in making these versatile counters...

... is yours.

Only Hewlett-Packard offers the versatility-economy combination represented by the new 5221A and 5216A Electronic Counters, using integrated circuits. Wide frequency range, high input impedance and sensitivity, long-life readout tubes with display storage, six measuring functions (in 5216A)...all this at prices as low as *one-half* that of comparable electronic counters available today.

The HP 5221A Counter has 0.1 and 1 second gate times (power line frequency time base), 1 meg/30 pF input impedance and an input signal sensitivity of 100 millivolts. It is the lowest cost frequency counter with a 10 MHz counting rate available. 4-digit readout is standard, 5 or 6 digits optional.

The HP 5216A Counter is an extremely versatile, 7-digit, 12.5 MHz counter for measuring frequency, time interval, period, multiple period average (in decade steps from 1 to 10^5), frequency ratio and totalizing. Gate times: 0.01/0.1/1.0/10 sec. Input sensitivity: 10 mV. Input impedance: 1 meg/50 pF. Time base: crystal with $< \pm 2 \times 10^{-6}$/month maximum aging rate. BCD output for operating data printers and other system elements. The price, even though the 5216A's frequency range is greater, is 30% below counters with similar functions.

Both counters feature HP's exclusive zero blanking, which makes reading easier and faster by suppressing any zeros to the left of the most significant digit. This unique benefit results from specially designed Hewlett-Packard proprietary integrated circuits used in both of the new counters.

Call your local HP field engineer for more details, or write Hewlett-Packard, Palo Alto, California 94304; Europe: 54 Route des Acacias, Geneva.

Courtesy: Hewlett-Packard

the demand for a particular brand of a product, such as RCA, Philco, or General Electric television sets. These two types of advertising are discussed at some length in Chapter 4.

Direct action and indirect action

Advertising designed to obtain some immediate response from the reader or listener is called direct-action advertising. Virtually all mail-order advertising is of this type, since it usually attempts to induce the reader to order the merchandise now. An advertisement that attempted to get the reader to send in a coupon for a sample of the merchandise would be an example of direct-action advertising. In contrast, indirect-action advertising is designed to influence the reader to have a favorable opinion or image of a brand so that when he does decide to buy that product he will buy the advertiser's brand rather than a competing one.

Product (and service) and institutional advertising

Most advertising, whether done by manufacturers of consumer or industrial goods, is done to increase the sales of a product (or service) or a specific brand owned by the manufacturer. Such advertising is called product advertising. However, some of the advertising done by such firms is not designed to promote specifically a certain product or brand of the manufacturer. Instead, it is designed to establish favorable attitudes toward the company as a whole on the part of present and potential customers, the general public or specific groups of people. It does not seek immediate action, but attempts to build up the reputation of the firm (by stressing the age and accomplishments of the firm, the skill of its employees, the extensive research carried on by the firm, the fine policies of the firm, etc.) so that consumers will trade with it rather than with other competing firms. This type of advertising is called institutional advertising. Some institutional advertising is used also for public relations purposes and for public service advertising, which involves sponsoring such public welfare activities as the prevention of forest fires, safe driving, and raising funds for various charitable programs. This latter type may also, on occasion, be defensive in order to dispel existing prejudices or to correct wrong impressions.

Miscellaneous classifications

Oftentimes, advertising is classified on the basis of the medium used, such as magazine advertising, newspaper advertising, outdoor advertising, radio advertising, television advertising, transit advertising (sometimes called transportation advertising), or direct-mail advertising.

Mail-order advertising is advertising in which the seller (the manufacturer or distributor) attempts to induce the reader to mail in his order for the goods advertised. This varies from national advertising, where the object is to persuade the consumer to buy the advertiser's brand when he goes into a store to buy that product, and from retail advertising, where the store attempts to induce the reader to come to that store to buy a particular brand of product, or to come to that store when he decides to shop for that line of goods.

Export advertising is that which appears in media that circulate in a foreign country. It is designed to stimulate demand among consumers (either ultimate individual consumers or industrial consumers) for the manufacturer's product.

These classifications are not mutually exclusive and much overlapping is involved, since many different bases are used for the purposes of classification. The advertisement of a manufacturer conducting a campaign for a new automobile via nationwide television networks might well be classified as national, consumer, selective, indirect-action, product, and television advertising all at the same time.

ADVERTISING EXPENDITURES

Some concept of the importance of advertising in the country's economy may be obtained by looking at the expenditures for advertising in recent years. Figure 1–4 shows the total expenditures for advertising during the years 1947–1970, with each year showing an appreciable increase over the preceding year in total dollar expenditures, except for a slight decline in 1958, when total expenditures for advertising declined by about $9 million from the 1957 figure, and in 1961, when the total declined by $87 million from the 1960 figure, due to the curtailment of advertising expenditures during the business recessions of these years. It is true that a part of this increase in advertising expenditures over these years may be explained by higher costs of media and production, or a cheaper dollar.

The high points of advertising expenditures as a percentage of Gross National Product were reached in the era 1955–60, with highs of 2.39 and 2.37 percent in 1956 and 1960, respectively. It might be of interest to note that of the $19,565 million spent for advertising in 1969, $11,460 million was for national advertising, and $8,105 million for local advertising.

This increase in the absolute and relative amounts spent for advertising is the result of several factors in our economy. In part it is due to our expanding economy and the fact that people are constantly having a greater amount of discretionary spending power, so that it is more and more important to stimulate the consumer to purchase goods and services by the use of advertising. Also, with changing trends in the services of retailers and the shopping habits of consumers, the importance of

FIGURE 1–4. Total United States advertising expenditures, 1947–70

Year	Advertising expenditures* (millions of dollars)	Total gross national product* (millions of dollars)	Advertising expenditures as a percentage of gross national product
1947	4,260	232,228	1.83
1948	4,864	257,325	1.89
1949	5,202	257,301	2.02
1950	5,710	285,067	2.00
1951	6,426	328,232	1.96
1952	7,156	345,445	2.07
1953	7,755	363,218	2.14
1954	8,164	361,167	2.26
1955	9,194	391,692	2.35
1956	9,905	414,686	2.39
1957	10,311	442,769	2.33
1958	10,302	444,546	2.32
1959	11,255	482,783	2.33
1960	11,932	503,800	2.37
1961	11,845	520,100	2.28
1962	12,381	560,300	2.21
1963	13,107	589,200	2.22
1964	14,155	628,700	2.25
1965	15,255†	676,300†	2.26
1966	16,670	749,900	2.22
1967	16,866	793,500	2.12
1968	18,127	865,700	2.09
1969	19,565	932,300	2.10
1970	19,715	977,000	2.02

* For years 1947–70: U.S. Bureau of Census, *Statistical Abstract of the United States: 1962* (83d ed.; Washington, D.C., 1962), pp. 312, 851; for years 1960–66: U.S. Bureau of Census, *Statistical Abstract of the United States: 1966* (87th ed.; Washington, D.C., 1966), pp. 320, 837.
† *Survey of Current Business,* Vol. XLVII, No. 5 (May 1967), p. 4.

preselling the consumer by means of advertising has increased. Hence, advertising is becoming a more important factor in the total marketing mix of most American firms.

In addition, some of the increase in expenditures may be due, partially, to the advent of a new and powerful medium, television. For some companies, at least, the expenditures in television advertising have been partly additional expenditures and not merely the substitution of television for expenditures in other media. Figure 1–5 shows advertising expenditures by media for the years 1950–1969.

It might be noted that the major relative increases in expenditures occurred in television, newspapers, radio, magazines and miscellaneous; while business papers and direct mail showed moderate increases; and transit, farm publications, and outdoor advertising showed smallest gains.

An indication of the expenditures of the 25 leading national advertisers in 1970 in six media may be obtained from Figure 1–6. The reader's attention is directed to the extreme variations in these advertising ex-

FIGURE 1–5. Advertising—estimated expenditures, by medium: 1950 to 1969 (in millions of dollars, except percent*)

	1950 Expenditures	1950 Per cent of total	1955 Expenditures	1955 Per cent of total	1960 Expenditures	1960 Per cent of total	1965 Expenditures	1965 Per cent of total	1968 Expenditures	1968 Per cent of total	1969 (prel.) Expenditures	1969 (prel.) Per cent of total
Total	5,710	100.0	9,194	100.0	11,932	100.0	15,255	100.0	18,127	100.0	19,565	100.0
National	3,257	57.0	5,407	58.8	7,296	61.1	9,365	61.4	10,883	60.0	11,460	58.6
Local	2,453	43.0	3,788	41.2	4,636	38.9	5,890	38.6	7,244	40.0	8,105	41.4
Newspapers	2,076	36.3	3,088	33.6	3,703	31.0	4,457	29.2	5,265	29.1	5,850	29.9
National	533	9.3	743	8.1	836	7.0	869	5.7	990	5.5	1,050	5.4
Local	1,542	27.0	2,345	25.5	2,867	24.0	3,587	23.5	4,275	23.6	4,800	24.5
Radio	605	10.6	545	5.9	692	5.8	917	6.0	1,190	6.6	1,270	6.5
Network	196	3.4	84	0.9	43	0.4	60	0.4	63	0.4	65	0.3
Spot	136	2.4	134	1.5	222	1.8	268	1.7	360	2.0	370	1.9
Local	273	4.8	326	3.5	428	3.6	589	3.9	767	4.2	835	4.3
Television	171	3.0	1,025	11.1	1,590	13.3	2,515	16.5	3,231	17.8	3,585	18.3
Network	85	1.5	540	5.9	783	6.6	1,237	8.1	1,523	8.4	1,675	8.5
Spot	31	0.5	260	2.8	527	4.4	866	5.7	1,131	6.2	1,245	6.4
Local	55	1.0	225	2.4	281	2.3	412	2.7	577	3.2	665	3.4
Magazines	515	9.0	729	7.9	941	7.9	1,199	7.9	1,318	7.3	1,375	7.0
Weeklies	261	4.6	396	4.3	525	4.4	610	4.0	657	3.6	660	3.4
Women's	129	2.3	161	1.8	184	1.5	269	1.8	284	1.6	310	1.6
Monthlies	88	1.5	133	1.4	200	1.7	282	1.9	342	1.9	373	1.9
Farm, national	37	0.6	39	0.4	32	0.3	37	0.2	35	0.2	32	0.1
Farm papers	21	0.4	34	0.4	35	0.3	34	0.2	33	0.2	33	0.2
Direct mail	803	14.1	1,299	14.1	1,830	15.3	2,324	15.2	2,612	14.4	2,680	13.7
Business papers	251	4.4	446	4.9	609	5.1	671	4.4	714	3.9	720	3.7
Outdoor	143	2.5	192	2.1	203	1.7	180	1.2	208	1.1	206	1.0
National	96	1.7	130	1.4	137	1.1	120	0.8	137	0.7	135	0.6
Local	46	0.8	63	0.7	66	0.6	60	0.4	71	0.4	71	0.4
Miscellaneous	1,125	19.7	1,836	20.0	2,328	19.6	2,959	19.4	3,556	19.6	3,846	19.7
National	610	10.7	1,040	11.3	1,368	11.5	1,750	11.5	2,035	11.2	2,145	11.0
Local	515	9.0	796	8.7	960	8.1	1,209	7.9	1,521	8.4	1,701	8.7

* See also *Historical Statistics, Colonial Times to 1957*, series R 99–102, R 110–113, and T 346–351.
Source: Compiled by McCann-Erickson, Inc., for Decker Communications, Inc., New York, N.Y. 1950–1965, in *Printers' Ink* magazine; beginning 1967, in *Marketing/Communications*. (Copyright.)

FIGURE 1-6. 25 leading national advertisers in six media: 1970

Company	Six media total	Magazines	Newspapers supplements	Network television	Spot television	Network radio	Outdoor
1. Procter & Gamble	$186,746,100	$ 7,364,800	$ 136,000	$128,444,500	$50,796,700	$ 4,100	$ 438,800
2. General Foods	109,299,600	11,993,800	2,463,800	44,642,000	49,259,200	502,000	458,900
3. Bristol-Myers	102,229,800	20,381,200	360,200	57,078,600	23,351,100	599,800	50,000
4. Colgate-Palmolive	90,267,300	5,018,400	140,200	46,507,800	36,860,900	1,690,000	246,000
5. R. J. Reynolds	77,843,900	9,986,100		52,405,900	14,401,200	804,700	222,200
6. American Home Products	76,542,400	7,382,300	430,300	40,791,800	26,355,800	1,360,000	4,938,500
7. General Motors	74,231,300	24,211,600	343,500	32,972,300	8,961,100	2,804,300	
8. Sterling Drug	67,807,100	10,122,800	444,700	41,324,000	12,940,100	2,975,500	1,700
9. Warner-Lambert	67,487,600	3,108,500	8,100	46,200,300	17,853,400	315,600	100
10. Lever Bros.	64,207,600	3,734,900	527,900	38,554,900	20,893,200	496,600	
11. Philip Morris	63,598,000	13,745,700	8,300	36,685,800	11,491,500	833,700	833,000
12. Ford Motor Co.	59,041,400	15,499,000		31,345,800	7,544,600	1,676,300	2,975,700
13. General Mills	50,061,300	7,023,700	544,900	24,152,400	17,940,000	386,700	13,600
14. American Brands	49,690,900	15,444,300	66,700	31,365,600	2,092,000	15,600	706,700
15. Gillette	49,598,200	5,383,600	28,600	27,479,300	16,320,300	382,900	3,500
16. Sears, Roebuck	48,132,500	13,399,100	7,200	15,273,500	18,960,900	59,500	432,300
17. British-American Tobacco (Brown & Williamson)	47,301,400	12,248,500	1,499,600	23,131,100	7,831,000	1,127,600	2,591,000
18. Loew's (inc. Lorillard Corp.)	41,481,300	5,364,900	1,969,300	15,903,600	15,536,200	108,800	1,579,700
19. Kraftco	41,076,700	8,897,400	221,300	18,359,300	13,181,100	168,800	308,800
20. Miles Labs.	40,546,500	1,845,800		28,937,600	9,594,300		1,439,200
21. Coca-Cola	40,024,700	6,064,600	48,500	15,527,800	16,944,600		334,200
22. Kellogg	37,419,200	2,970,100	689,900	24,934,700	8,490,300	930,500	646,900
23. Chrysler	36,616,300	9,570,600		21,541,600	3,926,700	468,000	812,700
24. PepsiCo.	35,019,000	2,966,200	110,100	16,864,300	13,797,700		1,071,000
25. AT&T	34,749,700	9,576,200		12,928,300	11,110,100	64,100	

Source: Data, Leading National Advertisers, Broadcast Advertisers Reports; chart, *Advertising Age*, May 17, 1971.

penditures in the six media. The explanation of such variations for advertising will be brought out in the later discussions of media.

It might be well to bring to the reader's attention a study of advertising expenditures by Kenneth H. Myers which indicates that, contrary to popular belief, there has been a decline in advertising expenditures over the long run in relation to national income. Figure 1–7 shows that the

FIGURE 1–7. Advertising expenditures as a percentage of national income

Year	Percent	Year	Percent
1880	2.7	*1960	2.9
1900	3.0	*1961	2.8
1920	4.3	†1962	2.7
1930	3.8	†1963	2.7
1940	2.6	†1964	2.8
1945	1.6	1965	2.7
1950	2.4	1966	2.7
1955	2.8	1967	2.6
1956	2.9	1968	2.5
1957	2.9	1969	2.5
*1958	2.8	1970	2.4
*1959	2.8		

* Percentages for these years calculated by authors from data taken from U.S. Bureau of Census, *Statistical Abstract of the United States: 1962* (83d ed.; Washington, D.C., 1962), pp. 316, 851.

† Percentages calculated by authors from data taken from U.S. Bureau of Census, *Statistical Abstract of the United States: 1966* (87th ed.; Washington, D.C., 1966), p. 320; and *Survey of Current Business*, Vol. XLVII, No. 5 (May 1967), p. 5.

Source: Kenneth H. Myers, "Have We a Decline in Advertising Appropriations," *Journal of Marketing*, Vol. XXIII, No. 4 (April 1959), p. 370.

volume of advertising expenditures in relation to national income had declined by over three fifths between 1920 and 1945, and that the increase in expenditures since World War II has raised the relationship to about two thirds of the level of the 1920's by 1955; and that it remained fairly constant from 1955 to 1966, but since then has begun to decline again.

Company expenditures

There is a wide variation found in advertising expenditures between companies. Within certain product groups, the variation is often wider than between the averages of one group and another. As a percent of sales, the range in the proprietary medicine group, as an example, varied from 31 percent to 64 percent; among food and grocery product manufacturers, from 0.25 percent to 47 percent; for agricultural equipment, from 1 percent to 20 percent.[1]

[1] Neil H. Borden, *Advertising in Our Economy* (Homewood, Ill.: Richard D. Irwin, Inc., 1945), p. 126.

There is also a range in advertising expenditures from 0.0 percent to 21.6 percent of sales among manufacturers of coffee, tea, extracts, and spices. Among industrial products, the average percentage of sales devoted to advertising varied from 4 percent for paper and paper products to 0.5 percent for chemicals.

Companies reflect the variations in the marketing strategy and planning of the organizations in deciding on the kind of marketing mix they believe is necessary to satisfy their specific sales problems.

Status of advertising

The status of advertising is changing, and, as a result, its future role will have to be reevaluated with a high degree of sophistication because business executives are beginning to consider it from a more and more critical point of view.

As an example, in Professor Stephen A. Greyser's survey findings in the May–June 1971 issue of the *Harvard Business Review* in which he studied 2,700 subscribers, he found that businessmen are becoming more critical of advertising and its function in society.

Professor Greyser pointed out that the main criticism of advertising is in the area of content which is most under the control of advertising and is more susceptible to change than other factors.

He went on to indicate that the businessmen surveyed question advertising's influence in the social area, and perceive a negative impact on public taste and an unhealthy effect on children.

A significant reason for the criticism, Professor Greyser stated, is that businessmen are assessing advertising not only in a business context, but also in terms of the societal implications. More than two thirds of the executives disagreed with the philosophy that advertising's sole justification should be returning a profit to the advertiser.

However, in the business area over 90 percent agreed that advertising is essential to business and that the public places more confidence in advertised products than in unadvertised ones. Over 93 percent think that advertising speeds the development of markets for new products; 67 percent say it helps raise the standard of living and 55 percent believe that it results in better products; while 70 percent believe that selling expense would increase if advertising were eliminated. However, about 50 percent believe that too much money is spent on advertising.

The repetition of ads was a frequent cause of irritation as well as hard-sell promotion and television and direct-mail advertising. Eighty percent believe that consumerism will lead to major modification in advertising and that advertising needs a code of ethics. Finally they believe that the primary responsibility for improving advertising rests with corporate top management.

While the survey yielded a wide range of findings, the business executives basically affirm a strong belief in the efficiency of advertising to perform a key role in our economic system. It is also clear that they question numerous aspects of the content of advertising.

HIGHLIGHTS

It is important to recognize that advertising depends on other marketing factors. In the first place advertising is only one phase of the marketing mix which includes not only the total promotion functions, but also those related to developing the product or service, to setting the price, and to planning the distribution.

The promotion functions include besides advertising both sales promotion and personal selling. In other words the promotion functions involve all the methods used in communication with the potential consumers.

It should also be remembered that the effective use of advertising is dependent upon such additional factors as competitive behavior, product characteristics, customer habits, retail availability, and environmental conditions.

Because of the complexities of consumer behavior and the problems in the evaluation of the marketing mix, it is difficult to set widely applicable advertising decision rules for the guidance of management. Nevertheless, it is important for management to take into consideration the following general concepts about advertising:

1. Advertising is only one part of the marketing mix.
2. It is nonpersonal and is directed toward a specific objective and appears in paid media.
3. It is difficult to separate advertising from the other components of the marketing mix.
4. It is of great urgency to develop a more systematic procedure for advertising evaluation.
5. Advertising is the most effective means available for specific forms of communication and education.
6. The responsibility for advertising policy should rest with the owner or chief executive of the firm.
7. Advertising must weed out those in their midst whose activities bring discredit upon advertising.
8. Advertising must keep abreast of the dynamic conditions in society which include problems of world hunger, of population growth, of economic developments and of environmental deterioration.
9. Advertising needs to do a more effective job of educating the public about its responsibility because, in many instances, much recent criticism stems from lack of knowledge.
10. Advertising communicates beyond its specific goal and is limited only by the total experience of the listener or viewer.

Finally, the work of demand creation depends upon a thorough understanding of the characteristics of the product and its market. A method of advertising successfully a cosmetic product may be a failure when applied to a different product.

The work of advertising requires the ability to understand all aspects of the psychology of consumer demand and to coordinate the advertising as an integral part of the marketing mix in order that the prospect will respond in a positive manner to the approach that is used.

Advertising is an important industry. Most of the 4,000,000 businesses in the United States do some kind of advertising, and in 1971 they spent over $20,000,000,000 for advertising.

QUESTIONS

1. In what ways does advertising influence or form a part of distribution?

2. How has the growth of mass production and mass distribution influenced the growth of advertising?

3. In your opinion, has advertising been an important factor in stimulating a desire on your part for the products you purchase? With what types of products have you been influenced the most by advertising?

4. Do you think advertising will become more or less important to the economy in the coming decades? Why?

5. Assume that a manufacturer of a branded grocery product can use either salesmen or advertising to introduce his product. Which would you consider better? Explain.

6. Bring to class six advertisements from your local newspaper, three which you consider to be examples of national advertising and three of local advertising. Explain the basis for your classification of these advertisements.

7. Bring to class two advertisements for the same product, one an example of primary demand advertising and the second an example of selective demand advertising.

8. What are some of the effects upon the nature of advertising which may come about because of the density of population in urban areas?

9. Contrast the significance of the use of advertising for industrial commodities versus ultimate consumer goods.

10. What do you believe will be the trend of the use of advertising in the next twenty years? Give your reasons.

11. To what degree can the overall selling functions be accomplished through advertising?

12. What are the necessary ingredients that a company's product should possess if the advertising of it is to be successful?

13. Should advertising that may conflict with the national goals of the economy be curtailed?

14. Indicate the reasons why some companies which sell almost identical products will use different advertising strategies.

15. Point out what you believe advertising can do for:
    a) A company manufacturing bearings which will be used in auto-
        mobiles.
    b) A wheat farmer.
    c) A department store.
    d) An office furniture manufacturer.
    e) An attorney in general practice.
    f) A soft drink bottler.
    g) A manufacturer of air conditioning units for the home.
    h) A major bank with a full line of services.
    i) An automobile manufacturer.
    j) A manufacturer of typewriters.

CASE 1.   ATLAS HARDWARE COMPANY
Considering advertising expenses

Atlas Hardware Company, a full service wholesaler, sold and distributed tools, builders' hardware, and a general line of shelf hardware,
plumbing and electrical specialties to the retail trade. It distributed its
merchandise to some five hundred accounts, and had a gross business of
$2,500,000 annually.

The company had not done much advertising to the trade and to
consumers but relied primarily on the manufacturers of the products it
handled to build demand. As a result, Atlas had a tendency to charge to
the advertising account a diversified list of items.

A new accounting firm had recently been hired, and, the senior ac-
countant of the firm found in analyzing the records of the company that
$52,963.86 had been charged to the advertising account in the prior year.

The following charges were included in the $52,963.86 advertising ex-
penses:

1.	Trade paper advertising	$ 3,500.00
2.	Purchase of mail order list	250.00
3.	Classified advertising for employees	835.00
4.	Miscellaneous printing for personal calling cards, and the like	196.42
5.	Photographers for publicity	112.35
6.	Folders and brochures	1,897.45
7.	Service club dues and expenses	562.32
8.	Country club dues	1,200.00
9.	Chamber of commerce dues	350.00
10.	Christmas gifts to retailers	2,500.00
11.	Postage on special mailings	475.00
12.	Convention expenses	2,175.00
13.	Subscriptions to trade magazines	95.15
14.	Printing and mailing of catalog	4,824.47
15.	Entertainment of customers in homes of executives	3,175.25
16.	Sponsorship of bowling team	1,750.00
17.	Promotional brochures for salesmen	1,115.45
18.	United Fund donation	750.00
19.	Ball-point pens with Atlas name on them	2,175.00
20.	Advertisement in high school year book	150.00
21.	Premiums for Atlas salesmen for sales contests	5,000.00
22.	Allowances to retailers for cooperating advertising	12,000.00
23.	Political advertising	750.00
24.	Salary of advertising secretary	6,250.00
25.	Special public service releases	875.00
		$52,963.86

Case questions

1. Is it important for Atlas to have a strict interpretation as to what items should be charged to the advertising expense account?

2. Develop the criteria which Atlas might establish to use in the future in deciding which expenditures should be charged to the advertising account.

3. Should these criteria be the same for companies that rely on advertising for the major part of the sales effort?

4. Evaluate each of the above expenses and indicate whether or not it should be charged to advertising.

CASE 2. M K RECORD STORE
Considering use of advertising

The M K Record Store is a small specialty record shop located in a midwestern city of 85,000 people. The store recently has been placed under new management, and the owner has inaugurated new policies and services to overcome the poor reputation which the original owner had created. The firm has attempted to inform previous and potential customers of these changes, and, at the same time, create an established clientele of satisfied customers.

The former owner opened the store 12 years ago as a record discount house which bought large lots of records from manufacturers and sold them at a discount. In conjunction with discount selling, trade-in allowances on old records were given, and these trade-ins were resold at reduced prices. Because the store was a high turnover, low margin retail outlet, no money was spent on the physical plant. The records were placed in open corrugated boxes on unpainted wood shelves. Facilities for auditioning records were very poor, and no attempt was made in building displays or developing a pleasing atmosphere.

The original owner developed a poor reputation with customers by frequently running misleading advertisements in newspapers. The salesmen were noted for being arty, rude, and sometimes insulting to the patrons. This behavior and the failure to have consistent store hours alienated many customers and made the store a one-time purchase place.

Sales policies

Against this background, the new owner took over the store three years ago, changing its name to M K Record Store and introducing a new set of policies and merchandising methods. The new owner discontinued the operation as a discount house and placed his emphasis on service.

He decided to change the store to appeal to a specific group of consumers. The appeal was directed to adult high-fidelity fans who enjoy classical music. As a result, the store specializes in records of high quality. The basic inventory consists of approximately 7,500 records, of which 50 percent are classical, 15 percent jazz, and 35 percent popular. The classical selection is broad in nature, and includes selections of both leading composers and recording companies. The jazz and popular items are also quite selective. These popular items are of the type which appeal primarily to an adult customer.

Along with the selective inventory, services are provided which appeal to the adult clientele. These include store hours from 10 A.M. to 10 P.M. seven days a week, and one-week delivery on out-of-stock items. The owner also offers to try to secure rare and out-of-print items. The records are guaranteed as to quality of the surface, and even records with the slightest defects are replaced without charge.

The interior of the store has been refinished. New display cases have been installed, the lighting improved, and an expensive high-fidelity system has been set up on which the salesmen will play any records for the customer. This is important for high-fidelity music purchasers who insist on perfect records and dislike shops where anyone can take a record into a booth and play it on an inexpensive, low-quality machine.

The owner believes that an important appeal of the store is the quality of the sales personnel. The strength of the sales staff lies in their courtesy and knowledge of classical music and recordings. Effort is made by the staff to preview new recordings in order to keep their knowledge of recordings current. Particular attention is paid to steady customers by learning their names, their likes and dislikes in music, and their current record libraries. With this backgound, the sales personnel are equipped to suggest recordings and selections which appeal to each customer. An effort is made to introduce customers to the various periods and kinds of classical music, thus helping the customer to develop a wider range of music appreciation.

As indicated above, the new owner has made a great effort to combat the reputation of the prior firm. The premises have been remodeled. The name was changed, though not radically, and the atmosphere and service were improved. However, the new management has not realized a substantial increase in gross sales.

Market situation

An informal survey of the current clientele by such means as asking customers where they live has shown the following distribution: 50 percent come from within a mile radius of the store; 40 percent come from within a radius of over 1 mile and less than 10 miles from the store, and 10 percent come from a peripheral area over 10 miles from the store. The distance a person will travel to the store appears to be correlated to the rarity of the records he is seeking and/or his interest in high-quality records to play on his high-fidelity system.

There are approximately five retail record outlets in the firm's basic marketing area. However, none of these competing stores offers a comparable selection of classical records, nor similar auditioning facilities. Few competitors offer the same service on out-of-stock or rare items, and none of them maintain a 12-hour schedule seven days a week.

Sales volume of the store is seasonal in nature, and appears to be affected by weather conditions. Sales are approximately 25 percent higher during the rainy and winter season than in the summer months. The peak is reached after the first heavy rain spell. It is believed that after people are forced to stay indoors, their interest in playing records is increased. In any given week, sales are highest on Friday, Saturday, and Sunday; however, sales on Sunday vary widely depending on the weather and "leader" sales which are advertised in the Sunday morning papers.

Occasionally, leader sales are made to stimulate business. Leader sales often are made by reducing the price on a major record or on various slow-moving items in the inventory. Sales usually run for a week. However, the management has not been particularly satisfied with the results of such promotions.

The basic purpose of these sales was to attract consumer attention to the store, encourage them to come and see the inventory, learn the store's location and the services offered. While the sales attracted satisfactory turnouts, the estimated return for further purchases by first-time customers ran only about 8 percent. Consequently, such merchandising methods were not used on a regular basis.

Advertising methods

The firm operates on a yearly advertising budget. The budget figure is arrived at by taking 3 percent of the previous year's gross sales. The owner believed that this amount gave him a starting point from which to work. Since this figure is fairly conservative, it was changed when sales anticipation was high or a good price was obtained on a particular purchase for stock. Last year's gross sales were approximately $90,000, thus providing a basic advertising budget for the current year of $2,700.

Several of the larger record companies, notably RCA-Victor and Columbia, offer cooperative advertising programs to dealers.

Under these plans, the dealer and the company share the cost of an advertisement on a proportional basis. In return for this allowance, the ad must feature the record company's products. M K Record Store takes advantage of these plans in its radio advertisements, but rarely uses them otherwise.

A substantial portion of the advertising budget is devoted to radio advertisements. These advertisements consist of spot announcements over the local radio station.

The only other form of general advertising used is the advertisement of sales in the local newspaper. These are run three or four times a year, once with each sale, at a cost of $200 per advertisement.

Occasionally, direct-mail advertising is undertaken by the store. This consists of sending newsletters to regular customers, announcing sales and enclosing catalogs of new releases by various recording companies. These newsletters are sent out once or twice a year. No effort has been made to test their effectiveness in stimulating sales.

It is the opinion of the manager that the most effective advertising the store receives is by word of mouth by a satisfied customer to his friends. Through conversation with new customers, he had found that many come on the recommendation of their friends. Consequently, the owner believes it might be more advantageous to put more emphasis on satisfying the people when they visit the store, and to curtail his advertising expenditure.

Case questions

1. Evaluate the importance of advertising for M K Record Store.
2. Should this advertising be primarily of an institutional nature? Give reasons.
3. Point out the pros and cons of the current advertising program.

CASE 3.   PHOTO, INC.
Evaluating advertising concepts

The President of Photo, Inc. emphasized some of the major aspects of advertising in addressing the owners of the retail outlets which handled the company's products.

The business of the company

Photo, Inc. is engaged in the wholesale distribution of a broad range of photographic equipment and supplies and a limited variety of sound ("audio") equipment. Most of the company's sales are made to retail outlets which cater primarily to amateur photographers but which also resell for industrial and professional use. The company itself operates no retail outlets.

In the last 20 years, amateur photography has developed rapidly into a hobby enjoyed by millions. Increased leisure time, the continuing rise in population and industry-wide advertising and promotion each have contributed to this growth. In addition, in almost every line of photographic products today's amateur can choose among several competing items suitable in quality to his level of skill and in price to his budgetary requirements.

Underlying the development of amateur photography are major technological advances in design and production affecting motion picture and still cameras and projectors and a wide variety of photographic accessories and supplies. Still cameras, for example, have changed from bulky apparatus with collapsible bellows and slow optics to easily operated, lightweight equipment which frequently incorporates range finders, flashguns, and light meters and which can now even set aperture and speed automatically. Similarly, motion-picture cameras have been transformed from single-lens devices, first to turret cameras and now to modern "electric eye" cameras.

Improvements in cameras have been accompanied by the development of many accessory and related items to facilitate or supplement their use. Faster films and better lighting and flash equipment have made possible indoor and outdoor still and motion picture photography under almost any conditions, and color photography has expanded the business in projectors, viewers and screens, and other projection accessories.

There are no published statistics showing the relative size of firms engaged in the wholesale distribution of photographic equipment and supplies, but, based upon estimates available from private sources, the company believes that it is one of the ten largest wholesale distributors of such products in the United States. However, sales by the company represent only a small portion of total sales of photographic products to retailers, since many retailers purchase directly from large manufacturers (such as Eastman Kodak, Bell & Howell, and Polaroid) who do not deal through wholesalers and who occupy a dominant position in the industry.

Sales and sales techniques

The company makes over 90 percent of its sales to retail outlets such as camera specialty stores, department stores, and retail mail-order catalog houses, and the balance to other retailers and wholesalers. The company has more than 9,000 customers, no one of which accounts for more than 3 percent of its sales during the last fiscal year. The 25 largest customers account for approximately 15 percent of such sales.

The business is somewhat seasonal in nature, the spring season extending from April through June and the fall season from August through December. Sales volume is usually lowest during January and February.

The company employs its own sales force, which includes over 60 fulltime salesmen. In addition, some accounts are served by the company's executive and supervisory personnel. The sales territory consists of the entire continental United States and Alaska.

Competition

The photographic equipment and supply business is highly competitive. In common with other wholesalers in the industry, the company operates on a small margin of profit and is therefore highly dependent upon volume sales. The company faces sales competition from other distributors handling one or more of the same products, from distributors handling competing products, and from manufacturers of competing products who make direct sales to the company's customers and potential customers. Also, in a few instances, manufacturers who supply the company sell the same merchandise, often under a different brand name, directly to some retail outlets.

In meeting sales competition, the company relies primarily upon its ability to provide its customers with more efficient service. It maintains substantial inventories in all product lines which it handles and is thus able to fill orders from customers promptly. Nationwide coverage by its sales staff and nationwide warehouse facilities enable the company to serve national retail chains as well as local retailers.

The company is also in competition with other wholesale distributors for sources of supply. In meeting such competition, the company depends upon its purchasing power, ability to provide national sales coverage, continuity of management, continuity of handling product lines over extended periods, and favorable credit position. In the company's opinion, its success in obtaining and keeping sources of supply has led to good relations with its customers and has therefore increased its ability to meet sales competition. The President believed, however, that if the business was to continue to grow and develop it was essential to get the retailers to advertise more extensively. In the past, the retail outlets handling Photo, Inc.'s products did very little advertising.

In his address to the owners, the President pointed out some advertising concepts. He said that advertising has had a major role in the development of this nation, promoting our high standard of living by making possible mass production and, consequently, lower prices. It has stabilized employment by creating all-year-around demand for products, such as canned soup, for example, which once was highly seasonal. But advertising the small business and the large industry are very different things. And it is important to bear in mind what advertising can do, how it may be used effectively, and the limits of what should be expected of it.

Basic factors to consider. There are several basic factors a businessman, particularly a "small" businessman, should bear in mind about advertising:

1. Advertising is much more than simply laying out an effective ad or writing a clever sales talk.
2. The kind of advertising which is best for some types of business may not be right for others.
3. Money can be wasted in advertising by failing to have adequate information about potential customers, by lack of experience or judgment, by spending too high a proportion of gross income, and in other ways.
4. And, finally, the purpose of advertising is to sell or help sell. Advertising which doesn't do this, directly or indirectly, should be avoided.

Retailer needs advertising most. The retailer, because he must wait for customers to come to his store, needs advertising more than does the wholesaler who sometimes can depend solely on salesmen.

Honesty in advertising. The retailer's advertising, like all his relations with customers, should be designed not only to get them, but to keep them. False or "sucker-bait" advertising should be avoided. It is better to get one customer who will come back than ten who come once and advise others to stay away.

The groundwork for advertising. The first step in advertising, as in anything else, is to do the groundwork. A businessman can begin by asking himself these questions:

1. Who are my potential customers?
2. How many are there?
3. Where do they live?
4. Can they get to me conveniently?
5. Should I plan to deliver to them?
6. Are they the kind of people who want charge accounts and delivery service?
7. Where do they now buy the things or service I want to sell them?
8. Can I offer them anything they are not now getting? How? What?
9. How can I convince them they should do business with me?

There are other questions which will emerge in the process of finding the answers to these. Honest answers will go far toward determining how, where, and how much a business should advertise.

Customer studies. A businessman should never cease to "survey" or study his customers. Neighborhoods change. Customers' habits change. If he finds that a customer has drifted away, he should try at once to learn why. Perhaps there has been a misunderstanding he can correct, or if he or an employee has given offense, there is a fault to correct before other customers are lost. If he finds he is beginning to get customers from an adjoining neighborhood beyond what he considers his logical area, he should find out why, then use that reason in advertising to attract others in the same area.

Direct-mail advertising. The retailer should see that the direct-mail advertising he uses has a specific thing to say which is of interest to specific people. Among the many ways to use mail advertising are enclosures that go with the bill (don't send bills alone; make the stamp do its full job), telling regular customers of sales ahead of time, announcing a new service or product, sending circulars or self-mailing folders cheaply at bulk mailing rates.

Door-to-door methods. Handbills, business cards, circulars, or other "throw-aways" have been effective, especially for announcements of sales. Like any other form of advertising, they should be used smartly and the pitfalls should be avoided. Responsible distributors should be used who will avoid placing circulars where they will litter premises and irritate possible customers. It is unlawful to put circulars in home mailboxes. Some communities have ordinances forbidding the distribution of handbills.

How much to spend. A safe policy for a retailer in the photography business is to set aside a conservative amount, perhaps 2 percent of expected gross sales, for advertising, and then watch results, increasing expenditures for those kinds of advertising which pay and cutting down on those which don't. Another factor to determine, either at the outset or gradually from experience, is whether activities such as memberships, civic activity, etc., are to be charged to the advertising budget.

In any event, there should be a definite advertising budget and it should be spent, for it is as bad to spend too little as too much. The budget should show how much is to be spent each month or each season.

The cost of advertising is part of the overhead the same as rent, light, or wages, is figured in the markup, and is part of the selling price of merchandise or services.

Essentials of advertising copy. There are certain things which every ad should do. These are: (1) attract attention, (2) secure interest, (3) produce belief or conviction, and (4) get the prospect to act. Another factor, which is leaving an impression on the memory or tying up with previous and subsequent ads, might be added to these fundamentals.

Mention the price. It's a safe bet always to mention the price in retail advertising. Whether a customer wants cheap or expensive things the price comes as close as anything to telling him whether it's what he wants.

What to advertise. In selecting items or specific services to advertise, there are several things to keep in mind: timeliness, buying habits, variety or novelty, and frequency of purchase. Although it is best to advertise the things people buy the most, often there also is strong appeal in offering something entirely new or novel.

When a store has window space it can become the most valuable selling space. The window deserves study, planning, thought, and work. Certain guides and principles to follow can be treated only briefly here:

1. The name of the store should appear in or on the window.
2. Glass and window display space should be kept spotlessly clean.
3. Displays should be changed frequently, even if only partly.
4. Tie-ins with seasons, holidays, local events, other advertising, etc. should be planned in advance so that the necessary materials may be obtained.
5. A display should not be cluttered up or scattered. Goods should be related to each other.
6. A window should present a simple, harmonious appearance, centering on one idea at a time—or at least one main idea.

The President concluded by stating that the primary purpose of retail advertising for photographic equipment was to produce immediate sales. It was his opinion that if the retailers followed his recommendations, all of them could improve their sales positions.

Case questions

1. What would you say are the major functions which advertising for the photographic equipment retailers should accomplish?

2. Should the cost of advertising be classified as part of the overhead, the same as rent or light?

3. Should advertising for photographic equipment retailers that does not sell or help sell be avoided?

4. If the retail stores spent 2 percent of sales on advertising, do you anticipate that marketing costs would increase or decrease? Give reasons.

CASE 4.   KELLOGG COMPANY
Growth of a company

Before Kellogg there was no such thing as a ready-to-eat cereal industry . . . when W. K. Kellogg in 1906 toasted, packaged, and sold his first box of Sanitas Toasted Corn Flakes, a new idea in U.S. manufacturing was born and a new habit in U.S. eating came into being.

Also, that early box of Corn Flakes was the inspiration for pioneering several principles of advertising and merchandising that are now considered basic and taken for granted. A few of them are: consistent advertising, test marketing, product sampling, packaging, and package display.

Today, the ready-to-eat cereal business in the U.S. alone amounts to nearly $700 million annually—of which Kellogg does almost half.

Early work in nutrition

Will Keith Kellogg and his brother, Dr. John Harvey Kellogg, worked together at the then well-known Battle Creek Sanitarium.

Dr. Kellogg had many new and radical ideas about food and nutrition including many that are taken for granted today. The doctor figured that just about everything a body needed could be obtained from ordinary grains, nuts, and fruits—including coffee.

In working to make some of the grain foods more appetizing-looking and better-tasting, W. K. Kellogg had hit upon a way to "flake" hearts of wheat, and later, hearts of corn.

In 1906, W. K. Kellogg decided to devote the greater part of his time and effort to his new firm, the "Sanitas Toasted Corn Flakes Company." A firm believer in the principle that if people tried a good product they would keep on buying it, W. K. Kellogg distributed four million sample boxes of Toasted Corn Flakes the first year.

By the end of 1906, its first year, the amount spent for advertising totaled $90,000, almost three times as much as the young company's initial working capital.

(It is interesting to note that within two years after Toasted Corn Flakes was introduced, there were 44 companies in Battle Creek imitating the product with their own versions. There was, in fact, an Indiana company that put on the market [it didn't stay there long!] a product called "Battle Creek Corn Flakes.")

Because there were so many imitations W. K. Kellogg soon decided to feature his signature on each package and in the advertising—even though personal modesty argued against it.

Thus the line "The package of the genuine bears this signature—W. K. Kellogg" became an important property of the company and contributed to its leadership.

However, though W. K. Kellogg never considered himself a merchandising expert, his basic sales premise included these three major basics:

1. That Toasted Corn Flakes should be sold as a delicious breakfast food rather than as a health food.
2. That it would "win its favor through its flavor."
3. That the W. K. Kellogg signature on every package would mark the genuine and original.
   —in making a good product and constantly trying to make it better.
   —in sampling it as broadly as possible.
   —in advertising extensively and intensively.
   —and in the principles of repetition and continuity in the advertising copy.

He believed in advertising broadly because, as he said, "Wherever you find people you'll find Kellogg's."

Early test market example

One of the food industry's earliest test market efforts can be credited to Kellogg's Toasted Corn Flakes.

The company bought $150 worth of newspaper advertising in Canton, Ohio.

It also had built an eight-foot, papier-mâché ear of corn and hired a man to get inside it and walk Canton streets.

On the strength of this test, the company "went national" (or relatively so) with that local campaign.

During the night before July 4, 1907, Mr. Kellogg was awakened with the report that his factory was burning.

He hurried to it. The ramshackle frame structure was a mass of flames—practically a total loss.

Before the day of July 4th was over, however, he had an architect over from Chicago starting work on plans for a new factory.

By the time of the fire, not 18 months since it was organized, the company had spent approximately $300,000 in advertising.

With production completely halted by the July 4 blaze, the natural question in top minds of the company was, "Would that advertising expenditure be a total loss?"

Here is what Arch Shaw, company adviser, director, and major stockholder, wrote to Mr. Kellogg: "The fire is of no consequence. You can't burn down what we have registered in the minds of the American women."

Within a few weeks, the boxes of Kellogg's Toasted Corn Flakes were rolling out of a new, more modern—and more fireproof—Kellogg factory! For nearly five years, Toasted Corn Flakes was Kellogg's one product.

In 1912, Shredded Wheat and Krumbles were added.

In 1919, All-Bran came into the line.

In 1922 the corporate name was changed to the Kellogg Company.

In 1927, the experimental lab brought to W. K. Kellogg two packages of a rather different-looking cereal.

He put sugar and milk on it, tasted it, and said, "You've got something there!" (That something was Rice Krispies, which were first marketed in 1928.)

In the early 1930's the depression hit.

It will be remembered that after the market crash of 1929 pessimism stalked the land. Wall Street brokers jumped from tall buildings; apple sellers cluttered the street corners.

"Blues" theme song of the times was "Run for cover. The dam has broken."

W. K. Kellogg was not restrained by the prevailing fear. Instead he told his executives, "Double our advertising budget! This is the time to go out and spend more money in advertising."

As Horace B. Powell, of the W. K. Kellogg Foundation, reports it: "Sales continued to accelerate, affected scarcely, if at all, by the Depression."

By 1940, the Kellogg Company had spent $100 million in advertising. The Burnett advertising agency began working with Kellogg in the late 1940s. Burnett's first assignment from Kellogg in 1949 was on a product named Corn Soya. Unfortunately, the public never would learn how good a product it was; so after a matter of time, it quietly disappeared.

However, Corn Soya made one big contribution; it got the agency acquainted with the Kellogg people in Battle Creek.

And Kellogg awarded Burnett the other products in the line which meant that it was in major league television almost overnight—for Kellogg was one of the pioneers in that medium as it earlier had been in radio.

Let's look at the record

Since the early 1950's Kellogg has been a major user of both spot and network TV.

It is interesting to make a quick survey of some of the shows Burnett has worked on for Kellogg from the time it started working with them.

The first effort was Colonel Tim McCoy headin' up a rootin', tootin' Western on local TV in California for Kellogg's Corn Soya, NBC's "All-Star Revue," on which the top star was most frequently Jimmy Durante.

Then there was "Space Cadet," the mythical Project Mercury of the early fifties for kids to watch and live, three afternoons a week on the now defunct DuMont TV network.

"Mark Trail," adapted from the comic strip, was a radio show that Kellogg was sponsoring then, too.

The first national property for Kellogg was "Howdy Doody," on NBC-TV. Then late in the fifties Kellogg pioneered a really new concept in TV: its syndication system, later called the Kellogg spotwork.

The big cereal company bought, financed, and produced an entire show, "Wild Bill Hickok."

An agency TV producer was sent out to Hollywood to supervise film production for both client and Burnett, and also to write and produce some of TV's earliest "integrated commercials." (These commercials used Guy Madison and Andy Devine, stars of the show, to sell the product, usually in settings related to the show story line.)

"Wild Bill Hickok" was the show that introduced Sugar Pops, Kellogg's first entry in the new presweet cereal field.

Kellogg commercials were spliced into the prints and shipped directly to the stations from the agency. Some stations refused to rerun the first 13 episodes right away. So hour-long features were bought on the open market, a print at a time, a subject at a time, cutting them down to 26 minutes, slapping in Sugar Pops, Rice Krispies, and Corn Flakes commercials, and racing them off to the stubborn stations.

"Superman" had been a Kellogg radio show, with Bud Collyer in the title role, in the thirties. Burnett brought it to TV for the introduction of Kellogg's Sugar Frosted Flakes . . . and the same shows relinquished by Kellogg are still running, 14 years later, on stations all over the country—and still getting good ratings, too.

"Super Circus" was a Chicago institution starring another Chicago institution, blonde Mary Hartline. It had Mary and Cliffy the Clown, and Scampy, and ringmaster Claude Kirschner. An hour of wild and square confusion from the Civic Theatre every Sunday afternoon.

Arthur Godfrey and Art Linkletter were Kellogg salesmen on their own TV shows, Art on "House Party," Arthur on his own "Arthur and His Friends."

Col. John Glenn was a very successful contestant on "Name That Tune" during Kellogg's cosponsorship.

In the late fifties the company bought into "What's My Line?" and stayed with it until late in 1965. It did the same with the "Garry Moore Show," a long and successful five-day-a-week strip on CBS. Both were long and happy associations.

Some shows hard to remember. There are some vehicles that are difficult to remember: "Hotel de Paree," "The Buccaneers," "The Deputy."

Then suddenly there was the Hanna-Barbera explosion of animated miracles: "Huckleberry Hound" and "Yogi Bear" and "Quick Draw Mc-Graw."

"Woody Woodpecker" also contributed his animated art to Rice Krispies. Then the company moved along to a delightful live-action film series based on the "Dennis the Menace" newspaper cartoon. "Captain Kangaroo" began helping out with the preschool moppets, the company bought "Beverly Hillbillies" in the pilot stage; "My Favorite Martian" replaced Dennis, and "McHale's Navy" came in 1965.

Flashback: start and growth

While Kellogg Company has been the leader of the ready-to-eat cereal manufacturers from the outset, it was not until about 1959 that Kellogg's share of market became greater than that of the combined shares of its two leading competitors, General Foods and General Mills.

It should be noted that the development by Mr. Kellogg of Corn Flakes started one of the greatest business revolutions in history: *the mass marketing of packaged food.* Until this happened, people generally bought their food items in bulk: barrels of flour and sugar, sacks of grain, wheels of cheese.

Getting people to buy a cardboard box, filled with light and airy delicate-looking corn flakes, was no easy task, and Mr. Kellogg finally, in desperation, invested the last dollar of his capital in national magazine advertising.

At the present time Kellogg Company and its subsidiary companies employ more than 10,000 men and women to produce and promote Kellogg products. It has 23 plants in 16 countries and a promising market for its product line in more than 150 countries. The packages are printed in many colors and many languages. Corn Flake cartons, for example, appear in twelve languages.

Since cereals are generally eaten by the spoonful, it is hard to visualize how many families would be required to consume one billion pounds of cereal, which is about what Kellogg produces annually. Most of its products are consumed as breakfast food or as snacks and many of them are used as ingredients in the preparation of other food.

While its share of the ready-to-eat cereal market varies from country to country, it is estimated that the company produces nearly half of the cereals sold in world markets.

According to market research, about 60 brands of ready-to-eat cereal are now being marketed in the United States. In many cases, these products are sold in packages of various sizes designed to give consumers the cereal they prefer in the quantities they find most convenient.

The average family consuming cereal in the United States has about three different packages of cereal on the kitchen shelf most of the time.

Every year a score of new products joins the parade from the plant to the grocery shelf. This makes the cereal business a highly competitive one, not only in this country, but in all countries where such products are sold.

The fact that ever changing preferences on the part of consumers can motivate the sale of a variety of cereals is one of the chief reasons why the industry has prospered. During the last 10 years, the annual per capita consumption of all ready-to-eat cereals has increased from 4.8 to 6.1 pounds in the United States. Comparable increases are on record in Canada, Great Britain, Australia, and many other countries. Australia is the one with the highest per capita consumption.

Generally speaking, the rate of demand for Kellogg's cereals has increased nearly twice as fast as the population in all countries where it does business.

For over 65 years Kellogg has been trying to convey to the public what it thinks is important about the nutrition, taste appeal, and convenience of its products. In its advertising, it tries to reach the younger children and teen-agers, as well as adults.

Marketing research shows that children and teen-agers consume about 50 percent of all the ready-to-eat cereal that is sold. Communicating the right sales messages to all age groups year after year with fresh impact is an absorbing task. Much depends upon the coordination of all aspects of promotion and distribution. Its advertising has to do what it is supposed to do quickly, effectively, and with great frequency.

Advertising and promotion of Kellogg products

A packaged food business such as Kellogg Company depends on a completely integrated process of manufacturing, distributing, and selling of low unit-cost products to millions of people every day.

In such a business, the key to volume manufacture (and hence to low-cost manufacture) is to keep the stream of goods moving off the grocers' shelves and into the hands of the consumers every day of the year. The decision to buy, or not to buy, Kellogg products is made millions of times each day by millions of people in thousands of stores. To maintain the constant high volume and low unit-cost it is necessary to continually remind consumers to buy Kellogg products and the principal means for keeping the Kellogg name in the mind of the consumer is advertising. This is especially true in the case of an institution such as Kellogg Company which distributes its products across the entire country.

From the beginning, Kellogg Company has advertised and promoted the sale of its cereal products through many advertising media. Mr. Kellogg recognized the importance of advertising and promoting and among his early promotions was the use of his signature on the package to indicate a guarantee of quality. Today consumers are constantly exposed to Kellogg products through newspaper, magazine, television and other forms of advertising.

Product lines

Kellogg Company and its subsidiaries produce a variety of products on an international basis in keeping with the local customs. The following products are marketed by Kellogg Company in the United States on a nationwide scale:

Corn Flakes	Special K	Variety
Pep	Froot Loops	Corn Flake Crumbs
Krumbles	Product 19	Bag and Bake
Rice Krispies	Puffed Wheat	Croutettes
40% Bran Flakes	Puffed Rice	Pop-Tarts
Raisin Bran	Concentrate	Danish Go-Rounds
Sugar Pops	Puffa Puffa Rice	Salad Mixes
Cocoa Krispies	Apple Jacks	Assorted Individuals
Sugar Smacks	Handi-Pak	Self-Serve Bowl
Bran Buds	Jumbo	Packages
All-Bran	Request Pak	Frosted Mini-Wheats
Sugar Frosted Flakes	Snack-Pak	

Case questions

1. How important do you believe the use of advertising was in the growth of the Kellogg Company? Give reasons.

2. Three companies, Kellogg, General Mills, and General Foods, account for four fifths of the cold cereal market. To what extent do you believe that the use of advertising has precluded other firms from entering the industry?

3. In a recent year, advertising expenditures were estimated to be 12.6 percent of the total sales of all products for Kellogg, 9.3 percent for General Mills, and 8.7 percent for General Foods. Comment.

chapter 2

CONSUMERISM

$\mathbf{C}$ONSUMERISM is rapidly becoming one of the more important issues confronting management. It has taken the form of the "consumer movement," a loose grouping together of various people and organizations to bring about a greater degree of protection for the consumer—who is unorganized, often ill-informed, and frequently without purpose or direction. Much of the agitation has been directly for legislation on behalf of the consumer.

Because the purpose of production is consumption, it is the consumer and the consumer's welfare which constitute the ultimate "good" in marketing. On the other hand, in our free-enterprise capitalistic economy, the hope of profit motivates the business executive. Many people are convinced that these two objectives set up a conflict—that the businessman, motivated by the prospect of profit, will fail to protect the interest of the consumer.

Background concepts

Although some individuals are prone to think of consumerism as basically a phenomenon of recent origin, careful study of all available sources indicates that the origins of consumerism are lost in the dim past, as is true of so many facets of modern life. But it is undoubtedly safe to assume that some type of consumerism has existed as long as one man decided to "sell" one idea or product to another. However, the term "consumerism" is associated primarily with the last decade.

Such literature as *The Affluent Society, The Waste Makers,* and *The Hidden Persuaders* contributed to the popularization of the concept. Also on March 15, 1962, President John F. Kennedy sent Congress a message asking for the strengthening of programs for the protection of consumer interests. The President stated that the consumer had four rights as such: the right to safety, the right to be informed, the right to choose, and the right to be heard. He proposed increasing the staff of the Food and Drug Administration to provide greater protection from, as the President put it, thousands of harmful substances now contained in common household items. The Federal Trade Commission, he hoped, would have its duties enlarged to allow it to protect the consumer from unjust and concealed interest rates on small loans and on time payments. Attention should also be given to packaging, and to the enforcement of regulations to prevent misleading packages. Various steps were suggested but not outlined in any detail.

Important among the proposals was one which did not require legislative sanction: the appointment of a Consumers' Advisory Council. The Council was appointed in July 1962. It was to report to the President's Council of Economic Advisors. Its duties were to examine and advise on issues of broad economic policy, on governmental programs protecting consumer needs, and on needed improvements in the flow of consumer research material to the public.

Although no specific directions were given to the Council, the members developed projects and procedures which they believed allowed the Council to be of maximum importance.

The work of the Council, during the ensuing years, has been reinforced by the dedicated efforts of Ralph Nader, interested legislators, and other leading writers and individuals who have kept the surge of publicity about auto safety, product ingredients, and various consumer problems in the forefront. As a result it would appear that consumerism will influence corporate activity to an even greater degree in the years ahead.

Protection of consumer

It would be naive to assume all businessmen are altruistic and virtuous. Much of the legislation which protects the consumer from adulterated and harmful products has been important to our public interest. The pure food and drug legislation, both national and state, has afforded protection in areas in which the consumer is particularly defenseless, and in which a small number of unscrupulous firms can cause great damage. Other legislation, such as the Wool Products Labeling Act, gives the consumer protection that he cannot himself provide, however vigilant and discriminating he may be. The ethical businessmen generally welcome such legislation, not only because it does afford the protection that the consumer needs, but also because it curbs unfair practices of competitors.

There are those, however, who believe that the consumer not only needs protection from the ills which he cannot determine or foresee, but also that he needs guidance in getting his money's worth. Implicit in this "Lo, the poor consumer" train of thought is the feeling the consumer is victimized by advertising and sales promotion and is, therefore, cajoled into buying more than he needs, into buying goods that merely pander to his whims, and into buying merchandise that is poor in quality and that is in poor taste.

Variations in demand

In considering consumerism, we should be particularly careful to avoid attempting to project our own value-judgments into criteria for the guidance of others. Some families prefer to live in low cost housing in order to be able to drive expensive automobiles. Some individuals prefer to take a trip to Europe instead of maintaining insurance programs. Some people prefer playing golf to attending a football game. But each person has made a free choice of those gratifications which please him the most. The concept of "plain living and high thinking" is preeminently suitable for those who are attracted to it, but is not to be forced on others. It is impossible to designate one person's consumption pattern as foolish and another's as sensible.

Each individual must draw up his own calculus of values which may weigh pride and pleasure more heavily than frugality. As a result, any attempt to guide the consumer in getting his money's worth should curtail any attempt to project someone else's set of values.

General considerations

Although, as pointed out above, the consumer occupies the central position in the economic system, he has not always received the attention to which he is entitled. Our government has been slow to provide him with the protection which the economic system failed to afford him. Businessmen often have put more emphasis upon short-term rather than upon long-run results. When legislators show an interest in the consumer, they usually approach it on an individual basis. Consequently, the consumer's position in the economic system tends to be weak. Among the causes of this weakness are such ones as:

1. It is difficult for the consumer to judge the quality of the products in the market.
2. The information about the products that is offered may be misleading and confusing.
3. The number of brands of the various items complicates his selection to an even greater degree.
4. Some sellers suppress pertinent information about their products.
5. Conflicting claims about products add to the confusion.
6. There is a tendency for some sellers to try to get the consumer to

purchase on the basis of emotion rather than on the use of factual data.

7. The consumer ends up by paying for a major share of the wastes involved in marketing.

8. Due to insufficient knowledge of consumer behavior, an accurate blueprint for defining products in terms of consumer choice is not available.

9. The consumer lacks the education and knowledge to judge what is the best buy.

10. It is too complex for the average consumer to evaluate the myriad conflicting claims of competing manufacturers.

Although the above list of criticisms is by no means complete, it includes a number of those which have been instrumental in spearheading "consumerism."

Outlook for legislation

Consumerism has never taken on a definite form of organization. It has involved the activities (largely uncoordinated) of a diverse group of individuals, associations and organizations. As a result, the goals toward which it may be moving are still ill-defined and uncertain. Before considering some of these goals, we would like to point out a few examples of some of the recent developments.

The Federal Trade Commission is moving quickly to initiate new regulatory proposals protecting consumers. At the same time some pre-existing FTC powers are being reactivated to provide fast relief and eliminate dangerous abuses.

The extent of these innovative regulations concerns all business. For example:

1. In an action against a California-based enfranchiser of a hair-replacement system the FTC is requesting an injunction, a remedy it has not used for the past ten years. The complaint charges the company with false advertising claims, failure to disclose possible medical risks and use of "high pressure" sales techniques. An FTC spokesman indicates that use of injunctions will increase, especially where health and medical dangers to the public might exist. One reason for the revived use of the injunction is that, unlike consent or cease-and-desist orders, there is no long delay while the administrative order is appealed through the courts. The protection given to the consumer is more immediate.

2. In another action, the FTC proposed that detergents carry warnings in advertising and on their labels (similar to cigarette package warnings). The warnings concern water pollution and would declare the quantity of "harmful" phosphorus in a given level of the product.

3. Another FTC proposal is aimed at getting new car list prices to reflect actual selling prices. It would require that "sticker" prices be no more than 3 percent higher than the lowest price at which most dealers' sales are made. Auto dealers and industry leaders oppose the regulation as an unworkable approach to the situation. They claim most consumers understand the list price is simply a starting point and also some cars must be sold at higher-than-average prices.

4. Cancellation of door-to-door sales is the subject of other regulation. It allows a three-day cooling-off period in which a buyer of goods or services worth $10 or more could cancel the purchase.

5. Greater protection of consumers who sign promissory notes in installment sales is the aim of another far-reaching FTC rule. If it becomes effective it would preserve buyers' claims and defenses in installment sales by (a) making any subsequent holder of a promissory note subject to defenses the buyer has against original seller, (b) barring agreements in which buyer consents to waive rights or remedies he may have, and (c) banning agreements by which buyer is prevented from making a claim or defense arising out of sale. The provisions would eliminate the traditional collection devices, used by sellers, known as "confessions of judgment" and "wage assignments."

6. The new credit card law went into effect January 25, 1971. It imposes limits on cardholders' liability and affects the way business by credit cards will be transacted. This law could affect the way credit card issuers, holders, retail stores, and others will do business. First, issuers will need a system which enables the retailer to establish quickly and efficiently the identity of a cardholder. Result could be more of the expense for losses being shouldered by retailers who have burden of ascertaining true ownership of cards. Some issuers may find the cost of complying with the regulations and sending notices to cardholders is not worth the cost when compared to possible losses. Of course the use of insurance protection will continue to be used by issuers as the best and safest way to guard against these "bad-card" losses.

7. In the first suit of its kind, the Attorney General of New York state has sued two of the largest soap manufacturers in the country. *Reason:* The manufacturers have failed to publish on the label of their products the amount of trisodium phosphate in the washing compound.

New Law—A New York State law, effective January 1, 1971, requires all detergent products to indicate on their labels the percentage of phosphate in the product. This is to let the consumer make a knowlegeable choice about whether he wants to use a potentially ecologically harmful soap product.

8. A company cannot contact or threaten to contact a debtor's employer in its effort to collect from the debtor, unless it first gets a judgment against him. That's the meaning of a New York State Supreme Court justice's decision, upholding New York City's regulation banning certain debt collection methods as unconscionable trade practices. The Court said harassment of debtors and loss or threat of loss of employment should be stopped.

9. Users of consumer credit reports (e.g., employers, insurance companies, retailers, banks, licensing agencies) now have legal responsibilities to the consumer. That's the impact of the Federal Fair Credit Reporting Act which went into effect April 25, 1971.

A company *must notify* anyone turned down for employment, insurance or credit because of an adverse report. It must (a) give the name and address of the credit bureau or consumer reporting agency making the report, and (b) tell the consumer of his right to request the specific information used.

10. The rights of financers holding consumer installment paper—already restricted by law in several states—may now be restricted nationwide.

Purchasers of such paper have usually been considered "holders in due course"—with good title, and no responsibility for seeing that the conditions of a sale were carried out. Now the Federal Trade Commission has just come up with this new Trade Regulation Rule that would take away an important right from purchasers of consumer paper—their immunity from certain "defenses" and claims made by buyers against sellers.

The rule would require the face of any note drawn up by a retailer to contain a statement in ten-point boldface type. This would declare that any third party buying the note is subject to legitimate claims the consumer has which result from the original transaction. The rule would also forbid any agreement whereby the consumer waives any legal rights he has to make such claims. Finally, it would prevent a buyer from agreeing not to assert claims or defenses against the seller or subsequent assignee of the note.

11. It is now illegal for a person to send unsolicited merchandise through the mails; and if he does, he not only will lose the products, but may also face heavy fines.

New postal reorganization act—The Federal Trade Commission will enforce the new law passed in 1970. It labels as an unfair practice the sending of unordered merchandise through the mails—with two exceptions: (a) free samples which are *clearly* and plainly *marked* as such, and (b) merchandise by a charitable organization asking for contributions.

12. If manufacturers, either by themselves or through their dealers and trade associations, do not take action to control warranty coverage and administration, there is strong likelihood that laws may be passed under which the various affected industries will find it hard to operate.

13. A company that manufactures drugs that doctors can prescribe will come under a new regulation of the Food and Drug Administration. The regulation requires that any drug judged less than effective by the National Academy of Sciences contain the NAS findings in its advertising.

14. Any employer, retailer, or creditor who uses consumer reports in any way is now affected by the Fair Credit Reporting Act. The Act imposes many new restrictions on all uses of such reports. One may be under a duty to tell applicants for jobs, credit, or insurance that he used a report and where he got it.

One must disclose to the consumer the fact that an investigative report is being made. Disclosure must be made not later than three days after the date on which one requested this report. Such advance notice is required if report concerns credit or employment for which the subject has applied.

The list above is not all-inclusive, but it shows the demand that is growing in Congress for government to (1) take a stronger stand protecting consumers from potentially hazardous products and (2) set tougher product-testing and standard-setting procedures. For business—manufacturers, distributors, retailers—government action in these areas will have decided impact on operations.

Recent disclosures by government agencies stating that various commonly used materials could produce serious health and environmental problems for users has prompted a flurry of activity in Congress to increase consumer protection. Legislation creating a government agency to regulate manufacturing and design of potentially hazardous goods—from kids' toys to chemical content of detergents—has been introduced. Supporters argue that existing federal agencies charged with protecting consumers from safety and health hazards are not doing a proper job. Product testing is also gaining popularity in Congress. Under such a procedure, prospective purchasers would know at a glance how a product performed and whether it would meet consumers' needs, because manufacturers using government test methods could print results of the test on a tag attached to the product. Similar systems, nicknamed "tell-tags" are in wide use in Great Britain.

Automobile and consumerism

The automobile is also a factor in the consumerism movement. The consumer no longer concerns himself merely with the immediate safety of the automobile, as in the days of Ralph Nader's "Unsafe at Any Speed," but is now also acutely aware of the potential danger which it may contribute to the environment.

Statistics indicate that the automobile produces 60 percent of all pollution and as much as 90 percent in some cities. Some critics of the automobile industry have claimed that auto emissions programs come close to being fraudulent. They mislead Americans into thinking that something is being done when in fact air pollution from automobiles is getting worse every day. Industry spokesmen counter by claiming that the effects of present controls are only beginning to be felt, and that no solution will be reached until older, uncontrolled automobiles are eventually phased out of use.

The industry sees profit making as a necessary industry goal. The consumer, on the other hand, believes that the industry can still make an adequate profit and, at the same time, solve the problem of pollution. This division in thought tends to create a conflict which often results in the consumer demanding from legislative bodies greater levels of control.

As an example of this, in 1970 the federal government informed the automobile industry that a continued clean-up of emissions must be established, and the Administration's Council on Environmental Quality set 1975 as a deadline by which it wanted to see working prototypes of two alternatives to the internal combustion engine. Based on this action,

Dr. DuBridge, Science Advisor to President Nixon, concluded, "Automobile pollution will decline steadily over the coming years."

Yet, because many of the consumers did not believe that satisfactory results would be attained by this order, pressure was placed on Congress and it passed a law requiring an essentially pollution-free automobile by 1975—a regulation which industry representatives claim will prove technologically unfeasible. The importance of this consumer pressure was pointed out by William Gosset, a former president of the American Bar Association, when he stated, "Private industry policy making and decision making that affects consumers is ultimately controlled in one way or another by the pressures that formulate public policy and inspire public decisions."

At the same time, as long as the industry also lacks a high degree of credibility with consumers, its actions may be misunderstood and misinterpreted. To improve consumer-industry trust, the automobile industry should, therefore, continue not only to work on solutions of environmental problems which concern the consumer, but just as importantly, to extend the policy of making the consumer more aware of the positive contributions that it is making.

Complexity of controls

What type of controls should be used and who should be responsible for these controls are only two of the complex questions that are involved in the solutions to the problems of consumerism. Indicative of this are the type of recommendations now being brought up concerning the Federal Trade Commission.

In a 1971 report submitted to President Nixon by the President's Advisory Council on Executive Organization the recommendation was made that the Federal Trade Commission be abolished. The Council further recommended that its currently combined responsibilities of consumer protection and antitrust enforcement be vested in two separate agencies.

The proposal suggested that the consumer protection responsibilities of the Federal Trade Commission be replaced with a new Federal Trade Practices Agency and the FTC antitrust activities be transferred to a new Federal Antitrust Agency.

The major reasons for dividing the responsibilities, according to the council were:

1. Antitrust cases are much longer and much more complex than consumer protection cases.
2. Antitrust cases are best served by a case-by-case approach; consumer protection problems would be better solved by more general rules and regulations.

3. Antitrust cases frequently require decisions which result in changes in industry structure, while consumer protection violations require less consequential sanctions.
4. Monitoring antitrust activity can best be performed in a centralized agency, yet consumer protection should be conducted on a regional approach.

According to the plan, judgment of consumer protection suits would be continued along lines similar to those used by the Federal Trade Commission. However, some of the responsibilities currently administered by other government agencies, such as the Department of Agriculture, the Department of Commerce, and the Food and Drug Administration, could ultimately be placed under the jurisdiction of the new agency. New consumer legislation would also be administered by the Federal Trade Practices Agency.

Future of consumerism

Consumerism is here to stay. Tomorrow's consumer will be better educated, more affluent, and more critical. He will probably be less concerned with status symbols and more anxious to get information about the product. He will expect management to accept greater social responsibilities even if this results in a decrease in short-run profits. For managements who fail to measure up to the desired standards, there will be increased government regulations, consumer boycotts, and employee dissensions.

Nevertheless, the authors wish to emphasize that there is no immutability about taste. Freedom of consumer choice is more important socially and economically than is conformity to one set of criteria. What is waste for one consumer may be wisdom for another.

We live in a competitive economy. Business prospers as it offers consumers what they want. So long as consumer protection is confined to shielding the consumer from dangers that he himself cannot foresee or avoid, and to the enforcement of contracts, and the curtailment of fraud and deception, there is greater merit in allowing competition to enforce the meeting of the consumers' wishes with respect to variety, quantity and quality of goods and services.

It is the opinion of the authors that through the mass production and mass distribution methods the average American consumer has been able to secure a great variety of products. Nevertheless, because of these techniques, it is inevitable that the inherent dangers involved in large-scale production and distribution processes may result in defective products, and misleading marketing strategies.

Therefore, the authors recommend that:

1. More effective quality control procedures be established by manufacturers.
2. Improved communication methods be developed at all marketing levels.
3. Pricing strategy be set on an objective unit basis to allow the consumer to make more realistic comparisons.
4. Manufacturers take the initiative in setting standards for safety, service, and certification.
5. Better procedures be instituted whereby customer-seller-manufacturer complaints can be handled.
6. Warranties for products be simplified and the distribution link closest to the consumer be given greater autonomy in rendering the service on these warranties.
7. Business organizations support policies and programs aimed at giving consumers more information and protection.
8. The marketing and advertising strategies be reevaluated in order to mirror more effectively the evolving social and ethical norms of the younger generation.
9. Business make a greater effort to prognosticate the social problems of the consumer.
10. Finally, the credibility of business in the eyes of the consumers be reenforced.

QUESTIONS

1. U.S. Public Health Service has estimated that in 1948 the average American threw away only two pounds of trash a day, but at present he discards over five pounds—and the population has increased by over 30 percent in the same period. The waste ranges from orange peels and beer cans to junked appliances and abandoned autos. The Automobile Manufacturers' Association indicates that, nationwide over six million cars and 900,000 trucks are junked each year. Comment on what advertising executives can do to help resolve this problem.

2. Farm crops from citrus to cereals are annually dusted with about one billion pounds of pesticides. Such massive spraying effects the environment and human health. An estimated 75,000 acute pesticide poisonings occur each year. What can business do, through advertising, to get more judicious spraying?

3. List some marketing and advertising changes that are occurring and are likely to occur as a result of consumerism.

4. Which buying motives should be emphasized because of the increased consumerism movement?

5. For which of the following products and/or services would consumerism movements have greater impact? Give reasons.

a) Furniture
b) Baby food
c) Lamps
d) Short term loans
e) Drugs

f) Women's shoes
g) Men's shirts
h) Hospital services
i) Dishes
j) Television sets

6. The state by protecting and enforcing competition will protect the interests of consumers. Discuss.

7. Who should be responsible for setting the standards for consumer goods?

8. Do you believe that the consumer movement will become a highly organized homogeneous course of action? Why? Why not?

9. Is it economical and socially sound to grant a manufacturer the privilege of using a brand name to differentiate his product from those of other manufacturers when in all other characteristics the products are identical?

10. Do you believe Congress should extend its jurisdiction to cover all clothing products under the Flammable Fabric Act which now makes sure that dangerous clothing is removed from the market?

11. It has been stated: "The consumer is king. What he wants, business will find it profitable to satisfy his demand." Comment.

12. Should legislation in protecting the consumer be directed primarily to regulating marketing and advertising? Discuss.

CASE 1. ASPIRIN ADS
Analyzing regulations

The Federal Trade Commission moved to halt deceptive advertising claims over which aspirin is better or faster. It said they were all about the same. Under proposed tough new rules covering advertising for non-prescription painkillers, the FTC could prosecute manufacturers who continued to make unfounded claims. The rules would require proof of significant differences to back advertising superiority and force manufacturers of "combination of ingredients" drugs to identify what is in them by their common names.

These products are known as analgesics, of which aspirin is the most common. Americans gulped $450 million worth of them during 1966. During that time, manufacturers spent more than $90 million advertising which is faster, lasts longer, or upsets the stomach less.

The FTC has known for at least seven years that its investigations cast doubt on the propriety of such advertising, tending to refute the various claims. But in proposing its new standards, the commission went much further. "It appears that each of the various analgesic products now offered to the consuming public is effective to essentially the same degree as all other products supplying an equivalent quantity of an analgesic ingredient or combination of ingredients," the FTC said.

It listed what it called unfair and deceptive practices being used by makers of these over-the-counter preparations:

1. Making effectiveness or safety claims which contradict or exceed directions for use given on labels.
2. Making false claims of comparative speed, strength, and duration of relief when actually the products are essentially the same.
3. Attributing beneficial effects to specified ingredients without substantiation or without identifying them by their common or usual names.

The FTC did not single out any companies in its report of deceptive advertising, but it now has cases pending against the manufacturers of four of the most widely known analgesics. They are Bristol-Myers Co., makers of Bufferin; American Home Products Co., producers of Anacin; Plough, Inc., manufacturers of St. Joseph's aspirin; and Sterling Drug Inc., makers of Bayer Aspirin.

James D. Cope, a spokesman for the proprietary association which represents over-the-counter manufacturers, said "The proposal will be given close study." He indicated the FTC rule would dovetail neatly with the association's own advertising code. Cope acknowledged that the code, revised last year, had not won wholesale endorsement by the industry. He also said that the association has only a few weak sanctions to force compliance.

The FTC rule proposal would work in concert with the Food and Drug Administration's drive to police the pills which are standard items in American homes.

The FDA also proposed a rule that would crack down on drugmakers in nearly the same fashion, except that the FDA rule is aimed at information on drug labels. FDA has truth-in-labeling responsibilities, while the FTC has the authority to move against users of deceptive advertising.

Case questions

1. Assuming that the companies realize that there are no significant differences in the various aspirin products, would it be ethical for them to continue to use the same appeals for their products? Why? Why not?

2. Would you set the same requirements for other industries, such as the paint industry, in which there is little major product differentiation?

CASE 2.   CHESHIRE COMPANY
Considering regulations

Cheshire Company in recent years has expanded its business to include, besides the manufacture and sale of cigarettes, cigars and smoking tobacco, a distilling operation, and a snack food products business. As the Cheshire products were distributed in over two million outlets in the United States, it was necessary for the company to use extensive broadcast promotion to attain customer acceptance. The executives were concerned with the regulations which required the substantiation of advertising appeals.

Tobacco products

Cheshire's domestic tobacco business includes cigarettes, smoking tobaccos, and cigars. About 95 percent of Cheshire's net sales of tobacco products consists of filter and nonfilter cigarettes. In recent years Cheshire's total unit sales of cigarettes have been declining, while total unit sales for the tobacco industry were relatively stable, although declining slightly. For several years up to 1968, industry sales of filter cigarettes grew rapidly, although this rate of growth has since leveled off. Cheshire's unit sales of filter cigarettes in 1968 represented only 11 percent of its total cigarette sales. At that time substantially increased emphasis was placed on the marketing of filter cigarettes, and by 1971 Cheshire had increased its unit sales of filter cigarettes to 58 percent of total sales. Its increased sales of filter cigarettes, however, have not been sufficient to offset the continuing decline in unit sales of nonfilter cigarettes, and even such increases in filter sales have leveled off in recent years.

Cheshire sells its cigarettes primarily in the U.S. market through distributors and directly to chain stores and other large retail outlets. The market for cigarettes is highly competitive, and all companies advertise their cigarettes on an extensive basis.

The Federal excise tax on cigarettes is 8 cents per package of 20 cigarettes. In addition, the District of Columbia and the 50 states had cigarette taxes ranging from 2 to 18 cents per package of 20. There were also about 260 municipalities and counties collecting cigarette taxes ranging from 1 to 7 cents per package.

Tobacco is an agricultural commodity subject to U.S. Government controls. In the ten years ended in 1969 the average market price per pound of flue-cured tobacco increased from 60.4 cents to 72.2 cents or 20 percent. From 1960 through 1968 the average market price per pound of Burley leaf increased from 64.3 cents to 73.7 cents or 15 percent. The average market price per pound of Burley leaf in 1969 was 69.7 cents. The decrease in price in 1969 was attributed to a poor crop year for Burley leaf.

The Federal Cigarette Labeling and Advertising Act, effective January 1, 1966, required that packages of cigarettes distributed in the United States bear the statement: "Caution: Cigarette Smoking May Be Hazardous to Your Health." A subsequent amendment, the Public Health Cigarette Smoking Act of 1969, requires that packages of cigarettes distributed in the United States bear the statement: "Warning: The Surgeon General Has Determined That Cigarette Smoking Is Dangerous to Your Health," and prohibits any other requirement of a statement relating to smoking and health on any cigarette package. The amended statute also prohibits radio and television advertising of cigarettes, and requires annual reports to the United States Congress from the Secretary of Health, Education and Welfare and from the Federal Trade Commission on the lethal consequences of smoking, cigarette labeling, advertising and promotion, and recommendations for further legislation.

Distilling operations

Cheshire owns and operates three plants with combined distilling capacity of 45,000 proof gallons of Bourbon whiskey per day, and bottling capacity of 17,000 cases of fifths per eight-hour shift, U.S. bonded warehouses with storage capacity of 900,000 barrels of whiskey and two water reservoirs with 150,000,000 gallons total capacity. Cheshire sells its products through various distributors and state liquor authorities. The market for the products is highly competitive.

Food products

Cheshire also manufactures and sells crackers, cookies, and snack goods. Sales are made through distributors and directly to retail outlets, hotels, restaurants, schools, and similar customers. The market for all of these products is highly competitive.

FTC regulations

The Federal Trade Commission informed the advertising business that in its capacity as a "data book" it would demand detailed documentation for advertising claims related to safety, performance, efficiency, quality, or price. The reasons for the decision were as follows:

1. Public disclosure can assist consumers in making a rational choice among competing claims which purport to be based on objective evidence and in evaluating the weight to be accorded to such claims.
2. The public's need for this information is not being met voluntarily by advertisers.
3. Public disclosure can enhance competition by encouraging competitors to challenge advertising claims which have no basis in fact.
4. The knowledge that documentation or the lack thereof will be made public will encourage advertisers to have on hand adequate substantiation before claims are made.

5. The commission has limited resources for detecting claims which are not substantiated by adequate proof. By making documentation submitted in response to this resolution available to the public, the commission can be alerted by consumers, businessmen, and public interest groups to possible violations of Section 5 of the Federal Trade Commission Act.

Appeals used by a number of companies

Some of the broad appeals which the Cheshire Company executives decided to evaluate are listed below:

1. *Anti-perspirant:* "This will roll on more protection than you can spray on."
2. *Tire company:* "You get the *best* combination of advantages—traction, strength, and mileage. They all add up to the *best* value."
3. *Aluminum wrap:* "There is no wrap which will compare to ours because it is oven-tempered for flexible strength."
4. *Household cleanser:* "Wipes out household germs in 15 seconds."
5. *Cereal:* "The leading high nutrition cereal."
6. *Cigarette company:* "America's favorite cigarette break."
7. *Cigarette company:* "Has less tar than any other cigarette."
8. *Cereal:* "John Unitas caught the wheat germ from Mickey Mantle."
9. *Toothache medicine:* "Stops pain on contact."
10. *Bourbon:* "Professional tasters say our bourbon is the best."
11. *Scotch whiskey:* "It never varies."
12. *Air Force recruitment:* "Find yourself in the job of your choice." "Guaranteed."
13. *Distilled dry gin:* "World's driest gin."
14. *Carousel projector:* "We've made it the most for your money."
15. *Balanced reducing formula:* "Guaranteed to lose 5 pounds the first week or your money back."
16. *Bath towels:* "The finest bath towel that is made of the finest combed cotton."
17. *Travel advertisement:* "There are no strangers in paradise."
18. *Avocado dip:* "Try an avocado love potion—the love food."
19. *National LP Gas Council:* "Gas makes the difference. A juicy steak melts in your mouth."
20. *Dry cleaning product:* "Just spray it on and brush away the spot—lifts spots, soup to sauce."
21. *Plastic baby milk bottles:* "This bottle saved my marriage."
22. *Computer company:* "No other computer company has as much to offer."
23. *Newspaper:* "San Francisco has no city limit."
24. *Crackers:* "Make your patio party perfect."

25. *Gasoline:* "Will hold exhaust emissions down, increase your gasoline mileage, keep your carburetor clean and keep your sparkplugs from misfiring."

Case questions

1. Evaluate each of the above appeals and indicate how the various companies might document these statements.

2. Do you believe that advertisers should be allowed to use general "puffery" statements?

3. In the event that there are no reliable tests that can be developed, what approach should the advertiser use?

4. What various approaches might Cheshire use in evaluating the kinds of appeals which will meet FTC regulations?

CASE 3.   COD SEA FOOD, INC.
Informing the consumer

Cod Sea Food, Inc. is a supplier of fresh and frozen sea food. Its offices and shipping center are located in Massachusetts. Cod maintained rigid quality controls; however, because of recent problems in the industry, it became concerned as to what it should do in informing consumers that Cod's products were safe. Cod recognized that there were inherent problems that existed in the sea food industry that prohibited it from being able to test every item in order to be 100 percent sure that no contamination or impurity existed.

Business

Cod deals in approximately 125 types of fish and other sea food items, including most of the well-known forms of seafood, and a variety of gourmet and specialty items, such as lobster and lobster tails, scallops, shrimp, king crab, clams, and oysters. Cod does not process or cook any of the products it sells, although in some instances, at customer request, fish are cleaned or cut into portions before delivery.

Sales are made by Cod's 10 salesmen to approximately 400 customers. Principal customers include several major supermarket chains, restaurants, hotels, country clubs, institutions, and steamships. No single customer accounted for as much as 10 percent of sales of seafood. Cod's five largest customers accounted for approximately 20 percent of its seafood sales.

Cod purchases most of its requirements of seafood directly from suppliers at the point of production, or, in the case of imports, through brokers. Cod relies on local wholesalers only for regional varieties of sea-food and to cover shortages which intermittently arise due to product scarcity or unexpected orders from customers. Certain varieties of sea-foods are purchased in bulk frozen form and stored by Cod in its own freezers and in public warehouses for later sale.

Cod's sources of supply are primarily in Canada, Massachusetts, Washington, Florida, Japan, South and Central America, and the Caribbean area. From time to time, Cod, along with most other suppliers of seafood, has encountered difficulty in securing sufficient quantities of certain varieties of seafood due to industry-wide shortages of fresh fish. The industry is currently experiencing such a shortage. The causes of these shortages have not been specifically determined. However, such shortages become most severe when weather conditions in catch areas or along transportation routes are particularly harsh.

Cod employs off-premises salesmen and performs the sorting, delivery, and other services which are not generally performed by wholesalers. Cod's salesmen telephone customers at prearranged times and receive orders for various quantities and varieties of seafood for delivery that day or the following day. The orders are filled beginning at 3:00 A.M. on the day of delivery and are delivered in the local area by its fleet of trucks and drivers. In addition, Cod has some customers with outlets spread throughout the continental United States, and deliveries to them are made by public truckers or by air or rail.

In recent years, as per capita U.S. consumption of both fresh and frozen seafood has continued to increase, there has developed a trend of sales in the industry toward frozen seafood products, and toward imported seafoods. Fresh seafood continues to account for more than 60 percent of Cod's sales; and sales of frozen seafoods, including certain shellfish and other specialty items, account for the other 40 percent.

Competition

The sale of seafood is a highly competitive business. Cod is one of the three largest in its area. While the company encounters competition from a large number of wholesalers and smaller companies specializing in one or two products, there are only a limited number in the area which handle the broad product lines maintained by the company and which provide the delivery and other service which is the keystone of the company's fresh seafood operations.

Government regulation

Cod's products, ingredients and facilities are continuously inspected by the U.S. Department of the Interior and the Department of Agriculture. The company is also subject to regulations by state and local health agencies. The company has never had any sanctions or penalties imposed upon it by any such regulatory agency.

Ocean dumping

Many businesses—large, medium, or small—have some of their wastes dumped in the ocean. Up to now boats carried the waste outside the 12-mile legal limit to discharge this waste cargo. Informed sources state that regulations are being prepared to force these vessels further out to sea— even up to 100 miles.

Quality control

It was the opinion of Cod's executives that the company maintained the strictest quality control standards for its products of any of the firms in the industry. Yet, they realized that because of the many unforeseen problems that might occur because of conditions that could develop with the discharge of waste cargo in the ocean, it was not feasible for a firm the size of Cod to develop the necessary tests which could avoid future problems. It was also necessary for the company to handle a number of its tests on a sampling basis.

Cod was also faced with a competitive situation which results from the nature of the industry. Small distributors are in the industry and do not always maintain quality standards. The procedure for many of these distributors is to operate at the lowest possible level of the minimum standards which the U.S. Department of the Interior and the Department of Agriculture set.

Cod, on the other hand, has attempted to look at these standards as only a starting point, and has set its own quality standards above the ones established by these government departments. Yet, the executives recognized that because of the limited inspection staffs which the two departments have, Cod was checked only on two occasions in the last two years.

Case questions

1. To what extent should Cod advertise to the consumer about its high quality standards?

2. Should Cod attempt to inform the consumers about the low quality standards of its competitors?

3. How can a relatively small company like Cod let the consumers know about the danger of ocean dumping and its effect on the sea food industry?

4. Do you believe Cod should make an effort to have the U.S. Department of the Interior and the Department of Agriculture establish more rigid standards for the seafood industry?

5. Is Cod obligated to let the consumer know that it uses the sampling procedure in conducting tests?

6. What can be done to alleviate the adverse publicity which the seafood industry received because of the banning of swordfish?

CASE 4. ENERGY, INC.

Energy, Inc. is a large bakery which carries on an extensive advertising program in the important media. It has put the main promotional emphasis on its bread and has used a variety of appeals. Among these are the following:

Energy's super-energy bread.
More than five times the vitamin B_1, 50 percent more minerals . . . than are present in ordinary unenriched white bread . . . the bread that baking experts judged the finest.
. . . Doctors say you need 200 to 300 vitamin B_1 units every day. To be sure of your daily B_1 quota, eat Energy's vitamin B_1 bread. . . .
Two or three delicious slices with every meal will assure you your proper B_1 supply.
So, for healthy nerves, fitness, and vitality eat Energy vitamin B_1 bread every day.

Energy's advertising director arranged to have a loaf of Energy's bread delivered without charge each day to the homes of 100 leading movie stars, and notified them that he would continue this as long as they wanted this service. Only four representatives of the stars indicated they did not want the bread. The company, shortly after it started the service, began to advertise as follows:

By appointment Energy's bakers have been selected as the official bakers of the movie stars, according to the formula and specifications approved by these stars.
The stars' own bread now baked for you. This extra nourishing bread is now a part of the stars' diet.
Now you and your family may enjoy this special bread, too.

Another advertisement which the company used was:

WHY BE FAT?
STARS TELL AMAZING NEW
WAY TO BE THIN
You don't have to starve yourself to a frazzle with violent exercise to have a trim waist. And you don't have to experiment dangerously with drugs. Lose weight and stay slender by using the same system as leading movie and television stars. . . . All you do is substitute at each meal two slices of Energy

bread for more fattening food. That way you fill up and avoid feeling hungry, but do not add excessively to your weight, for Energy bread has very few fat-making calories.

Streamline your figure.

Bring your figure up to date . . . . down in weight.

Energy bread is exceptionally high in energy elements yet extremely low in calories.

The easy pleasant way to slenderize.

Made of nonfattening vegetable flours.

Energy bread supplies necessary proteins to help keep your muscles from becoming soft and flabby while you are reducing.

Be slim the modern "hungerless" way.

Actually Energy's bread furnishes no more energy than many other competitive breads. Practically all the white breads on the American market are enriched with vitamin B_1 and minerals, and Energy's bread does not have a significantly greater amount than most competitive brands. No tests have been made by qualified experts which might justify the claim that this bread is the finest.

Although Energy bread is more digestible than whole wheat bread, it is not more digestible than white bread. It is slightly more nourishing than other brands of white bread, but not more nourishing than whole wheat bread. Since most white breads are enriched with vitamin B_1, Energy bread is only slightly richer in vitamin B_1 than most white breads. It is questionable if vitamin B_1 in bread will build healthier nerves or increase vitality. Other breads on the market are made from flour manu-factured by the same process as that used in Energy bread.

There is actually little basis for the designation of Energy bread as a reducing diet bread, because its consumption in sufficient quantities would tend to increase rather than decrease body weight. It contains only slightly fewer calories than ordinary bread. However, the slices are thinner.

The most authoritative medical opinion holds that the minimum daily requirement of vitamin B_1 is in excess of 300 units. The consumption of two or three slices of Energy bread a day at each meal will not provide the minimum daily requirement of this vitamin, nor will the daily con-sumption of this bread actually insure healthy nerves, bodily fitness, or vitality.

Energy bread has no unique properties in connection with the reduc-tion of excess weight. The flour from which it is made is no less fattening than flour used in other breads. Any reduction in weight which might occur in connection with the eating of Energy bread would result from the reduction of the person's total intake because the slices of bread were thinner. Bread as a part of an effective reducing diet will not prevent hunger; nor used in such a way will it prevent muscles from becoming soft and flabby.

While the management of Energy Bakery recognized these points, they continued to use the above appeals for the following reasons:

1. They did not believe the emphasis on the Bread of the Movie and Television Stars was any more misleading than the appeal which other major companies used in getting athletes and movie stars to endorse the products when, in many cases, these individuals never used the products. The management cited one particular case when an athlete was photographed with 50 different products in one day. The agent for this athlete went around to the various manufacturers of these products and was able to get 20 of these companies to give a stipend to the athlete for endorsing their products. These endorsements were later used in the advertising campaigns of the companies.

2. They had found that because of the tendency of a person to limit the number of slices of bread eaten at each meal, people who bought Energy bread actually began to lose weight because the slices of bread were thinner. Four slices of Energy bread were the equivalent of two slices of an ordinary loaf of white bread.

3. The emphasis of the company on the need for a minimum amount of vitamin B_1 was significant, because through this appeal it made the general public aware of the importance of using a sound approach to dieting. Many doctors recommended the use of Energy bread because it had a somewhat higher vitamin B_1 content. Tests indicated that it was difficult to measure the effectiveness of a vitamin in a product of this nature.

4. The executives also believed it was essential to have a rather dramatic appeal to get the public to buy its product.

5. Such terms as "finest" and "the best" have been used for such a long period of time by so many different manufacturers that these words are no longer misleading, because the public is aware of the interpretations they should place on these words.

Case questions

1. Comment on the advertising appeal which Energy uses.

2. Are Energy executives justified in their belief that it is essential to have a rather dramatic appeal to get the public to buy its product?

3. Is Energy's advertising approach ethical?

4. Can Energy alter its present advertising appeal and not risk losing its present clientele?

5. What method would you recommend that Energy adopt so the consumer would get more accurate data about bread?

CASE 5.   COUNTER-ADVERTISING
Controlling product claims

So-called "counter-advertising" to rebut controversial product claims made in commercials should be considered for television and radio. The Federal Trade Commission proposed that persons and groups be granted free, as well as paid-for, broadcast time to answer advertising claims involving such public issues as health, safety, and pollution. For example, the FTC would allow counter-ads to commercials advertising a company's antipollution efforts, those making auto-safety claims and food ads making nutritional claims.

The FTC statement was filed in response to a request for public comment by the Federal Communications Commission on its previously announced inquiry into the workings of the "fairness doctrine." The doctrine basically requires broadcasters to air positions opposing views broadcast on public issues. Among various problems the FCC wants to explore is how, and if, the doctrine should apply to commercials. So far, only cigarette commercials specifically have been ruled by the FCC to be under the fairness doctrine.

The FTC, whose proposal isn't binding on the FCC, likened the suggested counter-ads to the anti-cigarette commercials the FCC allowed. The FTC said such counter-ads also should be allowed to respond to advertising claims based on controversial scientific findings and to ads that don't say anything about the negative aspects of a product. The FTC would leave it up to the FCC to decide when counter-advertisements should be permitted. But it suggested that the FCC allow open availability of commercial time for anyone willing to pay for counter-ads at regular rates and that the FCC require broadcasters to provide some free time for counter-advertising.

Case questions

1. What criteria should be established to determine whether or not "counter-advertising" would be granted?

2. Who should decide as to whether or not this type of advertising will be done?

3. Comment on the pros and cons of this type of advertising.

chapter 3

SOCIAL AND ECONOMIC CONCEPTS

ADVERTISING is one of the most apparent or exposed aspects of business. The manufacture of machine tools, the manufacture of clothing, the buying for retail organizations, and the planning done to staff and operate our corporations are all carried on in such a manner that the general public does not fully comprehend how they are administered. Except as a person's own work and the work of his immediate circle of friends become evident to him, his knowledge of business frequently comes from what he sees when he buys at retail or through individual salesmen, and from what he reads, sees, and hears of advertising. Although the combined advertising expenditures for American business is about 2.2 percent of the Gross National Product in the United States each year, advertising is so conspicuous to so many people that they may tend to judge all business by advertising.

In general, there is a feeling among some who disapprove of our free enterprise, capitalistic society that advertising is blatant, uneconomic, and antisocial, as though advertising alone were responsible for what they consider an undesirable state of affairs. However, analyses will indicate that many of these negative comments are basically criticisms of the American system of economic organization.

In this chapter, we shall examine certain social and economic criticisms of advertising. In Chapter 20, present and desirable public policy in the area of control and regulation of advertising will be discussed.

SOCIAL CONCEPTS

In considering advertising from the point of view of some of the social concepts, advertising is by its nature so complex that it needs to be analyzed from various aspects. In the first place, it is conducted by both small and large companies, by advertising agencies, by advertising departments, by media of all kinds, by individuals, and with a hierarchy of sales organizations acting in complicated commercial relationships. These firms have office staffs, executives, contractual relations with other groups, and responsibilities toward these as well as toward the owners and the stockholders of the firms themselves. They are faced with the social problems of employer-employee relations, of civic responsibility, of compliance with tax and labor laws, of contractual compliance, and finally, of mass communication and sales promotion.

Waste in advertising

When people speak of waste in advertising, they do not generally refer to the offices of advertising agencies or the assignment to manufacturers' advertising departments of executives and clerical workers who possibly might be more productive assigned to other duties. When people speak of waste in advertising, they usually mean that more money is spent for advertising than they think is appropriate. This argument is advanced in spite of the fact that the percentage of Gross National Product devoted to advertising has varied little over the years, during good times and bad. Sometimes an advertiser may invest more in advertising than might be necessary. Sometimes an expensive commercial picture is ordered when a photograph costing but a fraction of the artist's bill might have sufficed. Sometimes a manufacturer may allocate funds for advertising a product for which there is no ready market because suitable marketing research was not done. While the above examples indicate some waste, one can find some superfluous expenditures in almost all business activities.

Social waste is a difficult subject to interpret. The expenditure of a million dollars for advertisements in the newspapers of a particular trading area, as an example, may be quite conspicuous. But if the stores in the area can save a greater amount in payments to retail sales personnel, it is difficult to determine that there is wastefulness without research to substantiate it.

General social criticisms

When we evaluate social problems in relation to the use of advertising, we are even more in the area of value judgments. How can deficiencies in our social system be corrected? How can things be managed so that people will get more of the essential necessities without giving up too much of their basic freedom of choice and action? What part does advertising play in helping to accentuate or relieve those conditions?

We find that there is a tendency for the critics of advertising to base their allegations of its social value on such statements as:

1. Advertising makes false statements which confuse and mislead consumers, and often these statements are made by implication.
2. Advertising forces customers to want goods and services they really do not need.
3. Advertising promotes the use of products which are inherently harmful.
4. Advertising, as it is exposed to the consumer, lacks aesthetic attributes.
5. Advertising (particularly the television commercials) is forced on the consumer.

The truth or falsity of a statement is difficult to ascertain. Automobile tires are sold with the help of advertising. In general each manufacturer will emphasize certain features of his tires. At first glance, it might seem that one tire must be best, another second best, and another third best. But actually, testing laboratories find difficulty in making such clear-cut demarcations. One tire will give a "softer" ride; another will last longer; a third will "corner" better. Each manufacturer attempts to emphasize the characteristics that he believes interest the most people. The advertising appeals will state, "This tire will last longer on rough roads," or "This tire will make your old car ride like a new car." Even the U.S. Bureau of Standards, which spends millions of dollars each year attempting to help the federal government select the "best" buys, has a hard time making its selections.

Let us consider another situation. A manufacturer of cosmetics uses the appeal that his cosmetics will make a young woman more lovable and will attract young men to her. Certainly, in her fantasy life, the young woman will probably want to be lovable and to attract a young man. And certainly she will be more attractive in real life if she is well groomed than if she is not. We learn, from advertising, that a particular brand of carpet will make a living room more attractive, or that this new lighting fixture will make a hallway brighter. These, and many other similar statements, are true. They do not, however, say that they will accomplish the impossible.

People want to look better, eat better, live in better houses, drive better cars—in fact, improve all aspects of their standard of living. Merchandise which may satisfy, entirely or partially, the wants of the consumer may be sold more easily through persuading the prospect with the right appeal. One finds that not only in the advertising for dentifrices but also in sermons from the pulpit, in lectures from the rostrum, and in directives from the government similar tactics of persuasion are used.

Let us consider the next criticism, that advertising forces consumers to want merchandise they cannot afford. The ubiquity of advertising does not give it compulsive force. Indeed, advertising cannot move people in directions contrary to social trends. One of the reasons companies use marketing research is to find out how to advertise goods and services to coincide with the demand of the consumers. At a time when women used leg makeup rather than hosiery, manufacturers of hosiery advertised heavily to get women to wear stockings instead of leg makeup. But no movement contrary to the social trend was started. When men decided that they did not need to wear hats, the hat industry tried to use primary advertising to reverse this trend, but the results were unsatisfactory.

When electric ranges were first developed, they were advertised heavily by leading manufacturers of electric appliances. Women, according to various marketing research studies, were afraid that the change from gas cooking to electric cooking would impair their cooking skill. Although extensive advertising was done, it required 20 years to get women to start using electric ranges. Then, as more and more women used electric ranges, advertising helped to speed the acceptance trend.

Dr. Lawrnce C. Lockley has said that advertising never brings about anything that would not occur without advertising, but that it does hasten product adoption and use. The number of instances which can be advanced to show that advertising has not been able to get consumers to buy products with a declining trend, or that advertising was not able to get consumers to adopt a product in advance of the time it seemed propitious, is great enough to dispel the belief that advertising has the ability to do more than advance effective suggestions.

Does advertising promote the sale of products which are harmful? There is a variety of legislation which is supposed to prevent the promotion of the sale of harmful products. There are many marginal questions here. Does one of the conventional shortenings build up the cholesterol content of the blood sufficiently to make it harmful to many people? We don't know. And in our confusion, we can find evidence suggesting that our conventional shortenings are entirely satisfactory. Are cigarettes harmful? Again, the evidence is not conclusive. So far as we can tell, smog is more harmful than cigarette smoke. And the studies attempting to show that cigarette smoking is harmful are not regarded as convincing by all statisticians. Are alcoholic beverages dangerous and immoral? Intemperately used, they are dangerous. Yet our one attempt to abolish them seemed to advance their use rather than restrict it. Again, conclusive evidence is not in.

Probably no product sold to the public causes more death and injury than the automobile. Yet few believe that it is immoral or that it should not be sold to the American public although federal laws now are requiring more safety and smog devices.

On the other hand, items whose disrepute is due to the adverse opinions of people who object to the American standard of living, or to the price system, should not, for those reasons, be banned!

Is advertising lacking in good taste? Laxatives, depilatories, liniments for aching muscles, and cemetery lots are all a part of the American scene. If the advertiser cannot advertise the goods and services that the American public openly buys, by what standard should he select what he is to advertise? Some radio and television commercials are obtrusive and irritating. If the public is offended by the appeals used, the advertiser may soon find out about their disapproval through his decrease in sales.

The first obligation of advertising is to communicate with the American public. Magazines, newspapers, television programs, and radio programs are molded to the public taste. Some people are more aesthetic and more sensitive than the general run of advertising readers, listeners, or viewers. If so, they may find some consumer advertising distasteful. That fact does not mean that the advertising now done is not gauged carefully to the level of most Americans. If it were not, it would indeed be wasteful.

Finally, we are told that advertising, particularly television advertising, forces its way into the American living room. Under our system of advertising, television comes to us without charge, at all times, and with a great variety of programs. Advertisers pay the costs of maintaining this service —evidently a service that the American public values—in order to advertise their products. The television viewer who is affronted by the television commercials is not obliged to keep listening to the commercials. If he wants to watch the programs, he may either submit to the commercials or he may turn the set off during the commercials. He is under no obligation to view the commercials or the television programs.

If he believes that the television service should be provided without the interference of commercials, then he must be willing to recommend that television programs be prepared at public expense and the taxpayer be assessed additional taxes to pay for this entertainment.

Some of the other social questions that are important are such ones as:

1. Does advertising contribute to a higher standard of living for society?
2. Does advertising cause people to place an undue stress on material possessions, to the neglect of their spiritual and cultural needs, their intellectual and aesthetic interests?
3. Does advertising persuade people to buy goods they do not need, that are not necessary for the satisfaction of the basic needs of life—food, shelter, and clothing?

Standard of living

Has advertising contributed to the ability of the masses to acquire and enjoy increased quantities and varieties of commodities? Most people would grant that advertising, through its contribution to more effective marketing and selling in the American economy, has made some considerable contribution to the present high standard of living of most

Americans. It has undoubtedly been a contributing factor, along with many others, in developing in people the motivation to work harder in order to acquire some of the many luxuries and semiluxuries made available by our productive economic system, and brought to the daily attention of people through advertising. The knowledge of such new products and improved products, and the potential enjoyment to be realized by their possession, has been brought to the attention of many individuals through advertising. Undoubtedly advertising has played a part in creating this desire among Americans to labor and to produce, and in turn to be able to acquire and possess and enjoy these goods and services which will lift their lives above the subsistence level.

The most exhaustive study that has been made of the economic effects of advertising reached the conclusion that advertising had made a major contribution to increasing the standard of living, as noted in the conclusion to the study:

Advertising's outstanding contribution to consumer welfare comes from its part in promoting a dynamic, expanding economy. Advertising's chief task from a social standpoint is that of encouraging the development of new products. It offers a means whereby the enterpriser may hope to build a profitable demand for his new and differentiated merchandise which will justify investment. From growing investment has come the increasing flow of income which has raised man's material welfare to a level unknown in previous centuries.[1]

Today's economy is geared to a high level of consumption, and if high levels of production and employment are to be maintained, and the economy is to continue to grow, consumers will have to continue to maintain, if not increase, their standard of living with reference to material goods. Certainly advertising fills a considerable role in stimulating this continued high standard of living among most Americans.

This is especially true in light of the fact that a large portion of today's production is of goods not required to meet human physiological needs, but is designed to meet psychological wants. Potential consumers of such new goods, which might be considered luxury or semiluxury by many, must be "educated" to desire such products, if the economy is to function smoothly. One of the key influences in such education is advertising.

Does advertising place an undue stress on material things?

In light of the discussion in the preceding paragraphs of the role of advertising in contributing to and maintaining a high standard of living, it is obvious that advertising does stress to a considerable degree the consumption of material goods. Does this mean that there has been a decline

---

[1] Neil H. Borden, *The Economic Effects of Advertising* (Homewood, Ill.: Richard D. Irwin, Inc., 1942), p. 881.

in the stress placed on people's cultural and spiritual needs? Have people's interests in intellectual and aesthetic pursuits declined because of advertising, or are they less than they would be if we had no advertising? Has interest in literature, music, painting, sculpture, the theater, creative pursuits, and efforts on behalf of the poor, the ill, and the unfortunate decreased, or is it less than it would have been, because of advertising?

Such questions are difficult to answer categorically. However, many think a reasonable standard of living in material things is generally a prerequisite to a great interest in cultural activities and the arts. And they would also say there is not necessarily incompatibility between a high standard of living and a high level of cultural and spiritual life. Also, some would cite statistics on the number of books sold, the number of symphony orchestras in this country, the growth of attendance at art museums, and increases in similar activities as evidence that the level of cultural interest is higher in the United States than at any time in the past; although it may not be as high as the critics believe it should be, or as it might be.

And, even if people's cultural and spiritual life is not as "high" as the critics feel it should be, is this lower standard due to advertising? Does the stress on material things automatically rule out attention to the cultural and spiritual values of life? Many would agree with F. P. Bishop when he says:

But in practice it is not easy to keep the conception of the ends of life separate from the problem of providing the means. Such is the constitution of human life that the satisfaction of the higher desires is only possible by means of the relative satisfaction of the lower. Thus the gratification of the desire for knowledge is only possible in a society and, in a sense, by an individual, on condition that the more primary instinct to acquire property and secure the means of subsistence has been satisfied. Man does not live by bread alone, but without bread or its equivalent he cannot live at all; and a substantial minimum of material comfort and security is necessary before he can attend to the consideration of the true ends of life to the attainment of which material possessions should be no more than a means. Of course it is wrong for the philosopher in his study, adequately clothed and warmed and fed, and equipped with all the material adjuncts of *his* ideal life, to pour scorn upon others who may seem to be excessively preoccupied with material desires which do not vex him.[2]

Does advertising cause people to buy goods they do not need?

It is certainly true that much of the advertising of today is designed to sell new products that are not "necessities" at present. However, many

---

[2] F. P. Bishop, *The Ethics of Advertising* (London: Robert Hale, Ltd., 1943), pp. 34–35.

of the products called luxuries or nonnecessities today become what people consider necessities for a reasonable standard of material living tomorrow, as was the case with the vacuum cleaner and the electric refrigerator. Actually, much of the criticism of advertising on this score, of its selling people things they do not "need," is directed more at the fact that people buy things the critic does not think they should want. The question naturally arises as to who is to make the decision as to what people should want. Many believe it is the consumer himself who should decide what he wants and needs, and not the critics or a government agency or any other authoritarian body. If the consumer's freedom of choice in the marketplace is taken away from him, he might soon lose many of his other freedoms also. To some it would appear strange that the legislators, economists, political scientists, and historians who are so often the ones who feel the consumer should not be allowed freedom of choice, and the advertiser freedom of advertising, are the loudest in their demands for the freedom of speech to say what they think, and the freedom to protest the causes they do not happen to approve. Since advertising (so long as it does not violate standards of good taste, ethics, and so forth) is one form of free speech for the business community, it would appear reasonable that it be permitted, and that the consumer have the privilege of deciding what products he needs and wants, whether or not they happen to be what critics call necessities or luxuries.

ECONOMIC ASPECTS

Another of the charges leveled against advertising by its critics is that there are inherent economic conflicts in its use. In an attempt to evaluate some of the economic aspects of advertising which have been the bases for much of the criticism, the following questions will be considered:

1. Does advertising limit competition?
2. Does advertising limit price competition?
3. Does advertising decrease the production cost of goods sold?
4. Does advertising increase the overall demand for products?
5. Does advertising create false company images which are misleading to the consumer?
6. Does advertising limit the number of products that will be offered?
7. Who pays for the advertising?
8. Is advertising a satisfactory yardstick for the consumer to use in buying products?
9. Are capital investments allocated uneconomically because of the use of advertising?
10. Does advertising perform a useful economic function?

Competition

The first question, "Does advertising limit competition?" has to be considered from several viewpoints. If, on the one hand, we weaken the effect of competition through advertising, then we must submit to some other regulating device. And yet, can small and big firms exist in competition with each other? Do the major firms take advantage of the public?

In the decision against the Atlantic & Pacific Tea Company, the judge stated there was no evidence that the company had attempted to put smaller rivals out of business, but it had the economic power to do so. What the decision came close to stating was that A&P was required to compete, but it would become illegal if it competed successfully.

Certainly to gain the necessary economies in many industries requires "bigness." Bigness is essential for large-scale production in automobiles, steel, aluminum, and atomic power. Bigness is necessary for large-scale distribution of cigarettes, gasoline, and other low per unit margin items. Bigness is necessary to have national distribution. Bigness is necessary to provide the funds for much of our basic research. Bigness is necessary to allow major changes in product design in a short-run period. Bigness is necessary to experiment with many new products. Bigness is more responsive to public opinion because the general concept of bigness tends to frighten the public.

In this economy with its tendency toward bigness, advertising is one of the forces which has been accused of weakening competition. And yet, with the ever continuing growth of business enterprises (as an example, there are about 315,000 food stores in the United States today as compared to 600,000 in 1939, and 9 percent of the 315,000 outlets do about 60 percent of the total food business), with the development of national markets, with the need for greater efficiency at all levels, with the expanding markets, with the continuous search for new products (as an example, in the drug industry only 45 percent of the products now sold were on the shelves of drugstores eight years ago), with the greater investment needed to start a business with a capacity great enough to gain adequate economies, and with the greater knowledge which consumers have about all products, the use of advertising has had to evolve to meet conditions in the ever changing market.

The tendency toward bigness is a composite of many economic factors. This bigness has brought with it many social dividends. It has also driven out the less efficient firms. To what extent has this bigness weakened competition? Has it intensified the competition among a few? Will increasing the number of outlets intensify competition, or will it cause the greater number to be more willing to maintain the status quo?

One way or another, we must develop a consistent policy in regard to the growth of a business. Until we can decide on what we mean by bigness, we cannot decide on whether or not advertising is intensifying or weakening competition.

Price competition

The second question, "Does advertising limit price competition?" is a difficult one to evaluate because of the complex price structure which we have in our economy and the variety of state and federal controls in effect. The degree to which a company may be able to control the market through such factors as product differentiation, brand name, company prestige, distribution economies, production economies, advertising appeals, and other methods of this type will vary from industry to industry.

In some areas of activity, such as in distribution of the services of utilities, regulations have been established to provide control of prices. In even such fields as law, medicine, accounting, and barbering, licensing arrangements have provided a means by which these groups have set prices for a number of their services. The federal enabling act and the state acts legalizing fair-trade agreements also made possible the elimination of price competition at the retail level for branded merchandise.

The U.S. government has interfered with the market prices for all major agricultural products. In fact, such groups as agricultural cooperatives and other associations are partially exempt from the federal antitrust laws. The Robinson-Patman Act puts barriers in the way of price flexibility. The states have "unfair practices" acts which prohibit sales below cost.

In industries where there are a few dominant producers, such as automobiles, steel, and cigarettes, price and production policies initiated by one company may be followed by the others. When General Motors decided to manufacture a small car to be sold at a price of $2,000, Ford and Chrysler also decided to produce a comparable car. While there may be an attempt to penetrate the competitor's market through price-cutting, in all likelihood the costs for each manufacturer will be such that no company will have significant production advantages.

In retailing where industrial concentration is not so great, there is a greater tendency for price competition. At the retail level, for example, the price appeal is used extensively. However, where artificial price controls have been put into effect in any segment of the economy, they will intensify rigidity in prices whether they are placed at the retail, at the wholesale, or at the manufacturing level.

By and large, however, there is not enough evidence to indicate whether or not the use of advertising has been one of the basic causes in the inflexibility of certain prices. As an example, the lack of price competition in the cigarette industry results as much from such competitive factors as the necessity of getting cigarettes into 1.25 million retail outlets, the taxes levied on the industry, and the low per unit margin earned, as it does from the extensive advertising which the companies use.

Production costs

In considering the third question, "Does advertising decrease the production costs of goods sold?" it must be kept in mind that advertising is only one part of the marketing mix. It is also important to understand that the responsiveness of the consumer to an advertising appeal will appreciably affect the per unit cost. As an example, if a cooperative decided to spend $1 million in an advertising campaign to increase the primary demand for its product, the expansibility or inexpansibility of demand would have a direct effect on the per unit cost. The elasticity or inelasticity of demand would also affect the unit cost. Furthermore, these costs are going to vary even within a given industry. The used or unused capacity of a company also will affect these overall costs.

As a result, it is difficult to show that advertising can be credited with decreasing production costs. As Neil H. Borden stated:

From an economic standpoint it is significant in these cases that the principle of decreasing costs does not continue beyond a certain point. Instead, a certain size of plant permits low manufacturing costs and, to attain a volume permitting this size of plant, competing firms may choose to use different marketing methods.

From this discussion, it is seen that the answer regarding the effect of advertising upon production costs cannot be given categorically and simply.

Where there is much affirmative evidence of striking economies in the costs of production which have attended the concurrent growth in the size of industries and in the use of advertising and aggressive selling, the sweeping claims sometimes advanced regarding production economies resulting from and maintained by advertising are not supported.[3]

On the other hand, some writers have credited advertising with lowering production costs through the process of increasing the demand for a product and thus making it possible for a company to operate on a larger scale, with resultant lower per unit costs. While there is merit in this viewpoint, nevertheless, the complexity of our economic system is so vast that it is difficult to pinpoint reduction in production costs to advertising through the use of any substantive data that are available.

Overall product demand

The fourth question, "Does advertising increase the overall demand for products?" is one which becomes extremely complex to resolve. The

[3] Neil H. Borden, *Advertising in Our Economy* (Homewood, Ill.: Richard D. Irwin, Inc., 1945), p. 164.

demand trend of the product, the environment and social conditions, and the characteristics of the people in the market are only a few of the variables which must be controlled in order to determine what impact advertising has on the overall demand for products.

Most studies have indicated that advertising has accelerated the time in which products will be accepted. The demand for such products as television, automobiles, and appliances can be cited as examples in which advertising hastened expansion because favorable market conditions existed. On the other hand, in situations in which there was a declining demand trend, such as in men's hats, advertising was not able to reverse the trend although it was able to slow down the decline.

As a result, we might conclude that advertising can help to get products accepted more readily if the other conditions in the market are favorable. We do not have evidence, however, to show that advertising can reverse a declining trend unless there is a change in environmental, social, or other factors.

Company images

The fifth question deals with a problem that has been popularized to a great degree during the past decade—"Does advertising create company images which are misleading to the consumer?" In other words, can a company create and maintain an identity which is not consistent with the general policy of the organization? Can General Electric continue to use successfully the appeal, "Progress is our most important product," unless General Electric actually makes the necessary progress to justify such an appeal? Or can Westinghouse emphasize, "You can be sure if it's Westinghouse," unless it maintains high-quality standards? How long can Cadillac use the appeal of "Universal symbol of achievement" unless it actually continues to build an automobile that will justify this appeal? Will Maytag be able to emphasize its appeal, "The most service-free automatics made!" unless its product standards continue to justify it?

Is it true that all advertising to some degree is institutional advertising? As an example, how can a product be divorced from the company which makes it any more than the executives of the company can be divorced from their opinions? Is it true that one of the most important advertising functions is the establishment of identity? In other words, is it possible to separate the advertising from the company? How many companies actually know what product they are really selling? Are they selling a particular product, or are they selling something else? Is a company selling electric typewriters, or is it selling a more economcial way of transcribing? Is the telephone company selling instruments, or a more economical way of doing something? Or is the company's image of even greater importance than the product?

In industry today, there is a growing belief on the part of many executives that the company image is becoming even more important to the total satisfaction the consumer derives from a product. As a result, the need to give a company a consistent identity appears to be more important. This identity, however, must be consistent in all aspects. As an example, a company cannot advertise its know-how for any period of time unless its product measures up to the required standards. Neither will a company find it economical to emphasize its progress unless it is actually a leader in the industry.

Number of products

The sixth question, "Does advertising limit the number of products that will be offered?" is another one of the broad criticisms that is sometimes advanced. At the same time, other critics will point out that the use of advertising is the major factor in having such a great number of brands in the market. Furthermore, they claim that there are meaningless product differentiations which exist between these brands, and as a result, the consumer cannot make wise selections.

In evaluating the position of the two groups of critics on the number and variety of products offered, there is available data to substantiate either position on the question. On the one hand, wholesale druggists point out that as late as 8 years ago, 55 percent of the products they now handle were not on the market; supermarket studies indicate that within the next 8 to 10 years, 50 percent of all the products they sell now will no longer be offered. The dramatic growth in the electronic and television industries which has resulted in many new products being manufactured are other examples which would seem to substantiate the fact that the use of advertising has not limited the number of products.

On the other side of the issue, however, the reluctance of manufacturers in the automobile, steel, and other basic industries to make significant instead of trivial changes is used as a criterion to judge that the use of advertising has limited the introduction of significantly new products.

In certain industries, like automobiles, cigarettes, and steel, there is a tendency for concentration in the hands of a small number of large companies. As a result, these firms are in a position during a short-term period, within the scope of the competitive conditions which they face, to decide on the number and variety of products which they will manufacture.

The fact is, however, that the use of extensive advertising cannot by itself maintain a company's position in the market for the long-term period unless the other ingredients in the marketing and productive mix are properly allocated. As an example, did the use of advertising protect the automobile manufacturers from having to produce a small car? Or were these same manufacturers able to maintain the automobile as a symbol of prestige? Will the automobile manufacturers be able to continue to produce a small economical car and through advertising have it attain the prestige of the foreign cars?

In a free economy, because of the preponderance and the extent of the economic factors which influence the number and variety of products offered, the use of advertising will be only a minor aspect in limiting the number of products in a few basic industries.

Cost of advertising

The seventh question, "Who pays for the advertising?" is one which critics point out to indicate that the sales price of goods might be lower if companies did not advertise. The cost of advertising, like all other expenses, is passed on to the consumer in one form or the other. However, the proper use of advertising can influence the unit sales volume and thus indirectly help to decrease the cost of production. In such instances, if the savings are passed on to the consumer in lower prices, the consumer will benefit even though he pays for the cost of the advertising.

It would be a mistake to assume that the above answer provides a sound solution to the basic problems indicated in the question. Such other points as the following are involved in the question: What is the result if the savings are not passed on to the consumer? What happens when the businessman does not properly appraise his market opportunities? What takes place when the firm does not effectively coordinate all other parts of the marketing program? What might happen to other sales costs if the use of advertising were decreased?

While these are only a few of the many questions which might be considered, the authors wish to point out that the cost of advertising is part of the sales cost and as such may be absorbed by our economic system in one of several ways. These include:

1. Advantages gained in production which may result in lower per unit costs.
2. Advantages gained in distribution which may result in lower per unit distribution costs.
3. Advantages gained in financing which may result in lower per unit financial costs.
4. Advantages gained in general management relations which may result in lower per unit managerial costs.
5. Advantages gained in price stability which may result in a decrease of the inherent dangers of cyclical influence.

From the cost viewpoint for the whole economy, therefore, the justification of the use of advertising depends on whether or not it performs its function more effectively than some other method.

Product information

The eighth question, "Is advertising a satisfactory yardstick for the consumer to use in buying products?" is one which the critics frequently answer by showing a variety of advertisements which they deem misleading. Advertisements such as the following are among those which they claim show how ineffectively advertising can be used as a guide for buying:

1. And the two extra doors don't cost a thing.
2. Be slim this modern "hungerless" way.
3. Made of nonfattening vegetable flours.
4. The finest costs no more.
5. Regularly $95 and $115 suits hand-tailored from the finest imported worsteds—now—$39.95.
6. Now you can have the finest hand-detailed coat of 100 percent imported cashmere for only $39.95—other stores normally charge $89.95.
7. Best value mattress in 59 years for only $35.95.
8. Special purchase—save 60 percent and more.
9. We've sold hundreds of these chairs at $139.50—now a special purchase makes one yours for only $78.
10. It is kindest to your taste.
11. It kills germs on contact, by millions!
12. Can do 75 cleaning chores better, faster, easier than any other cleaner.
13. Helps solve nine major beauty problems.
14. It's as easy to paint your home as cutting your lawn.
15. You can't get a more expensive taste than with margarine.
16. Fades horrid age spots with one application.
17. The toothpaste for people who brush their teeth only once each day.
18. There are 500,000 special filters.
19. Drains all eight sinus cavities in four hours.
20. Shoeshine lasts 14 days.

While some of the above advertisements might be classified as misleading and others might not give the detailed information that every consumer wants, it should be kept in mind that the function of an advertisement is to stimulate demand. While in some instances this can best be done by using specific data about a product, nevertheless, in the majority of cases, some other appeal may do a better job of persuading the public.

As a result, it appears necessary for the consumers to use the other means which sellers offer, to supplement the data that is included in advertisements, if they want more detailed information. The fact that some of them may be willing to evaluate complex tests of articles does not mean, however, that all consumers desire the same type of information.

In most instances, the purchaser is satisfied to rely on either the reputation of the manufacturer or the brand of the product. Consequently, there is a lack of uniformity on the part of sellers as to the amount of detailed information they provide.

Allocation of capital

The ninth question deals with capital allocation and is stated: "Are capital investments allocated uneconomically because of the use of advertising?" This is another one of those questions which deals with very broad economic concepts.

As to the question, therefore, of the part advertising plays in allocating investments in the economy, it is certainly true that whatever influence advertising has in helping a company succeed or in pointing out potential investment advantages, it is indirectly responsible for attracting venture capital to particular firms.

There is no concrete way, however, to place a universal value judgment on whether or not these activities are economically sound. It might be argued that in the patent medicine industry the use of advertising has played a major role in maintaining profits and, thus, indirectly attracting capital. While this may be true, is it the function of advertising to determine whether or not the manufacture of patent medicines is in the best interest of society? Is it not the responsibility of other groups in the economy to make this decision?

If these other groups decide that the patent medicine industry offers a satisfactory product, can it be said that because capital is attracted to the industry, it is not being used in the best interest of the economy?

By and large, therefore, the allocation of capital may be said to be only indirectly influenced by the use of advertising. And, as in evaluating any business investments, the investor is going to include in his analysis such other factors as market trends, risk elements, management's know-how, competitive conditions, and business conditions. In the final analysis, the flow of capital will be toward those industries where the risk and opportunities involved will be in balance insofar as the investor has the ability to judge.

Function

The tenth question is: "Does advertising perform a useful economic function?" In other words, can advertising perform a phase of the distribution function more economically than some other method?

As the businessman looks at these questions, he wants to know if the use of advertising will help him make a greater profit. The economist, on the other hand, although he is interested in the profit aspect, will also be vitally concerned with how advertising will contribute to consumption and how it will affect the whole economy.

In evaluating the effectiveness of advertising as an economic function, it must first be determined what the objective of the advertising is. This objective may be to shift the demand schedule to the right for a product, it may be to educate the public, it may be to keep the demand curve from shifting negatively, it may be to make demand less elastic, it may be to adapt the demand to the product, or it may even be to match the competitive advertising.

The advertising cost is part of the sales expense and, as such, is a cause and not a result of sales. Consequently, the effectiveness of the use of advertising must be judged on how well it performs a sales function.

As in all types of sales activities, the responsiveness to advertising will differ greatly with various products. For example, the sales of patent medicines are highly responsive to advertising. On the other hand, the responsiveness to advertising for the sale of major industrial equipment may be relatively low. The responsiveness to advertising will also vary during the life cycle of a product. The share of the market and the competitive position a company holds will sometimes be equally as important in determining the kind of responsiveness which will be secured. Both the long-term and short-term responsiveness will be other aspects which should be considered.

In judging the effectiveness of advertising, therefore, it is one thing to determine whether or not certain conditions exist in the market that would indicate the responsiveness to advertising. However, it is something else to measure the effectiveness of the use of advertising as compared to some other sales technique. While some excellent studies have been based on the incremental approach, there are such wide areas of responsiveness and economic activity that it has not been feasible to use control techniques that will give a satisfactory answer in all cases.

As a result, it has been necessary to deduce the effectiveness of the use of advertising from broad generalities which are based on general sales data. By and large, these studies have indicated that the use of advertising is, in most cases, an economical and effective sales tool.

In this chapter we considered the human values of advertising as compared with social values, and the effect of advertising on the level of competition. Ironically, we are still searching for a scientific method to furnish us the means of providing for a careful reassessment of the use of advertising. While some progress has been made the quotation below gives an insight as to the complexity of the problem.

Why, then, do so many intellectuals and moralists hold advertising in such contempt? It is because of a misunderstanding of the causal relationship between advertising and social values. Consider the source of social values and the effect they have on us.

We get our values from the family, play group, school, church, and other social institutions. As we grow up, these values are internalized, and we become socialized so that we can take our place in society. The function of advertising is to help socialize us so that we are prepared to play our role as consumers. . . .

Advertising is merely a means to an end, and the end is a consumption-oriented people. Thus, the question of whether or not advertising contradicts our value system hinges on the legitimacy of high-level consumption as a social goal.[4]

Finally, advertising is a part of the total marketing mix of a company. The potentials for waste are great because of the large sums involved. Yet, within the framework of a free economy, advertising must be judged on its ability to perform its part of the marketing job in a way more economical and efficient than some other means. At the same time, it must be kept in mind that advertising, like other businesses, is a competitive venture. Advertising is one of the better methods of providing a rapid means of communication to the public. In the final analysis, however, the expenditures for advertising should be appraised as one segment of the marketing costs and not as a separate entity.

QUESTIONS

1. From the social point of view, how would you justify product differentiation which is the direct result of advertising? How might this vary if the economic point of view is emphasized?

2. In the evaluation of the economc benefits of advertising, indicate the pros and cons of rising market share as a standard.

3. Is advertising the cause of the American belief in the merits of a high-level consumption economy?

4. If advertising is as effective in causing America's preoccupation with material things as critics say, should not the critics use advertising to raise the spiritual, cultural, and social levels of our society?

5. A leading advertiser has stated: "Advertising is vital to our economic and social growth." Comment.

6. Some writers have pointed out that in our economic system much of our advertising costs should be viewed as growth costs. Comment.

7. In what ways does advertising increase the cost of distribution? Decrease the cost of distribution?

8. A leading economist made the following statement: "Since advertising is

---

[4] Thomas A. Petit and Alan Zakon, "Advertising and Social Values; The World of Advertising," *Advertising Age,* Vol. XXXIV, No. 3 (January 15, 1963), p. 252. "Excerpted with permission from the January 15, 1963, issue of *Advertising Age.* Copyright 1963 by Advertising Publications, Inc."

accompanied by rigid prices, it prevents the price mechanism from taking up the dynamic shocks in our system." Comment.

9. Is it wrong for advertising to influence people to want so many luxuries and nonnecessities—things they really do not need to sustain life?

10. Select three companies in which you believe advertising costs may be viewed as being excessive, and give reasons.

11. What is the place of advertising in a capitalistic economy such as we have in the United States?

12. Is advertising necessary only in a "free economy" like the United States? Do countries like Russia need to use advertising?

13. Can a businessman divorce the interrelationships of ethical and economic issues in his advertising program?

14. Select three companies in which advertising budgets have been figured on a basis of sales, and indicate the policy each company followed in its advertising program during recent cyclical changes. Have the advertising policies of these companies had any direct effect in minimizing the cyclical fluctuations?

15. A social worker recently stated: "Advertising has broken down competition." Comment.

16. To what degree can advertising either change or influence customer behavior?

CASE 1. VALUE ADDED BY ADVERTISING
Considering important implications

The competitive enterprise system allows companies the right to produce and sell products which will satisfy the needs of the consumers. This right, however, has to be evaluated and controlled in the context of the conditions that exist in each situation. Some of the questions which arise include:

1. What is the importance of advertising in our economy?
2. To what extent should the decisions in the marketplace be the criteria used in determining whether or not certain products should be allowed to be sold?
3. How important is the concept of "freedom of choice" for consumers?
4. Will the product help the consumer attain greater total satisfaction?
5. How should new products be checked before they are offered in the market?
6. Should all manufacturers be required to inform the public in their advertising about the negative as well as the positive factors about their products?

The above questions are a few of the challenges which people in advertising must resolve as part of their social responsibility. Unfortunately, there are no easy solutions to these problems because a product that might be very worthwhile and valuable for certain groups could be harmful to other groups. As a result, the procedures to adopt for fulfilling this social responsibility are indeed quite elusive.

Consider the following two examples:

Example A. An advertising executive in addressing a college audience made the following comments about the value added by advertising:

The concept of "Value Added by Advertising" is derived from the more general concept of *value.* While theories of value differ in detail, there is general agreement on the basic idea. Value may be summarized as follows:

a) Value is fundamentally a subjective quality, since it depends on the capacity or *ability of a good or service to satisfy human wants and desires.* For this reason a good or service has value only with reference to human beings and only from their point of view. This is another way of saying that value is not objective and that unless a product or service is wanted by someone it has no value whatever. Such psychological valuations cannot, however, be measured directly, at least with any existing techniques.

b) Since we cannot measure psychological value, a practical measure of the value of a product is its *value relative to other goods and services,* as expressed by the quantity of a given product which exchanges in the marketplace for different quantities of other products.

The total value of a product, as measured by its price, may be regarded as the end result of the process of "production," which is defined as the *creation of economic value by the addition of utilities* to goods. In a highly developed economic system such as that of the United States, it must be recognized that almost all products pass through several stages of production before they are finally consumed.

Products also pass through several stages of distribution before they are available at the proper times and places and are finally transferred to a consumer. The entire process of mining, manufacturing, and distribution (which includes advertising) must be included in the term "production," since at each stage a certain amount of *value is added* to the product.

The value added by advertising is that part of the final price of a product which can be attributed to the advertising stages of the process. Similarly, the value added by a given marketing institution, such as the retailer, is that part of the price which is paid for the contribution made by him. These values added result from the performance of *marketing functions,* which are just as truly productive types of work as are agricultural, manufacturing, processing or factory assembling activities.

Value added by advertising may be defined, then, as the dollar value of the functions performed in the marketing process. The value of advertising functions comprises a part of the total marketing functions, usually estimated at about one half of the total value of goods and services produced in the United States.

The most difficult part of the value added concept is its relationship with the concept of *cost*. In one sense, price and cost must be identical. What an article costs the consumer is its price. Similarly, what advertising costs the consumer is also the value added by advertising. Thus, in a functional sense, value added by advertising is the same thing as part of the "social cost" of distribution. At this point, however, the difference in attitudes toward advertising, manufacturing, and agriculture begins to appear. One seldom hears of the "social cost of manufacturing" or the "social cost of agriculture." The values contributed by these forms of production are clearly recognized, and increases in them are hailed as social benefits. If the share of Gross National Product going to advertising increases, however, it is frequently considered undesirable and wasteful.

Much of the well-known public antagonism towards advertising stems from failure to recognize its role in the production process. There seems to be a cultural lag between economic development and public attitudes; and since advertising has only come to be of great importance in the last seventy years, it is not surprising that it has not yet been accorded its proper place.

The basic assumption underlying the many attacks on advertising costs is what might be called the "constant margin assumption." The reasoning runs something like this: Total production should be measured by the physical volume of goods produced, fabricated, and marketed to consumers. A certain percentage margin is necessary for advertising costs. If this increases, the consumer receives no more value, because he receives the same physical goods; but he is forced to pay more. The cause for the increased margin must be inefficiency in the advertising, and advertising, therefore, costs too much.

One need not be an economic theorist to see the fallacy of the foregoing argument. In the first place, much of the increase in advertising expenditures is due to increased specialization in the economic system.

Our economy has undergone a dramatic and far-reaching change in organization—a change which continues and apparently will continue in the foreseeable future. The full development of the production system, the application of mass production techniques, and the movement towards automation, all operate to shift much of the burden of production from manufacturing to distribution.

Example B. A leading M.D. was asked the question, "What do you think of the newly advertised remedies on TV for bad breath?" His answer was as follows:

It's sad to discover that a well-entrenched aphorism—a universally accepted tidbit of literary art—has at last bit the dust. Do you recall: "Even your best friend won't tell you"? In the past, think of the many completely oblivious to this personal failing: bad breath.

But these days such blissful ignorance is impossible. Whether you turn on the TV for news, your favorite Western, or a spy show, you are bound to hear the forceful reminder (by implication) that your breath is bad. Unfortunately, my bad luck is to hear these harangues whenever I am preparing for dinner.

You have bad breath! You have bad breath! These revelations are suddenly thrust on innocent, unsuspecting TV friends. These days they not only tell you; they shout it at you. It has gotten so bad that milquetoasts practice in front of mirrors so they can tell their bosses off.

I do not minimize the discomforts sometimes caused by one whose breath is not as sweet as a child's. It can be a problem. But in answer to your question, I believe the problem of bad breath should be attacked frontally by physicians and dentists. Removing the cause is often more important than experiments with various advertised agents. There's time for those later.

Here are some constructive points to remember:

People with chronic lung conditions and infections of the bronchial tubes (bronchitis, emphysema, etc.) have a tendency to have bad breath. Therefore, treat the underlying cause.

If you drink too much, smoke too much, it is not likely that your breath is sweet. Some patients with advanced kidney disease suffer from bad breath.

You may have no other reason for bad breath than food particles trapped between teeth causing decay and odor. Using the toothbrush after meals and finishing the cleansing process with dental floss is the best way to overcome the trouble. Are dentures clean? Do you make routine visits to your dentist or do you wait for a toothache to bestir you? It's possible that bad breath may be due to infection of your gums. Proper treatment will do much to improve the chronic complaint.

It is evident that mouthwash and gargles will be ineffectual unless you root out any infection like bad sinuses, tonsils, and adenoids.

It's not cricket to long for the good old days. But frankly, rather than have to listen to rudely overpowering TV commercials which deflate one's appetite like a pin in a balloon, I prefer the mildly Victorian approach. "Even your best friends won't tell you."

Case questions

1. How does advertising add value to the economy?

2. What value does the consumer receive as a result of advertising?

3. What economic value does the advertising effort actually have in order to get the consumer to purchase from one seller instead of another?

4. What social and economic value is there for advertising mouthwashes?

CASE 2.   GOLDEN HORN CO.
Evaluating use of advertising

Golden Horn Co. is engaged in the breeding, growing, processing, and marketing of poultry. Its activities consist of producing and hatching eggs, operating a feed mill, raising chickens, processing chickens in whole or cut in parts and marketing chickens and feed. Its 25 distributors at the annual meeting requested that Golden Horn begin an advertising program to the consumer in order to help them capture a larger share of the volume of national and independent food chains.

Breeding

Golden Horn has a two-thirds interest in Yak Poultry Co. which is engaged in the business of producing eggs. Under the terms of the agreement Yak is obligated to sell and Golden is obligated to purchase the entire egg production. Golden purchases day-old breeder pullets and cockerels from approximately ten nonaffiliated primary breeders. One such primary breeder supplies approximately 50 percent of such breeder pullets and another such breeder supplies approximately 50 percent of the breeder cockerels. The breeder flocks are sent to one of approximately 18 contract growing houses where they are kept for approximately 15 weeks. At such time they are transferred to one of approximately 12 contract breeder farms where they are kept during their entire productive egg-laying period (which period commences at about 26 weeks of age and may continue for 8 or 9 months). The contract growers are paid an average of 1.25 cents per chick housed, and contract breeders are paid approximately 12 cents per dozen hatching eggs produced. The contractors furnish all equipment, labor, and utilities while Yak's flocks are there, and supply the feed and technical assistance required. Yak's breeder flocks, which during the course of the year aggregate from 125,000 to 150,000 breeder hens in production at any one time, produce approximately 500,000 eggs per week.

Hatcheries

Hatching eggs are trucked by equipment from the contract breeder to the hatcheries where they are placed in incubators for 19 days, after which they are transferred to hatchers for two days. After hatching, the chicks are immediately delivered to grow-out farms. Golden currently purchases approximately 70,000 chicks per week from a nonaffiliated party.

Growing operations

Baby chicks are delivered by Golden to the contract growers who furnish houses, equipment, labor, and utilities during the eight to nine week period necessary to raise the chicks to marketable size. Golden's personnel supervise the growing process and Golden furnishes feed, fuel, and medical supplies required during the growing period. Golden generally has an average of four to five million chickens on grow-out farms at any given time. Golden maintains approximately 220 broiler flocks which average 21,000 chickens per flock and the contract growers raise an average of 4½ flocks per year. Each contract grower is paid on a performance contract under which the grower is guaranteed not less than $70 per thousand broilers started. At between eight and one-half and nine weeks the chickens are picked up and delivered to the company's processing plant.

Processing plant

The processing plant has a capacity on a one shift basis of approximately 500,000 chickens per week. The chickens, when delivered, are hung on overhead conveyors that carry them through the various processing steps which include slaughtering, picking, eviscerating, chilling, grading, sizing, and packaging. The entire process takes approximately one and one-half hours. Golden sells both whole and cut-up chickens, with whole chickens accounting for approximately 75 percent of total sales. Chickens are delivered to distributors within 24 hours after processing.

Sales and distribution

During the last fiscal year Golden produced and sold approximately twenty-two million chickens. It sells its poultry to approximately 25 independent distributors. Such distributors resell products to major national and independent food chains and neighborhood food stores. During the last fiscal year the largest distributor accounted for approximately 21 percent of total sales.

Competition

The broiler industry is subject to intense competition. The severity of competition increases during periods of overproduction when the supply of broilers exceeds market demand. The broiler industry is also in competition with producers of meat and other fowl. Golden is also subject to certain seasonal fluctuations, whereby people tend to eat meat in greater quantities in the late fall and winter, resulting in a decline in the consumption and price of chicken. The primary areas of poultry production are Georgia, Arkansas, North Carolina, Alabama, Mississippi and the Delaware-Maryland-Virginia area. Golden finds it difficult to sell fresh poultry on an interregional basis due to shrinkage, spoilage, and differences in shipping costs which prevent it from competing effectively outside of its region of the United States.

Evaluation of advertising

Golden's director of sales, John Aragon, was given the assignment to give a recommendation in regards to whether or not the company might find it economically and socially sound to begin a program of advertising. In his report to the directors he pointed out that the consumer, in making decisions to purchase, was faced with a number of alternatives. Generally, most of the decisions would fall into two categories: major purchases and minor purchases.

With major purchases there tended to be a gradual evolution which culminates in a concrete decision to buy the product. The stimulus to begin to evaluate the major product may be set in motion by both external and internal events. The washing machine may break down, a member of the family may be in an automobile accident, or the husband may be promoted to a new position. As a result, the consumer begins to question his friends about the product, checks the advertising more carefully, and visits the various stores to look at the models.

On the other hand, Mr. Aragon emphasized that in those purchases which would be classified in the category of minor decision making, the impact of advertising varies. Generally, however, advertising will place a minor purchase decision brand within the spectrum of what is acceptable. There is also the belief of many customers that one brand in particular is outstanding.

Recommendations

Mr. Aragon indicated that he believed Golden should advertise for the following reasons:

1. Advertising would provide a cumulative effect. Golden should not try to get immediate sales.
2. It was important from the social point of view to create a high degree of confidence in Golden's products.
3. Advertising would help develop a symbolic aura for Golden.
4. Although the purchase of Golden's products would generally be the minor decision type, for special functions the meat dish may actually become the equivalent of a major decision.
5. The emphasis of Golden's advertising should be centered on general reputation, quality, and value.
6. It is necessary to help the distributors gain a greater market share.
7. Advertising would be the most economical and fruitful method of giving the ultimate consumer information about Golden's products.
8. The consumer movement is going to continue at a faster rate and it is imperative for Golden to get involved in giving consumers product information.

9. Golden must keep abreast of the dynamic conditions in the broiler market.
10. Golden would have to make its products "familiar" before it could persuade the consumer to buy them.

Case questions

1. Evaluate the economical and social factors involved in getting the consumer to make decisions for:
   a) Major purchases
   b) Minor purchases
2. The average person, it is said, is exposed to 1,500 ads in a normal day. From the economic and social points of view, how can Golden justify spending funds for advertising?
3. How important is it for Golden to provide information to satisfy consumer needs for its products?
4. What effect would Golden's advertising have on the price which the retailers would charge?
5. From economic and social viewpoints, should Golden advertise?

CASE 3. SOCIOECONOMIC CONCEPTS
Value conflict

The outstanding feature of the American clothing economy during this century has been the gradual elimination of dress differences among the various socioeconomic groups. Clothing has become lighter in weight, simpler in style, more comfortable, and easier to care for. Certain items of the turn-of-the-century wardrobe are almost anachronisms. Today a skilled laborer may be required to wear a functional garment at his job, but his leisure-time wardrobe is as diversified as that of the average office worker. By the same token, a young secretary's style of dress is not too different from that of a young debutante's; while a Boston dowager may not even be as well dressed as the wife of a successful business executive. As for children, they are universally dressed in as little as the season permits, primarily with an eye to comfort, health, and easy care.

This equalization in dress habits is the result of interrelated social, technological, and economic changes, which were sharply accelerated during the last two decades, and which changed our society with previous periods and opened big new markets for types of consumer goods that were considered luxuries in the past.

It is a fact that, while total national clothing expenditures increased, they have not kept pace with the rise in consumer disposable income.

The textile and apparel industries have referred to this trend as a loss of their "rightful share" of the consumer dollar and have geared their promotional programs to try to recover this share.

The concept of a rightful or traditional share is based on a static view of the economy and denies the existing competition among industries to sell consumers all kinds of traditional and new products through all sorts of advertising media and other marketing devices. Fiber producers and textile industries—suppliers to the apparel trades—realized that they too must enter the competitive promotional fray if they were not to risk even further loss of their potential markets to other consumer goods. Today, clothing is being promoted with comparable budgets and the same techniques as are cars, refrigerators, and myriads of electrical appliances.

The major economic and social factors that have broadened the market base for consumer goods and services of all kinds, and put clothing into competition with these goods for the consumer dollar are:

1. Advances in industrial technology which permitted mass production of erstwhile luxury items at prices the growing number of middle-income families could afford.
2. The tremendous rise in total consumer disposable income and average family income which supplies the purchasing power for the products of advanced technology.
3. The widespread improvement of family living standards, crystallized in the movement to suburbia and accompanied by increased ownership of homes, cars, and other durable goods.
4. The commitment of important percentages of family funds for the repayment of mortgages and installment loans on types of durable goods which establish "status" in the community.
5. The increase of leisure time due to shorter working hours and increased paid holidays and vacations.
6. The trend toward informal living, encouraged and influenced by conformity among peer groups in homogeneous suburban communities—expressed, as regards dress, in a trend toward casual clothes.
7. An expanding volume of "discretionary income" which permits a wide and unpredictable choice of spending or saving out of total income over and above income required for essential consumer goods.

These factors, combined with the postwar shifts in the age composition of the population (which expanded the clothing market for the very young and the very old faster than for the intervening age groups) caused the nation's clothing expenditures to lag behind expenditures for other consumer goods and services.

An examination of total and per capita trends in the production of major outerwear items for men and women reveals two fundamental changes in the character of their wardrobes: (1) There has been an expansion of so-called separates represented by skirts, blouses, and sweaters in women's wear, and by slacks, sweaters, and sport jackets in men's wear; while the market for traditional tailored clothing—dresses, suits, and coats for women, and suits and coats for men—has remained stable or declined. (2) The switch from "big ticket" items, represented by tailored clothing, to relatively "little ticket" items, represented by separates, made it possible to increase the average number of items in the typical wardrobe without any significant increase in per capita clothing expenditures.

The implications for retail selling efforts may require more individual sales transactions to sell a blouse or a sweater and skirt, than a dress or suit; or in menswear, a pair of slacks and a jacket, than a suit. Furthermore, the character of the separates items more frequently than not represents "trading down" from the traditional single item in terms of the sales check. There is much talk regarding the ability of the consumer to trade up on clothing, but a continuation of the trend toward substitution of little ticket items for big ticket items will only increase retail selling costs at the expense of profit margins.

Because of technological advances in the production of textiles and the competition which prevailed in the textile and apparel trades, among competing firms as well as with other industries trying to get bigger shares of the consumer dollar, consumer apparel prices increased less than the prices of all other consumer goods and service. While the potential purchasing power saved on clothing enlarged the funds available for the purchase of other goods, the textile industry suffered low profit margins, excess capacity, and eventual contraction to a capacity more closely in line with the size of the market.

Outlook for the industry

A survey of family expenditures made by the United States Bureau of Labor Statistics evaluated the impact of changes on clothing expenditure patterns. It was found that in comparable income groups: (1) homeowners spent less than renters on clothing, (2) families with very young children and older members spent less on clothing than those with young and middle-aged adults, and (3) suburban families spent less on clothing than urban families. The dominant features of the consumer economy during the past two decades included an accelerated trend toward home ownership, and a movement out of urban centers to suburbs. These factors, which tended to depress clothing expenditures, may be somewhat less important during the next decade because of offsetting developments.

In addition to the economic changes which are expected to stimulate clothing expenditures, there is a less easily measured factor which may well come into play. And that is the matter of "status symbols"—a psychological term which has been popularized as a result of the extension of market research to the investigation of consumer buying motivations.

Leading psychologists believe that, in a dynamic economy, status symbols tend to change whenever large proportions of the population acquire the currently popular ones. Since it is no longer as unique to own a home, a car or two, and a large number of other types of family goods, the leaders of change will be looking for other ways of differentiating themselves from the group.

There are also signs that the simple life—the backyard cookout, the informal open house, the universal acceptance of the "come as you are, we're not dressing" attitude—may become more elaborate as the young suburban families mature both chronologically and economically. More elaborate settings and more formal social mores may demand careful grooming and more selective attire.

In urban centers, too, there is a trend toward more selective attire for special occasions such as dining out, going to the theater, and entertaining, as people seek to enhance the flavor of such special occasions by dressing up.

However, for clothing to take on the major status symbol in the years ahead, it will be essential to expand the promotional programs in textiles and clothing and to gear the themes to the special psychological auras of different sectors of the clothing market. This should dispel the monotony of uniform glamour and help the textile and apparel industries, in the future, come closer to achieving their objectives of increasing clothing purchases than they have in the past, for the very simple reason that consumers are ready for a change of pace.

Case questions

1. How do you justify, on a basis of social values, the attempt of the clothing industry to get the consumers to look upon clothing as a "status symbol"?

2. Why do consumers fail to invest more of their disposable income in clothing?

3. When a declining trend exists for clothing, how can you economically justify the industry adopting a more extensive advertising program?

4. Would the standard of living be improved if the consumer spent more of his income on clothing?

5. When a conflict exists between social and economic concepts, how should the decision of whether or not to advertise be made?

CASE 4. LARSON, INC.
Importance of advertising

Larson, Inc., a company that manufactures shoes which are sold under the brand names of its customers, has limited its yearly advertising budget to $25,000 in trade advertising. The company is considering the advisability of increasing the budget to $200,000 for the next year because it desires to secure a greater proportion of the shoe business.

Products

The company manufactures women's dress shoes, which are sold at retail in the medium-price range under the brand name or trademark of its customers. Shoes produced at Manchester and Lowell generally sell at retail in the $11.95 to $18.95 range. Style is an important factor in the merchandising of the company's products. The company employs designers who, together with its sales executives, work closely with the company's customers in the creation and design of new models. As indicated, the company manufactures against firm orders only, and thus, insofar as finished products are concerned, the company is subject to little or no inventory risk as a result of style changes. However, by the nature of its business, the company is frequently required to buy raw materials in advance of orders for finished products and, therefore, sometimes takes an inventory risk on its raw material inventory.

Competition

Approximately 375 million pairs of women's shoes are produced annually in the United States, about 55 percent of which are dress shoes, the remainder being flat-heel shoes, sandals, and similar casual types. Dress shoes, as a matter of custom, fall into several fairly well-defined retail price categories. Shoes which sell at retail under $11.95 represent the largest market and account for about 38 percent of women's dress shoes manufactured. Shoes which sell at retail above $18.95 represent the higher price market and account for about 29 percent of women's dress shoes manufactured. The $11.95 to $18.95 retail price range, in which Larson concentrates its shoe sales, is the medium-price market, and account for about 33 percent of women's dress shoes manufactured.

Larson, Inc. is among the five largest producers of medium-grade shoes, and produces approximately 4 percent of women's dress shoes of the grades it manufactures. Foreign competition is negligible in the price range in which Larson, Inc. sells its products to its customers and in which such customers resell such products at retail.

Production, distribution, and customers

As is customary in the industry, the company operates its factories on a single-shift basis. At normal operating levels the company produces at the rate of approximately 10,000 pairs per day. Actual production rates vary from time to time during the year as styles and seasons change. During the last fiscal year, the company produced 2,450,000 pairs of shoes, or an average of 10,000 pairs per day, based on a 245-day working year. The company considers that, on a one-shift basis, it cannot materially increase normal operating levels.

The company's business is seasonal in the sense that in some months of the year its production is less than in other months. Shoes are manufactured by the company for two principal seasons, one being fall and winter and the other spring and summer. Although there are no precise dates when production for each season starts and stops, generally speaking, production of spring and summer shoes begins around October 1, and production of fall and winter shoes around May 1. At the times of seasonal changeover, there are usually about two months of reduced production.

Larson presently has approximately 35 active customer accounts which include some of the major retail shoe chain stores. Such customers have at least 2,500 retail outlets. These outlets are located throughout the United States. Some of the largest shoe manufacturers have integrated the retail selling of their own products through their own chain stores. The company's four largest customers account for approximately 55 percent of the company's total sales. Sales by the company to wholesalers represent a minor part of its business. All prices to customers are f.o.b. Massachusetts, net 30 days. The company has no long-term contracts with any of its customers.

As indicated above, the women's dress shoe trade is highly competitive, both among manufacturers and among the company's customers themselves. In view of the well-defined retail price categories in the industry, style and quality are of prime importance within a price category. As a result the retailer works closely with the manufacturer, and the retailer's buyers call on the company at least as frequently as the company's representatives call on the retailer. Under these circumstances, all of the executives of Larson, in effect, are engaged in selling the company's products.

New designs are developed by Larson's own technicians, who utilize various sources for ideas. Frequently, customers will develop designs themselves, in cooperation with the company. Samples are prepared from such designs by hand at nominal cost and are presented to the customer or customers for approval. Larson manufactures against firm orders only, and it has been the company's policy not to put into production any new model unless sufficient orders are developed to justify it. Larson and its competitors who sell to retail chains generally follow this practice, whereas manufacturers who sell branded merchandise frequently maintain inventories of finished shoes.

Raw materials

The principal raw material purchased by Larson is leather, which constitutes between 25 percent and 30 percent of the cost of goods sold. Other materials purchased include such fabrics as cotton drills, sheetings, felts, flannels and failles, satins, nygen (leatherized fabric), tufsta (rubberized paper), composition sole material, and various components including plastic and wooden heels, steel shanks, tacks, and treated papers. The company also purchases various adhesives, paints, waxes, and cleansing materials. Total material purchases constitute between 50 percent and 55 percent of the cost of goods sold.

The bulk of the leather purchases is cattlehide and calf. Larson also purchases goat, reptile, and other leathers. Because of its cash reserves in relation to its size, it has been possible for the company in the past to take advantage of special price situations which have occurred in the leather market from time to time. Larson makes its purchases of raw materials from many sources and believes that these will be capable of meeting its future requirements.

Equipment

Until recent years Larson leased most of its principal shoemaking machines from the manufacturers under agreements in form usual and customary in the industry. As a result of a change in industry practice certain leased machines became available for purchase and it is the company's policy to purchase machines rather than lease whenever it considers it advantageous to do so. At the present time the company owns most of its stitching room equipment and more than two thirds of its other machines. Larson has the usual types and kinds of machinery used in the industry for the production of women's dress shoes. All of Larson's machinery is in good operating condition and is considered by the company to be suitable for the purpose for which it is used.

The executives of Larson, Inc., have decided to continue to limit the production to the firm orders which are received from retailers and to handle distribution on a direct basis.

The statement of income (in thousands of dollars) for the five years ended December 31, is as follows:

	A	B	C	D	E
Net sales	$5,500	$6,000	$7,000	$8,500	$9,000
Cost of goods sold	4,800	5,500	6,000	7,800	7,900
Gross profit	700	500	1,000	700	1,100
Selling, administrative, and general expenses	400	410	450	425	500
Income before taxes	300	90	550	275	600

Case questions

1. To what extent will the retail stores be influenced by Larson's advertising?

2. Is it important for Larson to do a limited amount of ultimate consumer advertising?

3. What procedures should Larson, Inc. follow to determine if it should increase its advertising budget?

4. Should Larson's primary purpose in advertising be to educate and inform the trade buyers?

PART II

Advertising strategy

chapter 4

BASIC DEMAND STRATEGY

THE STIMULATION of demand is normally the most impor-
tant function of advertising. A key question for the advertiser, therefore,
is "How do I stimulate or persuade the consumer to purchase my product?" And this brings him to the further questions of why consumers buy
particular products, why people change their attitude toward products
and brands, why people buy one brand instead of another, and why
they switch from one brand to another.

Man's basic drives or desires are inherent. These fundamental wants
and drives to action cannot be created by advertising. However, advertising can, by the use of the proper appeals to these basic desires,
activate latent or unrealized wants, stimulate demand so more of a
product will be used, or influence the consumer to satisfy his wants by
concentrating his purchases on a particular product or brand.

SELECTION OF APPEALS

It is necessary, therefore, in attempting to stimulate demand, to select
the "appeal" which will influence the present or potential customer to
satisfy his wants by using the advertiser's product and/or service. What
stimuli will be most effective in evolving the desired response on the part
of the prospect? Should it be one which appeals to only a select part of
the market, such as the appeal in Figure 4–1?

You need only to consider the appeals which are generally used to sell
automobiles to appreciate how complex they may be. In selecting the
appeals for advertising cars, the various companies have tried to assess
the importance of interest in engineering features, such as air conditioning, safety, upkeep, economy, trade-in value, and the like. However, to
know that a customer values comfort does not offer too much useful
information. What is comfort? Is it the upholstery? Leg room? Head
room? Good springs? Trunk space? Actually, the question is centered on
what the customer really means by comfort.

FIGURE 4–1

This nice young man is a gambler. His $24,000 home is insured for only $15,500.

Good luck, nice young man.

Please. Don't take chances. Protect your home for all it's worth. Against loss by fire. Tornado. Burglary. Vandalism. And more. With a State Farm Homeowners Policy. Naturally it costs money to increase your insur-ance as your home increases in value. But that's where State Farm has the edge on other insurance companies. State Farm offers a better deal than most. Same as State Farm does on auto insurance.

It's made us number one in both.

Whether you own or rent, it'll pay you to see your friendly State Farm agent about broad, low-cost coverage for your home and belongings. You can find him fast in the Yellow Pages. And maybe you'd better. Unless, of course, you have money to burn.

State Farm Fire and Casualty Company
Home Office: Bloomington, Illinois

In Texas, savings on State Farm Homeowners Policies have been returned as dividends. In Mississippi, we offer a Comprehensive Dwelling Policy similar to our Homeowners Policy.

Courtesy: State Farm Fire and Casualty Co.

To determine what appeal will be effective, the advertiser must determine which of the drives and motives to be discussed in Chapter 5 can be satisfied by his particular product and also, the specific qualities of his product which are of most importance to the consumer in satisfying his needs and desires. For instance, when the garbage disposal unit was first placed on the market, the manufacturer had to decide whether to make his basic appeal to health (eliminate the danger of diseases from flies that are attracted by a garbage can); to the mother's love of her children (protect your children's health from the diseases carried by flies that are attracted by garbage cans); to comfort (save all the steps and hard work of carrying out your garbage); to her pride as an efficient housewife (all the time and energy saved by the installation of this product can be devoted to other aspects of your duties as a mother and housewife); or to emulation (all the new and modern homes are installing these units).

APPEALING TO PERSON INFLUENCING DECISION TO BUY

It should be noted here that marketing research can be used not only to aid in selection of the most effective appeals, but also to determine who makes the decisions to buy and who influences the person who actually buys the product. In many cases, although the wife actually will buy the product in the store, the decision as to what to buy has been made or influenced by other members of the family.

The wife buys the package of frankfurters rather than the package of ground round steak (which she really prefers personally) because her youngster has expressed his desire for frankfurters. Or, although the mother buys the cereal, whether she buys a hot or prepared dry cereal and which brand or type of prepared dry cereal she buys is determined by, or strongly influenced by, the desires of her children.

So the advertiser must determine not only who buys the product but also who influences the decision to buy. For some products, such as certain food items, the children's desires will be influential factors in the mother's final purchase. However, for other products, such as major appliances, it may be a joint decision of husband and wife, and the desires of the children will not even be considered. No sharp dichotomy of the influence can be assigned in general terms for all products. As a result, an advertiser is faced with the continuous problem of analyzing who influences the decision to buy in the ever changing market environment in which his product is sold.

CONTRIBUTIONS FROM THE SOCIAL SCIENCES

In selecting his basic theme or appeal and copy strategy, the advertiser should attempt to utilize, as far as possible, the knowledge and contributions of the various fields of social science. The knowledge developed by the disciplines of anthropology (especially cultural anthropology), psychology, and sociology all can contribute much to this area of appeal strategy. The anthropologist can help select advertising themes through his understanding of themes in a culture. He can aid the advertiser by providing insights into the symbolic aspects of culture and the means by which culture can be changed. Also, the studies of family behavior can aid in developing a better understanding of buying influences. The knowledge of anthropology about the special subcultures of various racial groups would aid the advertiser in developing a strategy for reaching such groups effectively. This could also aid the advertiser in foreign advertising by preventing him from violating political, religious, or cultural taboos.

Psychology has developed a great body of knowledge that has application in the area of selecting effective copy themes. It has made great contributions to the field of motivation research, and has much to contribute in determining motivation. The theories developed by psychologists can be of great aid in selecting the proper appeal, and in adapting variations of this theme to special segments of the market.

Sociology has developed a great deal of knowledge regarding the importance of social classes, and the implications resulting from the different motivational patterns of various classes of society. Their contributions in this area of class and status can be of aid in the selection of the proper appeals to influence special groups.

It is thus obvious that the advertiser, in determining his advertising copy strategy, should attempt to utilize to the fullest extent possible the great bodies of knowledge developed by the behavioral sciences—knowledge of individuals, families, groups, social classes; and how they are motivated, how they influence others, and how they interact.

PRIMARY AND SELECTIVE DEMAND

Depending on the conditions surrounding the product, the consumer, and the market, there are two broad types of consumer demand that advertising attempts to stimulate. These two types of demand usually are called primary and selective demand.

Primary demand

Advertising designed to stimulate primary demand is that which is attempting to create demand for a type of product. For example, advertising which explains how the customer should enjoy the comfort of an air conditioner during the hot summer months, how much healthier the customer will be if she has cool air in her home, how much more work members of the family will be able to produce if they have the comfort, good sleep, and so forth, is advertising which attempts to convince the potential customer that she should buy air-conditioning equipment for her home. It points out the desires and drives that will be satisfied by having such a piece of equipment installed in the home. In other words, primary demand advertising tells the potential customer how her basic needs can be satisfied by a product, and does not attempt to sell a specific brand. (Figure 4–2 is an example of primary demand advertising.)

FIGURE 4–2

Courtesy: President's Council on Physical Fitness

Selective demand

Selective advertising is designed to stimulate the demand for a particular brand, style, or model of a type of product. Following up the above illustration of air-conditioning equipment, the General Electric Company, if it were using selective advertising, would not try to increase the demand for air conditioners as such, or the type of product as such. Instead, it would concentrate on those features of its brand that would cause people to buy a General Electric model when they purchase an air conditioner. The advertising usually would do this by pointing out those features of the brand that enable it to fulfill the customers' desires or needs better than any other air conditioner on the market. It would stress the distinctive features and qualities of the brand which make it the superior product—which make it the best solution to the customer's problems or desires. Such features might be: more accurate maintenance of desired temperature in the house; smaller, more compact size and hence a better appearance; more economy in operation; better quality so it will last longer or require less maintenance; or its lower price.

In the advertisement, Figure 4–3, as an example, the Carrier Air Conditioning Company stresses the advantages of its product and does not try to build demand for air conditioners in general. Its objective is to stimulate selective demand for its brand of products.

Combining primary and selective appeals

In practice, these two types of appeals are often combined in advertising. For example, although the main appeal of an advertisement might be primary (air conditioners will give you comfort, better health, make you a more efficient worker, etc.) it might go on with a selective appeal by ending with "and the air conditioner that will do this job most effectively is the General Electric model, because it has the most accurate temperature control, it is most efficient and economical in operation, etc." This usually is done during the early period after the product's introduction on the market, while it is still necessary to educate people to the want-satisfying qualities of a type of product, but with enough demand already created that companies attempt to obtain the major benefit of the demand they stimulate by advertising for their own brand. However, even after a product has been on the market for many years, it may be advisable for firms to do some primary advertising to hold their product's share of the consumer's dollar as against other and newer products that are appearing on the market. For instance, radio manufacturers might well do some primary advertising (use transistor radios while hiking, etc.) to show the want-satisfying qualities of radios. (See Berry Doors advertisement in Figure 4–4.)

FIGURE 4–3. The wall-to-wall air conditioner

For wall-to-wall comfort.
Carrier believes a room air conditioner
should cool the room, the whole room,
wall to wall. With no frigid zones
or hot spots. That's the idea behind
our exclusive 18-way air flow control.
Another reason why more people
put their confidence in Carrier
than in any other make.

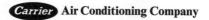

Carrier Air Conditioning Company

Courtesy: Carrier Air Conditioning Company

PRIMARY DEMAND ADVERTISING AS A CONTINUOUS PROCESS

It must be remembered that the stimulation of primary demand is to some extent a continuous process. For, although an extensive primary advertising program for a given product may have stimulated a desire for the product among most of the present adult age groups and income brackets that constitute the potential buyers for the product at the time, there is a constant shift in the makeup of these age groups in the population. As teenagers, for example, move into the adult age group to become

FIGURE 4–4. Contrast

Not if she has a Stanley-Berry Automatic Garage Door Opener!

Just a touch of the button—while sitting comfortably in your car—that's all there is to opening (or closing) your garage door the convenient Stanley-Berry way! Forget about wind, rain or snow. Wet feet, bruised knuckles and strained muscles are a thing of the past. And what a welcome sight on a dreary, dismal night to pull into your drive and have the garage door open and the light go on—all automatically! Don't wrestle another day! Have your Stanley-Berry Automatic Garage Door Opener installed now.

Portable transmitter and radio receiver are both completely transistorized and comply fully with F.C.C. regulations.

BERRY DOORS
DIVISION OF THE STANLEY WORKS
2400 E. LINCOLN RD., BIRMINGHAM, MICH. 48010

Berry Doors • Division of The Stanley Works
Dept. BHG-866, 2400 E. Lincoln Rd., Birmingham, Mich. 48010
Gentlemen: Please send me your descriptive literature on Stanley-Berry Garage Doors and Automatic Openers.
Name_____
Address_____
City_____State_____Zip_____

Courtesy: Berry Doors
Division of the Stanley Works

a part of the potential market, it may be necessary to educate them to the want-satisfying qualities of the product. Also, as people earn higher incomes and, hence, become potential buyers of a product for the first time, it may also be necessary to use primary advertising to stimulate their demand for the product. Similarly, changes in customs and buying habits of various groups may bring them into the market as potential buyers for a product.

The development of new uses for a product may call for the employment of primary advertising to point out these want-satisfying aspects of the product from this new angle. Hence, for most well-established products, periodically at least, emphasis must be placed on primary appeal advertising. These types of constant changes in the composition of an advertiser's potential market are the basis for the saying so often heard among advertising people: "You advertise to a parade, not to an audience."

The circumstances or conditions in which primary or selective demand advertising may be effectively used vary somewhat, so the two should be analyzed separately. These conditions might be divided into three groups or categories: the conditions relating to demand; the conditions relating to the product or service; and the conditions relating to the market.

THE STIMULATION OF PRIMARY DEMAND

Conditions relating to demand

There are several conditions relating to demand which must be favorable if a primary advertising campaign is to give prospect of success. There must be strong basic drives or desires that can be satisfied by use of the product or service. The stronger these desires that can be satisfied, the greater the probable response that can be obtained to any effective advertising which may be done. If the want that can be satisfied is the desire to sustain life or secure happiness or security, for example, then the prospects for success in stimulating demand through the use of primary advertising are enhanced.

Of equal importance is the answer to the question of how well these wants currently are being satisfied by other products already on the market. If the consumer can satisfy his desires and wants easily and well with products currently on the market and with which he is already quite familiar, convincing him of the desirability of changing to the advertiser's product to satisfy the want will be more difficult than if at present this need or want is not satisfied easily with products already available to him on the market.

And, as important as these two conditions relating to demand is the closely related one of the strength of the appeal, or appeals, that can be used to promote the product. How strong an appeal can be associated with the product? And how strong is it as compared with the same or similar appeals associated with other competing products? So the presence of a strong appeal to a basic buying motive is very important in evaluating the possibility of stimulating the primary demand for a new product.

Another significant condition is that of the potential expansibility of demand for this type of product. Are the buying motives to which the advertising for this product is directed such that the amount purchased and consumed at any given price can be readily increased?

What are the basic trends of demand for products of this general type? The demand trend for some types of products may be increasing, while for others it may be declining. Many reasons can account for these trends which are perhaps more basic than any promotional and selling activities of individual companies. Changes in the pattern of social life, changes in working hours and conditions, and similar deep underlying social, economic, and cultural changes will influence the trend of demand for various types of products. A favorable trend in basic demand greatly facilitates the possibility of using advertising successfully to increase the demand for a product.

Conditions relating to the product

The most important condition is that the product have some significant advantage over alternative products in its ability to satisfy the wants and desires of the consumer. Unless the product can satisfy certain wants better, more easily, or for a lower price, it may be difficult to stimulate demand to a sufficient extent to make primary advertising feasible from an economic standpoint. Also, if the product has certain notable weaknesses or disadvantages as compared with alternative products, the task of stimulating primary demand will be much more difficult.

Also, the outstanding characteristic of this product and its advantages over alternative products must be sufficiently great with relation to the price of the product or service. There must be what the prospective purchaser considers a reasonable relationship between the features and advantages of the product and its cost. For example, container companies attempting to stimulate primary demand for paper milk cartons when they were first introduced on the market had a product with significant advantages (less weight, elimination of bothersome return-the-bottle problem, elimination of glass breakage) but had extreme difficulty in stimulating demand for the paper carton among dairy firms because of the amount of cost differential.

Conditions relating to the market

Several conditions of the market are significant in determining the probable success of primary advertising in stimulating adequate demand for a product. Can the prospects for the product be identified and are their characteristics known? Advertising must use the right media and appeals to be effective, and the right media and appeals can be selected economically only if the market is identifiable. Similarly, how many of such prospects are there? Do they have sufficient purchasing power to buy an adequate amount of the product? On the basis of the number of prospects and their purchasing power, is it feasible to stimulate sufficient purchases to warrant the amount of advertising necessary to reach and influence these people? And is there sufficient margin between the cost of the product and its selling price to provide the funds that are necessary to support the amount of advertising that probably will be required?

Obviously, the above conditions are interrelated, and no one of them can be considered as an isolated condition. The significant characteristics and strength of appeals are related to the price of the product, and the price is related to and influences effective demand, and both influence the amount of advertising required. The importance of any of the above conditions will vary according to the circumstances surrounding any given situation, and in certain instances other factors may influence the feasibility of using advertising to stimulate primary demand. But these at least indicate the usual more important factors that must be considered when analyzing the possibility of carrying out a successful primary advertising campaign.

THE STIMULATION OF SELECTIVE DEMAND

As in the case of primary demand advertising, a number of factors or conditions influence the probable success of a firm's advertising designed primarily to stimulate increased demand for its particular brand of a generic product. It must be kept in mind that the opportunity to use advertising to influence selective demand profitably is dependent in part, in most instances, to the effect of advertising on primary demand. Hence, the conditions affecting selective demand must be considered against the background of the conditions influencing primary demand.

Conditions relating to demand

One of the most important conditions which influence the opportunity to stimulate selective demand by company brand advertising is the trend of the primary demand for the type of product. If the primary demand trend is favorable, the probability of successful selective advertising is much greater than if the demand trend is adverse.

Another condition of considerable influence in affecting the success of selective demand advertising by a company is the presence of strong basic buying wants or desires which the product is capable of satisfying, and the presence of strong emotional appeals that can be used to stimulate the potent basic wants and desires. It will be noted that these conditions of strong wants or needs or desires and potent emotional appeals used to stimulate demand are similar to conditions affecting primary demand. They are similar, but they are repeated here because they also appear to be equally significant conditions influencing the opportunity to stimulate selective demand through brand advertising.

Conditions relating to the product

A brand of product that possesses some significant individualizing feature of real importance to customers has a much better chance of being advertised successfully than one that possesses no such features. The advertiser who can point out real discernible differences between his product and those of his competitors has much better possibilities for stimulating selective demand for his brand than does the company whose product has no definite distinguishing features to differentiate it. At least it must be possible to convince the customer that the product has distinctly superior and distinguishing features or qualities. Also, this factor influences the price differential obtainable, the gross margin obtained, and hence, the funds available for advertising the brand. Sugar is a prime example of a product with virtually no significant differences among brands, while cosmetics manufacturers have convinced the customers that there are great and significant differences among the products of different manufacturers.

Another condition of real significance in determining the opportunity for a firm to stimulate selective demand through the use of brand advertising is the importance to the potential customer of the hidden qualities of the product as compared to the importance of those external qualities and characteristics which can be observed and appreciated by the customer by inspection. If there are such hidden qualities which are important to the customer, then the customer will tend to rely more heavily on the brand in buying, and so advertising can be used to build up the association of the brand with the desired qualities. But, if at the time of purchase the customer can judge by inspection the attributes of the product important to him, then brand name is not so significant and the customer will not be influenced so much by advertising. The customer is prone to rely more on his judgment of those characteristics than on associations that might be built up in his mind by brand advertising.

Conditions relating to the market

Of great importance in determining the ability to employ advertising effectively to stimulate selective demand for a firm's product is the amount of money the company's program will make available for its advertising and promotion program. There must always be sufficient funds available to a firm to permit an adequate advertising campaign if there is to be any opportunity for success. An inadequate campaign which cannot make an effective impression on the market will fail to get satisfactory results. The amount, obviously, depends on the number of units sold and the margin per unit, which margin per unit is dependent in part at least on the effectiveness of advertising in stimulating the consumer's evaluation of the special and differentiating characteristics of the product as produced by the advertising. The effectiveness of the advertising in creating this evaluation on the part of the customer depends not only on the differentiating characteristics of the product but also on the other conditions noted above. The amount of funds that will be available for advertising of a product would depend also on other conditions, such as the amount and type of competition existing in the industry, the absolute amount of the price of the individual unit, the frequency of purchase of the product, and the number of customers for the product.

These are probably the most important of the conditions to be considered in attempting to ascertain whether or not advertising designed to stimulate selective demand is feasible. If all these conditions were favorable, advertising would undoubtedly be successful in stimulating satisfactory selective demand, if carried out well. But it is not necessary that all these conditions be favorable. A failure to meet one condition may be offset by great strength in one or more of the other conditions. It is basically the combination of the above conditions that is determining. Hence, judgment must be exercised in weighing the situation for any given product at a particular time to determine whether or not it seems to meet the conditions sufficiently well to make advertising worthwhile.

RESPONSIBILITY FOR STIMULATION OF DEMAND

The manufacturer usually has the basic responsibility for stimulating demand for a new type of product. He cannot expect the channels of distribution, such as the wholesalers and retailers, to stock an unknown product with no existing consumer demand and try to sell it for him. So the manufacturer will generally have to do such advertising as is required to inform the potential users of the want-satisfying qualities of his product in order to stimulate the desire of the wholesaler and retailer to stock his item and offer it for sale to the customer. The manufacturer will usually not only advertise to the ultimate consumer to stimulate primary demand for his new product but also will coordinate with such advertising, personal selling effort, promotional activities, and advertising directed to the trade to induce them to stock his product. Thus, it will be available to the ultimate customer when his demand has been stimulated to the point at which he desires to buy the product, or at least inspect it on the basis of the interest created by the manufacturer's advertising. Another significant reason the manufacturer finds it necessary to assume the stimulation of demand responsibility is that during the past decade, impulse purchases have increased from 38 percent to 51 percent in food stores. As a result, the distributors are more willing to handle the nationally advertised products. These are the items for which there is usually a greater demand, and the retailer finds that generally he is able to make a more satisfactory profit when he gives such products preferred shelf position.

To a large extent, the same is true of a new brand of a product. Here again, normally the manufacturer will advertise both to the consumer to stimulate selective demand and also to the trade to induce them to stock this new brand of product. The appeals (as well as the media used, etc.) will be different for the consumer and the trade advertising, but both will have the same purpose—to induce purchase of his brand, in one case for consumption or use and in the other case for resale purposes.

FACTORS INFLUENCING NEED FOR ADVERTISING

The extent to which the manufacturer must bear the burden of "selling" or stimulating demand for his product by advertising varies with several factors.

Stage of market development

As is evident from the above discussion, the stage of market development for a product is one important factor in determining the dependence on the manufacturer's advertising for the sale of the product. When the product is new on the market, prime responsibility rests with the manufacturer to stimulate demand. After his product becomes well known and some degree of demand has been stimulated, the trade may be willing and may desire to carry on some of the advertising for the product as a means of increasing their sales of the product, and as a means of attracting customers to their stores. And, after a brand of product has built up a strong enough demand through advertising, retailers may feature its selective features very aggressively to the consumer in order to attract people to their stores. Or, they may use the appeal of price in their advertising and do a strong job of increasing selective demand in the form of sales through their price-appeal advertising.

Type of product as a factor

The type of product can be of great influence on the significance of advertising in the selling program. In the case of patent medicines, for example, where there is often a quite limited market potential and the retailer is not in a position actively to push the product, the manufacturer will find it necessary to carry almost the entire burden of stimulating demand. So he will advertise heavily to the ultimate consumer, creating in the consumers' minds a concept of the unique qualities of his product and its potent want-satisfying qualities, so that they will insist on having this particular product or brand of product. Thus, the trade is forced to stock it by the specific requests of customers, who ask for this particular product or brand of product and will accept no substitute. In turn, the retailer will insist on this particular product or brand from the wholesaler, and so the product is "pulled through" the channels of distribution by the demand stimulated by the advertising.

Or for some products that have a wide potential market and when the retailer believes people can be attracted to his store to shop for the product, the trade may also do some advertising of the product to aid in stimulating either primary or selective demand, although usually advertising by the trade tends to be selective rather than primary. In practice, the desire of the retailer to aid by advertising is enhanced if the product is being distributed on a selective or exclusive basis rather than on an intensive basis.

Actually, for most producers, advertising cannot stimulate a strong enough demand to cause people to insist on a particular product or brand of product. Thus, it is necessary to combine with consumer advertising, a good advertising, promotional, and personal selling program to the trade to induce them to stock the product and display and/or sell it aggressively. The more important demonstration and personal selling are to a product, the more importance the retail activity assumes in its sale, and the less actual insistence can be stimulated by advertising.

However, today, even products requiring demonstration and personal selling are being "presold" by means of advertising. One form of advertising that aids in this is television, a medium that can show and demonstrate the product in use as well as tell about its qualities. For some products, this enables advertisers to perform a larger share of the selling task than was formerly the case.

It must be kept in mind, however, that advertising media also include the point-of-purchase material and displays of merchandise and selling messages created and utilized in the store itself to influence the customer when he is in the store—nearest in place, time, and emotional mood for the actual purchase of the merchandise. And closely allied to the last forms of advertising and promotional materials furnished the retailer are such items as informative booklets for salespeople and various materials aimed to "sell" the salespeople on the product and stimulate them to active and enthusiastic selling of the product to the customer. All these forms of stimulation aimed at the consumer and the salespeople who are in a position to stimulate demand among the consumers must be closely coordinated with advertising and promotion efforts directed to the trade in order to obtain the desired distribution and the active cooperation of retailers in displaying and selling the merchandise.

QUESTIONS

1. Bring to class two magazine advertisements that you believe have utilized unusually effective appeals. Explain why you selected them.

2. Bring to class two advertisements you feel are using a weak or poor appeal. Explain the reasons for selecting them.

3. In most families the housewife, or mother, does most of the grocery shopping, and hence the actual buying of the product. However, many advertising people believe that for some of the items on her shopping list, she is strongly influenced in her selection of items or brands by other members of the family, so that advertising appeals should be selected to influence the husband or children. Do you agree? Why?

4. Name three products in the purchase of which you feel the children of the family have great influence on the mother's purchase. Explain why you selected them.

5. Which member, or members, of the family do you think have most influence on the brand decision for the following: (a) automobile, (b) refrigerator, (c) automatic dishwashing machine, (d) coffee, (e) sofa, (f) bread?

6. In what ways do you feel the knowledge borrowed from sociology and cultural anthropology can be of help to the advertiser in selecting effective appeals?

7. By means of an example, illustrate the difference between primary and selective demand.

8. Under what conditions might an advertiser combine primary and selective demand advertising? Give an example.

9. It is sometimes said that the stimulation of primary demand is a continuous process, so advertisers should always do some primary demand advertising. Do you agree or disagree? Why?

10. Name two examples of products that you feel should be supported with strong primary demand advertising at the present time. Explain why you selected them.

11. Name two products that you feel are especially suited to strong selective demand advertising. Explain your selections.

12. Should the manufacturer of a small executive airplane stress primary or selective appeals in his advertising at present? Why?

CASE 1. UNITED FRUIT COMPANY
The use of a selective appeal

Rising costs and declining revenue per hundredweight of bananas contributed to a diminishing earnings trend for the United Fruit Company.

Banana industry. The banana industry is highly competitive, because bananas are produced on an extensive basis in both the eastern and the western hemispheres. Asia was their original home, but they have been planted in many other warm parts of the world. The Hawaiian Islands produce a banana crop. In the continental United States, Florida grows small quantities of bananas. Some are also grown along the coast of the Gulf of Mexico.

The most important banana-producing region in the world is Central America; Mexico, the West Indies, Ecuador, and Brazil also have large banana plantations.

The bananas most commonly used as fruit in America are large, yellow, and smooth-skinned. They are known as *Gros Michel, Valery,* and *Cavendish* bananas, and there is no significant product differentiation regardless of the section of the world in which they may be grown.

Before 1860, most of the banana crop was consumed in the country where the bananas were grown. However, at about that time the first large commercial plantations were created. The activities required to build and operate these large plantations included the clearing of jungles and the building of roads and villages. As a result, only large companies with adequate financing were in a position to enter the banana industry.

The United Fruit Company was one of the major companies which concentrated its banana growing acreage in Central America. It was incorporated in 1899 and employs 49,000 persons in Latin America and the United States. It operates a steamship line to transport the crops to the United States; it also operates 13 hospitals and 250 grade schools in Latin America.

Use of bananas. While generally the only part of the banana plant that is used is the fruit, people use the leaves of certain kinds of banana trees to roof houses or to make mats, bags, and baskets. Cooked bananas are becoming increasingly popular in the United States, where they are fried, made into fritters, cooked with ham and bacon, and used in pies, cakes, and bread. Banana flour is also coming into wider use. The banana is one of the few fruits that can be bought fresh and in good condition at all times of the year.

Imports. When the fruit is to be shipped for considerable distances, workers pick it green, a whole stem at a time, cut it into clusters, and ship it in boxes. It is ripened at its destination market. The United States imports over 72 million bunches of bananas each year.

EXHIBIT 1

Now you *can* judge a banana by its cover

Meet Chiquita Brand Bananas

This seal outside   means the best inside

Some bananas come from the tropics unprotected ... get exposed to bumps and bruises. Now Chiquita Brand Bananas are shipped in heavy boxes, to protect them from bruises inside and out.

 Remember how it used to be? You could never really tell, whenever you bought a banana, whether you might be getting a peach—or a lemon. It might be bruised on the inside. But you couldn't always tell from the outside.

Now there's something brand new at your store: Chiquita Brand Bananas. Now you *can* judge a banana by its cover. Instead of coming up from the tropics in their birthday suits—on big stems—these bananas come in strong fiber boxes. To protect them from bruises, inside and out.

So next time you shop, make sure you get Chiquita Brand Bananas.

Look for the seal on the peel: It's the mark of a well-brought-up banana.

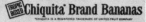

Courtesy: United Fruit Company

Competitive situation. The United Fruit Company found that its revenue was decreasing because its competitors had lower costs per hundredweight, and were selling their fruit at much lower prices. No consumer franchises existed for bananas, and, typically, the brokers in a commodity

EXHIBIT 2

The sign of a successful banana

That Chiquita Brand seal is a mark of achievement. Bananas that wear it have been rigorously inspected before they ever leave the tropics. Not just once, but six times. If a banana doesn't measure up, it doesn't make the boat.

Only after that are Chiquita Brand Bananas shipped. Shipped all the way from the tropics in strong, protective boxes. So when they arrive at your store, they're as sleek and golden and

tempting as bananas can be.
So to pick out the best of the bananas from the rest of the bananas, be sure to look for the seal on the peel.
It's the sign of a banana that's really a peach.

CHIQUITA BRAND BANANAS
THIS SEAL OUTSIDE ● MEANS THE BEST INSIDE.

*Chiquita is a registered trademark of United Fruit Company

Courtesy: United Fruit Company

market of this kind make their purchases on the basis of price rather than a consumer preference for a particular kind of banana.

Objectives. As a result of their analysis of the market, United Fruit Company executives set the following objectives for the marketing of bananas:

EXHIBIT 3

That Chiquita Brand seal says a lot about a banana. It says that *this* banana has been as pampered and protected as a banana should be. All the way from the tree to your grocer's.

It says that *this* banana was shipped from the tropics in a strong fiber box . . . to cut down on bruises.

You see, all bananas used to come up from the tropics right on their stems. Unprotected. Exposed to all sorts of bumps and thumps. And you know how it is with a banana: A bump on the outside can make a bruise on the inside. A bruise that may not even show up on the peel.

But Chiquita Brand bananas ride in comfort, because the *box* absorbs the bumps. So when the bananas arrive at your grocer's they're all firm and sleek and golden. As sweet and tempting and delicious as a banana lover could ask for.

So look for the seal on the peel. It's the one way to tell the best of the bananas from the rest of the bananas.

CHIQUITA BRAND BANANAS   THIS SEAL OUTSIDE MEANS THE BEST INSIDE

Chiquita is a registered trademark of United Fruit Company

Courtesy: United Fruit Company

1. To reduce its costs per sales unit in order to compete effectively in a commodity business.
2. To create selective demand for its product.

   Strategy. A cost improvement program was instituted to meet the first purpose. The second objective called for measures new to the company and unique in the banana industry. The first major step toward building selectivity centered on the product itself.

A comprehensive quality control program was adopted that included: (1) the planting of a new variety of banana more resistant to disease and wind damage, (2) a grading procedure which selected the best fruit, and (3) special packing and shipping methods to provide the bananas greater protection in transit.

The second step was centered on the methods to use to develop selective demand for United Fruit Company's product.

Execution. Consumer research indicated that United Fruit could fill a consumer need by providing a brand of banana with greater quality assurance. Specifically, 40 percent of all banana purchasers studied had purchased bananas at one time or another that looked good externally, but when peeled were inferior. Research results also pointed out that the company had a strong property in "Chiquita" from the old radio jingle. While brand identification had been achieved by labels affixed to the banana, the company recognized that it had to do more than label the product to stimulate demand. The fact that United Fruit shipped its bananas up from the tropics in fiberboard boxes rather than on the stem appeared to be a demonstrable advantage because the shipment in the boxes subjected the fruit to less handling and bruising.

A television and print campaign was launched promising "Chiquita bananas are shipped up in boxes to cut down on bruising." (See Exhibit 1.)

At the same time, the company continued its national selective brand advertising campaign in national media. Among the advertising appeals used were those in Exhibit 2 and Exhibit 3.

Case questions

1. What are the conditions necessary in the banana industry, if United Fruit can successfully use selective advertising?

2. Would it be economically advisable for United Fruit to emphasize primary appeals?

3. How important is "price" to the consumer in choosing between products like oranges, apples and bananas? Between different brands of bananas?

4. Give the reasons why you believe United Fruit emphasized its selective brand appeal?

5. Evaluate the plan used and give any changes in it that the company should adopt.

CASE 2.   TRIM PRODUCTS COMPANY
Expansibility versus inexpansibility of demand

The Trim Products Company, an experienced and successful milk processor, developed an instantly dissolving dry milk which it believed was more satisfactory than the milk powders of other manufacturers.

Although nonfat dry milk has been produced by dairy plants for many years, sale of the product at the retail level has been a rather recent innovation. Introduced in the early 1930s, it was not until after World War II that the product became acceptable to the home consumer. Sales of nonfat dry milk for use in the home increased from about 2 million pounds in 1948, to 30 million pounds annually. Consumption of nonfat dry milk is still only about 1.1 pounds per capita.

The dried product has both cost and storage advantages over fresh milk. The consumer who buys 5 quarts of fluid milk in paper cartons carries almost 11 pounds. She can bring home as much milk in a one pound carton of the instant product, and reconstitute it by merely adding tap water. The cost of the reconstituted milk is about 12 cents a quart, compared with a price of 20 to 25 cents for fresh skim milk. Furthermore, the dry milk product does not need refrigeration, and will keep indefinitely on the pantry shelf.

Many housewives also use powdered milk instead of liquid milk for cooking and baking and for making cream sauces and soups. Despite the continued growth in the use of the product, home use accounts for only about one fifth of the total domestic nongovernment sales of nonfat dry milk for food use.

Nonfat dry milk for human food is manufactured by about 450 plants located in 35 states. The greater proportion of the output comes from the dairy states of the Midwest, New York, Pennsylvania, California, and Idaho. The major portion of the output for instant nonfat dry milk, however, comes from plants in New York, Wisconsin, and Minnesota.

Three large dairy firms have supplied about 80 percent of the total nonfat dry milk sold in retail packages. While nationally known brands are few in number (these are primarily the brands of the above three large firms), regional brands are more numerous, as are the brands of small independents and cooperatives who put out the product under their own labels. It is important to recognize that the instantizing process is relatively simple, and the cost of equipment is low enough so that these factors do not stop small firms from entering the field.

In the early development of the market, the processors used relatively small packages with sufficient powder to make one to three quarts of milk. However, larger packages are now more popular, and the four- to twelve-quart equivalent is used more extensively.

There has been a tendency for the market in recent years to level off. Some processors believe there is need for extensive promotion if the retail sales are to attain the potential which they believe exists for the product.

The South continues to be the largest market for dry milk, with the lowest volume being the Northeast market. On an income basis, families in the lower- and middle-class groups are the largest purchasers. The greatest proportion of buying also is done among those families in which there are six or more members.

Trim Products Company has seven plants scattered in the Midwest and East, and distributes its products through various wholesale outlets. The company has little direct contact with consumers, and relies on its advertising to sell its products. Although the company has used spot radio and television announcements over stations in its trading area, the major portion of the advertising budget has been spent for newspaper and cooperative advertising with dealers and distributors.

The three major firms (which control 80 percent of the market) had national distribution, and used radio, television, and magazines in their schedules, as well as the local media which Trim emphasized. All three companies sold instantly dissolving dry milk, evaporated milk, and other products.

In a marketing test which Trim ran in several midwestern cities, it found that its instant dissolving product outsold the nationally advertised brands. The management recognized, however, that the cities in which the test was conducted were ones in which Trim's other products had strong acceptance. The management was also fully aware that the method which its research staff had developed for processing the dry milk was of such a nature that the major firms would be able to duplicate it within a relatively short period of time.

Case questions

1. List the inherent drives and impulses for the purchase of a dissolving dry milk.

2. To what degree will habit play a part in the purchase of a product of this nature?

3. Do you believe "selective" or "primary" motives are more important in the purchase of this product?

4. Is the market for dry milk an expansible one? Explain.

5. On the basis of the motives for purchasing point out the advantages and disadvantages of Trim's introducing the dry milk product on a local basis.

CASE 3.   NELSON COMPANY
Promoting a new product

The Nelson Company is a small chemical company located in New York. In the last ten years, sales have increased from $2,000,000 to

$4,850,000. Two years ago the company developed two new motor additives that were designed to clear the engine of harmful clogging gums, sludges, and other dangerous wastes. In tests that had been conducted, the additives seemed superior to the nationally advertised additives already on the market.

The products were marketed in two cans under the brand names of Nelson Additive A and Nelson Additive B. It was recommended that Nelson Additive A be put directly into the crank case of the engine to be treated. The engine was started and the additive was sucked through the oil line by the oil pump, eventually reaching the bearings and all of the movable engine parts. The additive dissolved and loosened the wastes. After the engine was run for about 20 minutes, it was stopped and the crank case drained.

It was recommended that Nelson Additive B should be poured into the carburetor air intake during this 20-minute period when the engine was operating. In this way, the additive entered directly into the combustion chamber and acted on the carbons, gums, and varnishes around the valves and piston rings. These wastes were then blown from the chambers through the regular exhaust outlets of the engine.

Nelson additives had been tested in different cars and were found to have no harmful effects. They were guaranteed to improve performance of the engine by giving it better acceleration and speed while reducing oil and gasoline consumption. The company offered to refund the sales price of $5.00 if the product proved unsatisfactory.

Nelson distributed the products to service stations and motor part outlets in the local New York area. These outlets seemed quite satisfied with the products and stated that the products were superior.

The products were also sold to a few diesel engine and locomotive manufacturers. Nelson believed the additives could be used extensively in the maintenance and care of these engines.

Nelson began its advertising campaign by direct mail to automobile owners in the New York area. Explanatory circulars were sent to service stations and garages and the company's three salesmen visited these potential outlets to try and get them to handle the additives. Point-of-purchase displays were also designed and were distributed to the retailers who agreed to sell the products. These displays consisted of streamers, signs, display racks, and other similar promotional devices.

The company had been established about ten years earlier, and, before one of the chemists had developed the additives, it had specialized in a variety of technical grade sodium phosphates and their by-products.

As a result of the favorable comments and the encouraging sales of the additives in the local area, the company began to call on the service stations and garages outside the New York area. However, in the wider area, the sales resistance was great. Dealers pointed out that although the Nelson additives might be equal to or even better than brands already established on the market, they were doubtful that the product would sell as well as the nationally advertised brands.

At the same time, although the diesel locomotive firms increased their demand for the additives, the quantity discounts given by the company left it with only a small profit margin. It was questionable if the company could profitably expand its sales to the diesel firms in other sections of the country because of high shipping cost.

On the other hand, the retail market among the service stations and garages appeared to have extensive potentials. One of the manufacturers of another additive in the first year of promotion sold well over 2,000,000 cans of its product. Another company sold over 1,000,000 cans in its first year. Both of these companies credited their high volumes to national distribution and advertising.

Independent surveys indicated that 80 percent of car owners were potential purchasers of a motor additive product. Sixty percent of these, however, stated that they would buy only a brand that had been well established and had been proved on a nationwide basis. They also indicated that they would hesitate to buy a local product.

The president of the Nelson Product Company suggested a promotion plan to increase sales. He favored a progressive method by which the advertising appropriations would be set for the first six-month period and would be increased by 25 percent during each successive six-month period. In this way, he believed that increasing sales would provide the revenue for advertising expenditures. He recommended that local radio, television, and trade papers be used in the marketing mix. He also recommended that five additional salesmen be added to the staff at once.

Four of the other five directors of the company agreed with the progressive advertising plan, but did not believe it would be necessary to increase the number of salesmen. They suggested that the three present salesmen could increase their territories. This would keep the salary expenses down and would provide more funds for advertising.

An advertising agent was asked to estimate the initial appropriation that the company would have to make for the first six-month period. After studying the problem, the agent reported that the company should appropriate $100,000 for advertising expenses.

When this recommendation was presented to the board of directors, the one dissenting director stated that the company should not attempt direct sale of the additives. He believed that the company could not obtain a large enough segment of the market in the face of the competitive brands that were already established. He thought that an additive was the kind of product that was very difficult for the consumer to judge and although Nelson had a somewhat superior product, there was not sufficient product differentiation to justify a large advertising appropriation.

As a result, he recommended that the company either continue to concentrate its efforts in the local area or sell the product to a large oil company.

Case questions

1. How important is it for a small company to have a major product differential before it attempts to introduce a product of this kind?

2. Contrast the type of product differential that faces Nelson with that of the Trim Products Co. How does this affect the approach to use in attracting customers?

3. How important is it that Nelson's competitors are selling on a national basis?

4. Point out what you believe should be Nelson's primary purposes in demand creation advertising.

5. Should the company follow the promotional program of the president? Why? Why not?

CASE 4.   SPEIDEL
Deciding on buying motives

Speidel, a division of Textron, Inc., was founded in 1932 as the Speidel Corporation through the merger of three companies which were then owned and operated by the Speidel brothers. Mr. Paul Levinger, now president of Speidel, assumed his position in 1961, having been with the company since 1934.

Speidel is the leading watchband manufacturer in the United States, and since 1965 has been the distributor for British Sterling, a line of "quality" men's toiletries.

In May 1964, the Speidel Corporation was acquired by Textron, Inc., a diversified manufacturing company. Although Speidel is a division of Textron, Inc., the actual operation of the company remained the same as before the Textron acquisition.

At its beginning in 1932, Speidel occupied two floors in the Providence, Rhode Island building which now, with other buildings in the area, is owned and occupied completely by Speidel.

Speidel has had many firsts in the industry. It was primarily responsible for getting the retailers to take the watchbands from under the counters and display them in attractive cabinets on the counters. It developed a beautiful package for the bands, which played a major factor in developing the bands as gift items. In 1940, it introduced the first ladies' expansion bracelet, the "Mignon."

In 1946, Speidel used full-page advertisements in *Life* and the *Ladies' Home Journal*—the first full-page national advertisements ever run for watchbands. In the spring of 1948, Speidel decided on a more spectacular approach and bought a portion of "Stop the Music," one of the more successful "giveaway" programs on radio. In 1949, the company became a pioneer television advertiser as sponsor of the first network television show to originate in California. Speidel was one of the first national advertisers to shift the major portion of its advertising budget into television.

Another of Speidel's most important breakthroughs was the development of the Twist-O-Flex watchband in 1959. The Twist-O-Flex is a band that conforms not only to the shape of the wrist, but also flexes in any desired direction. This band almost revolutionized the watchband industry and even further solidified Speidel's position as the country's leading watchband manufacturer. (See Exhibit 1.)

Speidel has relied heavily on advertising to build its market and, as early as 1947, it was spending $500,000 annually on advertising. The advertising budget now averages over $5 million, which includes the expenditures for British Sterling.

Speidel has attempted to see that through the combination of quality control, engineering, and effective advertising the name Speidel would be synonymous with quality and a name to be trusted.

Typical appeals are such ones as:

1. The Speidel Millionaires
    Obviously Speidel—Obviously Superior
2. Speidel Twist-O-Flex has become synonymous with quality metal watchbands.
3. Speidel improves on perfection with Romunda.
4. Speidel has spent hundreds of thousands of dollars researching, testing, and perfecting Romunda.
5. These new sophisticated Speidel Miniatures are the result of Speidel's continuing effort to bring women—in watch bracelets—the same fashion excitement they seek in other accessories and clothes.
6. Speidel's products are being presold on many popular network TV shows.
7. Did you know that Speidel products now account for more than 10 percent of the business of many jewelers who carry them?

A list of the shows which Speidel has sponsored is given in Exhibit 2.

EXHIBIT 1

Courtesy: Speidel, a division of Textron, Inc.

EXHIBIT 2. A partial list of the shows sponsored by Speidel since 1948

1. STOP THE MUSIC—1948–50
   (A nationally famous radio program)
2. THE ED WYNN SHOW—1949
3. SATURDAY NIGHT REVIEW—1950
4. WHAT'S MY NAME?—1950–53
5. MASQUERADE PARTY—1952
6. NAME THAT TUNE—1953–54
7. MAKE ROOM FOR DADDY—1953–54
   Danny Thomas
8. THE SID CAESAR SHOW—1954–55
9. THE BIG SURPRISE—1955–1956–1957
10. DOWN YOU GO—1956
11. THE ARTHUR MURRAY PARTY—1957
12. FESTIVAL OF STARS—1957
13. THE PRICE IS RIGHT—1957–60
14. AMERICAN BANDSTAND—1959
15. THE JACKIE GLEASON SHOW—1960
16. THE DEAN MARTIN SHOW—1960
17. THE ASPHALT JUNGLE—1961
18. TARGET, THE CORRUPTERS—1961
19. NAKED CITY—1961
20. SURFSIDE SIX—1961
21. CONCENTRATION—1962
22. THE PRICE IS RIGHT—1962
23. HAWAIIAN EYE—1962
24. SUNSET STRIP—1962
25. BEN CASEY—1962
26. THE DEFENDERS—1962
27. WHAT'S MY LINE—1962
28. THE ELEVENTH HOUR—1962
29. THE JACK PAAR SHOW—1963–1964–1965
30. PASSWORD—1963
31. THAT WAS THE WEEK THAT WAS—1964
32. GOLF CLASSICS—1964
33. PEYTON PLACE—1964–1965–1966
34. ALFRED HITCHCOCK—1964–65
35. HUNTLEY-BRINKLEY—1964
36. THE MAN FROM U.N.C.L.E.—1965
37. DANIEL BOONE—1965
38. THE LONG HOT SUMMER—1965
39. THE PATTY DUKE SHOW—1965
40. SHENANDOAH—1965
41. RUN FOR YOUR LIFE—1965–66
42. PLEASE DON'T EAT THE DAISIES—1965–66
43. THE VIRGINIAN—1965–66
44. WACKIEST SHIP IN THE ARMY—1965–66
45. NBC TUESDAY NIGHT AT THE MOVIES—1965–66
46. I SPY—1966
47. LAREDO—1966
48. HAWK—1966
49. GREEN HORNET—1966
50. CBS FRIDAY NIGHT AT THE MOVIES—1966
51. WALTER CRONKITE—1966
52. BIG VALLEY—1966
53. FUGITIVE—1966
54. ABC SUNDAY NIGHT AT THE MOVIES—1966
55. BATMAN—1966
56. JERICHO—1966
57. LOST IN SPACE—1966

Case questions

1. What are the important buying motives of the ultimate consumer for watchbands?

2. To what extent are these of a primary nature? Of a selective nature?

3. To what degree do you believe the demand for watchbands would be expansible? Inexpansible?

4. Indicate whether or not these motives are primarily of a direct or derived nature.

CASE 5.   ANALYSIS OF ADVERTISEMENTS
Evaluating the ads

The advertisements in Exhibits 1 through 4 have been used in national and local media in recent campaigns.

Case questions

1. To whom are the advertisements directed?
2. What are the objectives of the advertisements?
3. What other appeals might be used?

EXHIBIT 1

Courtesy: GMAC Corp.

EXHIBIT 2

STORE NAME

From Pendleton...

Get in on the fashion action — in Knockabouts
by Pendleton.® Bright, wild and woolly
virgin wool sportswear. Made to last —
and look terrific. Flannel western shirt,
$19; western pants, $26; zippered blanket
poncho, $20; hip pocket pants, $20; pattern
front turtleneck pullover, $18.

Courtesy: Pendleton Woolen Mills

EXHIBIT 3

"I didn't have the faintest idea you could save up to 87 per cent by dialing direct..."

Richard Clarke, President, Richard Clarke Associates, minority group consulting and recruiting, New York, Chicago, Atlanta.

"I used to place almost all of my Long Distance calls person-to-person. Then I found out how much cheaper it is to dial direct. I didn't have the faintest idea you could save up to 87 per cent by dialing direct rather than calling person-to-person."

For years, like Mr. Clarke, most businessmen have figured they save money when they place their Long Distance calls person-to-person through the operator. They felt they wouldn't be "wasting" a call.

But today's low dial-it-yourself rates have changed all that.

For example, from 8 a.m. to 5 p.m., Monday through Friday, a three-minute, coast-to-coast call placed person-to-person costs $3.55 plus tax.

But if you call station-to-station and dial the call yourself without operator assistance, the cost is just $1.35 plus tax.

You save $2.20 on that one call.

So whenever you can, dial your Long Distance calls yourself. It's good business.

Dial-direct rates do not apply on coin, credit-card, collect, person-to-person, and hotel-guest calls, or on calls charged to another number. Nor do they apply on calls to or from Alaska or Hawaii.

Courtesy: AT&T Long Lines

EXHIBIT 4

If you're convinced your investment program should hold more muscle than fossil

you'll hit it off with Hayden, Stone.

Sometimes an investor can't see the trees for the petrified forest. In this era of dynamic change, that can be an expensive myopia.

Hayden, Stone works with a creative, contemporary investment viewpoint. Based on vigorous, deep-probing research and on imaginative, insightful application of the results of that research. And, always, aimed at a close correlation between your unique investment goals and the emerging investment opportunities of today.

That kind of attitude can be refreshing. Even rewarding. We make no bones about saying so.

HAYDEN, STONE
INCORPORATED-ESTABLISHED 1892
MEMBERS NEW YORK STOCK EXCHANGE
25 Broad St., New York, N.Y. / 82 offices coast-to-coast and throughout the world

© 1966 Hayden, Stone Incorporated

Courtesy: Hayden, Stone, Inc.

EXHIBIT 5

"I like the new mini-skirt, Vera, but what have you done with your hair?"

Why do so many unknown products turn out to be bombs? For one thing, they don't have brand names the manufacturers have to stand behind. Brand names have to work hard to hold their reputation and your affection.

Just for fun, Vera, imagine what shopping would be like without brand names.

Imagine government grade labels on products. Grade A, Grade B, Grade C granulated sugar.

Sounds funny, doesn't it, But, it's not. There are well-meaning people today who make that very suggestion. They want the government to do your shopping for you.

Of course, that instant-dissolving sugar you're so fond of probably wouldn't exist. What manufacturer would go to the trouble of improving his product if he couldn't use it to compete with? However, you don't really *need* instant sugar. Or hair sprays. Or high heels.

And you could cook on a coal stove if you had to. But, do you want to?

Magazine Publishers Association
An association of 365 leading U.S. magazines

Courtesy: Magazine Publishers Assn.

chapter 5

COPY STRATEGY

To EFFECTUATE the basic demand strategy discussed in Chapter 4, it is necessary to convert the primary or selective demand appeal into copy strategy. In other words, to stimulate this latent demand, what appeals should be directed at what buying motives?

In developing the copy strategy in the first instance, it is essential to keep in mind that a multitude of needs and wants may be used to motivate consumer behavior. As a result, the advertiser must select the one(s) that is best in affecting the consumer's buying behavior, and which at the same time is adaptable to being most effectually incorporated in advertisements. And the creative copy strategist must also remember that normally the purchase of a product (as in the case of other types of behavior) is the result of several needs and wants, not a particular single one. Hence, he must study the wants and needs that motivate potential customers to buy, the manner in which people react to various stimuli, and how they arrive at decisions to buy.

Wants and needs

Human wants and needs are countless in number and are derived from many complex forces. Habit, custom, conformity, and distinctiveness are among these sources.

The demand for a new automobile might result from the need for more economical transportation. On the other hand, it might also be derived from the desire to keep up with one's neighbors, or to have the distinction of being the first person in one's group to have a new car.

In most cases, there will be an overlapping of a number of desires, and it may be difficult to isolate which specific one predominates. In some cases, the consumer may be able to identify readily these desires on his part, while in other situations it may be extremely difficult for him to indicate the motives.

Mason Haire's study on instant coffee is a good example of the inability of the customer to pinpoint these desires. Haire made up two "shopping lists" containing a series of everyday household purchase items such as hamburger meat, two cans of Del Monte peaches, and other similar products. The only difference between the two lists was that on one list Nescafe was listed, and on the second list Maxwell House regular coffee was substituted for the instant coffee. When he asked a matched group of housewives to describe the type of housewives who would purchase each list of products he found that a high proportion mentioned "lazy" housewives, "women who don't plan well," for the list containing instant coffee. Direct questioning had given no indication that this was a connotation associated with instant coffee.

Even an apparently simple product such as cigarettes had a variety of "meanings" and "desires." Some smokers, for example, see in a cigarette something to manipulate, a means of assertion; for others, a cigarette is a means of comfort—deep inhaling; for others, it means an outlet for nervous tension; and for others, a cigarette means primarily an oral sensation. In each case, a cigarette might be linked to basic tendencies or desires on the part of the smoker as well as to the interest in particular product attributes. However, because the individual is not always conscious of his needs, it is generally recognized that the wants of the individual must be stimulated.

NATURE OF HABITS

Habit is a quality in a person that helps him to perform an act well or poorly in relation to his nature or temperament. It is acquired by repetition, and shows itself in facility of performance or in decreased power of resistance.

Fortunately for man, the problem of making decisions is eased by the fact that he has a habit pattern. The considerate man finds it easy to be thoughtful because he has acquired the habit of consideration. The safe driver finds it easy to be careful because he has acquired the habit of safety. The housewife finds it easier to fulfill her many obligations because she has acquired a number of habits in buying, cooking, and cleaning.

Because a child has not developed fully his habit pattern, notice how difficult it is for him to decide what toy he wants, what kind of candy he desires, and how slow he is to let another child play with his toy. If all of our decisions were as difficult to make, our daily activities would be so complex that we would be weighted down by the burden of these decisions.

Habits are added to our nature and are related to human action either directly or indirectly. However, most habits are related directly with action because they are concerned with our powers to act. They help direct the powers of reason or the sense appetite to a specific type of action.

The most important natural cause of habits is human activity. It is by repetition that we acquire our operative habits. It is by repeatedly driving an automobile that we acquire the habits to make us skilled drivers.

The habits we acquire in this manner can be strengthened or weakened. The more frequently a person saves something each week out of his paycheck, the stronger becomes his habit of thriftiness. On the other hand, the same man may lessen or lose his habit of thriftiness by acting contrary to it and ceasing to save.

In deciding on the copy strategy, therefore, it is important to know what the buying habits of the consumers are. Why do they buy a product? Where do they purchase it? How do they want to buy it? Do they want to pay cash, or do they have the habit of buying on credit? Do they want a 30-day open credit account, or do they want to buy it on an installment basis? Are they willing to make a substantial down payment? Do they want to buy the product in a drugstore or a supermarket? Will they see our advertisement on television? Do they read the daily newspaper? Will they see the advertisement in the morning or afternoon newspaper?

Dynamic qualities

Habits and customs are not static. The variety of drives which exist is of such a nature that it is not possible to predict how long a habit or custom will predominate. As an example, technological advances may change our mode of living, which may cause us to adopt different habits and customs.

No longer is a housewife considered lazy and inefficient if she serves her guests a dinner which she prepared by opening some frozen food packages. No longer is it considered essential for a girl to be thoroughly skilled in all phases of cooking before she gets married.

The do-it-yourself trend in the United States has increased the sales of a variety of tools and equipment. The demand for hi-fi sets was a factor in improving the sales trend for phonograph records. The increased demand for air transportation has resulted in a decreased demand for railroad passenger services.

The consumer in the United States spends a smaller share of his income for food and clothing. Instead, he is budgeting a larger share of his income for education, medical care, recreation, and personal services.

The new pattern of his spending creates difficulties for some businesses and, at the same time, provides increased profits for others. Much of this change results from the rise in income. When the consumer earns more money, he needs a smaller proportion of it for the basic necessities. He has more money to satisfy other tastes.

New spending habits also have been influenced by changes in the makeup of the population. Larger families bring about a revamping of the family budget. Costs climb when a son or daughter enters college.

The sharp rise in the number of people over 65 affects the general spending pattern. These older individuals spend a larger portion of their incomes on medical care, special foods, and personal services. Clothing tends to be less important, and they are more interested in durability than in style changes.

How long will such trends continue? Have they become such an important phase of the American way of life that they will withstand the drives for other services? Will some other new development change our habits and customs?

Consumer behavior is inordinately complex. On the one hand, much of the consumer buying is so routine in character that the consumer buys more as a creature of habit rather than as a decision maker. Yet, when major purchases are made, the consumer must use decision making if for no other reason than to decide how to pay for the product.

Habit appears to dominate in the purchase of the items necessary to keep a normal household functioning. However, while these habits are being developed, decision making is more obviously at work.

At all times for major purchases, decision making takes place to a greater degree. In the purchase of a home or an electrical appliance, the consumer generally is influenced more by a pattern of motives instead of a single motive.

It is generally more economical for advertisers to use appeals to the consumer that will allow him to follow his established habit patterns than it is to try to change or develop new operative habits.

Inherent drives and impulses

Our wants are inherent and deep-seated. They can be either positive or negative. They may lead on the one hand to the motivation to buy a product, while, at the same time, be the reason for our not buying another article. They may lead to the motive to be first, or provide the reason why we refuse to be an innovator.

While these drives can be classified in a number of different ways, the following are among the important ones to consider. These are the drives for necessities, happiness, sex, security, recognition, and emulation. Although the relative importance of each of these drives will vary among different individuals, nevertheless each person possesses these drives to some degree.

Necessities. To sustain life is the first of the basic stimuli, because man must satisfy his needs for food, clothing, shelter, and health in order to exist. Needs and tastes may differ between people in the same social stratum, but the drive for minimum necessities is so great that man generally will give up other demands in order to get these essentials.

Environment is probably the most important factor in determining what these minimum requirements or standards will be. As an example, the nomads as they wander from place to place in search of their livelihood have evolved minimum standards which fall below the subsistence requirements of other groups.

Regardless, however, of what these standards may be, a person will labor to the fullest to get the necessities which make up his minimum requirements.

Happiness. A second drive is the one for happiness. It is an inherent drive with which each of us is endowed. Man is made for happiness. Every perfectly designed item of nature strains for that fulfillment.

Happiness is the goal of all human activity. It is the common ground on which all human desires, all human ambitions meet. The salesman trying to meet his quota, the engineer building a bridge, the baseball player hoping to improve his batting average, the wife preparing the meal for her family—all are seeking happiness.

Because the wants of man tend to be insatiable, no particular product can perfectly satisfy us. Not even health, strength, or beauty will satisfy all our longings. Nor can even absolute power completely satisfy this want, because it does not bring the peace which is a characteristic of happiness.

However, beneath the conflicting demands which man has, all men search for these things for one reason—they believe that the attainment of their desires will make them happy. Happiness is the ultimate end of all human acts.

Sex. The transitions from birth through the various age cycles characterized by departure from organized school life, home protection, and adolescent friendships into the adult world of life influence the individual's response to this drive.

During the first phases of the adult cycle, as an example, the focus of the drive will be on marriage and family life in which there will take place marked changes.

In the middle and last part of the adult cycle, the individual will tend to launch out from the family-centered cycles and will place more emphasis on leisure.

As a result, it is important to evaluate this drive not only in relation to the phase of the life cycle but also from the fundamental life objectives which the individual has set.

Security. A fourth drive is the one for security, and it will differ by the degree to which a particular person may think he needs it. Some men are more temperate than others. Some interpret security on the basis of an abundance of money. Others see it as the essence of an intellectual independence that can be achieved only by the spirit.

One man takes a job with a company because he analyzes the retirement plan and finds that it offers what he considers to be the highest in the industry. Another man studies the same company, concludes that his rate of progress will be too slow in the organization, and decides to gain security through casting his lot with a company which may not even have a retirement program but in which he has an opportunity to earn a higher salary.

Although we do not all interpret security in the same manner, experience shows us that security ranks high among the various stimuli. At the same time, because we do not completely understand the meaning of security, there is bound to be some obscurity in how different persons react to this drive.

In the search for security, man must choose the way in which he is to attain it by his own actions. However, the impact of advertising may be such that it will greatly influence the security goals which are set.

Recognition. The drive for recognition is another important stimulus, because people are very much alike and desire to be recognized for what they have accomplished. They want to be given credit for their ideas, and are disturbed when these are ignored.

Man is gregarious by nature, and much of his happiness is dependent on his relations with other people. In fact, some men even dissipate personal fortunes in an attempt to gain the esteem of their fellow man.

The prodigal man is a good example of this. He gives away his goods without prudence and deceives himself into thinking he can secure recognition by getting people to look on him as a generous man.

Again, in any group of men there must always be some who are willing to assume the duties of leadership. Frequently, the financial returns are below the levels paid by industry, but the honor and praise secured are great enough to offset any monetary loss.

In giving recognition to others, here are a few basic concepts to keep in mind:

Each person wants to feel important.
He wants recognition primarily by members of his own specific group.
He prefers giving advice to receiving it.
He wants to feel that his ideas and suggestions are of the utmost importance.
He leans more toward people whose interests are similar to his.

He wants others to judge him at a higher rather than at a lower level.
While he hates to be obligated to others, he prefers that those to whom he
is obligated are outside his own group.
He will accept flattery for only a limited period of time because he will
soon recognize that it is insincere.

The object of giving recognition is the purpose accomplished by it.
Just as the purpose of eating is for the maintenance of health, so the
purpose of giving recognition also should be sound. It is not enough to
provide a false type of recognition, because the individual will react
negatively toward it.

Emulation.   A sixth drive is one usually classified as the desire to
equal or excel others. Generally, the others whom we wish to equal or
excel are those in our own group.

In studies which *Fortune* and other organizations have made of executive behavior, it is interesting to note that when a man is promoted there
is a strong tendency on the part of both the man and his family to up-
grade the automobile, to move to a better section of the city, to join the
country club, to buy a mink stole, or to take a European cruise in conformity with the activities of those at the new level which he has attained.

This same drive is inherent in our desire to accomplish more than our
neighbor, to earn a higher wage, and to get a better home or television
set. In some instances, the drive may even lead men to change jobs. As
an example, 10 mechanics who had worked for a company from 5 to 10
years quit their jobs in a West Coast plant when they found that new
employees were being hired at the same pay rate old employees received.
As one of the mechanics stated: "The salary scale which the company
pays is above the level which competing firms in the area are paying. I
know it is going to be difficult to get a job at any higher wage than the
company is paying me here. It is a matter of pride with me, and I prefer
to get the same wage at another concern than to have these young guys
in this plant earning the same rate I do."

While the drive for emulation is primarily of an emotional nature, it
has to be aroused in many instances through primary and secondary
appeals. A picture in a newspaper of a person who is taking a trip frequently will result in some of his friends also taking a trip of some kind.

THE CONSUMER

Importance

Just as the drives and desires of the consumer must be understood in
order to know how to appeal to him, so must production be geared to
produce goods which will satisfy the consumer. Since in our economy
the ultimate consumer is free to make his decision as to what product(s)

he will buy, it is important for advertisers to understand the concept of freedom of choice in relation to the purchaser's desires.

Freedom of choice provides the means by which the consumer has the power to move himself to his acts with the knowledge that they will lead him to his objectives. As experience shows, the consumer must make innumerable free choices in the course of a lifetime.

The proper direction of these forces either can be hindered by opposing forces or given direction by the conditions which the advertiser sets in the situation where the consumer will make this free decision.

In other words, when an automobile manufacturer offers a new style and discontinues the prior model, he sets the conditions in the market place where the consumer must make his decision. If the consumer has to replace his old car because of a mechanical failure, he may buy the new model even though he might prefer a different style. In this instance, his freedom of choice in selecting an automobile is limited to the styles which are offered at a given time in the market.

If he doesn't have to buy a car immediately, however, he may postpone his purchase until a style is offered that will satisfy his demand. In most of these situations, the consumer does have latitude in timing his purchases and is in a position to forego buying a product until a later date.

Ignorance is a major enemy of the consumer's freedom of choice because it prevents him from seeking either the proper objectives or the right means to the objective. The consumer can refuse to learn or neglect to learn that the $5.00 product is superior in quality to the $3.99 article, and is a much better value. In this case, assuming the consumer buys the $3.99 article, ignorance results in the consumer failing to get the best value. Yet, it does not destroy his freedom of choice in any way. The consumer as he evaluated the purchase decided on the $3.99 article because, in his opinion, it produced greater personal satisfaction. Thus, the seller should offer the kind and quality of goods which the consumer believes he wants at the prices he can afford to pay.

BUYING MOTIVES

Definition

Man pursues happiness by proper use of the powers of reason, will, and the sense appetite. In this drive for happiness, even the intellect needs to be moved by the will to its activity. The will cannot move without reason.

The hunger pangs of a child force him to cry for food. Thus, at the beginning of reason in the child, he recognizes that there are such things as food which will satisfy him.

From then on in our lives we find the repeated interaction of the reason and will develop more and more by our desires. The end of this desire is always pleasure.

As we interpret these desires in terms of our buying motives, we find a tendency toward products which we do not possess. After we buy a product, we no longer desire it; we then enjoy it.

These buying motives are the energizing forces which set us into action to get the goods we do not have. While all men have natural motives for whatever is required to exist, yet, since we possess reason, we seek pleasure in many products which are not absolutely required.

Classification of motives

Among the ways in which buying motives may be classified are: (1) primary and selective, (2) emotional and rational, (3) patronage, and (4) direct and derived.

As discussed in Chapter 4, a primary motive is the stimulus that helps us decide whether we should buy an automobile, a television set, or a typewriter, whereas a selective buying motive helps us to select a specific brand of article.

Emotional and rational motives. Emotional and rational motives are so intermixed that it is difficult to isolate one from the other in many instances. This stems partially from the fact that they are grouped in contraries. Fear is contrary to bravery, love to hate, saving to spending, efficiency to inefficiency, joy to sorrow, and working to loafing.

The appetite, whether emotional or rational, also is stimulated by an object which attracts it or repels it. Yet, this attraction or repulsion cannot take place unless the object is recognized. When the sense appetite visualizes something that appears good to the senses, this is called pleasure. A man takes pleasure in eating a piece of apple pie. This is a sense pleasure and will generally seem stronger than the rational intellectual pleasures. This is caused by the fact that the emotional pleasures are better known to us and produce a feeling of satisfaction which the rational intellectual pleasures may not offer.

The consideration of these motives is complicated further by the fact that the objects of pleasure are so varied and some action must take place for every pleasure. Even change itself may be a cause of pleasure. What may be pleasure to us at one time, may not be at a later date. While we may decide on a rational basis today, we may be completely influenced by our emotions tomorrow.

Emotional motives are those which are influenced primarily by the sense appetites. Fear, anger, love, pride, joy, curiosity, comfort, and the other emotional impulses are the stimuli which get us to act.

The desires not to be outdone by our neighbors, to buy a more luxurious home, to buy the most expensive food, to be in style, to be a fashion leader, or to buy at only the exclusive shops are examples of emotional buying motives. In other words, emotion rather than reason is the principal motivation which determines "why" we buy a specific product.

Rational motives, on the other hand, are those which are based upon reason rather than upon the emotions. Efficiency, quality, dependability, economy, speed, convenience, and accuracy are among these types of rational impulses.

The rational buying motive predominates if when we select television set A instead of television set B, we do so because after checking the two sets we determine that Brand A is of better quality. We buy a product by mail order to get a 5 percent discount. We try to select the products which, in our opinion, are of the best quality relative to the selling prices asked.

For the rational motive to function, knowledge of the object need not be perfect. A man can make a decision on the basis of his reason and find that he did not select the most economical product. Yet, as long as he used a logical procedure rather than an emotional one, the decision would be considered as originating from rational stimuli.

Patronage motives. The patronage motives are the reasons which help determine the outlet from which a product will be bought. They are based on such factors as the reputation of the seller, the completeness of the stock, personal friendship with the dealer, and other services such as credit, delivery, and premiums which the seller may give.

The intensity of these motives will vary with individuals. In one instance, a consumer might pay a higher price for an article in order to purchase it from a store which is operated by a close friend. Yet, he might select another outlet if free delivery service was not extended. This same customer might shop at the corner grocery store as long as it held its prices at a competitive level, but would drive several miles to buy his food products at a larger supermarket if prices were not comparable.

These motives are under the control of the judgment of the individual and can be made on the basis of right reason. On the other hand, they can harm a man more than they will benefit him. Just as food is good for man, too much food at one meal is bad. So it may be if the patronage motives predominate. Buying from one outlet because of friendship with the owner is good, but too much buying on this basis may result in the individual not getting the best quality goods.

Patronage motives occupy a place between the desire for a product and the desire to buy from a specific outlet. To the degree that these motives will predominate when we decide to buy a product, they will determine the source we select.

The emphasis on patronage motives is also subject to change. What will hold customers today may not be the factors which will attract them at a later date. Just as the corner grocery store found that the services it offered to hold customers were no longer of primary importance, department stores are finding today that it is necessary to overhaul their merchandising techniques to hold customers.

Direct and derived motives. Direct motives stem from primary needs. These primary needs—to eat, to preserve life, to marry and raise children—are determined by nature. In order to preserve life, we have a direct stimulus for food. However, to make the food more palatable, we have a derived demand to use sauces and spices.

We have a basic need for some means of transportation. If we select an automobile to fulfill this demand, then a derived need for gasoline will exist. In other words, the motive to buy gasoline is derived from our decision to satisfy our basic need for transportation through the medium of an automobile. We could have selected any one of several other methods of transportation, such as a bicycle, a horse, or a train, to satisfy this need. If that had been the case, we would not have had a demand for gasoline.

Therefore, the derived motive stems from the demand we have for a primary product, while the direct motive originates from the desire to satisfy a basic need.

General limitations

In evaluating buying motives, it is important to recognize that man has complex tendencies and desires, and cannot be considered as a statistical unit. He will not react the same way to each appeal, and the intensity of his buying motives will vary from one time to another.

QUESTIONS

1. How would you differentiate between demand and need? Is this distinction of any importance to the advertiser? Explain.

2. In planning copy strategy, is it really important for the advertiser to know the buying habits of the consumer? Why?

3. Bring in three magazine advertisements that appeal to inherent drives. Explain your selections.

4. Analyze your buying behavior during your latest purchase of a major item of apparel. What motives influenced your purchase? Explain their significance from an advertiser's point of view.

5. Are emotional buying motives and primary buying motives one and the same type of buying motive? Explain.

6. Briefly compare the buying motives of a purchasing agent for a large corporation with those of the ultimate consumer.

7. If you were preparing an advertisement for the main department store

in a city of 50,000 population, what buying motives would you emphasize? Give reasons.

8. Do you believe the classification of buying motives as "emotional" or "rational" is valid? Explain.

9. Is this distinction of any value to the advertiser? Explain.

10. Can you give instances of your own or friends making purchases in which either emotional or rational buying motives were dominant? Describe.

11. List three products which you think people generally buy for "emotional" reasons rather than "rational." Explain your selections.

12. List three products which you think people generally buy for "rational" reasons. Explain your selections.

13. "To be a successful advertising executive you must be consumer-minded." Do you agree? Give your reasons.

CASE 1.   REEB
Meeting new challenges

Reeb is a manufacturer and marketer of a wide variety of grocery products as well as chemicals and industrial products. It is faced with selecting copy strategy for its various product lines for the current year in the face of the Federal Trade Commission's objective of advancing consumer interests in terms of nutrition, product information, safety, quality, and value.

Products

Grocery products have traditionally been the Reeb's principal business and account for over 75 percent of consolidated net sales. Reeb's grocery products are sold primarily to chains, wholesalers, and other distributors of food products. It maintains a network of 12 distribution centers throughout the United States, each of which carries an inventory of most of the company's grocery product items. Technical research, market research, test marketing, advertising, and promotion are important to growth through new products and continuance of well-established products. Reeb extensively advertises its grocery products, with an emphasis upon television. The company maintains a fulltime sales force in the United States of about 400.

Cereals. The company manufactures and sells both hot and ready-to-eat cereals in the United States and in foreign markets. Hot cereal products, most of which are sold under the Reeb brand, include regular and quick-cooking oatmeal, instant oatmeal, enriched cream of wheat, and rolled wheat cereal. Several new flavored varieties of instant oatmeal have been introduced in recent years. Principal ready-to-eat cereals are sold under the following names: King Kong, Energy, Ringo, Wheat-O, O-Puff, and Duol.

Reeb also manufactures prepared pancake mixes, frozen foods, and other mixes and table syrup under the Lucky brand, as well as pie crust and other mixes under the Delco brand. These products are marketed primarily in the United States and Canada.

Frozen waffles are also manufactured and sold under the Lucky brand. Frozen pizza and related products are sold under the Delco brand. Distribution of frozen products is concentrated in the United States and Canada.

Cookies and crackers. Reeb manufactures and sells cookies and cracker products under the Deluxe name. In an effort to improve the results of its cookie and cracker business, Reeb discontinued its high-cost store delivery system and now sells through distributors.

Pet foods. Reeb manufactures and sells a broad line of dog and cat foods. Principal brand names are Doggie for dog foods and Cattie for cat foods. The dog food line includes canned, dry and semimoist products, and the cat food line consists of canned products in the United States and of canned and dry products abroad. Pet foods are sold abroad either under the above brand names or under local brands.

Institutional and other foods. Institutional foods include many of the Reeb's regular grocery products suitably packaged for restaurants, hotels, hospitals, schools, and the vending trade.

Chemicals. Reeb manufactures and distributes chemicals which are produced from agricultural by-products and are used in the refining of petroleum and in the manufacture of a wide range of products such as plywood, rubber, plastics, and foundry molds. Chemicals are sold directly to manufacturers and through distributors, principally in the United States and Europe.

Industrial products

The company manufactures and sells to industrial markets certain grain products such as industrial flour sold to millers and corn grits sold to the brewing industry.

Raw materials and supplies

Raw materials used by Reeb for its grocery products include oats, wheat, corn, rice, sugar, meat by-products, and fish, most of which are purchased on the open market. The raw materials for its chemical products include corncobs, oat hulls and bagasse. The company purchases the major portion of its packaging materials, such as containers, labels, and shipping cases, from outside sources.

Regulation

Production and distribution of most of Reeb's grocery products are subject to the Federal Food, Drug, and Cosmetic Act and to various state statutes regulating safety and labeling of products.

The Federal Trade Commission (FTC) has initiated a study of the economic structure and effectiveness of competition in the breakfast cereal industry. At the request of the FTC Reeb is furnishing information in connection with the study. Recent press articles indicate that FTC economists have prepared a report critical of profits and advertising expenditures in the cold breakfast cereal industry.

Reeb also is participating in government hearings, investigations, and conferences which have the general objectives of advancing consumer interests in terms of nutrition, product information, safety, quality, and value. Reeb is unable to predict the effect of these trends on its business, but believes that its positive attitude toward consumer interests and the nature of its product lines are compatible with these objectives.

Deciding on strategy

As a result of the increased emphasis on consumerism and the fact that it was complex to evaluate on a truly scientific basis the nutritional benefit which the consumers derived from the grocery products line, Reeb's executives believed that it was essential to decide whether or not the copy strategy which had been used should be changed.

The executives were particularly concerned with the cereal advertising. They had found that placing emphasis on nutritional, health, and testimonial appeals had proved to be successful. They had also utilized the fewer calories appeal on various occasions and had found this to be quite successful.

Some of the general copy appeals which had been suggested for the current period, included:

a. It's the real food.
b. Breakfast delight.
c. Start the day right.
d. How to get a great shape and be right.
e. The cereal of the stars.
f. Eat up, America.
g. Keep young and fit with Reeb.
h. You can maintain a busy schedule with Reeb.

    i. The easiest-to-digest breakfast.
    j. The cereal that is all wheat.
    k. Reeb can give you the edge.
    l. Want to lose pounds fast?
    m. How to be sure you get enough nutrition.
    n. Star athlete says, "Win with Reeb."
    o. "Mom, get me a package of Reeb."
    p. How to fight the bulge.

Case questions

    1. How can Reeb develop a selective copy strategy?

    2. To what extent should Reeb expect to adopt a primary advertising copy strategy to counteract some of the pending regulations?

    3. Some children play an important part in the decision as to which cereal to purchase. How important are the concepts of health, nutrition, etc.?

    4. Evaluate the suggestions of the advertising department and develop a copy strategy for Reeb's cereal products.

CASE 2.   UNITED OIL CO.
Overcoming customers' desires

United Oil Company is one of the leading marketers of gasoline and other refined petroleum products in the East, and also markets through its subsidiary, New Oil Company.

United was one of the first companies to introduce no-lead/low-lead gasoline. It believed that it had come out with the product too early and was then faced with which type of copy strategy to use.

United supplies a total of 12,000 retail outlets of which approximately 4,000 are owned or leased by it. In its entire marketing area, United owns and operates 550 bulk plants and terminals which supply its dealers and distributors as well as its industrial, commercial, agricultural, and governmental accounts.

Products

The principal products manufactured and marketed by United Oil Co. are gasoline, motor oils and lubricants, diesel fuel, jet fuel, heating oil, kerosene and industrial oils, lubricants, asphalt, and coke.

United owns and operates 1,500 miles of gathering lines located in 12 states and 600 miles of trunk lines. It also owns and operates 4 refineries with a rated total capacity of 400,000 barrels of crude oil per day.

Low-lead gas

The executives of United believed that the way in which they introduced the low-lead gas resulted in mass hysteria and panic marketing. For more than two years, United has been pushing this new fuel with expensive, high-octane ads, trying to convince motorists that using low-lead/no-lead gasoline would help clean up the air. Though many of the 1971 American cars and all the 1972 and 1973 models are engineered for these fuels—as well as for conventional leaded gasoline—motorists simply are not buying them.

What is more, even motorists who try to buy low-lead/no-lead gas often find that it is hard to secure. Consumer demand has been so sluggish that United and other refiners are converting stations at a much slower rate than might have been expected if demand were stronger.

Though the Big Five national gasoline marketers have either a low-lead or a no-lead offering available, many of the 129,000 company-owned and the 146,000 independent stations do not have them yet. The reasons are the long lead time and high cost necessary to set up a third-grade system—pumps, lines, storage tanks, etc. Industry sources hasten to add, even where the no-lead/low-lead gases are available, sales account for less than half of the volume expected for them.

By the end of the 1973 model year, a theoretical 30 percent of the cars on the road will be engineered to use them. This does not mean that 30 percent of gasoline then available will be no-lead/low-lead, though. Production of these fuels is picking up slowly, partly because the demand for them really is not there yet—and will not be until all cars are equipped with sophisticated new pollution-control devices that will require a leadless gas, no earlier than 1975. Meanwhile, United and the other refiners are being forced to market a commodity that the public is reluctant to buy and, in fact, really does not need.

What is making matters worse from United's standpoint is that older cars probably should not use these new fuels at all. Chrysler Corporation, among others, does not recommend unleaded gasoline for pre-1971 models, because the lead compounds in leaded gasoline act as a lubricant for valves and valve seats, helping to prevent excess engine wear and exhaust emissions. Pre-1971 cars can operate on the new low-lead fuels, however, if the octane rating is high enough to prevent engine "knock," the uncontrolled combustion of gas in the cylinders. But until authoritative studies say that some lead is not needed to protect engine parts, people may not risk engine damage, even to cut emissions. From a promotional standpoint, American Oil has a competitive edge in the no-lead/low-lead sweepstakes. It has had a no-lead gasoline, once called "white gas," on the market since 1915.

Getting the lead out has been particularly costly for the companies.

Shell, for example, estimated that the switch to its no-lead fuel, Shell of the Future, cost the company $60 million just for distribution and new equipment at the retail level.

While the petroleum industry generally still is not sold on the no-lead idea, most refiners seem resigned to it. The president of United stated,

It is only a matter of time before all gasoline will be unleaded. Unleaded, probably; cheaper, probably not. Refining costs will continue to be high in direct proportion to the octane requirements of future engines. That is the real issue. Many companies believe that the public will not put up very long with Detroit's new low-compression, less-efficient and, therefore, more expensive to operate automobiles, and will again start demanding "high-performance" engines. The higher the performance, the higher engine compression. The higher engine compression, the higher octane the gasoline necessary to feed it. And the higher the octane, minus the lead, the higher the cost of gasoline.

Case questions

1. Give the reasons why individuals will purchase low-lead gasoline. Indicate reasons why they are not purchasing the product.

2. List as many appeals that you believe have potential in advertising low-lead gasoline.

3. How would various motivational theories play a part in deciding which appeal to use?

4. To what extent should United use primary and/or selective appeals in its advertising?

5. What copy strategy would you recommend for United?

CASE 3.   MARSHALL FIELD & COMPANY
Deciding on customers of a store

In the course of its long history, Marshall Field & Company has been engaged in a wide variety of activities that have included retailing, wholesaling, manufacturing, and real estate. Until about 40 years ago, it was principally a wholesale operation. Since 1953, it has confined itself almost entirely to the operation of retail stores. It now has ten of these. Much the most important, both in sales and earnings, is the main store in downtown Chicago. Second in importance is the main Frederick & Nelson store in Seattle.

The Chicago operation includes branches in Evanston, Oak Park, Lake Forest, Skokie, Oakbrook, Calumet City, and Park Forest, all suburbs of the city, and in Wauwatosa, a suburb of Milwaukee. The Seattle store has three suburban branches.

It is an ironic fact that the founder, Mr. Marshall Field, is remembered mainly as a great retail merchant. Throughout his life dry goods whole-saling was the principal part of his business, and his interest in retailing was distinctly secondary, particularly in the early years of his career.

Mr. Field arrived in Chicago from Pittsfield, Massachusetts, in 1856. He was 21 years of age and had been reared in a strict New England farm family. After four years as a clerk in a country store, he decided to head west with his savings of something less than $1,000.

His brother Joseph helped Marshall obtain employment as a clerk in the largest wholesale dry goods house in Chicago—Cooley, Wadsworth and Company. His salary was $400 a year. He slept on the premises and at the end of the year had saved $200.

As a result of his seriousness of purpose, his selling skill, and his keen interest in merchandising, young Field progressed rapidly, becoming a partner in 1860. In 1863, the firm name was changed to Farwell, Field & Company, John V. Farwell having become a partner some years earlier. Also in 1863, Levi Z. Leiter joined the firm.

Two years later both Field and Leiter left Farwell, Field & Company and bought into the dry goods store of P. Palmer, changing its name to Field, Palmer and Leiter. In 1867, the two men bought out Potter Palmer and his brother, and the firm name became Field, Leiter & Company.

Potter Palmer had come to Chicago from Lockport, New York, in 1852. He established a dry goods store on Lake Street with his $5,000 capital. At this time Chicago had a population of 40,000. Its streets were unpaved. Its sidewalks were of wood, many of them on stilts. It was indeed a rough frontier town.

Potter Palmer was the first to bring quality and fashion to the city. He branched out into the wholesale business and introduced many innovations in advertising, personnel, merchandising, and customer relations. His business grew rapidly and was profitable. At the time he sold out to Marshall Field and Levi Leiter, its sales volume approximated $8 million, nearly as much as the combined sales of its two leading competitors.

The center of Chicago's dry goods trade was then on Lake Street near Clark. State Street was a narrow road flanked by rows of more or less dilapidated shacks. In the mid-1860s, Palmer came to the conclusion that State Street could be made into a more satisfactory retail center than Lake so he quietly began buying property on the street. In due course he owned most of it. He then proceeded to move the buildings back far enough to allow for a street 100 feet in width. With this project completed he constructed a six-story building at the corner of State and Washington, and the first Palmer House a few blocks south.

With the signing of a lease by Field, Leiter & Company on Palmer's new building, State Street was on its way to becoming one of the great shopping streets of the world. With the leading dry goods firm in the city located there, most of its competitors were soon forced to follow.

The decade of the 1870s proved to be a period of great trial for Field,

Leiter & Company. Its beautiful new store on State Street was totally destroyed by the great Chicago fire in 1871; it was caught in the financial panic of 1873; its State Street store again burned to the ground in 1877.

The 1871 fire, on October 9, devastated practically all of the central business district. After the fire the only evidence that a store had stood on the corner of State and Washington was a crude sign reading: "Cash Boys and Work Girls will be paid what is due them Monday 9 A.M. Oct. 16th at 60 Calumet Ave. Field, Leiter & Co."

Three weeks after the fire, the company reopened its business in an old car barn at 20th and State Streets. Meanwhile, it had decided to construct a building on Madison Street just west of the present Loop in which to house the wholesale division. This building was completed in March, 1872. For the first time the wholesale and retail branches were housed at different locations.

The retail division moved back to its old site at State and Washington on the second anniversary of the fire, October 9, 1873. It occupied a new and somewhat larger five-story limestone structure leased from the Singer Company, which in turn had bought the land from Potter Palmer.

In 1873, the country entered a severe depression which lasted six years. Despite a decline in the price level, Field, Leiter & Company maintained its dollar sales volume during the period. Its earnings averaged nearly a million dollars annually on a capital investment of between $2.5 million and $4.5 million.

In November, 1877, a second fire destroyed the new State Street store. Thirteen days later the company was open for business in an exposition building at Adams Street on the lakefront. In March, 1878, it moved once again, this time into a row of buildings on Wabash Avenue, near Madison.

In the meantime, the Singer Company had proceeded with the construction of a new six-story building on the old site at the corner of State and Washington. Mr. Field and Mr. Leiter offered $500,000 for the property but the Singer Company refused to sell for less than $700,000. During this impasse the building was leased to an important competitor, Carson Pirie Scott & Company. Faced with this dilemma, Mr. Field and Mr. Leiter bought the building for $700,000 and paid Carson's $100,000 to cancel its lease. Field and Leiter than proceeded to lease the building to Field, Leiter & Company. The new store opened for business in April, 1879. The company's main store has been at that corner ever since.

Despite two devastating fires and a serious depression, the company not only survived the 1870s but in 1880 was a flourishing and highly profitable enterprise. While Mr. Field was its dominant figure, he had shown great skill in the development of younger men, several of whom had become junior partners. However, serious differences had arisen between Mr. Field and Mr. Leiter. Field therefore agreed to buy Leiter's interest in the firm or offered to sell his own interest to Leiter. Since the junior partners were clearly loyal to Field, Leiter had no choice but to sell. The transaction was consummated in 1881 at a price of something over $2 million. Thus Marshall Field became practically sole owner of the business. Thus, too, there came into being for the first time the name Marshall Field & Company.

During the next 25 years, the company enjoyed a remarkable growth. Sales increased from $25 million to $73 million. Retail sales, which in 1882 had been 16 percent of the total, increased to slightly more than one third in 1906. Annual net profits in the 25-year period increased from $1.7 million to $4.8 million.

The steady growth in sales of course necessitated the acquisition of additional space. In 1887, the wholesale division moved into a new building constructed on the block bounded by Adams, Quincy, Wells, and Franklin Streets. In 1893, the retail division was enlarged by the construction of the building which still stands at the northwest corner of Washington and Wabash, adjoining Holden Court on the west. In the years between 1893 and 1914, Mr. Field or his estate acquired the entire block bounded by State, Wabash, Washington, and Randolph. New buildings were constructed from time to time as the business grew, until in 1914 the main store occupied the entire block. Also, the old Singer Building, built in 1878, had been replaced in 1907 with a modern structure. The building housing the Store for Men, across Washington Street from the main store, was completed in 1913.

Since 1914, there have been no basic changes in or additions to the downtown store properties in Chicago. They have been kept in excellent physical condition, however, through the expenditure of many millions of dollars on maintenance and modernization.

Harry Selfridge was hired by Mr. Field in 1879 as a stock boy in the wholesale department. Four years later he was transferred to the retail division and in another four years was its general manager at the age of 29. Selfridge was a man of terrific energy and soaring ambition. He was extremely creative and imaginative. He also possessed great promotional skill. He more than anyone else deserves credit for transforming the retail dry goods store into a full-line department store, by adding many lines of merchandise not previously carried.

Mr. Selfridge's personal ambition probably was responsible for his departure from the company in 1904, and, two years after the departure of Selfridge came the death of Mr. Field. He had been one of the great businessmen of his day. Coming to Chicago as a youth with less than $1,000 in his pocket, he died a multimillionaire. Not only did he build a great commercial enterprise but in his mature years he played an active role in the affairs of numerous other industries, notably transportation, steel, banking, and real estate. Without question he was one of the most influential and powerful men in Chicago.

It might be useful at this point to examine the principles and policies which Mr. Field applied to his business. One of these had to do with integrity. He would tolerate no deception of any kind in his relationships with customers and employees. His extremely liberal treatment of customers is reflected in the well-known phrases: "Give the lady what she wants" and "The customer is always right." In practice this meant that the customer could return merchandise for full credit for practically any reason whatever.

Mr. Field had several very strong convictions with respect to merchandising. He constantly stressed quality and would have nothing to do with cheap or shoddy merchandise. He was a pioneer in the field of fashion, something which Chicago women had hardly heard of prior to the days of Potter Palmer. He believed in assembling the widest possible assortments of merchandise not only from domestic sources but from countries around the world. He was a pioneer in the establishment of European buying offices, having opened the first such office in Manchester, England, in 1871. Mr. Field also was one of the first to offer merchandise for sale at only a single, clearly marked price.

Mr. Field probably had as much to do with the development of the customer service concept in retailing as any merchant in America. He employed good people and saw to it that they were thoroughly trained in the art of courtesy in dealing with the public. Full satisfaction was to be given to all customers regardless of the nature of their requests.

As a result of his emphasis on service to the public, the company was among the first to make available to its clientele many facilities not usually then found in retail stores: tearooms; waiting, writing, and rest rooms; nurseries; information desks; theatre ticket offices; travel bureaus; and numerous other conveniences.

Finally, Mr. Field believed in providing his customers with the most attractive physical facilities obtainable. He felt that people responded to beauty and good taste in the design of buildings and interiors just as they admired beauty and good quality in merchandise.

Meanwhile, back in 1901, the company had begun to interest itself in manufacturing and converting. Between that year and 1929, some 30 mills were acquired, most of them producing or converting textiles. Much of their output was sold to wholesalers, and for a period of time, the company undoubtedly gained important advantages from this course of action. However, as the wholesale trade started its long decline in 1924, the ownership of the mills presented the company with many new and serious problems. All the mills were eventually sold or liquidated.

The decade between 1920 and 1930 was marked by four important events: the purchase of the Davis Store on south State Street in Chicago in 1923; the opening of three suburban stores in the Chicago area in 1929; the purchase of Frederick & Nelson in Seattle in the same year; and the building of the Merchandise Mart in 1929–30.

The Evanston, Oak Park, and Lake Forest stores were among the

first department store branches built in this country. They were successful from the start and still are.

The company had entered the depression of the early 1930s a sprawl-
ing enterprise comprising a group of retail stores, a wholesale operation,
an assortment of mills, and the largest commercial building in the world.
One of the stores—the Davis Store—the wholesale division, the Merchandise Mart, and at times the mills, were all sources of substantial operating
losses. In fact, through a period of eight years starting in 1930, these
losses approximately offset the rather satisfactory earnings of the Marshall Field and Frederick & Nelson stores.

The process of transformation began with the liquidation of the wholesale division. Some of the mills and converting operations were disposed
of at about the same time. The wholesale had been on the decline since
the early 1920s, due mainly to the growth of retail chains and the practice of direct buying. Its liquidation was recommended by a business
consultant, James O. McKinsey, who was elected chairman and chief
executive officer of the company in 1935. The Davis Store on south State
Street was also sold during the McKinsey regime, which was terminated
by his sudden death in late 1937.

By 1943 the feeling was beginning to develop that the company should
confine itself to the operation of quality department stores. To this end,
it began to work toward the sale of the Merchandise Mart. This was
accomplished in 1945 and resulted in a substantial strengthening of the
working capital position.

The Merchandise Mart had been conceived in the early 1920s as a
grandiose scheme to save the wholesale division. Not only the company's
own wholesale unit but competitive establishments as well were to be
housed in one gigantic center. The plan has never been realized to this
day, due in part to the depression, but mainly because of the continued
rapid decline of the wholesale dry goods industry.

The last of the mills were finally sold in 1953. The mills were originally
acquired as important sources of supply for the wholesale division. Following the disposal of the wholesale, the relationship of the mills with
the rest of the company was of negligible importance. It was believed
that the capital derived from the sale could be put to excellent use in
retail expansion.

With the company once again in strong financial position due in part
to improved earnings in the 1940s, it was able to move forward aggressively on the retail front. Up to this time the reputation with the public
had rested largely on the State Street store in Chicago and the Frederick
& Nelson unit in Seattle. True, it had opened three rather small suburban
stores in the Chicago area back in 1929, but they were no longer adequately serving the suburban market. The population explosion into the
suburbs was already well under way.

Despite this fact, the company still regarded the two main stores as the principal bulwarks of the business. In the years following the war, therefore, it spent many millions on improvements in the State Street store and on the modernization and enlargement of the Seattle store, the latter alone at a cost of $10 million.

Meanwhile, the company again turned its attention to the suburban problem. The first modern shopping centers had begun to spring up in the late 1940s, and automobile transportation was well on the way toward revolutionizing customer buying habits. While the downtown stores were doing well, and still are, the only way to maintain or improve its position in the market was to expand further in the suburbs.

The first move in this direction was the opening of a small store at Bellevue, east of Seattle, in 1946. This was replaced by a much larger unit in 1956 which was expanded in 1964. A second suburban unit, Aurora Village, was opened in 1963 with the third Frederick & Nelson suburban store, Southcenter, opening in 1968.

In 1950 the company completed the acquisition of over 100 acres of land in Skokie, north and a bit west of downtown Chicago. It then undertook to create what it hoped would be the most beautiful shopping center in the world, Old Orchard. The company store in that center opened for business in 1956, and has been very successful. The store was enlarged in 1963 and again in 1967.

In the meantime, in 1955, the company had opened a somewhat smaller store than Old Orchard in Park Forest, south of Chicago. This unit also has proved to be successful and was enlarged in 1957.

In the mid-fifties, the company decided to go into the Milwaukee market and opened a store in the new Mayfair center in Wauwatosa in 1959. This store is approximately the size of Old Orchard. After a slow start, it has grown rapidly.

Oakbrook Center, in the western suburbs of Chicago, was patterned after Old Orchard and was ready for business in March, 1962. The size of this unit was increased in 1964 and again in 1968. Many people now regard Oakbrook, with its gardens, trees, and fountains, as the most attractive shopping center in the country.

In 1966 another Chicago suburban unit was added. River Oaks, located southeast of the city in Calumet City, is similar in design to the Oakbrook and Old Orchard stores. With the opening of this store the ring of regional shopping centers north, west, and south of the city was complete.

Mr. James L. Palmer stated the following principles of the company: "In all of our business relationships, we believe in integrity of the highest order. We believe in rendering the finest possible personal service to our customers. We feel that our main function is the assembling, from all corners of the globe, of the widest, deepest, and newest assortments of quality merchandise to be found anywhere. We believe in the fair and generous treatment of our employees, and as a matter of policy, we pay higher wages and grant more liberal benefits than the average firm in our industry. Finally, we believe in operating only full-line, quality department stores so designed and equipped as to achieve the maximum in beauty and good taste."

Case questions

1. In what ways do the customers of the branch stores of Marshall Field & Company differ from the customers of the main store in Chicago?

2. Would you find the same kind of quality merchandise in Marshall Field's as you would be able to secure in high-price specialty shops?

3. What classes of customers does Marshall Field attempt to reach?

4. To what extent should department stores be leaders in fashion?

CASE 4.   CNV, INC.
Planning strategy

CNV, Inc.'s principal products are the component parts—mufflers, exhaust pipes, tail pipes, and related fittings—of replacement exhaust systems for automotive vehicles. In all road vehicles using internal combustion engines, the exhaust system performs the important functions of conducting exhaust gases safely from the engine to the outside atmosphere and muffling engine noises. Eighty-five percent of the company's annual sales are accounted for by component parts of replacement exhaust systems.

As a result of new technological developments and the fact that sales had only increased by 1 percent during the last fiscal year, the executives of CNV decided that it was important to consider whether or not it should develop new copy strategy.

The exhaust system parts are sold under the trade-marked brand names—Protect, Special, and Last. The mufflers are made in more than 350 models and the exhaust and tail pipes in more than 1300 models, to fit practically all makes and types of domestic cars and the more popular makes of imported cars.

CNV manufactures most of its requirements of mufflers, less than 25 percent of its requirements of exhaust and tail pipes, and about half of its requirements of related fittings; and purchases the balance of its requirements of such products from outside sources.

CNV also distributes other automotive parts, such as gears, automatic transmission parts, shock absorbers, safety belts, engine parts, fan belts, oil filters, clutch parts, and brake parts, which are all purchased from outside sources.

Distribution

Protect division. Exhaust system parts and miscellaneous automotive replacement parts bearing the Protect brand name are sold to automotive parts jobbers and automotive accessory stores throughout the United States and Canada, and in various foreign countries. These customers in turn sell principally to filling stations, independent repair shops, and automotive dealers. This division accounts for 40 percent of the company's sales.

Deliveries to the company's customers are made from the CNV's warehouses. All warehouses carry a complete line of automotive exhaust system parts and serve CNV's customers in their respective territories.

Special division. CNV established franchised dealers who specialized in the sale and installation of automotive exhaust systems. Under the franchise the dealers are licensed to use the Special brand name in the advertising and sales of the company's products. At present there are approximately 300 franchised dealers operating approximately 400 Special muffler shops. This division accounts for approximately 46 percent of the company's sales.

CNV has a staff of eight advisors who conduct negotiations with prospective dealers in desirable locations and who advise dealers on installation methods and shop-operating procedures. Generally, a dealer can open a Special muffler shop with an investment of $25,000 to $50,000. Company subsidiaries operate 25 Special muffler shops. Some of these will be disposed of when qualified dealers can be found to acquire them.

The merchandising program of the franchised dealers encompasses: the sale of exhaust system parts at competitive retail prices; courteous and rapid installation service by specialists in clean, spacious shops; and a guarantee on each muffler sold, so long as the customer continues to own the automobile in which the muffler is installed. CNV sponsors strong national advertising and promotion of the Special muffler shops through radio and television network programs as well as magazines. These efforts have been supplemented by similar advertising and promotion on the local level by the franchised dealers. In the past six months the company's expenditures for national advertising were $950,000. Of this amount, the company received $200,000 reimbursement for national advertising from its dealers. CNV believes that the most effective use of its funds for national advertising is through the use of network radio rather than network television—the latter being much more expensive than the former.

Additional products, including shock absorbers and safety belts for passenger automobiles, have recently been added to the Special line. Some of these products have heretofore been merchandised successfully by some Special dealers in local markets.

CNV has undertaken certain preliminary and experimental work with a view to determining whether or not to expand the Special line to include tires, brakes and component parts, possibly meriting establishment of additional shop outlets of the type described above.

Last division. Mufflers and other components of exhaust systems bearing the Last brand name are sold to automotive jobbers and to large automotive parts distributors who sell principally to jobbers. The jobbers in turn sell principally to filling stations, independent repair shops, and automobile dealers. This division accounts for approximately 14 percent of CNV's sales.

Deliveries to the company's customers are made from its warehouses in Chicago and Canada, and from approximately five independent automotive warehouses strategically located in various parts of the United States.

Guarantees

Mufflers bearing the Protect and Special brand names are sold with written guarantees to the original consumers against all defects, so long as the vehicles on which the mufflers are installed are owned by such consumers. The guarantees cover the cost of the replacement mufflers but not replacement service and installation charges. The guarantee must be validated by the company and the defective muffler must be presented, with the validated guarantee, by the original consumer. The guarantee will be honored at any authorized dealer upon presentation of the defective muffler and the written guarantee. The company allows its customers full credit for the cost of mufflers used to replace defective mufflers. The company and the dealers share equally the cost of new mufflers used to replace defective mufflers. The cost to CNV of mufflers replaced during the last fiscal year was approximately $1,250,000.

Technological developments

Automobile manufacturers have focused efforts on extending the life of mufflers by use of steel coating to resist more effectively external rust caused by the elements and internal corrosion caused by exhaust acids and condensation. For the past several years all domestic manufacturers have used zinc-coated steel or aluminized steel in mufflers for original equipment, and one car manufacturer is using a ceramic coated muffler on its models. The opinions of automotive design and test engineers regarding the effect of coated steel on muffler life are inconsistent because of the difficulty of developing reliable and uniform test standards. CNV has developed a ceramic coated muffler which is being distributed on an experimental basis.

There has also been a decline in the number of dual exhaust systems in new car installations from a high of approximately 40 percent to practically none, as standard equipment on the current models. This has tended to restrict the number of mufflers introduced into the market each year on new cars.

Competition

Competition in the replacement exhaust system parts business is extensive at both the wholesale and the retail levels. CNV has three principal competitors each of which has greater total sales volume. These competitors sell under various brand names and furnish private brands to oil companies, rubber companies, mail-order houses, installation chains, and automobile companies for both original and replacement sales.

Competition among those engaged in the installation of replacement exhaust system parts has increased substantially in recent years. Several other national chains of muffler installation shops have been or are in the process of being formed. Local muffler installers, generally with one shop, are springing up in a number of metropolitan areas. Other competitors include automobile dealers, gasoline stations and independent repair shops.

Advertising strategy

Since the development of its franchised system for the Special division, the company had centered its advertising strategy around the two major concepts of "the Guarante" and the "Speed" in which the job could be completed.

However, with the technological developments and the decline in the dual exhaust system, CNV executives began to question whether or not this type of strategy was as significant as some other approach which it might adopt.

CNV had concentrated over 90 percent of its advertising on the Special division. It had relied primarily on a limited amount of trade advertising along with its emphasis on the use of salesmen to develop sales for the Protect and Last divisions.

In evaluating its overall advertising policy the executives evaluated several strategies which they might use for the Special division because it was their opinion that advertising could not be used to any great degree for either of the other two divisions.

Among the strategies considered were the following:

a. Continue to place major emphasis on guarantee and speed of service.
b. Discontinue use of guarantee approval and reduce price. Emphasis would be placed on a very low price concept.
c. Quality of the products at a low price.
d. Testimonial approach using professional athletes.
e. Certified professional dealer emphasis.
f. Most effective product.
g. Develop new warranty plan so that it would be good for the first 100,000 miles, regardless of whether or not the car was sold to another person.
h. Put emphasis on the brand name and ignore service and other features of this nature.
i. Emphasis placed on the need for a safety check or a "performance" outlet.
j. "We try harder because we are number four."
k. Emphasize the dealer name instead of Special.

The executives wanted to become more than just a "low No. 4" and decided that if they could create a more effective copy strategy, they would be willing to increase substantially the advertising budget.

Case questions

1. Evaluate the reasons why individuals will purchase the Special products.

2. When does the consumer begin to take a serious interest in advertising for automotive exhaust systems? Give reasons.

3. To whom should the advertising be directed?

4. Consider the various copy strategies listed and indicate what approach you would recommend for CNV, Inc.

chapter 6

IDENTIFICATION METHODS

For advertising to be effective, some means must be used that enables the prospective buyer to identify the advertiser's product. If such means are not used, the prospect will not know what to ask for, nor will he know that the goods offered are the same as those which were advertised. Since the earliest days of trade, sellers of goods have placed identifying marks or brands upon their products. The early Greek potters used marks, trade guilds had guild marks, and public houses and business establishments used identifying signs from the earliest times.

Today, in order to meet the demands of our mass-production and mass-distribution oriented economy, the seller must generally have a suitable form of identification for his products.

As a result, most products have some identification, either in connection with the product itself or on the package. Although historically these identification marks, such as trademarks and brands, were used largely for the purpose of identifying the manufacturer or source of origin of the product (so that he could be held responsible in case of poor quality or fraudulent practices), today the primary significance of identification is as a means of attracting and building patronage.

The identification used may be the name of the company, or trade name, especially used to associate in customers' minds the family of products. For the retailer and service organization, the firm name is also an important means of identification. But, for most other firms, it has been found that the individual product brand name or trademark is a more important means of identification than the name of the company.

Some basic definitions[1]

Patent: Applies to new and useful inventions or discoveries or improvements. Owner has exclusive rights for 17 years from date of issue

---

[1] Reprinted with special permission of Charles A. Holcomb, of the Kudner Agency, Inc., New York, and the American Association of Advertising Agencies.

whether or not he actually uses or takes advantage of the patent himself.

Copyright: Protects the owner against others copying "artistic creations" such as books, articles, music, paintings, and drawings. (Advertisements can be admitted to copyright, particularly if they show a degree of originality or artistic and literary merit.) Copyright is effective upon publication with copyright notice. Protects against copying by others for 28 years and can be renewed once for a similar period.

Trademark: A word, symbol, or device used to identify a manufacturer's goods or services and distinguish them from those of others. Must be in use in interstate commerce before it can be registered with the Patent Office. The certificate of registration remains in force for 20 years and may be renewed without limit for additional 20-year periods. Registration accords a degree of protection against another's use of the same or similar mark if confusion is likely to exist but in itself does not give exclusive ownership, as does a patent or copyright. Patent and copyright could be considered a reward for something done, whereas trademark rights have to be earned, as shown later in this report.

Service mark: Applies to the advertising of services rather than products. Includes marks, names, symbols, slogans, and other distinctive features that distinguish the services of one company from those of another (Greyhound).

Certification mark: Used by persons other than the owner of a mark to certify geographical origin, grade or quality, material, mode of manufacture, or other characteristics of goods or services (Underwriters' Laboratory Seal).

Collective mark: A trademark or service mark used to indicate membership in a union, association, or other organization (Shriners' emblem). Also to identify goods or services of a collective group (Sunkist).

Brand name: Synonymous with *Trademark.*

Trade name: (also known as *commercial name*): Many people assume that "Trade Name" and "Trademark" are synonyms. In rare cases they are (Johnson & Johnson), but in general usage the terms are quite different. A trademark is the brand name of a product; a trade name is the name of the company that makes it (Cadillac-General Motors Corporation). A trade name cannot be registered as such although the trademark itself may be a part of the company name.

Principal Register: As its name suggests, this is the trademark register that affords greatest protection and should be used wherever possible.

Supplemental Register: This accords less extensive rights, although it accepts a broader variety of marks. Marks which are nonregistrable on the Principal Register, for instance, because they are descriptive may be acceptable on the Supplemental Register if they have or may have possible trademark significance, i.e., be capable of distinguishing the applicant's goods or services. To be acceptable the mark must be used exclusively for at least one year before application. A supplemental mark which has been used exclusively for five years may be promoted to the Principal Register by affidavit showing such exclusive use. Distinctive slogans may be registered but may not qualify if used solely in advertising.

Secondary meaning: This is an important ingredient in the trademark mix. The term generally is used with reference to words that are descriptive of some characteristic of the product, but have been used so extensively as a trademark by a single company that they have come to be generally recognized as such (Holeproof hosiery, Nu-Enamel paint). The same principle applies to place names and family names (Waltham watches, Ford automobiles). To begin with, they are not good trademarks because by their very nature they do not belong to any one business concern. But long-continued, exclusive use by a single company can give them an additional (secondary) meaning. If this happens they are entitled to protection as trademarks. There is no inflexible rule to use in determining whether a secondary meaning has been acquired. The Patent Office or courts decide each case on its own merit. However, the exclusive and continuous use for five years may under the law be accepted as prima facie evidence that the mark has become distinctive. (Depending on circumstances a shorter period may be acceptable.)

House mark: A primary mark of a business concern producing a variety of products usually used in association with another or secondary mark (Du Pont—primary; Lucite, Dacron, Zerone—secondary).

Coined word: An invented or manufactured word, i.e., the product of a person's imagination, having no previous meaning (Kodak).

Generic term: Used to designate a general type, class, or name of a product (electric shaver, aspirin). Such a term cannot serve as a trademark for that product. But it can be perfectly satisfactory as a trademark for another *type* of product.

Descriptive: A word or term which describes one or more characteristics of a product, e.g., what the product is, what it is made of, or what it does. Descriptive marks cannot be registered (unless secondary meaning has been established).

Suggestive mark: Suggests rather than describes one or more of the characteristics of the product it is to identify (Ivory soap, Arrid deodorant). Is registrable.

Arbitrary mark: Connotes nothing about the product (Camel cigarettes, Shell oil).

Laudatory term: Word or words that indicate general superiority (premium, blue ribbon, supreme). Such words usually make weak trademarks because they lack distinctiveness, being used by many companies for a variety of products.

Infringement: The use by one of a mark which is so similar to the existing mark of another that confusion is likely to occur.

Dilution: The use of another's mark in a manner which tends to deprive it of distinctiveness. For instance, the slogan, "Where There's Life —There's Bugs," was held to be a dilution of the beer slogan, "Where There's Life—There's Bud."

Abandonment: A trademark is ordinarily considered abandoned after two consecutive years of nonuse unless there is no intent to abandon it and good reason exists for failure to use it.

Trademark registration

Contrary to popular impression, registering a trademark does not confer the status of ownership, as does a patent. Trademark rights are recognized at common law as property rights, aside and apart from registration under the trademark statutes. Such rights come from priority of use, continuous use, and due diligence in proper use and protection. You might say registration is like a birth certificate; it merely provides official recognition of what has already been created. But it is a constructive step toward protection. It puts all on notice that the trademark has been registered; no one can plead ignorance of your claim. It means that in all probability any case involving it will be tried in a federal court, and that the burden is shifted to the other party who must prove that the registration is invalid or that you do not own the trademark. Two very imporant points should be understood: (1) A trademark applies only to the specific article of merchandise to which it is affixed and (2) "mark" is a common legal synonym for "trademark," and it may apply to a picture, device, or other symbol as well as a word.

The purpose of a trademark is to protect the owner from unfair competition and the public from being deceived. The legal attitude toward it is based on the principle that a man cannot sell his own product under the pretense that it is the goods or services of some other firm. Therefore, he cannot be permitted to use names, marks, or letters by which he may make purchasers believe the goods he is selling are manufactured by some other company.

The party first to use a trademark in the United States is considered its owner for that class of commodity. Common law, founded on custom and usage, works to prevent unfair methods of competition. Our trademark laws represent an accumulated body of legal acts tempered and revised by the courts to meet changing requirements. The present federal trademark act, the Lanham Act, was passed in 1946 and went into effect in 1947. This act probably represented the most drastic change of all inasmuch as it opened up new areas for trademark registration by creating the Supplemental Register. Note the point made above for the two registers in the section on basic definitions.

Registration gives a trademark the following advantages:

1. The burden of proof in litigation is placed on the other party if it did not register its mark.
2. It helps to prove the exact nature of the trademark in case a question should arise as to whether or not there is an infringement by a second mark.
3. It gives federal courts jurisdiction in action against infringements. An injunction issued by this court is enforceable anywhere in the United States; that of a state court in only one state.
4. Domestic registration is now necessary in only a few foreign countries. These countries require that the trademark be registered in the United States first before accepting registration under their respective laws.

When a man sells merchandise under his own name, he may experience difficulty in protecting that name if a second person with the same name enters the same type of business. Even in cases of serious misuse of a family name, the courts have allowed a person to use his own name, while they will generally stop the use of a trademark in similar circumstances. The second party may not necessarily have to stop using that name, as the courts may only compel him to use his name in connection with a distinguishing mark. This distinguishing mark may consist merely of a line of copy to point out the difference, as:

Henry Ford
(Distinct from Ford Manufacturing Company)

or

*Smith Manufacturing Company
(Not connected with original Smith)

In view of these facts, it is important to distinguish between a trademark and a trade name. In advertising, words used for trademark purposes often are spoken of incorrectly as trade names. Though this practice is a common one, it is incorrect.

State registration

It is not necessary to register a trademark in any state in order to use the mark within a particular state. While each state has its own trademark laws and procedures, trademark rights are a matter of common law, and neither state nor federal registration takes precedence over the facts of priority of adoption and use.

However, state registration may be valuable because some state trademark laws impose criminal penalties for deliberate and knowing infringement of locally registered marks. State trademark procedures usually permit registration without previous official search for conflicts or prior use. The cost of such registration is nominal.

Nonregistrable marks

Following is a broad picture of what the Patent Office will not accept for registration. It does not include certain exceptions,[2] but is an indication of what to avoid when creating a new trademark.

1. A mark which so resembles another existing trademark for the same or similar goods as to be likely to confuse or mislead purchasers.
2. Anything merely descriptive, geographically descriptive, or deceptively misdescriptive.
3. Generally, marks which primarily are surnames since others having the same name are entitled to use it. Unusual surnames may be registrable but difficult to protect.
4. Anything contrary to good taste or public policy: (a) immoral, deceptive, or scandalous matter; (b) anything that disparages persons, beliefs, institutions, etc.; (c) flags or other insignia of the United States or any state, municipality, or foreign nation; (d) name, portrait, or signature of any individual now living, except with his written consent.

Trademark in conflict

A mark is considered in conflict if it is ruled that there is too great a similarity to another trademark in look, sound, or meaning. The question always comes up when registration is applied for. And it is the basis for infringement actions.

Conflicts occur in three areas: identical (or substantially identical) products, the same class of product, and completely unrelated products. The following examples are typical.

Identical items. Lemon-Up was held to sound too much like Seven-Up, as was Nidol analgesic too much like Midol.

Trademarks can conflict because of similar meaning even though quite different in appearance and sound. Hence, Canned Light paint was considered too much like Barreled Sunlight. For the same reason, I Wanta for biscuits was turned down because it conflicted with Uneeda

---

[2] For instance, trademarks used during the ten-year period prior to 1905 may be continued for the same class of goods. For example, there exist some 30 registrations for the Red Cross name or symbol which is not now registrable.

(the marks also looked somewhat alike). On the other hand, Hava for biscuits was approved.

No conflict was found between Easy-Carve and Morrell E-Z Cut—both for boned hams; Milk-O-Seltzer and Alka-Seltzer; Omicron watches and Omega; or Canadian Crown whiskey and Canadian Club.

Same class of goods. "Same class" is broadly interpreted. It includes products which in the mind of the buyer might come from the same source represented by the owner of the original trademark, whether or not such is the case. It has even been applied to goods because they are sold in the same type of outlet, although of a different character.

Sweetheart paper towels and tissues was held to conflict with Sweetheart soap; Quick Tea conflicted with Nestle's Quik powdered cocoa; Jantina shoes with Jantzen beachwear; Comet floor wax with Comet cleanser; Buffagum antacid, analgesic chewing gum with Bufferin.

However, no conflict was found between Rose Hall and Robert Hall —both clothing; nor Goldenrod shelled pecans and Goldenrod ice cream; nor E-Z Krinkles raw potato product and Krinkles breakfast cereal.

Unrelated products. In general, it is unusual and difficult to prevent the use of a conflicting trademark in fields completely outside the activities of the original owner—even if such protection is wanted. However, there are exceptions. Kodak, for instance, was refused registration for something as far afield as cigarette lighters; Johnny Walker was enjoined for cigars—more evidence of the strength of these marks!

Each question of conflict is decided on its own merits by the Patent Office or court. Rulings are a matter of judgment, and, as the above examples show, it is not always easy to follow the line that separates the sheep from the goats. The deciding factor is the degree of confusion which is, or might be, caused by the mark in question.

The Seven-Up Company once sued a competitor using the mark Fizz-Up for its lemon-lime drink. Evidence offered by the plaintiff included a public reaction survey in which approximately 25 percent of the persons interviewed indicated some degree of confusion because of the similarity between the marks. The court held this was sufficient to warrant infringement, and the injunction was granted. (The fact that Seven-Up had become an extremely well-known mark probably also played a part in this decision.)

Another factor is the trend of the courts to prevent a newcomer from exploiting the reputation already established by another firm's trademark. This is sometimes known as the "free ride" doctrine which, while not universally accepted, is gaining judiciary support.

It is obvious that the questions of conflicts is strictly a legal one. But the Trademark Committee (see page 168) can help by submitting alternate suggestions for marks in case a search invalidates for registration the number one choice.

Requirements for a good trademark

It is difficult to select a good trademark. Every effort should be made to develop a strong one with unique identity and broad protection. A coined word, such as Kodak, is a strong mark, well identified as Eastman's property. Examples of marks difficult to protect are such nondistinctive words as Gold Label, Superior, and Premium. The owner of a Blue Ribbon trademark, for instance, was not able to prevent the use by another company of Blue Ribbon as a trademark for a closely related product. The court pointed out that Blue Ribbon was registered over 60 times in the Patent Office for all kinds of goods; hence, it could not recognize "a large measure of distinctiveness" in the name. To some degree this also applies to the design. Common shapes slow up quick identification. In one year alone 429 circles were registered in the Patent Office, 293 oblongs, 272 ovals, and 123 squares.

When challenging another's adoption of the same mark, the owner of a weak mark may be offered only limited relief by the courts, such as merely preventing its use by another on goods that may be practically identical. If you are creating a new trademark, why start with that handicap?

Distinctiveness is the prime ingredient in a trademark. Over a half-million trademarks have been registered at the Patent Office. Replacing those that for one reason or another are dropped from the registers are some 20,000 new ones each year.

Yet these are only those used in interstate commerce. Each state has its own registrations. And there is a large body of locally used trademarks that are not registered anywhere. Worse yet, any of these state and local marks may prevent registration of a new mark at the Patent Office on the basis of prior use. There are many trade and private sources available for trademark search in addition to the files at the Patent Office. (The U.S. Trademark Association publishes a list of 125 principal reference sources.) *Printers' Ink* maintains what is said to be the largest file of slogans.

What are the characteristics that make a trademark strong and distinctive? It should be instantly recognized, easily remembered, and able to be reproduced effectively in any size, color, or medium. It should be dissimilar from other marks in appearance, sound, and meaning. It should resist time changes. It should have no unpleasant connotations and be suitable for export commerce. Do not worry about relevancy. A trademark becomes accepted as a symbol, and eventually the public reads no meaning into it except that of brand identification. What, for instance, could be less pertinent than Frigidaire kitchen range, Hotpoint refrigerator, Chock Full O'Nuts coffee? Actually, the more apt a trademark seems to be, the harder it may be to protect.

Classifications of trademarks

Coined word. Coined words make good trademarks if easy to pronounce and remember. They may be meaningless: Raytheon, Yuban, Zonite. Or suggestive—that is, the mark suggests a feature benefit or function of the product itself: Certo, Kleenex, Zerex. Mechanical means of trying various combinations of prefixes and suffixes with pertinent roots can be helpful in searching for a suitable mark. Misspelled common words: Arrid, Kromekote, Ennds (if not merely descriptive) are included in this category. Through popular usage, some trademarks in a sense have been coined by the public: Coke, Bud, Luckies.

Arbitrary. This includes the large number of trademarks where an existing word or symbol is selected arbitrarily, without relevance to the product: Camel, Arrow, Admiral. Others might be termed "semiarbitrary" in that they aim to establish a favorable impression of the product —a connotation of quality, prestige, economy, or whatnot: Pall Mall, Prudential, Partner's Choice. When combinations of common words are used, this line should be pursued with caution lest the mark becomes descriptive.

Pictorial. Good, if distinctive and kept simple, because it has strong identification and recognition values: Log Cabin, His Master's Voice, Four Roses. Often capsules a sales message: Bon Ami, Shaw-Walker. Characters make strong trademarks with added merchandising values. Many types are used. Distinctive people: Old Grand-Dad, Quaker man, Chef Boy-Ar-Dee, Campbell kids. Mythical: Green Giant. Historical: G. Washington, Lincoln, Webster. Animal: Elsie, White Owl, Hartford Stag.

Geographical. Usually will be refused for registration if the name denotes merely a place of origin rather than the brand of a specific owner. Thus Grand Rapids for furniture, Herkimer County for cheese would not be acceptable because the localities are well known for those products. However, secondary meaning established by long use makes Waltham and Elgin OK for watches, Paris for garters.

Surnames. Family names generally may not be registered as trademarks, since others with the same name are entitled to use them. However, many surnames have acquired trademark status through historical association by the public with specific products: Whitman, Gillette, Wrigley. Full names of individuals—baptismal plus surname—are entitled to registration if used as trademarks: Elizabeth Arden, Robert Hall, Fanny Farmer.

House mark. This is an overall trademark used by a company with multiple brands. It may be used as the brand name of various items that make up the company line (Toastmaster appliances) or used in connection with the individual brand marks (Westinghouse Laundromat washing machines, Westinghouse Magnalux electric lamps). Many house marks are contractions of the company name (Sunoco, Nabisco, Alcoa) or initials (GE, RCA, A&P). Before adopting a mark consisting of initials, consideration should be given to the difficulty people have in remembering arbitrary letters and numbers. Such combinations are almost certain to resemble other trademarks, and it may take a long time to make them distinctive and recognizable as referring to specific products and companies.

In choosing a new trademark one thing is certain: The more descriptive it is, the harder it will be to protect. If it is "merely descriptive," it cannot be registered in the first place. If it is "highly suggestive" (this distinction is made by the Patent Office), it may be registrable. If it has trademark significance, it may be registered on the Principal Register. Or one may have to settle for a listing on the Supplemental Register, hoping that it can be transferred to the Principal Register later.

It sometimes happens that individuals concerned with the selection of a new trademark will fall in love with a word that is descriptive enough to be difficult to protect. It should be pointed out that the risk of losing exclusive rights—especially after years of promotion—outweighs almost any advertising or sales advantages of such a mark. One might say this is a case where "it is better never to have loved at all than to have loved and lost."

Loss of trademark

Exclusive ownership rights in a trademark can be lost for several reasons. The trademark may be abandoned voluntarily or through neglect. The last can happen when goods withdrawn from the market are reinstated after a lapse of several years, or when the sale of a business fails to assign trademark rights. Dilution can lead to the loss of trademark rights, as can failure to maintain the quality requirements of a licensee. Rights can be lost by adverse decisions on conflict or prior use.

But a principal reason for the loss of trademarks is that they become generic. Some were descriptive (shredded wheat, dry ice, milk of magnesia, mineral oil), others semidescriptive or suggestive (cellophane, escalator, zipper). Some were meaningless when introduced (aspirin, kerosene, celluloid); but eventually all got into the language as common words.

Cellophane lost out largely because it was introduced as a new *type* of product. By the time competitive products were on the market, "cellophane" was the only name by which this type of product could be identified by the public. The court ruling (1936) is significant—"It therefore makes no difference what efforts or money the du Pont Company expended in order to persuade the public that 'cellophane' means an article of du Pont manufacture. So far as it did not succeed in actually converting the world to its gospel, it can have no relief."

This is the same philosophical rock on which Thermos was wrecked, the difference being that Thermos had been established as a trademark for half a century and was widely known. In fact, it was so well known that according to the trial court it finally became generic in spite of frantic efforts by its owner to protect it. The judge felt that the company itself contributed to the consequent loss of exclusive ownership. From the beginning the advertising objective was to popularize the term Thermos bottle. The company's 1910 catalog states that "Thermos is a household word." In the recent trial, the court pointed out that, intentionally or not, this was "an encouragement for generic use of a synonym for *vacuum insulated.*"

This line was pursued vigorously by the company until 1923 when it brought a trademark infringement action against the W. T. Grant Company. It won—on a technicality—but the judge who decided the case expressed the thought that Thermos might have become the name of the product, hence, invalid as a trademark.

With this warning, the company changed its advertising policy by associating "vacuum" or "vacuum bottle" with Thermos. It also began to police the misuse of the trademark by others. But at the trial, the judge found that the number of such protests from 1923 to the early 1950s was "infinitesimal" compared to the great number of generic uses that had appeared in print during the same period. He ruled that the company had failed to use reasonable diligence in protecting its mark.

About 1954, the company intensified its protective measures. The name of the company was changed to include the word "Products." Again, to strengthen the brand connotation, the line was diversified to include such items as camp stoves, tents, bottle openers—all labeled as Thermos products. Policing activities were stepped up.

But such measures were ruled too little and too late. Referring to them, the judge said, "The plaintiff's extraordinary efforts, commencing in the middle of the 1950s and carried on into the time of the trial, came too late to keep the word 'thermos' from falling into the public domain; rather it was an effort to pull it back from the public domain—something it could not and did not accomplish."

Thus, the American Thermos Products Company lost its exclusive trademark rights. Aladdin Industries, against whom the infringement action was taken—or anyone else, with certain restrictions—is now free to use "thermos" for vacuum bottles.

What steps to take in protecting a trademark

Set up a trademark committee. Establish the responsibility for the many steps in trademark procedures, from creation of a mark through the continuing "due diligence" necessary to maintain its exclusive brand status. Create a "strong" mark. See earlier notes on how and why.

Meet basic requirements. The trademark must be placed physically on the product, its container, point-of-sale displays closely associated with the product, or tags and labels attached to the product. The more types of exposure, the better. The product must be sold or transported in interstate commerce before federal registration is applied for. Principal Register offers more protection than Supplemental Register.

Use properly in advertising. A trademark is an adjective. Do not use it as a verb or noun. A trademark is not a *thing* or a *kind* of thing. It is a *brand* of a thing. To maintain this proprietary status (the objective of all protective measures), the trademark should always be associated with the generic name of the product. Ask for "Wamsutta sheets." Do not use as a possessive. Say, "The wonderful smoothness of Wamsutta sheets," not "Wamsutta's wonderful smoothness."

Sometimes the combination of trademark and product is cumbersome, especially when repeated several times. But how much repetition of the trademark is really necessary? One mention in the copy (plus logotype or prominent display element) may be enough. Repeating the brand name is good in broadcast media, but can easily be overdone in print.

How should the trademark be shown in print? There is no hard and fast rule about this. The legal objective is to make it distinctive from common words. This can be done with quotes, italics, boldface type, and so on. But it should start with a capital letter—it is a proper name.

Cap initials and lower case is by far the most popular treatment. Some advertisers like to see the trademark name stand out from the rest of the text matter by running it boldface, all caps, or reproducing the trademark itself, if distinctively lettered. While this might have some legal advantages, they could well be outweighed by marketing disadvantages —a jumpy layout and interruption of fast, smooth reading. This, of course, does not apply to the use of the trademark as a display element.

Nor is there a mandatory way to show that the trademark is registered. Trademark law gives three choices:

1. Registered in U.S. Patent Office
2. Reg. U.S. Pat. Off.
3. "R" in circle.

Most popular use by far is the "R" in circle positioned close to the trademark. It not only satisfies legal requirements, but is easiest to handle mechanically. However, several other types of notification are in common use. Eastman Kodak for many years has used simply "trademark" with Kodak. Some companies asterisk the trademark, referring the reader to a footnote showing trademark ownership.

Do not show a trademark as registered before it is actually so registered. This can be considered by the courts as a purposely false claim of registration; trademark suits have been lost because of it. "Trademark applied for" is not recommended. Prior to registration, many companies simply use the notation "Trademark" or "TM."

Avoid statements that, while designed to enhance exclusive rights, may have just the opposite effect. For instance, the Whosis Company advertises its Yanko bottle opener with such phrases as, "If it isn't a Whosis, it isn't a Yanko." Or, "Get the genuine Yanko." This not only misuses the mark as a noun, but implies the existence of more than one Yanko bottle opener.

There is no rule that specifies how many times the notice of registration should appear in an advertisement. Some companies have definite policies about this—to use it the first time the trademark is shown, to use it only in display or logotype, or to use it wherever the trademark appears. However, the objective is to make clear that the trademark is registered, and there is not much point in overdoing it or setting up arbitrary specifications that may diminish the sales impact of the advertisement.

In addition to protecting the trademark in product or corporate advertising, many companies run special advertisements for the sole purpose of identifying their trademarks—Coca Cola, du Pont, Ethyl, Eastman, to name a few. Some car campaigns run over an extended period; others are of the one-shot variety. This is not only beneficial from a merchandising viewpoint but could be helpful in a legal action in showing "due diligence" in protecting a trademark.

Police misuse of trademark. A trademark is valuable property—a visual symbol of a company's or product's reputation. If the owner is to maintain exclusive rights to it, he must do everything possible to prevent or correct misuse in print or broadcast media.

The law makes it very clear that trademark rights are lost by acts of omission as well as commission. Whether the misuse is innocent—due to ignorance or apathy—or deliberate infringement, prompt action should be taken by the trademark owner.

The most common cause of trouble is the trend of a trademark to become generic. Once the public thinks a word is the name of a thing rather than the brand of a thing, it gets into the public domain. For words mean what people understand them to say.

Keep records. Proofs of advertising should be maintained in the trademark file (one for each mark), showing first use of the mark and enough subsequent evidence to demonstrate consistent use. A brief history of how the trademark came into being and pertinent data covering earliest plans for marketing should be filed to establish priorities. Copies of labels, invoices, and shipping documents should be in the files to support the first use of the mark in commerce. Of great importance is a record of all policing correspondence as well as notes on actions taken.

All decrees and judgments of the Patent Office and courts should be bound together. Registration, renewal dates, and other legal specifications should be preserved in the trademark file.

If possible, apportion sales figures for various trademarks; they could be important in assessing damages. For instance, one company was awarded $239,000 when another firm's mark was found to infringe on its well-known trademark.

Watch those licenses. Licensing the use of a trademark carries with it two responsibilities for the owner. First, he must make sure the standards of quality of the licensed product are consistent with the quality which is assured by the reputation of the original trademark. This applies especially where several companies are licensed. The following agreement is typical: "The Creslan trademark may be used only in accordance with the provisions of a trademark agreement with American Cyanamid on fabrics the quality of which has been approved by American Cyanamid in writing as having met its standards of quality."

Second, licensing must be carried out in such a way that the trademark continues to indicate a single source of goods. The owner must make sure his trademark is not misused, either through generic designation or promotion (intentionally or not), as a grade mark. For instance, from a current ad, "Dacron is du Pont's registered trademark for its polyester fiber. Du Pont makes fibers, not the fabric or dresses shown." Nor should it be used by the licensee in a manner that could be construed as unfair competition. This is a matter of original contracts and rigorous supervision.

If these many protective steps seem burdensome, keep in mind the fact that someday your company may have to take the risk of proving in court that it has taken every reasonable measure possible to protect its trademark. U.S. courts decide nearly 1,000 trademark cases annually!

QUESTIONS

1. Why is it important for an advertiser to be able to identify his product?

2. What is a trade name? A brand name? A trademark? Give an example of each.

3. What are the important conditions a trademark must satisfy in order to be registered?

4. What are the main advantages of having your trademark registered under the Lanham Act?

5. Should a trademark be registered in every state? Why or why not?

6. What are some of the important requirements for a good trademark?

7. How may a trademark be "lost"?

8. What steps should be followed to protect a trademark?

9. List what you consider three very good trademarks and three you consider weak. Give reasons for your selections.

10. Give what you consider would be a satisfactory trademark and brand name for the following products:

    a)   Sweater.

    b)   A new brand of soup.

    c)   A ball-point pen selling for $1.95.

    d)   Hair tonic.

    e)   Toothpaste.

    f)   A special wafer for acid indigestion.

11. The manufacturer you represent distributed an inferior branded product during the war. This impression has been left with the buying public, and your sales have dropped to 25 percent of what they were prior to the war. What action would you recommend that this manufacturer take, and why?

12. Comment on the following statement: "Doctors and nutrition experts always have known that skim milk retained the life-giving proteins and minerals in milk after the fats were extracted. Thus 85 percent of the very small demand for fresh milk was on doctors' orders for people who could not use the fat content but who needed the other factors in milk. The hundreds of millions of gallons of skim milk annually left behind during cream and ice cream production had to seek a market in very low recovery products like cheese, animal feed, and even, experimentally, a synthetic cloth. Today, there is a mounting duction had to seek a market in very low recovery products like cheese, animal Francisco, was a simple little word—'SLIM.'

"The public can be told that something is good for its health, but it takes a word that appeals to the weight-consciousness of people to get the fire started."

13. Indicate how you believe the cases listed below should be decided.

    (*a*)   During 1965, a number of cases involving attempts by business firms to protect their business reputations and trademarks were taken before the courts.

            Perhaps the most significant cases have been those relating to product simulation problems, where the courts have attempted to apply the principles set forth in the 1964 Supreme Court decisions in *Sears, Roebuck & Co.* v. *Stiffel Company* and *Compco* v. *Day-Brite Lighting Inc.* There the Supreme Court indicated that while state law could not prevent the imitation of the appearance of a product, it could require copiers to identify their products as their own.

    (*b*)   In a case before the Court of Appeals for the Seventh Circuit, the owner of the trademark DUM-DUMS for a peculiarly shaped lollipop sought an injunction against a competitor marketing under the mark POP-POPS a lollipop which duplicated plaintiff's. The defendant's managing partner testified that in designing the packaging he tried "to get as close to (plaintiff's) as I thought good ethics and good taste would allow me to."

CASE 1. THE COCA-COLA COMPANY
Value of trademarks

In the Mishawaka opinion Justice Frankfurter observed that "If it is true that we live by symbols it is no less true that we purchase goods by them." He could have added that there is scarcely a social custom, or a generally recognized rule of conduct, or a basic principle of literature, law, or philosophy that is not frequently associated with, or interpreted by, or made more effective through, some well-known symbol.

At the top of the list, the *Cross* of the Christian Church before which billions of people have bowed in the last 1900 years.

The Sickle and the Crescent, emblem of the faith of 250 million followers of Mohammed who twice a day turn their faces toward Mecca to offer up a prayer.

The Golden Bough, with its countless suggestions of superstition, of fear, of spiritual yearning, and of tragic ignorance.

The *Red Cross,* with its promise of relief and of mercy.

The *flag* of every country, with all that each means to the citizen or subject in terms of patriotism, national ambition, and desire for security.

The *Lion* of Great Britain, the *Bear* of Russia, the *Lily* of France, the *Eagle* of the United States, the G.O.P. *elephant,* the Democratic *donkey,* and the picture of *Uncle Sam,* each synonymous with a whole library of human history and human experience.

The blind goddess balancing the *scales* of justice, the *laurel wreath* on the brow of the victor, the *crown* of royalty with its uneasy glory.

No wonder the Egyptians and Chaldeans imprinted a sign on their bricks, or that the Greeks marked their pottery, or that the artisans who built Solomon's Temple left their characteristic sign on it, or that the Romans and Etruscans made symbols familiar companions of the work of the craftsman. Admittedly, the beginning of commercial symbols is hidden in the long past, but they are of "ancient lineage" and boast a "long pedigree."

In the use of trademarks the businessman has merely imitated what all have done in all fields of activity. An illiterate person went into the leather business and made an "X" as a substitute for his signature, and the combination of this "X" and the man's name came to be "Mark Cross," the best known of all of the manufacturers of leather goods.

A bookkeeper in a drugstore searched for a name for a new beverage, wrote the compound word "Coca-Cola" in a flourishing script, and gave to commerce the mark which was to travel oftener and farther than any other word mark known to man.

"His Master's Voice," "Kodak," "Smith & Wesson," "Ivory Soap," "Winchester," "Frigidaire," "Old Dutch Cleanser," "Waltham," "Arm & Hammer," "Steinway," "Coca-Cola," and "Green's Fuel"—these trademarks and 400,000 more chaperon 50 million shoppers daily to the marts of trade in North America. At least 850 of these marks now serving our economy have been with us continuously for more than 50 years.

Much has been written about the legal characteristics having to do with "The Value of Trademarks from a Merchandising Standpoint," but before this boon to the trader came of age in the sight of the law, it had established itself with the manufacturer and merchant. The law concerns itself with brands because of their availability and their special usefulness in expanding and conserving consumer goodwill.

Prior to the Middle Ages, these marks served only to identify the product of the particular workman or of his group.

The 12th and 13th centuries discovered new reasons for putting them on manufactured products. Merchants earmarked their wares to provide evidence of ownership in case of shipwreck or loss. The guilds required their members to place the adopted seal on the output of their labor to fix responsibility for faulty work. These brands were the forerunners of the merchant's and the manufacturer's marks of today, but at that time the one served only as evidence of title to property and the other insured the liability of the careless craftsman. Here we come upon the basis of the modern theory that a trademark distinguishes the origin or ownership of goods—the manufacturer's mark pointing to the origin and the merchant's mark connoting ownership.

In England such marks had become quite common as early as Edward III. Notable among these were the swan marks, the printers' and publishers' devices, the cloth marks, and the marks in the cutlery trades.

Not until 600 years later did the businessman in the Western world wake up to the selling qualities of brand names and marks, and these names and marks acquired stature only with the arrival of the power machine. When factories began to turn out goods in volume they generated the necessity for mass consumption, since the mill had to find more and more buyers if it was to keep on running.

The trademark of the 20th century has matured into an indispensable servant of the production and distribution of goods, a direct response to a practical need, a utility in great demand in this latest phase of the industrial revolution.

One authority has described trademarks as "The cornerstone of the multibillion-dollar advertising business, the foundation of marketing policies in consumer goods industries, a powerful influence on the buying habits and cultural pursuits of people all over the world, and a force to be reckoned with in evaluating the state of our competitive economy."

Edward S. Rogers considered them a necessary support of a free economy; observing that " 'free enterprise' rests on the practice of identity and personal responsibility on the part of the producer for the goods he sells," which are documented by his marks and brands. He did not believe "we can have competition if we do not distinguish the competing goods and give the purchasers a chance to choose between them." "Trade-marks stake the reputation of the seller on the character of his goods," and underwrite his responsibility to the purchasing public.

Wherein does society at large share in the economic gain which flows from a wide and intelligent utilization of marks and brand names by manufacturers and sellers of goods?

In some sense a brand serves as a guarantee of the quality of the goods to which it is attached; but it is not so much a legal warranty as it is a moral representation that the goods are of equal merit to those purchased before under the same name, and that their identity is vouched for by the owner of the mark.

These symbols also act their part in advertising. The highly profitable service commercial marks are performing for American business is in the field of institutional and merchandising publicity intended to enlarge and intensify mass goodwill, with bigger sales as the ultimate target. When properly cast in advertising, the mark becomes a lodestone, an effective psychological pull that brings buyers to the owner's place of business. The trademark has been called the "silent salesman," but in fact it speaks with decisive voice everywhere in our commercial life.

The dealer, the distributor, and the factory look to advertising to bring customers. The nexus, the spark of the advertising matter is the trademark. It is the reflector of reflectors of the goodwill, the popularity of the merchandise, and the reputation of the company. As the institution and its product acquire a good name, the mark somehow gathers to itself this public approval and becomes a magnet to would-be buyers.

Responsible management and quality product are cornerstones of sound public relations; but the third element must come into play before that valuable intangible asset known as goodwill can be crystallized, consolidated, and turned into dividends. This goodwill expresses itself in the fact that the business holds its customers—plus the favorable report these customers circulate about it in the community. This expectation that former customers will also be future customers may for a particular company acquire a huge value. The goodwill of The Coca-Cola Company has for long been worth several times as much as all of the tangible assets it owns.

Advertising has been relied on primarily to carry the message for Coca-Cola to its dealers, consumers, and potential consumers. The trademark "Coca-Cola," since 1886, has dominated this advertising in whatever media it appeared and whatever form it took. What the Coca-Cola business has done has been repeated in one degree or another by every other successful business that looks to the public for customers. Everyone recognizes the essential part played by advertising, but not everyone appreciates the work done by the trademark, especially in getting sales and holding fast to customers. A trademark will bear endless repetition without becoming stale and without losing its selling power with the marketgoers. Wherever a mark appears in a paper, in a magazine, or on a poster, it should be given a prominent place. It rates a high seat, and it can use profitably all of the light, color, and sparkle you can give it.

The grade labelers, the consumers' leaguers, and the innocent tools of the promoters of state socialism are striving to discredit trademarks and brand names in the minds of the masses. Their argument implies that our shoppers are incapable of choosing intelligently between competing goods and that our marks and brand names are a hindrance to smart purchasing. They would place all of us in the hands of a government employee who would tell us where, when, and what to buy, through grade labels which are to be substituted for human experience and individual preference as the one basis for the buyer's choice.

No mark can possess a character superior to the goods it sells, and the reputation of both mark and goods must be supported by true worth. Thus supported, a mark acquires a just fame and becomes a real convenience to the buying public, a sign they can trust, a badge of a successful business. The dealer and the distributor share with the owner the impressive merchandising advantages of the mark, the consumer favor that follows it, and the selling power of the goodwill it symbolizes.

Case question

Evaluate the importance of trademarks in our present merchandising strategy.

CASE 2.   ROBERTS, INC.
Considering brand policy

Roberts, Inc. manufactures lines of domestics, consisting of blankets, towels and other bath fashions, sheets, and bedspreads. It also sells rugs and carpets through its RC Division.

Approximately 60 percent of Roberts' sales are made under its own brand name *Robo*. The remaining 40 percent of sales are made in quantity to chain stores, department stores, and other retail outlets for marketing under their private labels.

Sales under the brand name *Robo* have declined 5 percent during the past year where the sales to the chain stores and other outlets have increased 6 percent. Roberts' vice president of marketing believes that the customers are beginning to recognize that the chain stores are handling the "Robo" line at substantial discounts under private brands. Since

Roberts sold the products to the chain stores at a price differential of 7 percent, the vice president was concerned about the inherent dangers if this trend of declining sales under the "Robo" brand continued.

Roberts' central marketing division

The central marketing division, with headquarters and principal showrooms in New York City and district offices in nine other major marketing centers, places its principal marketing emphasis on Robo brand products which are sold primarily to leading department stores in major metropolitan areas and also to distributors, for resale to other retail accounts located in secondary markets. The division's marketing program emphasizes related product selling through "One Vision" promotions of matched and coordinated sets for bedroom and bath. Special store fixtures, developed by the Roberts Co. are supplied to retail department stores which set up "Robo Shops" within their own domestics departments for operation by store personnel.

The company's merchandise is displayed on these fixtures, and a cooperative advertising and display program featuring the company's seasonal products is employed. These shops have been installed in over 125 leading stores throughout the country and have resulted in a sales increase in past years of Robo's highly styled and most profitable merchandise. The Division carries substantial stocks of finished merchandise at the mills and also operates warehouse "Service Centers." In addition to direct sales to retailers under its own labels, the Roberts Co. sells a broad line of domestics in quantity to leading mail-order and retail chains, buying groups and jobbers for resale under their private labels. Private label sales are made principally by the central marketing staff, and two private label customers accounted for approximately 12 percent of Roberts' volume.

Blankets. Roberts manufactures regular and electric blankets of wool, acrylic fibre, rayon, cotton, and blends of these materials. Blankets, including automatics and shells, account for approximately 28 percent of the company's sales. Roberts has a line of printed blankets and, in addition, has developed improved finishes for synthetic blankets.

Towels and bath fashions. Roberts' marketing emphasis on style and fashion has been particularly effective in its lines of towels and bath fashions. Printed towels have grown in popularity and now represent an important and profitable portion of the towel volume. The overall product line was strengthened by the addition of other bath fashions consisting of bath rugs, shower curtains, and lid covers. The latter articles which are purchased from outside manufacturers are coordinated with towels and are styled by Roberts exclusively for its distribution. The addition of these bath fashions has given it the advantage of offering coordinated styling for all textile products normally used in a bathroom. Towels and other bath fashions account for approximately 24 percent of Roberts' sales.

Sheets and bedspreads.   Roberts also manufactures and markets a quality line of fitted and hemmed combed-cotton bed sheets and pillowcases. The line is marketed in white, solid colors, stripes, and printed patterns which coordinate with the printed patterns of the Roberts' other domestics. The Roberts Co. also manufactures and markets a wide variety of woven bedspreads both under the Robo label and private labels of chain stores, mail-order, and other bulk customers. The bedspread mill is equipped to manufacture yarn-dyed box-loom and jacquard spreads, plain piece-dyed spreads and colonial and heirloom styles, both in spread and coverlet sizes. Matching draperies for bedrooms and bath are fabricated from the same materials and sold with the spreads as matched sets.

Screen printing.   The use of matching and coordinated printed patterns on bedroom and bath products has made an important contribution to Roberts' development of fashion in domestics. These patterns are printed principally by a silk-screen process requiring skilled techniques.

RC marketing division

The RC marketing division is responsible for styling and marketing rugs and carpets manufactured by Roberts. The division's sales, which during the last five years have increased from approximately 26 percent to 30 percent of the company's total volume, are made to four principal types of outlets: department stores, furniture stores, carpet specialty stores, and interior decorators.

Advertising

Roberts uses national advertising in leading home furnishings and general media and offers a cooperative local advertising program and promotional help at point of sale to all Robo customers.

In the advertising copy, Roberts stresses quality products, advanced styling, and points out the widespread acceptance by leading department and specialty stores in the United States.

Case questions

1. What are some of the inherent problems that Roberts will face if it continues to sell 40 percent of its products under private brands?

2. To what degree is the "brand" important to the ultimate consumer in the purchase of Roberts' products?

3. How can Roberts build the "Robo" brand loyalty and still sell to chain stores who will sell under private labels?

4. Point out whether or not Roberts will be able to sell the products under the "Robo" brand at a higher price than what the company charges the chain stores. Is this a satisfactory policy?

5. Give the broad strategy which you believe Roberts should adopt.

CASE 3. HUNT-WESSON FOODS, INC.
Developing of brands

Twenty years ago most housewives had never heard of tomato sauce. Today, 28 million of them—more than 50 percent of the homemakers in the United States—use it regularly.

What happened? It started in 1943, shortly after Hunt Brothers Packing Company merged with ValVita Food Products. Searching for a product with potential mass appeal, the company chose tomato sauce (then often described as "Spanish Style"), a minor commodity product sold primarily in California, New York, and the Gulf states and almost totally unknown in the middle regions of the country.

The company poured millions of dollars into a nationwide campaign that introduced tomato sauce as a recipe ingredient for meat, fish, and spaghetti dishes. Working chiefly through full-page, four-color ads in consumer magazines, the company enticed the housewife with large, colorful photographs of food, then showed her how to duplicate the results. It created a market where none had existed—a market which it proceeded to dominate (today the company continues to sell more tomato sauce than all its competitors combined).

What is particularly fascinating about the tomato sauce campaign is the thinking behind it. For here was the outgrowth of a marketing philosophy that played a major role in transforming Hunt Foods and Industries, Inc., from a small, local cannery (1943 sales: less than $10 million) into a diversified, nationwide industrial complex with sales of over $500 million. In 1964, all of the company's food operations were consolidated under the Hunt-Wesson Foods Division. In 1966, this business was established as a separately incorporated subsidiary under the name "Hunt-Wesson Foods, Inc." Today, this company accounts for over 70 percent of Hunt Foods and Industries, Inc., sales.

To understand that marketing philosophy, it is important to understand Hunt-Wesson's attitude toward advertising. To Hunt-Wesson, advertising is not an expense but an investment, an indispensable tool for selling Hunt-Wesson products and building a reputation for the company and its brand names. But indispensable as it is, advertising is still just one ingredient in the marketing mix. Director of Advertising Fritz Ohliger explains it this way: "Advertising is one means of communication—one link in a chain of sales motivators. There are so many factors that convince people to buy or not to buy: price, packaging, point-of-sale material. If you stopped to think about it," he says, "you could make up a list of 20 or 30 factors that affect sales—like, 'How good is your distribution system?' 'How effective are your salesmen?' 'What's the competition doing?' Any one of these could help counteract a bad advertising campaign or help ruin a good one."

"Then of course, there's your most important factor," Ohliger says, "and that's quality. All your advertising and pricing and packaging, all your skills as a salesman aren't going to do you one bit of good if your customer doesn't think your product is first rate, if he doesn't come back for more. So, at the heart of this philosophy is an insistence on quality."

Hunt-Wesson advertising itself is a notable example of this desire for quality. "The look of quality has always been a primary requirement," says Ohliger. "Fine illustrations and reproduction, clean layouts, full-page color advertising with appetite appeal and with very strong impact. In order to achieve this look, we've always gone first class. The best photographers. The best copy. The best engraving and printing. We'll produce a dozen ads, go right down the line on them, test them thoroughly, then use only the best ones."

Right from the start, Hunt-Wesson's quest for strong advertising impact has guided a choice of large circulations and dominant schedules. In 1947, when the company began advertising nationally, it bought 52 successive full-page color ads in *Life*. All 52 ads concentrated on the same product: tomato sauce. This was a new approach—a kind of strategic bombing designed to build sales volume and brand franchises quickly. Hunt-Wesson intensified the advertising even further by concentrating virtually all its fire on certain "spearhead" items (sauce, paste, catsup). These items, Hunt-Wesson figured, had the greatest growth potential; they were economical, they could be used by broad segments of the population, and they were in categories where there was no single dominant national franchise.

Here then were several radical departures from what was considered sound marketing strategy. Other canners were spreading out their advertising, distributing it among various products in their lines, and continually trying to add more products to those lines. Hunt-Wesson, on the other hand, was eliminating a number of low-volume items and focusing production and promotion efforts on the spearhead products.

This business of bucking tradition is nothing unusual for Hunt-Wesson. Throughout its rapid climb, the company has flouted old bugaboos. Take, for instance, Hunt-Wesson's approach to the relationship between advertising and distribution. According to some experts, when you promote a new product you start with regional advertising and expand it as brand strength develops. Yet, in promoting tomato sauce, Hunt-Wesson let advertising precede a product into an area; that is, the company advertised the product nationally before it achieved national distribution and thereby created a demand that expedited wider and faster distribution.

Many of Hunt-Wesson's marketing innovations have, by now, become standard practice in the industry—but not for Hunt-Wesson. It is constantly changing, constantly shifting to meet specific product needs. What has remained constant is the overall philosophy and the overall goal: to develop strong consumer brand franchises, franchises which Hunt-Wesson regards as "our real earnings and our real assets."

The development of Hunt-Wesson's brand franchises has been entirely compatible with the narrow focus on spearhead products. The spearhead ads have helped to sell immediate use of the product; at the same time, they have added, bit by bit, to the total public personality of the Hunt brand. As people have become familiar with the widely advertised spearhead products, the name "Hunt's" has transmitted a stronger quality image. In this way, the spearhead products have paved the way for the others and for new products yet to come.

Today, Hunt-Wesson has some of the nation's most successful food products: Hunt's tomato sauce and tomato paste are the largest selling brands in the U.S.; Wesson is the top nationally distributed vegetable oil; Hunt's catsup and Hunt's peaches both rank among the best sellers; Snowdrift is one of the leaders among solid vegetable shortenings; and Ohio Blue Tip matches are strong number two sellers in their field.

Some of these brands were nurtured and developed by Hunt-Wesson. Others are comparatively new arrivals in the Hunt-Wesson family (arrivals who share one common trait: strong, quality brand names). Hunt-Wesson magazine ads currently appear in consumer magazines and in hotel, restaurant, institutional, bakery, and professional magazines. Hunt-Wesson has always relied heavily on national magazines because of appetite appeal possible with quality, full-color reproduction and because of the large female audience of such publications. Television, radio, and newspapers also have been used effectively, particularly in regional advertising campaigns designed to supplement the national magazine coverage.

There is a tendency among advertising and marketing people to feel that the longer the list of magazines you are using for a given product, the better the campaign. The attitude at Hunt-Wesson tends to be the converse. It is convinced that the concentration of an advertising message in a few magazines has a greater effect than simply the sum of the number of impressions. It likes to dominate an audience . . . to bring its message home to them with real power . . . to convert them to Hunt-Wesson. For example, it will run an advertisement for a single product in every issue of a monthly magazine, in every issue of even a weekly magazine. And what is more, it will regularly run more than one advertisement for a single product in the same issue of the same magazine. Hunt believes that the advertising dominance will be reinforced by the power of reaching the consumer with as much frequency as the particular magazine provides—be it monthly or weekly. Further, it reasons that the added power upon the consumer's mind of more than one ad per issue will drive home its message much more forcefully than will a single impression each time.

Hunt-Wesson was a pioneer in the use of the broadcast medium and especially television at the time when it was particularly exciting because of its novelty. In fact, in 1950, Hunt's Tomato Sauce was the first product to be advertised five days a week on a single network. During the next 10 years, however, broadcast dollars were concentrated in local television. But it did not use local television in the usual way. Many advertisers will run campaigns of moderate weight in a relatively large number of markets. In an effort to find the best way to use the medium, Hunt-Wesson has always run long-term campaigns of extremely heavy weight —that is, a very intensive schedule of commercials—in a relatively small number of markets. Its philosophy of dominance comes into play once again, because Hunt-Wesson believes that the power stemming from concentration of its messages against a few number of consumers would tend to impress more efficiently Hunt-Wesson's communication in their minds. And Hunt-Wesson is not afraid to repeat the same message by using the same commercial once it finds the one that best communicates its message.

Hunt-Wesson Foods, Inc., products include: Hunt's (tomato products, fruits, and vegetables), Wesson and Snowdrift (vegetable oils, mayonnaise, and shortenings), Pride of the Farm and Snider's catsup, Blue Plate (mayonnaise, margarine, salad dressings, preserves and jellies, and coffee—all distributed primarily in the South), and Ohio Blue Tip Matches.

Case questions

1. Why, in your opinion, does Hunt not use a single brand name for all of its products? Give the advantages and disadvantages of such a policy.

2. In some instances Hunt does not identify itself with the products in its advertising. Why is this policy followed?

CASE 4.   ECONOMY CORPORATION
Evaluating and identifying merchandise

Economy Corporation is engaged in the sale of merchandise at retail through 185 company-owned stores and at wholesale to 221 affiliated retail stores. The stores are operated under the name "Economy General Stores."

The management of Economy is considering whether or not it might be advisable for them to change the policy of not using any advertised brand names on the merchandise they sell, as a result of the request of the managers of a number of its stores to adopt such a policy.

Merchandise

During the last fiscal year approximately 75 percent of Economy's total sales through its general and affiliated stores were of soft goods, primarily wearing apparel. Of such soft-goods sales, approximately 65 percent were irregular and "close-out" merchandise, the balance being regular "first quality" merchandise purchased by Economy needed to fill out inventory lines. Irregular goods purchased by the Economy Corp. contain minor flaws not affecting usefulness and not readily apparent. Close-out merchandise is first quality goods sold to Economy at discount prices for reasons unrelated to quality, such as style changes and seasonal factors. The manufacturer's label is removed and irregular merchandise is appropriately marked. The company's General Stores guarantee the satisfaction of their merchandise and will exchange the merchandise or refund the purchase price upon return of the goods.

Most irregular merchandise is purchased in volume on a continuing basis from 85 manufacturers at previously negotiated discounts ranging generally from 35 percent to 50 percent below the manufacturers' regular prices. Although Economy has no long-term contractual arrangements, it has for several years purchased all of the irregulars of some manufacturers and all of the irregulars in specified lines from others, regardless of such factors as color and size. Economy also purchases close-out merchandise from these manufacturers and from a large number of other suppliers at prices negotiated at the time of purchase. Irregular and close-out merchandise is sold at substantial discounts from regular retail prices. Successful operation is, to a large extent, dependent upon its continued ability to purchase such irregular and close-out merchandise on such terms.

During the last fiscal year, purchases from the single largest supplier of irregulars and close-outs represented less than 10 percent of Economy's total purchases of such goods. Although no manufacturer has ever terminated arrangements for sales of irregulars, Economy has other alternative sources.

All of the Economy Co.'s stores and affiliated retail stores sell a variety of merchandise, including men's, women's, boys', girls' and infants' wearing apparel; shoes, sheets, pillowcases, blankets, curtains, bedspreads, piece goods, toys, gifts, school supplies, housewares, and paint. About 60 percent of the stores carry health and beauty aids through rack service merchandising provided by others. Some of its larger stores carry small appliances such as electric irons, toasters, and hair dryers. About 5 percent of retail sales of its stores are of nationally advertised, brand-name merchandise.

The following table shows approximate percentages of sales by product categories:

Product category	Percentage of sales
Soft goods	72
Housewares	12
Shoes	11
Health and beauty aids (through rack service)	4
Other	1

Most of the stores are operated in rural communities with populations ranging from 5,000 to 60,000. Generally, they are located on the ground floor of older store buildings in downtown areas. Economy's policy is to lease its store properties for relatively short terms, usually three to five years, with renewal options when available. Rental costs are approximately $1.00 per square foot of selling space. Selling space ranges from 1,700 to 12,000 square feet, with the average being approximately 3,600 square feet. The typical store has annual sales of approximately $150,000. The stores are all air-conditioned and similar in appearance. All sales are cash and carry.

The affiliated stores purchase almost all of their merchandise from Economy and are afforded quantity discounts. The stores are independently operated and are not subject to any reporting requirements. Economy advertises in local newspapers and over local radio and television stations. It also uses direct-mail promotions from time to time. It is the policy of Economy to operate its stores six days a week and at least one night a week. The company has no plans to establish leased departments in any of its stores or to expand rack service merchandising, presently limited to health and beauty aids, to other types of merchandise.

Competition

The business in which Economy is engaged is highly competitive. It is in competition with discount stores, which also sell popular-priced merchandise, and with all types of retailers, including department stores, variety stores, mail-order chains, and specialty stores. Some of the largest retail merchandising companies in the nation have stores in some of the same areas where the Economy and affiliated stores operate.

The managers of the stores requesting a change in the policy of using advertised brand names, believed that customers' buying habits had changed. It was their opinion that their competitors had shifted to using price appeals on advertised brands to such a great extent that it would be difficult for Economy to continue to meet this competition in the future.

They contended that in the past it was satisfactory to emphasize the fact that Economy stores specialized in quality merchandise (irregulars and close-out merchandise), but that this appeal had lost is credibility. They further believed that Economy would have to exploit and promote the specific brand of merchandise, instead of relying on the general patronage appeals for stores.

Case questions

1. If Economy adopted a policy of "brands" for its products would this create a more flexible or a more rigid price structure? Explain.

2. Mail-order houses do not market most of their items primarily on brand reputation since products are purchased because of the reputation of vendor. How does this compare to Economy's operation?

3. How could Economy maintain its present buying policy and still use a brand policy?

4. How important are individual brands for the products which Economy sells?

5. What brand policy would you recommend for Economy?

PART **III**————————

Preparation of the advertisement

chapter 7

COPY PREPARATION

In chapters 4, 5 and 6, the emphasis was placed on the important aspects of demand creation and the techniques of product identification. It was pointed out that the attention of the prospect must be attracted and drawn to the product or service to be sold, his interest in it must be aroused, and, after he is induced to desire it, this desire must be converted into a buying decision.

Setting objectives

Before the copy can be prepared, however, it is important to evaluate the overall marketing objectives to be sure that they are in harmony with the economic and social aims of society. If the company, as an example, has a marketing objective to increase its market share by 1 percent by selling to a new market segment, then, the decision as to the degree to which the company believes it should concentrate its advertising on this segment will have to be made before preparing copy. At the same time the social implications should also be checked to determine if there are conflicts which might exist. Consider a cigarette company that decided to increase its market share by concentrating more advertising on the 18-year-old market. The social implications of the marketing objectives and the morality of advertising cigarettes to the above market segment should not be overlooked.

The authors have found that preparing copy by objectives is an effective base from which to develop practical advertising appeals. Such a procedure accommodates the correlation of the copy to the overall marketing program, and, at the same time, assists the copywriter in presenting his material in clear and concrete terms.

Before going into the details of preparing an advertisement, it is advisable to discuss briefly the objective(s) of the individual advertisement. That is, what must the individual advertisement accomplish to be an effective one?

Various advertising people will describe somewhat differently the specific objectives. Some will divide the requirements into gaining attention, arousing interest and obtaining readership, stimulating desire, establishing conviction, and securing action. Others will express requirements for effective advertisement in terms of obtaining initial attention, arousing and holding interest, and creating an effective and lasting impression on the audience that will result in current or future favorable action.

Although the ultimate objective of the advertisement may be to obtain action in the form of a sale or to create a lasting "brand image" in the mind of the potential buyer, these ends obviously cannot be achieved unless the immediate objectives of having the advertisement noticed and read are achieved. That is, unless the advertisement attracts the attention of the potential customer and holds that attention (by arousing and maintaining interest) long enough to have the advertisement read and understood, the ultimate goals cannot be achieved. Hence, in preparation, these immediate functions of the advertisement must be kept in mind and planned in such a manner to achieve these specific purposes. For example, the headline, the layout, the illustration (including the use of color), and/or the typeface used, among other things, should be planned with the primary objective of attracting the initial attention to the advertisement, but in such a manner that this initial attention will aid in arousing and holding interest and creating a favorable lasting impression.

It is also important to keep in mind that in writing copy which is to appear in newspapers, magazines, and other publications of this nature, a somewhat different approach is used from that used in preparing the script for radio and television.

The script for radio advertising must put primary emphasis on the audio aspect. In television advertising, on the other hand, the script should complement the picture and, at the same time, appeal to the sense of hearing of the viewer. Because television appeals to both sight and sound, development of the advertising message may be more complex.

Furthermore, the commercials on radio and television are of a temporary nature, because the listener or viewer cannot bring them back. The advertiser has to decide on the degree of repetition he wishes to use. With a printed advertisement, however, the reader decides how many times and to what degree he wishes to read it.

DEFINITION

Copy includes the word messages, whether for print, radio, or television. In the printed advertisement, it consists of the printed words except, perhaps, for those words forming part of the registered trademark. In other words, copy is defined here as the word message of the advertisement.

For example, in the March 1971 issue of *Reader's Digest* appeared a Pinto advertisement. The headline was: *New Pinto—3-door Runabout.* Then followed an illustration of the Pinto with a couple loading hunting gear in the storage compartment. Following this was the copy:

Now you can pack more fun and games into a little car than you ever thought possible. Because now there's Ford's new Pinto 3-door Runabout— to go along with the fast-selling Pinto 2-door.

Just flip down the Runabout's rear seat, open the big back door, and the big back room makes the packing easy. Pack in your golf clubs, bulky packages, those big pieces of luggage. Pack it all in. There's big room in your little Pinto.

But that's not all. You get the regular Pinto goodies like a gas-saving 75-horsepower engine for more "go" on hills and freeways. And a wider stance than any little import so the Pinto hugs the road better.

The servicing? It couldn't be easier. And Pinto is still priced down with the little import cars.

Take a good look at the new Pinto 3-door Runabout or the Pinto 2-door. And take your pick. At your Ford Dealer's.

APPROACH TO WRITING COPY

Before any copy is written, the copywriter should answer three basic questions. "What am I advertising or selling?" "To whom am I advertising or selling?" and "How can I best convey this message, or concept, to my reader?" The answers to these three questions provide the basic idea for the copy.

"What am I advertising or selling?"   The copywriter must determine what there is in the product or service he is selling that appeals to a desire of the potential buyer. At first glance, it might seem obvious that he is selling a certain product, such as a hi-fi set, a soft drink, a face cream, or gasoline. But, in actuality, he is not selling the product but what the product can do for the prospective buyer. For the buyer is not interested in the product as such, but in what the results will be for him if he buys and uses the product. So the advertiser of a TV dinner would not sell a unit with so many well-cooked, well-flavored items, but a quick, easily prepared meal, proficiency as a hostess, a quick nourishing meal when you are on a camping trip, etc. Similarly, in the case of the soft drink, he sells the refreshment provided during a break in the workday, or after a hard tennis match. The advertiser of a jar of face cream does not sell the ingredients, but a lovely skin or the way to become a beautiful girl and be popular. And the advertiser of gasoline sells more mileage, a faster pickup, or better engine performance.

In each case, the advertiser is selling something of self-interest to the buyer and showing how his product will satisfy or gratify that desire or self-interest of the buyer. So the advertiser of life insurance shows how insurance is a way to educate the buyer's children, provide security for his wife, or provide travel and enjoyment in old age. Even in advertising oranges good health was emphasized. So copy should generally sell something the product will supply or accomplish, and that the customer wants or needs.

"To whom am I advertising or selling?" The copywriter must ascertain who are the prospects for the product, what their wants are, who influences the prospects in making their decisions to buy, and what the wants of these people are. In addition to determining who the prospects are, the copywriter must determine what these prospects will consider as evidence that will make them buy the product.

"How can I best convey this message, or concept, to my reader?" Having decided on the prospective customer, his wants and motivations, the want-satisfying qualities of the product, and how these will satisfy the desires and self-interest of the prospect, the copywriter must decide how best to bring these two—the product and the prospect—together. In other words, he must decide on the best way to get his idea across to the prospective customer.

IMPORTANT COPY ATTRIBUTES

The copywriter should keep the overall plan of the advertisement in mind when considering the actual wording to be used to convey the want-satisfying qualities of his product to the prospect and to show him how it will satisfy his desires. He must also keep in mind the medium in which the advertisement is to appear. That is, if the particular advertisement is to appear on a billboard along a highway, the copy must be brief and concise; whereas if it is to appear in a monthly magazine which will be in homes for some months and be read at leisure, the copy does not have to meet the same rigid restrictions as to length and brevity.

If the copywriter is preparing copy for radio he must keep in mind that the ear cannot assimilate as much material as the eye and that the message is very fleeting. If he is writing copy for television he has to develop the script in a manner similar to that of a person writing plays for motion pictures. In other words, he should visualize the scenes and write the script for what the characters are to say, with instructions to the technicians and performers who are responsible for producing the television commercial.

The matter of special functions to be accomplished by the advertisement also must be kept in mind by the copywriter. For example, if an attempt is to be made to induce immediate action and sales, he may wish to include specific suggestions in the copy as to when the product is available, the price, terms of sale, or other special conditions. Good copy should be brief, clear, apt, interesting, and personal. To write copy of this nature, it is important to keep the following observations in mind.

Be brief

A copywriter must write briefly, yet effectively. Therefore, read the rough draft slowly. Study each sentence. Consider its meaning and importance. Eliminate unnecessary words; weigh each word. At times one word, if properly selected, can be made to take the place of several without weakening the sentence. A sentence with slight alterations can frequently be made to take the place of two, sometimes of several, sentences, and occasionally an entire paragraph can be cut.

Some individuals believe that no one reads long advertisements. Certainly an advertisement should never be longer than is necessary. However, if the success of the advertisement is jeopardized by dropping even one word, then that word should be included.

Two men spoke at Gettysburg. One of these men spoke for two hours, and very few persons could quote a single sentence from his talk. The other man spoke about 300 words. That address, 300 words, has become one of the nation's recognized literary gems. This speech of Abraham Lincoln's is an excellent example of what advertising copywriters should understand by brevity. Be brief, but tell it all—leave nothing worthwhile untold.

Be clear

When advertising lacks clarity, it will be ineffective. Even a slight vagueness will cripple advertising copy. The authors' analysis of several thousand pieces of advertising discloses that most frequently clarity is clouded by one or more of the following three faults: (1) the use of words whose meanings are not understood by the prospect, (2) the incorrect selection and use of words, or (3) ambiguous phraseology.

Local tradition, habit, custom, and nationality are among the factors that play a part in determining the manner in which copy will be interpreted. Some people in some sections of the country still believe that white eggs are superior to brown, while the reverse is believed by persons in other sections. Manufacturers of certain products have found it necessary to package identical products under several different labels so as to meet the copy emphasis that must be used to satisfy the wishes of their customers in different sections of the country.

Be apt

Copy must be apt—it must fit the needs or wants of the prospects. The influencing power of copy depends greatly on the correlation that exists between the desire of a prospect and the quality or feature of the product. The ability to show this relationship is the art of making copy apt.

To write copy that is apt, a copywriter must continuously study human nature. While the appeal to vanity and pride in personal appearance may influence some, nevertheless the consumers' ever changing method and mode of living and their financial condition may make other appeals more important.

If the product is to be sold to a manufacturer, study the needs of manufacturers. If automatic equipment is to be advertised, the manufacturer will be interested in knowing that one man can do as much work with this piece of equipment as ten men could do with some other product. Such information will be apt because the cost of labor is an important problem with the manufacturer. He will be interested in knowing that the equipment can be adjusted readily, that it is strongly built, and that it is easy to purchase parts.

In the sale of baby food, the copy should be written so that it will appeal to mothers. The mother's pride in the health of her child and her natural concern for his general welfare must be studied if the copy is to be apt. To be apt, copy must be specific. Generalities create vagueness.

In Figure 7–1 A.T.&T. uses an illustration and copy that may be difficult for the reader to correlate with its line of products although it possesses a strong attention-attracting device.

Think of the copy as speaking to one specific individual; think of one man or one woman; think of a girl getting dressed for her first date; think of a woman preparing a meal for her children; think of the product that flashes through their minds. Think of that momentary flash, followed by a warm feeling of approval. It comes, it goes, but it has registered. That friendly thought has been stored away; it will rise to the surface again when the occasion demands. There is a predisposition there in favor of the product, a preference for a specific product.

The art of writing advertising copy that is apt is the art of putting into words that which creates in the minds of prospective purchasers a desire to possess the article, in which the need of the prospects will be satisfied by a feature or quality in the product.

To write interesting copy, one must share the problems and hopes which are those of the prospects. To be genuinely human is to be emotional. Emotion or feeling is a most vital feature in good advertising copy. People want to learn about individuals who live on their street; men and women who had to work hard in their childhoods; folks who are human enough to have budget problems and know what it is to make a small income go a long way. They are the kind of people the public understands.

FIGURE 7–1

And we were glad to share them—with hundreds of people from over 40 nations who visited us last year to learn about the telephone business.

They came from places like Chad, Dahomey, Malawi, Togo and Bechuanaland; and from France, Germany, Japan, India and Australia.

All these people had one thing in common. They wanted the latest information about modern telecommunications and we gave it to them. They saw how our fast nationwide switching system works. Learned how scientific breakthroughs are converted into better means of communications. And studied the day-to-day work of our operating companies.

We're glad to do everything we can to help people improve their telephone service as we keep improving our own.

We may be the only telephone company in town, but we try not to act like it.

AT&T and Associated Companies

They came to get our trade secrets

Courtesy: American Telephone and Telegraph Company

Customers enjoy being told of a girl who prepares a special meal because her boyfriend likes it that way. They like to hear about a dad repairing a toy for his son with a tool he purchased at the hardware store. They respond to the little boy who cried every time he played with his friends until a tonic improved his health.

The reason the boy on the street enjoys football is that he knows about it. He knows the names of the players. He is interested in football because it is constantly being interpreted to him in an interesting way. Copywriters are dealing with human nature, not dead commodities. They are interpreting worthwhile commodities to the prospects.

Be personal

Copy should be written from the prospect to the product, not from the product to the prospect. Visualize this scene: A city street is lined with people out to greet a new governor; they crowd along the sidewalk; they stand on window ledges, boxes, and anything that will raise them above other spectators; they wait the coming of the governor. Finally, he appears. The crowd shouts its greeting. The governor rides in his car with head uncovered. How dramatically he picks out one group along the curb, smiles, and raises his hand unmistakably to them. Then his eye alights on a party nearby. He greets them all along the route; he picks out a definite face or particular group of faces when he bows to return a greeting. The governor has left the impression of having addressed them personally, man to man! He is remembered because he was personal.

The great temptation that confronts copywriters is to preach to the prospects. The difference between the personalized advertisement and the group preachment may be seen in the following copy:

A. *Group-appeal copy:*
Housekeepers know it is necessary to select carefully a good brand of coffee.
A. *Personalized-appeal copy:*
Find out, at no cost, how really good caffein-free coffee can be!
B. *Group-appeal copy:*
Here is America's first forgettable tire. Forget it for 40,000 miles.
B. *Personalized-appeal copy:*
Brace yourself! You will get a 40,000-mile guarantee.
C. *Group-appeal copy:*
Our machine is an incredible vacuum cleaner.
C. *Personalized-appeal copy:*
Take over the controls of the vacuum cleaner that floats on its own air stream and. . . .

Personalized copy is centered on the prospect. What is the first thing a man looks for when he examines a picture? How often will he buy a picture of a group unless he recognizes one of the faces as either his own or the face of some friend? The same personal factor measures a man's interest in an advertisement. Personalized copy, therefore, presents something of interest to the reader. The two personalized steps in effective advertisements are illustrated in the following examples:

Do you need money? Write for this booklet.
Cool off with this fan.
Guard your health by washing with this soap.

In each of the foregoing statements, two elements are present. The first, the idea of interest to the reader, serves as the entering wedge for the second idea, the use of a specific product.

The real salesman counsels—he shows ways of doing something better —he imparts suggestions which will be to the prospect's advantage. Insulating concerns have advertised for years that their salesmen are practical counselors in matters of heat insulation.

The personalized advertisement is developed from an idea within the scope of the reader's personal interest. It may be taken from the physical qualities or the satisfaction derived from the product. To get the reader to appreciate what the product may mean to him, advertising seeks to awaken his imagination.

Every interpretive approach translates a statement of fact into one that means something to the prospect in his own sphere of thought. It matters not what the product is; one can, by visualizing the wants of the prospect, develop a personal copy theme. The correct theme may appear frequently to be deeply hidden; but, in fact, it is often a situation so obvious that it is easily overlooked.

Other methods

Emphasis also may be secured through a number of mechanical devices, as well as through direct description, description by effect, by detail, by analogy, by suggestion, and by narration.

Direct description tries to picture the article in words. It endeavors to describe the product in such a way that the reader can see it as vividly as if he had it before him. Direct description is important where the satisfaction it may give already has been established.

Description by effect gives the effect of using the product, or tells what the product will do, as in the following examples:

Serve Hostess Fruit Pies—made with more fruit filling than crust—
Now you can fly a Cessna . . . for $5,
The seven-minute cigarette time
Feel this fresh all day long!
You cannot brush bad breath away—reach for Listerine!

When it is important to emphasize what the product will do, a description by effect can be employed to advantage.

Description by detail is useful in the advertisement of products for which primary demand already has been stimulated, because it permits emphasis to be directed to a distinct useful feature of the advertiser's particular brand of product. In describing by detail, points of difference between the advertised product and competitive ones should be chosen. Where little difference exists, any detail which has not been emphasized previously may serve the purpose.

Description by analogy draws a parallel between the idea to be conveyed and one that is already established. A well-chosen analogy, metaphor, or personification has strong descriptive power. For example: "Mennen presents a 'Swaddling Powder' as new as your baby. . . . Once upon a time . . . mothers swaddled their new-born babies in soft silks and linens. Today—you can wrap your baby in even greater luxury and in the newest protection of New Mennen Baby Powder." A precaution to observe, however, in using this device is to be sure to base the analogy on an idea which is well known, and not to use an analogy that is far-fetched.

Description by suggestion starts the thought process and then lets the reader's imagination finish it. It plays on his emotions, his recollections, and his imagination; the advertisement need say very little to suggest a great deal.

Epigrammatic copy is a higher form of description by suggestion, implying its entire meaning in very few words. Of all the forms of suggestion, it is the most subtle. "The office safe isn't" and "It's a wise hammer that never loses its head" are examples of this type of copy. Epigrammatic copy is terse and succinct. It may lack conviction but is rich in suggestions. Because it is subtle, its point may be too vague for its readers to grasp.

Description by logic depends on facts to prove why a prospect should purchase the product. It is not what the advertiser says but what the facts show; not what he thinks but what the evidence is. The facts may be secured from impartial tests; they may be established through satisfaction of customers expressed in testimonials and endorsements, through samples, trial offers, and guarantees; or they may be demonstrated through logical argument based upon other facts especially compiled.

In addition to the aforementioned kind of descriptive copy there is another type called the narrative form. Generally it is written in the first person and has both sincerity and convincing qualities. Because it seems to come from a specific person, it carries its point directly and vividly. Narrative copy can assume the form of monologue, of dialogue, or even be in the third person.

The story in narrative copy should get under way immediately, for the entire effect depends on getting the reader absorbed in its action. This may be accomplished by opening in the middle of the conversation. The prelude may be disposed of either by omission, if it appears self-evident, or by caption, by illustration, by explanatory note, or by doubling back after the start of the copy, like a motion picture which has a scene cut in, showing what happened prior to the opening of the story.

The story should illustrate a definite point, and once it establishes this point, the scene should be shifted to the prospect. A good transition is a delicate piece of copy craftsmanship which draws the reader into the advertisement quite naturally while his interest in the story is at its height. The last step of the narrative copy is to tell the prospect what he should do.

THE HEADLINE

The headline is that part of the copy which has been made to stand out in the advertisement by the size or style of type in which it has been set, the prominence of its location, or the white space surrounding it.

The function of a headline is to attract the favorable attention of prospective purchasers and to interest them so that they will read the advertisement. Subheadlines are subordinate headlines. They are used in a wide variety of ways and for many reasons, such as to complete the meaning of the headline, to bring out related but additional or different appeals, or to break up lengthy copy.

It is not possible to say that the headline is more important than the illustration, or that one is subordinate to the other. As an example, in a recent advertisement of a large oil company, the principal illustration was the picture of a mushroom and a toadstool standing side by side in their native habitat. The caption read: "Which is the mushroom and which is the toadstool? Would you eat one to find out?" The copy brought out the point that if it was foolish to take a chance of being poisoned by eating mushrooms when they could not be identified simply by looking at them, it would be equally foolish to buy and use oil of unknown lubricating qualities.

Without the headline, this illustration, the picture of the mushroom and the toadstool, was meaningless. The headline, "Which is the mushroom and which is the toadstool? Would you eat one to find out?" is almost as worthless if used alone. When used together, they make a forceful comparison.

It is questionable whether the writer of this advertisement got the idea for the illustration or the headline first. It is quite probable they came simultaneously. His visualizing efforts perhaps drifted toward apt comparisons, and knowing of the close physical likeness of toadstools and mushrooms, he recognized a similarity in the difficulty people have in telling them apart and the difficulty they have in differentiating between brands of oil.

When a salesman tells a customer about the merits of his product he already has the ear of his prospect. While there are a number of factors that might prevent him from closing the sale, he does have the attention of the buyer.

In advertising a product, however, the advertiser does not have this exclusive attention. The television program, the music on radio, the articles in the magazine, and the news in the newspaper are generally more important to the prospect than the advertisement. These special features are the reasons why people watch television programs or purchase newspapers and magazines. As a result, it is necessary to attract the prospects from their prior interests for a long enough period to get them to listen to or read a message. It also becomes important to distract them in such a manner so that whatever attention-attracting device is used will lead logically ino the message and will appeal to the prospect.

Types of headlines

Headline appeals may be classified into two broad categories, direct or indirect. The direct-appeal headline attempts to use a primary sales feature of the product for both the attention-attracting device as well as the sales appeal. An indirect-appeal headline attempts only to stop the reader and to get him to read or listen to the body of the appeal.

An example of the direct appeal is found in Figure 7–2. Mennen points out: "MENNEN SPEED STICK. It actually builds up a resistance to odor." This is direct selling emphasizing one of the main features of the Mennen Speed Stick.

An example of the indirect approach is the Blue Cross Advertisement in Figure 7–3. "This is all the profit we need." This appeal doesn't sell anything other than a general interest concept.

In deciding whether to use the direct or indirect appeal, one should analyze the product to determine what specific advantages it has over those of competitors. If these advantages are such that lend themselves to a direct appeal, then, as a general rule the advertiser is more likely to make the sale if he uses this approach. There is always greater danger of attracting the attention of those who may not be interested in the product if the indirect selling appeal is used. There is also the additional danger of antagonizing even the actual prospects if the indirect approach results in their believing they were misled in reading the copy.

Specific headline classifications

Among the ways in which headlines may be classified are the following:

1. Directive
2. News
3. Slogan

THIS IS ALL THE PROFIT WE NEED.

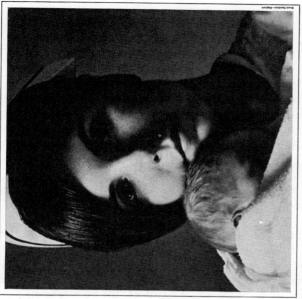

Bruce Davidson—Magnum

It better be.

We don't make a nickel of the other kind. But when 63 million people know they can enter hospitals and simply present their Blue Cross cards, we think our business is a rip-roaring success.

And that's exactly what Blue Cross is. People who never know when they might need a hospital's services, so they all put a little into big emergency funds called Blue Cross.

When the need comes, the money is there.

Making sure that your hospital bill gets paid and that you and yours are well cared for is what Blue Cross management does.

Now, with all that to do, you might well ask why we also take the time to advertise. Our answer is this. One-third of America already has Blue Cross.

We feel that the other people have a right to know about it.

BLUE CROSS®

Courtesy: Blue Cross

FIGURE 7–2 (left).   **FIGURE 7–3 (above).**

MENNEN
Speed Stick

It actually builds up a resistance to odor.

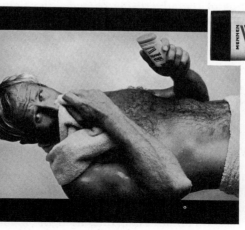

This deodorant's special bacteria-fighting ingredient builds in a resistance that lasts even through a hot, soapy shower. You don't have to settle for protection against odor anymore. **Now you can build up a resistance with...Mennen Speed Stick**

Courtesy: The Mennen Company

4. Rational
5. Curiosity
6. Emotional
7. Gimmick

It is difficult to make sharp distinctions between the classifications because there is overlapping in the divisions, and a given headline or appeal may embody two or more of the above types.

The *directive approach* is used more often in retail advertising. The objective with this appeal is to get the prospect to act now. An example of this is found in the Whirlpool advertisement in which it gives the telephone number to call in an emergency:

"IN CASE OF EMERGENCY CALL (800) 253–1301"

A *specific news* item headline is given by *Datsun* in an advertisement:

"HOW TO BUY A SMALL CAR"

How important is this news item in getting prospects to read the body of the text? Will this news item attract the people who buy cars? Does the news item drive home the selling points? Does it attract attention while starting to sell? These are some of the questions that should be considered whenever an appeal of this kind is used.

The Bank of California incorporates its *slogan* in the headline:

"COME TO THE BANK FOR ACTION"

It should be kept in mind that when a slogan is used, it should embody the most significant message of the advertising campaign, and that if the theme of the advertising changes, the slogan also should be changed.

The *rational appeal* is an important approach to consider using because prospects have a tendency to envision themselves as being intelligent individuals and desire to rationalize their decisions. DENTU-CREME uses this approach in its headline:

"ARE YOU SPENDING MORE THAN 45 SECONDS CLEANING YOUR DENTURES? IF YOU ARE, YOU'RE WASTING YOUR TIME."

Institute of Life Insurance uses the *curiosity appeal* in:

"WIFE INSURANCE IS FLOWERS ON HER BIRTHDAY, RIGHT?"

The danger of the curiosity appeal is that it may attract readers who are not interested in the product, and, it is also difficult to correlate the "sales" message to this type of headline.

Foster Parents Plan, Inc., used the *emotional appeal* effectively with the headline: "You can dry his tears." This type of headline is effective in situations where we wish to attract the readers through the sense appetites.

While the *gimmick approach* is somewhat similar to the curiosity approach, it is one that goes beyond mere curiosity by presenting an appeal that is completely an attention-attracting appeal. Dayton uses this appeal—"$2 against your life. . . ."

General recommendations

In the final analysis, the suitability of the headline rests upon its ability to get the prospect into the main copy in a positive frame of mind.

There are four major characteristics in most good headlines: (1) brevity, (2) clarity, (3) aptness, and (4) interest.

Brevity. A caption that is not brief and concise fails to perform its first and most important task. Each advertisement has been prepared to attract the favorable attention and hold the interest of the reader. This means that each advertisement is silently but skillfully attempting to attract the eye of the prospect. The reader, on the other hand, may not be particularly interested in the advertisement—to him it may even be an intrusion—he knows what he wants and where to find it. In his own opinion, his time is both limited and valuable. Recognizing this picture of the competition and handicaps that confront an advertisement, it is important that the headline be sufficiently short to be read at a glance.

Clarity. Little advantage will be gained from the use of a headline sufficiently short to be read at a glance if its meaning is not clear. It is important that the advertiser state his headline in a clear and concise manner so that it will appeal directly to the prospect. Unless this is done, there is danger of a vague headline attracting the attention of persons who may not be in the market for the product, but missing those who should be reached.

Aptness. Aptness is developed by showing that the product advertised has the particular feature or quality that fills or satisfies the prospective purchaser's needs or wants. Attempts to prepare cute or clever advertisements may result in vague and irrelevant headlines that are not appropriate. Such statements as "Why not?" or "Would you?" do not particularly mean anything to anyone. The caption "We announce" is vague and has little meaning, for who cares for what anyone else wishes to announce? "Look at this offer" is entirely too vague. Tell the prospective purchaser what the offer is, and if it is sufficiently enticing, he will stop and read the advertisement.

Interest. There is perhaps no easier way to make a headline interesting than to make it speak directly to the individual reader in a personal manner. This does not mean that one must eliminate the necessary dignity that an advertisement should possess.

When preparing a headline do not address the prospect like a man giving a talk by saying, "Ladies and gentlemen." The use of the word "you" usually will help make the headline personal. An interesting headline is a sincere and personal message prepared for an average prospect.

There are several things that may nullify a prospect's interest in an otherwise interesting headline—seeming exaggeration, insincere or misleading statement, and antagonism. Whether the caption should be a declaration, question, command, or a part of an unfinished sentence in the form of a phrase will depend entirely on the objectives of the specific advertisement.

Below are listed several captions and illustrations which have been used successfully in advertisements:

1. Tire advertisement:
   Illustration: An automobile tire superimposed on a man's hand gripping into the soil.
   Headline: "The Armstrong grip."
2. Cough medicine advertisement:
   Illustration: Young mother giving little boy a spoonful of medicine.
   Headline: "For fast relief of cough and cold miseries."
3. Shampoo advertisement:
   Illustration: Mother and daughter, both with beautiful hair, very similar in appearance.
   Headline: "Now! Wash those years right out of your hair!"
4. Advertisement for long-distance telephone calls:
   Illustration: Young woman beaming as she listens on telephone; while a question mark appears in another equal-sized panel next to her.
   Headline: "Can you picture the other half of this long-distance call?"
5. Camera advertisement:
   Illustration: Charming young couple sitting on park bench, the man giving instructions to smiling policeman holding camera.
   Headline: "Just press the button, Chief—it'll come out fine!"
6. Advertisement for hearing-aid glasses:
   Illustration: Young girl talking to her grandmother, who is wearing a pair of glasses.
   Headline: "Grandma, did God give you new ears?"
7. Advertisement for encyclopedia:
   Illustration: Two women and a man listening attentively to a man talking at a party.
   Headline: "When you talk . . . do people listen?" (Copy theme: people listen to you if you have a command of words.)

In each of the above advertisements, the headlines are brief, clear, apt, and interesting. At the same time, an inherent personal appeal also is present. The chief weakness of many headlines is that they are not specific and, as a result, may not attract the right prospect.

SUMMARY

There is no easy road to copywriting. It is an exacting activity which requires the ability to use basic human appeals and to recognize the differences that exist in the writing style that should be used for the different products and media.

Good advertising strategy makes the copy conform to the advertising plan. All necessary provisions should be made so the reader will be put to the least amount of trouble. Frequently the reader is told to ask for a product "at your dealer" when the goods may not be stocked in his store. Instructions should be precise and complete. All questions which might possibly arise should be anticipated. "Get the summer catalog: out soon" leaves the reader wondering when it will be out, where he can get it, whether he will have to pay for it. "Go to your dealer—there is one in every town" is less effective than "Go to the dealer that shows this sign" or "For sale at ———" (where the local address can be given in the advertisement).

An advertisement can at times be closed with a suggestion such as: "Some day soon when you're feeling adventurous, match your mood with a drive in the new Plymouth; the car is ready for inspection at Plymouth showrooms." "If your background qualifies you to work in any of these areas, we would be pleased to hear from you." This gentle suggestion is a refined type of closing, stronger than the implied, but possessing a courteous, gracious charm which is effective with some people and necessary in advertising some products.

The closing part of the advertisement generally should help to overcome the tendency to procrastinate. The reader may be quite sincere in believing that he will carry out the suggestion contained in the advertisement the next time he is in the market for the advertised product. However, as soon as he turns from the one advertisement to the next advertisement or story, he starts to forget the message. The best way to be certain he does take the desired action is to urge him to do so immediately—now.

Although many devices exist for inviting action or for assuring early attention by means of urge lines, the concluding message in advertisements still offers opportunity for further improvement. The urge line may tell how restricted the offer is, for example: "Since the number of albums available for this special offer is limited, orders will be filled in the sequence received, and this offer may be discontinued at any time. We sincerely urge you to mail the coupon now" (Columbia Record Club); or "Stocks limited! Act now!" Or it can stress the value of that which is being offered, for example: "If you act now—this coupon is worth $4.55." "Buy now for extra values." The urge line can reiterate the convenience of acting and the subsequent satisfaction, as "Get a jar of Kava today and prove it tonight" or "Start feeding your pet Puss'n Boots today. In just three weeks—or even less—see if you aren't delighted with an amazing improvement in her health, appearance, energy."

When writing copy, try always to use the present tense. Keep in mind the illusion that you are using the appeal for the first time—it will almost add news value to the statement that the Eastman Kodak Company manufactures Kodaks! Keep constantly in mind the prospect's likes and dislikes; write about these things as the situation may require, but never allow any other point to dominate the advertisement. Visualize the product as an article which the reader needs and stress how it will benefit him.

While new copy slants are constantly being sought by advertisers, one will find that frequently these innovations will be short-lived. The important aspect to keep in mind is that the advertisement should be unified and where possible it should concentrate on one main idea.

QUESTIONS

1. Indicate how you would use a specific strategy and translate it into dynamic advertising for print media for the following products:

 a)   Bell & Howell 16mm movie camera
 b)   Polaroid camera
 c)   General Electric vacuum sweeper
 d)   Norelco electric shaver
 e)   Farberware 12-cup percolator
 f)   Philco 8-track stereo
 g)   Frigidaire upright frost-proof freezer
 h)   Ford Pinto automobile

In what manner would you translate differently if broadcast media were being used?

2. Many companies do not actually know the product they are selling. Explain.

3. Compare a letter to your parents asking for money with the copy in an advertisement.

4. Select five advertisements from any current magazine and comment on the copy in regard to: clarity, aptness, interest, and personalization.

5. Select from any current media two advertisements in which the headlines are satisfactory; select two in which you believe the headline might be improved. Rewrite these and give reasons why you believe they are better.

6. What are some of the major advertising problems involved in getting the attention of the prospect?

7. When might it be advisable for an advertising copywriter to leave out some of the basic information?

8. Indicate when you believe *humor* can be used successfully in advertising. Contrast the use of humor in print and broadcast media.

9. What is meant by "unfair advertising"? How would you evaluate the appeal, "Quieter than a Rolls Royce!"

10. In what ways may the scripts for radio and television be the same? In what ways may they differ?

11. A leading advertising executive made the following statement: "The major emphasis today is on arresting and visual concepts, jarring headlines, terse copy, elimination of the secondary, sharp focus on a single selling point." Comment.

12. Copy writers were advised to adopt the following strategy: "Get the attention of the customer any way you can and then embark on your selling story!" Today the advice is frequently given, "your attention getter today has to make our selling point." Comment.

13. How might an advertiser get the appeal to radiate from the culture into the product?

14. Give some of the consumer resistances that a copywriter should keep in mind in writing copy.

15. A regional distributor of *Freeze Dried Coffee* has decided to sell the product on a national basis. Develop a slogan which you believe could be used successfully in both print and broadcast media. The distributor wishes to emphasize that the quality of his product is superior.

CASE 1.   RINGLING BROS.–BARNUM & BAILEY COMBINED SHOWS, INC.

Deciding on copy

History

The Company traces its history to the circus organized by P. T. Barnum in 1871 at a time when the American circus was emerging from a period of inactivity during the Civil War.

In 1881, James A. Bailey, who had operated a circus for sometime prior to 1873, combined his circus with Barnum under the name " P. T. Barnum's Greatest Show on Earth, Howe's Great London Circus and Sanger's Royal British Menagerie." In 1888 the name of the circus was changed to "Barnum & Bailey's Greatest Show on Earth" and Bailey became sole owner of the circus after Barnum's death in 1891.

In 1882, five Ringling brothers—Al, Otto, Alf T., Charles, and John—introduced their first show entitled "The Ringling Bros. Classic and Comic Concert Company," and by 1890, the Ringling brothers' circus had become a serious competitor of the Barnum & Bailey circus. After a period of intense competition and the death of Bailey, the Ringlings in 1907 acquired the Barnum & Bailey circus from Bailey's estate. After operating the two circuses independently until 1919, the Ringlings combined the two circuses. The resulting circus was incorporated in 1932 as "Ringling Bros.–Barnum & Bailey Combined Shows, Inc." (sometimes referred to herein as "Former Ringling Bros.").

John Ringling, the last surviving brother, died in 1936. Shortly after his death, operation of the circus was taken over by John Ringling North and his brother, Henry Ringling North, sons of Ida Ringling, the Ringling brothers' only sister.

In October 1967, Roy Hofheinz, Irvin Feld and Israel S. Feld founded Hoffeld Corporation under the laws of the state of Delaware ("Hoffeld") for the purpose of acquiring all of the outstanding capital stock of Former Ringling Bros. In November 1967, Hoffeld acquired all the stock for $8,000,000 in cash.

Hoffeld held the circus as a wholly-owned subsidiary corporation from November 1967 until December 31, 1968, at which time Former Ringling Bros. merged with and into Hoffeld and the name of the Company was changed from "Hoffeld Corporation" to "Ringling Bros.–Barnum & Bailey Combined Shows, Inc."

General

The principal business of the Company is entertaining "children of all ages" through the staging of circus performances in various cities throughout the United States and Canada. Shows are staged 2 or 3 times a day and performance time is between $2\frac{1}{2}$ and $2\frac{3}{4}$ hours. Admission prices range from a low of $2.00 to a high of $7.50 and vary depending upon the location and arena in which the circus is performing. In every city, at certain performances, reductions from regular price are given to children under 12 years of age.

In 1971, for the first time in its 101-year history, Ringling Bros. operated two separate but comparable circuses called "Ringling Bros.–Barnum & Bailey Red Unit" and "Ringling Bros.–Barnum & Bailey Blue Unit." The Red Unit toured for 47 weeks before returning to winter quarters in Venice. The Blue Unit toured for 36 weeks. It is anticipated that the Blue Unit will tour for 40 to 42 weeks or longer in subsequent years. With the addition of the Blue Unit, each circus will now play a two-year itinerary, visiting approximately twice as many cities as played in the past. Under this new arrangement a completely different circus will be shown in every city in successive years. Each unit stages two or three shows per day during the touring season except during those days when the circus is traveling. The shows include a variety of traditional circus acts and five theme production number extravaganzas.

Acts

Forty to fifty acts are presented in each circus performance and are supplemented by numerous clown routines. With the exception of wild animal, high wire, and specialty acts, performances are staged simultaneously in three rings. The circus includes traditional circus acts such as clown acts, high wire and trapeze acts, a variety of animal acts, teeterboard and perch acts, and various other acts such as jugglers, unicyclists, tumblers, horsemen, etc. Each act performs for a period of two to twelve minutes, and performers frequently participate in more than one act.

The quality and variety of the acts are important features in the business of Ringling Bros. and new acts must be found annually in order to keep performances fresh and interesting to the public. To insure a variety and quality of new acts, the circus is continually on the outlook for new talent. Many trips a year ranging from two days to three months are made abroad to book acts. Last year, as an example, approximately 50 to 60 circuses were visited in Europe, Mexico, and other parts of the world. In addition, the talent search is extended to circus schools which are part of the cultural mores of many eastern European countries. Of the 275 to 300 performers comprising the circus casts, approximately 150 are citizens of foreign countries, principally European. Many acts are family units in which the father or mother is responsible for training the children in circus routines.

Pursuant to the terms of an agreement between Ringling Bros. and the American Guild of Variety Artists all acts perform under contract with the company. These contracts range from one to five years, and, as a minimum, guarantee the act one season of work. Frequently, Ringling has an option to renew performers' contracts for periods of one, two, or three additional seasons, in most instances under the same terms and conditions as included in the original agreement. All foreign acts, to qualify for acceptance under the Company's agreement with the American Guild of Variety Artists, must be classified "unique" and the quota of foreign performers may not exceed 55 percent of the total performers of the circus.

Production numbers

In addition to the acts, each circus performance includes five production number extravaganzas. These numbers combine musical selections with a parade of circus performers in various costumes built around a central theme. For example, one of the production themes two years ago featured a trip to the moon by a performer-astronaut and included the complete cast dressed in a wide variety of lavish costumes, utilizing many different floats and sets. Other theme productions include an aerial ballet and an elephant spectacle.

Discussion of production numbers begins in the March preceding the calendar year in which the numbers are to appear. Themes are suggested, discussed, and finally chosen, after which costumes are designed and ordered from the circus costume manufacturer.

Music for the production numbers, as well as music for the acts, is provided by the circus band comprised of the circus bandmaster and traveling musicians, augmented by local musicians.

Concessions

In addition to paid admissions, Ringling Bros. also derives revenues from a variety of concessions. The company has an agreement with a concessionaire for the sale of program books, food, (snow cones and candy floss) and circus novelties. The company's concessionaire also operates a food service on the circus trains and a restaurant which is located at the circus winter quarters in Venice, Florida, from which the company also derives some revenue.

Many of the arenas played by the circus have their own concessions, such as hotdogs, soft drinks, popcorn, etc., which are normally sold by the arena's concessionaire with no payment to the circus for these sales. However, the company's concessionaire is usually afforded the opportunity to vend program books, snow cones, candy floss, and circus novelties in most arenas. Ringling Bros. also derives income from the sale of advertising space in its program books.

Royalties

Ringling Bros. also receives revenue from theater and television reruns of the motion picture entitled "The Greatest Show on Earth." The company recently entered into an agreement with an independent firm to design products and license the use of the circus name. The agreement covers a broad variety of products including toys, childrens' books, food, clothing, etc. While no licensing agreements have yet been signed, negotiations are substantially completed for 17 agreements covering numerous products bearing two-year terms and providing the company with an aggregate guaranteed minimum compensation of approximately $100,000 against a percentage of sales of licensed products.

Television program

Pursuant to an agreement with the National Broadcasting Company, a one-hour television program is scheduled featuring highlights of the circus. This show, packaged in full by the company, is hosted by a prominent show business personality and features approximately 35 minutes of circus performances.

Arenas

The circus has operated indoors in arenas or auditoriums since the "big top" was discontinued in 1956 in Pittsburgh, Pennsylvania. Ringling Bros. enters into contracts or leases with the various arenas for the dates during which the show will be played. Typical arrangements provide the arena with either a guaranteed minimum rent against a percentage of the gross revenues derived from ticket sales (excluding admission taxes) by the company from the engagement, or a fixed rental without a percentage.

Most contracts bear one-year terms, although arenas customarily reserve circus dates many years in advance. The longest single engagement of the circus has been at Madison Square Garden, New York City, where one of the units annually plays six consecutive weeks. The company also entered into an agreement with Houston Sports Association, Inc. providing for a 13½ week circus engagement in the Houston Astrohall.

Transportation

The principal means of transporting the circus between cities is by Ringling's own trains. The company presently owns two trains, one for the Red Unit and another for the Blue Unit. Twenty cars are assigned to the Blue Unit and 24 to the Red Unit. The Blue Unit uses fewer cars because of the purchase by the company of four "piggyback" cars which are used with the Blue Unit train and can carry greater loads of material and equipment than the customary type of equipment (see "Property"). The circus enters into agreements annually with a number of railroads which agree to move the circus trains from location to location. The railroads furnish engines, cabooses, and crews and coordinate the scheduling and logistical work with a representative of Ringling Bros. Prior to entering a city, the circus advance agent has arranged for water and sanitary facilities, siding facilities and has attended to the myriad of other details which must be observed before the arrival of the circus train.

Advertising and promotion

The circus uses all media in its advertising campaign including television spot commercials, radio, billboards, newspapers, magazines, and direct distribution of literature. Approximately six to eight weeks before the circus arrives at any given community, representatives of the circus' advertising staff, supplemented by local advertising agencies and public relations firms, commence advertising for the circus performances. Advertisements for a particular city are carried in media up to a radius of 100 miles from the arena. Two clowns are sent in advance of the circus as part of the promotional efforts, and bus cards and press manuals are also utilized. Approximately 10 percent of the expected revenue in each community is reserved for publicity.

The name "Ringling Bros.–Barnum & Bailey Circus" and the service mark "The Greatest Show on Earth" are featured in all advertising and no individual performer or group of performers are named as stars or featured attractions. In prior years the company relied substantially on advertising and promotion efforts of outside independent promoters. The company now assumes all advertising and promotional activities for 31 engagements and supervises such activities for the other 13 engagements.

Competition

Although there are other circuses operating throughout the United States, Ringling Bros. is the largest, employs more performers than any other circus, and guarantees the longest continuous period of employment. Other entertainment and recreation attractions may be considered competitors of the circus as they compete for leisure-time dollars. Management believes the loss of any act would not cause a serious disruption in its performances and believes further that it will be able to compete successfully with other entertainment and recreation attractions by continuing to offer a variety of fresh acts, productions, and other attractions.

Case questions

1. Assume that you are asked to prepare the copy for the local media in your city advertising the appearance of Ringling Bros. How would you proceed in solving the following problems:

    a)   To whom would you direct the appeal?
    b)   What general appeal would you use?
    c)   To what extent would you vary the appeal in the following media: television and radio spot commercials, newspapers, and billboards?
    d)   Prepare the copy to be used in your local newspaper.

CASE 2.   LEVER BROTHERS COMPANY
Identifying the manufacturer

The Lever Brothers Company executives are faced with the decision of determining to what degree they should identify the name of the company with the variety of products which they advertise.

Among the major consumer products which Lever manufactures are the following: laundry detergents (Breeze, Rinso, Silver Dust, Cold Water Surf, Advanced All, Fluffy All, Wisk, Cold Water All, and Vim); all-purpose household cleaner (Handy Andy); fabric softener (Final Touch); Lux Flakes; Dove-for-dishes; Lux Liquid; Swan Liquid; Dishwasher All; toilet bars (Dove, Lifebuoy, Phase III, Lux Beauty Soap, Praise); toothpastes (Pepsodent, Pepsodent Fluoride, Super Stripe); Pepsodent Tooth Powder; toothbrushes (Pepsodent, Life Line, Life Line Professional); Pepsodent Antiseptic; and a number of food products, such as Imperial, Sof-Spread Imperial, Good Luck, and Golden Glow Margarine, Spry Shortening, Mrs. Butterworth's Syrup, and Lucky Whip Dessert Topping.

Lever Brothers Company is the second largest company in the industry and is also a leading member of the worldwide Unilever organization, which includes more than 500 operating companies. The company over the years has emphasized individual brand advertising. It has used virtually all media—magazines, newspapers, supplements, direct mail, radio, and television. Its largest expenditure goes into television because the executives believe this medium is very effective in reaching millions of people.

History

Greeting visitors at the entrances of Lever House and Lever Brothers manufacturing plants throughout the country is a stainless steel plaque stating the mission of the company as its founder, William Hesketh Lever, saw it: ". . . to make cleanliness commonplace; to lessen work for women; to foster health and contribute to personal attractiveness, that life may be more enjoyable and rewarding for the people who use our products."

The business began in 1895 when Mr. Lever opened a small office in New York City to handle the sale of Lifebuoy and Sunlight soaps, both then manufactured in England. Sales for the first year barely reached 50,000 cases. Manufacture of these products was started in the United States three years later, following the acquisition in 1897 of Curtis Davis & Company, a small soap concern in Cambridge, Massachusetts. In 1899, the sales office was transferred from New York to Cambridge, and the new company was incorporated in the state of Maine as Lever Brothers, Ltd. (Boston Works). The present name, Lever Brothers Company, was adopted in 1903.

Progress during the early years was steady but slow. Originally, only about 50 people were employed. The country was divided into 2 sales districts: the New England Territory, served by 12 salesmen working out of the Cambridge plant, and the so-called General Territory, which took in the rest of the country and was serviced first by jobbers and later by an exclusive sales agent.

These formative years played an essential role in the company's future success. One significant development was the establishment of a laboratory primarily concerned with testing the quality of raw materials. This was the forerunner of the present Research and Development Center in Edgewater, New Jersey, which serves as a continuous source of new and improved products.

In 1912, the company established a national sales organization and entered an era of rapid growth. Three still famous products were introduced: Lux Flakes in 1914; Rinso, the first granulated laundry soap, in 1919; and, in 1924, Lux Toilet Soap, the first white, milled, perfumed soap made and sold in this country at a popular price. Supported by strong advertising and promotional campaigns, each moved into a position of market leadership. Sales soared to millions of cases! By 1929, the company had become the third largest manufacturer of soap and glycerine in the United States.

The growing demand for Lever Brothers products sparked a period of major expansion of manufacturing facilities. In 1930, the company constructed a major new plant at Hammond, Indiana. Another new plant was opened in Edgewater, New Jersey, in 1933, to manufacture shortening. Covo, a bulk shortening for commercial use, was produced at first; then, in 1936, Spry was introduced as a consumer product. These were Lever's first entries in the edible products field. In 1939, plants in Baltimore and St. Louis were acquired through purchase of the Hecker Products Corporation's soap interests. Among the products acquired was Silver Dust, a granulated laundry soap.

The end of World War II ushered in a new period of diversification and expansion of the Lever product line. This was achieved primarily through the purchase of other companies already established in related consumer goods fields. In 1944, Lever acquired the Pepsodent Company, a leading manufacturer of dentrifices, toothbrushes, and oral antiseptics, with a plant in Chicago. This established Lever Brothers as a major factor in the oral hygiene field. Four years later, the company achieved an important position in the food field through purchase of the John F. Jelke Company, a pioneer manufacturer of margarine and related food products. Within a few years, both Pepsodent and Jelke were completely integrated with the Lever organization and product lines.

During the early 1950s, the company again expanded its physical facilities and laid the groundwork for another period of growth. Manufacturing operations were extended to the West Coast in 1951 with the opening of the Los Angeles plant. Two years later, a new plant was constructed at St. Louis to replace the Hecker Products facility acquired in 1939.

To meet the growing business needs of expanding operations, more office space and a more convenient business location were required. The company accordingly in 1949 moved its headquarters from Cambridge to New York City. Lever House, the new headquarters building on Park Avenue, was opened in 1952. Designed to provide ideal working conditions, the 24-story glass and stainless steel structure has received many awards for building excellence and is considered "one of three most significant buildings in the past 100 years of architecture in America." It has been called "the most honored office building in the world."

Of special importance to the company's growth in modern times was the opening in 1952 of the multimillion-dollar Research and Development Center in Edgewater, New Jersey. This scientific center united the research groups which had previously worked at separate plant locations and put at their disposal the facilities of a complete and modern laboratory. As a result of the steady stream of new and improved products that have come out of this laboratory in recent years, Lever Brothers has maintained a rapid pace for new product introductions.

Significant firsts have been scored by a number of its products in their respective fields. Notable among these are Imperial, the first premium margarine with the taste of the "high-priced spread"; Dove, a completely new type of beauty bar containing cleansing cream; Wisk, the first heavy-duty liquid laundry detergent; Lux Liquid, a pioneer liquid dishwashing detergent; White Lifebuoy, the first pure white deodorant bar; and Lux Beauty Soap, the first popular soap to offer consumers a variety of colors and the first to offer the sealed protection of an aluminum foil wrapper.

Another major development of recent years was the acquisition in 1957 from the Monsanto Company of the "All" family of controlled-suds powder detergents, which include Advanced All, Fluffy All, and Dishwasher All. The newest member of the "All" family is Cold Water All, introduced in 1963, the first nationally distributed heavy-duty liquid detergent that launders the entire family wash in cold water.

Other new products, all introduced since 1958, include Super Stripe Tooth Paste, which added a new visual appeal to dental hygiene habits; Life Line Toothbrushes; Lucky Whip Dessert Topping and Topping Mix; Mrs. Butterworth's Syrup, the original pancake syrup with butter in it; Golden Glow Margarine, a soft margarine containing liquid corn oil; Praise, a deodorant beauty soap; Pine Green Lifebuoy; Pink Dove; Vim detergent tablets; Warm Water Swan, a liquid dishwashing detergent; Handy Andy with Ammonia, an all-purpose liquid household cleaner; Cold Water Surf, a laundry detergent that works effectively in hot or cold water; Final Touch fabric softener; Dove-for-Dishes, a new light-duty liquid; Phase III, a completely different toilet bar combining cream bar mildness and deodorant protection; and Sof-Spread Imperial, a soft margarine and companion product to Imperial Margarine.

In April, 1966, Lever acquired the nationally distributed Glamorene line of rug cleaners, cleaning appliances, and other household specialty cleaning products, which are sold through a network of brokers and in-store rental appliance franchises. Headquarters, research, and principal manufacturing facilities of the Glamorene Products Corporation, operated as a subsidiary of Lever Brothers Company, are located at Clifton, New Jersey. The Lever unconditional guarantee has become a trademark for quality products and dependable performance.

Case question

To what extent should Lever Brothers Company place emphasis on its company name in its advertising?

CASE 3.   O'BRIEN FROZEN FOODS COMPANY
Selecting a brand name

The O'Brien Frozen Foods Company, for many years packers of frozen vegetables and fruits for private brands, had no firmly established brand of its own, and was considered to be one of the smaller frozen food packers in the United States.

Although the company cultivated the private brand business aggressively, it faced keen competition from the major packers in the industry who competed for private brand business in addition to marketing their own advertised brands of frozen foods. Because of their larger scale manufacturing operations, these companies had on a number of occasions been able to underquote the O'Brien Company in competition for private brand orders.

O'Brien packed primarily for large grocery chains, cooperative wholesale grocery companies, and had on several occasions secured orders from government sources. All the products were packed under private brands which were owned by others, and O'Brien never had made any effort to stimulate consumer demand for its line of frozen foods.

Although operations showed a profit during the past year, earnings were down from the year before, due in large measure to generally lower profit margins. Sales, also down slightly, declined in dollar volume about 5 percent, and in unit case volume somewhat greater than 1 percent.

O'Brien maintained a small staff of salesmen who were paid on a commission basis, but were allowed a drawing account and traveling expenses. These men sold about 80 percent of the total pack. The balance was sold by brokers and other middlemen.

Mr. Thompson, president of O'Brien, had been reluctant to develop the company's own brand name because he did not want to risk losing the private brand business. It was his opinion that once O'Brien began to push its own label, the customers would seek other sources of supply.

The sales manager argued that while O'Brien had an adequate volume of business at present, there was no public acceptance of the company's products by name, and, therefore, the market could be cut overnight if brokers, wholesalers, and retailers placed orders with the other packers. He also believed that unless the company attempted to develop a brand of its own, growth of the company would be very limited.

It was his recommendation that the company should continue for the present time to pack for the private brand market all the products except frozen strawberries. The srawberries had proved to be one of the best sellers, not only for the O'Brien Company, but also for the entire frozen food industry. Last year they accounted for more than a third of the total frozen fruit pack. (One reason for the popularity of frozen strawberries is that they are much more closely comparable, in flavor and other characteristics, to fresh strawberries than are the canned products.)

In a recent Consumers Union's test of 44 brands of sliced frozen strawberries, the brand of the company for which O'Brien had packed the product was one of the 25 which met the standards for Grade A. The samples had been graded by CU's consultants on the basis of conformance with U.S. Department of Agriculture standards which call for properly ripened fruit that has been divested of stems and caps, washed, and sorted. Grade A (U.S. Fancy) frozen strawberries must have, in addition, bright, almost uniform, red or pink color, depending on the variety, must be practically free from such defects as stems and leaves, and must consist for the most part of fleshy and reasonably firm fruit.

The sales manager believed that O'Brien could establish its own brand name by using an advertising campaign on a modest scale, because it could promote the delicious flavor of frozen strawberries and, at the same time, make full use of the colorful background of the California area where the product was grown. He also indicated that the fruit is a good source of vitamin C, and since O'Brien's strawberries rated high in overall quality and could be sold at a competitive price, there would be a number of other appeals which the company could use in advertising its own brand. The sales manager felt that a big market for the company's other products by brand name would open. The company would then be able to shift from a private label business to its own brand name business.

The president was reluctant to accept the sales manager's recommendation because he did not believe that it was possible to promote frozen strawberries under the company's own label on a small advertising budget. He stated: "There is no particular advantage to a company like O'Brien's to have its own label. It would be impossible for us to advertise on a large enough scale to get the consumers to ask for O'Brien's products in competition with the General Foods Corporation's Birds Eye promotion. Libby's, SnowCrop, Pictsweet, Top Frost, and Polar are other brands which are well established and have over the years earned high consumer acceptance. If O'Brien attempted to promote its own brand, our present outlets might shift to other sources of supply, not only for frozen strawberries but also for their other frozen foods. We have built our business on a private label basis and have too much at stake to attempt to develop our own brand."

Case questions

1. Assume that O'Brien decides to promote the strawberries under its own label. Develop five brand names which you would recommend, taking into consideration the various legal requirements.

2. How important are specific brands of frozen food?

3. If O'Brien decided to promote its own brand, what procedure would you recommend?

CASE 4.   GENERAL DRUG, INC.
Preparing the copy

General Drug, Inc. develops, manufactures, and sells products classified by it into three general categories: denture (false teeth), dental care, and oral hygiene products; proprietary drug products; and ethical pharmaceutical products. A number of the company's products are sold in over 100 foreign countries. During the last three fiscal years, international sales accounted for approximately the following percentages of net sales: year 1, 10 percent; year 2, 11 percent; and year 3, 14 percent.

Denture, dental care, and oral hygiene products

General produces a number of specialized products intended for the cleaning of dentures, as aids in denture retention, for the greater comfort of the denture wearer, and for general dental health and oral hygiene. "Lasting" is the brand name of its mouthwash. This product has been the major profit maker in this category.

Proprietary drug products

General manufactures a number of proprietary drug products among which are headache powders and tablets, sleeping tablets and capsules, and medicated shampoo.

Ethical pharmaceutical products

General also produces a number of ethical pharmaceutical products which include a digestant tablet containing simethicone, a prescription product for the control of pediculosis and scabies, and a line of products for the treatment of the symptoms of psoriasis.

Marketing

General spends a substantial portion of its gross income on advertising, promotion, market research, and test marketing. Substantially all of its products in the denture, dental care, and oral hygiene category are promoted through advertising and also through professional channels to the dental profession by means of a staff of trained professional representatives. Other promotional methods used for products in this category include distribution of professional literature and samples, advertising in professional journals, displays at dental conventions, and mailings to dentists. General's proprietary drug products are advertised directly to the consuming public.

General sells its denture, dental care, oral hygiene, and proprietary drug products through a sales force of sales representatives and regional managers who make regular calls on the company's accounts, consisting of approximately 9,000 active customers—including wholesalers; drug and food chains; and food, drug, and variety stores.

Ethical pharmaceutical products are promoted only to the medical profession through professional channels. A separate specially trained staff of professional representatives is maintained to call on physicians, hospitals, and governmental installations to describe these products and their uses and to present samples and product literature. General also advertises these products in professional journals, conducts periodic mailings of professional literature, and maintains exhibits at medical conventions. Sales of these products are made through these representatives, principally to wholesale and retail drug outlets and to hospitals and governmental agencies.

In its advertising, the largest expenditure by General is for the purchase of television time. In addition, the company uses other media including radio, magazines, and newspapers. During the last fiscal year General's domestic expenditures on these advertising media were approximately $19 million. General also uses point-of-sale promotions and in-store displays for its products.

Lasting mouthwash

The advertising director of General wished to develop a new approach in advertising Lasting mouthwash, and pointed out the following general recommendations. He believed that the copy appeal for Lasting mouthwash should be to convince mouthwash-users that Lasting is the best product for good, clean breath. At the same time he wished to emphasize that a very real "breath problem" is present in the morning right after waking up—a problem that is sometimes called or referred to as "morning mouth." Research had indicated that consumers are particularly aware of this feeling because the bulk of mouthwash usage occurs either right before or after breakfast. He wished to take the familiar problem of "morning mouth" and dramatize the feeling to capture consumer attention. With the "morning mouth" problem established, then, it would be possible to show as the solution the great personal satisfaction resulting from use of Lasting mouthwash.

Case questions

1. Develop a central appeal that could be used for Lasting mouthwash advertising.

2. Write the copy for a one-minute television commercial and indicate what type of setting you would use.

3. Prepare the copy for an advertisement to be used in *Life* magazine.

4. How might this copy be different for a publication such as *Good Housekeeping?*

chapter 8

LAYOUT CONCEPTS

DURING the past decade there has continued to be a greater emphasis on the use of television and other broadcast media. As a result, in considering the concepts of layout and advertising production, it is important to keep in mind that the principles involved in the arrangement of the advertising elements for print media can be adapted in part to broadcast media. In Chapters 8 and 9, however, the emphasis will be placed upon the application to the print media. By concentrating on this type of media the reader should be able to derive an insight into the methods which may be used to attain distinctive visual styles and consistent production techniques.

Functions

An effective layout must satisfy a number of requirements. It must not only satisfy the laws of orderly structure, but it must also present the units in the advertisement in a manner that will get across the sales message.

While a layout may be defined as a working drawing or blueprint for an advertisement showing the sizes, positions, and color-weight values of the different units (headline, text, illustration, logotype, border, and white space) that make up the completed advertisement, it is important to keep in mind that a layout is in the final analysis directed to a selling display.

THE BASIC PRINCIPLES OF LAYOUT

To develop a layout, the following six points should be considered: (1) first impressions, (2) atmosphere, (3) artistic design, (4) variety, (5) space division, and (6) unit placement.

First impressions

The appearance of an advertisement makes the first impression on a reader. If this first impression is favorable, the reader's attention may be held and he will read the advertisement.

This generally can be accomplished somewhat more effectively by having all the parts of the layout organized in such a way that they will point toward one specific objective.

As an example, in an advertisement in which the headline stated here was a new wall paint, each part of the advertisement pointed to this basic concept. On the other hand, in an advertisement for an electrical cooking unit, the basic appeal was that this appliance cooked everything better. However, the individual parts pointed to a number of other appeals, such as where the product might be purchased, how the busy housewife could use it, and how the product could be washed. As a result, the first impression was like looking at a smorgasbord.

In Figure 8–1, Volkswagen creates an interesting first impression by the manner in which the one line is placed in the layout to get across the message of how the shape of its cars remain the same.

Atmosphere

It is in the layout that one should try to highlight that intangible—atmosphere. In many instances it is the atmosphere in the advertisement that attracts the reader's attention.

In automobile advertising, as an example, emphasis frequently is placed on atmosphere. In checking various media, one will see advertisements during the fall months illustrating cars being driven through the open country with fall-colored foliage scenes. In the winter, cars are shown in snow scenes; in the spring, the advertisers will attract prospects with illustrations of picnics and fishing trips. An intriguing atmosphere carried properly into the layout will do much toward creating interest.

Artistic design

It is important that the layout be arranged so that the reader will be able to follow the appeal that is used. If the headline states that this is the most reliable television set, then each part of the layout should be arranged in a manner to develop this theme. If the appeal used is that ready-mix cake can be made with the ingredient, the proper arrangement of the step-by-step procedure will provide the type of orderly layout needed for artistic design. Proper arrangement is the basic quality that will make an artistic layout.

FIGURE 8–1

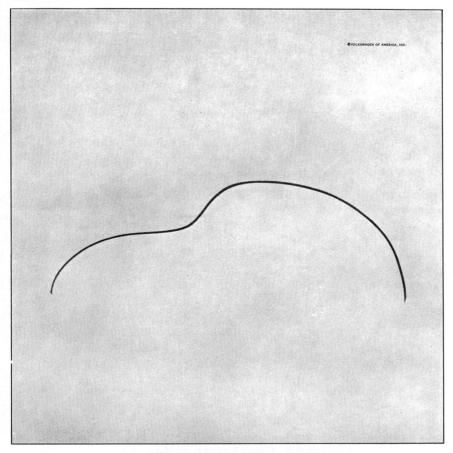

©VOLKSWAGEN OF AMERICA, INC.

How much longer can we hand you this line?

Forever, we hope.
Because we don't ever intend to change the Volkswagen's shape.
We play by our own set of rules. The only reason we change the VW is to make it work even better.
The money we don't spend on outside changes we do spend inside the car.

This system gives us an immense advantage: Time.
We have time to improve parts and still keep most of them interchangeable.
(Which is why it's so easy to get VW parts, and why VW mechanics don't wake up screaming.)
We have time to put an immense amount

of hand work into each VW, and to finish each one like a $6,000 machine.
And this system has also kept the price almost the same over the years.
Some cars keep changing and stay the same.
Volkswagens stay the same and keep changing.

Courtesy: Volkswagen

Variety

One of the ways to attract the attention of readers is to make use of the principle of variety. By varying the approach from the standard form, an advertisement will stand out, and a higher readership rating may be attained. Variety may be secured in a great many ways, such as by using different color combinations, leaving more white space, providing con-

FIGURE 8–2

We've evolved a new kind of brain cell.

The seven men around this table in Hong Kong are nationals of six different countries.

Two of these men are experts in communications technology. Four have broad experience in such areas as manufacturing, international finance, on-the-job training, international law.

And since they're discussing a communications network for a Far East country, one man is an expert on that country's problems and goals.

These men make up what we call a "brain" or management cell— a group with a unique approach to problem-solving.

Our "most valuable asset"

Next month some of these same men may be part of another group— larger or smaller—that will work on Europe's need for more hotels in the age of the jumbo jet. Or how better to train poorly educated Americans so that they can get and hold jobs.

Multiply this group of seven by four hundred and you have an idea of why our worldwide management group has been described by an independent financial analyst as our "most valuable asset."

New training methods

Because we're in fields as diverse as home building and satellite communications, we've had to develop new executive training programs.

One of our key programs centers around an intensive 3-day workshop where executives improve their ability to function effectively as members of ad hoc working groups. Here executives sharpen their skills by bringing them to bear on problems that parallel those they face in everyday work.

ITT and you

Business Week magazine has stated editorially: "The great corporation is perhaps the most effective device ever invented for getting things done in a free society. When there are jobs to be done, the American people turn instinctively to the corporations to do them."

But before anything worthwhile can happen, there must first be men, like ours, who can make the most efficient and resourceful use of available money, material and manpower. Which results in better products and services—and, in the long run, a safer, more comfortable life for you and people everywhere.

International Telephone and Telegraph Corporation, 320 Park Ave., New York, New York 10022.

SERVING PEOPLE AND NATIONS EVERYWHERE

trast, varying the direction of the pointing devices, using different type-faces, and utilizing different proportions for the parts of the layout. (See the ITT advertisement in Figure 8–2.)

Space division

While it is difficult to give an exact definition for the division of space, it is, however, this proper dividing of space that satisfies an indefinable inner sense of proportion and causes the reader to be pleased with the harmonious structure of the advertisement.

Among the divisions into which artists classify themselves are two—conventional and modern. The conventional artist lays out his picture on the canvas before starting to paint, for the purpose of getting satisfying proportions. His layout dictates to him where certain objects must be located in order to get a pleasing effect in his finished picture. He paints to obtain realism—to portray his object or scene graphically. He accepts the law of space division as fundamental, but does not make it his first and only consideration.

The modern artist accepts the law of space division not only as a fundamental rule of art but as the principal objective of the finished picture. Modern artists do not, strictly speaking, attempt to paint realistically or to portray their objects faithfully. They divide the space on their canvas for the purpose of producing a picture which is ostensibly a pattern or design created by the objects and the spaces between the objects.

The division of space leads into a wide variety of complicated designs or patterns. However, at present it is more important to consider the fundamental divisions and their comparative values in order that the different units (illustration, headline, copy, trademark, signature, etc.) may be placed and divided effectively.

Examine Illustrations 1 and 2 in Figure 8–3. Number 1 is divided at the center by a vertical dotted line. Number 2 is divided into equal parts by a horizontal line. Both spaces have been cut exactly in half, leaving two equal divisions of space. This is the least complex of any possible division. Such divisions, which are equal, have a tendency to be uninteresting and monotonous. Monotony may result from equality or uniformity. As an example, if one part of an electrical cord is broken, a person's attention generally will be attracted to that spot. One could take a hundred individuals past a fence with a broken picket, and if they remembered having seen the fence at all, the one fact that would stand out would be the broken picket. Thus, to avoid monotony or sameness, it is usually better not to divide the space into equal parts.

Illustration 3 presents a simple, yet graphic picture of life's great drama. Men, animals, and other creatures of nature do not attack a foe of equal strength. They are constantly seeking the more timid and weak

FIGURE 8–3. Space division illustrations

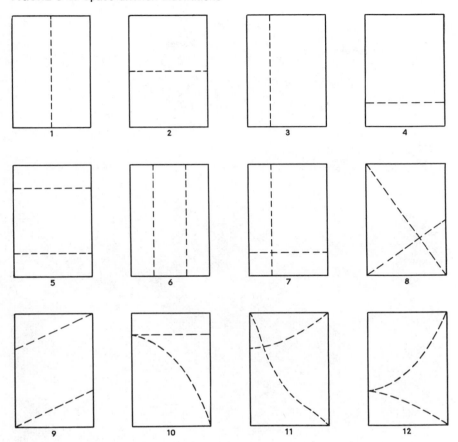

as an antagonist. Illustration 3 depicts inequality—the struggle for life in a simple form. It illustrates a dramatic, unequal, interesting situation. The smaller space battles against the larger space for its place. One might visualize an illustration similar to a large boy fighting with a small youngster. One's natural tendencies and inclinations are to sympathize immediately with the smaller boy. A situation of this kind is interesting and stimulating. These situations are the kind that generally will attract attention.

Illustration 4 gives a dramatic situation similar to the one found in Number 3, except in the fourth drawing a horizontal dotted line is used to make the division, while in the third a vertical line is used. GMAC used this method of space division in Figure 8–4. This situation creates an impression of a large object crushing a smaller one. A comparative analysis of the mental reactions to these kinds of space divisions usually

FIGURE 8–4

Taking a car pool to work is one thing.
Getting there on time is another.

Car pools are great if they arrive when they're supposed to. But if there's a Late Late Show in your office every morning, and you're the star, we have a suggestion.

Form your own car pool. And if you have to buy a car, we can help. We're GMAC. General Motors Acceptance Corporation.

And General Motors Dealers who use GMAC make it less complicated for people to buy cars. By financing your car, car insurance and creditor life insurance. (We also finance trucks and appliances.)

Right where you buy. Quickly. At a cost you can live with. Anywhere in the country.

That way, you won't be waiting for someone at your front door. While the boss is waiting for you at his.

GMAC
FINANCING
We uncomplicate things

In your own best interest—always remember, the most economical way to buy on time is to pay down as much as you can and pay the balance as soon as you can.

indicates that while Illustration 4 may not create the interest that Illustration 3 does, it is nevertheless superior in attention-attracting qualities to either Illustrations 1 or 2. Illustrations 5 and 6 are similar to 3 and 4, except that each has been divided into three spaces instead of two. These divisions give dramatic situations which, for attracting interest, are probably greater than those found in 3 and 4. The three spaces enlarge the field of activity and enable one to get greater variety. The vertical spaces will, of course, get different reactions than the horizontal.

Illustration 7 gives a more complex division of space. None of the four spaces is equal in area. It broadens even further the possible fields of activity which enable a layout man to produce greater variety. It has the advantage of oblongs, both horizontal and vertical. The intersecting point of the two divisional lines also results in an "X." This provides another device for attracting attention. In Figure 8–5, the Carrier Air Conditioning Company advertisement utilizes this principle on an effective basis.

Illustration 8 provides a space divided into four unequal parts, three of them forming triangles of different sizes. The division is brought about by two diagonal lines crossing each other, producing the "X." The crossing of two opposed diagonal lines is symbolic of crossed swords, and creates the atmosphere of duels, battle, etc. This dramatic action attracts attention and creates interest.

Illustration 9 is another of the many possible uses of diagonals. This is similar to Illustration 5, but possesses an appeal with greater dynamic force than straight horizontals. Here one gets the feeling of the power required to pull something uphill and the effect of coasting down at a high rate of speed.

Illustration 10 portrays a combination of straight and circular lines bringing about two curved space divisions. Curves create soft fluid designs, lacking in force and directness when compared to straight lines, but making up for this deficiency in beauty.

In Illustrations 11 and 12, the divisional lines are curved. It is the opinion of many artists that straight lines are masculine in feeling and curved lines are feminine. Men usually are attracted by advertisements that go straight to the facts in a logical manner; beauty in advertising is not as important to men as it is to women. Women, on the other hand, are usually attracted by advertisements that tend toward the artistic and consider logic and facts as secondary. It should not be overlooked, however, that curved divisions of space develop an atmosphere of ease and quiet, while divisions of space made by straight lines create a feeling of power, speed, and excitement. Aetna Life Insurance uses curved lines in Figures 8–6 to create a feeling of love and softness.

Unit placement

After the space has been divided, it is necessary to determine how the different units of an advertisement will be placed within these spaces. The units themselves, or the white spaces between them, should, by their position in relation to each other, create a pattern or design which will be attractive.

FIGURE 8–5. Space division (7)

We can take about 10 pounds off our air conditioners. But we won't.

That's the way we like them
and build them. Heftier. Stronger.
Carrier uses heavier components,
thick Weather Armor® coating,
more insulation. So they'll last longer,
run quieter. Maybe that's why more
people put their confidence in Carrier
air conditioning than in any other make.

Carrier Air Conditioning Company

Courtesy: Carrier Air Conditioning Company

FIGURE 8–6. Space division (12)

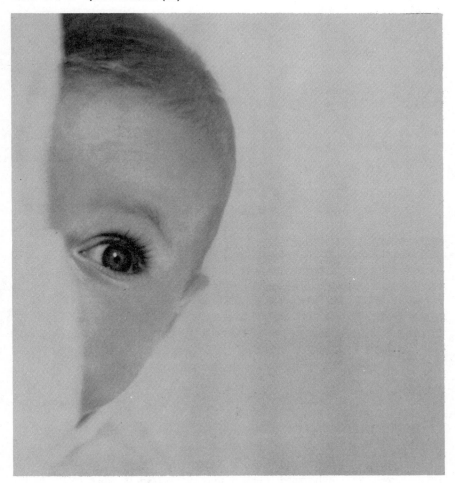

Your business judgment now may determine his outlook forever

Not just today. Or tomorrow. But for all the days of his life. The future of everyone in your family will be more secure if you approach your insurance needs in a businesslike manner. To make sure you do, to avoid mistakes and waste, consider Ætna—the insurance company respected by businessmen for its sound business judgment. It's a fact that more businesses are group insured by Ætna than by any other company. This is confidence well placed. Confidence you will experience when you discuss protection for your family with the Ætna representative. Call him today, so he can help you make a sound business decision for your family.

ÆTNA LIFE INSURANCE [ÆTNA]

THE CHOICE OF BUSINESSMEN LETS YOU CHOOSE WITH CONFIDENCE

ÆTNA LIFE INSURANCE COMPANY, Hartford 15, Conn. ■ Affiliates: Ætna Casualty and Surety Company, Standard Fire Insurance Company, The Excelsior Life, Canada

Courtesy: Aetna Life Insurance Company

The selection of particular units for specific spaces in the advertisement is of importance because the advertisement must have the appearance of being clear and easy to read. If not properly located, the shapes and color-weight values of some units may have an effect of blocking the vision.

Because it is difficult for the eye to obtain a photographic impression of a complete scene or entire subject at a glance, it is advisable, whenever possible, to locate the units in the layout so that they will be seen in the order of their importance.

Path of the eye: Illustration 1 in Figure 8–7 shows the normal path

FIGURE 8–7. Illustrations

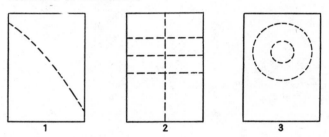

traveled by the eye when looking at an advertisement. Notice that the eye enters the page on the left near the top and passes down and across the space in the form of an arc, leaving the space on the right side near the bottom. Although the eye will follow this particular path under normal conditions, it can be diverted by pointing devices, barriers, and the like.

Various tests indicate that the eye wanders while following the natural course. There is a place, however, along the path where more will be seen at a short distance from the path than at any other point. In other words, it can be said there is one place that is more likely to be explored by the eye than any other. This point is called by some the optical center; by others it is known as the focal point; and by others it is referred to as the visual point.

In Illustration 2, the focal point is slightly above the center of the space. Usually it is located, for all practical purposes, by dividing the upper half of the space into thirds and then drawing a vertical line dividing the spaces equally. The focal point will be at the center of the intersection of the vertical and horizontal lines.

At this point, the unguided eye generally will wander. It has been found through experimentation that an area around this point, about one third of the width of the space, has the greatest potential for advertising purposes.

Examine Illustration 2. If the space were six inches wide and nine inches high, the optical center would be approximately two inches in diameter. From this optical center area there is a gradual but declining value. The second most valuable area surrounds the optical center and is called the "field." The field can be estimated to include a circular space which in the overall width (including optical center) is about five sixths of the width of the space under consideration. As an example, if the space under consideration were six inches wide, the field, including the optical center, would be five inches in diameter. All space not included in the optical center and field is called the fringe.

Generally, the unit which has been designed for the purpose of creating interest, should be placed in the optical circle. However, when conditions exist which may make it impractical to do this, it is then advisable to place the unit as near the focal point as possible. Location for all other units should be selected according to the order in which it is desired they be seen or read. Copy panels should be located also with this thought in mind. Trademarks and slogans usually are placed in locations to complete the pattern, for ordinarily they are not an important part of the sales appeal. The firm's name usually comes at the bottom or end of the copy unless, for cause, it is placed elsewhere.

When a coupon is used, it is generally placed in one of the lower corners. To spur a prospect to act, it should be made easy for him to clip the coupon. As a result, the outside corner of the page is used because it requires only two cuts, one vertical and one horizontal. Some advertisers even use a triangle-shaped coupon because it requires only one diagonal cut.

There are certain situations, however, where it may not be possible to place the main appeal near the optical center. In cases of this kind, some pointing device may be used to guide the eye from its natural course to another path or route so that the reader will be more likely to see and read the basic appeal.

Pointing devices. Many techniques can be used to guide the eye, such as arrows, rising smoke, trailing vines, pencils, and other devices.

In a recent soup advertisement, the pointing device employed to carry the eye from the headline to the product was a cluster of peapods on a leafy stalk. The lower pod was open and displayed a row of peas, slanted conspicuously toward the bowl of steaming soup. It formed a pointing means, and yet, because it fitted into the complete advertisement, was not readily recognized as such a device.

A soft-drink distributor used an illustration of the beverage being poured from the bottle as a pointing device. A ribbon on a package, a man pointing to a product, different intensities of colors, a curving highway, or a wire stretching from a pulley are a few of the devices which can be used.

Background unit. One of the ways to place a product in the foreground and make it stand out is to place a background behind it. When this is done, it creates a third dimension. This illusion may be created by leaving white space around an illustration which becomes as much a background as the picture of distant hills or mountains.

A background which creates a third dimension has the advantage of making the advertisement stand out in bold relief, bringing it out into the foreground in front of other units, and thereby giving it display prominence.

In an advertisement of batteries for portable television sets, a battery was placed in the immediate foreground, standing out against white space. Back of the battery was a picture of three persons on the beach viewing a television program. The scene was a little grayer than the illustration of the battery and was vignetted into the white space at the bottom. Superimposed on this background, in an upper corner, was the company's trade name. In this advertisement, the treatment of the background harmonized with both the copy idea and the scheme of the design.

A television advertisement for a color television set also made a similar use of backgrounds to help illustrate visually what the product does. The theme of the campaign was "The Theater of the Home." The illustration depicted a scene of a show in color.

Reasons for dual background. Below are listed several reasons for using a dual-purpose background. These do not represent all the reasons, nor do they indicate that any one of these is more important or valuable than another. However, they indicate a number of instances in which a dual-purpose background can be used effectively:

1. To show uses of the product or to form a pattern, thus uniting a number of small illustrations in a decorative design that does not detract from the boldness with which the main illustration or picture of the product is to be treated.
2. To make specific appeals to various occupational classes by using scenes behind the product that will interest each group—an office building, golf course, fishing stream, hunting scene, a factory, and so on.
3. To contribute to or symbolize an atmosphere of luxury, refinement, and strength.
4. To construct an allover pattern either of the product or trademark against which an illustration or copy can be made to stand out.
5. To suggest what is likely to happen if the product is not used—the skeleton is an effective device to use as background for an insurance policy, a sheet of fireproof wallboard, or a set of automobile tires.
6. To place a trademark or some other unit in the distance so that it does not cut into the scene depicted.

QUESTIONS

1. "The worst thing about today's cult of creativity in advertising layout is that it puts the emphasis on spectacular individual ads instead of campaign success." Comment.

2. "Many of the bad layouts in print media today can be blamed on broadcast media." Discuss.

3. It has been stated that original layout forms come from creative thinking, not from previously conceived formulas. Comment.

4. Explain what is meant by the focal point and select an advertisement in which this has been used effectively.

5. Select an advertisement from a magazine in which the main appeal was not placed in the optical center. Explain why.

6. Where is the best location in the layout to place a coupon in the following cases:

    a)   Full-page advertisement.
    b)   Upper one-half page advertisement.
    c)   Column advertisement near the gutter corner.

7. Select and clip from some newspaper or magazine an advertisement which, in your opinion, has made good use of the focal, field, and fringe spaces. Make a layout of that advertisement showing, with light circles and optical center, the field and fringe. Make a second layout using a different arrangement of the parts. Indicate whether or not you believe there is improvement.

8. Select and clip from some publication the advertisement that in your opinion excels all others in "favorable attention-attracting" and "interest-creating" qualities. Base your judgment upon the ability of the advertisement's caption, illustration, and general typographical appearance to "atttract favorable attention" and "create interest." Before making your selection, be sure you understand what is meant by the terms "attracting favorable attention" and "creating interest." The quality of the copy is not to be considered. Make a layout of this advertisement, exact in size and similar in color-weight values; letter in the captions and signatures—the lettering to be similar in style, size, and weight; try to make illustrations recognizable.

9. It has been stated that in a layout pattern, one element must dominate in order to get the reader's attention. Comment.

10. How can the layout express the ideas of the advertiser?

11. Indicate some of the methods for securing distinction in a layout.

12. What information do you need before a layout can be started?

13. Point out the layouts you would recommend for the following products for print media:

    a)   Retail discount house
    b)   Swift's Premium franks
    c)   Salem cigarettes
    d)   Dial soap
    e)   Bulova watch

f)   Shrimp cocktail
g)   Hathaway shirt
h)   Coca-Cola
i)   Leslie salt
j)   New York Life Insurance

14. Indicate how layouts would vary between the following media: Newspapers, magazines, trade publications, direct mail, transit advertising, and outdoor.

CASE 1. ANALYSES OF ADVERTISEMENTS
Considering layout principles

In Exhibits 1 through 4 evaluate the advertisements on following bases:

1. Favorable attention-attracting qualities.
2. Interest-creating qualities.
3. Effectiveness of layout to direct the eye.
4. Use of contrast, proportion, balance, and unity.

CASE 2. EVALUATION OF DIFFERENT LAYOUTS
Preparing layouts

1. Make two thumbnail sketches of the advertisements for each of the exhibits in Case 1.
2. Rearrange the units in your sketches in several ways.
3. Compare your recommended sketch with the original advertisement and give reasons why you believe your layouts are better or worse.

EXHIBIT 1

Let's face it, not every youngster can earn a fortune in the major leagues. Or even win a college scholarship. But as a college graduate, chances are he'll earn $100,000 to $200,000 more, in his lifetime, than a high school graduate.

So play it safe and prepare for the expense of his college education now, with the help of American United Life's Sentinel policy. By the time he's ready for college, your Sentinel policy can be worth more cash than the total you've paid in premiums. And you'll have life insurance protection all the while.

Talk with your A·U·L agent. He'll show you how a Sentinel policy can guarantee your child's education, even if you're not here to see him graduate.

The Company with the Partnership Philosophy
AMERICAN UNITED LIFE INSURANCE COMPANY
FALL CREEK PARKWAY AT NORTH MERIDIAN
DEPT. S-47, INDIANAPOLIS, INDIANA 46206

Courtesy: American United Life Insurance Company

EXHIBIT 2

Cluett, Peabody & Co., Inc., permits use of its trademark "Sanforized" only on fabrics which meet its rigid shrinkage requirements under its regular inspection. Such fabrics will not shrink more than 1% by the Government's standard test. Use of the Company's trademark "Sanforized-Plus" is permitted only on fabrics which pass its regular tests and inspection for smoothness after washing, crease recovery, tensile strength, and tear strength, as well as meeting the "Sanforized" shrinkage requirements.

Be suspicious!

Don't ask. Look.

Look for it on the label or tag.

If it's not there, you are risking your money.

You can't be sure the fabric won't shrink unless you see *SANFORIZED*

You can't be sure of the best wash-and-wear performance unless you see *SANFORIZED plus*

Right there. On the label.

Don't fall for a glib "It's the same thing."

If it is, why doesn't it say so?

You're entitled to "Sanforized" and "Sanforized-Plus".

Get them.

Courtesy: Cluett, Peabody & Co., Inc.

EXHIBIT 3

Will something always be missing from his life?

Yes, unless you start him on the piano now, and give him the gift of music. For a lifetime. And the best way to start is a Yamaha piano. Its tone is clear and brilliant. The touch is sensitive and fast. The tune holds longer. For Yamaha gives you *truly* professional quality at family-affordable prices.

Yamaha is the world's largest manufacturer of pianos (more than twice as large as the next largest). See and hear a Yamaha soon. For *his* sake.

YAMAHA Since 1887
INTERNATIONAL CORPORATION
7733 Telegraph Road, Montebello, Calif. · 685-5135
Eastern Branch: 200 West 57th Street, New York, N.Y.

Courtesy: Yamaha International Corporation

EXHIBIT 4

Anytime...but not just for any man!

Cologne:
$5.00 and $8.00
After Shave:
$4.00 and $6.00

CLARION DIV., NEW YORK

Available only at fine drug, department and men's stores.

Courtesy: Clairon Division

chapter 9

ADVERTISING PRODUCTION

BY ITS very nature, advertisement production for broadcast and print media is a complicated activity because it calls for the efficient utilization of the specialized talents of a number of individuals. Here the usual problems of communication, timing, planning, decision making, and human relations assume a new dimension of challenge.

With new concepts being placed before them, with their desires being aroused, and, with competition subtly encouraged, the consumers have also raised their sights. Ironically, companies have found that to keep the consumer seeking higher and higher economic levels, it has been advantageous to presell their products using dynamic emotional appeals.

There is growing evidence, however, that consumers are getting tired of many of these symbols of rising aspiration appeals that have been used and are demanding more rational strategy. As a result, it is now even more important for advertising production techniques to be developed in correlation with the current economic and social setting.

As an example, in visualizing the production of the advertisement, the overall appeal should be focused on one sales point which can be reinforced by an exciting headline, succinct copy and convincing visual concepts. All of these parts must also be considered as a unit.

ENVISIONING

Envisioning may be defined as "the process of forming a mental image, picture, or representation of an object not before the eyes." As an example, consider this situation. During the past year, a reporter, while driving across a bridge, saw a woman stop her car in the middle of the bridge, get out, walk to the side rail, deliberately climb over, poise herself momentarily on the outer ledge in a diving position, and jump into the water. Now, stop a moment; analyze this scene clearly and distinctly. What is the mental picture of this tragedy?

The picture includes many details; an artist could paint a detailed picture of this scene as it appears. This picture would clearly show this woman jumping off one side of the bridge. One might envisage the Golden Gate or Brooklyn Bridge, or some other familiar bridge—undoubtedly the particular bridge visualized is the one which is the most familiar. One might see the color of the coat she wore, or perhaps in the mental picture she wore no coat—perhaps she wore a robe. The mind pictures her as either wearing a hat or being bareheaded; it pictures her as being tall or short, old or young. What was the expression on her face? What kind of car did she have? Did she leave the motor running?

To envisage is the ability to develop a mental picture of a thing or situation, and then present this mental picture to another person in a vivid and graphic manner. Perhaps the chief difference between the ability of the average person to interpret and that of an advertising man or woman, is the difference in the ability to translate a visualization into action. The inherited type is not self-starting, because it requires an explanation or a story to start it into action, while the one that creates advertising ideas must be self-starting. It has no story to envisage, but must develop the concept or situation and then see it so clearly that it can be explained to the artist or photographer.

A sound example of visualization is found in Ernest Hemingway's *The Old Man and the Sea.*

He saw him first as a dark shadow that took so long to pass under the boat that he could not believe its length . . . he came to the surface only thirty yards away and the man saw his tail out of the water. It raked and as the fish swam just below the surface the old man could see his huge bulk and the purple stripes that banded him. His dorsal fin was down and his huge pectorals were spread wide. . . . He made the fish fast to bow and stern and to the middle thwart. He was so big it was like lashing a much bigger skiff along-side. . . .

Now the man watched the dip of the three sticks over the side of the skiff and rowed gently to keep the lines straight up and down at their proper depths. . . .

The results which can be secured from envisioning a situation are as numerous as are the minds focused on the subject. As an example, en-visage the act of fishing. If twelve artists were asked to illustrate the act of fishing, one would probably receive twelve different mental pictures transferred on paper. The first artist might see a small, barefoot boy in patched trousers and straw hat sitting on the bank of a small pond with a crooked stick for a pole; the second artist might visualize a fisherman standing in a boat, dressed appropriately in fisherman's sport clothes, wielding a fly rod in an expert manner; the third might visualize a family fishing scene which includes mother, father, and several children on a day's outing, with fishing as an incident in the day's happenings; the fourth might picture a deep-sea fishing scene.

Abraham Walkowitz, an artist and the world's most prolific portrait sitter, held an unusual one-man show—130 portraits of himself by 109 U.S. artists. The walls of one of the main galleries of the Brooklyn Museum were all but concealed by Walkowitz in oil, watercolors, pen and ink, photography, stone and clay.

The fact that it took Mr. Walkowitz over 700 hours of posing is not of the greatest importance. What is, however, is that every one of the 100 artists saw in Walkowitz something entirely different. One depicted him as a man of great determination; another saw him as a leader; another portrayed him as an old man; another put emphasis on his eyes; another saw him as a ruthless individual; still another saw in him a person who had great understanding of his fellow man. In fact, every artist put emphasis on some different characteristic. It was difficult to recognize in many of the portraits that Walkowitz was the one who had posed.

The variety of results of the artists' attempts to envisage a specific situation, and unacquainted with the facts, indicates the necessity of finding out through an analysis of the prospects what features and qualities of the product will appeal to them.

It is also important to keep in mind that an artist will generally not be as well qualified to visualize an appeal as effectively as the person who has studied and evaluated the market for a product. One need not be an artist to visualize ideas successfully. It is the ability to interpret and to convey the concepts to the artist that is essential.

IMPORTANCE OF BROAD ANALYSIS

Afer studying the consumer, it is important to envisage a variety of situations wherein the wants and needs of the prospects will be filled by the features and qualities of the product or service.

If the product to be advertised is paint, and it is determined that the best appeal would be one that would emphasize the beauty of a home, then the illustration might enhance that beauty by the use of the latest and most artistically lighted photographic reproductions. There should also be the proper kind of setting arrangement and background atmosphere that would intensify and multiply the beauty of the product.

In advertising a product it may be advisable to find out what it does that no other similar product can do. It may be that it operates more economically due to some new or exclusive feature. If so, that is a particular feature that could be emphasized.

Assume that in advertising a toothpaste distributed on a national basis, a study of the market indicates the importance of getting the prospects to remember the name of the product and how the package looks. In this case, one might consider an illustration which would say pictorially: "This is the name of your favorite toothpaste. Ask for it by this name when you make your purchase. See, this is the package. Remember how it looks." A pleasing inviting picture of the package in a colorful setting might help make an indelible impression.

A manufacturer of insulating material showed a man with a blazing blowtorch in one hand and the insulating material in the other to emphasize that this product would not burn. An insurance company used an illustration of a pair of open scissors to show that a family's income hangs by a single thread—the husband's ability to work at his job. Kellogg pictures a little girl with a curl in the middle of her forehead with a big bowl of Kellogg's Corn Flakes to emphasize its product:

> There was a little girl and she had a little curl
>   right in the middle of her forehead.
> When she was good, she was very, very good
>   and her mother gave her—Kellogg's.

Planters used a peanut dish with only one peanut in it to show the rapidity with which peanuts are eaten. Bell Telephone depicts the visits by long-distance telephone by showing a husband talking to his loved ones at home.

There is an almost unlimited number of ways to interpret any appeal. To envisage effectively, however, is not easy. As one studies and analyzes each situation, one generally will find an ability for this creative work. Creative imagination is not an inherent gift—it can be acquired through constant practice of visualizing what illustrations to use for specific market conditions.

THREE ASPECTS OF DEMAND

In selecting the approach to use, it is important to consider on which of the three aspects of demand to place emphasis. A prospect may have his attention focused on a product in several ways. In evaluating whether to purchase an automobile, a person might think of the hours each day he must spend in waiting for public transportation. On the other hand, he may think only of the satisfaction to be had from driving a new car; or he may concentrate on an obstacle, such as the price, which might prevent him from buying it. These three fundamental aspects of demand are called the negative, the positive, and the obstacle appeals. It is possible to use illustrations that will stimulate the thinking of the prospect in any of these directions.

Negative aspect

The negative appeal involves the use of the unpleasant, and it is generally more difficult to use than a positive appeal. The danger in its use lies in the fact that it may produce a negative reaction which may be transferred to the product. When it is effectively used, however, it may depict a situation in which the prospect might find himself, and directly or indirectly provide a way of conquering the difficulty. Patent medicines are sold frequently through the use of negative appeals. Cosmetics, insurance, soaps, toothpaste, mouthwashes, and other such products continue to use the negative approach. It is important, however, whenever the negative appeal is used that the positive result from the use of the product be given somewhere in the advertisement. As an example, when an illustration portrays a man with a serious cold or backache, the advertiser should also point out how his product will relieve this condition. Unless the advertiser has a unique objective, the negative appeal should not be used without also providing the positive solution to the problem.

Positive aspect

The positive appeal places emphasis on the result to be derived from use of the product. It portrays the satisfaction secured; the peace of mind in driving because of the premium automobile tires; the healthier, happier living for you and your family; the flawless fit and beautiful wear; the unsurpassed natural color of a new television set; the friendship, rich and warm and strong, that can be secured through serving good coffee; the fun in flying to Hawaii and enjoying the island paradise.

Regardless of what specific appeal is used, the positive aspect generally should be implied in every advertisement. Never permit the prospect to forget that he will find satisfaction through the use or possession of the product. The positive appeal also differs from the negative and obstacle appeals because it may be used alone.

In many instances, the positive appeal may emphasize the satisfaction to be derived to such a degree that it may be more effective not to cloud the issue by indicating either a negative or obstacle aspect. The beauty of the automobile, the speed in getting the work completed, the healthy youngster, the pause that refreshes, and the security from a planned investment program are examples of situations in which the advertisers limited their appeal to the positive phase.

Obstacle aspect

The obstacle appeal attempts to stir up a man's fighting spirit, to arouse his determination, and, through this approach, bring an action that might otherwise be delayed. As an example, manufacturers of limited-production runs have used an appeal indicating the small number available.

Retail advertisers use special sales in which such statements as "limited quantity," "while they last," "will be available only from 6—9 P.M.," "first come, first served," "no returns allowed," "will meet any competitive price," "if you can get a better deal," "compare the prices in other stores," "only our special customers will be admitted," and "special closeouts" will be used in order to place some impediment or hindrance in the way of the buyer.

Setting for envisioning

As a result of the greater emphasis on the use of broadcast media and the shifts in stress on various social values along with other dynamic changes in the past decade, there has evolved a more complex combination of circumstances that require new insights into the process of visualization.

The changing cultural patterns have brought about a different interpretation of conformity to characteristic goals and institutional means. The reluctance of society to measure success in terms of heavy emphasis on financial attainment is but one example of a symptom of this attitude.

Yet, at the same time is the inherent drive on the part of the consumer to have an identity. The dynamism in society, however, makes this more and more difficult to attain. The demands on the individual by an affluent society, the outgrowth of leisure as a problem in society, the stress on large-scale organizations, and the decrease in individuality have lessened his chance of developing this unity of personality.

It should also be kept in mind that each consumer is unique and that there is no one else exactly like him. Each consumer's primary function is the realization of his unique potential.

Although these individual drives are important, nevertheless, despite all of the contradictions, the consumer has a great sense of attachment to society as a whole and an attraction to his fellows. In other words, the value of the experience of society relationships is needed and essential.

National advertising market

The segmentation that has taken place has also eroded what was at one time considered to be a national advertising market. National advertising is now frequently designed and placed on a regional basis with the retailer and distributor having an ever growing voice in the process. This has resulted from a number of factors which include:

1. Increased cost of network advertising.
2. Failure to develop a yardstick to measure adequately the national advertising.
3. Desire on the part of large distributors to participate in the advertising planning.

4. Need to use specific appeals for different sections of the country.
5. Use of spot advertising on a basis that appeared to be as effective as network promotion.
6. Availability of special regional and metropolitan rates for media.
7. Segmentation of market potential.
8. Potential of correlating advertising to meet needs of various markets.
9. Decline in expenditures for advertising as a percentage of Gross National Product.

Clues to preparation

In selecting the procedures which should be used in formalizing the appeal there are many facets which should be included. It is also important not to underestimate the complexity of the total situation. Keep in mind also that no detail is ever too small to be considered.

Some of the questions that might provide an insight into the clues for firming the approach are the following:

1. Who makes the decision as to the class of product to purchase? (primary appeal)
2. Who makes the decision as to the brand to buy? (selective appeal)
3. Who influences the buyer?
4. Where will the product be purchased?
5. When will the buyer purchase the product?
6. How will the buyer arrive at the decision to purchase it?
7. What type of budget is available to stimulate demand?
8. Will the appeal have to differ for the various market segments?
9. Are there any contradictions about the product characteristics that need to be overcome?
10. How do customers relate to the product?
11. What kind of self-enlargement or self-expression might result from purchase of the product?
12. How can the communication be best advanced? Will it be confined to a verbal expression? A pictorial approach?
13. Are there any incongruous or inappropriate presentations for the product?
14. What media are available for the presentation and can the same appeal be used in all of them?
15. Is the approach geared for short-term or long-term goals?

It would be incorrect to say that this list of questions is complete. Nevertheless, they give some indication as to the complexity of what is involved in broad visualization.

Consider the Vicks VapoRub advertisement in Figure 9–1. The mother probably makes the decision as to the product and brand which will be

FIGURE 9–1

Sniffles,
congestion,
coughs,
tears . . .
so sick
with
a cold!

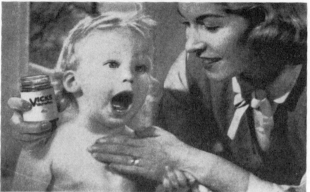

Comfort your baby with soothing relief that acts faster, works longer than aspirin or cold tablets

ATOM TRACER TESTS PROVE VAPORUB ACTS IN 7 SECONDS, WORKS 10 HOURS

Your loving hands massage Vicks VapoRub over chest, throat, back — and right before your eyes, the stuffiness starts to clear, the cough calms. That's because soothing vapor medications reach cold-infected nose, throat, and chest in just 7 seconds . . . keep working for 10 hours — startling facts discovered by laboratory atom tracer tests. Medical literature shows that pills and tablets which go through stomach and bloodstream act slower and for shorter periods. And VapoRub relieves stuffiness, coughs, congestion . . . symptoms aspirin does not help. For sniffles, sneezes, as well as croupy coughs . . . for grown-ups and children — use VapoRub for every cold. Use as a rub, in steam, in the nose.

Doctors prescribe medicated steam for colds and croupy coughs. To make steam most effective, add VapoRub to bowl of boiling water or vaporizer, as directed.

VICKS VAPORUB ®

WORLD'S MOST WIDELY USED COLDS MEDICATION

Courtesy: Vicks Chemical Company

purchased. When the youngster comes down with a cold, the child becomes the influential factor. As a result, the decision to show the benefits derived from the use of the product becomes an effective appeal. This appeal can be dramatized in a number of ways and can be used both in broadcast and print media. It is also an appeal that will reach the segment of the market in which families have children. On the other hand, there is the danger of getting some negative reaction on the basis that a

FIGURE 9–2

Are kids stronger today? No. Boats are aluminum.

You don't have to be a weight-lifter to carry an aluminum boat.

An 11-year-old can hold up his end with ease. Aluminum is so light (one-third the weight of steel) and so strong (some aluminum alloys are stronger than structural steel), the role it plays in all forms of transportation keeps getting bigger.

Today's jetliners are 75% to 85% aluminum.

There are 2,000 *tons* of aluminum on the *S. S. United States*, world's fastest ocean liner.

The most modern railroad cars are aluminum. So are the newest buses, trucks, mobile homes, travel trailers.

Aluminum makes automobiles look better, perform better, wear better than ever.

Aluminum is a wonderful homebody, too. Alumi-

num siding is rustfree, practically maintenance-free, and hardly ever needs painting.

A great deal of the frozen food you buy comes packaged in aluminum. And every woman knows how good aluminum foil is.

Aluminum is big today. And it's going places. Come on along.

May your future be as bright as aluminum's.

easy-care
aluminum

The Aluminum Association

The mark of aluminum: symbol of the world's most versatile metal. © The Aluminum Association 1966

Courtesy: The Aluminum Association

product that can be used by youngsters will not be strong enough for adults.

Two other approaches that are of interest are the ones found in Figures 9–2 and 9–3. Again both of these advertisements not only use illustrations effectively to dramatize the general appeal, but they also pinpoint rational factors that are of importance to the potential consumer.

FIGURE 9–3

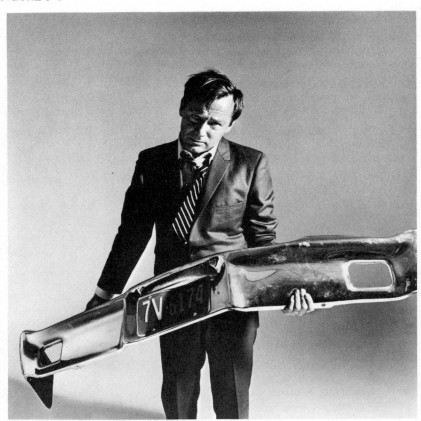

If you need competitive bids to get your car fixed ...maybe you need a new insurance company

Like MIC.

We think it's a waste of your time to get competitive bids. It's bad enough your car is damaged. Why make things worse?

So we simplify. When you have a claim, you just take your car to a Chevrolet or

Pontiac dealer. Or a Buick, Olds or Cadillac dealer. Or any reliable repair shop.

That's all you do—and Motors Insurance Corporation arranges the repairs. Saves you time and trouble.

Service like this doesn't cost you a

penny extra. MIC's rates are competitive.

And you can buy our insurance from over 10,000 licensed insurance agents at General Motors dealers in the U. S. and Canada.* Stop in and find out—insurance can be convenient.

*Available only on time purchases in Mass., Mich., Ohio, N.Y., Ontario and Quebec.

MOTORS INSURANCE CORPORATION
Subsidiary of General Motors Acceptance Corporation

Courtesy: Motors Insurance Corporation

GENERAL SUGGESTIONS

In pointing out some of the different procedures in envisioning an idea, it is important to determine not only what the product is technically but also how the consumer sees it. The concept of the "psychological environment" includes the notion that what people "see" depends not only on the appeals used, but, also on such factors as the type of persons they are, the environment in which they live and the ideology which they have. People "see" things in the way their culture and the particular social group in which they move have induced them to visualize these things.

As a result, each appeal has certain advantages. In a television advertisement, several devices may be used, each serving its own purpose; thus, the person who failed to use the product may dramatize a situation while another person who did use the product may show the benefits derived. In print media a package may be placed with a before-and-after scene.

While the combinations are extensive, the following points are some which might be considered in deciding on the appeal to use:

1. A single sound appeal is better than a poor one supported by mediocre ones.
2. Continuity in a series of advertisements can be secured by employing the same technique of visualization in each advertisement, and allowing the ideas to provide distinctiveness.
3. The test of an appeal is whether or not it conveys the idea which underlies the advertisement.
4. The illustrations, script, text, etc., should complement each other.
5. People like to look at illustrations. As a result, good illustrations will arouse interest.

MECHANICAL TECHNIQUES

Because by its very nature advertising is also dependent upon the mechanical means by which the message will be presented in a sound and economical manner, the authors have included basic introductory concepts and principles. An understanding of this material will provide the nomenclature that is essential in considering the recommendations of the production staff.

Printing

Although a number of new processes have been developed, these new techniques are generally adaptations of one of the three basic printing processes. These three processes are called: letterpress printing, intaglio printing, and lithographic printing. Letterpress printing, or relief printing, is transferring to the paper from a raised surface. Intaglio, or rotogravure, printing is transferring to the paper through an etched or depressed surface. Lithographic, or planographic, printing is transferring to the paper from a flat surface which has been specially treated. The three processes of printing are shown in Figure 9–4.

FIGURE 9–4

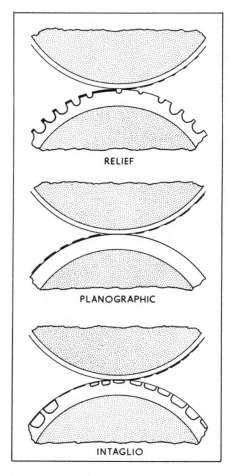

RELIEF

PLANOGRAPHIC

INTAGLIO

Lithographic printing may be either direct or indirect. Indirect lithography is referred to as offset lithography. The main difference between direct and offset lithography is that in direct lithography the plates touch the paper. In offset the plates do not touch the paper but deliver the ink to an intermediate cylinder which is covered with a thin sheet of rubber. It is this thin sheet of rubber that prints off, or offsets, the ink on the paper. The upper cylinder carries the paper receiving the impression and the lower shows the printing plate in a magnified cross section (line and Ben Day).

Type measurement

The point system is the standard method of measurement used by printers for type, rules, and borders. The basis of the point system is the "point." A point is approximately 1/72 of an inch in height, or, the vertical measurement. There are 72 points to the inch. Only the height of type is measured in points; the width is not measured by points and will vary, depending on the face of type used. When type is spoken of as 6-point and 8-point, it means that the body—not the face—of the letter is 6/72 or 8/72 of an inch high. The height of the face is usually less than the height of the body. The face of an 8-point capital M, for example, is only about 6 points high, the other 2 points being taken up by the shoulder.

Line of type per inch

Another problem in selecting type is to determine the amount of type that can be set in a given space. Figure 9–5 gives the number of lines

FIGURE 9–5. Lines of type per inch

Size of type	Set solid no. of lines	2-point leaded no. of lines
5-point	14	10
5½-point	13*	9*
6-point	12	9
8-point	9	7*
10-point	7*	6
12-point	6	5*
14-point	5*	4
18-point	4	3*

of various sizes of type that will set within an inch. The asterisk (*) means that the size of type does not divide evenly into 72 points (number of points per inch) and that a fraction of a line is left over.

Classes of type

For practical purposes, the various styles of type are divided into two classes: "display type" and "body type." Display type is heavier in the face than body type, and is used where emphasis is needed in an advertisement, as for example, in captions, subcaptions, prices, signatures, and addresses. Body type is used in setting those portions or units of an advertisement that do not require display, such as the body or text matter in an advertisement.

Text or body type

Type for text or body matter should have one important quality, that is, legibility. Generally, either Old Style Roman or Modern Roman will fit the requirements for text or body matter. If at any time these two faces are not available, pick a face that has their general characteristics for legibility.

Faces of type

While legibility is generally the most important single factor to be considered in choice of a typeface, other factors also should be evaluated. As an example, one of the other more important factors is color or weight. Some faces print very dark and some print very light; between these two extremes are a whole series of different degrees of lightness or darkness which can be attained by the careful selection of a typeface.

In the selection of a typeface, there are thousands from which to choose, and additional ones are being developed each year. However, there is no reason to know the names of all these, as each printer has only a limited number of typefaces, depending on the kind of equipment and facilities he might have. As an example, Lanston faces are made by the Lanston Company for use on the Lanston monotype machine. This is also true with the Ludlow machine and some of the other kinds of monotype equipment.

Some of the other major type manufacturers are: American Type Founders, Neon Type Foundry, Mergenthaler Linotype Company, Baltimore Type and Composition Company, Bauer Type Foundry, Inc., Los Angeles Type Foundry, and Intertype Corporation.

Measuring advertising space

Two units are used in measuring advertising space in publications: (1) the column inch, (2) the line. A column inch is a space one column wide and one inch deep—not a square inch. It must be borne in mind that a column is not an exact unit, because different publications have different column widths. The "line" is actually an agate line and is equivalent to a space 1/14 inch deep and 1 column wide. It is derived from the agate size of type. There are 14 agate lines to the inch. When one speaks of a 100-line advertisement, it is necessary to divide 100 by 14 in order to determine the column depth in inches. The "column inch" and the "line" are units used for measuring the depth of advertisements. Publications may use either of these two measures for quoting prices for space. The "12-point em," also called a "pica em," is sometimes used as a measurement of width, 1/6 of an inch square. When the width of a column is stated to be a certain number of ems or picas, 12-point picas usually are meant. Thus, if a column is said to be 12 ems or picas wide, the column is 2 inches wide.

ENGRAVINGS

Relief printing plates

There are two main kinds of relief printing plates: (1) line engravings or zinc etchings, and (2) halftone engravings. Line and halftone engravings are classed as photoengravings, or process engravings. Photoengraving is a process by which a design or image is transferred, by means of photography, to a metal plate by having portions of the surface etched or cut away by chemical and mechanical actions.

The general principle of making photoengravings for printing purposes is to put a design or image on a metal plate and to cut away—by hand, by machinery, or with acid—such portions of the plate as are not to appear in the finished illustration. This leaves the design standing in bold relief.

Line engravings or zinc etchings. Line engravings, often called zinc etchings, can be made by the photoengraving process from any drawing or print that consists of distinct lines, dots, or masses of solid black such as pen, crayon, or charcoal drawings. Each line, dot, or solid mass in the drawing is represented by a line, dot, or mass of exactly the same shape and relative size on the printing surface of the plate. The best copy for the zinc etching process is made with black ink on a white surface. Illustrators generally use India ink for their drawings, as it produces clear black lines even when drawn fine. Gray or shaded effects must be obtained by numerous lines or dots placed closely together, but each line or dot must be a distinct black character in itself. Strong red, dark green, or dark blue lines or dots can be reproduced. However, these colors are considered poor copy by the engraver because they are not sufficiently intense to photograph clearly.

Combination line and halftone plates. There are advertisements which, by their very nature, demand illustrations which can only be produced by combining line engravings and halftones in the same plate. As an example, it might be necessary to use several products in which it is desired to reproduce exact photographic likeness. In order to get the desired atmosphere around these photographic illustrations, it might be easier to use pen-and-ink drawings and then combine the halftone with the line engraving. These combinations also can be satisfactorily used in a variety of situations, such as in fashion drawings and ornamental decorations in which photography might be inserted for background effect.

The Ben Day process. Many mechanical methods have been devised for the purpose of reproducing shaded effects and backgrounds in extended areas of space. One of these mechanical methods is that known as the Ben Day process. Through the use of the Ben Day process, tints are transferred from a celluloid film to the surface of paper, metal, or lithographic stone. By means of this process, line spaces can be given the necessary highlights which will give the appearance of halftones. A wide variety of textures and designs may be secured with the Ben Day process.

Electrotypes. Electrotyping is a process by which type forms and engraved plates are duplicated. The original line engravings and halftones have a limited life when put on the printing press, and eventually must be replaced. To save this expense, it is often advisable to make electrotypes and use these on the printing press, saving the original engravings which are more costly. It is also desirable to have more than one engraving of an individual illustration.

In electrotyping, an impression of the type form or engraving is made in wax or other material, and on this impression the metal is deposited by an electrical process, thus making an exact reproduction of the original. Unlimited numbers of electrotypes may be made from an engraved plate without injury or wear to the original.

Plastic plates. Plastic printing plates are made from a granular plastic material. They can be made in large quantities at a relatively low cost and are not so expensive to mail as electrotypes. They are quite durable, are not easily scratched, and require less ink than metal plates.

Mortises. A mortise is a hole cut through, or a notch cut in, the edge of the plate to permit the insertion of type matter. The first type of mortise is known as an inside mortise; the notch on the edge of the plate is called an outside mortise.

When a drawn border is used to add to the effect of an advertisement, the border is usually engraved on the plate, and the part intended for the type is mortised out. In advertisements carrying coupons, the electrotype often is mortised out so that different identifying characters such as box or street numbers may be inserted.

Matrices or "mats". Matrices or "mats" as they are called, are a cardboard-like composition material on which has been impressed, under high pressure, a faithful reproduction of the original plate. The original plates and electrotypes cannot be bent without damage. They are made for "flat bed" presses. However, newspapers and other media often use rotary presses. Therefore, when rotary presses are used, the plate must be capable of being curved so that it can be fitted on the rotary press. National advertisers also find it more economical to have matrices made and sent to the newspapers instead of plates.

COLOR

The vivid reproductions that can now be secured through the use of color combinations have resulted in getting advertisers to use color more extensively in their advertising. However, the media charge a premium when color is used.

With so many advertisers using color in some publications, a black-and-white advertisement will sometimes prove to be a real contrast and may get a higher readership rating.

Selection of colors

Decide on the purpose of the design and choose the colors accordingly. Choose colors that have proper association. In choosing colors, be prepared to make some sacrifices. The combination that has the greatest legibility may not be the most pleasing (black letters on yellow have the greatest legibility).

If one desires a pleasing combination, it may be necessary to sacrifice distinct legibility (yellow and blue combinations are generally preferred).

As a single color, blue is the favorite with men and red is the favorite with women. For example, in choosing a color for advertising a refrigerator, note that while red is the favorite with women, it may have the wrong association. The ideal dominant color to use might be blue. It has the proper association and ranks second with women and first with men.

Remember that colors may look totally different under artificial illumination than when viewed in daylight. At night, dark blues and purples may appear nearly black, red and yellow may appear more yellow, and yellow will be added to greens. Use large light areas in illuminated advertisements, and remember that value difference between letters and background is of utmost importance for legibility.

As a general rule, complementary color combinations are more satisfactory to use for television and outdoor advertising. They are the most attractive combinations and are preferred by the greatest number of people.

Color process

When the four-color process is used, a separate halftone plate is made for the three primary colors—yellow, red, and blue—and also one for black. (See Figure 9–6.) In the three-color process (which is seldom used) no black halftone plate is needed, and in the two-color process work, any two colors can be used.

In making the plates which are used for the color process, a photographic method of color separation is used. The colored illustration is photographed with different filters in order to get the negative from which halftone plates are made. When these plates are printed in their respective colors and superimposed in the proper manner, the same colors in the original illustration will be reproduced.

Use of color

The use of color in all advertising media will continue to grow because:

1. The mechanical techniques in the reproduction of color in all media have improved.
2. Color provides a more accurate picture of how the product actually appears.
3. It can be used in an effective manner to get greater sales results.
4. It will attain generally higher readership ratings.

FIGURE 9-6. Reproducing the full-color illustration

There are many advantages in using four-color reproductions for advertising purposes. Among the more obvious is the ability to show the product, or person, in "living color"! But beyond this there is a further advantage in that a color illustration not only has variations in lights and darks (which do show up in a black and white) but also a variation in intensity of color which produces much more depth than can possibly be achieved in black and white.

It is possible to take a color photograph and by color correction create a negative which will give a passable print. In general, this process does lose a great deal of the sharpness of detail found in the original.

To produce the full-color illustrations as are typically used in magazines today, four plates must be made. This process is known as four-color lithography. A color print or transparency is broken down by means of a camera and halftone screen into the three primary colors, red, yellow, and blue. A new negative is produced for each of these separate colors and one for black is also made to enhance the detail.

- Panel A shows the black-and-white illustration produced by the use of a color-corrected negative.
- Panel B shows a proof of plate created from the negative made for the yellow color.

- Panel C shows how the plate carrying the red color tones will appear.
- Panel D shows the result when the yellow color plate is over-printed by the red color plate.
- Panel E shows how the plate carrying the blue tones appears when printed alone.
- Panel F shows the three primary colors combined by over-printing the blue plate on the red and yellow proof.
- Panel G shows the black plate alone.
- Panel H shows the completed four-color reproduction when the plate for black has been over-printed on the three primary colors.

Note the resulting depth of contrast, vividness and depth shown in this illustration as compared with the color-corrected black-and-white reproduction illustrated in Panel A.

In the four-color lithography process it is possible to achieve almost every conceivable color hue and value. It requires the skill of a trained camera technician and color-dot etcher, and is, therefore, considerably more expensive than black and white.

This is the process which makes possible the excellent color reproductions which we see every day in our magazines and in other advertising material.

Panel A

Panel B

Panel C

Panel D

Panel E

Panel F

Panel G

Panel H

5. The additional cost of using color is not excessive in relation to the results which can be secured.

QUESTIONS

1. Briefly describe the illustrations you visualize which might have the best impact for the following products, and give your reasons:
   a)   Cologne for men
   b)   Hearing aid
   c)   Sterling silver
   d)   Portable TV set
   e)   Safety glass for the home

2. A large paper manufacturer used the same illustration of a girl examining a new type of paper in *Life, Reader's Digest, Time, Business Week,* and *Fortune.* Evaluate this policy.

3. Indicate some of the points to keep in mind in selecting an illustration if the advertisement is to appeal primarily to teen-agers.

4. In what way will the advertising appeal and the media affect the typography that should be used in the advertisement?

5. Select advertisements from current newspapers or magazines in which the following production techniques were used:
   a)   Halftone
   b)   Line engraving
   c)   Silhouette finish
   d)   Color halftones

6. Indicate when a company should use the four-color process in its advertising.

7. In the selection of color combinations, does it make any difference whether the advertisement is pointed to men or women? Explain.

8. Select from a newspaper or a magazine advertisements in which the illustrations used appealed to the negative, obstacle, and positive aspects of the prospect's wants. Indicate whether or not some other appeals might have been more satisfactory.

9. Select three advertisements in which there are no illustrations. Give possible reasons in each case why no illustration was used, and indicate several illustrations that might have been used.

10. Continuity in a series of advertisements can be used by employing the same method of visualization in each advertisement and allowing the ideas to provide distinctiveness.

11. Explain how a person's background might affect how he would interpret an illustration used in an advertisement.

12. In the production of print and broadcast advertising what can be done to avoid the problems of which the consumers frequently complain. These include: intrusiveness, exaggeration, high-pressure selling and offensive advertising.

13. Point out what techniques might be used to get the consumers to have a positive conscious impression towards the advertisements to which they are exposed.

14. Interview a number of retailers and manufacturers in your area. Ask them to show you how they prepare their advertisements for both print and broadcast media. Also visit the advertising department of your local newspaper and ask the manager to give you the details of the production techniques used.

15. Write a brief statement of what you would tell an artist of the visualization you interpret for the following:

   a) *Automobile battery:* Where the good ideas on starting, start.
   b) *Trucking company:* We move families, not just furniture.
   c) *Home air conditioning unit:* It is so compact your neighbors won't even see how comfortable you are.
   d) *Soft drink company:* Open a bottle and springtime breaks loose.

CASE 1. ORAL B COMPANY[1]
Suggesting illustrations

The executives of the Oral B Company requested that its advertising agency prepare an advertisement which was to appear in a 1969 issue of *Reader's Digest.*

The Oral B toothbrush was placed on the market in 1949 by a young San Jose, California, dentist. Since the end of World War II, he had pondered the need for a brush which could not only clean teeth but could cleanse and stimulate an area equally important to sound dental health —the gums. What he wanted was a "mouthwash" rather than a toothbrush. Hence, the name "Oral B."

Digesting complaints about existing brushes and suggestions for improvement solicited from dentists and dental schools, he proceeded to redesign a product which had not undergone a basic change in 150 years. By mounting 2,500 (three times the usual number) flat-trimmed, medium-soft synthetic bristles on a straight handle, he produced a remarkable brush. It could reach easily into heretofore inaccessible crevices and could clean teeth more effectively. The same brush could also massage gums without injury to delicate tissues. This was a vital point in tooth care which had never before been emphasized to the public. It was this feature which established Oral B as a new standard in toothbrush design.

Initially, the young San Jose dentist had a small supply of the brushes

---

[1] Used with permission of Clark Lawrence, President, Long Advertising, Inc.

made for some of his patients and a few fellow dentists, who were enthusiastic. As a result, they began prescribing the new brush for their own patients. Requests became so numerous that it was decided to manufacture them in quantity.

Detailing by mail

The fledgling company was on the threshold of a highly competitive field, operating on a very limited budget, and the new toothbrush was just catching on with dentists. Long Advertising, Inc., was then contacted, and a modest advertising program was directed toward the dental profession. This effort included informative folders, catalog sheets, letters, a heavy detailing operation, and attendance at as many dental conventions as the time of Oral B sales representatives would permit. Using prescription pads bearing the product name, dentists began sending patients to drugstores for the new Oral B toothbrush.

Dentists force distribution

Consequently, wholesalers began to stock the product, and druggists, who normally would be reluctant to add a new product to the thousands already in stock, began to display and sell Oral B. From the start, a policy was established to win over the druggists as well as the dentists. This was done by establishing a fair-trade price which provided an ample profit on each sale. Another attractive feature was the small quantity which druggists could purchase, as contrasted with other similar products. The small compact displays took up very little room and sold rapidly, keeping inventory at a minimum. Thus, with simple methods and minimum expense, Oral B successfully moved into the toothbrush market through the side door.

Advertising starts with the dental profession

In 1950, a small advertising campaign was launched in state dental journals, and even more emphasis was placed on attendance at all major dental meetings. As sales rose sharply, exhibit booths were maintained at all major conventions. In 1967, over half a million professional samples were sent out to dental hygienists, assistants, dental students, and dentists. Scholarships and grants to dental colleges and the American Dental Association are also a part of the Oral B Company's continuing cooperation with the profession.

In 1951, the dental journal program was expanded to include national coverage, a step which combined with dental and drug detailing to bring about three results: (1) a sharp incense in sales, (2) the interest of larger wholesalers, (3) the appearance of major competition.

Since 1951, nearly all major toothbrush manufacturers have entered the market with some version of the soft-bristle brush. However, with the advantages of being first with the brush, plus marketing lead time and strong professional support, the original promotion plan was continued and intensified.

Consumer advertising initiated

Starting in 1952, consumer advertising got a modest start after a careful survey among dentists to confirm the hope that they would approve this step. Most dentists questioned were enthusiastic, and so a consumer campaign was launched. Every precaution was taken to keep the dentist and his philosophy clearly in mind while developing the consumer approach.

Although national magazines have been the backbone of the consumer program, radio, television, and newspapers also have been used effectively to achieve special marketing objectives. The policy has been to evaluate all major media annually and make changes whenever greater advertising effectiveness would result.

While the Oral B toothbrush has moved up to the number one position in California (the nation's top drug market) and the West, and joined the top three brands in drugstore sales nationally, the Oral B Company learned these valuable lessons:

1. Good distribution can be achieved without huge cost. The device in this case was seeking sales for a good product through dental prescription.
2. Ethical groups (dentists, in this case) are not so opposed to consumer advertising as is often supposed. They object mainly to misleading and fraudulent claims, but will back an educational approach placing them and their profession in a good light.
3. The low-pressure, ethical type of approach in both trade and consumer advertising can get good results, even in a highly competitive field.

Current promotion plans call for adherence to the policies which have served so well in the past. This includes effective soft sell, relying on advice of the dentist as final authority, avoiding exaggerated or otherwise questionable statements, and a strong program of dental contact through attendance at more than 70 dental conventions annually.

Suggest five illustrations to accompany the following copy A or copy B in a full-page advertisement which was to appear in an issue of *Reader's Digest*.

COPY A.   The right brush protects your gums, too!

Take the guesswork out of choosing a toothbrush and ask your dentist about Oral B. This brush does something about the fact that over 37 percent of all tooth troubles start with gum troubles.

The gentle message of 2,500 smooth-top Oral B fibers stimulates circulation to help you keep gums firm and healthy. The same flexible fibres polish teeth and clean hard-to-reach crevices.

Insist on Oral B for the entire family.

COPY B.   The 2nd best thing you can do for your teeth

First visit your dentist regularly. Second, use the best toothbrush you can buy.

Ask your dentist about Oral B. Let him explain how effectively it protects gums as well as teeth. Oral B has three times as many smooth-top flexible fibers, to massage gums gently, clean teeth thoroughly. The double action of Oral B is the best mouth care you can have between dental checkups. The Oral B habit is easy to acquire. And so pleasant! Try Oral B today!

Case questions

1. To whom should Oral B direct its appeal?

2. What should Oral B Company try to attain through its illustration?

3. Should the illustration be used to bring out special features in the tooth-brush?

4. What should Oral B emphasize in the illustration of its product?

CASE 2. CREATING ILLUSTRATIONS
Preparing descriptions

For each of the six advertisements in which the copy is given below, write a description of the kind of illustration you believe should be used to accompany the copy.

COPY A.   Cluett, Peabody & Co. Inc.

(this advertisement is to appear in *Ladies' Home Journal*)

She started slowly.

First we let her check all Daddy's shirts for the "Sanforized" label.

Then she could go to the store and do the same thing when Mommy shopped for blouses.

After a while she even bought a fitted sheet.

See, everybody in our family follows these two rules:

You can't be sure the fabric won't shrink unless you see "Sanforized." You can't be sure of top wash and wear performance unless you see "Sanforized-Plus."

But I think Melissa's going to be the best shopper of us all.

Last week she was looking for some new blue jeans.

And the salesgirl said, "Well, they aren't actually labeled 'Sanforized.' "

Melissa bit her.

"WE'RE RAISING MELISSA TO BE SUSPICIOUS!"

COPY B.   Polaroid Color Pack Camera

(this advertisement is to appear in *Life* magazine)

You can get color prints like this in 60 seconds with a Polaroid Color Pack Camera. Is there any other way to take pictures? Prices start at under $60.

COPY C.   Manpower

(this advertisement is to appear in *Time* magazine)

Ready vacation replacement
skilled, experienced, specially trained office help
Call for the GIRL IN THE WHITE GLOVES from MANPOWER
The very best in temporary help

COPY D.   Mutual Benefit Life

(this advertisement is to appear in *Business Week*)

THE 7-MINUTE INTERVIEW:

The limit our agent will stay unless you ask him to stay longer.

We invented the 7-minute interview to give you a chance to size up our man.

In that seven minutes, a Mutual Benefit agent can outline the work he's prepared to do for you.

In seven minutes, he's not about to solve your problems, though he may very well spark a couple of ideas to save you money. The important thing is you'll have a chance to see for yourself that he knows his stuff and to find out whether he's the kind of man you find it easy to talk to.

If you want, invite him to stay. Otherwise he'll be on his way at the end of seven minutes. If you're too busy to see anyone right now, write for our free booklet, "What you can expect a Mutual Benefit agent to do for you."

COPY E.   Kodak

(this advertisement is to appear in *Seventeen*)

NO KNOW-HOW NEEDED:

Since Kodak introduced "super 8" there are no mysteries left in movie-making. No good reason why you shouldn't be shooting and proudly showing your own movies. The KODAK INSTAMATIC M8 Movie Camera loads instantly with the super 8 film cartridge. No midpoint flip-over. No edge fogging or doubling exposure. No winding, either —this camera is battery driven. The CdS electric eye operates through the lens for precise exposure accuracy.

The M8 even adds a few frills (and thrills): choice of four shooting speeds—from fast to slow motion—for special effects. 5 to 1 power zoom lens—goes from extreme wide-angle to telephoto close-ups at the touch of a button. Or zoom manually, if you wish. Reflex viewing through the lens lets you see exactly what you'll get on the film.

The superb M8 camera is less than $225. See it and the complete line of super 8 KODAK INSTAMATIC MOVIE PROJECTORS at your Kodak dealer's.

COPY F.   Dictaphone

(this advertisement is to appear in *The Wall Street Journal*)

ARE YOU A DICTATING DROPOUT? (Maybe you met the wrong machine. We make two right ones.)

If you're one of the people who tried a dictating machine once and found it too complicated, it's time you tried the Dictaphone Time-Masters. You'll notice we use the plural because we're the only people who make both a visible belt machine and a magnetic belt machine.

Two kinds. One is faster.

The Dictaphone Time-Master with the visible Dictabelt is the fastest recording device you can use, because you don't have to back up to correct mistakes. Touch a button on the mike to indicate an error or change, then give your correction. When your secretary sees the mark, she listens ahead for your correction.

Right your own wrongs.

Dictaphone's magnetic Dictabelt system lets you back up and correct your own errors. You give the word and the error is automatically erased. And Dictaphone's new automatic place finder, "Forward Memory" (a tiny arrow just below the Dictabelt) indicates precisely where you stopped dictating, so you can quickly get going again. Your girl will never know that you're not perfect.

You don't need an engineering degree

You can be all thumbs. The Dictaphone Time-Master controls are under one of them. All the working controls are on the mike. You can work them without looking. And both of our machines use a simple belt. You slip it on without wrestling the machine.

The lightweight heavyweight.

You could call the Time-Master a "desk top portable." It's light enough to take home with you at night. Fits in your attaché case. Now that you know a good many of the facts about modern dictating, try it again. Try BOTH Time-Masters. One of them is made for you.

The name that started the whole business: DICTAPHONE.

PART IV

Media mix

chapter 10

MEDIA SELECTION PRINCIPLES

$\mathbf{A}$FTER the advertising strategy has been determined, and the advertising copy and layout have been selected, the advertiser faces the important problem of bringing his message, or advertisement, to the attention of the proper prospects. It is apparent that the finest advertisements can be of no value to the advertiser unless they are seen and read, or heard, by the potential buyers or users of the advertiser's product, service, or idea. If enough money were available, one approach would be to place advertisements "everywhere" and present them to everyone who might be a prospect, so that no matter where a potential prospect turned he would be exposed to the firm's advertising message. However, the amount of money that can be spent for advertising is limited, so this suggestion is not economically feasible. Hence, it is important that the advertising be placed where it will reach the largest number of real prospects and influence them most effectively at the minimum cost. This task of deciding on the proper placing of the advertisement is called the selection of media.

Definition

An advertising medium is the means or conveyance by which the sales message is carried to prospective customers. A newspaper is a medium, as are magazines, streetcar cards, poster boards, matchboxes, television, radio, and the like.

Generally, no one medium will suffice in reaching all potential customers and, as a result, it may be necessary to use a combination of several media in an advertising campaign.

TYPES OF MEDIA

The major types of advertising media can be divided into the 12 principal classes listed below:

1. Newspapers
   a) Metropolitan
      Daily
         Morning
         Evening
      Sunday
   b) Rural
2. Magazines
   a) Consumer
      (1) General
      (2) General with specialized interest
      (3) Women's magazines
      (4) Home and shelter magazines
   b) Industrial and trade
   c) Service and professional journals
   d) Technical journals
   e) Farm publications
3. Television
   a) Network
   b) National spot
   c) Local
4. Radio
   a) Network
   b) National spot
   c) Local
5. Direct mail
6. Outdoor advertising
   a) Billboards
   b) Signs
7. Transit advertising
8. Motion pictures
9. Point-of-purchase displays
10. Novelties
11. Containers
12. Miscellaneous (programs, directories, timetables, house organs, annuals, menu cards, registers, etc.)

ADVERTISING EXPENDITURES IN MAJOR CLASSES OF MEDIA

Some idea of the overall significance of the various classes of media can be gained from the allocations of total advertising expenditures as shown in Figure 10–1. In 1970 the advertising volume was $20.8 billion,

FIGURE 10–1

ADVERTISING REVENUES BY MEDIUM

| | | | | | | ADVERTISING REVENUES BY MEDIUM | | | | ALLOCATIONS | OTHER | |
Year	Total	Newspapers	Magazines	Business Publications	Farm Publications	Television	Radio	Direct Mail	Outdoor	Point of Purchase Displays	Agency Income	Other Expenditures
1947	4,241	1,192	434	150	41	2	365	566	113	187	265	926
1948	4,907	1,410	482	163	42	9	408	671	115	194	309	1,104
1949	5,331	1,503	463	162	43	34	415	724	115	199	338	1,335
1950	5,864	1,641	481	164	42	106	444	739	132	202	373	1,530
1951	6,497	1,747	545	182	44	236	450	833	137	235	414	1,674
1952	7,161	1,879	592	210	46	324	470	907	145	262	459	1,867
1953	7,784	2,002	650	220	48	432	476	1,003	158	290	501	2,004
1954	8,080	2,059	646	228	48	593	449	1,040	172	288	520	2,037
1955	8,997	2,320	668	250	50	745	453	1,229	176	311	597	2,198
1956	9,674	2,476	680	275	53	897	480	1,308	189	345	675	2,296
1957	10,313	2,510	695	319	56	943	517	1,324	201	318	737	2,693
1958	10,414	2,459	652	302	55	1,030	523	1,419	219	344	757	2,654
1959	11,358	2,705	718	354	58	1,164	560	1,597	223	362	815	2,802
1960	11,900	2,821	769	383	55	1,269	598	1,658	242	387	859	2,859
1961	12,048	2,818	774	384	53	1,318	591	1,687	232	405	870	2,916
1962	12,919	2,930	797	378	50	1,486	636	1,758	230	416	955	3,283
1963	13,639	3,087	832	413	47	1,597	681	1,760	229	490	1,005	3,498
1964	14,824	3,411	873	451	47	1,793	732	1,890	241	554	1,085	3,747
1965	16,175	3,658	924	475	47	1,965	793	2,057	251	574	1,194	4,237
1966R	17,511	4,130	997	528	47	2,203	872	2,277	270	597	1,293	4,297
1967R	18,004	4,175	990	545	46	2,273	907	2,323	279	666	1,317	4,483
1968R	19,054	4,446	1,020	560	46	2,521	1,023	2,434	310	706	1,441	4,547
1969R	20,507	4,858	1,063	609	42	2,796	1,086	2,488	325	777	1,575	4,888
1970P	20,838	4,936	1,019	579	42	2,853	1,128	2,548	362	839	1,597	4,935

RRevised   PPreliminary

Source: *Advertising Age*, June 7, 1971, p. 28.

approximately $330 million above the 1969 level. This 1.6 percent increase was the smallest since 1961.[1]

The small gain for 1970 was unevenly distributed among the media, as noted in the following paragraphs.

Newspapers. Expenditures in 1970 were estimated to have increased 1.6 percent over 1969, in line with the average for all media.

Magazines. Magazine revenue declined by 4.2 percent.

Business publications. This medium had the greatest decline relatively, dropping 5 percent below 1969.

Farm publications. The preliminary 1970 estimate for this category was 0.5 percent above 1969.

Television. The medium had a small increase. Network increased about 2.1 percent; national spot, less than 1 percent; and local spot was up over 5 percent, yielding an overall increase of 2 percent for the medium.

Radio. Network radio was down slightly in 1970, although national spot and local spot registered a slight gain. The overall increase for the medium was 3.9 percent.

Direct mail. The medium recorded another good year in 1970, with an increase of 2.4 percent over 1969.

Outdoor. This medium had the best percentage increase for 1970, with an increase of 11.5 percent.

Point-of-purchase. Preliminary point-of-purchase data indicate that this medium scored an increase of 8 percent over the 1969 figure.

SELECTION OF MEDIA

The problem of selection of the best medium or media for a particular advertiser will vary greatly, depending on the particular situation and circumstances in which he is conducting his individual business. A small manufacturer of an industrial product that is a component or fabricated part of one particular industry in a field with only one trade publication would have a relatively simple media selection problem. He would use the trade publication going to the people in that particular industry, and his problem would be to decide on the size and frequency of his insertions. In addition, he might use direct-mail advertising.

In contrast, the large manufacturer of a nationally distributed consumer product that is widely used by many types and classes of people faces a complex problem in selecting media. He could conceivably reach his market through any one of the major mass media—television, radio, newspapers, magazines, and outdoor advertising. And even after he de-

---

[1] Source: *Advertising Age,* June 7, 1971, p. 27.

termines the basic type of media to use, he has a problem of selecting the specific class of individual publication or station within the type. For instance, should he decide that magazines are his best medium, he must decide whether to use general magazines, general magazines with special interest, women's magazines, or home and shelter magazines. And if he decides to use home and shelter magazines, he must decide whether to use *Sunset, Better Homes and Gardens, House Beautiful, Ladies Home Journal, Good Housekeeping, American Home,* or *Home & Garden.*

It should be apparent from the above discussion that there is no simple formula or rule for solving the problem of the selection of media. Each advertiser faces a unique situation with respect to his particular market and marketing program. Each type of medium possesses certain characteristics, advantages, and weaknesses from the individual advertiser's standpoint. Hence, in general, it can be said there is no medium that is the best for all similar firms. The individual advertiser must determine on the basis of his specific needs in a given situation which medium or media are best for him.

FACTORS INFLUENCING SELECTION OF MEDIA

A number of factors influence the decision of the advertiser and must be considered in the selection of media. The most significant of these factors are: (1) the product; (2) the potential market; (3) the extent and type of distribution; (4) the objectives of the campaign; (5) the type of message or selling appeal; (6) the budget available; (7) competitive advertising; (8) the character of the media (a) circulation or coverage, (b) the audience reached, (c) relative cost, and (d) miscellaneous factors. These factors will be discussed individually in the following pages, but it should be kept in mind that in many cases it is the combination of these factors that determines the selection of media, and not any one individual factor taken by itself.

The product

The characteristics of the product exert an important influence on the decisions involving which media shall carry the advertising message. Certain consumer products of an intimate nature may find it difficult to employ certain of the mass media without encountering the danger of antagonizing large portions of the public, including those who are potential customers. Certain individual media will not take advertising for certain specific classes of products. For example, some family-type magazines do not carry liquor advertising. Restrictions may also prohibit use of certain media by advertisers of specific items.

The general character of the product also may strongly influence the type of media used. That is, if the product has a certain personality or image, certain media may be appropriate to maintain or develop that image; whereas other media may tend to diminish or distort this personality or image.

Similarly, product personality would influence very strongly the decision as to the class of broadcast program or magazine selected to carry the advertisement.

The potential market

The characteristics of the potential market are of primary importance in influencing the selection of media. Since the principal object in selecting media is to find a vehicle that will carry the advertiser's message to the potential buyer most economically and effectively, it is quite apparent that this statement is true. It is evident that one of the first aspects of the selection of media is the proper identification of the potential users of the product or service, or in other words, the market. The marketing research studies conducted by the advertiser should have collected data regarding the nature of the market and a profile of potential users. And considerable data is available on the audiences reached by the various types of media and by the individual media within these types. However, it will be found that it is usually quite difficult in practice to match closely the market the advertiser's research has delineated, and the audience reached by any of the media, particularly in the case of mass media.

If the advertiser's product is one which goes to a limited and easily identified segment of the market, the problem of media selection may not be too complex. For instance, if the product is one sold only to poultry raisers, or to yachting enthusiasts, or to superintendents of hospitals, there will be one or only a limited number of magazines reaching the bulk of members of these groups, and the magazines normally are subscribed to only by prospects.

However, for most products, the market is not so easily identified and is not such a specific segment; and the media reaching prospects also reach many somewhat similar people who do not fit closely the profile of the advertiser's market. Most mass media reach a rather diversified group of consumers and, hence, involve a considerable amount of waste circulation for any particular advertiser. The individual media do, of course, reach somewhat different groups of consumers. In the case of newspapers, the audience will vary with the editorial and news policy of the paper. Although television and radio for the most part are also mass media and reach a broad spectrum of consumers, the individual stations in some instances do vary in the audience they attract. The general character of the programs presented by the station is a determinant of the type of audience it attracts. Some radio stations emphasize symphonic and classical music, high-quality plays, and educational programs; some feature popular music; some stress news; others will strive to cover a wide range of popular programs. Each may attempt to attract a somewhat different audience, and often will conduct studies of the character of its audience in order to provide the advertiser with the information to match against a profile of his potential customers.

Some magazines are also more selective in the audiences they reach. The trade and professional journals reach rather specific and specialized audiences. There are consumer magazines that go to groups interested in specific hobbies or sports or other special interest groups. Others appeal especially to women, to homeowners, to youth, to specific racial groups, or to certain religious groups.

Outdoor advertising is basically selective from the standpoint of geographic location only, although the specific location of posters within a city may enable some selectivity with respect to income groups.

In summary, it is evident that since the advertiser wishes to reach his prospective customers most efficiently, his problem is to identify them as accurately as possible in order to select a medium that will carry an effective message to them most economically.

Extent and type of distribution system

Another factor that must be considered in the selection of media is the extent and the type of distribution the advertiser has for his product. Generally speaking, there is no point in advertising a product to consumers and creating a desire to buy the product if it is not possible for the interested consumer to find the product in the outlets where he normally shops. There is little point in the advertiser's using national media if he does not have national distribution. Hence, an advertiser with regional distribution will generally not use national network radio or television. However, in some areas, regional networks are available. He may be able, in a number of magazines, to buy the regional editions if the regional edition coverage conforms quite closely to his distribution pattern. Generally, an advertiser with regional distribution will use various combinations of local media, such as newspapers, spot radio and television, outdoor, and car cards. The same is true for an advertiser who has national distribution, but whose distribution varies widely in intensity. He may find it better to use local media so that he can exert more intensive advertising effort in those areas with the best distribution coverage.

Even on a local basis, the distribution pattern may influence media selection. An advertiser with good outlet coverage within a large city may have rather weak distribution in the suburbs and surrounding area, and find that some of the local media such as particular radio and television stations have a large share of their audience in the outlying suburbs. In this case, the advertiser might decide that the purchase of time on these stations would involve too much waste circulation to make them effective media from a cost standpoint.

The objectives of the campaign

This factor, the objectives of the campaign, is in some respects quite closely related to the preceding factor. For, in those cases when the advertiser uses a medium to advertise to consumers in an area where retail distribution is not adequate, so that he can use the effect of the advertising to obtain distribution, his decision on media selection is influenced both by his distribution pattern and the objectives he has in mind. His decision on media is influenced by what he hopes to achieve with this particular campaign of advertising. Where the objective of the advertising campaign is primarily to influence consumers, the factor of the potential market is of primary importance. In those cases where the objective is to gain distribution in an area where distribution is weak or where the advertiser now has no distribution, the advertiser must consider the media which will be of maximum value in achieving the dual purpose of influencing the consumer and the potential dealers. In some instances, advertisers have used costly television spectaculars because of the impact on dealers, realizing that, although the program will obtain a fairly good consumer audience, it is not the most efficient medium for reaching the potential customers. Also, in some cases an advertiser may use a specific medium solely for its impact and effect on dealers. In the case of products for which the dealer is very important in the ultimate sale to the consumer, and far more significant than the influence of consumer advertising, the advertiser may select media primarily for the effect they will have on dealers and their support of his product. In this instance, the objective of influencing dealers will be the prime factor in the selection of the medium to use.

The objectives of the campaign also influence media selection from a somewhat different standpoint. An institutional advertising campaign may be run in different media than would a product advertising campaign for the same company. Some large companies sponsor high-quality television programs to carry primarily institutional messages, whereas they do not use this medium for their regular product advertising. A firm carrying on what Neil H. Borden classifies as public service institutional advertising might well use a general interest magazine to carry such an advertisement, although it would not find such magazines a good medium for its product advertising.

In a similar vein, firms sometimes wish to create a better climate or market for their securities, and run advertisements in media reaching security analysts, brokers, bankers, and other financial people who are of influence in this field, although such media do not reach the potential buyers of their product.

Also, if the objective of the advertising is to create a certain image of the product in the minds of consumers, the media selected should have the status or personality to help develop and sustain that product image. Certain magazines are prestige magazines, and products may gain some reflected prestige by appearing in their advertisements. Similarly, certain television programs are prestige or "highbrow" in nature and, therefore, would tend to increase the effectiveness of advertisements designed to enhance the image of the product.

These illustrations should suffice to indicate that the specific objective of an advertising campaign will be of great influence in the selection of the media to carry the particular message.

The type of message or selling appeal

The type of message or appeal believed most effective in selling the product or service will, in many cases, dictate the type of media used to carry the advertising campaign. For example, if it is believed that fine color illustrations are significant in the effectiveness of product advertising, then magazines are the first choice as a print medium, since their quality of color reproduction is generally superior to that in newspapers. If the feeling of timeliness and newsworthiness is an integral aspect of the appeal, newspapers, radio, and television are particularly appropriate media. For this reason, they are often used in advertising the introduction of a new product, a new model of a product, or a special promotional offer. If demonstration of the product in use is of particular value, television is the especially appropriate medium. If the product is one requiring a rather detailed explanation or long directions, print media have the advantage over broadcast media. If the product sells to a mass market and is so well known that the main objective of the advertising is to keep the name and package before many people, outdoor advertising would be an appropriate medium, with its advantages of large size and excellent color reproduction. Should the strategy of the appeal involve the desire to inspire confidence in the product and its quality, the advertiser might well select those magazines that have developed a high dgree of reader confidence in the accuracy of their editorial content, such as *Sunset* and *Good Housekeeping* (which also has its respected Seal of Approval).

The budget available

Another factor that must be considered in planning the selection of media is the amount of funds available for advertising. For instance, a product might be one for which actual demonstration would be highly desirable, as would the prestige of a quality network television program at a prime evening hour, but yet the advertiser would be unable to sponsor (or even cosponsor) such a program because its cost exceeded his total advertising budget. Or the advertiser might believe it most desirable to use four-color, full-page advertisement in *Life* or *Reader's Digest*, not only to reach desirable prospects, but also to influence the trade, yet finds that his budget does not permit the use of these magazines. In the last case, his budget might be sufficient to enable him to buy, say, one four-color page ad in *Life*, but he might feel that this would be of insufficient impact to accomplish his purpose, and that he could not afford the minimum effective schedule of advertisements. Thus, the advertiser must turn to a medium in which he can get sufficient participation or a sufficient schedule of insertions to achieve an effective program.

Competitive advertising

The pattern of competitive advertising in the various media is frequently a factor that should be considered in planning the media strategy. By analyzing the expenditure pattern of competitors in the various media, the advertiser can determine the relative evaluation of the different media by these competitors. Advertisers normally will place considerable weight on the fact that successful competitors place the bulk of their advertising in particular media. It is assumed they have done so on some sound bases, not only of evaluation of the product and the market, and other pertinent factors, but also of successful experience over time with these media.

Hence, unless there are good reasons to select other media, many advertisers normally will follow the industry pattern. In some cases, however, the advertiser may decide it is advisable to depart from the industry pattern. One of these cases often occurs when the advertiser's budget is so much smaller than that of the competition that he feels his advertising would be overwhelmed in those media being used by competitors. In this case, the advertiser should carefully analyze the possibilities of using alternative media that would reach his audience and in which his smaller expenditures might give him a dominant position for his product line. For example, the advertiser might, on the basis of other factors, have decided that magazines would be the preferred medium, but evaluation of competitors' advertising showed they all placed the bulk of their advertising in these same magazines and took a heavy schedule of dominating space. The advertiser might decide that his infrequent small-space advertisements would exert little impact. As an alternative, he might use outdoor and transportation advertising for his advertising program. However, the advertiser should be certain that the alternative media he selects do provide a satisfactory means of reaching his audience with an effective message.

The characteristics of the media

The preceding sections have discussed those factors involved in media selection that are of a rather broad marketing nature and involve the general strategy of media selection. In the following several sections, the discussion will consider factors that bear more specifically on the nature of the media themselves.

Circulation or coverage

The advertiser must consider the circulation or coverage of the media being considered in his media strategy. In the case of magazines and newspapers, this is a very clearly defined concept—the number of copies of the publication that are delivered to people, either to regular subscribers (usually by mail in the case of magazines, and by delivery boys in the case of newspapers) or by newsstand or street sales. Or in the case of some trade magazines of the controlled circulation type, the circulation is the number delivered to their lists of recipients. The advertiser is interested not only in how many copies are distributed but also in how closely this distribution fits the pattern of his distribution geographically, and how closely the type of people receiving it fit the profile of his buyers and potential buyers.

Reliable data on the circulation of most magazines and newspapers is provided by the Audit Bureau of Circulations (ABC). For the controlled circulation trade magazines, data is provided by the Business Publications Audit of Circulations, Inc. (BPA). In the case of broadcast media, the above concept of circulation is not considered applicable. (The usual basis of considering coverage of broadcast media is the audience, which will be discussed in the following sections).

One concept used today is that of the number of radio or television sets owned. One aspect of sets owned is in terms of the number or percentage of homes having at least one set in the home, while another aspect of sets owned is from the standpoint of the total number of sets owned by consumers in the geographic area being considered. In most areas of the United States at present, virtually all homes own at least one radio and one television set. As a result, the most significant factor is the multiple ownership figure.

Currently, the average radio ownership in the United States is more than three sets per home and approximately one and one-half television sets per home. This multiple ownership is particularly significant in the case of radio. With this great number of radios, 230 million in households and 91 million in automobiles and public places, the listening habits of Americans have changed. Instead of the family listening to the radio set in the home, as is still largely true in the case of television, each member of the family listens to his or her own set. This is particularly true in the summertime, when car radios and portable sets are used most extensively because of the pattern of living occurring during that season.

The audience reached

A factor that has become more significant in recent years is the number of people actually reached by a medium. More consideration is being given to the concept that the most significant aspect of coverage from the advertiser's viewpoint is in terms of the total audience potential, indicated not by the number of copies of a print medium circulated or number of radio or television sets owned, but by the total number of readers of the print medium or total number of sets tuned in, in the case of radio and television.

With regard to print media, this total audience potential is measured by the circulation of the medium multiplied by the average number of readers per copy. This factor has been stressed particularly by the magazines, many of which have conducted comprehensive studies to determine the total readership of their publications, both by those within the home receiving the copy and the pass-along readership by people outside the subscriber's or purchaser's home. This total readership figure in some cases varies appreciably even for magazines with comparable circulation. One other additional value of these readership studies conducted by or for the magazines has been the information they have provided on the characteristics of the readers of the magazines.

These data can be of great value in ascertaining how closely the readership characteristics parallel the profile of the advertiser's potential buyers. In the case of the broadcast media, the audience concept is normally expressed in terms of total number of sets tuned in to the particular station or program. Normally, this measurement is done with reference to a particular program, a portion of a program, or a time period, rather than a general one for a station or network as a whole. Here again in evaluating particular programs or time periods, the advertiser should not be dominated by the total audience rating alone, but should, to the extent possible, also consider the characteristics of the audience being reached. For example, an advertiser whose potential market was of a certain sophisticated nature, might well consider a program with a rating of 12 featuring a symphony orchestra superior, for his purpose, to a western program with a rating of 20.

It must be kept in mind in considering this factor that the audience of the different types of media cannot be compared directly because of the differences in the kind of advertising message reaching the consumer and the somewhat different terms in which audience is measured. The potential customer views (or watches and/or listens to) television, listens to radio, reads magazines and newspapers, and sees and reads outdoor and car-card advertisements. Hence, they are receiving different forms of communication in somewhat different circumstances. In most magazine readership studies, anyone who has read one item in a given issue is defined as a "reader" in measuring the total audience, which in a sense implies he has been exposed to all the items in a magazine. In the broadcast media, the audience is the number of sets turned on at a particular time. In the case of outdoor advertising, the audience is defined in terms of the people who pass the location of the billboard during a period of time from a direction enabling them to see the advertisement; and in car-card advertising, the number of passengers who rode in the vehicle during a given period of time. Thus, it is obvious that the audiences for different types of media are not directly comparable.

It should also be noted that the advertiser must use extreme care in using audience studies even when using data concerning only one type of medium. This is true because various studies measuring the total audiences of magazines may use different techniques and definitions of what constitutes a reader, and different studies of radio listening and television viewing use different techniques for measuring the audience of a particular program or station. Hence, the person evaluating media must be aware of these differences in the data being used.

Relative cost

The relative cost is another factor which influences the selection of media. As noted earlier, the total budget available and the ability to do an effective job of advertising with that budget in a particular type of medium is significant. When the type of media has been determined, then the cost factor becomes a matter of the relative cost of the individual media. In the case of newspapers, this relationship is determined by the use of the milline rate, and in the case of magazines, the cost per page per thousand.[2]

In the case of radio and television, when data are available, the comparison can be made on the basis of the cost per commercial minute per thousand listeners or viewers. However, it should be stressed that relative cost is only one factor to consider, and that usually many other factors will be more significant than this matter of relative cost. But in those cases where several media appear approximately equal on the basis of all other criteria used, then the advertiser probably would select the medium which is most economical on the cost comparison basis.

Miscellaneous factors

Several other factors sometimes enter into the selection of media, but are not of general enough significance to warrant lengthy discussion,

---

[2] Explained in more detail in the chapter on newspapers and magazines.

although they may be of great importance in individual situations. For instance, in some cases the interest and confidence the readers have in a publication can be of real importance to the advertiser. This may be particularly true in the case of some trade papers, when no readership studies are available and where the quality of the editorial material may influence the attentiveness and care with which the editorial material and the advertisements in the magazines are read, and the influence they may have on the readers. The editorial content should be studied carefully to see if it provides a good atmosphere for the advertiser's particular product and advertisement.

The advertiser must also check on the availability of the time he desires, in the case of radio and television. In network television, for instance, there are only so many prime hours of broadcasting time. If the particular time or program the advertiser desires is not available, he obviously is precluded from using that medium in that manner. The same might be true in the case of spot commercials at certain times of the day.

When considering magazines, the advertiser might well check on the mechanical requirements, including such items as the use of color, the availability of bleed pages, the closing date for the advertisement to be in the hands of the publisher, the ability to handle inserts, the possibility of securing certain preferred positions in the publicaton, and the amount of premium charged for such preferred positions.

In some cases, the advertiser may also be influenced in selecting media by the amount of merchandising aid and assistance the media will provide for the advertiser in working with the trade in the area involved.

Responsibility for selection of media

A brief note regarding the question of who assumes the responsibility for the selection of media may well be in order at this point. The overall decisions for the general types of media are the responsibility of the top management people responsible for planning the marketing and advertising strategy and program of the advertiser. Since the question of the media to be used is so significantly influenced by the decisions on other aspects of the total marketing program, in terms of the objectives established, the funds provided, and others, the decision must be made by management people at this stage of the planning. The marketing and advertising executives should, of course, avail themselves of all the specialized knowledge the media people in the advertising agency possess, regarding the qualities, coverage, costs, etc., of the various media in arriving at their decisions as to the basic pattern of the media to be used.

Once the basic decisions as to types of media to be used have been made by management, the detailed decisions concerning which particular stations, programs, magazines, or newspapers should be made by the technically competent people in the media department of the agency or company, if the advertising is handled entirely by the company itself.

Use of computers in selecting media

In the last few years, several of the large national advertising agencies have been devoting a great deal of effort and considerable sums of money to the development of a more scientific approach to the selection of media. Much of this effort has been directed to the development of mathematical models that will be applicable in making decisions regarding media, along the same general lines that models are being developed in many areas of business activity to aid in the decision-making process. Once the model has been developed, the use of high-speed computers enables the mass of relevant data to be processed, thus obtaining the media and media schedules that best fit the criteria laid down by the media people.

Several different approaches have been used in these programs. In at least one case, the system is primarily the adaptation of linear programming to media scheduling. Other organizations have developed somewhat different systems and programs. The general concept is to develop a model which includes all possible pertinent data relative to the media selection decision. Among the data incorporated in the model are all available information on the media themselves (such as rates, audience size and composition, duplication and accumulation among media), data on consumers and their buying habits (such as demographic data on consumers, purchase rates, brand share figures, any data available on probable consumer rates of brand switching), and any data on the effectiveness of advertising in influencing the consumer (such as effect of repetition or number of exposures, size of advertisements, and probability of switching brands).

A general decision system is also developed. The data and decision system are the inputs for the computer. The computer will then select the media or media schedule that would give the optimum results for a given expenditure of funds.

To date, limited information is available on the various applications of media models and computer use to media selection. The firms using such an approach apparently are pleased with the results to date, although granting that much data on consumers, their buying habits, and reactions to varying types, amounts, and frequencies of advertising are still lacking. In the present state of the use of models and computers, it should be noted that the computer merely processes the data and the decision system that the operator feeds into it, albeit much faster than could be done by humans (and in some cases the bulk of work is so great it probably could never be done except with the use of computers). The media people must still tell the computer how to do its work and make its selection. However, this quantitative approach to media selection and scheduling holds much promise, and will quite probably become a much more significant factor in the whole area of media selection in the years ahead.

SUMMARY

In the selection of media, the following questions are among the more important ones which the advertiser should consider:

1. Does the medium reach the right audience?
2. Is the environment of the medium one that will produce interest and confidence in the products which are advertised?
3. What is the image of the medium in the minds of the prospects?
4. What is the purchasing behavior of the media audience?
5. What type of exposure can the advertiser hope to secure in the media?
6. How many people does it reach?
7. What is the accumulation of audience members by successive programs or issues of the printed publication?
8. How much duplication is there among the different media?
9. What will be the cost of reaching prospects in the different media?
10. What merchandising services are provided by the media?
11. How is the distribution of the product correlated to the circulation of the media?
12. What data are available to judge the media?
13. Will the budget of the advertiser justify the use of the media?

Since media charges generally represent the largest expenditure in the advertising budget, and the success of a campaign rides on sound media choices, advertisers increasingly are concerned with objective methods of evaluating media in their selection.

QUESTIONS

1. Would you agree with the authors' statement, "There is no simple formula or rule for the selection of media."? Why?

2. State in general terms the objective desired in the selection of media for an advertising campaign.

3. What is the significance of the changes that have taken place in advertising expenditures in the various media since 1962 as noted in Figure 10–1?

4. Give an example of a product being advertised in a particular magazine because of the nature of the product and the appeal used.

5. Give examples of advertisers using certain media because of the characteristics of the potential market.

6. Discuss the influence of the advertising budget on the selection of media.

7. How might the amount of competitive advertising influence your selection of media? Give examples.

8. Why do advertisers distinguish between the "circulation" of a medium and its "audience"? Under what circumstances do you think this distinction is important? Give examples.

9. Is it possible to compare one medium with another on the basis of cost? Explain.

10. What influence has the widespread use of computers had on media strategy?

11. If you were selling space for *Reader's Digest,* what data would you want before contacting a space buyer for a food account? For an automobile account?

12. An FM radio station in a metropolitan area, a "good music" station, stresses in its advertising that, although its audience is rather small, it is highly selective. It says most of its listeners are in the upper income brackets, and are two-car families, and hence its advertising cost per prospect is low. If you were the Cadillac distributor in that city, would this station be a more effective medium than the television station that reached almost everybody in the city? Why?

13. A salesman for space in *Playboy* magazine tells you that more women read his magazine than read either *Glamour* or *Vogue.* Assuming he is correct, would you, as advertising manager for a manufacturer of expensive, fashionable women's apparel, switch your advertising from *Glamour* and *Vogue* to *Playboy?* Why or why not?

14. A salesman for magazine space tells you, "Many people recall the magazine advertising campaigns for Volkswagen and Avis Rent-a-Car, but do they recall any television campaigns as well? No! This is because print advertising is more effective and is remembered longer than broadcast advertising." Do you think this is true? Discuss.

CASE 1. PHILLIPS-VAN HUESEN CORPORATION
Developing media factors

The Phillips-Van Heusen Corporation, having marked its centennial year in 1959, has had an interesting history. In addition, it has been responsible for many of the innovations in the men's furnishings industry.

Phillips-Van Heusen came into existence as a result of the merger of two companies: D. Jones and Sons, founded in 1859 (who operated a chain of factories in Lebanon County, Pennsylvania), and M. Phillips and Sons, founded around 1887 (who at first operated a small plant located at the corner of Center and Norwegian Streets in Pottsville, Pennsylvania). In 1907, D. Jones and M. Phillips joined forces, and the new firm became known as Phillips-Jones Corporation. In July, 1957, this name was changed to its present one, the Phillips-Van Heusen Corporation.

To understand the development and growth of Phillips-Van Heusen requires some knowledge and background of the evolution of men's shirts during the first half of the 20th century.

Around 1840, or just prior to the Civil War, the era of the starched collar, front, and cuff gave rise to the dickey bosom. The dickey bosom, with separate detachable cuffs, was an innovation in itself. Even the well-dressed gentlemen of that era, with a good supply of these separate bosoms and cuffs, had need for only a very few shirts. A further innovation was to have the necktie or bow tie sewn right in as part of the dickey bosom, so that the whole neck ensemble was of one piece. By 1850, this style of dress had all but vanished. However, its influence has persisted right up to the present day, and a shirt with a bosom and cuffs of a different color from the body is still sold as an item of high-fashion men's wear.

By around 1890, the collar attached shirt began its rise in popularity. At first, its use was restricted to what would now be called a work shirt for use in factories and mills. As this era progressed, a man wore either a work shirt with an attached collar or a neckband type shirt which required a separate white stiff collar. Usually the neckband shirt was colored, striped, or some fancy type of patterned design. All-white shirts did not become popular until after the first World War, when fine broadcloth fabric began to be imported from England. Following the armistice in 1919, almost five million men who had the experience of wearing collar-attached military shirts were mustered out of the armed forces. The old-fashioned neckband shirt was definitely on the wane in popularity. As with other changes in popular taste, many old established companies refused to see this oncoming trend and suffered accordingly. One of the exceptions was Phillips-Van Heusen, the first major brand house to make and feature collar-attached dress shirts.

The year 1920 was a historic one for the Phillips-Van Heusen Corporation as well as for the menswear field as a whole, for it was then that Phillips-Van Heusen brought out the Van Heusen collar and, as *Time* magazine stated recently, "revolutionized the entire dress shirt industry." The product was named for its inventor, John M. Van Heusen, who discovered and perfected a method for weaving cloth on curve and applied this discovery to the manufacture of men's collars. By the use of this curvilinear cloth, he was able to achieve a graceful fold line, avoiding the unsightly gaps that occur when a straight piece of cloth is forced into a curve. In addition to this curving process, Van Heusen also perfected a method whereby a man's collar could be woven entirely in one piece, whereas normally, men's collars ar manufactured from three separate pieces of cloth—a top and bottom piece of fabric with a liner between them. Thus was born the Van Heusen Century, the soft collar that "won't wrinkle ever."

Those men who still desired a neckband type shirt could wear a collar with the *look* of the old stiff formal collar, but which had all the *comfort* of a soft collar. Thus, 40 years ago, the Van Heusen brand name came into existence. It was some time before this, of course, that Phillips-Van Heusen began its expansion into other areas of the men's furnishings field. As far back as 1912, Phillips-Van Heusen became the first major brand manufacturer to produce men's sport shirts, and even earlier, around the turn of the century, they began to manufacture and produce pajamas. This was followed over the years by the addition of the other product lines that today make up the Van Heusen roster—1937, Van Heusen neckwear; 1950, Van Heusen handkerchiefs; 1951, Van Heusen swimwear and beachwear; 1956, Van Heusen sweaters; 1959, the company entered into retailing by acquiring a large chain of fine men's stores in the northeast; 1961, Van Heusen slacks.

By 1939, Phillips-Van Heusen had fallen from a once highly respected position as an industry leader to a low point in the company's history. Beginning in 1929 and throughout the depression, the company had been in a steady decline. Promotion was spotty, sales slumped, distribution was careless, and little thought was given to the types of outlets that were carrying the Van Heusen line. Prestige dropped to a low ebb; the company had lost about $1 million and was operating at a deficit.

In 1939, Seymour Phillips became president of the company, and through his leadership revitalized the company so that it regained its former position as an industry leader. Since 1939, the company has never failed to show a profit. A high point on this road back was the winning of the coveted Army-Navy "E" award during World War II. Van Heusen was the first company in the industry to achieve this distinction.

Among Mr. Phillips' first steps as president was the improvement of the styling, quality, and durability of the Van Heusen products. To insure a continuing high standard of quality control, a testing laboratory was established in the Bronx, New York, plant.

Distribution was completely overhauled. The 11,000 accounts of *all* types then on the books were slashed to 1,000, and the job of rebuilding distribution with class menswear and department stores was begun.

In 1939, the advertising budget was $9,775. Under the leadership of President Phillips, this amount was systematically increased until the year 1949, when it passed the $1 million mark. It now surpasses $2 million.

Phillips-Van Heusen today employs over 3,000 people at its 12 factories and depots in Illinois, California, Washington, Georgia, Pennsylvania, and Arkansas. Last year's sales were over $55 million.

Advertising and sales promotion

In 1908, when national advertising in the United States was practically unknown, the Phillips-Jones Company ran a one-column, three-inch ad in the *Saturday Evening Post* for its Princely and Emperor shirts. Small and almost insignificant by today's standards, this advertising was, nevertheless, quite revolutionary for its time. This was an era when few manufacturers could envision the potential of brand advertising and brand selling.

The advertising department together with Van Heusen's advertising agency is responsible for a complete advertising and sales promotion program which includes everything from television commercials to packaging. The preparation of a Van Heusen national advertising campaign begins a full 12 months in advance. The first step is a preliminary meeting between the advertising director, the general merchandise manager, and the various merchandise and sales department heads. The purpose of this meeting is to select the promotions that are to be advertised and promoted nationally. The advertising director then meets with the agency's creative group to determine specific advertising concepts. The full-time job of organization and layout of the campaign then begins. There are many more meetings, and each progressive step is cleared with the merchandising and sales departments to minimize errors and eliminate possible deviation from the original concept.

The agency then prepares roughs or storyboards of the proposed ads and commercials, and presents these together with media recommendations to a special advertising executive committee consisting of the advertising director and representatives of Van Heusen's top management team. Once approval is obtained, the agency proceeds with the preparation of the finished commercials and places orders for the desired time and space.

All this effort finally culminates at a general meeting of the entire Van Heusen selling force who assembles to view for the first time the merchandise and the advertising they will be working with during the coming months.

This presentation is made twice yearly—one presentation for the spring–summer and another for the fall–winter season. Each complete campaign is geared to the specific season in question and to the specific merchandise to be brought forth that season.

The Van Heusen sales promotion program is an extension of its national advertising and is based on the promotional themes or ideas developed for that national advertising. Sales promotional material is prepared simultaneously with art and copy from the campaign used, modified and tailored to serve the needs of local retail selling. This is a completely integrated advertising-sales promotion effort starting with Van Heusen selection of media, deciding on the appeal, and continuing right through to the all-important point-of-sale materials.

Case questions

1. What are the major factors which Phillips-Van Heusen should consider in selecting its media?
2. Analyze the Phillips-Van Heusen product line and marketing situation as it relates to the major factors that influence the selection of media.
3. What particular media would be most effective for the Phillips-Van Heusen corporation?
4. Which of the factors discussed above seem most important to Phillips-Van Heusen in selecting media?

CASE 2. TRANS-WORLD LEASING CORPORATION
Deciding on media

Trans-World Leasing Corporation, an Alabama-based company, is interested in increasing the number of its dealers. In considering the approach to use, the company wanted to determine how it should evaluate the various media that it might use.

The industry

Transportation leasing is one of the fastest growing industries in the country with a volume increase of over 800 percent in the past decade. Trans-World Leasing Corporation has designed a leasing program that enables every qualified person with a driver's license to become a potential customer for a leased vehicle from a Trans-World Leasing dealer.

Major corporations, trucking companies, car rental agencies, bus companies, and many other business organizations plus a wide range of individuals are leasing over two million vehicles. The "Car & Truck Renting and Leasing Association" states that the industry had gross revenues of over $2 billion in 1966 and the anticipated volume for 1967 will be in excess of $2.4 billion. It is estimated that by 1970, 55 percent of all vehicles will be purchased through the lease method!

Why? Leasing is the easiest, and perhaps the best, way of automotive ownership with a minimum of investment. One fact speaks for itself— the leasing industry has increased 800 percent in the past 10 years.

1. Today: Auto and truck leasing is one of the country's largest industries.
2. Tomorrow: It will be the dominating influence in car sales.

Definition of lease.   Essentially, a lease is a form of financing that permits the lessee to use an automobile under specified conditions, and over a predetermined length of time, *without tying up his capital.*

The lessee pays for the use of the vehicle at regular intervals during the lease period, and upon expiration of the lease he returns the car to the lessor. All manufacturer's guarantees and warranties are available for the benefit of the lessee.

Trans-World Leasing

Trans-World Leasing Corp. provides complete training, assistance, and full support necessary for the successful operation of a sound business venture. Trans-World Leasing endeavors to free the dealer from burdensome routine tasks so that nearly 100 percent of his available time may be utilized for lease procurement through tried and proved methods.

Trans-World Leasing purchases and delivers all vehicles, performs the duties of credit check, monthly billing, collections, and the final disposition of each vehicle, in addition to record-keeping, financing, vehicle licensing and tax records.

Trans-World Leasing seminar training

When a person becomes Trans-World Leasing dealer he is advised as to when he will attend a New Dealer Seminar. At this initial seminar he is introduced to the company's simplified methods of securing leases, completing forms, and obtaining a general knowledge about his new business and its operational procedures. He also meets the key personnel and those people with whom he will be in contact.

In addition, all training and education is continued, with the dealer receiving bulletins, reports, lead procurement brochures, and pertinent information relative to the leasing industry. With this continual flow of up-to-date information, the dealer is prepared to answer questions or objections to the lease program with facts!

It is company policy that one of its field representatives be scheduled periodically for each dealer's territory. In addition, immediate assistance is available at all times, by phone or field consultation, in regard to the company's business. Trans-World Leasing provides a continually expanding knowledge of its dealers' business—leasing.

Dealership procurment

Trans-World Leasing is now selecting dealers on a national basis, based on its successfully proven marketing techniques. The complete Trans-World Leasing dealership program, with its services and materials, is available only to its leasing dealers.

National surveys show that a standard Chevrolet dealer averages about $138 gross profit per car sold. In the Trans-World Leasing program, a dealer can earn $300 to $450 gross profit per leased car. It is generally easier to lease a car than sell one and Trans-World Leasing shares with the dealer on an equal 50/50 basis *all profits*. Trans-World Leasing assumes all major losses.

The Trans-World Leasing dealership program is a planned working operation, complete with adequate funding, experienced and competent personnel and administrators, and, most importantly, a parent company with full experience in leasing both to the individual and to business accounts.

Full or part-time

Initially a Trans-World dealership program may be started as a part-time operation. The prime, key feature of the leasing dealership is that even through part-time effort, using the available advertising materials, mailings, and home office support, a dealer can build a profitable business.

Any dealer may start his leasing program on a limited basis and expand to a full-time operation encompassing additional sales personnel as his visions of dealership potential and time element allow.

Marketing analysis

Trans-World Leasing has developed a dealership program based on population and potential, consisting of individual dealership within each prime marketing area. All available statistical data has been compiled prior to its evaluation of each area and its potential.

The Trans-World Leasing dealership program

No special or technical knowledge is required, since Trans-World Leasing fully trains the dealer and assists and supports him through its backup program. A dealer receives his training, literature, all forms and stationery, special quotation service, lowest price leasing plans, latest information and data, publicity and advertising aids, special bulletins and reports, and a continual working relationship with the home office to assure rapid and reliable operations throughout all phases of the dealer network.

Trans-World Leasing dealer's programs

Dealerships may be awarded on either an exclusive or nonexclusive basis. The nonexclusive, or area, dealership costs $2,500. The exclusive dealerships vary in cost according to area population and potential.

The company's experience indicates that a dealer, using the prescribed methods of lease procurement and with the company assistance provided, should produce a minimum of 100 leased vehicles per year. National figures show an estimated renewal rate for leased vehicles is 84 percent.

Four-Year Table (based on two-year lease programs)

First year	100 cars
Second year	100
Third year	100
Plus first year renewals	84
Fourth year	100
Plus second year renewals	84
Total estimate	568 cars

The preceding figures and table represent an expected minimal number of leases procured by a dealer working by himself following the company program. This projection should improve as each dealer becomes more familiar with his territory and prospects.

Dealer's profits and return of investment

A Trans-World Leasing dealer receives approximately $300 as his equal share of the "built-in" profit for each vehicle leased. The dealer receives $25 from Trans-World Leasing for each vehicle leased as a "return of investment." This $25 refund continues until the leadership investment is fully returned.

After each lease termination any profit realized from the sale of each vehicle is shared annually with the dealer. The dealer may also exercise his "right of first refusal" on the purchase from the company of any leased vehicle and may then receive an even greater profit.

All manufacturers' rebates and any rebates from insurance or financing are also shared equally with the dealer.

There are no hidden fees or charges attached to the dealer program and every dealer can earn satisfactory profits and have his entire investment returned in a very short time.

Using the low figure of only $350 per leased vehicle as profit for the 568 cars projected for a four-year period, there is a gross income in excess of $200,000—*An annual average of* $50,000.

It is important to remember that the company and the dealer actually comprise a "working partnership," with both parties sharing equally in all profits received from each lease. (See Exhibit 1.)

EXHIBIT 1. Trans-World Leasing system dealer (*examples*)

1972   Chevrolet Impala—$99.11 per month*

Two-door hardtop—Equipment: front and rear seat belts with front retractors; padded instrument panel & visors; 4-way hazard flasher; windshield washer & two-speed wipers; backup lights; outside rearview mirror; energy-absorbing steering column & instrument panel; heater & defroster; foam-cushioned front seat; front & rear armrests (ashtray in rear armrest); glove compartment light; automatic front door dome light switches; electric clock; luggage compartment light on sedan and coupe; standard V8-283 ci, 195 hp; air conditioner (4-seasons); glass tinted (all); power brakes; power steering, radio am push button; 8.25 x 14 whitewall tires; powerglide transmission.

1972   Pontiac Bonneville—$110.24 per month**

Hardtop Coupe—Equipment: anchors, shoulder belts (front seat); armrests, ashtray; belts, seat w/front retractors & push-button buckles; brakes, dual master cylinder w/warning light; directional signal w/lane change feature; door locks, safety 4-way; heater & defroster; instrument panel & visor padded; lighter, cigarette; lights, backup; mirror, outside rearview & inside day-night; steering column & wheel, energy-absorbing; windshield washer & dual-speed wipers w/reduced glare arms & blades; carpets; wood-grain styling instrument panel; lights ashtray, glove box, lighter; recessed windshield wipers; electric clock; decor group; fender skirts, deluxe wheel discs; engine V8-325 h.p., power steering; power brakes; custom air conditioner; glass tinted (all); radio am push button; Turbo-Hydramatic transmission; 8.55 x 14 whitewall tires.

1972   Lincoln Continental—$164.00 per month***

Coupe hardtop—Equipment: armrests, folding center, brakes power, disc front, dual-system w/warning light; electric clock; emergency flasher, 4-way; engine V8-462 w/4 BBL. carburetor & dual exhausts; instrument panel, padded; heater; lights; ashtray, backup, courtesy, low-fuel warning; glove box, map reading; rear door open (front on hardtop); trunk; mirrors; vinyl-back breakaway (or ball-joint windshield mount), inside rearview, remote control sideview, vanity; seat, 2-way power, seat belts, front & rear w/front retractors & warning light; steering, power steering wheel, deep-dish w/padded hub; wheel covers, windshield washers & variable speed wipers, air conditioner, automatic; glass tinted (all), radio am w/power antenna; tires 9.15 x 15 whitewall.

* Prices quoted are for one vehicle only.
** Prices subject to change without notice.
*** Prices above do not include maintenance and insurance.

Case questions

1. What factors should Trans-World be considering in deciding upon the media to use?

2. How important is circulation of the media? Composition of media audience? Message content?

3. Compare the importance of the media factors that you would recommend to Trans-World to those that might be used seeking dealers for:
   a)   Franchised coin car wash.
   b)   Franchised home furnishings store.
   c)   Franchised pancake house.
   d)   Franchised automatic transmission company.
   e)   Franchised food store.

CASE 3. PINDAR COMPANY
How diminishing returns affect selection of media

Pindar Company is a leading manufacturer of sleeve-type bearings and bushings for use principally in the automotive industry. Its products are also used extensively in the aircraft, farm equipment, diesel engine, and locomotive industries.

The principal products of the company are:

1. Bearings, bushings, and related products.   Lined bearings and lined, plain, and graphited bronze bushings are manufactured in a wide variety of types and sizes for use as original equipment and for replacement purposes in internal combustion engines and in many other applications. Rubber-and-metal bearings are manufactured for use primarily in automotive chassis applications.

2. Electronic components and devices.   Artifically grown piezoelectric crystals are produced and sold for use in phonograph pickups, microphones, headphones, hearing aids, sonal and underwater listening devices, and other acoustical products. Analyzing and recording instruments, including direct-writing oscillographs, amplifiers and strain, surface and general purpose analyzers, are manufactured for industrial and research use.

The customers of the company include manufacturers of automotive original equipment, aircraft engines and equipment, railroad locomotives, engines and engine parts, agricultural machinery and equipment, and electrical machinery and equipment. The company sells directly to manufacturers, as well as through distributors, wholesalers, and jobbers of automotive parts and electrical products.

The following tabulation gives the percentages of total sales represented by sales to the principal classes of customers:

Manufacturers of:	Percent of total sales
Automotive original equipment	31
Aircraft engines and equipment	15
Railroad locomotives	5
Other engines and engine parts	11
Agricultural machinery and equipment	10
Electrical machinery and equipment	9
Distributors, wholesalers, and jobbers	19
Total	100

A major portion of the total sales of Pindar has been made to a relatively small number of customers. In the past year, sales to the three largest customers (manufacturers of automotive vehicles) accounted for 25 percent of total sales, while sales to the ten largest customers accounted for 46 percent of the volume. Sales outside of the United States amounted to 3 percent of total sales.

The bearing and bushing business is highly competitive. Pindar's competitors include not only other independent manufacturers of bearings and bushings but also certain manufacturers of equipment using such items who produce substantial portions of their bearing and bushing requirements. Automotive manufacturers will also sell bearings and bushings for replacement through their own outlets.

As a result, because of the intense competition, the advertising manager of Pindar had followed the policy of dividing his advertising budget so that the leading industrial magazines would be included for each of the major customer classifications. For every classification, he used three or more magazines.

It was his opinion that while such a policy resulted in some duplication of the reading audience, nevertheless Pindar was able to make a greater impact on its potential customers by advertising in the most important specialized magazines for the various groups. In the selection of the magazines for the automotive classification, as an example, he divided his budget in automotive trade publications as follows:

Publication	Percent of advertising budget
A	40
B	30
C	15
D	15

The representative of *Publication A* was dissatisfied with this division because his magazine was recognized as the leading publication in the industry. To show the Pindar advertising manager how he might be able to make his advertising dollar more effective, he prepared a chart (Exhibit 1) on "How the law of diminishing returns affects advertising media." He pointed out that it is uneconomical, under average conditions, to select more than one or two publications to cover the important

EXHIBIT 1. How law of diminishing returns affects advertising media cost for each additional publication

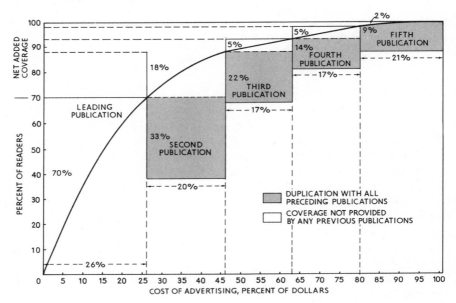

potential buyers, because, as was indicated in the chart, the number of additional readers becomes smaller as each successive publication is added, and the cost of reaching these extra readers becomes proportionately higher.

He believed that with a limited budget, to divide an advertising schedule between the number one and two magazines in any industrial field resulted in too thin a coverage to obtain good returns from either publication. It would only be when two trade magazines had practically equal circulation, market coverage, editorial acceptance, and space cost that a split schedule on an alternate-month basis would deliver as much, or more, effectiveness than a full schedule in one magazine. It would have to be a very exceptional situation, in his opinion, that would justify a policy whereby a company would advertise in more than the two leading publications.

Pindar had followed for the last ten years a policy of using the same copy for each of its principal product categories in the industrial magazines which were used for that specific line.

As an example, in the media selected for the automotive classification the advertisements featured an illustration of an engineer looking through a microscope examining a bearing with a headline, "A Pindar Engineer is Your Best Friend." The copy then stated that no other sector of the industry rendered equal service and know-how.

During the past year the advertising manager had received some negative feedback from a number of purchasing executives who said that it was annoying to them to see the same advertisement time and time again in several different industrial magazines. It was their contention that repetition turned them off and that no industrial ads were so brilliant and intellectually acceptable that they justified this excessive repetition. I was also their opinion that this practice of repetition resulted in significant diminishing returns because it discouraged them from reading any of Pindar's advertising.

Case questions

1. Evaluate the advertising policy which the advertising manager of Pindar has been using.

2. On what hypotheses do you believe that the representative of *Publication A* developed the chart for the "law of diminishing returns"?

3. What policy should Pindar follow in deciding on the number of trade magazines to use?

4. What should be the policy of Pindar in repeating the same advertisements in several different industrial magazines?

5. Would this law of diminishing returns operate the same way for TV, radio, and outdoor boards if similar studies were made for those media?

CASE 4. NADAB STORES, INC.
Evolving principles of media selection

Nadab Stores, Inc. operates a chain of 56 discount stores which are located in the eastern and midwestern sections of the United States. The stores vary in size from 40,000 sq. ft. to 125,000 sq. ft. All of Nadab stores are air conditioned and well maintained and are located near major highways.

Merchandising policy

Nadab sells a broad selection of merchandise with emphasis on items selected to appeal to persons of middle incomes. The merchandise carried includes women's, children's, and men's wearing apparel, linens, draperies, shoes, and such hard goods as housewares, hardware, home furnishings, and small appliances. It also sells sporting goods, cosmetics, toys, phonograph records, and jewelry. Twenty-five of the stores carry cameras, hi-fi and television sets. About 55 percent of the sales of the company stores are made up from the sales of wearing apparel.

Nadab spent 2.25 percent of its $30 million sales on advertising. Nadab has limited this advertising to newspapers, circulars, and spots on television and radio stations. Its primary emphasis has been on promotional or direct-action advertising. The dominant appeals have been on price and specials. The policy of the company has been to use only a token amount for institutional promotion.

It was the opinion of Nadab's executives that the growth of its operations to date was in large part due to the ability of the individual stores to offer discount prices. They believed that Nadab's customers were astute bargain shoppers and were not too concerned about the "image" of the store. As long as Nadab stores could offer a satisfactory selection of quality merchandise at a relatively low price, the company would be successful.

During the past five years, however, there was increased competition from additional discount stores which were opened in trading areas competing with Nadab. As a result, the Nadab executives decided that they should reevaluate the policy of concentrating the advertising in local media and consider using media in which institutional appeals could be used.

In his analysis, the vice president of marketing pointed out that Nadab was in competition with the conventional department stores, auto accessories outlets, specialty stores, variety stores, drugstores, supermarkets, mail-order houses, and other discount department stores in each of the markets in which the company stores were located. He also stressed the fact that there were other discount stores which were substantially larger and that these stores had built a broad image for the stores in all of the markets in which they operated through institutional advertising in national and regional media.

To date Nadab had followed a basic principle that in selecting media it had decided on the basis of the number of potential customers in the immediate market. The major appeals had also centered on facts that would attract attention quickly and convey the sales messages with brevity.

While this approach had been successful in the past there was concern that if Nadab were to reach its overall market potential it would be necessary for the company to develop appeals that would enhance the image of the company. In other words, it seemed important to consider, in developing the store appeal, the *character* of Nadab versus the kind of outlet which merely offered a wide selection of quality merchandise at a discount price. At a meeting of the store managers which was held the first part of August each year, the managers recommended that the current policy be maintained in selecting media. It was their belief that local media provided the best means to reach and maintain the position that the stores had in each of the areas. They also emphasized that building a broad image for Nadab was not too important because, in the final analysis, the zeroing in on the discount price of commodities actually pulled the individuals to the specific stores. They further stressed that they were not in favor of spending additional funds for institutional advertising.

Case questions

1. Do you agree with the store managers that the major function of Nadab's advertising should be for immediate sales of goods?

2. If one decided to build the image of the Nadab's discount operation, what principles do you think should be considered in the selection of the media?

3. Contrast the principles of selecting media for a discount chain operation such as Nadab as compared to Federated Department Stores.

4. Point out some principles that you think should be considered in selecting Nadab's local media which would include newspapers, circulars, television, and radio.

5. Since discount stores generally appeal to people belonging to the middle class, what impact would this have on the type of media which should be used?

chapter 11

NEWSPAPERS AND MAGAZINES

THE SIGNIFICANT FACTORS involved in the selection of media were discussed in the preceding chapter. In this, and the following two chapters, the salient features of the most important media will be discussed briefly. This chapter will include the publication media, newspapers and magazines; chapter 12 will cover the broadcast media, television and radio; and chapter 13 will cover other media forms.

NEWSPAPERS

The position of the newspaper as an advertising medium seems secure. The newspaper has for many years been the leading medium in terms of advertising revenue. In 1970, advertisers spent $4,936,000,000[1] on newspaper advertising, approximately 24 percent of all advertising dollars. About 8 of every 10 adults will read a paper any given day. Approximately 1,600 daily newspapers are published with a combined daily weekday circulation of about 62 million. There are about 575 Sunday newspapers, with a circulation of 49.7 million. In addition, there are over 8,000 weekly newspapers, with a total circulation of approximately 25 million.

Classification of newspapers

Newspapers are usually classified as morning and evening daily papers, Sunday papers, the Sunday supplements, weekly or rural papers, shopping news, and specialized newspapers.

Daily papers. Most daily papers are evening papers, carrying news of that day's important national and local events, including business, entertainment, financial, social, and sports activities. Usually they have a

---

[1] *Advertising Age,* June 7, 1971, p. 28.

larger relative readership by women than men. The morning papers usually have a wider geographical circulation (covering more of the suburban areas around the city) than do evening papers. They carry the news of the preceding day, with news coverage comparable to evening papers, and have a larger male readership than female. Individual circulation and reading audience characteristics should be studied carefully by media men, however, rather than selecting papers purely because they are morning or evening.

Sunday newspapers. One of the main characteristics of the average Sunday newspapers is its bulk. It has special sections with longer articles of specific class interest; the circulation of Sunday newspapers is ordinarily greater than that of dailies. Although the rates are higher, the per unit cost may be lower.

In using Sunday newspapers, the advertiser should check circulation figures to be sure this edition reaches the desired market. Since only 5.25 percent of the 10,800 weekly and daily papers publish a Sunday newspaper, this edition usually has a wider and more extensive circulation.

The Sunday supplements. Some 300 newspapers also have magazine supplements, or Sunday magazines, which they publish or distribute as a part of their Sunday papers. There are two kinds of Sunday newspaper magazines. The first type is the independent Sunday magazine, individually edited and published by a particular newspaper. There are approximately 90 such magazines. The second type is the syndicated magazine, which is distributed to many newspapers although it is centrally edited and published. These magazine sections use smoother paper stock than the rest of the paper and provide for superior color printing.

Some newspapers also have comic supplements that appear in the Sunday editions. These comic sections usually are edited and published on a syndicate basis, and the printed copies sent out to the subscribing newspapers. The advertiser can reach all the papers on the list of any syndicated comic supplement by placing one insertion order and preparing one set of plates.

The weekly newspaper. The weekly newspaper usually serves a small community and, on the average, has a circulation of only about 3,000 copies per issue. Because they serve a local and homogeneous population, and cover thoroughly the news concerning the local people and their problems, they usually have a very high readership—considerably above that of the average metropolitan daily paper. Thus, although their advertising rates usually are higher than daily papers on the basis of circulation, the thorough reading and longer life of the weekly may well justify such higher rates. As a rule, the bulk of their advertising comes from local advertisers.

The shopping news. In some respects, the shopping news is not a true newspaper. As a rule, such papers carry very little news of the type characteristic of the newspaper, and a limited amount of editorial matter. For the most part, they carry only advertising. They are usually distributed free on a controlled basis, with the publisher determining to whom the paper will be distributed. Usually the publisher attempts to deliver copies of his shopping news to every dwelling unit in the shopping district of the area he serves.

Specialized newspapers. Although these papers are either dailies or weeklies, they are usually classified separately because they do have a unique feature for newspapers due to their high selectivity in terms of type of audience. They serve special groups of people who usually have some close and common bond of interest. For example, some are published for certain religious or racial groups, or in a foreign language. Others are designed for specific labor or trade groups, or to cover special fields of business, such as finance. Many are published by high schools and colleges for the students and staffs of their respective institutions.

Appeals

Newspapers are read hurriedly and have a short life, although they reach all classes of people. An advertisement in a newspaper is usually read but once, with the average reading time estimated to be less than 30 seconds. In this short space of time, the appeal must stimulate the reader into action. As a result, since one of the funtcions of this type of advertising is to produce immediate sales, the copy appeal is based generally on quantity, quality, and/or price.

On the other hand, the purpose of general or national advertising in newspapers is to create goodwill and acceptance—first for the product itself, and then for the merchants who sell it. Such copy generally should be direct and terse, because the average newspaper reader is not going to spend much time reading the advertisement.

Flexibility

Daily newspapers have great flexibility for an advertiser. The advertiser can reach his audience as often as he likes. It is possible to concentrate the sales efforts during the most profitable season, and then to thin out his efforts during slack periods. Copy can also be inserted, withdrawn, and changed within a few hours before the newspapers are printed.

Because of this flexibility, copy can be correlated to recent important news or local events. A sudden storm might necessitate a change in the advertisement a department store was planning, or the announcement of the passing of a new city ordinance might provide an appeal which would be more effective than one that had been planned for an advertisement.

In addition to this flexibility of timing, the newspaper also has the advantage of great flexibility from a geographic standpoint. That is, the advertiser can place advertising in only the particular area or areas he desires to reach. He can also adjust the amount of advertising he desires to use in a particular market to meet his particular needs.

The newspaper has people on the staff who can help the small retailer or local business firm who wishes to advertise with them. The services may include planning the advertising, writing the copy, preparing the layout, and providing illustrations. These services are available for all local advertisers, but are used primarily by the small retailers, since larger firms usually will have their own advertising departments or may use local advertising agencies.

Many newspapers also conduct research studies, the results of which can be helpful to local retailers as well as to national advertisers. These studies may be general compilations of pertinent data relative to the population and buying power of a trading area. Studies are also made of the newspaper readership and the coverage it provides of the population of the market area. Other studies sometimes made include surveys of consumer buying habits and brand purchase studies.

Many of the larger newspapers also provide merchandising aids for national advertisers. Frequently, this involves attempting to obtain more retail cooperation in displaying the products of the advertiser, using the point-of-purchase display materials provided by the advertiser, encouraging retailers to place advertising to tie in with the advertising of the manufacturer, or to push retailer use of the cooperative advertising allowances of the manufacturer.

Classified and display advertising

The advertising appearing in newspapers is divided into two major categories—classified and display. Classified advertisements are the small statements of fact that appear in special columns which have been set aside for that purpose. The columns are headed according to the class of advertisements appearing in them and from this get their names, classified advertisements. Display advertising, on the other hand, includes all advertising matter not included in the classified sections.

Advertising space and rates

Newspaper advertising space is sold by the agate line or column inch. The agate line is one fourteenth of an inch deep and one column wide. The standard newspaper is eight columns across and approximately 21 or 22 inches (300 lines) deep. The width of the column differs according to the publication, but is usually about two inches. The column inch is one inch in depth and one column wide. A column inch contains 14 agate lines. Hence, a full-page advertisement in a standard newspaper is approximately 2,400 lines. A flat rate is a rate of so much per agate line, regardless of the amount of space used or the frequency of use. Most newspapers also have a contract rate, in which the cost per line decreases as the number of lines used in a year increases, or with the frequency of insertion.

Short rate

If the advertiser contracts with a newspaper to use 5,000 lines within 12 months at a rate of 59 cents per line, he would be billed monthly at that rate for the amount of linage he used. If at the end of 12 months the advertiser had actually used only 1,000 lines, he would be billed for the difference between the 5,000-line and the 1,000-line rate. If the 1,000-line rate were 60 cents, he would be billed 1 cent per line for the 1,000 lines used. This is known as the short-rate method. This method often proves unsatisfactory because of the misunderstanding that may develop.

Long rate

The long-rate plan ordinarily is more satisfactory. Under the long-rate plan, a contract is made for the minimum amount of linage to be used. Then, if more linage is used, the difference will be rebated by the publisher.

The advertiser in the above case would sign a contract to purchase 1,000 lines. He would be billed each month at the rate of 60 cents per line. If, at the end of 12 months he had used 5,000 lines, the newspaper publisher would give him a rebate of 1 cent per line, which is the difference between the 1,000-line and the 5,000-line contract rate.

Preferred positions

Newspaper advertising is ordinarily sold by the publisher on a run-of-paper or ROP basis. Run-of-paper means the advertisement will be placed in the position in the paper that is most satisfactory to the publisher. The publisher naturally will attempt to use good judgment in placing advertisements, since he desires that the advertiser obtain good results from his advertising. However, except for certain special pages, such as amusement pages, the newspaper representative will not make definite commitments as to the exact placement of advertisements at the time the advertiser places the insertion order.

If the advertiser definitely wants a special position in the newspaper, he can obtain it, assuming it is available, if he is willing to pay extra for it. Oftentimes, however, it is possible to obtain a specially desired position without paying extra by merely indicating on the insertion order "run ROP, this particular position requested." Then, if the advertising makeup man finds it feasible, he will give the advertiser this preferred position at no extra charge, although the publisher still has the right to run the advertisement where he desires.

If the advertiser insists on a special position, he may secure it in most papers by paying extra for it at a preferred position rate. An example of a preferred position often offered by papers is "full position," which provides reading matter all across the top and down one side of the advertisement, or places the advertisement at the top of the column with reading matter down one side. Such full position commonly costs from 25 percent to 50 percent above the ROP rates. Another commonly offered special position, for a usual rate of 10 percent to 20 percent extra, is known as NR, or next to reading matter. This guarantees reading matter all along one side of the advertisement. There are other special positions available in most newspapers. These often include pages 2, 3, and 4, and the sports, society, or women's page.

Readers

Some publications allow advertisers to set their copy in the same type style as the news matter. This gives the advertisement the general appearance of being a regular news story. Advertisements of this sort are run next to news columns. These advertisements are usually followed by the word "Advertisement" in small type. A higher rate is usually charged for this privilege. Because "readers" rely heavily on subterfuge to get attention, some newspapers refuse to accept this type of advertisement.

Local and national (general) advertising

The two principal classes of newspaper display advertising are designated by the terms "local" and "national," or "general." Local or retail advertising is that done by an advertiser when he sells directly to the consumer through one or more local retail stores which he alone owns and controls. National, or general, advertising is that placed by an advertiser—not a local or retail advertiser, but usually a manufacturer—advertising his brand of merchandise.

Most newspapers have a different set of rates for the two above classes of advertising, with the general or national rate usually averaging from 35 percent to 50 percent higher than the local or retail rates. Also, the national advertiser usually is charged a flat rate, whereas the retailer is offered a contract rate.

The justification for this difference in local and general rates advanced by newspapers is that the sale of general or national space involves high commissions or brokerage fees and other costs. Much national advertising space is sold through publisher's representatives who receive a 15 percent commission. Also, most national advertising is placed by advertising agencies who also receive a 15 percent commission for their work in creating and handling the advertising they place in the newspaper. In addition, the newspapers have extra costs in handling the national advertising which originates out of the city. This double system of rates has long been the subject of discussion and debate, but it still persists. It has caused advertising agencies placing national advertising, as well as national advertisers, to use all legitimate methods to take advantage of the lower local rates.

Special and color rate differentials

Newspapers in most cases also vary the rates charged for different types of advertising. For instance, the rate charged for political advertisements is usually different from that charged for an advertisement of a general nature.

Newspapers also charge extra rates for the use of color. In recent years, the use of ROP color in newspaper advertisements has developed rapidly, and most daily and weekly papers now will provide color. Some provide only black and one color, some black and two colors, and a few provide black and three colors. Usually there is a minimum size space required if the advertiser wishes to run a color advertisement, the minimum commonly being 800 to 1,000 lines. Color advertisements above the regular rate for black alone will in most instances amount to the following: 25 percent for black and one color, 35 percent for black and two colors, and 45 percent for black and three colors.

The national advertiser who desires color reproduction comparable to that in good magazines can obtain such in most newspapers by the use of preprint color. This involves the advertisement printed on large rolls by a firm specializing in color printing, shipping the printed rolls to the various local newspapers which print the black impression, cut the roll to page size, and insert the preprinted advertisement in the paper. This normally requires a full-page ad, and costs the advertiser the paper and color production costs plus the regular space rate in the newspaper. There are several types of preprint production, varying somewhat in the special technique involved in the printing and insertion in the local paper.

The milline rate

When selecting advertising media, it often is necessary to compare the rates of the media. Assume that the rates of two newspapers are to be compared. Each charges 50 cents per line. One paper has a circulation of 50,000, while the other has a circulation of 45,000. The rates are the same, and if all other points are equal, the one with a circulation of 50,000 is a better buy than the one with 45,000 circulation. However, in actual practice, the rates per line will be in odd cents, and the circulation figures will be complex. Therefore, in order to compare the rates of different publications, the milline rate is used. The milline rate of a publication is the rate per line per million circulation. This can be figured in two ways.

Example:

A publication has a rate of $1 per line, and its circulation is 500,000. $1 divided by 500,000 equals $0.000002 multiplied by a million equals $2. $2 is the milline rate.

The above method involves the use of small fractions. The following method eliminates the small fraction or large decimal:

$$\frac{1,000,000 \times \$1}{500,000} = \$2 \text{ milline rate}$$

In figuring the milline rate of the newspapers listed above with circulations of 50,000 and 45,000 and a line rate of $0.50, the following procedure would be used:

$$\frac{1,000,000 \times \$0.50}{50,000} = \$10 \text{ milline rate for newspaper with circulation of 50,000}$$

$$\frac{1,000,000 \times \$0.50}{45,000} = \$11.11 \text{ milline rate for newspaper with circulation of 45,000}$$

In case some of the circulation of one or both papers being compared is considered undesirable, or "waste" circulation, the "trueline" rate should be computed. This is done by using only the effective circulation of the papers, rather than total circulation, as follows:

$$\text{trueline rate} = \frac{1,000,000 \times \text{line rate}}{\text{effective circulation}}$$

Advantages and disadvantages

The advantages of using newspapers include: (1) they provide intensive coverage of the cities and surrounding area; (2) they have geographical selectivity; (3) they are very flexible, and copy can be tied in with latest developments; (4) they are relatively low cost in comparison to other media; (5) they reach all economic classes; (6) they can be tied in with the sales appeals in specific localities; (7) they can be used effectively in a cooperative advertising plan; (8) they can emphasize the local news appeal; (9) they can be used even when the advertising budget is quite modest; (10) they can be used on a daily basis; (11) they appeal to the entire family; (12) they are one of the media in which great numbers of people look for information about merchandise which they are about to purchase; (13) they await the convenience of the reader to read; (14) they are the major local medium for which readers pay; (15) they can be used effectively for test campaigns and to check results; and (16) they are *news* papers.

The main disadvantages of using newspapers are: (1) for products purchased by a restricted class, there is considerable waste circulation; (2) the paper and printing techniques may make them unsatisfactory for products which require special color and other mechanical features to show qualities of the products; (3) they are read hurriedly and the impact of the advertisements may be relatively brief; (4) there are complex difficulties in selecting a satisfactory schedule of newspapers in a campaign and in deciding which newspaper to use in a specific market; (5) there are so many advertisements in some newspapers that it is easy for an advertisement to get buried; (6) when an extensive list of newspapers must be used, it may be more economical to use the "low cost per-thousand" broadcast media for continuity; (7) there is overlapping of newspaper circulations in many sections of the country; (8) many newspapers employ publishers' representatives to represent them nationally, which results in the national advertiser having to place his advertising through an intermediary.

MAGAZINES

Whereas newspapers as a rule reach the people in a city or shopping area, magazines reach a particular segment of the national market. They normally select special interest groups and design their editorial content for such groups. Virtually any segment of the population can find one or more magazines to appeal to its particular interests.

Influence of magazines

There are more than 7,000 periodicals published and distributed in the United States. The total per-issue circulation of all the members of the Audit Bureau of Circulations is about 235 million.

Nearly 7 out of every 10 adults 15 years of age and over in the United States are regular magazine readers. Over 8 out of every 10 U.S. families are magazine-reading families. Magazines are read regularly by 85 million adult consumers.

When the Audit Bureau of Circulations was founded, the total circulation of its 54 general and farm magazines was 17.5 million copies per issue, against the present circulation of 160 million. Since 1947, magazine circulation has increased 64 percent, a growth more rapid than the growth of the population or the number of homes with radio sets, or the circulation of the country's daily newspapers. Magazine advertising expenditures were $1.64 billion in 1970.[2] Magazines exert their influence in two ways— through their editorial content and through their advertising. So closely are the editorial and the advertising pages welded in magazines, that it is difficult to divorce one from the other. They combine to make a total effect.

Classification of magazines

The more important classifications used for magazines include the following: general consumer, women's magazines, shelter magazines, industrial, trade, service, professional, technical journals, and farm publications. This classification could be much more detailed, since, for instance, Standard Rate & Data Service divides consumer magazines into some 49 classifications, business magazines into 159 classes, and farm publications into 11 classifications. There is no need to give all these classifications here, but the detailed breakdowns possible indicate the high degree of specialized interests served by magazines, and the fact that many consumer groups and virtually every professional, industry, and trade group has its own special magazine. In the following paragraphs, a few of the most important classes of magazines will be discussed briefly.

General consumer magazines. These magazines are edited to appeal to the general consumer, rather than to any special interest segment of the population. Generally, they do tend to be read by higher income consumers, who buy them either for entertainment or information, or both. The editorial content of these magazines consists of fiction, articles, pictures, and special features that are selected to appeal to the so-called general reader.

Women's magazines. There are several different classes or categories of magazines published primarily to appeal to women. These include women's fashions, women's service, romance, society, dressmaking and needlework, and home service. The women's service magazines and home service, or shelter, magazines are probably the most important classes. The women's service magazine is an important source of fiction and information about family and personal problems as well as fashion news, with most of the editorial material featuring information about the family, home, and housekeeping. Thus, the publications are aimed

---

[2] *Advertising Age,* June 7, 1971, p. 28.

at reaching and influencing millions of housewives who do a large part of the buying for the household and who also influence the purchase of many other items bought by the family. The women's service magazines include such leading publications as *Good Housekeeping, Ladies' Home Journal,* and *McCall's.*

The other important class of women's magazines is the so-called shelter group. These are magazines similar to those discussed above, except that they concentrate their editorial appeal almost entirely on the home, covering the areas of food preparation, home building and remodeling, home decoration, and gardening. Good examples of this category are *Better Homes and Gardens, The American Home,* and *Sunset* (which also includes a strong section on travel).

Business publications.   Approximately 2,400 business magazines are listed in Standard Rate & Data Service. The Audit Bureau of Circulations classifies this large number of publications into four categories, which for our purposes are more meaningful than the 159 classification groupings given by Standard Rate & Data Service. The four ABC categories are: industrial publications, which are published for all kinds of industry; institutional papers, edited for clubs, colleges, hospitals, hotels, schools, etc.; professional publications, published for architects, artists, doctors, engineers, lawyers, professors, etc.; and merchandise publications, which go to retailers, wholesalers, and other types of distributors.

Some of the features of these publications should be noted briefly. They have very high selectivity, going to groups that are specifically interested in the particular field or subject covered. The publications usually have a good knowledge of their readers in terms of positions held, type of firms by which employed, and interests. The magazines usually contain editorial matter of a rational nature, often quite technical, and usually of a type designated to help the reader to do a better job, to familiarize him with new developments in the field, to give the features of new products being introduced, and to tell how products and services might enable the reader to increase his returns from his business or profession. Because the copy of advertisements run in these magazines usually attempts, like the editorial content, to tell the reader how to increase his profits or income from the use of the advertised product or service, the advertisements have very high readership. These magazines usually have small circulations, and their advertising rates on a per page basis are low. In many cases, subscriptions for these magazines are paid for by business firms, and the copies are routed to several members of the firm for reading.

Some of these publications attempt to reach all of a certain type of reader in many or all industries, and are called horizontal magazines. Examples would be *Purchasing,* which is designed to reach purchasing agents and others interested in purchasing in all industries, and *Sales*

Management, which reaches sales executives in all industries. Other publications are designed to reach all levels of readers within a single industry or field, such as *Modern Textiles Magazine, Appliance Manufacturer,* or the *American Drycleaner,* and are called vertical magazines.

Farm magazines. As indicated by their category title, these magazines are edited for the farm market or specific segments of that market. Some are edited to reach the general farm market, such as the *Farm Journal* and the *Progressive Farmer.* However, more of them are designed to reach particular segments of the farm market, such as those edited for the fields of dairy farming, livestock, poultry, or fruits and vegetables, with examples being *Hoard's Dairyman, Breeder's Gazette, American Poultry Journal,* and the *American Fruit Grower.* Within these detailed classification groupings as given by Standard Rate & Data Service, there are very specialized publications. For instance, in the poultry class there is a magazine, *Turkey World,* aimed at those specializing in turkey raising, and within the fruits and vegetables class there is a magazine, *California Citograph,* aimed at citrus fruit growers.

In some cases, farming magazines are selective on a geographical basis rather than (or in addition to) a specific interest basis. For example, the Cowles Publishing Company, Spokane, Washington, publishes the *Idaho Farmer,* the *Washington Farmer,* and the *Oregon Farmer,* each magazine edited to cover the agricultural interests of the particular state, with the bulk of subscriptions going to that state.

Advantages and disadvantages of magazines

Advantages. Magazines offer high selectivity, national and local coverage, use of excellent mechanical techniques, prestige, longer life, and a relatively low cost.

Whether an advertiser wishes to reach executives, homeowners, farmers, women, college students, teen-agers, or any other specific group, there will probably be several magazines available for him to use. For business groups, there are such publications as *Nation's Business, Fortune, Forbes,* and *Business Week;* for literary groups, such magazines as *Harper's* and *Atlantic Monthly;* for parents, such magazines as *Hygiene* and *Parents' Magazine;* for juvenile groups, *Seventeen, Boys' Life,* and *Scholastic;* for fraternal groups, such magazines as *Rotarian, Christian Herald,* and *Columbia;* for farm groups, such magazines as *American Pigeon Journal* and *Successful Farming.*

Another advantage which magazines have over newspapers is that an advertiser can get national circulation. Since magazine circulation tends to follow population trends, for most general products the circulation of the national magazine may be closely correlated to the advertiser's market.

A third advantage is that because of the higher quality of paper in magazines, it is possible to use a variety of colors and mechanical techniques. Illustrations may be done in opaque and transparent watercolors; photoengravings and four-color halftones are some of the other methods which can be used effectively.

A fourth advantage is that advertising a product in such magazines as *Life, Vogue, Good Housekeeping, Esquire,* and *Town and Country* helps to enhance its prestige and at the same time, provides a means by which the manufacturer can prevail on local dealers to make use of the national advertising in local tie-ins. Point-of-purchase displays, window displays, and local advertising are a few of the methods a retailer can use to point out that a product he sells was advertised in a national magazine.

A fifth advantage is that magazines have a longer life than most other media and are read more thoroughly. A magazine usually will be picked up to be read a number of times by the subscriber as well as by members of his family.

A sixth advantage is that magazines provide a low per unit cost of reaching potential customers. Even a small company may find that by properly choosing a magazine that will reach its selective group of customers, this medium will be an economical one to use.

There are several other advantages in addition to the six discussed above. The great strength of magazines lies in their believability, acceptance, authority, and editorial vitality. Magazine readers come more from the prosperous and middle-income class home and represent above-average prospects for nationally advertised products. Magazines have extensive "pass-along" or "secondary" readership. The loyalty to some magazines is so great that they may create in the minds of their readers a feeling similar to belonging to a special, select class. Magazines may also reach buyers who are out of range geographically as well as buyers who are hard for the salesmen to approach.

Disadvantages. One of the main disadvantages in the use of magazines has been the necessity of buying space and preparing copy for the advertisement well in advance of the date on which it is to appear. In some cases, weekly magazines require that the plates for the advertisement be in their hands seven weeks prior to publication date in the case of four-color advertisements. After this closing date, no changes in the advertisement or cancellation of space may be made.

Many magazines are making all possible efforts to shorten this period between closing date and publication date, but it is still in most cases such a period of time as to constitute a timing disadvantage for the advertiser.

A second major disadvantage of magazines is that of waste circulation if the advertiser does not have complete national distribution, or has wide differences in distribution and sales strength in different markets of the country. That is, magazines as a rule did not possess geographical or market selectivity. This weakness is still true in many cases. However, a number of magazines now issue regional editions of their magazines, so that an advertiser can advertise in only those regions of the country which he desires, or can advertise different products in different regions. They have 10, 26, 59, and up to 70 regional and local editions; a number have from 10 to 20 major market editions; some have editions defined by metropolitan market areas, and some have up to 50 test market editions.

Approximately 60 consumer magazines which do not publish regional editions attempt to reduce their territorial selectivity weakness by providing for split-run insertions of advertisements. This split-run system means that by making special arrangements (and paying for extra production costs involved) an advertiser may advertise different products in different regions of the country to fit his needs, or two different advertisers can run advertisements for their respective products in different regions. Each advertiser would pay for that share of the magazine circulation delivered into his region.

In rare instances, a consumer magazine will limit the geographic area it serves. For example, *Sunset* (one of the leading shelter magazines), accepts subscriptions essentially only in the far western states and in Hawaii. Even in this restricted area it publishes three regional editions, with a large share of the editorial matter changed for each edition. However, it is still true that for the most part magazines do lack the geographic selectivity possessed by other media.

There are several other limitations in addition to the two discussed above. Closely allied to the disadvantage of a lack of geographic selectivity is the need to use an appeal in the advertising that is broad enough to be satisfactory in every section of the country (or of the region) and yet specific enough to persuade the prospects to act. Since in many instances there are significant differences in demand and in conditions in different markets, this is often a serious handicap to the copywriter. Since magazines are as a rule published weekly or monthly, the advertiser cannot communicate with his buyers as frequently as he can with newspapers, radio, or television. Also, the cost of mechanical preparation of advertisements for magazines, especially for four-color advertisements, can be quite high.

Special services provided to advertisers

As is true of newspapers, magazines do offer some special services to advertisers. Some of the magazines have specialists in merchandising in certain fields of retailing, such as food, drug, appliance, or department stores. Many offer merchandising material such as display and special letters to dealers at cost to aid in tying in the product at the point of sale with the magazine advertising. Some magazines will provide help to the advertiser and his advertising agency in handling the sales force, broker, wholesaler, and retailer meetings at which the advertiser's national advertising and sales program is explained and sold to the trade. Several of the fashion magazines publish advance editions for the trade to help coordinate the selling programs of the stores with the national advertising in the magazines. Most publishers conduct considerable research in the areas of readership, brand preference, consumer attitudes, and general market conditions, and provide the results of such studies to advertisers and potential advertisers in running test programs by publishing advertisements only in the issues going to the test market.

Space rates

Magazine advertising space generally is sold by the page or fraction of a page, although in some cases it is sold by the agate line. Many magazines quote rates for one page, one-half page, one-fourth page, and one-eighth page, and some quote rates for full, two-third, and one-third pages. For advertisements of less than one-half page, most magazines will require the advertisement to be in multiples of 14 agate lines. Some magazines also sell "junior" units which have editorial material above and along one side. These units are usually offered as junior pages and half pages, the junior units containing about 60 percent of the number of lines in the regular units.

Rates are quoted on two bases: flat and open. Flat-rate magazines charge the same rate regardless of how much space the advertiser uses during the year.

Discounts. Open-rate magazines, on the other hand, will charge on the basis of the volume of space used and/or the frequency of insertions of advertisements during the year. Monthly magazines will often quote a discount for 6 advertisements run during a year, and a still larger discount for 12 advertisements run during the year. Weekly magazines in many cases will quote a successively larger discount for advertisements inserted 13, 26, 39, or 52 times during a period of 12 months. The Standard Rate and Data Service provides rate and circulation information about magazines as well as about newspapers.

Other factors influencing rates

Several other factors besides the amount of space and frequency of insertion influence magazine rates. As is indicated in the schedule above, magazine-rate quotations normally refer to the rates for black-and-white printing, and color rates normally are quoted separately for each multiple of colors offered by the magazine. Also, as is true of newspapers, most magazines make an extra charge for certain preferred positions. Because of the greater attention-getting value of the cover pages, they are particularly desired by advertisers. Although the premium charged for these preferred positions (cover pages) varies by magazines, the following example would be fairly typical. The second cover (inside front cover) and the third cover (inside back cover) are required to be in four colors, the rate for which is usually about 40 percent above the black-and-white page rate, but it is often the same rate as for a four-color page in the magazine. The fourth, or back cover, usually must be in four colors and will carry a premium charge of from 25 percent to 40 percent above the regular four-color page rate. In consumer magazines, the first, or front, cover is not sold to advertisers, but trade and industrial magazines often sell space on the front cover to advertisers, usually at a premium rate somewhat higher than the fourth-cover rate.

Most magazines which make bleed pages available also charge a premium of about 15 percent above the regular rates. A bleed page is one on which the advertisement is printed fully to the outside edge of the page, with no margin. Another position for which special rates are applicable is the center spread, which consists of the two facing pages in the exact center of the magazine. On these two pages, the printing can be done on a single sheet of paper, and the advertisement can run across the gutter—the usual margin space between the pages—without a break. Usually the rate for the center spread is the same as for two facing pages in four colors, regardless of whether or not the advertiser uses four colors in his advertisement.

Another basis for a rate differential is the use of inserts. If the advertiser desires to have a distinctive advertisement, he can elect to use special stock for printing it instead of the regular paper stock used by the magazine. To do this, the advertiser has his advertisement printed and forwards it to the magazine, which inserts it in the publication. This permits the advertiser to make his advertisement as distinct as he desires in terms of paper stock, colors used, and printing process. The distinctiveness of such inserts usually results in great attention and impact for the advertisement. If the paper stock is quite different than the usual magazine stock, the magazine will often tend to open at the insert, giving it even greater attention value.

Cost comparisons

As is the case with newspapers, it is often desirable in the case of magazines for the advertiser to compare the rates and cost of the media. In newspapers, the unit of measurement used is the milline rate. In magazines, the basis of comparison is the "cost per page per thousand," based in large part on the fact that the most common unit of space for which magazine advertising rates are quoted is a page or fraction thereof, rather than the agate line as for newspapers. The two figures used in computing the cost comparisons for magazines are the one-time insertion cost of a black-and-white page and the net circulation of the magazine.

The formula for the cost per page per thousand circulation is:

$$\frac{\text{page rate} \times 1,000}{\text{circulation}} = \text{cost per page per thousand circulation}$$

For example, if the rate for magazine X is $12,500 per black-and-white page, and the net circulation is 2.5 million, the cost per page per thousand would be $5, computed as follows:

$$\frac{\$12,500 \times 1,000}{2,500,000} = \$5 \text{ cost per page per thousand.}$$

As was noted in the preceding chapter on selection of media, many advertisers today analyze carefully the figures for audience, or readers, of magazines (as determined by marketing research studies) as well as the net circulation figures. In such cases, the advertiser may well compute a cost per page per thousand readers, using the same formula as above, except that total audience or readers would be used in place of circulation in the denominator of the formula.

In many cases, the advertiser is interested in reaching a particular identifiable group of readers of the magazine, specially in the case of the business publications where the circulation is usually broken down by special groups. When such is true, the advertiser often compares costs on the basis of the number of real potential prospects reached by the media. To do this, he takes the figure of real prospects in the circulation or readership, and by substituting this figure for net circulation computes an effective cost per page per thousand. It is obvious that this is a more meaningful figure for the advertiser when it is possible to identify clearly the real prospects among the circulation or audience of the magazines being compared.

The warning indicating the care that must be taken in the use of cost comparisons for selecting media should be repeated here, particularly in the case of cost per page per thousand circulation. This figure does not indicate how many people will read a particular advertisement, or how many real prospects will read the advertisement. The cost per page per thousand will vary widely among magazines. Usually, the greater the selectivity of the magazine in terms of the interests of its readers, the purchasing power they represent, or the positions they hold, the higher its cost on a page per thousand basis. For instance, the cost per thousand rate for *Skiing* is about 4.33 times higher than for *Life*, while for *Esquire*, it is about 1.6 times that of *Life*.

In attempts to justify their particular rates and cost, magazines today use a number of different bases for indicating the quality and/or quantity of their circulation and audience. In addition to quantity of readership, they conduct studies to indicate the quality of readers, the amount of time the reader spends with the magazine, the number of different days he reads in it, the length of time he keeps the magazine in the home, and the confidence he has in the editorial and advertising material appearing in the publication. Such data should be studied carefully by the advertiser along with the comparative cost ratios.

Statistical reports

Magazine publishers offer a wide variety of different types of statistical reports. These analyses give detailed information on income of readers, percentage of different kinds of advertising carried, circulation according to market areas, and other such factual evidence.

Among the more important independent studies is the Starch Advertisement Readership Service which points out such data as number of readers, age of readers, occupation, reader duplication, and to what extent the advertisements in the magazines checked were seen or read thoroughly.

W. R. Simmons & Associates also makes an extensive analysis in its annual audience report, "Study of Selective and Mass Markets and the Media Reaching Them."

AUDIT BUREAU OF CIRCULATIONS

During the early days of advertising, the circulation figures issued by some publishers were open to question. Unreliable statements were made and affirmed with such glibness that advertisers could not rely on the circulation figures. This condition placed a handicap on the publishers who sought to give only the exact figures of their circulation, as well as on the advertisers and agencies attempting to use the figures in planning the selection of media. As a result, the Audit Bureau of Circulations (ABC) was established in 1914 under the sponsorship of advertisers, advertising agencies, and publishers of newspapers and magazines, all of whom were anxious to protect themselves against the publishers whose circulation figures were not dependable. The membership of the board of directors of the ABC consists of representatives of advertisers, advertising agencies, and publishers of newspapers and magazines, with the buyers of advertising space having a majority on the board. The Audit Bureau of Circulations will not accept for membership and audit any publication that has less than 70 percent paid circulation. (Those magazines distributing the bulk of their circulations on a free or controlled basis may become members of the Business Publications Audit of Circulation, which audits the controlled and paid circulation of its member publications.)

The Audit Bureau of Circulations makes independent audits of the circulations of its member newspapers and magazines. In the case of newspapers, it reports the net paid circulation for three geographical areas: the "city zone," the "retail trading zone," and "all other."

Its statements of circulation also indicate the breakdown by "street-vendor sales," "dealer sales," "carrier-delivered circulation," and "mail subscriptions." This information is of interest to advertisers, since a high home-delivered subscription circulation is considered an indication of continuing readership by entire families. Its reports also indicate what share of the subscription list is "in arrears" (overdue in payment for the paper or magazine) and what share of the circulation was obtained by means of special inducements (such as contests and premium offers). Both these items are of interest to advertisers as reflecting on the desirability of the circulation.

In addition to auditing the circulation figures of member publishers and certifying to their accuracy, the ABC also establishes standards for reporting on circulations and serves as a clearing house for circulation reports. Approximately 90 percent of the daily newspapers in the United States and Canada belong to the organization. ABC has also influenced those publishers not members, since advertisers have become skeptical of circulation figures not certified by some accredited agency. As a result, many nonmembers now issue sworn statements of their circulation figures, compiled in a manner similar to that of the ABC. This organization has had a most beneficial effect in the advertising field.

STANDARD RATE AND DATA SERVICE

The Standard Rate and Data Service provides detailed information about the various major media. It offers rates and data information for daily, Sunday, and weekly newspapers; business publications; consumer magazines and farm publications; spot radio; spot television; national radio and television; films for television; transportation advertising; and Canadian media.

With the exception of the data for weekly newspapers, the bulletins for the other media are published on a monthly basis. The weekly newspaper bulletin is published in March and September.

The content of each of the ten Standard Rate and Data Service publications is arranged in such a manner as to provide the important data for buyers of advertising time and space.

QUESTIONS

1. Why do you think newspapers are the leading medium in terms of advertising revenue?

2. If the circulation of the three were approximately equal, should it make any difference to an advertiser whether he uses a morning, evening, or Sunday newspaper? Explain your answer.

3. Newspapers usually quote a lower rate for retail advertising than for national advertising. Do you think this practice is justified? Why or why not?

4. Give examples of three products that you think could justify paying the premium for preferred position in the newspaper. Why?

5. Check the advertisements in your local newspaper for a week. Give reasons why certain advertisers and certain product advertising seem to be concentrated on certain days of the week.

6. In some cities, most supermarkets run their big one and two-page "special" advertisements on Thursdays, and so most national advertisers of food products schedule their advertisements for Thursday to reach all the people who will be reading the paper for the supermarket specials. The advertising manager for a rather new food product with a limited budget decided to run his small-space ads in the paper on a day other than Thursday, when he said the competition for readership would be much less severe. Comment.

7. Do you think the adoption of regional editions by magazines is a threat to newspapers in competing for advertising? Why?

8. For what types of products do you think the newspaper is a better medium than magazines? Magazines than newspapers? Why?

9. The rates for television advertising are normally reduced during the summer months. A magazine is considering reducing its rates for summer months about the same relative amount. Is this a sound move? Why?

10. Do you think the adoption of regional editions gives magazines competitive selectivity? Explain.

11. What is the difference between vertical and horizontal industrial magazines? Under what circumstances is this difference of significance to an advertiser?

12. In theory the cost per page per thousand gives a basis for comparing magazines. Is it sound to select magazines on the basis of the lowest cost? Explain.

CASE 1. MASON COMPANY, INC.
Deciding on the use of magazines

The Mason Company of New Jersey was contacted by a representative of *Life* and asked to consider his proposal including this magazine in the selection of advertising media for the following year.

The Mason Company is a diversified company and has four major groups of products:

1. A general line of paints and enamels which are sold nationally through hardware and paint stores.

2. Linoleum, felt-base floor coverings, and industrial floor coverings which are sold nationally through retail outlets.
3. Heat-insulating materials which are sold nationally by local building supply firms.
4. Building materials, such as roofing, shingles, and plasterboard lath, which are sold primarily in the eastern market through building supply firms. At different times the Mason Company has used television, radio, outdoor boards, direct mail, trade publications, and national magazines in its advertising mix. However, the company has put greater emphasis on outdoor boards, trade publications, and such national magazines as *House Beautiful, Life,* and *Good Housekeeping.* In the past, the executives had selected these media because they could use a variety of colors in these publications.

As one executive stated: "In order to sell Mason's products, it was our opinion that it was essential to portray them to the consumer in vivid colors." However, at the time the representative of *Life* called, the company was considering the advisability of a change in emphasis on media. Exhibit 1 shows the percentage of the total advertising budget of $2 million as it was allocated to the media at the present time.

EXHIBIT 1. Important media used by Mason Company by percentage of total advertising budget

Media used	Percentage of total advertising budget
Magazines	35
Trade publications	15
Outdoor boards	12
Direct mail	11
Radio	10
Television	10
Other	7
Total	100

Exhibit 2 gives the allocation which the company is considering for the ensuing year's advertising budget of $2.25 million.

EXHIBIT 2. Proposed allocation of advertising budget to media

Media used	Percentage of total advertising budget
Television	45
Trade publications	15
Magazines	14
Direct mail	14
Radio	5
Other	7
Total	100

Under the proposed allocation, the major change was that greater emphasis would be put on television, with a more limited amount being used for magazine advertising.

The representative of *Life* pointed out the following ten tenets of magazine advertising:

1. Appearance. Magazines are always modern, presentable, exhilarating in their own format, design, style; always the antithesis of old-fashioned; always a clean, young, vibrant personality.

2. Color. Magazines are alive with color, replacing the drab monotone, work-a-day mood with exciting overtones.

3. Content. Magazines put the advertiser in company with the very values he is selling, surrounding his story with fiction and articles and illustrations that stimulate and encourage the use of new products and news ways of using old products.

4. Flexibility. Magazines give the advertiser complete freedom to do the advertising job he decides he needs to do, when he needs to do it, presenting him with a long menu, a wide variety of magazines and markets, so he can shrink or expand his list or space size to increase or decrease pressure, for one product or another, or in one or another kind of market, or on whatever combination of buying or selling factors he determines.

5. Authority. Magazines place the advertiser's product in the greatest show window in America, among thousands of other quality products of American business large and small.

6. Display. Magazines give the advertiser's product invaluable package display, imprinting on the mind's eyes of the prospect a perfect picture of his product, for ready reference at the point of purchase, identifying the package in color, shape, and trademark, with an image that can be made indelible against substitution and confusion.

7. Volume. Magazines furnish the advertiser the greatest potential in sales he can find anywhere, in groups of however many millions of prospects he may decide upon—multiplying his opportunities by however many times he may want to sell to them during his sales year.

8. Economy. Magazines give the advertiser extremely low-cost advertising—low in cost of preparation, low in cost per prospect; but high in quality of prospect, high in merchandisability.

9. Selectivity. Magazines deliver nation-wide and regional audiences already prepared and selected from the great public mass, each gathering together its own group of readers who are considerably above the average in being able to buy and alert to try, and on intelligence levels that are economically right for the product.

10. Exposure. Magazines give the advertiser time to sit down and talk to his prospects, extending his time with them to however long he can interest them with what he is picturing and saying, remaining in the

EXHIBIT 3

Life

A Time Inc., Publication

 MPA

Media Code 8 377 0100 2.00
Published weekly by Time Inc., Time & Life Bldg.,
1271 Ave. of the Americas, New York, N. Y.
10020. Phone 212-586-1212.
For shipping info., see Print Media Production Data.

I. PERSONNEL
Publisher—Garry Valk.
Adv. Sales Director—Worthington S. Mayer.
Asst. Adv. Sales Dir./Sales Mgr.—Arthur Hecker.
Asst. Adv. Sales Dir./Operations—Charles D. Hogan.
Asst. Adv. Sales Dir./Sales Analysis—Herbert
Breseman.

2. BRANCH OFFICES
Chicago 60611 — Robert J. Gilfert; Assoc. Mgr.,
Edwin C. Kidd, 401 N. Michigan Ave. Phone 312-
467-9700.
Detroit 48202—J. Burns Cody, Assoc. Mgr., Frank
X. Gaughen, Fisher Bldg. Phone 313-875-1212.
Los Angeles 90005—W. Pendleton Tudor, 3435
Wilshire Blvd. Phone 213-385-8151.
New York 10020—N. Y. Mgrs.: Joseph E. Corr,
William S. Myers, John D. Howell, Franklyn
Theis, Ernest M. Walker. Time & Life Bldg.,
Rockefeller Center. Phone 212-556-4336.
San Francisco 94104—Philip A. McDonnell, Shell
Bldg. Phone 415-982-5000.
London, W-1—Robert Dumper, Intl. Adv. Dir., U. S.
Editions, New Bond Street. Phone Grosvenor 4080.
Tokyo—Yasushi Ogawa, Life U. S. Editions. Time &
Life Bldg., 3/6, Ohtemachi 2-Chome, Chujoda-Ku.

3. COMMISSION AND CASH DISCOUNT
15% to agencies; 2% 10 days from billing date.
Bills rendered 20th of publication month.

4. GENERAL RATE POLICY
Orders beyond 13 weeks at rates then prevailing.

ADVERTISING RATES
Rates effective January 8, 1971 issue. (Card No. 49.)
Card received November 30, 1970.

5. BLACK/WHITE RATES
1 page	36,500.
1/2 page (vertical)	20,700.
1/2 page (horizontal)	21,500.
1/4 page	11,300.
1/8 page (vertical)	5,900.
single line	78.00

All line space must be in multiples of 14 lines. Line
space added to vertical 1/8 page (84 lines) or square
1/4 page (168 lines) charged basic 1/8 or 1/4 page
rate for first 84 or 168 lines plus line rate for each
additional 14 line multiple.
Full pages or units-of 3 or more consecutive
full pages will be given a discount of 3% and the
resulting rate considered the basic rate for discount
purposes.

5a GEOGRAPHIC and/or DEMOGRAPHIC EDITIONS
50 SPOT LIFE MARKETS
Effective January 8, 1971 issue.
Patterned after basic television marketing area definitions. Page, multi-page and vertical half-page
units in black and white, black and 1 color and 4
color available. (The number of vertical half pages
accepted per market per issue may be subject to
availability.) Any single Spot or combinations may
be purchased. Minimum circulation requirement:
200,000. If the circulation of the Spot Market or
markets used is less than this minimum, the base
rate for those minimums applies. A 5% margin must
be allowed for the circulation and distribution of
Spot forms by market.

50 SPOT LIFE MARKETS

Spot:	Average Circulation	Spot:	Average Circulation
Albany	55,000	Milwaukee	65,000
Atlanta	65,000	Minneapolis-St.	
Baltimore	95,000	Paul	100,000
Boston	220,000	Nashville-	
Buffalo	50,000	Chattanooga	35,000
Charlotte, N. C.	55,000	New Orleans	35,000
Chicago	275,000	New York	830,000
Cincinnati	50,000	Oklahoma City	40,000
Cleveland	170,000	Philadelphia	310,000
Columbus	55,000	Pittsburgh	110,000
Dallas-Ft. Worth	100,000	Portland, Ore.	55,000
Dayton	35,000	Providence	35,000
Denver	55,000	Raleigh	35,000
Detroit	195,000	Richmond-Norfolk	65,000
Fort Wayne-So.		Sacramento	65,000
Bend	30,000	St. Louis	75,000
Fresno-Bakersfield	40,000	San Antonio	55,000
Grand Rapids-		San Diego	65,000
Muskegon	75,000	San Francisco	220,000
Harrisburg	50,000	Scranton-	
Hartford-New		Wilkes Barre	25,000
Haven	150,000	Seattle	85,000
Houston	70,000	Syracuse-	
Indianapolis	90,000	Rochester	90,000
Kansas City	65,000	Tampa-St.	
Los Angeles	420,000	Petersburg	60,000
Louisville	30,000	Toledo	40,000
Memphis	35,000	Washington, D.C.	165,000
Miami	90,000	Wichita	35,000

Canadian circulation (150,000) available only to
advertisers who use a greater amount of U. S.
circulation for the same.
Publisher states: Effective January 8, 1971 issue,
"Rates based on circulation figures shown above."

ADDITIONAL RATES PER M
Circulation:
Full page:

	b/w	b/w 1 c	4 color
200,000— 500,000	6.40	7.90	9.20
500,000—1,000,000	6.18	7.51	9.15
1,000,000—2,000,000	6.10	7.43	9.05
2,000,000—3,000,000	5.98	7.30	8.88
*3,000,000 and over	5.82	7.10	8.64

1/2 page (vertical only):

200,000— 500,000	3.70	4.55	5.60
500,000—1,000,000	3.34	4.26	5.54
1,000,000—2,000,000	3.25	4.17	5.48
2,000,000—3,000,000	3.18	4.03	5.40
*3,000,000 and over	3.13	4.00	5.30

(*) The amount paid for any Market Area insertion will not exceed the price that would be
paid for that insertion if run in entire circulation.

An advertiser buys 1,785,000 circulation in Spot or
States markets, or in a mix of the 2 programs.
Figure his basic rate for a black and white page as
follows: Rate for first 1,000,000 circulation: 7,060.
Rate for additional 785,000 circulation is 6.10/M
times 785, equaling 4,788.50. Total basic rate 7,060,
plus 4,788.50 equals 11,848.50.

6. COLOR RATES
	b/w 1 c	4 color
1 page	45,000.	54,000.
1/2 page (vertical)	25,500.	32,400.
1/2 page (horizontal)	26,500.	33,700.
1/4 page	14,350.	19,000.

6b DISCOUNTS (Gross Expenditures)
SCHEDULE A
CORPORATE DISCOUNTS

Dollar Vol. Groups	Volume Discounts
400,000— 699,999.	4%
700,000— 799,999.	5%
800,000— 899,999.	6%
900,000— 999,999.	7%
1,000,000—1,099,999.	8%
1,100,000—1,199,999.	9%
1,200,000—1,299,999.	10%
1,300,000—1,399,999.	11%
1,400,000—1,499,999.	12%
1,500,000—1,599,999.	13%
1,600,000—1,699,999.	14%
1,700,000—1,799,999.	15%
1,800,000—1,999,999.	16%
2,000,000—2,999,999.	17%
3,000,000—3,999,999.	18%
4,000,000—4,999,999.	19%
5,000,000—5,999,999.	20%
6,000,000—6,999,999.	21%
7,000,000 and over	22%

BRAND DISCOUNT WITHIN A PRODUCT CATEGORY
In addition to the Corporate Dollar Volume Discounts, a Brand Within a Product Category using 13
pages or more will earn additional discounts. To
qualify, all space must run within the same 52 consecutive issues.

13 pages or more:
One brand at this level earns	2%
Two or more brands at this level each earn	5%

26 pages or more:
Any brand at this level earns	8%

39 pages or more:
Any brand at this level earns:	
On first 26 pages	8%
On next 13 pages or more	12%

51 pages or more:
Any brand at this level earns:	
On first 26 pages	8%
On next 13 pages	12%
On next 12 pages or more	16%

Definition of page: a full page unit in Life's total
circulation or its equivalent, regardless of coloration.
Fractional pages and all market area space can be
used to build national page equivalents.

Brands Within a Product Category: defined on the
basis of a combination of consumer interpretation of
a brand name or names, and generally accepted industry definitions within each Product Category.

Brand Discount Year: like a Corporate Contract Year,
may not exceed 52 consecutive issues. However, the
year selected to qualify for the Brand (or Brands)
Discount need not run concurrently with the Corporate Contract Year. Both Brand and Corporate Dollar Volume
Discounts must be based on the same Discount
Schedule.

SCHEDULE B
CORPORATE DISCOUNTS
Effective September 6, 1968.

Dollar Vol. Groups	Volume Discounts
297,500.— 599,999.	4%
600,000.— 949,999.	6%
950,000.—1,299,999.	8%
1,300,000.—1,899,999.	10%
1,900,000.—2,599,999.	12%
2,600,000.—3,499,999.	14%
3,500,000. and over	16%

BRAND DISCOUNT WITHIN PRODUCT CATEGORY
Effective September 6, 1968.
In addition to the Corporate Discount, a Brand
Within a Product Category, employing pages as
described, will earn additional discounts as follows:

7 pages or more	1-1/2%	2%
13 pages or more	3%	4%
19 pages or more	7%	9%
26 pages or more	10%	12%
39 pages or more	13%	15%
51 pages or more	16%	18%

(*) Discount earned with 1 brand at this page level.
(†) Discount earned with 2 or more brands, each
at this level.

SPACE RENEWAL CREDIT PROGRAM
Companies using 5 or more national pages or equivalents or spending 250,000.00 or more in a corporate
contract year can earn advertising credits towards
space in Life in the following contract year as
follows:

	Following Year's Usage
Previous Year's Usage:	(*) (†)
Under 500,000.	4% 6%
500,000.—1,000,000.	4% 6%
1,000,000. and over	5% 8%
	6% 10%

(*) On matching dollars.
(†) On added dollars.

7. COVERS
4th cover (4 color) .... 70,700.

8. INSERTS
Special units as gatefolds, small size multi-page sections, insert cards, special inks, etc. available. Illustrations of these space units and others available.
Basic rates quoted on individual specifications.

9. BLEED
Bleed available at basic rate plus 15% for pages,
spreads, half pages, quarter pages, 5- and 6-column
units in all colorations. No extra charge for bleed
across gutter for facing pages or 5- and 6-column
units if regular outside margins are maintained.

12. SPLIT-RUN
A1 and A2 NATIONAL SPLIT
Advertisers offered option of buying 1/2 of national
circulation. By dividing total circulation within all
ZIP Code areas, 2 equally representative parts of
national circulation are obtained. Each Life subscriber has been assigned for the duration of his
subscription to part A1, or part A2. Newsstand copies
also divided equally. A 3% circulation and distribution margin must be allowed for this market separation.
Advertiser may buy part A1 only or part A2 only
or he may choose to alternate insertions using A1
in one issue and A2 in another. Page units only
in any coloration are available but may be subject
to availability by issue.
Rates:
50% of prevailing national rate based on coloration
plus 3,000.00 production charge. If one advertiser
uses both parts in one issue, production charge is
5,500.00.
COPY CHANGES
A national or Market area advertiser may change
copy as many different times as desired. Production
charges per copy change, as follows:

	b/w	2 color	4 color
Pages	525.	700.	1,150.
Spreads	900.	1,200.	2,000.

TEST MARKET FACILITIES
In addition to Life's standard Spot and State markets, test markets are available on a limited basis
to advertisers of new products and services. Contact
sales representative for rates and availabilities.

14. CONTRACT AND COPY REGULATIONS
See Contents page for location—items 12, 14, 16, 20,
24, 35.

15. MECH. REQUIREMENTS (Letterpress)
For complete, detailed production information, see
SRDS Print Media Production Data.
Trim size: 10-1/2 x 13-1/4; No./Cols. 4.
Binding method: Saddle Stitched.
Colors available: 4-Color Process (AAAA/MPA);
Metallic: Simulated Metallic.
Cover colors available: 4-Color Process (AAAA/MPA).

DIMENSIONS—AD PAGE

1	9-3/8	x 12-1/8	1/4	4-5/8	x 12-1/8
1/2	4-5/8	x 12-1/8	1/4	4-5/8	x 6
1/2	9-3/8	x 6	1/8	2-1/4	x 6

16. ISSUE AND CLOSING DATES
Published weekly, dated Friday; issued Monday
preceding.
Black and white and black and one color national
units close Monday, 25 days preceding date of publication. Four-color units close Monday, 46 days
preceding date of publication.
Fast close: black and white, black and 1 color and
crash 4 color close 11 days preceding date of publication. 4 color fast close will close 24 days preceding date of publication. Rates: Regular fast close,
unit rate plus 5%; special crash color, regular unit
rate plus 10%.
Market area and Split run closing date for Spot or
State markets and Split run (regardless of coloration)
is Monday, 46 days preceding date of publication.
All regional ad: Space contract and complete physical material are due on the Monday, 46 days preceding issue date.
Cancellations not accepted after closing date.

17. SPECIAL SERVICES
A.B.C. Supplemental Data Report received 10/9/69.

18. CIRCULATION
Established 1936. Single copy .50; per year 10.00.
Summary data—for detail see Publisher's Statement.
CPM—B/W 4.29.
A.B.C. 12-31-70 (6 mos. aver.—Magazine Form)
Tot. Pd. (Subs.) (Single) (Assoc.)
8,510,686 8,300,798 209,888 ....

TERRITORIAL DISTRIBUTION 11/70—8,638,991
N.Eng. Mid.Atl. E.N.Cen. W.N.Cen. S.Atl. E.S.Cen.
612,883 1,829,633 1,662,636 641,194 1,107,099 267,518
W.S.Cen. Mtn.St. Pac.St. Canada Foreign Other
628,724 363,282 1,311,724 152,253 17,854 44,189

Rate Card No. 49, effective January 8, 1971 issue
states: "Circulation base 7,000,000."

home for days and weeks and months with a chance to sell time and again, in sharp contrast to the glimpse-and-run or mention-and-run action of newspapers or radio or television.

The representative then emphasized the advantages of *Life*, pointing ou the number of copies sold at newsstands and the circulation, the cost per page, and the like.

He further went on to stress that it was possible to pinpoint the advertising in any one of 50 spot *Life* markets as well as the 50 states and the District of Columbia. See data for *Life* in Exhibit 3.

Case questions

1. Should the Mason Company put more or less emphasis on the use of magazines in its advertising mix?

2. Evaluate the tenets of magazine advertising as presented by the representative of the magazine.

3. If the company adopts the new proposed budget, what magazines would you recommend that it use? Would your recommendation be different if the current allocation plan was adopted again?

4. Which of its products should the company advertise in *Life?*

5. To what extent should the fact that *Life* plans to limit its circulation and increase the cost of advertising be considered in deciding upon the use of this publication.

CASE 2. HOME PRODUCTS CO.
Deciding on newspapers

Home Products Co. is engaged principally in the purchase, manufacture, processing, and distribution of dairy products in the United States. Home is one of the largest companies engaged in the dairy-products industry in the United States. It is also a major manufacturer and distributor of ice cream. An important characteristic of these activities is that they are essentially local in nature involving a large number of marketing areas. Home is also in the manufacture and distribution on a national scale of a substantial number of other food products and a variety of chemical and other nonfood products. Home's business is highly competitive. Profit margins vary not only among products but also in respect of the same products by reason of differing local conditions. Products are advertised and promoted extensively. At present the executives are concerned with how they should allocate a $350,000 newspaper budget for the milk, ice cream, and other food products. The respective sources of net sales of the Home Products Co. during the last fiscal year were as follows:

```
Fluid milk and ice cream fluid milk......................  38 percent
Other products sold in fluid milk operations.............  12
Ice cream.................................................  16
Food products............................................  19
Chemical products........................................  11
Other products...........................................   4
                                                          ___
                                                          100 percent
```

Fluid milk and ice cream division

The principal products in this division are fluid milk, cream, butter, cottage cheese, eggs, buttermilk, non-fat milk, chocolate-flavored drink, bulk and packaged ice creams, ice-cream novelties, and sherbets.

These products are sold at wholesale to stores, schools, restaurants, hotels and hospitals. Products, other than butter and eggs, sold in this division are, with a few exceptions, processed or manufactured in this division and marketed under the name "Home," although local brand names are used in some areas. Butter and eggs generally are purchased for sale under Home's brand names. The principal source of supply of milk is the local dairy farm, in many instances selling through a cooperative association. The products of this division are distributed mainly by a fleet of motor vehicles. Ice-cream products are distributed in 42 states. Fluid milk and related products are distributed in 35 states.

Food products division

Products in this division include cheese; evaporated milk; condensed milk; nonfat milk powder, other brands of whole milk powder; malted milk, cakes, cookies and similar products; and powdered lemon and orange juice.

In the cheese line are bulk American and Swiss type cheeses, process loaf cheese, packaged process cheese, cheese foods, cheese spreads, cream cheese, and specialty cheeses. Most bulk cheese is purchased from local cheese factories and assemblers and is sold in bulk unbranded or processed and sold primarily under the name "Home."

In recent years this division of operations has expanded to include, among others, the following items: refrigerated ready-to-bake products such as biscuits and rolls; instant potato products and clam products. The products in this division are sold directly or through food brokers to wholesalers, stores, food processors, and institutions.

Chemical products division

Products in this division of operations include synethetic resin adhesive for the manufacture of plywood and furniture, household glues, packaging film, medical tubing, and lacquers. Products are sold to industrial users, to distributors, wholesalers, jobbers, and dealers.

Special products division

Products manufactured or processed in this division of operations include animal and poultry feed supplements, soybean oil, soybean meal, bakers' ingredients, and vitamin-mineral fortifiers. Products are sold to feed mills, pharmaceutical makers, drug supply houses, food processors, and confectioners.

Newspaper coverage

Exhibit 1 gives the cumulative line rates and b/w page costs necessary to attain 60 percent metro coverage in the top 100 markets. Studies

EXHIBIT 1. Cumulative line rates and b/w page costs necessary to obtain 60 percent metro coverage in top 100 markets

A)

	Metro markets	Number of papers	Line rate	Cost of 1 page b & w
Top	10	18	$ 37	$ 75,000
Top	20	34	54	114,000
Top	30	46	66	142,000
Top	40	58	76	165,000
Top	50	70	84	184,000
Top	60	82	91	201,000
Top	70	92	98	218,000
Top	80	104	103	232,000
Top	90	114	108	243,000
Top	100	125	113	254,000

Note: Morning and evening newspaper combination counted as one.
Source: SM Survey of Buying Power, 1969; ANM Circulation '69; SRDS, Sept. 1969; BBDO estimates.

B) *Market Groups*

		Daily circulation and rate costs—60% household coverage—major newspapers		
Markets	Number of papers	Total circulation	Line rate b & w	Full page b & w
		(000)		
1–10	18	12,000	$ 37	$ 75,000
1–20	34	16,000	54	114,000
1–30	46	20,000	66	142,000
1–40	58	22,000	76	165,000
1–50	70	25,000	84	184,000
1–100	125	35,000	113	254,000

EXHIBIT 1—*Continued*

C) *Daily papers (ROP color—one-time rates)*

Page b & w and 1 color

Markets	Top paper in the market			Major papers in the market		
	No. of papers	Total cost	Total circ.	No. of papers	Total cost	Total circ.
			(000)			(000)
1–10	10	$ 47,300	6,860	16	$ 78,600	10,750
1–20	20	79,600	10,170	33	122,500	15,570
1–30	30	108,100	12,930	45	154,800	19,310
1–40	40	132,100	15,580	56	180,100	22,090
1–50	50	150,700	17,610	68	200,700	24,300
1–100	99	212,500	23,190	114	266,300	30,020

Page b & w and 3 colors

1–10	9	52,600	6,160	15	81,100	9,630
1–20	18	83,300	9,290	30	128,100	14,310
1–30	28	114,900	12,550	43	164,200	18,050
1–40	37	140,100	14,970	53	190,900	20,620
1–50	45	157,200	16,550	62	209,400	22,320
1–100	84	222,300	21,880	104	279,800	27,780

Source: SRDS, September 1969; SM Survey of Buying Power, 1969.

D) *Cost of one page b & w in sunday newspapers with at least 5% penetration in top 100 metro markets*

Markets	Top paper in market	Major papers in market
1–10	$ 52,200	$ 75,000
1–20	76,500	106,100
1–30	98,600	133,200
1–40	117,200	151,700
1–50	130,700	164,600
1–100	181,800	220,000

Source: SRDS, September 1969; SM Survey of Buying Power, 1969.

show that 73 percent of Home's fluid milk, ice cream, and other food products distribution was in the top 100 markets in the United States. As a result, the advertising director of Home had recommended that it might be more economical to shift from the current policy of placing the newspaper advertising for Home on an area by area basis and to limit the newspaper advertising to the metro coverage in the top 100 markets.

Case questions

1. Point out the major problems which Home might face if it began to limit its newspaper advertising to the top 100 metro markets.

2. On what days of the week should Home advertise in the newspapers? Give reasons.

3. How does one judge the value of the newspapers in the top 100 metro markets?

4. To what degree should Home use cooperative advertising for its products?

5. How could one control the "timing" of the advertising if these major metro areas are used?

6. How would you advise Home as to how it should use its $350,000 newspaper advertising budget?

CASE 3. HARAPAHOES, INC.
Considering use of newspapers

Harapahoes, Inc., is engaged in the manufacture and sale of linoleum, asphalt tile flooring, corks, corkboard insulation, and cork-type covering. It also manufactures felt-base rugs and flooring. During the last fiscal year it had sales of $80 million.

The company had limited its use of newspaper advertising to 10 percent of its annual advertising budget. The percentage breakdown for the Floor Division media was as follows:

a)	Magazines..........................	50%
b)	Television..........................	20
c)	Radio..............................	15
d)	Newspapers.........................	10
e)	Direct Mail & Other.................	5
	Total	100%

The company today is made up of the Floor Division, the Building Materials Division, and the Industrial Division.

Floor Division: From its origin in 1920 the Floor Division expanded rapidly. Within 15 years it became Harapahoes' highest sales volume division, and it still is. According to the company, several new ideas introduced in 1938 were important factors in the Floor Division's consistent expansion: published price lists, a wholesaler-retailer distribution system whose pattern is still followed, and national advertising. The company reports that there are two major markets for the Floor Division's product line, and that considerable homogeneity exists within each: (1) the residential market. Customers are interested in Harapahoes' linoleum for use in their homes. (2) the commercial market. Customers are business and professional men. In such a market Harapahoes' linoleum is considered as a means of improving the appearance and services of stores and offices.

As might be expected, there is a corresponding split in the division's sales and advertising programs: One major effort is directed to the residential, the other to the commercial market.

Underlying all Floor Division advertising is the conviction that people buy floor covering only after deliberate, rational thinking. Linoleum, for example, is not a snap-judgment item; often it is purchased as part of a costly remodeling or redecorating project. Altogether, according to company executives, Floor Division advertising should be calm, believable, and editorial in nature. Incidentally, Harapahoes' advertising director tests the "editorial nature" of each proposed Floor Division ad by asking himself, in effect, this question: If the logotype and sales plug were deleted, would the ad be informative enough and provocative enough to make a good editorial feature in the magazine for which it is scheduled?

Early in 1967 Harapahoes and its advertising agency had occasion to review and evaluate the Floor Division's campaign. It had been appearing in national magazines for several years, with illustrations and copy based on testimonials obtained from successful users of Harapahoes' floors.

Although the Floor Division's sales curve had been healthy during the testimonial campaign, the company evaluated its advertising as only a "pretty fair effort." Letters of inquiry traceable to it were disappointing in number. Results in general seemed neither good nor bad. Further, satisfactory testimonials were becoming scarce. The client and its agency, therefore, decided that they must change—and improve—the campaign. In evaluating the campaign of one of its competitors, the company found that the two campaigns were similar in several respects. Each was aimed at a specific market and showed the application of linoleum floors. Both were major advertising efforts, involving the consistent use of full-page, full-color ads in national magazines, but the competition put more emphasis on newspapers. Harapahoes also observed that the two campaigns differed sharply as to their basic themes:

1. The Harapahoes ads had been built around statements from satisfied users. Illustrations and copy featured the interiors of existing establishments.

2. In contrast, the competitor's campaign featured *ideas developed by extensive research*. Each advertisement showed a variety of new "ideas for homeowners" and offered, at a nominal charge, pamphlets giving further details.

The Harapahoes Floor Division concluded that an honest contribution of ideas—really helpful ideas, and a variety of them—would be the key to successful advertising.

The new campaign began with research in building design. Ideas were gathered from many sources: designers, associations, equipment manufacturers, and food merchandising experts. Information was then checked with officials of the National Association of Architects. Finally, ideas reached the drawing board stage, to serve as the basis for designing a complete interior. Each business classification featured in the commercial campaign was to be selected with an eye to its potential as a market for *Harapahoes'* floors. Late in 1967, the Floor Division's advertising department made out a production schedule, allotting time for creative work, illustration, and production of the ads.

Selection of media

One of the company's executives questioned the 50 percent of the budget that was being spent for magazines and indicated that he believed the company' major competition was probably getting more mileage by allocating about 45 percent of its budget for newspapers.

He stated that the consumer could be influenced to a greater degree if the name of the local distributor was associated with *Harapahoes*. He also believed that it would be possible to develop a rather extensive cooperative advertising program with the dealers if the newspapers were used to a greater degree.

In further emphasizing the reason why he believed the company should allocate more of its budget for newspapers, he stated:

1. Newspapers are the most widely consumed form of communications in the United States, with over 60 million copies distributed daily and over 50 million on Sunday. Over 80 percent of all adults read some newspapers during the average day.
2. Newspapers throughout the years have received a larger share of the country's total advertising investment than any other medium.
3. Their major advantage to advertisers stems from the fact that they are *news* papers and people read them to find out what happened today.
4. Newspapers form a perfect environment for the *news* advertising which we are planning for the current campaign.
5. Our Floor Division depends upon "merchandisability" to sell its products, and local retailers favor using this medium. As a result, we should get better sales effort from the dealers if we allocate more of our budget for newspapers.
6. We will be able to make a deeper penetration of individual markets.
7. ROP color is now available in most papers, and while the quality of reproduction is not as good as what we get in magazines, it is more than adequate for our product.
8. Newspapers will have greater flexibility and we will be able to tie in the appeal to the local news.
9. The people we are trying to reach with our advertisement can be reached more directly through the newspaper.
10. We will be able to use more specific appeals in the newspapers.

Case questions

1. Evaluate the reasons that the Harapahoes executive gave as to why newspapers should be used to a greater degree.

2. What would be the disadvantages of Harapahoes putting more emphasis on newspapers?

3. The company spends 6 percent of sales on advertising. How much would you allocate to newspaper advertising? Give reasons.

CASE 4. UNITED STATES STEEL CORPORATION
Selecting magazine media

United States Steel carries on a wide variety of advertising and sales promotion programs, including product, merchandising, and corporate campaigns involving different media such as magazines, radio, motion pictures, exhibits and displays, direct mail, creative sales aids, merchandising kits, and product literature of all kinds.

The advertising director decided that there would be merit if a humorous approach would be used in providing the quality and dependability of United States Steel pails and drums.

Working with King Features Syndicate, Inc., he had Jimmy Hatlo of the famous "They'll Do It Every Time" cartoon prepare the four cartoons in Exhibits 1, 2, 3, and 4.

Case question

Indicate in what magazines you believe these advertisements should be used.

EXHIBIT 1

They'll Do It Every Time
By Jimmy Hatlo
THAT'S THE FOURTH SCRATCHED PAIL I'VE REJECTED THIS YEAR! CAN'T YOU GUYS BE A LITTLE MORE CAREFUL?
YOU SCRATCH MY PAIL··· I'LL SCRATCH YOURS···
OL' EAGLE EYE COULD SPOT A SCRATCH ON A PAIL INSIDE A TUNNEL OF LOVE WITH HIS EYES CLOSED···
LAST MONTH HE SAW A SCRATCH ON A COMPETITOR'S PAIL AND HE LAUGHED FOR TWO WEEKS!
ONE SCRATCHEE, NO SHIPPEE!
USS U.S.STEEL PRODUCTS
DUNN+ SCADUTO
NO MATTER WHAT KIND OF DRUM OR PAIL YOU NEED, YOU CAN GET IT FROM U.S.STEEL PRODUCTS AND BE SURE OF CONSISTENT QUALITY····
USS U. S. Steel Products
Division of United States Steel
© King Features Syndicate, Inc.

EXHIBIT 2

EXHIBIT 3

EXHIBIT 4

chapter 12

TELEVISION AND RADIO

SINCE television and radio have many similarities, they will both be discussed in this chapter. Both broadcast via the public airwaves and operate under a license from the Federal Communications Commission. They both present programs and commercials on a similar time basis, and sell the same general classes of time: network, national spot, and local. Both have national organizations of stations (networks) to provide for simultaneous broadcasting. And both have the same trade association, the National Association of Broadcasters.

However, since they also exhibit some marked differences, they will be covered individually, albeit with some cross-references as material is analyzed and developed.

TELEVISION

Advertising volume

Television has exhibited the most rapid growth of any advertising medium. In approximately 25 years, the total advertising expenditures have gone from zero to $2,853,000,000 in 1970.[1] Since a major portion of this is national advertising, television is now the leading medium for national advertisers. The expenditures for network television (which gives simultaneous coverage of the national market) amounted to about 47 percent of total television advertising. The amount spent on national spot television (national advertisers using individual stations to reach specific markets) represented about 35 percent of the total. Expenditures for local television (use of local stations by retailers) amounted to 18 percent of the total.

---

[1] *Advertising Age,* June 7, 1971, p. 28.

The organization of the television field

The physical facilities which television provides for carrying the advertising message to potential customers are of prime importance to the advertiser. First is the number and type of stations available to reach the market. Second is the organization of these stations to facilitate their use as an advertising medium, namely the network setup. Third is the number of receiving sets in use, and the number of homes having television sets, since the advertisement presented by a television station cannot reach a potential customer unless he has access to a television receiving set to view the advertisement.

Number and types of stations

The basic unit in the television field is the individual local station. In 1971, there were 511 commercial VHF (very-high-frequency) stations and 185 UHF (ultra-high-frequency) stations or a total of 696 television stations.[2] (This represents a dramatic growth when it is recalled that commercial television stations did not actually start operations until the end of World War II. In 1947, the five stations that had been licensed by the Federal Communications Commission when World War II started finally began broadcasting. By mid-1950, there were 104 television stations in operation in approximately 50 major cities.)

In addition to the 696 commercial stations, there were 196 educational television stations in 1971. However, since these last do not carry advertising, they need not be considered at any length here. But it should be noted that the programming may have a distinct influence on some segments of the potential listeners for commercial stations and, hence, in one sense cannot be totally ignored by the commercial stations and the networks. There were also 2,799 community antenna television systems, with 4.5 million CATV homes.[3]

These TV stations broadcast at designated frequencies, which are commonly referred to as channels. The channels are designated by the Federal Communications Commission, and the plan of channel allocation provides for 12 channels (channels 2 through 13) between 54 and 216 megacycles. These frequencies are known as very high frequency band (VHF), while the channels between 470 and 890 megacycles (channels 14 through 83) are known as the ultra high frequency band (UHF) or channels. On the whole, the VHF stations have been much more profitable than the UHF stations, largely because they were established first

---

[2] *1971 Broadcasting Yearbook,* p. 11.
[3] *1971 Broadcasting Yearbook,* p. 14.

in the major markets (no UHF stations were licensed until 1952), and partly due to being favored by the networks.

Networks

At the present time, virtually all the commercial VHF-TV stations are affiliated with one of the national television networks. These three are the American Broadcasting Company (159 primary affiliated stations and 96 secondary), the Columbia Broadcasting System (192 stations), and the National Broadcasting Company (221 affiliates).[4] A fourth network, the United Network, was established and operated briefly in 1967, but failed after only a few weeks of operation. (Each of the three networks also operates a radio network.) There are also 11 regional television networks.

The networks provide a means for national advertisers to reach a national audience, since the network normally has an affiliate in each major market area. They have negotiated affiliation agreements with the stations to give a good coverage of the national market, and arranged for facilities with the American Telephone and Telegraph Company (coaxial cables and microwave relays) which enable the stations affiliated in the network to be interconnected for simultaneous broadcast of programs and commercial announcements. The networks also provide the facilities for originating programs, and in some instances, producing the programs. They also have the organization and facilities to handle the sale of network programs and time periods to advertisers and advertising agencies.

The network, which enables the advertiser to reach the national market through television, can charge a sufficiently high rate to the advertiser to permit the hiring of the best of talent and the production of expensive programs, which would be impossible for the individual station from an economic standpoint. Since the cost of such expensive programs and talent is spread over the entire national market, the cost to the advertiser of reaching a thousand viewers can still be a reasonable one when he uses the network setup.

Community Antenna Television (CATV) is becoming a more important segment of the field. It enables homes in poor receiving areas, or where there are no local stations, to get TV reception. It uses a master antenna to receive signals from television stations located at some distance, and distributes the signals to the subscriber homes by cable. There are now some 2,799 such systems, with 4.5 million subscribers, and with a dollar volume of approximately $200 million. It is strongest in rural and mountain areas where few stations are available and where regular television reception is poor.

---

[4] All from *1971 Broadcasting Yearbook*, pp. 11, E-9, E-12, E-15–16.

The Federal Communications Commission in 1971 did announce a set of rules designed to permit the rapid growth of effective cable systems all over the United States. In general, the rules conceived of cable as a potential source of original programs, two-way communications, and specialized programs for individual markets.

The FCC banned cross-ownership of CATV and television stations in a market, and ordered networks out of CATV entirely. The rules also required that: Cable systems help subsidize noncommercial television; copyright owners be paid for use of their material; and CATV systems with more than 3,500 subscribers begin originating programs in 1971.

TV receiving sets available

As mentioned earlier, of prime importance to the advertiser is the number of TV receiving sets in the homes of potential customers (or in public places) that can receive the advertising message as it is broadcast by the stations and networks available. (Although a number of sets in various public places enables people to view television, it is believed they constitute a minor segment of the TV viewing audience today and will for the most part be omitted from this discussion.) As of September 1971, out of a total of 65,507,300 households in the United States, the American Research Bureau estimated there were a total of 62,969,100 "TV households." That is, approximately 96 percent[5] of all U.S. households have at least one TV set available for viewing advertising broadcasts by the above television stations.

More than 40 percent of households own two or more sets; more than 45 percent own one or more color sets; 50 percent own one or more UHF sets; and 7½ percent are CATV subscribers.[6]

There is only a slight variation geographically in the share of households equipped with one or more television sets. The New England and East North Central areas have 97 percent; the Middle Atlantic, South Atlantic, West North Central, and Pacific areas have 96 percent; the West South Central and Mountain areas have 95 percent; and the East South Central 94 percent.

Types of TV advertising

Television advertising is commonly classified as network, national spot, or local advertising.

Network advertising. This is using the facilities of one of the three networks in which the program and commercial are produced, or origi-

---

[5] "Estimates of U.S. Television Households," American Research Bureau, September 1971–August 1972, p. 3.

[6] *BBDO Audience Coverage and Cost Guide,* 10th ed., 1971, p. 9.

nate, as a central station, or studio, from which the broadcast is sent out to the other stations of the network. This obtains wide and simultaneous coverage of the country with a single telecast.

Several of the advantages to the advertiser in using network advertising have been alluded to in the previous discussion. Often they permit the production of top-quality shows which attract large audiences and enhance the prestige of the advertiser, both with the consumer and the trade. The networks usually have the best hours for broadcasting on the stations in the network. The arrangements for network advertising are much simpler than for spot campaigns, and the cost is lower on a network basis than it would be for the same time bought from the individual stations involved. Even though the network time cost is high, it may actually be quite economical on the basis of cost per thousand viewers, assuming the distribution of the advertiser's product parallels fairly closely the pattern of the network stations.

There are some weaknesses of network advertising which the advertiser must consider with respect to his individual needs. Some stations in the network may be relatively weak in their market areas. If the advertiser has weak distribution in some areas, he may not gain full benefit from some of the stations included in the network. The show that carries a commercial must be the same for all markets, whereas the tastes of people do vary by areas of the country. Programs vary widely in their popularity in different parts of the United States. The advertiser usually must make fairly long and costly commitments on network advertising.

National spot advertising. All nonnetwork broadcasting and advertising, that which originates in the single station broadcasting it, is called spot broadcasting and spot advertising. Any such nonnetwork advertising paid for by a general (national) advertiser is "national spot" advertising. The advertiser who uses national spot advertising may use the sponsored program approach or the announcement approach. He may have a program filmed or taped and then have it used on selected individual stations in the various markets he wishes to reach at the time he selects in each market. Or the advertiser may prepare his commercial announcements and have them aired during participation shows or during station breaks on the stations and at the times he buys. In either event, he can buy the stations he desires in each market and the times he desires on each station (subject, of course, to the availability of the desired times).

It is obvious that this procedure has certain real advantages for the advertiser. In the terminology used with regard to print media also, spot advertising is highly selective. The advertiser can choose exactly which markets to cover with his advertising and can omit all others. He can also select different programs for different markets if such procedure is believed to be desirable, and he can schedule his program or announcements for what he considers the best time of day and the best day of the week for each. The advertiser can also, of course, vary the commercial announcement itself for each market, should he so desire, including the appeal used and the personality delivering the advertising message. If the advertiser has a line of products, he can also advertise different products in various local markets as deemed desirable.

The other main advantage of spot advertising is its flexibility. The advertiser can gear the amount of advertising he places in any market to what he believes the current situation there demands. He can meet varying seasonal needs easily with spot advertising. It is possible to run intensive campaigns in each individual market as he introduces a new product or special promotion there. The advertiser can vary the type and amount of advertising in terms of both time and market. He can adjust all facets of his program to meet the conditions of the individual markets. In a sense, spot television advertising fits the adage so often used with respect to newspaper advertising (as contrasted with national magazines not having regional editions), "All business is local."

Local. Local television advertising is done primarily by retailers. It may utilize programs produced and sponsored by a retailer, or, it may be a network show which is sponsored in part by a local advertiser. It may be a syndicated series which a retailer sponsors. Much of local advertising consists of spot announcements, and much of it is cooperative advertising which is sponsored by the retailer but paid for in part by the manufacturer.

Planning use of TV advertising

In planning for use of television as an advertising medium, the advertiser must consider several general aspects. Among these are: the type of program he will sponsor or use as a vehicle for his advertisement (if any); whether he will use spot announcements or sponsor a program; and the day and the time of day he will utilize the medium.

The advertiser must consider whether to use a regularly scheduled national show, to share a program by cosponsoring or using alternate sponsorships, or a participating program. And he must decide what type of program or show he will sponsor (comedy, drama, sports events, etc.). He will try to select a program appropriate to the product, that will attract the largest possible audience of potential customers, and that will also influence his dealers and sales organization favorably.

The advertiser must also decide whether to sponsor a program or use spot announcements. There are several advantages to sponsoring a TV program. He can conceivably tailor it to fit his special desires. Sponsoring a good-quality, popular program gives prestige to both consumers and the trade. Often the program and its stars can be used effectively as a merchandising device. Also, the advertiser can control the placement or timing of his commercials, and can integrate them into the program if he so desires. Due to high costs, advertisers will often cosponsor a program or sponsor it on alternate weeks.

As noted earlier, the spot announcement approach gives the advertiser much more flexibility. He can run a "saturation" campaign, concentrating his expenditures in a short time period, or in certain areas. He can run a very strong introductory campaign for a new product, and then change to a normal sustaining campaign later.

Due to the high costs of one-sponsor shows, and the risks involved in selecting a popular show, fewer advertisers are sponsoring programs, but instead are either buying participations in a number of programs or using the spot announcement approach.

The current trend in programming is for networks to plan the pattern of the programs on their networks, particularly during the prime evening hours, in an attempt to obtain the largest possible audience in competition with the other networks. This approach is called the "magazine concept," with the network or station planning the programs (like the magazine plans the editorial material in its publications) and selling only spot announcements. The advertiser controls merely the advertisement itself.

Another trend which is evolving is a reduction in the number of half-hour series shows. Instead, there are more lengthy shows, many of them movies and specials. The networks believe the longer programs—60 to 90 minutes are the best approach for the time from 7:30 P.M. to 11 P.M. They feel the longer shows give more time for plot development, which enables them to hold an audience for the whole evening, especially if they follow the long programs with a movie. Also noticeable is the tendency to use shows that appeal to a broad cross section of audience, particularly a large share of the younger audience, where much of the buying power is concentrated.

The TV audience

Obviously, when the advertiser considers television as a medium for his advertising, he is interested in the questions of size and composition of the audience he can reach.

FIGURE 12–1. TV audience composition

	Homes using TV	Number of viewers per home	Men	Women	Teens	Children
Mon.–Fri.:						
M–F, 10 a.m.–1 p.m.	24.0%	1.39	17%	53%	5%	25%
Mon.–Fri.: 1–5 p.m.	32.0	1.45	16	53	8	23
All nights: 7:30–11 p.m.	64.3	2.12	32	40	10	18

Source: *1971 Broadcasting Yearbook*, p. 64.

The average American home views TV for a total of 6 hours and 18 minutes a day.[7] Figure 12–1 gives an idea of the general composition of the audience by time of day and days of the week.

Measuring the TV audience

Several methods of measuring this audience of individual stations and of specific programs have been developed and are being used currently. They are all based on the same general basic concept. That is, all systems use some method of contacting a sample of television homes to determine their viewing habits, at what hour the television set was turned on, and to which program or station it was tuned. This data collected from the sample is then expanded to give figures for the total statistical universe or market for which the specific study is being made. Hence, figures on viewing habits are estimated for the particular city or market or for the whole United States, and for all viewers or viewers of a particular station or a specific program.

A number of different measures of the television viewing audience ordinarily are used. The *sets-in-use* (sometimes called "households using television") measure is a figure showing the percentage of all homes in the sample (city, market, or country) in which the television set was turned on at the time the measuring was done. For example, if the measurement was made of the U.S. audience at 8–8:30, Saturday night, and 50 percent of the sets included in the sample were turned on at the time, the national figure for sets in use would be 50 percent. For the United States, that would mean that 50 percent of the sets, or approximately 31.5 million sets, were turned on.

Another very important measure used is the *program rating,* or the percentage of all homes in the sample involved tuned in to the particular program being rated. In the above example, if 15 percent of all sets in the study were tuned in to the program X, the program *rating* would be 15 percent, or, as usually expressed, 15.

The *share-of-audience* is a frequently used measure of comparison. This is the percentage of those homes having the television set turned on that are tuned in to the particular program being measured. In the above hypothetical illustrations, since 15 percent of the stations were tuned to program X, and 50 percent of all television households had sets turned on, the *share-of-audience* would be 15/50, or 30 percent. The *total audience,* a measure also used, is the total number of homes the study indicates is listening to the program. In the above case, it would be 15 percent of the total U.S. TV homes, 63 million, or approximately 10 million homes.

Audience composition is also an important measurement. This refers to the distribution of the audience by demographic factors.

[7] *1971 Broadcasting Yearbook,* p. 11.

A number of different techniques or methods are being used currently to obtain these measurements of the size of television audiences. One method involves placing a recording device on the television set in a carefully selected sample of television homes. An example of this is the *audimeter* method used by the A. C. Nielsen Company. The audimeter records on a continuous basis the time the set is turned on, to what station it is tuned, and the time the station is tuned in and out. In this way, an accurate measure is obtained of the time a set is turned on, the program to which a set is tuned, and what dialing and shifting of stations is done during the commercials on the station break. The sample of 1200 homes can be drawn scientifically from the entire population of television homes and then expanded to the total universe. Accurate trends of the above type of information can be obtained, since the same sample is used over a period of time. The chief criticism of this method is that it measures only that the set is turned on, and gives no indication of who was viewing the program or whether they were viewing and listening during the commercials. Also, it gives no indication of whether viewers can identify sponsors or the message carried by the commercials. Recordings are made on a two-week basis, but reports to clients are not made until approximately three weeks after the end of the two-week measuring period. This method is rather costly, and occasionally mechanical failure of the audimeter eliminates a few members of the sample.

A second method of measurement is the *coincidental telephone* method. This involves telephoning a sample of homes during the broadcast to determine whether or not the television set is turned on and, if so, to what program and station the set is tuned. With this method, it is possible to ask additional questions, such as who is viewing the program, the product advertised, and the sponsor of the program. This method is used extensively for measuring local market areas. It has the following advantages: it is fast, since ratings can be supplied the day following the broadcast; it is relatively inexpensive; it does not rely on the accuracy of people's memories; it can check on actual viewing and people's awareness of the advertiser and the product or service or idea he is advertising. The chief disadvantage of this method is that it can include only households having telephones. In addition, it is used only in large cities and is limited in the hours during which calls can be made to approximately the span, 8 A.M. to 10 P.M. It obtains information at only the instant the telephone call is completed. As in any telephone interviewing, the number of questions must be limited, and it must be assumed the respondent is giving accurate information.

A third method of measurement is the *roster-recall* method. This technique consists of having personal interviewers call at homes to show the respondents a roster, or list, of the stations in the area and the programs being broadcast. The interviewees are asked to indicate which stations and programs they recall having watched. Usually, the interviews include only a few hours of programs and are conducted shortly after the broadcasting period involved. This method can include all homes, including nontelephone homes, and has the usual advantages of personal interviewing. On the other hand, its use is restricted normally to larger cities, it does depend on the accuracy of the interviewee's memory, and it is subject to possible bias in that the interviewee may check more of the better programs in order to make a favorable impression on the interviewer.

The *diary* method consists of giving to a selected sample of television people or television homes a diary form requesting them to keep a record of all their viewing of television programs. They are asked to record their viewing at the time it takes place to minimize dependence on memory. This method can cover viewing time outside as well as in the home, and can supply information about viewers similar to that obtained in the methods using the automatic recorder and the roster-recall. It is also a relatively low-cost technique. The usual criticisms of this method are based on the question of the accuracy with which people will keep such a diary.

Since these methods vary considerably in the techniques involved, it is not too unexpected that their results in program ratings sometimes vary considerably. There is much discussion regarding the accuracy of the ratings and the amount of influence they have on the programs that are sponsored on television, particularly on national networks.

The program rating figure is the most widely publicized and used of the measurements discussed above. However, the advertiser should exercise care in the use of the program rating figure. This figure does not give consideration to the average number of people who may be viewing the program on each set, nor does it provide information on the composition of the viewing audience.

And, to the advertiser, even more important is the question of whether or not the people actually viewing the program are potential users of his product. Also, he is highly interested in knowing whether or not the viewers are actually viewing his commercial message as well as the program itself, and how many saw, understood, and were influenced by his commercial. Hence, it is obvious that the advertiser should not be ruled by a program's rating, although trends in program rating may well be very important to him. He should also use the other reports on television audiences offered by some of the research services, and study the local market reports to ascertain the variations in viewing by area.

Cost of television advertising

The advertiser who sponsors his own program on television has two basic cost elements—program costs and time charges. The television advertiser also must pay such expenses as those required for studio rehearsal time and production. The cost of an individually sponsored program can be very high. In a few instances, a single hour-and-a-half spectacular has cost a sponsor over a million dollars for the program alone. Many of the regular network shows cost up to $100,000 per broadcast for the talent alone.

This factor has led to the increased use of alternate sponsoring and cosponsoring of programs, and, more recently, wide use of the scatter plan —buying participations in a number of different network programs or station break periods.

Rate structure

Television rates are quoted on the basis of periods of time and vary according to the time of day involved. The usual time periods are one hour, a half hour, a quarter hour, ten minutes, five minutes, one minute, twenty seconds, and ten seconds. In some cases, a one-and-one-half-hour period will be sold for special shows, or spectaculars, and for unusual events, longer periods of time may be arranged and shown. The periods of one minute and less are called announcements, and are placed at the breaks between programs or in participating programs. The basic rate which the television station charges for its time periods is set according to the time of day the program is shown or the commercial announcement is given.

A typical time division and hourly rate structure for programs is given in Figure 12–2. A typical time division and schedule of charges for announcements is given in Figure 12–3. It will be noted that stations vary their rates depending on the time of day or night involved, reflecting the normal differences in the size of the audience attracted at those hours. In Figure 12–2 it is seen that the station charges $1,170 for a one-half hour program period in class "AAA" time, from 7:30 P.M. to 11:00 P.M. Monday through Friday; 7 P.M. to 11 P.M. Saturday; 6 P.M. to 11 P.M. Sunday. The charge is $315 for a one-half hour program in class D time, sign-on to 10:30 A.M. Sunday through Friday, and sign-on to 9 A.M. Saturday, with charges for in-between times, AA, A, B, and C running $921, $852, $630, and $519 respectively.

The basic rates given in Figures 12–2 and 12–3 generally include transmitter, film facilities, necessary film rehearsals, and studio facilities (except audience participation). Rates quoted ordinarily do not include special production services, art department, talent, staging, and others.

The national and regional television networks set their rates on the basis of the time of day the program is shown, the number of stations of the network which the advertiser includes, and the amount of time for which the advertiser contracts in a given period.

Some examples of the cost of one minute of network television commercial time on well-known programs might be of interest. One minute of commercial time on the average professional football game broad-

FIGURE 12–2

PROGRAMS
Time Classifications

Class "AAA" — 7:30 p.m. to 11:00 p.m. Monday through Friday; 7:00 p.m. to 11:00 p.m. Saturday; 6:00 p.m. to 11:00 p.m. Sunday.
Class "AA" — 7:00 p.m. to 7:30 p.m. Monday through Friday; 6:30 p.m. to 7:00 p.m. Saturday.
Class "A" — 6:00 p.m. to 7:00 p.m. Monday through Friday; 5:00 p.m. to 6:00 p.m. Sunday; 6:00 p.m. to 6:30 p.m. Saturday; 11:00 p.m. to 11:15 p.m. Sunday through Saturday.
Class "B" — 5:00 p.m. to 6:00 p.m. Monday through Friday; 9:00 a.m. to 6:00 p.m. Saturday; noon to 5:00 p.m. Sunday; 11:15 p.m. to conclusion Sunday through Saturday.
Class "C" — 10:30 a.m. to 5:00 p.m. Monday through Friday; 10:30 a.m. to noon Sunday.
Class "D" — Sign-on to 10:30 a.m. Sunday through Friday; sign-on to 9:00 a.m. Saturday.

	1 hr.	1/2 hr.	1/4 hr.	10 min.	5 min.
CLASS "AAA"					
1 ti...	1,950.00	1,170.00	780.00	685.00	585.00
26 ti...	1,853.00	1,112.00	741.00	651.00	556.00
52 ti...	1,755.00	1,053.00	702.00	617.00	527.00
104 ti...	1,658.00	995.00	663.00	582.00	497.00
156 ti...	1,560.00	936.00	624.00	548.00	468.00
CLASS "AA"					
1 ti...	1,535.00	921.00	614.00	538.00	461.00
26 ti...	1,458.00	875.00	583.00	511.00	438.00
52 ti...	1,382.00	829.00	553.00	484.00	415.00
104 ti...	1,305.00	783.00	522.00	457.00	392.00
156 ti...	1,228.00	737.00	491.00	430.00	369.00
CLASS "A"					
1 ti...	1,420.00	852.00	568.00	497.00	426.00
26 ti...	1,349.00	809.00	540.00	472.00	405.00
52 ti...	1,278.00	767.00	511.00	447.00	383.00
104 ti...	1,207.00	724.00	483.00	422.00	362.00
156 ti...	1,136.00	682.00	454.00	398.00	341.00
CLASS "B"					
1 ti...	1,050.00	630.00	420.00	368.00	315.00
26 ti...	998.00	599.00	399.00	350.00	299.00
52 ti...	945.00	567.00	378.00	331.00	284.00
104 ti...	893.00	536.00	357.00	313.00	268.00
156 ti...	840.00	504.00	336.00	294.00	252.00
CLASS "C"					
1 ti...	865.00	519.00	346.00	303.00	260.00
26 ti...	822.00	493.00	329.00	288.00	247.00
52 ti...	779.00	467.00	311.00	273.00	234.00
104 ti...	735.00	441.00	294.00	258.00	221.00
156 ti...	692.00	415.00	277.00	242.00	208.00
CLASS "D"					
1 ti...	525.00	315.00	210.00	184.00	158.00
26 ti...	499.00	299.00	200.00	175.00	150.00
52 ti...	473.00	283.00	189.00	166.00	142.00
104 ti...	446.00	268.00	179.00	156.00	134.00
156 ti...	420.00	252.00	168.00	147.00	126.00

FIGURE 12–3

ANNOUNCEMENTS
Time Classifications

Class "AAA" — 7:29 p.m. to 10:30 p.m. daily.
Class "AA" — 6:59 p.m. to 7:29 p.m. and 10:30 p.m. to 11:00 p.m. daily.
Class "A" — 4:59 p.m. to 6:59 p.m. and 11:00 p.m. to sign-off daily.
Class "B" — 8:59 a.m. to 4:59 p.m. daily.
Class "C" — Sign-on to 8:59 a.m. daily.

SECTION I
(Units per week)

60/30 seconds:	Class "AAA"	Class "AA"	Class "A"	Class "B"	Class "C"
1 time..	160.00	140.00	100.00	60.00	40.00
2 times	160.00	119.00	85.00	51.00	34.00
3-4 times	160.00	112.00	80.00	48.00	32.00
5-6 times	160.00	98.00	70.00	42.00	28.00
7-9 times	160.00	84.00	60.00	36.00	24.00
10-11 times	160.00	77.00	55.00	33.00	22.00
12+ times..	160.00	70.00	50.00	30.00	20.00
20 seconds:					
1 time..	140.00	120.00	100.00	60.00	40.00
2 times	140.00	102.00	85.00	51.00	34.00
3-4 times	140.00	96.00	80.00	48.00	32.00
5-6 times	140.00	84.00	70.00	42.00	28.00
7-9 times	140.00	72.00	60.00	36.00	24.00
10-11 times	140.00	66.00	55.00	33.00	22.00
12+ times..	140.00	60.00	50.00	30.00	20.00
10 seconds:					
1 time..	70.00	60.00	50.00	30.00	20.00
2 times	70.00	51.00	42.50	25.50	17.00
3-4 times	70.00	48.00	40.00	24.00	16.00
5-6 times	70.00	42.00	35.00	21.00	14.00
7-9 times	70.00	36.00	30.00	18.00	12.00
10-11 times	70.00	33.00	27.50	16.50	11.00
12+ times..	70.00	30.00	25.00	15.00	10.00

40-SECOND ANNOUNCEMENTS
40-second rate is twice the 20-second rate in Class "AAA" time; all other times the same as minute rate.

SECTION II
The purchase of 1 Class "AAA" spot weekly on Section I earns 50% discount from the 1-time rate on all Class "AA," "A," "B" and "C" spots, except in special participating features where a flat rate exists. Spots non pre-emptible.

	Class "AA"	Class "A"	Class "B"	Class "C"
60/30 seconds	70.00	50.00	30.00	20.00
Station break	60.00	50.00	30.00	20.00
Identification	30.00	25.00	15.00	10.00

cast costs $65,000; on National Collegiate Athletic Association games, $50,000; and on the Superbowl game, $200,000. One minute of commercial time on a World Series baseball special broadcast costs $82,000. An idea of relative costs involved is obtained when it is noted that 40 percent of TV households are reached by a Superbowl game, or an advertising cost of $8.60 per thousand; whereas the average Monday night professional game reaches 19 percent of households at a cost of $5.70 per 1,000; and the World Series delivers 24 percent of households at a cost of $5.70 per thousand.[8]

Discounts

As a rule, television stations offer a cumulative quantity discount rate based on the number of time units the advertiser uses during a given

[8] Source: *BBDO Audience Coverage and Cost Guide* (10th ed.; BBDO Media Department, 1971), p. 15.

period. Common patterns are to quote discounts based on cycles of 13 times, 26 times, 39 times, 52 time periods, and so on. And in the case of 60-second announcements, 20-second station break spots, and 10-second ID's, discounts often are given based on the quantity bought during a week. Some offer lower summer rates (June through August).

Advantages of TV as an advertising medium

The obvious and chief advantage of television as an advertising medium is that it makes full use of both sight and sound. Print media rely on sight only, and the ability of the potential customer to read the advertisement.

TV can attract the attention and interest of the potential customer through both sight and sound in combination. In addition, it has a great advantage of being able to use motion. This permits the actual demonstration of the product in use to be made by a living salesman. Since the salesman can discuss and explain the use of the product and its advantages and features as he demonstrates it in use on television, the commercial is the nearest thing to personal selling that can be achieved in advertising or promotion.

Also, while the commercial is on the screen, there is no competition from adjacent editorial material, as is true of print media. And it permits the use of the human voice, which many consider more effective for numerous purposes than the printed word because of its intimate nature. Television also permits the use of color, which can add greatly to the effectiveness of the advertising, and permits the commercial to do an excellent job of package identification.

Another important advantage of television, although not inherent to the medium, has developed. Because of its tremendous popularity, it has proven to be a true mass medium. Since 96 percent of all homes have television receiving sets, and the average home has a set turned on over six hours a day, the advertiser using television can reach almost all the people in all parts of the United States with his message. As a result, many advertisers of widely used items employ television as a medium even though they make little use of the demonstration advantage of television, but do basically much purely reminder type advertising. Closely tied in with this factor of television's effectiveness in reaching and influencing such a large proportion of the people is the advantage of television advertising's effectiveness in influencing the trade.

Television also has the advantage of being relatively selective and flexible in several ways. By the selection of type of program, the advertiser can gain a relatively selective type of listening audience. Also, the selection of time of day and day of the week permits a certain selectivity of audience. He can select only those markets and areas in which he wishes to advertise and those stations he wishes to use. The television advertiser can use as much or as little time as he desires. He can use spot television to run seasonal advertising programs, and can run saturation programs for special occasions such as promotions or introduction of new products. The advertiser also can use different appeals in various local markets as he deems desirable, and, in the case of spot television, can make his message timely.

Limitations of television

As is true of all advertising media, television does have certain limitations or weaknesses. The advertising message lasts only as long as it is being presented on the receiving screen. If the prospect is not viewing or listening at the exact moment the advertisement is presented, the message is gone forever and wasted as far as that prospect is concerned. This is quite a contrast to print media, where the message may be available to the prospect over quite an extended period of time.

Also, since in most markets several television stations are broadcasting at the same time, the message of any advertiser can reach only that portion of the total viewing audience tuned to a particular station at that time. And, in the case of announcement advertising on station break time, his audience may be further reduced, because many viewers may be twirling the tuning knob, selecting a new station for the next time period. Even during sponsored programs, viewers may leave the set during the commercial to do other things, thus missing the commercial message.

The cost of good programs is very high, eliminating this form of television advertising as a medium for many smaller advertisers. Also, the advertising message must be brief.

Another problem or handicap in the use of television is that of different time zones existing in the United States. A program broadcast on the East Coast at the prime time of 8 p.m. would be heard at 5 p.m. on the West Coast, during the childrens' hour, if broadcast simultaneously on a national network. To compound this problem, various areas of the country have different daylight saving practices. Advertisers can and do overcome this timing problem by using electrical transcriptions or delayed broadcasts. Possibly a greater time handicap is that there are only so many desirable hours available on a television network, so that the number of advertisers who can use desirable time is limited.

RADIO

The organization of the radio field

As is true with television, the advertiser considering the use of radio as an advertising medium is interested in the facilities provided for broadcasting and receiving his advertising messages. Similar to television, three segments of facilities are of interest to the potential advertiser. These are the individual stations, the network system, and the number of receiving sets owned.

Number of stations. The basic unit in the radio field is the individual local station. As of February 1, 1971, there were 4,327 AM radio stations licensed, and 2,303 commercial FM stations.[9]

The networks. As is true in television, many of the leading radio stations are organized into networks. These were formed early in the history of radio to provide programs to the affiliated stations in local markets covering the country, which could be broadcast simultaneously by telephone cable. This enabled advertisers to broadcast their advertising messages to most parts of the country through one organization, as is done in television today. There are 4 national networks and 53 regional radio networks.

Before television reached its present great popularity, the radio networks were important, and most radio advertising was network. Since the present wide viewing of television, the radio networks have declined in relative importance, and only a small percentage of radio advertising is network, compared with national spot and local.

For selected years the expenditures for the three types of radio advertising have been as shown in Figure 12–4:[10]

FIGURE 12–4

	National network	National spot	Local
1945	125,671,834	76,696,463	99,814,042
1950	124,633,089	118,823,880	203,211,000
1953	60,268,000	120,393,000	272,011,000
1960	35,026,000	202,102,000	385,346,000
1965	44,602,000	247,942,000	535,238,000
1969	50,900,000	349,604,000	799,900,000

Sets available. According to latest Radio Advertising Bureau estimates, there were over 321 million radio sets, or over $1\frac{1}{2}$ sets for every man, woman, and child in the United States as of January 1971. The average American household has over three radios. Almost every household owns at least one radio.

Of the 321 million sets, 230 million are in households, while the remaining 91 million are in automobiles and public places. (Estimates are that 80 percent of automobiles have radios). Approximately 80 million sets are FM—bringing the FM household penetration to nearly 75 percent.[11]

---

[9] *1971 Broadcasting Yearbook,* p. 11.

[10] *1971 Broadcasting Yearbook,* p. 13.

[11] *BBDO Audience Coverage and Cost Guide,* 10th ed., 1971, p. 21.

Literally millions of people own either regular portable radios or the small transistor radios which they carry with them in their pockets. Thus, the average American is physically in a position to listen to radio at almost every hour that he is awake. In one day, 92.1 million U.S. adults (18 years and over), or 75.1 percent, are reached by radio; and in seven days (the cumulative reach of radio) 111 million adults or 90.5 percent, are reached.[12] Although the amount of family listening to radio in the evening has declined drastically since the advent of television, the great number of sets of various types in use indicates that the average American, as an individual, still spends considerable time listening to radio.

Radio programs. The advertiser using radio must decide whether or not to use a sponsored program. However, in recent years, with the television's taking over the main big-show entertainment aspects of broadcasting, the number of sponsored programs has declined drastically. Although many of the comments made earlier about the advantages of the sponsored show on television are true of radio, it must be remembered that the sponsored radio show does not carry the same amount of prestige today that it did in the past. Also, the radio show is much less costly to produce. Production costs are much lower than for television shows, because they are much simpler to produce, usually calling for less expensive talent, much less rehearsal time, and do not call for the staging and costuming required on television.

Today the majority of advertisers using radio do not use sponsored shows. Most radio stations and the networks have adopted what is often referred to as the "magazine format" of programming. That is, the network or stations plan the programming for the day and week to develop a listening audience for the station, much as a magazine develops a particular editorial content to appeal to a certain audience. This involves the use of many participation programs, with the station responsible for the production of the program. A large portion of the programs in radio today consists largely of news and music, following a planned general format. The advertiser's commercials are interspersed in the participation shows or inserted in the station breaks, as is done to a more limited extent on television.

Audience measurement in radio. Basically, the same general approach is used in the measurement of the radio audience as is used in television, that of determining the listening of a sample of homes and expanding this percentage to determine the number of homes in the universe that are listening. In doing this, radio uses the same four techniques for determining listenership as are used to determine viewing in television. However, there is one additional serious problem in the case of radio. As noted earlier, a very large share of the radio listening is

---

[12] *1971 Broadcasting Yearbook*, p. 65.

done outside of the home (while driving in automobiles, at the beach, or on picnics in the case of portables, and at various times and places with the use of transistor sets), and it is difficult to measure the actual amount of such listening. This audience can be measured by the use of personal interviews and diaries, but it still makes extremely difficult the accurate determination of the size of the radio audience.

The cost of radio advertising. As is true of television, the advertiser using radio as a medium must consider two basic elements of cost—time charges and program costs. However, unlike television, studio rehearsal time and production expenses are relatively low, particularly today when few of the high-salaried performers are employed in radio. In the case of sponsored programs, the advertiser will find the same time unit structure on radio as in television. If he decides to use the announcement approach rather than a sponsored program, he will have basically the same selection as in television, except that he may find available a somewhat wider choice in short commercial times. Radio time charges have continued to decrease in many areas as station owners have tried to meet the competition of other media, especially television. Spot announcements, cooperative sponsoring of special programs, special concessions, and other inducements have been used.

Radio stations today generally set their rates on the basis of three classes of time. The periods indicated in Figure 12–5 are typical of the classification definitions.

A sample of the costs for announcements can be obtained from Figure 12–7.

A typical table of time charges for programs is indicated in Figure 12–6.

FIGURE 12–5. Three-class time breakdown (usually used for program time purposes)

Class AA: 6 a.m. to 10 a.m. and 3 p.m. to 7 p.m., Monday through Friday.
Class A: 10 a.m. to 3 p.m. Monday through Friday; 6 a.m. to 7 p.m., Saturday.
Class B: 7 p.m. to midnight, Monday through Saturday; 7 a.m. to midnight on Sunday.

FIGURE 12–6. Station time rates

	1 Hour	½ Hour	¼ Hour	10 Minutes	5 Minutes
Class AA.................	$265.00	$160.00	$110.00	$90.00	$55.00
Class A.................	225.00	135.00	95.00	75.00	45.00
Class B.................	155.00	90.00	65.00	50.00	30.00

Discounts

13 consecutive weeks..	5%
26 consecutive weeks..	10
39 consecutive weeks..	15
52 consecutive weeks or more..	20

FIGURE 12–7. Spot announcements

Regular announcements (rotate 6:00–10:00 a.m. and 3:00–7:00 p.m.)
Annual frequency

Per wk: 1 minute	1–25 ti	Class AA 26– 103 ti	104– 155 ti	156– 311 ti	312– 467 ti	468 or more ti
1 ti.............	110.00	99.00	93.50	88.00	85.25	82.50
5 ti.............	104.50	94.05	88.83	83.60	80.99	78.38
10 ti.............	99.00	89.10	84.15	79.20	76.73	74.25
15 ti.............	93.50	84.15	79.48	74.80	72.46	70.13
20 ti.............	88.00	79.20	74.80	70.40	68.20	66.00
25 ti.............	82.50	74.25	70.13	66.00	63.94	61.88
30 second						
1 ti.............	100.00	90.00	85.00	80.00	77.50	75.00
5 ti.............	95.00	85.50	80.75	76.00	73.63	71.25
10 ti.............	90.00	81.00	76.50	72.00	69.75	67.50
15 ti.............	85.00	76.50	72.25	68.00	65.88	63.75
20 ti.............	80.00	72.00	68.00	64.00	62.00	60.00
25 ti.............	75.00	67.50	63.75	60.00	58.13	56.25
1 minute		*Class A*				
1 ti.............	60.00	54.00	51.00	48.00	46.50	45.00
5 ti.............	57.00	51.30	48.45	45.60	44.18	42.75
10 ti.............	54.00	48.60	45.90	43.20	41.85	40.50
15 ti.............	51.00	45.90	43.35	40.80	39.53	38.25
20 ti.............	48.00	43.20	40.80	38.40	37.20	36.00
25 ti.............	45.00	40.50	38.25	36.00	34.88	33.75
30 second						
1 ti.............	54.00	48.60	45.90	43.20	41.85	40.50
5 ti.............	51.30	46.17	43.61	41.04	39.76	38.48
10 ti.............	48.60	43.74	41.31	38.88	37.67	36.45
15 ti.............	45.90	41.31	39.02	36.72	35.57	34.43
20 ti.............	43.20	38.88	36.72	34.56	33.48	32.40
25 ti.............	40.50	36.45	34.43	32.40	31.39	30.38
1 minute		*Class B*				
1 ti.............	35.00	31.50	29.75	28.00	27.13	26.25
5 ti.............	33.25	29.93	28.26	26.60	25.77	24.94
10 ti.............	31.50	28.35	26.78	25.20	24.42	23.63
15 ti.............	29.75	26.78	25.29	23.80	23.06	22.31
20 ti.............	28.00	25.20	23.80	22.40	21.70	21.00
25 ti.............	26.25	23.63	22.31	21.00	20.35	19.69
30 second						
1 ti.............	30.00	27.00	25.50	24.00	23.25	22.50
5 ti.............	28.50	25.65	24.23	22.80	22.09	21.38
10 ti.............	27.00	24.30	22.95	21.60	20.93	20.25
15 ti.............	25.50	22.95	21.68	20.40	19.76	19.13
20 ti.............	24.00	21.60	20.40	19.20	18.60	18.00
25 ti.............	22.50	20.25	19.13	18.00	17.44	16.88

20-second announcements—80% of 1-minute rate.
10-second announcements—50% of 1-minute rate.

Selecting the program and station

Although in general the discussion of television program selection holds true for radio, it should be stressed that since relatively few advertisers sponsor programs today, this problem does not have the importance in the radio field that it does in television or did formerly in radio. However, if the advertiser using radio does wish to sponsor a program, the same concept of selecting a program that will appeal to his potential customers is the dominating consideration. For instance, a number of advertisers still sponsor sports contests on radio, since it is believed they attract a large listening audience with certain characteristics and can, therefore, be a very effective vehicle for many products. Because of the emphasis on the so-called magazine format approach and the heavy emphasis on news and music, the advertiser must decide what type of participation program attracts the best audience for his product.

The criteria for selecting the station are the same in radio as in television. Probably the main difference is that there are many more radio stations than TV stations, and so the alternatives are increased. Too, with the greater number of stations, including commercial FM stations, and their attempts to develop special audiences through their programming, it may be possible in some cases for the advertiser to obtain a station appealing more specifically to his segment of the market, giving him greater selectivity of audience.

Advantages of radio

The chief feature of radio as an advertising medium is that it depends solely on the spoken word. Thus, the listener can hear the programs and the commercials while doing other things, such as driving a car or doing housework. It does not require the effort and concentration required by other media. And the human voice is probably the most natural way for people to communicate with each other. The human voice has a warmth and persuasiveness in conveying a message that can be most effective. It permits the listener to develop his own image of the program or store or setting, and to involve himself in the situation in his own preferred way, since he does not see the setting or action or announcers. In many instances, such mental imagery can be much more effective than any actual setting and performance.

Also, radio can and does reach almost everybody. As noted earlier, virtually every home and most automobiles have radios, and many individuals have a portable set, so that most people have sets available to them at almost every hour of the day. Thus, people can listen to radio at almost any time and any place, regardless of their other activities.

Hence, radio can reach a mass market. With the great number of sets in the hands of the population, the potential audience of radio is greater than that of television, all magazines combined, or all newspapers combined.

Radio is a selective medium in the sense that the advertiser can advertise in only those markets he desires. He can vary his messages, and the intensity of coverage of different markets to meet local conditions. He can obtain also, by proper selection of programs, time of day, and stations, selectivity of type of listenership. In the case of FM radio with its features of high-fidelity music reproduction and static-free reception, stations often develop quite a selected segment of the market with excellent musical programming.

Radio is also flexible and timely. The advertiser can run as many commercials in an area or during a period of time as he believes desirable. And news events and special occurrences can be aired on radio almost as soon as they happen. For this reason, many people listen to radio habitually to "keep up with the latest news." This same effect of timeliness can be brought into commercials when announcing special promotions or the introduction of a new product.

As a result of the lack of concentration required in listening to radio, it is probable that a larger percentage of listeners hear the radio commercials than is true with television viewers. A study conducted by the authors indicates this may well be so. In this study, made in a metropolitan area on the West Coast, 52 percent of the respondents indicated that during the television commercial they regularly left their television sets to do other things such as to make telephone calls, work in the kitchen, or get refreshments. Of this same group who responded, only 27 percent said they left their radio sets during the commercials.[13]

Radio advertising is much less costly than most of the advertising media. A single announcement on a station in a small market will cost usually only a few dollars, and on a station in a large metropolitan market will cost usually less than $100. On a national network, such a commercial announcement often will cost the advertiser less than $1,000. As a result, the advertiser can reach a market with a budget much smaller than is needed for television.

Disadvantages of radio

As is true of other media, radio has its real weaknesses as an advertising medium. Like television, the message that radio delivers is a perishable one. If the person is not listening to the advertiser's message at the time it is broadcast, it is gone forever. Also, as is true of television, with

---

[13] C. J. Dirksen, *Listening Habits of TV and Radio Audiences in Santa Clara County* (Santa Clara, Calif.: University of Santa Clara Press, 1957).

the great number of television and radio stations on the air, the advertiser's message can reach only that share of the population listening to his particular station at the time of the broadcast.

The advantage of being able to listen to radio while doing other things means that many people are hearing the radio program only as a background effect, and are not listening attentively. Hence, although they may be listening to the music, they may not actually grasp the content of the advertising message delivered between musical numbers.

Radio is the one medium in which it is impossible to illustrate the product, so it is not a good medium for products which must actually be seen by the potential customer. However, for many products, a verbal description can still be a very effective selling device.

Another current problem in radio, while not inherent as a feature of the medium, is the tendency for many of the stations to crowd in too many commercials—more than the industry codes recommend. This condition has arisen because of the efforts of stations to bolster declining advertising revenue. The result may well be to make all commercials less effective, as well as to cause much criticism of the broadcasting field in general and bring on the distinct possibility of actual government regulation of the number of minutes that commercial announcements may be permitted.

Radio also poses the problem of selecting the station and program that will obtain the desired number and composition of audience the advertiser desires.

QUESTIONS

1. Do you believe television is a better medium for advertising certain types of products than others? If so, give examples and explain why this is true.

2. Does the present wide use of color television add to its suitability for more types of products than when it was "black and white"? Explain.

3. Describe briefly various measures of the television viewing audience that are frequently used. Which do you consider best? Why?

4. What do you understand by the term "magazine concept" as applied to broadcast media? What is its significance to the advertiser on television and radio?

5. Television and radio rates to advertisers are normally established on a time period basis—Class A, Class B, etc.—although the size of the audience within that time period may vary considerably. Would it be better to set rates on the basis of program ratings? Why?

6. Why is the advertiser so interested in the television program on which his advertisement appears?

7. What is a participating program? What are its significant features from an advertiser's standpoint?

8. What are the important factors for an advertiser to consider in determining whether or not to use radio as an advertising medium?

9. Is it possible to use television and radio to reach particular consumer groups or market segments effectively? Explain.

10. How would you use television and radio, on an effective cost basis, to reach farmers? Businessmen? Housewives? Teen-agers?

11. With virtually every American home having at least one television set, and most of them having color, do you believe it possible for radio to compete successfully with television for the advertisers' dollar in the future? Explain.

12. Watch your television programs from 7 to 10 P.M. one evening. List all ads appearing during that time. In your opinion, how many and which ones utilized effectively the features of television as an advertising medium? Explain.

13. Listen to your favorite radio station for one hour. List the ads you heard. How many utilized effectively the features of radio as an advertising medium? Explain.

CASE 1.   RADEK, INC.
Deciding on the use of television advertising

Radek, Inc. one of the leading department stores in a midwestern city, is considering the advisability of putting a major percentage of its advertising budget into television advertising.

The Radek store had used a few spot announcements, as well as special programs, like its competitors, but the amount spent on television had never exceeded more than 2 percent of the annual advertising budget. In the past, Radek's advertising had been concentrated in newspapers, radio, and direct mail.

It was the opinion of the general manager of the store that television would now be a preferred medium for promoting merchandise in its market. He recommended that the advertising department apportion 35 percent of the current budget for this medium.

Radek's yearly sales averaged about $35 million, and the company budgeted 2.75 percent of sales for advertising. Of this amount, the company had been spending about 65 percent for newspaper advertising, 15 percent for radio advertising, and the remaining 20 percent for direct mail and all other forms of advertising.

The general manager, in recommending a greater emphasis on television, pointed out some facts about the medium.

Home audiences

In Radek's trading area 45 percent of the TV sets are owned by the top-third income group. In the middle economic group, ownership is

39 percent, and 16 percent in the remaining economic third. As a result, television advertising could reach all segments of Radek's market.

Television results

It was the opinion of Radek's general manager that the response to television advertising was superior, as indicated by the results shown by local advertisers who have used the medium. The examples covered products or offers in different classifications of advertising: high-priced products, medium-priced products, low-priced products, and free offers (booklets).

High-priced products

Air-conditioning unit. A 12-week local spot campaign at a time and film production cost of $12,700 brought in approximately 800 inquiries for a $400 air conditioner. These inquiries resulted in $160,000 worth of business.

Low-priced products

Product with dual adult and juvenile market. A test survey was conducted one month before the product was advertised on TV, and again after the schedule had been on TV for 13 weeks. Five hundred television

EXHIBIT 1

	Before campaign	13 weeks after start of campaign
Percentage naming advertised product	12.2	23.4
Men	17.4	21.6
Women	10.5	22.2
Children under 18	41.7	62.5
Percentage naming advertised product as		
last brand bought	1.6	5.0
Men	1.4	2.3
Women	1.4	5.3
Children under 18	8.3	12.5

families were visited, and one member in each family was asked what brands or makes he could name and what was the last brand purchased. Increased mention of advertised product and increased sales showed that the five-a-week TV spots had had major impact. (See Exhibit 1.)

Free offers

Cookbook offer. In a given month, thirty-three 40-second free-cookbook offers following an 80-second film playlet in two markets brought in

55,276 requests. Cost of the TV spots was $7,265.43. The unit cost per request was 13 cents. The printed media offer cost, on the other hand, $92,687.77 and brought in 36,541 replies at a unit cost of $2.54 per reply.

In another instance, an advertiser desiring response in order to distribute a booklet about a vacation resort found a careful analysis of inquiries from various media—newspapers, magazines, and television—to reveal the following cost-per-inquiry comparison: television, 27 cents; printed media, 62 cents.

Retail advertising

Radek's advertising manager argued that he was well aware of the impact of television for national advertising, but he did not believe that it could do as good a job at the retail level as could be accomplished with newspapers. He said that the newspaper is the best medium of advertising in which great numbers of people, as a matter of custom, look for advertisements of merchandise or service which they are about to purchase.

He also mentioned that the newspaper is the local medium which is sure to reach daily the interested attention of an audience in excess of the circulation for which the advertiser pays. The newspaper's advertising rate is based generally upon copies sold rather than upon the number of readers. On the other hand, he stated, "that a television message must be received within a fleeting moment. An advertisement in the daily newspaper lives for many hours—and sometimes for days."

The women's market

The advertising manager also believed that television did not penetrate the major important women's market. He stated that there are two major markets: housewives devoting full time to running a home and raising children, and working housewives with a full-time job who run their homes after business hours. More than half of the working housewives are in the 25 to 44 age group and are considered by many to be among the most desirable prospects. These women cannot be reached by daytime TV. About 90 percent work in business or industry an average of 40 hours a week. Their evening TV viewing has to be selective, because evenings are spent catching up on the many household duties. Daytime TV cannot reach many widowed, divorced, or separated women who must also work. There are almost five million women who fall in this category, along with the six million single women who work during the day and cannot be reached by daytime TV.

Cost

The advertising manager stressed that television is an expensive medium for retailers and presented the rates in Exhibit 2 for the local station to indicate the significance of this (see Exhibit 2).

The data for the county in which the Radek Department Store is located is given in Exhibit 3.

EXHIBIT 2. TV rates in Radek's market

ANNOUNCEMENT CLASSIFICATIONS

Most announcements are assigned two prices. Announcements offered at the higher price (fixed rate) may be purchased on a fixed position non-preemptible basis. When purchased at the lower price (preemptible rate) advertisers may be preempted on 2 weeks' notice.

PARTICIPATING ANNOUNCEMENT PROGRAMS
When network or local programming delays the News, Weather and Sports block (including announcements) or other regularly scheduled 10-10:30 pm programs and announcements, regular rates will apply except in instances when the start of the News, Weather and Sports block (including announcements) is delayed until after 10:30 pm.

	Pre-
	Fixed empt

		Fixed	empt
CBS News—7-8 am Mon thru Fri.			
1 min.		22	18
30/20 sec.		14	10
Channel 3 News At Noon—noon-12:30 pm Mon thru Fri.			
1 min.		120	110
30/20 sec.		72	66
Dialing For Dollars/Early Show—3-5 pm Mon thru Fri.			
1 min.		90	80
30/20 sec.		54	48
Perry Mason—rotating 10:30-11:30 pm Sun & Mon.			
1 min.		90	80
30/20 sec.		54	48
It Takes A Thief—9-10 pm Mon.			
1 min.		130	120
30/20 sec.		80	70
Late Show—rotating Tues thru Sat.			
1 min.		54	46
30/20 sec.		32	28
Wackiest Ship in the Army—11:30 pm-concl Sun.			
1 min.		12	10
30/20 sec.		8	6
Channel 3 News At 6—6-6:30 pm rotating Mon thru Fri.			
1 min.		230	200
30/20 sec.		138	120
Thursday & Friday Night CBS Movie, rotating.			
30/20 sec.		200	186
Theatre 3—8:30 pm-concl Sat.			
1 min.		300	240
30/20 sec.		150	120
Channel 3 News At 10—10-10:30 pm approx rotating Sun thru Fri.			
1 min.		220	190
30/20 sec.		132	114
Munsters—5-5:30 pm Mon thru Fri.			
1 min.		120	100
30/20 sec.		72	60

PROGRAM RATES

AA—Daily 6:30-10 pm.
A—Daily 10-10:30 pm; Sat & Sun 6-6:30 pm.
B—Mon thru Fri 5:30-6:30 pm; Sat & Sun 5-6 pm; daily 10:30-11 pm.
C—Mon thru Fri 11 am-5:30 pm; Sat & Sun 11 am-5 pm; daily 11 pm-concl.
D—Daily sign-on-11 am.

CLASS AA	1x	52x	104x	156x
1 hr.	1300	1170	1105	1072
1/2 hr.	780	702	663	644
CLASS A				
1 hr.	1000	900	850	825
1/2 hr.	600	540	510	495
1/4 hr.	400	360	340	330
10 min.	320	285	270	260
5 min.	250	200	190	180
CLASS B				
1 hr.	800	720	680	660
1/2 hr.	480	432	408	396
1/4 hr.	320	288	272	264
10 min.	260	234	221	215
5 min.	240	190	180	170
CLASS C				
1 hr.	650	585	553	536
1/2 hr.	390	351	332	322
1/4 hr.	260	234	221	215
10 min.	185	167	157	153
5 min.	130	105	100	95
CLASS D				
1 hr.	420	378	357	347
1/2 hr.	252	227	214	208
1/4 hr.	168	151	144	139
10 min.	125	113	106	103
5 min.	90	81	77	74

SPOT ANNOUNCEMENTS

AA—Daily 6:30-10 pm.
A—Daily 10-10:30 pm.
B—Daily 6-6:30 pm & 10:30-11 pm.
C—Daily 3:30-6 pm & 11 pm-midnight.
D—Daily sign-on-3:30 pm & midnight-sign-off.

CLASS AA	F	P	Q	I	R
30/20 sec.	190	160	140	120	100

F—Fixed position.
P—Preemptible on 2 weeks' notice.
Q—Preemptible on 1 week's notice.
I—Immediately preemptible.
R—Immediately preemptible without notice.

	—60 Seconds—		—30/20 Seconds—		—10 Sec—	
	F	P	I	F	P	I	F	P
A	145	125	110	87	75	66	52	......
B	95	80	70	57	48	42	30	25
C	85	70	50	51	42	30	26	21
D	50	35	20	30	21	15	15	11

Announcements between rate classifications take the rates of the higher classification except:
3:30 pm Mon thru Fri, takes Class D.
6:30 pm & 10 pm take the following rates:

	M	T	W	Th	F	Sa	Su
60 sec F	115	115	115	115	115	115	......
P	100	100	100	100	100	100	......
30/20 sec F	75	75	75	75	75	75	......
P	60	60	60	60	60	60	......
10:00 PM: 60/30/20							
10 sec F	150	150	150	150	150	150	150
P	130	130	130	130	130	130	130

F—Fixed position.
P—Preemptible on 2 weeks' notice.
I—Immediately preemptible.
The following programs rotate horizontally and vertically:
Late News—Sun thru Sat.
Dragnet—5-5:30 pm Mon thru Fri.
Tonight—Mon thru Fri.

360Advertising principles and problems

EXHIBIT 3. TV market area for department stores

Total households.....................................	275,200
TV households......................................	262,900
Consumer spendable income.....................	$2,724,275,000
Total retail sales..................................	$1,712,387,000
Consumer spendable income per household.......	$10,378

Case questions

1. Do you believe the Radek Department Store should invest 35 percent of its advertising budget in television advertising? Why or why not?

2. If the company decided to use television, what type of programs should it use and at what hour of the day should it advertise?

3. Assume that the company apportions 35 percent of the budget to television, how should the rest of the budget be divided?

4. Evaluate the points which the general store manager and advertising manager give for the two media.

CASE 2. GLAMOR, INC.
Television merchandising

Glamor, Inc., is engaged in the design, manufacture, and distribution of a wide assortment of hair care items and accessories, including hair curlers, hair rollers, wave and pin-curl clips, chignons, hairnets, combs, and barrettes. At the present time, the company's line of products, including variation of size, decoration, and color, consists of over 400 items. During the last year, various types and styles of hair curlers and rollers accounted for approximately 85 percent of the company's dollar sales volume, and various types and styles of barrettes, novelties, and other items accounted for the remaining 15 percent.

The higher cost of professional hair care and the widespread marketing and use of home permanent kits in recent years have broadened the market for the company's line of hair care and hair accessory items as more women have become aware of the simplicity, effectiveness, and economy of styling and curling their own hair. Women who do receive regular professional hair styling may also use the Glamor, Inc.'s, hair care items for nightly pinups and day-to-day styling as a means of complementing and caring for the professional styling. In addition, the company believes the increasing teen-age awareness of style and appearance has been an important factor in its sales growth.

Periods of general business recession have not noticeably affected the company's business in the past. It is the opinion of management that during recession periods more women style their own hair in order to save the higher cost of professional hair styling.

Each year, the company generally produces new styles in certain lines, which it categorizes as its seasonal lines. As new hair styles have come into vogue, the company has developed or adapted different lines of hair accessories to complement such stylings, thus broadening its line of products beyond that of the standard type hair accessories. Changes in women's hair styles have had no material adverse effect on the company's business, since its basic product of hair curlers and rollers is used regardless of hair style. Hair styles requiring medium length to long hair are most favorable to the company's business in that a limited number of hair styles may be employed with short hair and, hence, a fewer number of hair care and accessory items. Medium length to long hair may be styled in a number of different ways, using many different types of hair accessory items.

Glamor, Inc., for the most part, designs its products and manufactures them from the raw material into the finished product. It also does its own packaging and ships to its customers. The principal raw materials used are plastics, aluminum, wire, brushes, cards, and cartons. Sources of such materials are many and varied. None of the raw materials used is in short supply, and the company does not see any difficulty, in the foreseeable future, in obtaining sufficient raw materials at competitive prices.

During the past several years, Glamor has developed self-service, combination merchandise racks, both counter and floor, designed primarily for self-service stores. These racks, which hold a wide assortment of the company's products, have been found useful in introducing such products to new retail outlets. As new products are introduced, the company adds them to its combination rack assortment. It has been Glamor's experience that after introduction of the company's products by means of combination racks, many retailers have devoted regular counter and retail space to such items.

In order to broaden its line of hair care items, the company has placed on the market bobby pins, wave nets, slumber caps, and bandeaus, which are manufactured by other firms on a purchase order basis, packaged in the company's cards and containers and sold with its regular line of products.

The volume of net sales has increased steadily over the past 12 years. Sales for the past year amounted to about $15 million.

Distribution

The company's products are sold throughout the United States and in Canada, and in a number of other countries. The United States is divided into 10 sales areas, each area served by several company salesmen. Changes in retail merchandising in recent years have widely increased the number and type of retail outlets for the company's products. Initially, the company's line of hair care items was sold almost exclusively in variety stores. Food stores, department stores, drug stores, discount stores, and mail-order houses are now equally important outlets. The company sells its products to approximately 4,000 jobbers who, in turn, each sell to a large number of retail outlets, and to approximately 500 chain store systems, having approximately 40,000 retail outlets.

Advertising

Glamor had concentrated its advertising in trade journals, women's magazines, and in *Reader's Digest*. However, one of its major competitors began to use daytime women's shows on television with theater audiences so that samples could be distributed in the audience while the commercial was being aired.

During the commercial lead-ins, the hostess of the show explained that the audience had been invited to try the competitor's products, and then asked the home viewers to try the product. In some markets, the competitor distributed these samples through drug and food stores.

It was the opinion of the executives of Glamor that this competitor had made significant market gains as a result of using television. They recommended, therefore, to their advertising director that he should point out to them what kind of merchandising services they might expect to receive from television stations. The advertising director gave the following report.

SUGGESTED MERCHANDISING ACTIVITIES

Television campaigns

Television networks and stations place considerable emphasis on assisting advertisers throughout their television campaigns. It is their belief that any advertising campaign can be a great deal more effective with proper merchandising assistance.

Product sales will fall short of their *potential goal* if the key people behind the scenes are not properly prepared. These key people must be fully aware of the campaign. Salesmen and retailers should have the full story to insure an adequate supply of stock and be given that extra "boost" to stimulate interest and demand.

Our product, like every product advertised, requires special attention for its specific needs. With a fresh approach, television will tailor a merchandising plan designed to fit our needs.

As a television advertiser, we will have the advantage of full assistance from their merchandising departments. The following activities are merely suggested ideas:

In-store spectacular.   Many television stations will offer animated displays to be used in stores at the advertiser's discretion. These displays will be designed exclusively for our product. Fully animated, these displays are effective tools for product sales. They are designed, constructed, installed, and serviced at no cost to the advertiser.

Counter cards.   As an added help in emphasizing the campaign and pointing up sales, an attractive counter card tying in campaign and product will be produced in quantity for distribution by sales representatives to stores that stock our product.

Sales meetings and brochures.   When advisable, they will prepare a sales brochure to include various advertising tools—advertisers' campaign, success stories, map of coverage area, etc. They will be glad to discuss plans for a television representative to speak to the sales staff, highlighting the important facets of their campaign. This meeting can be either at the regularly scheduled sales meeting or perhaps it might be held in the TV studios.

Nightletters.   When time is essential and an extra plus is needed to help kick off an important TV campaign, a night letter or telegram to the right person can be very valuable in increasing distribution and opening the door for the local sales representative.

Mailers.   There are various forms of effective mailers which can be sent to key buyers, to people of the advertiser's choosing. A mailer sent at the proper time can play an important role in announcing or reminding the right people of your product's television campaign.

Contests.   We can partake in various contests which can be of tremendous benefit; a contest will stimulate viewership, create added attraction to the product, and provide an emphasis on the product's advertising messages.

Personal appearances.   Special activities, such as store sales, product introductions, and sales meetings can be highlighted with the appearance of the television personality that gives our product's commercials.

Trade ads.   In further support of our campaign, an ad can be placed in trade publications, thus giving an added reminder to key buyers about your television campaign.

Gimmick attractions.   There is an inexnaustible list of special gimmick attractions available. Favors, imprinted messages, promotion pieces, etc., can be cleverly used to attract attention. These can be as store giveaways or sent to key people of the advertiser's choosing.

The executives were impressed with the variety of merchandising services and studied the programs of one of the stations they thought they might use in the television campaign. These programs for the period under consideration are given in Exhibit 1.

Glamor, Inc., had spent $750,000 for advertising in the prior year and had decided to increase this to $850,000 for the current year.

EXHIBIT 1

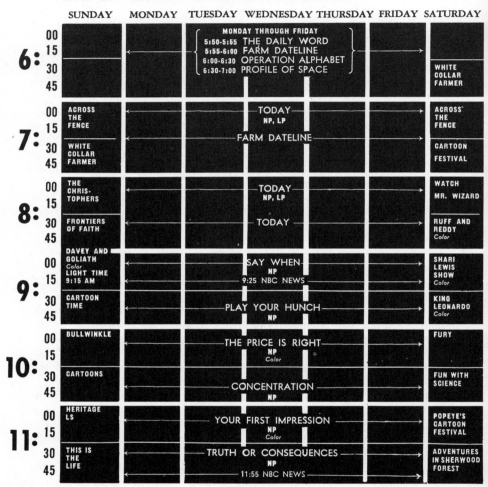

MORNING

		SUNDAY	MONDAY	TUESDAY	WEDNESDAY	THURSDAY	FRIDAY	SATURDAY
6:	00 15 30 45			MONDAY THROUGH FRIDAY 5:50-5:55 THE DAILY WORD 5:55-6:00 FARM DATELINE 6:00-6:30 OPERATION ALPHABET 6:30-7:00 PROFILE OF SPACE				WHITE COLLAR FARMER
7:	00 15 30 45	ACROSS THE FENCE WHITE COLLAR FARMER			TODAY NP, LP FARM DATELINE			ACROSS THE FENCE CARTOON FESTIVAL
8:	00 15 30 45	THE CHRIS-TOPHERS FRONTIERS OF FAITH			TODAY NP, LP TODAY			WATCH MR. WIZARD RUFF AND REDDY Color
9:	00 15 30 45	DAVEY AND GOLIATH Color LIGHT TIME 9:15 AM CARTOON TIME			SAY WHEN NP 9:25 NBC NEWS PLAY YOUR HUNCH NP			SHARI LEWIS SHOW Color KING LEONARDO Color
10:	00 15 30 45	BULLWINKLE CARTOONS			THE PRICE IS RIGHT NP Color CONCENTRATION NP			FURY FUN WITH SCIENCE
11:	00 15 30 45	HERITAGE LS THIS IS THE LIFE			YOUR FIRST IMPRESSION NP Color TRUTH OR CONSEQUENCES NP 11:55 NBC NEWS			POPEYE'S CARTOON FESTIVAL ADVENTURES IN SHERWOOD FOREST

Case questions

1. What are the advantages of television as a medium for Glamor, Inc.?

2. What merchandising services are beneficial enough to Glamor to warrant the use of television advertising?

3. Should Glamor use television in place of some of their magazine advertising?

4. How can Glamor best use television advertising?

5. Which of the programs listed in Exhibit 1 would be suitable for Glamor?

CASE 3. SPOT TELEVISION AND RADIO

Planning using spots

1. A leading detergent manufacturer had selected as the central appeal for its TV and radio spot advertising the following central theme (the product is purchased and used primarily by women for washing dishes): "It softens your hands as no other detergent can. You can discard your expensive hand lotions the day you begin using this detergent."

That company planned to spend $2 million in spot TV and radio advertising during a six-month period, emphasizing the above appeal.

2. A major cereal company had selected for its TV and radio spot advertising appeal: "Get the energy of champions with the breakfast of the stars." This cereal is one that appeals to children because it is sugar-coated. The company had allocated $1.25 million for TV and radio spot advertising for a six-month period.

3. An international soft-drink beverage company budgeted $2 million for spot TV and radio advertising for a six-month period and decided to emphasize the appeal: "Get that special refreshing sensation."

The soft drink is sold in bottles and easy-opening cans and is purchased by children, teen-agers, and most other groups.

Information in regard to market coverage, time periods, and costs is given for spot television and spot radio commercials in Exhibits 1 and 2.

Case question

1. For each of the companies listed above, develop a six-month budget in which you indicate how the allocations for spot TV and spot radio commercials should be used. The products are sold on a national basis in all markets of the United States.

EXHIBIT 1. Spot television (TV market coverage)

The number of TV households tuning at least once a week to one or more stations originating in a given TV market. Below is shown the percentage of U.S. TV households viewing stations in each group of markets. The top 10 markets combined cover 38 percent of the United States; the top 20, 50 percent, and so on.

Time periods

The time periods used in this section are defined as follows:

Prime evening—7:30–11:00 p.m., Monday to Sunday
Early fringe—5:00–7:30 p.m., Monday to Sunday
Late fringe—11 p.m.–sign-off, Monday to Sunday
Daytime—Sign-on to 5:00 p.m., Monday to Friday

Note: Ten- and 20-second commercials are available during all time periods for network and independent stations. Sixty-second commercials are available only on independent stations during prime time when sponsored network programs are broadcast. Central Time Zone classifications are one hour earlier, local time.

EXHIBIT 1—*Continued*

TV market coverage and costs

Markets	% U.S. TV HH covered	Day "60" 9 a.m.– 5 p.m.	Early fringe "60" 5–7:30 p.m.	Prime "20" 7:30–11 p.m.	Late fringe "60" 11:30–1 p.m.
1–10	38%	$2,800	$ 6,100	$11,800	$ 4,900
1–20	50	4,000	8,400	15,800	6,500
1–30	60	5,000	10,700	19,100	7,700
1–40	67	5,900	12,600	21,700	8,700
1–50	74	6,700	13,900	23,800	9,500
1–60	80	7,400	15,200	25,900	10,200
1–70	84	7,900	16,300	27,400	10,800
1–80	88	8,400	17,300	28,600	11,200
1–90	92	8,900	18,100	29,700	11,700
1–100	95	9,400	18,900	30,800	12,100

Note: Although Spot TV prices have gone up, the prices in the above table are lower than those reported in prior years. This is due to a change in the base used to compute costs.

Costs are based on the average of all network stations in each market. Five plan rates were used when they were available—otherwise 6, 10 or 26 plan rates were used.

Source: BBDO estimates.

Average rating levels for spot TV announcements in the top 100 markets by program type (fall)

Program type	HUTV	Average rating levels					
		HH	Men	Women	Teens	Children	Total viewers
Daytime	22%						
Local movie		5.0	1.5	3.0	2.0	3.0	2.5
Network		6.0	1.5	4.5	1.0	2.5	2.5
Early fringe	37%						
News		13.0	9.0	9.5	5.0	4.0	7.5
Movie		7.5	3.5	4.5	6.0	5.0	4.5
Syndicated		8.5	5.0	5.0	5.5	7.0	5.5
Prime time	55%						
Network		18.5	13.0	15.0	10.0	8.0	12.0
Independent		5.0	3.5	3.5	2.5	2.0	3.0
Late fringe	23%						
News		11.5	8.0	9.0	2.0	.5	6.0
Movie		5.5	3.5	4.0	1.5	—	2.5
Tonight		6.0	3.5	4.5	.5	—	3.0

Source: BBDO estimates.

EXHIBIT 1—*Concluded*

Cost efficiency (representative CPM's for spot announcements in the top 100 markets)

	Homes	*Men*	*Women*
Daytime "60"	$1.00–2.00	$5.00–10.00	$1.25–2.50
Early fringe "60"	2.00–3.00	3.60– 5.50	2.85–4.30
Prime time "20"	2.50–3.50	3.60– 5.00	2.80–3.90
Late fringe "60"	2.50–3.50	3.85– 5.40	2.95–4.10

Source: BBDO estimates.

EXHIBIT 2. Spot radio (ownership)

Latest Radio Advertising Bureau estimates indicate that there are 242 million radio sets in the continental United States. Of these, 172 million are in households, 60 million are in automobiles, and 10 million are in public places. About 15 percent of all radios are FM. There are 4,034 AM stations and 1,408 FM stations (Fall 1966).

Hourly U.S. radio total adult audience by sex

N.Y. time, hour beginning	*Percent total adults listening during the average quarter hour*			
	Weekday		*Weekend*	
	Men	*Women*	*Men*	*Women*
6 a.m.	9.0	11.0	4.0	4.5
7 a.m.	13.0	16.5	7.0	8.0
8 a.m.	13.5	19.0	10.0	12.5
9 a.m.	13.5	19.5	12.0	15.5
10 a.m.	12.0	18.5	13.5	16.5
11 a.m.	11.5	16.5	14.5	17.5
12 NOON	12.0	15.0	15.0	16.5
1 p.m.	12.0	13.5	16.0	15.0
2 p.m.	12.0	11.5	16.0	14.5
3 p.m.	12.5	11.5	15.5	14.0
4 p.m.	13.0	11.5	13.5	13.5
5 p.m.	12.0	11.0	12.5	12.0
6 p.m.	10.0	10.5	10.0	9.5
7 p.m.	9.5	8.5	9.0	8.0
8 p.m.	9.5	7.5	8.5	8.0
9 p.m.	9.5	6.5	8.0	7.0
10 p.m.	8.0	5.0	6.5	6.5
11 p.m.	5.5	3.5	4.5	4.5

Source: Sindlinger (September 1966).

EXHIBIT 2—*Continued*

Network radio costs

	5-minute*	1-minute	30-second
ABC	$ 900–1,850	$700–1,350	$400–1,000
CBS	1,700–2,500	750–1,350	550– 900
MBS	1,065–1,540	615– 895	450– 645
NBC	1,800–2,125	630–1,350	470–1,000

* 1½–2 commercial minutes
Source: BBDO estimates.

Spot radio costs

Markets	Cost per spot		
	Drive time (6–9 a.m.; 4–7 p.m.)	Housewife time (9 a.m.–4 p.m.)	Evening (7 p.m.–mid.)
1–10	$1,000	$ 800	$ 600
1–20	1,500	1,200	800
1–30	1,900	1,500	1,000
1–40	2,200	1,800	1,200
1–50	2,600	2,100	1,500
1–60	2,800	2,300	1,600
1–70	3,100	2,500	1,800
1–80	3,300	2,600	1,900
1–90	3,400	2,800	2,000
1–100	3,600	2,900	2,100

These estimates represent the costs of one 60-second announcement on a single station in each market and are based on 12 plan rates for 13 weeks.
Source: BBDO estimates.

Household and adult audience ratings by market groups average for top 3 stations per market in metro area only (Monday–Friday)

Markets	Drive time (6–9 a.m.; 4–7 p.m.)			Housewife time (9 a.m.–4 p.m.)			Evening (7 p.m.–mid.)		
	HH	Men (18+)	Women (18+)	HH	Men (18+)	Women (18+)	HH	Men (18+)	Women (18+)
1–10	4.0	2.0	2.5	3.5	1.0	2.5	2.5	1.5	1.5
11–50	5.0	2.5	3.5	4.5	1.0	3.5	3.0	1.5	2.0
51–100	5.5	3.0	4.0	5.0	1.5	4.0	2.5	1.5	1.5

Source: BBDO estimates.

EXHIBIT 2—*Concluded*

Demographic peaks of appeal by station type

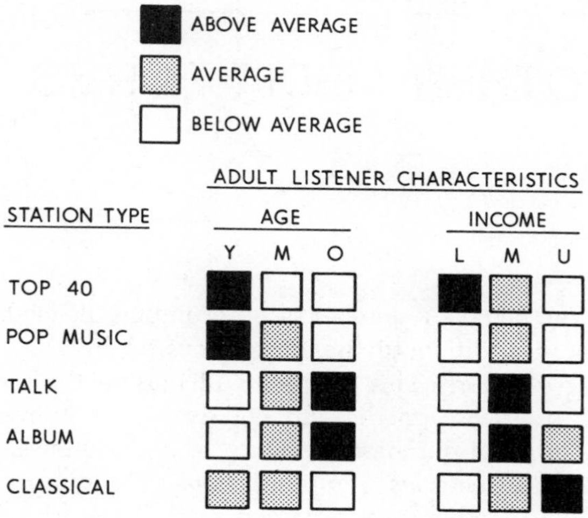

■ ABOVE AVERAGE

▨ AVERAGE

□ BELOW AVERAGE

ADULT LISTENER CHARACTERISTICS

STATION TYPE	AGE			INCOME		
	Y	M	O	L	M	U
TOP 40	■	□	□	■	▨	□
POP MUSIC	■	▨	□	□	▨	□
TALK	□	▨	■	□	■	□
ALBUM	□	▨	■	□	■	▨
CLASSICAL	▨	▨	□	□	▨	■

chapter 13

OTHER MEDIA FORMS

THERE ARE a number of other important media available to the advertiser in addition to the four discussed in some detail in the two preceding chapters. This chapter will outline the most significant aspects of the following media: direct advertising (direct mail); outdoor; transit; point-of-purchase; exhibits or trade shows; specialty advertising; screen; directories; sampling; house organs; packages; labels; and inserts. Some of these are classified in the area of sales promotion rather than in advertising; but, since they are important in the overall aspects of media planning in the advertising campaign, the authors discuss them briefly here under the heading of media.

DIRECT ADVERTISING

Direct advertising is one of the oldest methods of reaching the consumer. It consists of printed matter that is sent by the advertiser directly to the prospect. This material is usually sent out by mail, but it may be distributed by house-to-house or personal delivery, handed out to passersby on the sidewalk, placed in automobiles, or stuck under windshield wipers of automobiles. That portion of direct advertising that is sent through the mail is called direct-mail advertising.

Direct-mail advertising differs from mail-order advertising in that mail-order advertising seeks to complete the sale entirely by mail, while direct-mail advertising is supplementary to other forms of advertising and selling. Direct mail is usually a part of the general marketing plan, whereas mail-order advertising is a complete plan in itself.

Direct advertising takes many forms, such as letters, postcards, announcements, catalogs, folders, envelope and package enclosures, novelties and goodwill reminders, cards, or blotters.

Use of direct advertising

One of the principal functions of direct advertising is to supplement general advertising in magazines, newspapers, television, radio, and other media. Proofs of advertisements that are to be used in mass media can be sent to dealers. Jobbers can be shown the advertising campaign in a broadside. Circular letters, folders, or postal cards can be sent to prospects, calling their attention to a specific advertisement.

Direct advertising may be used also to pave the way for salesmen. In most instances where a series of letters or folders has been sent before the salesman's call, it takes less time and effort to complete sales. The retailer also can use direct advertising effectively. By the use of carefully planned material, he can tie in his personal appeal with the general advertising campaign of the manufacturer or wholesaler. The retailer may either mail, or distribute his direct advertising on a house-to-house basis. However, some cities forbid house-to-house distribution, so it is well to look into the local laws before adopting such a method.

Virtually all advertisers use some form of direct advertising. For many small firms, it is the only form of media used. Direct advertising is estimated to rank third among all media in volume.

Some idea of the specific objectives for which it is frequently used can be obtained from Figure 13–1.

FIGURE 13–1. How is direct mail used?

To obtain orders by mail	14,813
To obtain prospects for personal contact by salesman	9,484
To obtain outlets, distributors, members or subscribers, or to keep them informed	5,468
To provide advertising literature for franchised or other dealers or outlets, mailed under permit number	3,425
To provide advertising literature for franchised or other dealers or outlets, mailed by those dealers or outlets	2,121
For general advertising purposes	33,043
To distribute (i.e., to move or to transport) the product	2,521
Other uses	9,795

Source: Department of Commerce survey of 56,417 users of bulk third-class mail.

Forms of direct advertising

A number of forms are significant to many advertisers and will be discussed briefly in the following paragraphs.

Form letters. In direct advertising, form letters are used most frequently. These are standard letters used alone or with other advertising matter, such as with catalogs, folders, or in answer to inquiries. No matter how attractively a catalog or booklet is prepared, its selling power is strengthened by sending a good form letter along with it, because a letter has a special appeal all its own. It may be used not only to give direction to the selling effort but to emphasize as well particular features of the product.

Circulars.   Circulars and leaflets, as defined here, include advertising literature not mailable under their own covers. These include dodgers, package inserts, bulletins, and pieces of printed matter that are not properly classified under any of the other forms.

The uses of circulars vary. They are not intended primarily as envelope enclosures, though they are often mailed in envelopes. Some circulars, for instance, may be given to workmen as they leave the factory. They may be used to introduce a new product at a supermarket or even solicit votes for a certain candidate.

Circulars are also inserted in packages. For instance, in a cereal package an advertiser may put a circular advertising a brand of cakes. Circulars may be used by a manufacturer to inform the dealer about advertising plans or some other information of mutual interest, or for distribution.

Catalogs.   Catalogs are used as a source of purchasing information as well as to stimulate a desire for the goods described. In many instances, the products are illustrated in colors, and the catalog may carry a major share of the sales effort. Because the cover of a catalog is so important to its success, it is well to choose the cover with a great degree of care. It must be strong enough to go through the mails undamaged and last as long as the catalog is useful. It should also be designed to get attention as well as to convey the atmosphere of the goods advertised in the catalog.

Booklets.   In a catalog many items are listed, while in a booklet only a limited number of products might be explained.

Many manufacturers furnish booklets for distribution with or without the imprint of their local representatives. Special products, new lines, and services may also be treated effectively in booklets. In fact, in many national advertisements it will be suggested that the reader write for a booklet. Booklets are cheaper than catalogs and can be used as a supplement to give general information about specific requests.

Postcards.   The postcard is a widely used form of direct advertising, because it has high attention value and may be produced cheaply. It is intended to get direct and immediate action. When the article advertised is small and inexpensive, it pays to make ordering convenient by using a double postcard which may be detached easily and filled in with the name and address. Postcard messages should be brief and direct.

The postcard can be used effectively to call to the attention of customers other advertising material such as a catalog or samples, to give the date when salesmen will arrive, or announce such information as new dealers or new styles.

Broadsides. Another form of direct advertising is a broadside, or a large advertising folder. It differs from the folder in that in a folder each page may be a separate unit, while a broadside when opened constitutes one advertisement. The large size of a broadside makes it possible to use a variety of typography and illustrations.

As one of the objectives of a broadside is to get immediate reaction, high attention value is important. For this reason, it is well to use more than one color.

Portfolios. A portfolio is a portable case for keeping, usually without folding, detached material, loose papers, prints, and booklets, and can be used effectively in direct advertising.

Manufacturers who advertise nationally, as an example, may send portfolios to the dealers to show the extent to which their products are backed up by advertising. Such portfolios will include full-page advertisements from various publications, booklets, letters, folders, and all other forms of advertising employed.

The mailing list

The success of any direct advertising will depend primarily on having the material go to the right people—those who are potential customers for the advertiser's product or establishment.

In the case of direct-mail advertising, this list of names of prospects is called the mailing list. Ideally, the advertiser would like to have his list include all those people he wishes to influence with his advertisement —those who are prospects for his product or establishment—and no others.

There are a number of means of obtaining desirable mailing lists. For firms already in business, probably the best single source is the list of present (and past) customers of the firm. Retailers' lists should include both cash and credit customers. Names for the lists are often obtained from those responding to the firm's advertising, from coupons in advertisements inviting requests for information or booklets, from public records such as building permits, and directory membership lists and rosters of professional organizations.

A manufacturer can often obtain desirable names for his mailing list from his dealers and from his sales force. An advertiser who wishes to reach all the people in an area (rather than a selected group) can do so by addressing his material to the *occupants* of the street address in cities and boxholders on rural free delivery routes.

One of the principal means used by many firms to obtain lists is either to buy or rent them from list firms, to rent them from other business firms, or to exchange lists with appropriate noncompeting firms.

The most common way to obtain the ready-made lists is by rental. The advertiser never actually sees the list, but arranges for its use through a list house or a broker and is merely informed where to send his cards or envelopes to be addressed. Many classes of lists are available. For instance, Dartnell's *Directory of Mailing List Sources* has information on 1,200 lists that are available in 239 classifications. Probably the largest and best known of the individual list houses is R. L. Polk and Company.

For those compiling their own lists, it is very important that they be kept up to date and accurate. This means that the list must be checked constantly for the accuracy of names and addresses. This can be one of the costly aspects of direct-mail advertising.

Advantages of direct advertising

The advantages of direct advertising may be summarized as follows:

1. If the right list of prospects is secured, there is limited waste circulation; each prospect receives the material.
2. The potential consumers can be reached in a short period of time.
3. There is a personal touch in direct appeals. An advertisement on television or in a magazine is directed to a group; a letter or mailing piece is directed to one man either at his home or in his office.
4. Through the more personal appeal of direct advertising, the advertiser can correlate his appeal in many ways to national, class, or trade advertising.
5. The sales campaign is hidden from competitors.
6. Advertising can be released at the right time; the advertiser can also take advantage of opportune markets, business conditions, or unusual circumstances of any kind.
7. Returns can be keyed more effectively than in general media because there is better control of the distribution of the material.
8. It is possible to divide the list into natural units and treat each unit separately.
9. It is the most selective of all media.
10. It is the most flexible of all media.
11. There is a wide variety of forms available to the advertiser.
12. It avoids distracting competition for attention from other advertisements and editorial material.

Limitations of direct advertising

1. In terms of the cost of reaching a thousand people, it is a high-cost medium. This feature can, of course, be offset by the careful selec-

tivity of the mailing list and by the effectiveness of the results obtained.

2. If the mailing list is not carefully selected, there may be low readership and interest.

3. It is often difficult to obtain good mailing lists, and it takes a great deal of effort to keep a mailing list up to date and accurate.

4. Among some people, direct mail has a poor reputation and has been referred to as "junk" mail. This is usually the result of much direct mail being sent to people who are not good prospects for the item or service involved.

5. Direct mail also requires careful preparation in order to insure readership, since there is no editorial material or progam to aid in obtaining attention and interest. Thus, specialized skills are required by those preparing direct-mail advertising.

OUTDOOR ADVERTISING

Although outdoor advertising accounts for only about 1.1 percent of the U.S. advertising expenditures by media, it is an important form of advertising for many national advertisers and for many local firms. Its significance has been increased in the last decade with the great increase in the number of automobiles and the amount of driving that people do (both in everyday life and on vacation trips), combined with the large suburban movement of the population and growth of suburban shopping centers. These trends have resulted in an increase in exposure of the potential customer to outdoor advertising.

Not all the advertising signs appearing along streets and highways are considered to fall into the category of outdoor advertising by the industry. Only those posters and painted displays that meet the standards set up by the industry, through the Outdoor Advertising Association of America, are considered as being part of the medium as such. Miscellaneous signs and posters not conforming to the organized industry standards are called *signs* and do not fall within the industry's technical definition of outdoor advertising. The most important aspect of this technical distinction arises in connection with the criticism of outdoor advertsing and the attempts to legislate against it.

Types of outdoor advertising

There are a number of different types of outdoor advertising. Among the more important types are posters, painted displays, and electric displays.

Posters. The most important form of outdoor advertising is the poster which accounts for over 75 percent of the national outdoor sales volume. It consists of the advertisement lithographed, or otherwise printed, on sheets of paper, placed on a background.

The standard poster is known as the "24-sheet." This term is derived from the original unit of poster-size measurement. Copy area of the 24-sheet poster is 8 feet 8 inches high and 19 feet 6 inches long. The panels or structures on which the posters are placed are generally uniform and standard in size and construction. There are intermediate sizes, but 3, 8, and 24 sheets are the popular sizes. Three-sheet posters are used principally on the sides of retailers' stores. Eight-sheet posters are used mainly for theatrical signs, while the 24-sheet variety is the standard poster on which advertising may be placed along streets and highways.

The 30-sheet poster offers a display area 9 feet 7 inches by 21 feet 7 inches, although posted on the same size structure. New posting techniques now allow an even larger posting area, called a bleed poster, giving the advertiser approximately 40 percent more printed area than the 24-sheet poster copy. There is generally no additional space charge for the larger size.

Painted displays. Painted displays account for approximately 20 percent of the volume of all standardized national outdoor advertising and may be classified as bulletins or wall panels; these in turn may be either illuminated or nonilluminated.

Illuminated bulletins and wall panels are erected by the outdoor advertising companies who usually repaint them two or three times a year, with a change of copy at that time, if desired.

Nonilluminated bulletins and wall panels are of many types, and are placed on roofs, along highways, and on the sides of store buildings.

Painted displays are bought on an individual basis. The advertiser may order one display or many. The price varies with the size of the display and the position of the individual sign. Usually, these units are designed and built to fit the special requirements of a specific location, so they vary in size. The advertiser buys these on an individual basis, and the bulletin remains on display at the same location for the period of the contract. Each bulletin is priced on the basis of the merits of the specific location.

However, in some cases the bulletins are physically moved by the plant operator periodically to new locations in a market to give the advertiser wider coverage and the impact of the large printed display. This is called the rotary plan, versus the permanent plan described above.

Painted bulletins of both of these types are usually sold on a one-year (base rate) or three-year contract, the latter carrying a 10 percent discount. Shorter terms are available at higher monthly rates.

They can be individualized by using unusual designs, shapes, and sizes. By using cutout designs with the cutout feature extending in front or behind the surface of the bulletin itself, a third dimension can be added to increase its effectiveness and attention value, or to stress the product package or other features of the advertiser's message. The use of various special fluorescent and phosphorescent paints, beaded plastic, and black light enables the advertiser to achieve unusual and striking effects with painted displays.

One frequently used, popular variation of the painted bulletin is known as "trivision," or "multivision." In this variation, a portion of the face of the bulletin is made up of vertical triangles which turn at intervals, showing three different messages on the same panel.[1]

Electric spectaculars. Electric displays are individualized night spectacular bulletins with special lighting and action effects. They are erected at important traffic centers such as Times Square, New York; Michigan Avenue, Chicago; Campus Martius, Detroit; the Public Square, Cleveland; on the piers at Atlantic City; on Canal Street, New Orleans; in Union Square, San Francisco.

Electric spectaculars are designed, erected, and maintained by outdoor advertising companies. Space on them is sold usually for a period of from one to five years. Such displays are sold individually.

Characteristics of the medium

The outstanding feature of outdoor advertising is that it stands still and the reader is exposed to it as the result of being outdoors and traveling to some destination. Since his rate of travel is determined by his desire to arrive at a destination and not by the attractiveness of the various outdoor billboards he may pass, the outdoor advertisement must tell its story in the short period of time it takes the person to walk or ride past the poster.

Since virtually every person goes outdoors almost every day, outdoor advertising is truly a mass medium. In turn, it is difficult for the advertiser using this medium to select his audience or to direct his advertising to a given segment of the market or type of consumer. Hence, it serves best for the national advertiser who has a product of wide appeal, or for local business firms that wish to reach a large share of the local market with their message. Outdoor advertising is flexible in that the advertiser can choose the areas or markets in which he wishes to advertise. He can use the number of boards where they will be most effective for him. He can easily adapt his use of outdoor advertising to meet the requirements of his particular distribution pattern and competitive conditions. Another feature of outdoor advertising is the penetration it can achieve by frequent repetition. If the advertiser uses a 100-showing in a market, most people will see his advertisement many times during the month, so that the number of impressions is great.

---

[1] Source: "This is Outdoor Advertising," (New York: Institute of Outdoor Advertising, undated), pp. 11, 12.

Outdoor advertising permits the use of color in a very effective manner. It enables the advertiser to reproduce his product or package exactly as it appears on the store shelf. The large size of the bulletin gives great impact and impressiveness to the advertisement. The message reaches the consumer on his way to the market and, hence, can influence him at a most important psychological moment. Since the advertisement is seen often by the dealer as well as by the consumer, outdoor advertising can be merchandised to the trade very effectively. It can be used well in cooperative advertising with local dealers by placing the name of the local dealer at the base of the bulletin.

Outdoor advertising does have its limitations. The message that can be included must be very brief, so the medium is not particularly appropriate for some advertisers and certain types of advertising. Normally, it is not appropriate for telling a long story required to introduce a product, unless the advertiser might possibly use teaser type introductory ads. Basically, this requirement of such brevity of message makes the medium best for reminder type advertising. Thus, national advertisers generally use outdoor advertising as a supporting medium for their campaigns using other media, or to get extra support in selected markets. The outdoor advertisement faces keen competition for attention from the scenic attractions, the traffic, the buildings, and other billboards along the route of travel. And, of course, once the person has passed a particular billboard, he cannot possibly read the message until he again passes that particular spot.

The outdoor advertisement

Since in outdoor advertising the potential customer must virtually grasp the selling message in a matter of a very few seconds and virtually at a glance, it is essential that the advertisement contain but a single idea. This should be a simple concept that can be put across with an illustration and few words of copy.

Generally, it is advisable to limit the advertisement to no more than the following:

1. The picture or illustration.
2. Brief text to reinforce the picture.
3. Name of product.
4. The package.
5. The selling phrase.

Outdoor advertising rates

In the case of posters, outdoor advertising is sold on the basis of showings. A 100-showing, consists of that number of posters (strategically located in various parts of the city or market) required to give complete coverage of the market or to expose the advertiser's message to all the people in that market during a 30-day period. The number of posters required to constitute a 100-showing will obviously vary with the city. This is determined by the plant operator, and will depend on the population and area of the city, the arrangement or layout of the industrial, commercial, and shopping areas within the city, the pattern of streets and highways and the traffic flow thereon, the network of public transportation, and other factors. The actual number of posters in a 100-showing will vary from only one poster in a small town to 472 posters in the largest outdoor circulation market—Los Angeles Metro Market. Normally, there will be a number of 100-showings available in a market, each equal to the other not only in the number of posters (illuminated and nonilluminated) but also having such locations that an equal amount of traffic will pass during any given period of time.

The advertiser may also buy fractional showings if he does not believe he needs the intensity of coverage provided by the 100-showing. A 50-showing is one in which the poster locations are as evenly distributed for purposes of covering the market, but with only one half the intensity of a 100-showing. The advertiser who wishes to saturate a market may buy a 150-showing which would provide one and one-half times the coverage of a 100-showing. Foster and Kleiser, in the *1971 Rate Schedule,* offers showings in the following showing intensities: 150, 100, 95, 90, 85, 80, 75, 70, 65, 60, 55, 50, 45, 40, 35, 30, 25, 20, 15, and 10. The charge for a 100-showing will vary from city to city. Figure 13–2 gives a few illustrations of the number of posters required for a 100-showing and the rates for such showings in selected markets. These rates are for the space only; they do not include the cost of designing or printing the advertisement.

Public relations problems of outdoor advertising

In addition to the usual criticisms of advertising the outdoor field faces a serious problem in the criticisms leveled at it because "its signs mar the landscape, and hide scenes of beauty along the highway from the motorist." A second argument is that posters and bulletins are a traffic hazard. The claim advanced is that since the driver of the automobile must take his eyes off the road to see the outdoor advertisement, the posters and bulletins act as a distraction and will cause more accidents. Several studies have been made which indicate there is no evidence to show that outdoor advertisements do cause accidents and, in actuality, they may well reduce accidents.

However, despite these counterarguments, the trend has been for more legislation to be passed to restrict outdoor advertising. A provision was included in the 1958 Amendment to the Highway Revenue Act of 1956

FIGURE 13–2. Number of 24-sheet posters on no. 100 showing and rates in selected markets*

	Number of panels		Price per
Market	Unillumi-nated	Illuminated	month
Brooklyn metro—zone #2 (Queens/ Kings counties)		148	$23,680
Chicago metro market	96	176	32,512
Cincinnati metro market	14	44	6,572
Cleveland metro market	24	104	14,752
Long Beach metro	20	40	7,240
Los Angeles metro market (Los Angeles, San Bernardino, Orange, and Riverside Counties)	114	358	58,688
New York metro market		232	37,120
Oakland metro—zone #2 (including Alameda, Contra Costa, and Solano counties)	42	70	13,258
Portland metro market	32	44	8,000
Sacramento metro—zone #4	24	30	6,246
San Diego metro market	34	36	7,984
San Francisco metro—zone #1 (including San Francisco, San Mateo, and Marin counties)	68	68	9,044
Seattle metro market	32	48	8,480
Tacoma metro market	18	18	3,690

Courtesy of the Foster and Kleiser, Division of Metromedia, Inc. "1971 Rate Schedule."
* Thirty days is the normal display period. In some cases, operators offer special short-term rates. In one instance—Foster and Kleiser—the company offers poster displays of 15 days' duration, with the rate being 70 percent of the monthly price.

(Highway Beautification Act), which provided additional federal funds to those states forbidding or at least severely restricting placement of outdoor advertising on highways constructed under the act. Some states have passed legislation restricting outdoor advertising in order to gain this additional federal support. In addition, many localities pass zoning ordinances that restrict the use of outdoor advertising markedly in certain areas of cities or counties.

Users of outdoor advertising

Outdoor advertising is used by both national and local advertisers. It is estimated that approximately 75 percent of the outdoor advertising is national and 25 percent local. Local advertisers use outdoor advertising often to remind people coming into the town to trade at the advertiser's establishment. In areas where tourist business is important, outdoor advertising strategically placed on all major approaches to the area constitutes an excellent way to reach the tourist and inform him of the facilities available. Large local users of outdoor advertising include hotels and motels, restaurants, souvenir stores, garages, and resorts. In towns depending essentially on the population of the surrounding area, virtually all types of stores, entertainment, and service facilities may use outdoor advertising as a medium. National advertisers normally use outdoor advertising as a supplement to other media. The message type advertising will be carried in magazines or newspapers, on television, or radio, and outdoor advertising will be used largely in a reminder capacity. It may also be used to gain greater impact and penetration in selected markets.

Outdoor advertising is a good medium for widely used impulse-type goods which are already well known. It is used often by food manufacturers and soft drink firms to remind the housewife of their products when she is on her way to shop. Other heavy users of outdoor advertising are firms manufacturing products closely allied to highway use, such as automobiles, gasoline, or tires, and also breweries and distillers.

TRANSIT ADVERTISING

Transit advertising is the term used for all types of advertising signs on or in trains, subways, streetcars, buses, taxicabs, and other such public transportation vehicles, or the stations from which they operate. The volume of transit advertising is estimated to be approximately $40 million. Although people generally think only in terms of car cards when referring to transit advertising, there are actually three major basic types or forms of transit advertising. These are:

1. *Car cards.* These are the advertisements placed inside streetcars, buses, and the cars of subway, elevated, and suburban trains.
2. *Traveling displays.* There are the larger signs posted or painted on the outside of buses, streetcars, and cabs.
3. *Station posters.* These are the posters and displays of varied size which are placed inside bus and railway stations and airport terminals, and on station platforms.

There are also several miscellaneous types of advertising handled by the transit advertising companies. In a few instances, public transportation systems have their buses or streetcars equipped to broadcast radio programs and commercials in the vehicles received from a local FM broadcasting station. Some companies sell advertising space on dining car menus, on timetables, or spectacular displays on stations. Although in a few instances the transportation companies themselves sell the advertising space in their vehicles and stations, in the great majority of cases special independent transportation advertising companies buy an exclusive lease on the advertising space in, on, or around the vehicles and stations of the one or more transportation companies in the city, and then sell the advertising space. The advertiser using transportation advertising must supply the car cards and posters to the operator, as in the case of outdoor advertising (with enough extra copies to take care of normal replacement needs).

Transit advertising and rates

Car cards. Car cards are the most important form of transit advertising; the estimate is that about 70 percent of the volume of transit advertising is spent on this form. Car cards are sold on the basis of: (1) double run, which means two cards in each car; (2) a full run, which is one card in each car; (3) a half run, a card for every other car; and (4) a quarter run, which is a card for each fourth car. In some instances, the terms "showing" or "service" are used instead of run.

The standardization of card size has been accomplished to a considerable extent by the Transit Advertising Association, Inc. All car cards are now 11 inches in height. The length may be 14, 21, 28, 42, 56, or 84 inches. The most commonly used sizes are the 11 by 28 inches and the 11 by 21 inches.

As a rule, car cards are sold on a basis of 6 months to a year of service, the rates being discounted for longer contract periods. The contracts normally provide for the transit advertising firm to place, change, and maintain the cards in the cars, although the cards themselves must be provided by the advertiser.

In 1971, it would have cost an advertiser $18,710 a month for a half showing in the top ten U.S. markets, giving him 9,640 bus and subway displays.[2]

Advantages of car cards

1. Advertisers in cars and buses get the last chance at the buyer, as the housewife can be reminded of the advertiser's product on her way to the store.
2. The cost is reasonable.
3. Cooperative tie-ins with local retailers can be arranged.
4. The car cards are before the prospects for a considerable length of time. Studies by the National Association of Transportation Advertising, Inc., point out that the average length of ride is over 25 minutes per one-way trip and that the average rider will be in a position to see between 6 and 15 cards during most of his trip.
5. Small advertisers are not overshadowed by large competitors. A well-

---

[2] Source: *BBDO Audience Coverage and Cost Guide,* 10th Edition, 1971, p. 48.

designed card, although there may be only one to each four cars, will not be overshadowed by a competitor who is using even two cards per car.

6. Readership of the cards is high. Dr. Frank J. Charvat, of Emory University, in an actual Georgia study found that 62 percent to 90 percent of the group studied, saw, read, and remembered the car cards included in the analysis.
7. Color can be used very effectively.

Disadvantages of car cards

1. Copy is limited. Ten to twenty words is about the maximum that should be used.
2. It is difficult to quote daily prices, because the copy usually runs for a period of 30 days.
3. Car cards are so numerous in each car and tend to look so much alike that they are confusing.
4. Automobiles are used by many potential customers in major markets. As a result, car advertising will reach only those who use public vehicles.
5. Shift of stores to suburban areas decreases the number of trips which the housewife makes to the downtown sections of the city.
6. Car cards are primarily an urban medium and are not effective in reaching rural and small-town areas.

POINT-OF-PURCHASE ADVERTISING

The term is defined to include all advertising materials—signs and displays—placed in, on, or around retail stores (excluding the labels, packages, or containers of the merchandise itself). Various other terms are sometimes used such as dealer displays, dealer aids, and point-of-sale materials. Point-of-purchase is now the more generally used inclusive term, since it tends to put the emphasis on the consumer or buyer rather than on the dealer or seller. Also, the trade association of the industry uses the designation, Point-of-Purchase Advertising Institute, so we shall do so in this discussion.

In recent years the point-of-purchase medium has become increasingly important in the advertising picture. The trend to self-service and self-selection at the retail level has made it more important for the manufacturer to have some means of bringing his product to the attention of the consumer at the point where the final purchase is consummated. Since in many instances there is little or no personal selling, the manufacturer feels he must try to get his final suggestion or sales story to the prospective customer at the point where the buying decision is being made through some type of advertising display. Many studies have shown a great increase in impulse buying in recent years at the self-service outlets, and point-of-purchase materials can do much to stimulate impulse buying of a manufacturer's brand. With the increased competition of new brands and new products coming on the market, the manufacturer has found it increasingly necessary to devise some means to hold or enlarge his share of the market, and has found good advertising materials at the point of purchase to be an effective aid to sales.

This medium of point-of-purchase advertising has grown rapidly in recent years, and it is estimated that advertisers are now spending approximately $700 million annually for point-of-purchase merchandising materials.

Organization of the industry

The bulk of the materials included in the point-of-purchase advertising used by the retailer is provided by the manufacturers or advertisers of the products being sold by the retailer, although some of the display materials will be provided by the individual retailer, particularly in the case of the large department and specialty stores. In some instances, the agency or the advertiser plans the point-of-purchase materials and handles its production. However, much of the material is produced for the advertisers by firms specializing in the production of point-of-purchase display materials. Some 250 such firms are members of the Point-of-Purchase Advertising Institute (usually referred to as POPAI), and most of them are in a position to advise and aid advertisers in the planning of materials as well as in the actual production. Since the work of these firms is not commissionable, they usually try to work directly with the advertiser rather than through the advertising agency.

Forms of point-of-purchase advertising

A wide range of actual materials and devices, signs and displays are included in this medium—so wide as virtually to defy classification. They range from simple cardboard shelf strips or cloth banners to elaborate illuminated and animated spectaculars. They may be made of paper, wood, cardboard, metal, or plastics. Many are temporary in nature, such as paper banners and posters, while others are quite permanent, such as metal signs, self-merchandising display stands, and clock advertisements. Some are designed for exterior use and some for interior use. A list prepared by POPIA included 40 kinds.

Use of point-of-purchase advertising

Generally speaking, the advertiser uses point-of-purchase as a part of his entire advertising and promotion program, to increase the sale of his brand of merchandise. But specifically, he wishes to have this form of advertising in use so that it will remind the shopper of his product and brand at the moment she is in the store at the point of buying. A second basic purpose of point-of-purchase advertising is to stimulate impulse buying.

The third purpose the manufacturer has in mind in using point-of-purchase advertising is to influence the dealer to stock his merchandise and cooperate in increasing the sale of his merchandise through its effective display. In the same way that the advertiser's salesman "merchandises" other media advertising when selling the retailer on why he should stock the product, he uses the story of the good display material he furnishes and its influence in obtaining good sales and stock turnover to aid in getting the retailer to stock the product initially. Also, after the retailer has stocked his line, the salesman uses the point-of-purchase materials to aid in getting better display positions, more display, and more pushing of his product by the retailer.

Considerations in creation and use of point-of-purchase advertising

One of the main problems the advertiser faces is to create point-of-purchase materials that will be effective in maintaining to the point of sale his message and the brand image created by his mass media advertising, and which will stimulate impulse and reminder buying by his prospective customers. A number of factors should be considered in developing this material. These include:

1. The material must attract attention and must compete effectively in the store to catch a prospective buyer's eye and hold it. Design, shape, and color are methods which can be used in attaining this objective.
2. The material must build confidence. It must indicate that the product is a quality one and that the manufacturer is reliable.
3. The material should give the product information briefly and succinctly. The customer wants to be able to get in a glance all the information about the product.
4. The material should create the proper atmosphere for the product. It must be appropriate and suitable. Depending on the company whose products the point-of-purchase advertising is attempting to sell, it may be humorous or sophisticated, traditional or modern.
5. The appeal should create the impression that the product advertised is of good value. Housewives are trying to make their dollars go as far as they can. As a result, the appeal that stresses this fact will result generally in greater impulse sales.
6. The material must be attractive enough to deserve a preferred place in the store. Because of the competitive battle for space in the store, material that adds to the beauty of displays, etc., is much easier to

get into a position where it will have a maximum chance to be seen by the customers.

EXHIBITS AND TRADE SHOWS

The exhibit has two unique features as a form of advertising. It is the only one where the product can be made available for actual inspection and demonstration, and where the prospects come to the place of the advertising so the advertiser's salesmen can "sell" the product's features on the spot.

There are various types and categories of exhibits or trade shows. Some are designed for consumers, either to reach the general public or specific segments of the buying public. General type shows include the exhibits at county, state, and world fairs. Those aimed at special segments of the market include such exhibits or shows as automobile, boat, garden, hobby, and home furnishings shows.

However, a larger proportion of the shows are industrial, and restrict the attendance to people who are directly connected with that particular field. The bulk of these shows are in connection with the annual meeting of the trade association involved, and usually sponsored or run by the particular association. The limitation on attendance at these shows insures to the exhibitor that all who inspect his exhibit are potential customers. Thus, in essence it is a form of controlled circulation for his advertising and sales effort.

The advertiser who plans to use the exhibit must plan the design of his booth in the exhibit with the thought of attracting the attention of those attending, and also maximizing the sales impact he will achieve with his exhibit. The exhibit may be very simple, consisting merely of tables with samples of the advertiser's product displayed thereon, or they may be very complex and costly, with elaborate cutout working models of large pieces of equipment. Usually the advertiser will also have special sales literature and materials to hand out to those who stop and inspect the exhibit.

The exhibit can be a costly form of promotion. The exhibitor must pay rent for the space at the show; he must pay for the design and construction of his booth and the contents thereof, and for moving the exhibit from one trade show to another; and he also must consider the costs of providing salesmen and other people necessary to man the booth during the show. Rental costs will vary from as little as $50 for a booth in a small, local show to an average figure of $4.50 per square foot for a major industrial show. The cost of the booth and its contents will vary widely, but some exhibitors estimate that to do an effective job today involves costs varying from a minimum of $200 per running foot of booth frontage to $600 per running foot to do a creditable job of advertising. Most firms exhibiting in only a few trade shows will use the services of special companies specializing in the design and construction of exhibits. There are approximately 115 companies of this nature, most of which belong to the trade association of the industry, the Exhibit Producers & Designers Association. They usually work on a fixed fee basis.

SPECIALTY ADVERTISING

As defined by *Advertising Age,* "An advertising specialty is a useful product with an advertising message imprinted on it. It is usually distributed to customers and prospects by businessmen to promote goodwill, with no specific obligation attached." It is always distributed free. The advertiser does hope, of course, that the recipient of the specialty will be influenced to buy his product in the future by frequently seeing the advertising message on the specialty. It is believed that over half of American business firms use some form of advertising specialty, and it is estimated that approximately $650 million is spent annually for specialties by these firms. All forms of advertising specialties are sold through advertising specialty distributors or firms, whose salesmen in the field vend this form of advertising in the same manner that other media have sales forces for their media.

The variety and range of items included or used as advertising specialties is virtually endless. However, for discussion purposes, we shall classify them into the three groupings usually used by the industry—novelties, calendars, and executive gifts.

Advertising novelties

An advertising novelty is any relatively inexpensive item which is mass-produced for wide distribution as an advertising specialty. Literally thousands of items would fall into this category. Among the more common ones intended to be carried are ball-point pens, bottle openers, coin purses, cigarette lighters, emery boards, key rings, pocketknives, and wallets. For use on the recipient's desk are such items as ashtrays, blotters, letter openers, pencils, pens, memo pads, and rulers. For use in the home are such items as ashtrays, bottle openers, drink stirrers, pencils, ice picks, and thermometers. Every reader can think of many items he uses in his everyday life that are such advertising novelties.

There are several reasons why advertising novelties are so widely used as a form of advertising. Since the object is normally a useful item, it cultivates goodwill for the advertiser, and it gives the recipient a value for looking at the advertiser's message. The novelty provides for excellent repetition of the advertising message, since the user of the item will be exposed to the message each time he uses the article. For many novelties, this will be every day, and often many times each day. Another important feature of novelties is that they are inexpensive, and the cost per exposure is very small. The advertiser can select his prospects, and use novelties in such areas and with such groups of prospects or customers as he desires and selects. They fit in well with any regular campaign of advertising the firm may be using.

In selecting the novelty, the advertiser should be certain it is a useful item, one that the recipient will use or handle or consult frequently. It should have a long life, to get the benefit of long use by the prospect to whom it is given. The item should be such that the advertiser's name and message can be displayed effectively on it. It should be inexpensive so that it is economical to provide all those prospects the advertiser would like to reach. The advertiser should also try to select a novelty that is appropriate, or that ties in with his particular business. A bottle opener is good for the brewery; a key ring for car keys is particularly suitable for a service station or gasoline company.

Calendars

Calendars are the most commonly used of all forms of specialty advertising. A high percentage of individuals look at a calendar at least once every day of the year. It is thus no wonder that estimates are that at least one half of the money expended for specialty advertising is spent for calendars. Probably the most important problem facing the advertiser who decides to use calendars is the selection of an appropriate and attractive form and design for the audience to which the calendars are to be sent.

Executive gifts

Executive gifts is the term applied to advertising specialties that are expensive, in contrast to inexpensive trinkets or items that are usually classified as advertising novelties. In most instances, the executive gift is not imprinted with the advertiser's name or an advertising message. Hence, it probably should not be included as a form of advertising and not allocated to the advertising budget, although it frequently is so charged. The category is included here as an advertising specialty since it is usually so considered in the industry. And, of course, the gift is often designed or selected to be such that the executive will use it often, with the hope that each time he uses or sees the gift he will have a feeling of goodwill toward the giver and tend to buy his product. They are given in the industrial and commercial fields where the potential purchases by the recipient for his firm are appreciable in quantity, and so can easily justify a large expenditure per prospect.

There are crucial problems connected with the use of the executive gift—both moral and legal. For when an expensive gift is given to an executive who is in position to influence the purchases made by his firm, the question of commercial bribery arises. Hence, the advertiser may create more ill will than goodwill by offering such an executive gift. In many firms today, executives are prohibited by company policy from accepting gifts above a certain value.

SCREEN ADVERTISING

Some advertisers use short motion-picture films shown in regular movie houses as a part of their advertising program. Although theater-screen advertising is an important medium in many other countries of the world, it is only a very minor medium in the United States in terms of relative expenditures involved. While no comprehensive statistics are available, it is estimated that approximately 12,000 to 13,000 (including 4,000 drive-ins) of the some 16,000 movie theaters in the United States make their screens available for screen advertising.

Users of screen advertising

Screen advertising is used by both national advertisers and by local advertisers. National advertisers use it in manufacturer-dealer campaigns, in that the national advertiser produces and pays for the film advertisement, and the local dealer pays for the showing of the film, which includes a trailer identifying the local dealer as the place to buy the advertised product. The largest users of this medium on the above bases are the automobile manufacturers and the petroleum companies. Many of the local advertisers who utilize screen advertising do it as a part of their cooperative programs with their manufacturers. Among these are the automobile, petroleum products, and farm implement dealers. In addition, local service firms and retailers use screen advertising as an important medium for their local advertising. Among the heaviest users are banks and insurance agencies. Also, firms who naturally cater to after-theater business, such as restaurants, coffeehouses, pizza parlors, and ice-cream parlors are logical users of film screen advertising. In some instances, these local advertisers may merely use slides rather than movie films to present their advertisements.

Features of screen advertising

One of the major advantages stressed for screen advertising is that it has great impact, due to the large size of the screen and the fine picture presented to the viewer, and is able to use action and color, and actually demonstrate the product in use.

In addition, it has the advantage of selectivity and flexibility. Another advantage of screen advertising is that almost everyone in the audience for which the advertiser is paying is virtually certain to see and hear his message. The disadvantage of screen advertising is that some patrons of movie theaters resent the interjection of advertising messages during the entertainment.

Costs of screen advertising

The charge for theater screen advertising is based on weekly showings in the various theaters. Rate books are published which show the average weekly attendance for each theater, and the local and national advertising rates for a week. The actual rate on a cost-per-thousand viewers basis would appear to be high, as compared with other mass media, averaging in the neighborhood of $6 or $6.50 per thousand (the range being from $5 to $7).

DIRECTORIES

Another medium used to quite an extent by many advertisers is the directory. There are more than 4,000 directories in current use in the United States. These are published by directory publishers, magazines, trade associations, chambers of commerce, and city, state, and federal government agencies. Most of these directories are published to serve the trade, industrial, and professional fields. One of the most widely used consumer directories is the classified section (Yellow Pages) of the telephone directory. The Yellow Pages usage is a direct outgrowth of telephone usage. The long-established habit of looking up telephone numbers in the alphabetical (White Pages) directory carries over to the Yellow Pages when consumers are trying to find where to call for a particular product or service. Companies that encourage telephone shopping and use "tie-in" advertising (in which their TV, radio, and print ads carry the "Find it in the Yellow Pages" reference) reinforce the directory usage. To advertisers, one of the most significant features of the classified directory is that it is as available as the telephone itself. Over 150 million Yellow Page directories are distributed each year, blanketing a large segment of the population. In some large cities, because of size, the Yellow Pages forms a separate volume. But in most cities, the White and Yellow Pages are bound together. Every household or business having a telephone receives at least one Yellow Pages directory. For those few persons without telephone, or those on the move, directories are available at public telephone locations.

The familiarity and availability of the Yellow Pages make it an effective tool for the advertiser who seeks transient, seasonal, or infrequent customers, as well as general market customers.

For customers wishing to be represented in markets in a number of geographic areas, the National Yellow Pages Service provides a convenient way to order Yellow Pages advertising. One transaction can provide for advertising in 5,000 Yellow Pages sections. (See Figure 13–3 for some Yellow Pages costs.)

FIGURE 13–3. National Yellow Pages Service (NYPS) (circulation and annual costs within top 100 markets)

Selected market, regional, or national coverage can be purchased in local telephone directories with one centralized order. Practically all directories have a 12-month issue life.

Annual costs shown below include primary city and suburban directories circulated within specific market areas, where applicable. Space units range in size from quarter-pages to two-line bold listings.

Selected space units

Markets	Directory area population	Trademark heading	Boldface listing	1 column inch informational listing	Quarter column display
	(000)				
1–10	47,150	$21,420	$ 5,360	$16,480	$ 36,460
1–25	69,100	34,280	8,750	26,780	58,190
1–50	90,350	48,930	12,570	38,520	81,060
1–100	111,750	67,470	18,230	50,470	111,450

Source: *National Yellow Pages Service Rate and Data Book.* Reprinted in BBDO Audience Coverage and Cost Guide, 1971, p. 45.

SAMPLING

Sampling is a procedure by which a sample of the product is given to prospective consumers so that they can test the product, on the assumption the product "will sell itself" if once used.

There are four general types of sampling:

1. Delivered packages.
2. Delivered through cooperation with dealers.
3. Sent directly in answer to advertising coupons.
4. Sold through dealers and vending machines.

Delivering samples from door to door is one of the oldest forms of sampling. When advertising was not used to such a great degree and any new item distributed to the home was the center of a family discussion, almost any goods distributed from door to door received attention.

But with the change in living habits and the advent of laws and ordinances prohibiting the littering of streets, distributing samples from door to door has become less feasible. In addition to the cost of samples, delivery expenses tend to be high. It is sometimes advisable to use advertising to prepare a reception for the sample. Regardless of the cost, with many products like foods, house-to-house sampling can still be a profitable means of advertising.

One of the methods of sampling that has been tried in many different ways is that of supplying samples for retailers to give to their customers. This has been criticized because some dealers may sell the samples instead of giving them away. Some advertisers do not object to this. They say that the purpose of the campaign is attained, and perhaps those who pay for the samples use them with greater care and appreciation than if they were handed out gratis. Or, samples can be given out by demonstrators in the stores.

Another form of sampling which has worked out well in some fields is selling a small package of the product. Vending machines also may be used in a limited way to distribute sample package goods of low unit value. To arrange with dealers to redeem coupons which are used either in national or local advertising media is a common practice. In past years, a few advertisers have taken advantage of dealers by advertising that a dealer would supply a free sample or one at a reduced price on presentation of a coupon. However, the advertiser who uses this form of advertising should give the dealer sufficient notice so that he will be familiar with the campaign.

HOUSE ORGAN

Another medium for a company to use is a house organ. This is a magazine or bulletin published by a company and sent to its dealers, customers, or employees for the purpose of promoting goodwill, increasing sales, or for molding public opinion. House organs are distinct from publications for which a subscription price is charged because they are sent without charge. While the mortality rate for such publications is high, they can render a real service to the company. A well-edited house organ can do much to get customers to feel they know the people who are in the company. Owing to the cost of editing, printing, and mailing, a first-class house organ is expensive and requires close attention if results are to be profitable.

House organs for customers

When the magazine is for the consumer or user, the material in it must be of a different nature from that of a publication intended for salesmen, agents, dealers, or employees. If house organs are sent to prospective consumers, it is important that the publication be interesting and informative. The prospective consumer does not have the same interest in the manufacturer that the employee has, and, therefore, the material must get attention and create interest if it is to be effective. The house publication when properly used can be adapted to almost any business and is a valuable adjunct in building and maintaining goodwill.

Packages, labels and inserts

Although normally the package is considered as the container for the product (to protect it and to facilitate its handling) it also serves as a means for carrying a message about the product. Hence, in a sense, it is a type of advertising medium.

For best results, the advertising message on the package should be brief. A picture of the product, or the product in use, is desirable. The brand name and trademark should, of course, be prominent. Brief copy may include some information about the quality of the product, the contents and the methods of preparation. For food items, this may include recipes. If there is an inside container (glass bottle inside the cardboard box), the label on the bottle might have similar information on it.

Of almost equal importance is the package insert, often neglected by advertisers. Although it does not reach as many people, since normally seen only by the actual buyers and users, it still presents an opportunity to get a message across to the prospect. It is an inexpensive means of direct advertising to the prime prospects.

The insert can be used to convey various advertising messages. It can include more detailed information than the appeal on the package as how best to use, or care for the product, or, it can advertise other items in the firm's line.

QUESTIONS

1. It has been said that almost every business, regardless of size, uses some direct advertising. Do you agree? Explain.

2. With the recent criticism leveled at "junk" mail, and the advent of the consumers' movement, do you think the outlook for direct-mail advertising is bleak or promising? Explain.

3. Direct mail is often described as the most selective of all media. Is this true? Discuss.

4. Are specific forms of direct advertising more suitable for some retailers than others? Explain.

5. What are some of the recent trends and developments that have influenced outdoor advertising—some tending to increase its importance and

some tending to diminish its use? From your analysis of these, what do you think the future holds for outdoor advertising? Why?

6. Are there any circumstances under which an advertiser might use outdoor advertising as his primary medium? Explain. If yes, give examples.

7. Is outdoor advertising suitable as a medium for reaching particular segments of the market? Explain.

8. For what types of products, and for what advertisers, do you think transit advertising is more appropriate? Why?

9. How important is transit advertising as a medium in your city? Why is this true?

10. Study the advertisements in the Yellow Pages of your local telephone directory. Describe what you consider the most effective ads you found there. For what types of advertisers do you think this medium is most appropriate? Why?

11. How often do you use the Yellow Pages as a source of information for shopping? Do you think this is really a good advertising medium? Explain.

12. For what types of products would you consider sampling a particularly good means of advertising? Discuss.

13. Visit one department store and one supermarket in your city. Describe the point-of-purchase advertisements you saw there. Which of the stores made more effective use of point-of-purchase materials? Describe what you considered the two best pieces of point-of-purchase advertising.

14. Why do you think it is becoming increasingly difficult for an advertiser to obtain wide use of his point-of-purchase advertising materials?

15. For what types of advertisers, and under what circumstances, are exhibits an important form of advertising?

16. Bring to class three examples of "specialty" advertising. Do you consider them effective advertising? Why?

17. Bring to class a package that you consider an effective advertising vehicle, and one you consider a poor one. Explain your selections.

CASE 1.   PRECISION INSTRUMENT, INC.
Evaluating decreasing European sales

Precision Instrument, Inc. is a New York firm which is engaged principally in research, design, development, manufacturing, and sales of differential pressure-measuring devices and related instrumentation for industrial and commercial use where accurate and reliable measurement and control of liquid and gas flow are required.

Approximately 60 percent of the company's sales are made in the United States to a broad base of commercial industry, including oil and gas production companies, gas transmission and distribution companies, chemical and steel companies, public utilities, and to the military.

The other 40 percent of sales are made to countries throughout the world (except in South America, where the company has granted exclusive manufacturing and sales license), through 35 firms which act as manufacturer's representatives.

Precision had never advertised in the European market and had relied completely on the direct selling efforts of its sales representatives. Over 70 percent of the company's foreign sales were concentrated in Western Europe. Sales in this section, however, declined 7 percent in 1971, and 9 percent in 1972.

Company executives believed that declines in overseas sales were probably due to the economic alliances established in Europe, and the increased cost of manufacturing goods in the United States. The chief executive officer of Precision indicated that he believed the threat of a monetary or trade crisis was over and that now the manufacturers in the United States had a good currency environment in which to go forward. He stressed that because of the expertise of Precision in its product line, it would continue to excel over foreign competitors in the foreseeable future. At present Precision and 15 other U.S. based companies sell over 65 percent of these special pressure-measuring devices which are used in the Western European market.

Another problem that existed was that duties on imported merchandise from countries outsides of the Common Market were set high enough to protect the industries of member countries. Thus, each group constituted a self-contained Common Market allowing trade freely within the group and protecting the industries of member countries from outside competition.

Since the Common Market had come into existence, Precision Instrument, Inc. believed that its major foreign competitors were able to sell their products throughout the market duty-free. As a result, the prices which these companies charged were about 2 percent below Precision's prices.

The average duty levied by the Common Market group against Precision's products averaged 20 percent. Precision's standard products ranged in price from $300 to $5,000 per unit. In 1971 Precision did business with 920 customers in Western Europe. In 1972 the number of customers in Western Europe with whom it did business decreased to 850. Precision was unable to obtain accurate data on the cost of production of the European competitors. However, the executives believed, on the basis of a general analysis they had made, that better products could be produced more effectively in the United States.

In prior years Precision's prices had been competitive in Europe. Precision's sales figures for the period of 1967–1972 are given in Exhibit 1.

The executives were satisfied with the sales representatives who represented them throughout Western Europe, and had made arrangements

EXHIBIT 1. Precision instrument, Inc.,
annual sales (1968–1972)

1968	$43,944,688
1969	47,623,796
1970	48,526,488
1971	47,235,697
1972	46,976,025

with them to maintain inventories of standard products manufactured by Precision in order to provide faster service to the European customers. A number of these representatives maintained multiple offices in their territories.

At the last meeting of the European agents, the sales representatives from West Germany, France, England, and Italy recommended that to counteract the declining European sales, Precision should allocate 2 percent of its sales to an advertising program that would include media listed below in Exhibit 2.

EXHIBIT 2. Magazines (selected U.S. publications with international editions)

		Rate base (000)	Page b & w	Page 4-color	Percent sub.
1.	Business and news magazines				
	a. Business Week Int'l.	35	$1,160	$ 1,850	100
	b. Fortune Int'l.	31	1,290	1,940	100

Locally published major magazines	Type	Circulation (000)	Page b & w	Page 4-color	
2.	England				
	a. The Economist	Business	100	$ 768	$ 2,016
	b. The Guardian Weekly	Business	36	264	N.A.
3.	France				
	a. Express	News	460,000	$2,610	$ 4,500
	b. Paris Match	G. Edit.	1,170,038	4,500	7,110
4.	Germany				
	a. Neue Revue	News	1,670	$6,854	$12,338
	b. Der Spiegel	News	884	5,081	8,893
5.	Italy				
	a. L'Espresso	News	153	1,290	2,194
	b. Panorama	News	145	871	4,481

Case questions

1. Discuss the functions of manufacturer's foreign agents and indicate to what extent they should be responsible for the total marketing activity.

2. Point out what you believe will be the short-term and long-term effects of the Common Market.

3. What part can an advertising program play to correct declining sales in the European market?

4. Evaluate the media recommendations which the sales representatives made.

5. What media would you recommend for Precision in the European market?

CASE 2. ANALYSIS OF THREE COMPANIES
Deciding on media

Indicate the importance of using outdoor, transit, and direct mail in the selection of advertising media for each of the companies listed below and give reasons as to how and why they should or should not be used.

DIRECT WHOLESALERS, INC.

The company's business consists primarily of the procurement, warehousing, and sale of groceries and nonfood items to independent supermarkets, discount stores, and neighborhood grocery stores. In 1961 the company instituted a method of selling which was unique at the time in the wholesale grocery business and which is still followed by the company. At that time all salesmen were eliminated and today no salesmen are employed by the company. Instead, lists of products and prices are circulated weekly among the company's customers and potential customers and orders are taken by telephone clerks and processed on IBM equipment. The company's business has approximately 5,000 active customers throughout the eastern metropolitan area. Approximately 125,000 cases of groceries and nonfood items are moved in and out of the company's warehouse each week. Delivery is made in trucks leased by a company subsidiary, which leases trucks almost exclusively to the company. Sales are substantially on a cash basis with accounts receivable collected within an average of 3½ days after billing, which occurs 1 or 2 days before delivery of merchandise. The amount of the average invoice during 1966 and 1967 was approximately $300. Most of the items distributed are nationally advertised brands and are purchased directly from manufacturers or through food brokers. The company believes it has adequate alternative sources of supply for such items.

Competition

Since the company's business consists primarily of supplying independent retail outlets other than chain stores and cooperative groups, its success depends upon the ability of such outlets to compete successfully with chain stores, cooperative groups, and other independent operators. The principal chain stores operating in the area served by the company are A & P, Grand Union, Food Fair, First National Stores, and American Stores. The company competes at the wholesale level with many other wholesale grocery distributors, independent and cooperative. The wholesale grocery business is, thus, competitive and has been characterized historically by narrow profit margins. Although comparative figures are not available, the company believes it is among the larger independent wholesale distributors of groceries in its area.

DISCOUNT STORES, INC.

The company, a pioneer in the self-service discount department store field, opened its first store in 1950. This store has since been expanded and the company in 1967 operates a total of 12 stores with approximately 900,000 aggregate square feet of floor space in five states. Leases have been executed and construction commenced on three additional stores with approximately 325,000 aggregate square feet of floor space, one of which is scheduled to be opened later this year. The company's expansion program also contemplates the opening of additional stores.

Discount Stores, Inc., offers a wide range of first quality, popular-to-medium-priced department store merchandise at discount prices. The following policies have permitted the company to reduce (and in some instances eliminate) conventional retail operating costs and overhead.

1. All sales are on a cash-and-carry basis, thus eliminating delivery, credit sale bookkeeping, and collection and accounts receivable financing expenses.
2. The company's "Unconditional Money-Back Guarantee" policy is intended to assure customer satisfaction.
3. Customers serve themselves by rolling conventional self-service shopping carts through aisles of merchandise and paying at check-out counters.
4. Merchandise is delivered directly to the stores by vendors. This eliminates warehousing and reduces inventory, stockroom, and merchandise handling costs and facilitates more effective space utilization (i.e., greater selling space to total floor space ratio per store).
5. Simple self-service fixtures, which replace more costly counters, permit the display of a broader selection of merchandise and render it readily accessible to the customer.
6. Major thoroughfare locations in outlying, residential, or neighborhood shopping centers or areas result in more reasonable occupancy costs, better parking accommodations, and shorter travel time for

customers within the trading areas served by the company's stores, than for downtown stores. Only one of the company's present stores is located in a downtown area.

7. Single-story buildings eliminate elevator and escalator operating and maintenance costs, reduce housekeeping and merchandise handling expenses, and facilitate traffic flow within the stores. Customers are exposed to the merchandise from the moment they enter the store until they leave. Periods of nonexposure while in transit between floors, traffic congestion at elevators, escalators and stairs, and delays while waiting for sales clerks are thus eliminated. Counter and merchandise arrangements direct the traffic flow throughout the stores and facilitate both impulse and intended purchases (i.e., the merchandise "sells" itself).

8. Centralized planning, control, administration, and quantity buying for multiple operating units reduce overhead and unit merchandise costs, as compared with single-unit department store operations.

In addition to the foregoing, all stores are well lighted, spacious, and are open from 10:00 A.M. to 10:00 P.M., six days a week. Two stores are open seven days a week. All stores are air-conditioned. Advertising has been conducted through all local media, including radio, television, newspapers, billboards, circulars, and transit.

Discount Stores, Inc., competes with all other national and local retail establishments which handle similar lines of merchandise within its trading areas, including conventional department stores, variety and auto accessory chains, clothing, drug, hardware, home furnishing, furniture and appliance stores, and specialty shops, as well as supermarkets, other self-service discount department stores, and some of their cotenants in residential shopping centers.

LASTING PAINT COMPANY

The company is primarily engaged in the manufacture and retailing of a complete line of paints for interior and exterior home decorating. The company also sells in its own retail outlets linoleum, floor tile, wallpaper, stepladders, rollers, brushes, and a line of accessories and items used in decorating the interior and exterior of residential and commercial buildings.

The company pioneered the principle of selling paint and decorating supplies directly to the public through large discount retail stores, and its sales have grown to $25 million in the last fiscal year. This method of merchandising results in operating economies by avoiding the expenses of a credit or mail-order department and shipping or delivery service, as well as the financing of customer receivables. This sales method has made it possible for the company to offer both the amateur painter and decorator paint supplies at prices which are lower than those of competitive products of the same quality. Although the bulk of sales is made to "do-it-yourself" householders, professional painters also make purchases in the company's retail stores. The company believes that its retail prices are lower than the net prices charged by most of the larger paint manufacturers to professionals after deducting a trade discount from retail prices. The company has continued to operate on this basis and presently operates 25 stores in the midwest area, concentrating on catering to do-it-yourself property owners and tenants.

The paints sold by the company include interior and exterior oil base paints and enamels, rubber base paints, both oil and water emulsion paints and enamels, vinyls and acrylics, as well as varnishes, lacquers, etc. Paints account for approximately 60 percent of the total sales of the company. Sales of various types of linoleum, tile, and other floor covering constitute approximately 25 percent of the sales of the company. Wallpaper, stepladders, rollers, brushes, and other lines of items and accessories, the sale of no one of which is significant in itself, constitute the remaining 15 percent of sales.

Competition

The paint industry is competitive and the company competes with a large number of major paint manufacturers and retailers and with the paint departments of department stores, mail-order, and discount houses. However, the company has concentrated its efforts in the field of paint and related products sold primarily to the do-it-yourself and amateur painter. The company is one of the largest in the country.

With respect to its floor coverings and other products, the company competes with numerous other merchandisers in its area.

CASE 3.   MASTER FOOD, INC.
Considering promotional methods

Master Food, Inc.'s products include beef stew, corned beef hash, chili with beans, ham salad spread, beans and bacon, beans and ham, and Vienna sausage. The products are sold under its brand name "Tasty Master" as well as the nationally known brand names of firms for which it custom packs products. One third of Masters pack is sold under the company's brand name.

Master Foods did only a limited amount of advertising in newspapers to promote the Master label. It relied primarily on the salesmen to get shelf space in order to retain the desired sales.

Recently, the Yancey Company, a large national firm, notified Masters that it planned to purchase its products from another packer. In the past fiscal year, Master also experienced a decrease of 3 percent in sales of Tasty Master products. As a result, the company is faced with the problem of deciding whether or not to change its advertising strategy.

Process

Raw materials, consisting principally of meat, are readily available at commercial sources and, in order to alleviate the risk of market fluctuations, usually are procured upon the booking of orders. Except in a few instances, Master does not stock raw materials for which it does not have orders. The large percentage of meat is brought to the plant from packing houses located in the Midwest. Upon arrival, the raw materials, in the case of fresh meat, are placed immediately in freezer or cooler facilities preparatory to further processing. Depending upon the particular product, the meat is then ground, cut, or taken in its boneless state to batching areas where it is weighed according to predetermined formulas. Next, the meat is transferred to a processing area where other ingredients and spices are blended with it, according to specification, and it is precooked and preformed. Finally the entire formulation is transferred to mechanized canning lines (designed specially to accommodate the particular item being packaged), pressure-cooked, labeled with the respective customer's brand, packaged in cases, and stored preparatory to shipment.

Quality control

Master's plant operates under continuous inspection by the U.S. Department of Agriculture, Meat Inspection Division. The company maintains a separate department in which a quality control staff checks and tests products withdrawn from production runs to determine their compliance with predetermined quality control standards.

Research and development

Master maintains a separate research and development department at its plant. The department is engaged in developing and evaluating new food products and improving those presently produced both independently and in conjunction with customers.

Recommended strategy

The president of the company, Carl Grey, indicated that the company should not increase its general advertising but should put more emphasis on increasing the shelf space for Tasty Master products. It was his opinion that among the reasons that Yancey discontinued buying from Master was because the executives of that company were disturbed because of the fact that Master's own label was in direct competition with Yancey products. (Master's sales to Yancey had amounted to 2 percent of its total volume.)

While Master's president was concerned about the loss of the account, he believed that it was possible to offset this by increasing sales to its other accounts and, at the same time, increasing sales of Master's own brand.

The marketing manager, on the other hand, did not believe that more shelf space would build demand for Tasty Master products. He contended that Master's products were of the slower selling food varieties and would not respond economically to the effort that would be necessary to get more shelf space. He also stated that most supermarkets would generally not carry more than three brands of the items sold under Master's label.

Furthermore, he believed that the length of time between the purchase of Master's products was generally as long as two weeks or more. It was essential, therefore, in his opinion, that to increase sales of Master's products, one had to build brand loyalty through media, such as television, radio, and newspapers.

Need for shelf space. The president replied by stressing that purchase of Master's products was largely of an impulse nature. He stated, "even with paper products it has been shown that two thirds of these are bought on impulse." He went on to point out that it was his experience in merchandising that there was a direct relationship between shelf space and sales. He also argued that by Master's putting its promotional dollars into getting more shelf space, it would not alienate its other major customers.

Case questions

1. How important is the amount of shelf space which can be secured in the sale of Master's own brand?

2. If one found it was important to get shelf space, how should Masters attempt to service it?

3. Evaluate the comments of the president and marketing manager.

4. Should Masters plan its major promotional emphasis on securing more shelf space? Give reasons.

CASE 4.   RAWTON COMPANY, INC.

Importance of a dealer program

At the annual meeting of the directors in June, it was decided to reappraise the effectiveness of the dealer program which the company had used for its roofing material during the past year.

The Rawton Company was located in Salt Lake City and manufactured paints, roofing materials, industrial floor coverings, linoleums, and composition rugs. All the products were distributed throughout the United States under the corporation's family brand "Rugged."

For many years prior to 1953, Rawton sold its products through 30 wholesale distributors. However, as a result of a study which the marketing research department made of the trend in the distribution methods of its competitors, the Rawton executives decided to discontinue the use of wholesale distributors and to sell the products directly to retail outlets. This policy had been in effect since January 1, 1955.

Rawton sold its roofing materials through hardware stores and lumberyards. These outlets, as a whole, had proved to be the most satisfactory ones the company had been able to secure. Neither the lumberyards nor the hardware stores devoted much sales effort to the roofing material because they regarded the item as a staple and carried it only to fill customers' requests. It was left to the various manufacturers to develop their own market for their respective brands.

As a result of the lack of sales effort on the part of the outlets, Rawton's advertising agency produced a number of expensive, attractive dealer displays which were given to dealers without charge. It was the opinion of the company sales manager that this was the best way in which to make the distributors "roofing conscious."

In the checks which the company made, it found that the displays were not being used properly in many instances. Sometimes, it was because the dealer did not know how to put the display together. In other cases, the dealer was just too busy to put up the display. Frequently, after the dealer requested the material, he changed his mind and decided that he would use his display space for some other product that he considered had greater sales appeal.

The company approximated that only 50 percent of the material which it sent to dealers was actually put up in a final display. In the opinion of the executives, this was unsatisfactory. Therefore, they notified the sales manager that, because of the ineffective use of the dealer displays, they were going to discontinue the use of such displays and would in the future spend the advertising budget for more productive advertising.

The dissatisfaction among the retailers as a result of this policy was so pronounced that the officials of the company offered a special contract specifying the dealer-help materials the company would make available and the amount of cooperation the retailers would have to give in order to secure these materials. The contract offered retailers required their agreement to:

1. Handle the Rugged lines of roofings, shingles, building paper, sheeting papers, and roof coatings exclusively for one year.

2. Purchase from the Rawton Company during the year a minimum of 700 squares (or rolls) of the company's roofing materials.
3. Place a carload order immediately with the company. This order could include other merchandise than that stipulated under the quota, but such merchandise was not to be regarded as completing a part of the quota.
4. Follow Rawton's merchandising suggestions month to month, and give continued merchandising support to all the company's products.

The retailers who signed the contract were to be supplied with the following materials:

1. A large metal sign for the retailer's store front.
2. All the essential counter display pieces.
3. Two large floor mats on which the name Rawton was prominently printed.
4. Easel display boards and posters.
5. Counter and instruction books on Rawton's products.
6. A series of 12 monthly merchandising bulletins which offered various sales ideas, suggestions on developing mailing lists, instructions on displays, and other merchandising aids.
7. Cuts, mats, and electros for advertising done by the retailer.

As first planned, this contract was to be offered only to 250 retail outlets, the "cream" of the company's retail accounts. Soon after it was offered, however, requests from retailers not included in the selected list convinced the company's officials to widen the scope of the plan so that by the end of the first year a total of 321 outlets had signed the contract. A number of dealers whose business was so small as to preclude acceptance of the minimum stipulated in the contract were allowed to purchase the materials for $100.

On the acceptance of this contract by the retailers, there was an immediate increase in Rawton's sales of roofing materials because of the stipulation which required the retailer's immediate placing of carload order. The executives, however, were unable to tell whether this increase constituted a genuine increase in net sales, or whether it merely was an anticipation of orders that would ordinarily be spread out over a longer period of time.

Case questions

1. How important are dealer displays in the sales of roofing materials?
2. Do you believe that Rawton used the best outlets in selling this product?
3. Did Rawton have a sound policy regarding the use of its dealer aids?

4. Should the company plan to continue the contract with its dealers? If so, are there any changes that you would recommend be made in it?

5. Was it sound policy for the company to limit the contract to only the "cream" of the retail accounts? What legal problems might be involved?

6. What procedure should the company adopt to get its dealer displays properly used in the event it was decided to discontinue the use of the contract?

PART **V**——————

Advertising

Research

$$\text{--- chapter } \mathbf{14}$$

RESEARCH TECHNIQUE

As TECHNICAL RESEARCH has increased the number of new products being brought to market and has shortened their life cycle, as competition in the marketplace has increased, and as the sheer volume of advertising has made it more necessary and yet more difficult to make advertising effective, the need for and the importance of research in planning advertising has increased. Its use has grown markedly in recent years, as advertising people have found that in many cases research can be of real aid in arriving at the correct or best answer, or can at least develop a great deal of factual data to aid in reaching better decisions.

THE NEED FOR RESEARCH

In order to have advertising achieve its maximum effectiveness, it is necessary that the proper message reach effectively the greatest number of potential prospects at the minimum practical cost. This means it is of paramount importance to know the answers to such questions as who the prospects are, where they are located, what features they like in the product, what appeals will be most effective in inducing them to buy or in stimulating demand, what are the most effective means of presenting these appeals, when and how often advertisements should be run to maximize economical effectiveness, what media are best for carrying the messages to the prospects, and how much can justifiably be spent on advertising as compared with other parts of the marketing mix?

Changes are taking place so rapidly in the market today that determining the answers to the above questions by intuition or on the basis of the general knowledge and experience of the advertising man is virtually impossible. Even through the extensive use of research in its present stage, many of the questions cannot be answered. However, marketing research will almost always provide data that will enable the advertiser to arrive at a much better solution than would have been possible without such research.

Advertising research

In addition to these general types of problems that lend themselves to handling through marketing research, there are a number of problems, specifically in the field of advertising, that should not be answered by the advertising executive without using research to the extent that is deemed economically justifiable.

Among the specific advertising problems which research can aid in solving are the following:

1. What is the degree of consumer acceptance for the product?
2. At which market segments should the advertising be directed?
3. What should be the advertising strategy?
4. What appeals are best to stimulate demand among the various groups of prospects? What should be the campaign theme? What copy and headlines should be used?
5. What media will be most effective in reaching particular groups of potential customers?
6. In print media, what layout, illustrations, and size will be most effective in gaining consumer attention and in inducing effective readership of the advertisements? Should the ads be in color or black and white?
7. In radio and television, what program and copy will be most effective in obtaining listenership and viewing, and what message will be most effective in stimulating demand?
8. What timing and frequency of insertion will provide maximum return for the cost?
9. What tests can be made to predict the readership, listenership or viewing and effectiveness of the ads?
10. What should be the amount of the advertising budget?
11. How should the consumer advertising be merchandised to the advertiser's sales force, and to the trade?

GENERAL PROCEDURE IN MARKETING RESEARCH

Finding the answers to problems such as those listed above is the purpose of advertising research. Basically, marketing research is merely the application of the scientific method to problems in the field of marketing and advertising. In following such a systematic search for the facts and the solutions to problems, the researcher finds it advisable to follow a particular methodology which is designed to obtain accurate results. This treatment of the general procedure of marketing research is not intended to be an exhaustive analysis of the techniques of marketing and advertising research, but will be a brief discussion of the major steps involved in virtually every research project, regardless of its particular nature. Later in this chapter and in chapter 15, some of the specific tests and methods of research applicable to special problems in advertising will be discussed briefly. The student interested in research as a field should realize this presentation is merely an introduction to the subject and should consult the references in a good bibliography for further details on various phases of the subject.

Planning the study

The first step in any marketing research study is to define the problems accurately. To do this, the researcher should make a thorough analysis of the situation in order to define exactly the objective or objectives of the study. It is essential there be a clear statement of the objectives in order that the researcher can determine exactly what specific data is required. If the objective is not clearly defined at the start, much unnecessary data may be collected, while essential data may be omitted, resulting in an unsatisfactory study.

In making this analysis and definition of the problem, the researcher will conduct a background study, in which he will obtain basic information about the environment. With this the researcher is in a position to determine the real problem that should be studied. Although it may be believed that the problem is always obvious, this is not the case. In a number of instances, the apparent problem is found to be erroneous, and another aspect of the situation is the important one, the one that should be investigated. When the researcher has ascertained the real problem involved in the proposed study, he should write it down in a concise statement. For, unless the researcher can do this, it is evident that he does not have a clear understanding of the problem himself. Without an exact understanding of the problem he is to study, the researcher obviously has no clear objective for the further steps of his research work.

The preliminary investigation

The next step is to make the preliminary investigation (sometimes called the exploratory investigation or the informal investigation). The purpose of this step is to ascertain the possible solutions to the problem and to eliminate all except those that are the probable correct ones. If this is not done, much time and effort may be expended on possible, but improbable, solutions rather than concentrating all effort on the few most promising solutions to the problem. Also, in the conduct of this step the researcher obtains a practical familiarity with the actual conditions existing in the various areas on which his study will touch, eliminating the chance that his approach will be too theoretical and out of keeping with actual conditions.

In this preliminary investigation, the study is limited to matters pertaining to the specific problem as defined in step one. There is no formal outline of the procedures to be followed in making the preliminary investigation. The researcher must be flexible, for he is in reality an explorer attempting to find possible solutions to the problem he has defined. The usual search involves interviews with consumers (or industrial or commercial users) of the product involved, as well as with wholesalers and retailers who sell and service the product, specialists or experts in the field, and executives and personnel of the company involved in the study. In addition to such primary sources, this step will usually involve some limited evaluation of the secondary material in the field.

The interviews made in this step are not the formal planned interviews used in a regular field survey. The researcher usually will do the field work himself, and will merely talk to the above people. He normally will write up the results of each interview at its conclusion, and when he feels he has sufficient information, he will consider the ideas and suggestions contained in the individual interviews. It is then necessary to exercise judgment as to which of the original hypotheses seem to be pertinent ones. The final result of this study should be a clarification of the hypotheses and a list of the possible solutions that have real potential of solving the problem.

EXECUTION OF THE RESEARCH PROGRAM

In general, data useful in solving the problems of marketing research may be said to be available from two main sources—primary and secondary.

Sources of primary data

The principal sources of primary data can be classified in the following manner:

Consumers. The people or firms who buy and/or use the product or service under study are usually the best sources of information. It is necessary to determine the extent to which the buyer differs from the user, which of the two is most significant for the problem involved, and who influences the decision to buy.

Dealers. In many instances the wholesalers and retailers who handle the product are good sources of data regarding their own particular operations, reactions, and opinions. The salesmen may also be a good source of information about buyers.

Specialists. For certain types of research studies, various experts and specialists in the field may be a good source of data bearing on the solution of the problem. They are used more frequently in the preliminary and background phases of the study than in the final collection of data.

Sources of secondary data

There are many kinds of secondary data and sources from which it may be obtained. Here, only a few points will be made to indicate leading sources of data. A frequently used distinction of types of secondary sources is that of *internal data* and *external data.*

Internal data refers to information found within the records of the company itself. Sometimes the proper organization and manipulation of information contained in the accounting and sales records of the firm provides the answers to some of the research problems. Figures such as sales by type and size of product, prices, sales by consumers and classes of customers, sales by territories, and selling and advertising expenditures are indicative of the type of data that may well be analyzed in the study of a problem involving some facet of marketing. In some instances, important qualitative information may be obtained from customers' correspondence, salesmen's reports, and analysis of adjustments and complaints.

External data refers to materials that have been published in some form or that are compiled and sold by various types of organizations. It includes both writings of all types and statistics that have been compiled by government and public agencies, associations, and private firms of various types. The research man should know the general sources of marketing information and how to locate and evaluate the information acquired from such sources.

The main sources of secondary data are the following:

Libraries. One of the first places to look for published data is the library. Most public libraries contain a great deal of business information and many business publications, and contain the various indices and source books that make possible an organized search for available material on the subject under study. Most universities and many large business firms and institutions maintain libraries that contain good collections of materials on business in their special field of interest. The addresses and descriptions of the collections in special libraries may be found in *Special Library Sources,* available in any good public library.

Reference bureaus. There are also certain other institutions that function to provide business information. One of the most useful is the "Inquiry Reference Service" of the U.S. Department of Commerce in

Washington, D.C., which will provide service on specific requests from business firms. The Department of Commerce also maintains field offices in the principal cities which keep stocks of the department's literature and publications and also offer reference assistance on request.

Federal government. The largest collector and publisher of information in the world is the U.S. government. It is a source of much valuable information for the researcher, since its data are comprehensive and impartial and are available in many instances free of charge, or otherwise for a nominal cost. The researcher should familiarize himself with the types of data available from the federal government and the different publications and sources of government publications. Lists of such publications may be obtained from the Superintendent of Documents in the Government Printing Office in Washington, D.C., or from the special government agency involved.

The following government departments are among the major sources of data valuable to the field of marketing research:

Department of Agriculture:	Bureau of Agricultural Economics
	Production and Marketing Administration
	Office of Administration, Research and
	Marketing Act
Department of Commerce:	Bureau of the Census
	Bureau of Foreign and Domestic Commerce
	Bureau of Standards
Department of Labor:	Bureau of Labor Statistics
Federal Communications Commission	
Federal Reserve System	
Federal Power Commission	
Federal Trade Commission	
Securities and Exchange Commission	

State governments. Various agencies of state governments are engaged in gathering data on subjects of interest to the researcher, usually covering only the state involved. Data are particularly good in the fields of agriculture, retailing, and labor. Information on the data published by the states can be obtained through the *Monthly Check List of State Publications,* published by the U.S. Government Printing Office.

Publishers. Some of the large publishers of general magazines and newspapers have been active in conducting marketing research studies and collecting data. This is usually done to serve their advertisers, but much of the information is valuable for the researcher and can usually be obtained on request. Publishers of the many magazines in the industrial and trade publication field are specialists in their fields of interest, and valuable information in the technical and business fields often may be obtained from such trade publications. A well-known and widely accepted source of secondary data for use in estimating territorial market potentials is *Sales Management* magazine's "Annual Survey of Buying Power." This index is designed to reflect the relative buying power of the counties and cities of the United States, and is based on the area percentage of national disposable personal income (weighted 5 times), national retail sales (weighted by 3), and national population (weighted by 2).

Trade associations. Virtually every important field of business has its own trade association, and most of them collect statistics in their field. The pertinent trade association should always be contacted for data and can be located through the comprehensive directory published by the Department of Commerce, entitled *National Associations of the United States.* Somewhat similar in nature are the chambers of commerce of states and cities which often have local current data on activities in their areas.

Private sources. There are a number of specialized marketing research and statistical collection agencies that make a business of compiling information, and charge a fee for providing the data. The charges may seem high, but often it is less costly to buy the information desired from such firms, if they have it available, than to collect it firsthand, and it usually is much less time consuming. Some of these are:

Source	Data
A. C. Nielsen Company, Chicago.	Current sales in retail stores for various drug and grocery products by brands, etc.; index of television and radio listening.
Daniel Starch and Staff, New York.	Magazine and newspaper readership surveys.
F. W. Dodge Corporation.	Statistics on actual and contemplated construction.
Dun and Bradstreet, Inc.	Credit ratings and information about companies.
Gallup Robinson, Princeton.	Magazine and television impact ratings.
Market Research Corporation of America, New York.	Continuous consumer panel data, showing purchases by brands of selected commodities.
R. L. Polk Company.	Auto registrations and mailing lists.
Audit Bureau of Circulations	Paid circulation data on newspapers and magazines.
Standard Rate and Data Services.	Advertising rates and publication data for all publications and stations of the major advertising media. The SRDS Consumer Market Data provide estimates on population, number of households, consumer spendable income, and retail sales for counties and standard metropolitan statistical areas.
Publisher's Information Bureau.	Monthly expenditures by advertisers in various magazines and in radio and television.
Media records.	Newspaper advertising linage by advertisers.

Great care should be taken in selecting and using data from secondary sources, since the researcher is depending on other people's having done accurate and unbiased work in the collecting, compiling, and reporting of the data involved. The data must be very carefully evaluated before being accepted and used as the basis for solving the problem under study. Usually it is better to use the figures compiled in a study than to use the findings and conclusions which may have been drawn from them. A few of the things to keep in mind in evaluating secondary data are: the character and integrity of the organization collecting the data or making the study, the objectives of the study, the research methodology employed, the definition of terms used, and the time covered in the study.

Methods of collecting primary data

After the researcher has determined what data is available from secondary sources and, thus, what further data must still be obtained from primary sources, he must decide what methodology to employ. Basically, there are three methods of obtaining primary data. These are the observational method, the experimental method, and the survey method. These techniques vary in their approach and, in cases, in the accuracy of the data obtained. Since in some instances any one of the three could be utilized, it is necessary for the research man to decide which one is best in the particular conditions of a specific study.

Observational method. The observational method is having an observer (a person or a machine) watch what is taking place and record it. If the observer perceives accurately what is taking place and records it accurately, this method will obtain factual data. Obviously, only overt behavior can be studied in this manner. But, in those instances where it can be used, it has the advantage of greater objectivity than surveys, and so there are many valuable applications of this technique in marketing research.

An example might serve to clarify what is meant by the observational method. If a hat manufacturer desired to know just what the average retail clerk said and did while waiting on a prospective customer for a hat, he would post an observer in the store and have him record what the retail clerk did and said while waiting on the hat customer.

The observational method is more objective and accurate than the survey method. It eliminates the human element of the respondent which is uncontrolled in the survey method, and although usually the observer is human, he is one that is trained and controlled to a high degree by the researcher. However, he can observe only what people actually do, and this is sometimes not sufficient for the researcher. Also, this method is usually much more costly than the survey method. Further, it is not applicable at present in many instances. But when it is applicable, the researcher should give the method serious consideration because of its objectivity.

In some cases the observing is done by a machine. For example, the sales talk may be recorded by tape or wire recorder; traffic may be counted by one of several electric devices; and the users of radio and television sets may be recorded by the "audimeter" of the A. C. Nielsen Company.

Experimental method. The experimental method is, in essence, the procedure of carrying out, on a small scale, a test solution to a problem; so this method is used primarily to determine whether the tentative conclusions reached will prove to be right in actual conditions. It is essential that the conditions in which the test is conducted be essentially the same as the conditions that will be found in the total operation to which the conclusions are to be applied. In the conditions normally holding for marketing research, it is obvious that the environment of people, and market conditions, are ever changing and cannot be controlled by the researcher. However, by conducting the experiment simultaneously in different conditions and by repeating the test in rotated conditions of the different sets of variables, it may be possible to isolate the effect of different factors. Also, the experiment is used to try out different selling, advertising, and promotion programs in small areas, where the conditions of the test are selected to be as near those of the entire market as possible.

An example of the experiment would be the following procedure. If a package for a soap product has been selected, and it is decided that either blue or pink is the desirable color, an experiment might be used to select which of the two colors is best. Putting up equal displays of the two colors of packages in a carefully selected sample of stores, a record would be kept of the actual sales of the two colors of packages. At the end of the selected period, the color which had sold most in actual conditions would be presumed to be the better color from a sales standpoint.

Survey method. In marketing research terminology, the survey method refers to all methods of obtaining information through asking questions of others. Because a series of questions, when combined, is called a questionnaire, this method is sometimes referred to as the questionnaire method. The essential element in this method is that the information is furnished by an individual or respondent in a conscious effort to answer the questions. An example of the survey method could be given by referring again to the problem of selecting the preferred color of package, blue or pink. In the survey method, investigators or interviewers would show a blue and a pink package to a sample of people and ask each, "Which color of package do you prefer?" The survey method is probably the most widely used of all research techniques, since much more information can be secured by this method than by the others. Attitudes, motives, past actions and experiences, and much factual information that cannot be observed can be obtained only by the survey method. Two significant factors affecting the survey method should be mentioned here. First, the questions must be worded in such a manner as to obtain the desired information in an accurate and unbiased form. Also, the person giving the information, usually called the respondent, must be able and willing to give the desired information in response to the questions asked, accurately and without bias.

There are three principal methods of conducting the survey insofar as reaching the respondents are concerned, and when electing to use this means for gathering primary data, the researcher must plan on which of these three methods to employ. The three methods are by mail, by personal interview, and by telephone. The two most widely used are by mail and by personal interview. Each of these has its advantages and disadvantages, and they should be understood so that the preferred method can be used for the particular study involved.

1. *The mail survey.* The mail survey has several important advantages. It eliminates the personal element and possible bias introduced by the field investigator or interviewer. The entire country can be covered even though respondents are spread all over the country and in remote areas, all at the same cost per respondent. It may be possible to reach people by mail who would be very difficult to find at home or in the office for personal interviewing. Since the questions appear in print, they are the same in every questionnaire. The respondent may take more time in preparing answers to questions, will be able to confer with others if he so desires, and may hence take more care in his responses. The respondent is anonymous and may feel freer to give frank and confidential information.

This method has some serious disadvantages. There is always grave danger of having the returns represent an invalid and biased sample. It may be difficult to obtain a truly representative mailing list. The persons who return the questionnaire often represent a highly selective group of those receiving it, which results in a distorted sample. Often only a small percentage of the questionnaires mailed out are returned completed, so that the assumed low cost becomes an actual high cost per usable return. It is difficult to plan the timing for a mail survey. Since respondents may take some time in returning the completed questionnaire, often it takes more time to complete a mail survey than one using the personal interview method. It is impossible to observe anything about the respondent and his surroundings. Also, for obtaining information that requires extensive discussion and some probing, personal interviews have great advantages. And, if a specific order of questions is essential for obtaining the desired information, this cannot be achieved by a mail survey.

2. *The personal interview.* In general, the advantages and disadvantages of the personal interview method of making a survey are the opposite of those just enumerated for the mail survey. The sample can be

much better controlled in the personal interview method. The interviewer can obtain the required number of interviews within the time limits set, so that work can be completed quickly if that is necessary. The interviewer can observe the person and his surroundings, and so obtain much significant information not included in the actual questionnaire. The interviewer can explain questions if doubt arises in the respondent's mind, can probe further information, and can stimulate the respondent into supplying further information. The interviewer asks the questions in the desired order and records the replies in a standardized and clear manner, simplifying greatly the editing and tabulating of the data.

This method does have limitations that must be considered when determining which survey method should be used. The personal bias of the interviewer cannot be avoided. And the mere presence of a person may cause some respondents to alter their answers to avoid embarrassment or to try to please the interviewer. If it is desired to include remote areas in the study, the costs of using interviewers may be prohibitive. It is very difficult to find some people at home or at the place of the interview, and this either results in higher costs for return calls or distortion of the sample for the final study. People may refuse to answer questions of a highly personal nature when asked in person. The interviewee may be in a hurry, or in a state of excitement, and this may prevent him from giving accurate replies to the questions.

3. *The telephone survey.*   Use of this means of obtaining information by the survey method has increased greatly in recent years. The chief advantage of this method is that it is possible to obtain a large number of interviews quickly and at a relatively low cost. It may be possible to reach people who would not care to be interviewed personally, and also at times when interviewing might not be feasible.

One of the most significant disadvantages of this method is that it is limited to telephone subscribers, which is a selective group, with different characteristics than that portion of the population without telephones. Generally speaking, only a relatively small amount of information may be obtained from answers to questions of a simple and nonconfidential nature. It is virtually impossible to obtain vital classification data about the respondents. It is difficult to get the cooperation of the respondent, since setting up a desirable rapport between the unseen respondent and the interviewer is most difficult. Recently, with so many firms using the telephone for direct selling, it is becoming more difficult to obtain the cooperation of selected respondents. Usually, due to the cost and time involved in attempting to place toll calls to outlying areas, the method is confined to urban areas and ignores outlying areas. For most survey purposes, the disadvantages of the telephone method far outweigh its advantages, so its use is confined to special types of studies and information.

Executing the collection of primary data

After the method of collecting the primary data has been selected, the actual execution of the plan may begin. Several aspects of such execution will be discussed briefly.

Sampling. Since in most studies it would be virtually impossible from a standpoint of time, cost, and practicality to interview (or observe) every individual person, firm, or household possessing data involved in the study, in most instances only a sample of the total number of people or firms, known as the universe or population involved, is contacted. Sampling is the science of selecting a relatively small group from a larger group in such a manner that the small group accurately represents the larger group from which it is drawn. A good sample must fulfill two basic requirements: It must be representative of the population from which it is drawn; and it must be reliable, or adequate.

The sample is representative when its characteristics provide an accurate cross section of the characteristics of the entire population from which it was selected. Within limits, the larger the number of cases included in the sample, the greater the accuracy of the results.

The reliability of a sample can be controlled by taking a sufficiently large sample and by using proper sampling techniques. In marketing research, usually the researcher has made some decision about the degree of accuracy that he requires in his study. On the basis of sampling theory, it is known that there is a sample size which will yield accurate results about the entire population within stated limits of error. To use a sample larger than one that will yield the required degree of accuracy is wasteful for the researcher, since it reduces the chances of error more than is necessary for his particular study, and the costs of increasing the size of the sample increase much faster than does the increase in accuracy of the results obtained.

Preparing questionnaires and forms. The design of proper forms and questionnaires to be used in the field work is of great importance. Properly designed forms insure that the proper data will be collected, and that it will be recorded in an accurate and readily usable form. Generally the forms for observation studies are not unduly complicated or difficult to design. Their functions usually are to provide or indicate exactly what is to be observed, to provide a standardized and simple manner of recording the observations, and possibly to facilitate the tabulation of the results obtained. Normally the form should make provision for identifying the observer and the place and time the observations took place. Such a form should be well pretested before the final collection of data begins on any large scale.

Questionnaires. The questionnaire (the term for the form used in the survey) involves considerably more problems than the usual form for observation studies. For, in addition to having the functions of the form noted above, it includes the problem of asking the right questions in the correct form and in the sequence that will result in maximizing the amount of accurate information obtained. And the proper arrangement of questions and their correct wording is one of the most difficult arts of marketing research.

Basically, the questionnaire will consist of three parts: the identification information, including usually the name and address of the respondent and the name or initials of the interviewer; the classification data, including descriptive information about the respondent (such as age, sex, income); and the actual questions designed to obtain the information bearing on the problem under study. The questions should be relevant, clear, specific, and arranged in proper sequence. Care should be taken to word questions in such a manner that they do not induce bias. Proper design of the questionnaire is a difficult art, and experience is more important than following any set of rules that might be listed. It is important to pretest the questionnaire prior to its use, to eliminate as many weaknesses as possible.

Interviewing. With the sample selected and the questionnaire designed, the next step is the actual interviewing. In outline form, the important steps here include the following:

1. Providing an adequate number of well-qualified and well-trained supervisors.
2. Selecting and training a good staff of field investigators or interviewers.
3. Providing complete written instructions for the guidance of the interviewers.
4. Adequate supervision of the work of the interviewers.
5. Checking of the work of the field staff.

Tabulation and analysis. When the completed questionnaires are received, the first step is to edit them carefully. This involves checking carefully the reports of each interviewer to appraise the accuracy of his work, checking for inconsistent answers within the questionnaire, rejecting obviously inaccurate replies, standardizing answers involving units of measurement, filling in incomplete answers where possible, and sorting general answers into the desired classifications. Then the answers from the questionnaires are tabulated; that is, all the answers in the same classification are consolidated into totals and summarized in orderly tables. The data is then in shape for analysis. This involves studying the data and arranging it in such ways as to make its nature and relationships clear. It is often helpful also to summarize the data by applying appropriate statistical measures, such as computing measures of central tendency and dispersion.

Interpretation.   At this point, the researcher must study the data obtained above, including the various statistical measures that have been computed, and draw from them their meaning with regard to the specific problem under study, and decide what conclusions can be drawn from the data. Usually this would involve deciding which of the original hypotheses set up as possible solutions for the problem was the correct one. This step calls for clear logical thinking, the use of judgment, and a constructive imagination.

Presentations of the findings.   The final step is to present the findings of the study to the responsible executives involved. This may be done orally or in writing. There are a number of somewhat different types of reports, depending on the person or persons for whom the report is intended. Regardless of the type of report, those intended for the sponsors of the research must be well presented, otherwise the results may be ignored regardless of their accuracy and value. In a very real sense, research results must be "sold" if action based on the findings is to be taken.

SOME SPECIAL FORMS OF RESEARCH

The above discussion has in a brief manner discussed the general field of marketing research and its methodology. The attention of the student should now be drawn to certain special fields or types of research.

Motivation research

The type of survey described previously in this chapter is of a nature designed to determine many facts about the characteristics of the present or potential customer, such as how many and what kind of people buy a certain brand or product, where they buy, and where they live. However, it has long been realized that this type of survey did not obtain accurate answers to questions such as: "Why do people buy my product?" and "Why do they act as they do?" A new type of research known as motivation research, has been developed in recent years which does attempt to discover and explain why the consumer behaves as he does, and what appeals and sales programs will best influence his decision to act and buy.

Motivation research has been defined as "the use of psychiatric and psychological techniques to obtain a better understanding of why people respond as they do to products, advertisements, and various other marketing situations."[1]

The two main groups of social scientists contributing most to the development of motivation research are: the psychologists and psychia-

---

[1] Charles J. Dirksen, Arthur Kroeger, and Lawrence C. Lockley, *Readings in Marketing*, (Homewood, Ill.: Richard D. Irwin, Inc., 1963) p. 439.

trists, who basically study the personality of the individual as such; and the sociologists and anthropologists, who study the social framework or environment in which the individual lives. Its principal use to date has been to aid the advertising man in selecting the best appeals and the best words, symbols, and concepts with which to influence the consumer. However, since motivation research ascertains the basic needs and desires (conscious or unconscious on the consumers' part) which are most important in influencing his buying decisions, it can aid in many business decisions. Hence, this type of research should prove to be of great value not only in determining the proper promotional and sales programs and the proper advertising appeals, copy, and advertising presentation but also should prove of great value in product planning and design, in packaging, and in the selection of brand names and trademarks.

Motivation research is basically the application to the specific problems of business of the theories and generalized observations developed by social scientists about how individual consumers and groups in the society behave, and why they behave as they do. On the basis of this knowledge of why people act as they do, and about their feelings, wants, and motives, the motivation researcher narrows down the marketing or advertising problem to a manageable set of hypotheses. After he has done this, he determines what field study may be necessary to determine the correct hypothesis or the answer to the particular problem. It is then that he decides which of the several techniques of motivation research will provide him with the information he needs to solve this particular problem. This aspect of motivation research is stressed here because so often discussions of the field place so much stress on the unusual techniques of this method, such as depth interviews or projection tests, that readers come to believe these techniques constitute motivation research.

The projective test. The use of this technique involves stimulating the interviewee to project himself and his own personality into an artificial or ambiguous situation. For example, if the researcher wanted to learn about the interviewee's attitude toward shopping in a supermarket, he might show her a picture of a housewife shopping in a supermarket and then ask her to tell a story about the housewife in the picture. Without realizing it, the interviewee normally will weave into the story she tells her own feelings, attitudes, and values. There are several types of projection techniques, including the above picture response, free-word association and sentence completion.

Depth interviewing. In contrast to the regular interview, no formal questionnaire is normally used in the depth interview. Instead, the interviewer, who must be a highly trained person, merely asks questions to encourage the interviewee to talk as freely as possible about the subject in question. Rather than trying to solicit factual information, the interviewer is merely asking questions to draw out the emotions, the feelings, the opinions of the interviewee, and he develops his pattern of questions as the interview proceeds in such a way as to bring out the interviewee to the maximum extent possible. The interview will normally last from one to two hours. The information gathered in such interviews must be analyzed and interpreted by a highly trained social scientist. Usually only a rather limited number of interviews is sufficient for the motivation researcher, since the studies are more qualitative in nature than quantitative, as is true of the ordinary surveys.

Motivation research has now become an important form of consumer research done by most agencies, advertisers, and marketing research firms. It is especially valuable for discovering and identifying the "subconscious" or hidden attitudes, feelings, and motives of the consumer. Hence, because it can be used to bring out the inner determinants of proper behavior, it is most useful and valuable for determining alternative appeals which can be used as the theme for an advertisement or a campaign.

Use of mathematics in the decision-making process

It is apparent from the above discussion that the ultimate object of all marketing and advertising research is to aid the executive in making sounder decisions. In recent years rapid developments have taken place in the application of various tools of mathematics to the decision-making process, including the fields of marketing and advertising. And, although a certain amount of quantitative analysis has always been involved in marketing and advertising research, it usually involved only basic statistical applications. Currently, far more sophisticated methods of quantitative analysis are being developed and applied in advertising to aid in making better decisions.

A good discussion of the techniques involved, some applications, and the implications involved in a more quantitative approach to decision making are included in the article by Philip Kotler which appears in the October 1963 issue of the *Journal of Marketing*. If the student will read this article carefully, while keeping in mind that the general concepts as applied to marketing can be applied equally well to advertising research and advertising decision making, he will gain a good idea of the possible use of quantitative methods and mathematical models in advertising. If more information is desired, recently published books on quantitative methods and marketing research should be consulted.

QUESTIONS

1. What specific advertising problems do you think research can aid in solving?

2. Do you think the step, the preliminary investigation, is essential and warranted, if time is very short for the complete research study?

3. Under what circumstances would the retailer and wholesaler be your best source of primary data?

4. For what types of data would you use your local chamber of commerce ʰs a main source of secondary data?

5. How would you proceed in determining whether or not the information contained in secondary data was valid and appropriate for your purposes?

6. Do you consider government agencies and government reports sound sources of secondary data? Why?

7. Give examples of conditions under which you would consider the observational method a particularly appropriate form of research.

8. Describe a specific problem in which you think the experimental method would be especially appropriate.

9. Interview a member of the staff of a local marketing research firm. Ascertain their relative use of the survey, observational, and experimental methods. How do you account for this relative use of the three methods?

10. Indicate under what circumstances it might be advisable to use the telephone survey method.

11. How would you judge whether or not a sample was a "good" sample?

12. How do advertising research practitioners often justify the use of a relatively imprecise sampling procedure?

13. What do you consider the most important uses of motivational research? Explain.

14. In your opinion, how will the newer methods of quantitative analysis and the use of the computer influence advertising research?

CASE 1. PESTO COMPANY

The Pesto Company is engaged in processing and packing food products, consisting principally of peeled tomatoes and tomato products, such as pizza sauce, catsup, tomato paste, tomato puree, tomato juice, chili sauce, and tomato sauces, and of asparagus, peaches, fruit cocktail, pears, apricots, and cherries. The company also has an extensive line of low-calorie food products, which includes the same kinds of fresh vegetables and fruits as are packed in the regular canning operations of the company, and, in addition, low-calorie dressings, toppings, sweeteners, jellies, preserves, puddings, and gelatins. Modern, efficient methods and equipment are utilized in the processing and packing operations to maintain grade and quality control of the products of the company and of the products purchased from other producers.

The executives of the company are considering the introduction of a group of canned vegetable products that are children-oriented. The brand name, package design, and advertising would be attuned to children. The products would have an additive that would make them appeal to childrens' tastes.

The low-calorie food products which the company has been producing and marketing since 1958, were developed for those who must eliminate or restrict the intake of natural sugar and salt in their diet, as well as for those who must reduce daily calorie intake. The volume and line of low-calorie foods has steadily expanded, particularly as people have in recent years become more weight and health conscious, and now constitutes one of the most important phases of the company's business.

The period of heavy production for the company each year is between the months of June and November, when most crops become available for canning.

Sales

Apart from sales to the government, approximately 55 percent of the company's sales of its food products are made under the company's own brand names and the remaining 45 percent is marketed under the customers' brand names. The low-calorie line is sold exclusively under the company's own brand name. The company has expended substantial sums of money to advertise and otherwise promote the sale of its products under its own brand names so as to develop consumer recognition and acceptance of such names. During the fiscal year 1967, such promotional expenses amounted to approximately 1.4 percent of total sales.

The only products which accounted for more than 15 percent of the company's total sales for the year 1967 were tomatoes and tomato products, which together represented approximately 43 percent of such sales, and peaches, which represented approximately 18 percent of such sales. Low-calorie foods accounted for approximately 15 percent of the total sales for that year. In proportion to sales, however, the low-calorie foods made a greater percentage contribution to the profits of the company than the other two lines of products.

The company's products are sold directly to about 3,000 customers, consisting of wholesale grocers, chain stores, restaurants, institutional and industrial customers, and certain governmental agencies. Approximately 6 percent of the company's total sales for 1967 were made to the government. Sales to no other single customer accounted for more than 5 percent of such total sales. Approximately 60 percent of such sales were made through food brokers to whom a commission is paid by the company. All but a few of such food brokers also handle competing lines of products. The company employs 15 salesmen who call on direct customers.

Exports have not up to the present constituted a significant portion of the company's sales. However, the company has, within the last year or so, expended considerable effort to develop its export trade and intends to continue such efforts. The company has already entered into agency arrangements for the exploitation of the markets in those other countries.

Competition

The canning industry is very competitive and is subject to many inherent risks, such as major production during a comparatively short harvest season, the unpredictable raw material supply that is dependent to a great extent on weather and crop results, and the adverse effects of either excessively small or excessively large packs. Since there is considerable diversity as to the products handled by different companies in the canning industry, it is difficult for the company to determine its relative position in the industry in general on any comparable basis. Certain competitors of the company are much larger and have substantially greater financial resources than the company. In its particular line of canning and processing, however, the company believes that it is among the 15 largest producers.

A number of farmer cooperatives have recently acquired cannery plants with a view to giving their members the benefit of a manufacturing profit on the fruits and vegetables grown by them in addition to the profit on the sale of raw materials. Such enterprises furnish competition to independent food canners and processors not only in the sale of their products but also in the acquisition of raw materials. There has also been a recent tendency for different chain stores to merge or otherwise integrate their operations. While this reduces the number of available customers for the products of the various food canners and processors, the company has not to date been adversely affected by such combinations, since loss of individual chain store customers in some combinations has been offset by acquisition of additional outlets for its products in others.

The statements of income for the three years ending December 31, 1967, are given below:

| | Year ended December 31 (in thousands of dollars) | | |
	1965	1966	1967
Income:			
Net sales	$20,000	$22,000	$23,000
Other income	1,000	300	1,200
Total	$21,000	$22,300	$24,200
Loss:			
Cost of sales	$17,000	$17,500	$18,200
Selling & gen. exp.	2,000	2,100	2,500
Interest expense	200	300	300
Provision for fed. income tax	900	1,000	1,300
Total	$20,100	$20,900	$22,300
Net income	$ 900	$ 1,400	$ 1,900

EXHIBIT 1

Can you trust us with your wife on tire-buying day?

Absolutely.

You say she doesn't know anything about cords and plys? You say she can't tell a retread from a radial?

Fine. We say she doesn't have to. (Neither do you, if you'd rather keep the dubious pleasure of buying tires all to yourself.)

Because, at B.F.Goodrich, we talk straight talk. Not a lot of technical tire gibberish.

All you've got to know to get the right tires from us is a few simple facts about how you drive. How much, how far, how fast and so on.

Then you reach for one of our BFG Tire Value Calculators. Feed it the facts, as you know them. And it will tell you which BFG tire will suit you best, cost you least.

Would we try to sweet-talk anyone into buying the wrong tires?

Nope. We're the straight-talk tire people.

The straight-talk tire people. B.F.Goodrich

Courtesy: B. F. Goodrich Company

EXHIBIT 2

Are four-ply tires going the way of inner tubes?

It looks like it. Almost all the tires we ship to car makers now are two-ply rather than four-ply. Matter of fact, nearly all new cars have come with two-ply tires for the past three years.

But we've been asked: How can we take something out of a tire and make it better?

People asked the same thing when B.F.Goodrich introduced tires without inner tubes: How could they be as strong? But they were. Today almost every car rides on tubeless tires.

Sure, two-ply tires have only two plys (layers) of cords while four-ply tires have four. But every cord in two-plys is twice as big and twice as strong as the cord in four-plys. So, two-ply tires are every bit as tough as four-plys. And, in some ways, they're better. They run cooler. And give a softer ride.

Who says so? Test experts on car-proving grounds. And millions of car owners who've racked up billions of miles on two-plys.

Next time you need tires, ask a BFG dealer about two-plys. He'll give you straight talk. It's a specialty of the house.

The straight-talk tire people. B.F.Goodrich

Courtesy: B. F. Goodrich Company

Case questions

1. Indicate the procedures that should be followed in testing the children's line of vegetables before they are introduced.

2. How would the company determine the nature and size of this market?

3. How would the company determine what trade channels to use?

CASE 2.   B. F. GOODRICH COMPANY
Pretesting advertisements

The B. F. Goodrich Company plans to use the advertisements in Exhibits 1 and 2 in its "straight talk" campaign for passenger tires.

Exhibit 1 ("Can you trust us with your wife on tire-buying day?") is scheduled for *Sports Illustrated, U.S. News & World Report,* and *Newsweek.*

Exhibit 2 ("Are four-ply tires going the way of inner tubes?") is scheduled for *Business Week.*

Case questions

1. Recommend a plan for pretesting the two advertisements. Describe the size and composition of the sample and how you would obtain the information.

2. To what extent would your procedures be changed, if B. F. Goodrich asked you to compare the effectiveness of the "straight talk" appeal to one which emphasized some other appeal, such as safety or durability?

CASE 3.   ROSE OVENWARE COMPANY
The pretesting of advertisements

The Rose Ovenware Company, a large manufacturer of pottery ovenware of such various types as casseroles, baking dishes, bean pots, and custard cups, had developed recently a new type of glazed china ovenware which had a much finer appearance of quality and style than did their traditional lines of pottery ovenware, since it could be manufactured in much lighter weight and could be designed along smarter and finer lines. At the same time, it was equal to the old lines of ovenware from the standpoint of durability and quality of its baking results. The company selected the name "China Roseware" for the new line.

The company had decided to do a thorough job of pretesting their advertising and promotion program for the new line before beginning their national advertising campaign and marketing program.

The company marketed their regular lines nationally through hardware stores, department stores, and houseware specialty stores. It was a leading firm in the field and had very good distribution through most of the leading stores of the above types.

The Rose Company planned to market their new line of glazed china ovenware, "China Roseware," through the same types of stores, although it was thought it might be advisable to add gift shops as a channel for their new line, since it was believed that the smarter appearance and better styling would make it very attractive for wedding and shower gifts, as well as for Christmas gifts, as was true of their traditional lines.

In their regular lines of ovenware, the Rose Company sales records indicated two retail sales peaks—one during the last part of November and in December before Christmas, and the second (a slightly smaller sales peak) in April and May. The company had for many years carried on a consistent program of advertising in national magazines, using women's service magazines primarily, and the appeal of "the finest quality in ovenware" as the major theme.

The Rose Company's advertising agency had from time to time carried on surveys to determine consumer usage of Rose Company's products and their opinions of Rose ovenware. These surveys had indicated that Rose ovenware enjoyed a fine reputation among most housewives, who considered it one of the finest quality lines of ovenware on the market.

While discussing plans for marketing the new "China Roseware" line, the advertising agency recommended the Rose Company conduct an area sales test to select the advertising approach to use in their national campaign. Since the Rose Company planned to invest several million dollars in promotion of the new line during the next few years, the agency deemed it advisable to protest the main advertising theme. The agency had developed three different copy approaches from ideas submitted by various members of the agency.

The three themes developed by the agency were: copy theme 1, stressing "the beauty and style of China Roseware"; theme 2, "the convenience and attractiveness of serving food at the dining table directly from the utensils in which the food was cooked"; and theme 3, "the better baking results from China Roseware." Although the Rose Company advertising manager was somewhat dubious as to the ability of any firm to conduct a really sound area sales test because of the many problems involved, he finally approved the plan for the agency to conduct such a test.

For the test, the agency selected nine cities (as nearly comparable as possible for all important factors), all of which met the usual criteria for good test cities. The Rose Company had very good distribution of their regular lines in all these nine cities. In the two months prior to the conduct of the test (July and August), a team of three Rose Company salesmen covered the nine test cities with an intensive sales effort, and were able to get over 90 percent of all the company's regular outlets to stock the new line of ovenware, with only very minor variations among the nine cities in the percentage of stores stocking the China Roseware line.

For the test, the advertising agency developed three sets of advertisements, each set based on one of the three copy themes. The sets of advertisements were considered comparable in quality and attractiveness. In conducting the test, the advertisement series 1, using the theme "the beauty and style of China Roseware," was run in cities A, B, and C. The second series of advertisements, based on theme 2, "convenience and attractiveness of serving food at the dining table directly from the utensils in which it was cooked," was run in cities D, E, and F. The third series of advertisements, based on theme 3, "the better baking results from China Roseware," was run in cities G, H, and I. Sales in all the hardware and department stores in all the nine cities were audited weekly for a period of six weeks before the advertisements were run, and for the six weeks of the actual advertising campaign. Since the new ovenware was fair-traded, no cut-price sales took place during the period of the test, and no unusual promotions were held by any of the stores which were audited. Half-page advertisements were run twice a week for the six weeks in the leading evening newspaper published in each of the nine cities, always in preferred positions in the women's section of the paper, and on the same day of the week.

Sales results for the two periods involved were as shown in Exhibit 1.

EXHIBIT 1

	Sales, 6-week period preceding advertising, Sept. 1– Oct. 15	Sales, 6-week period of advertising, Oct. 16– Nov. 30	Percent of increase due to advertising
Cities A, B, & C. Advertising theme 1, "The beauty and style of China Roseware."	2,000	3,000	50
Cities D, E, & F. Advertising theme 2, "The convenience and attractiveness of serving food at the dining table directly from the utensil in which it was cooked."	1,800	2,800	56
Cities G, H, & I. Advertising theme 3, "The better baking results from China Roseware."	1,600	2,600	62.5

The agency was very pleased with the results, which indicated all three appeals were very good. Although the agency believed the results were sufficiently significant to make advertising theme 3, "the better baking results from China Roseware," the obvious theme to use, they decided to follow the sound procedure of double testing, so obtained the approval of the Rose Company's advertising manager to run an inquiry test to check the results of the area sales test.

For this purpose, they decided to use the Chicago *Bugle*,* a newspaper which provided facilities for running a three-way split-run test. In its Sunday edition, the *Bugle* published a "local news" section, varied for different areas served by its circulation. This section had excellent readership in all areas, and had often been used by food and drug companies for inquiry tests, with excellent results in the way of response. The *Bugle* showed them the results of several of these tests, and the enthusiastic letters received from the agencies which had conducted them.

For the inquiry test, the agency prepared new and improved advertisements, using the same three basic appeals which had been tested in the area sales test previously. The same sized advertisement, in the same position on the same page of the special section, was inserted for each appeal. The advertisement using advertising theme 1, "the beauty and style of China Roseware," was run in the section of the paper which went to the North Side. The advertisement using theme 2, "the convenience and attractiveness of serving food at the dining table directly from the utensils in which the food was cooked," was run in the section which went to the South Side, and the advertisement using theme 3, "the better baking results with China Roseware," appeared in the section distributed in the towns and rural areas of downstate Illinois. Although the circulation varied slightly for the three areas, the inquiry results were corrected to allow for this discrepancy. The offer, a recipe book (*One Hundred Delicious Casserole Dishes*), was in the form of a buried offer, and was equally prominent in all three advertisements. The advertisements all appeared on Sunday, January 8, since it was believed housewives spent more time reading the newspaper on Sundays.

The corrected results of the inquiry test were as follows: advertising theme 1, using "the beauty and style of China Roseware," 127 inquiries; advertising theme 2, stressing "the convenience and attractiveness of serving food at the dining table directly from the utensils in which the food was cooked," 108 inquiries; and advertising theme 3, incorporating the idea of "the better baking results from China Roseware," received 181 inquiries.

Since this test so definitely marked advertising theme 3 as the superior appeal, and also confirmed the results of the first test, the agency now

---

* Fictitious name.

was positive it had the best appeal, and recommended to the advertising manager of the Rose Company that he authorize them to plan its campaign around advertising theme 3, the appeal of "the better baking results from China Roseware."

Case question

If you were the advertising manager of the Rose Company, what would be your reaction to the agency's recommendation, and how would you evaluate the testing procedures used?

chapter 15

TESTING ADVERTISING EFFECTIVENESS

B<small>ECAUSE</small> of the large sums of money invested in advertising, and the highly competitive nature of today's market, media owners and advertising agencies are all vitally interested in determining the effectiveness of advertising.

Because of the complexities of testing advertising effectiveness, many advertisements are not tested. That is, some people engaged in advertising doubt the validity of tests designed to measure advertising effectiveness. Or they feel the qualities of advertising that can be tested do not truly measure the value of the advertisement to achieve its ultimate goal, the sale of the product or service, and so it is not worthwhile to test. Some feel that the creation of good advertisements is an art, not a science, and the use of tests and research tends to stifle the creativity of advertising people. Others feel the costs of good testing outweigh its value. On occasion, due to the pressures of time, testing and research may be omitted because good research does require adequate time and cannot be rushed. Some advertising people are confident they have the ability and experience to create effective advertising without measurement or testing.

However, the use of testing and measuring of advertising effectiveness has increased in recent years due to several factors. One is the increased interest of top executives of advertisers in getting the best possible results with the larger advertising appropriations required today, so that they support expenditures for testing. The development of scientific methods of testing has also helped in getting more agencies and advertisers to budget sufficient funds for the proper testing of a good share of their advertising.

Most advertising people will agree that it is wise to make judicious use of testing. They would agree that all methods of testing do have certain limitations. However, they believe that careful and adequate use of testing can be a real aid to producing better advertisements and advertising. Also, it should be stressed that generally speaking it is not always possible to measure the effect of an advertisement or advertising on sales and profits of a company (because of the difficulty of isolating the effects of advertising from the effects of all the other elements of the marketing mix). Hence it is usually necessary to establish other criteria of effectiveness for advertising, and test these. Other objectives may be established for advertising and tests are devised to measure the effectiveness of advertising in achieving these more specific and narrower objectives. Among these objectives are the extent to which print advertising is noticed, seen, or read, the extent to which the message is understood, the extent to which it is believed, and so on.

Some tests are designed to determine the effectiveness of advertisements prior to running them, and are known as "pretests." Other tests are designed to evaluate advertisements or campaigns while they are being run or at completion of the campaign. The major forms of both these types of tests will be discussed briefly in the following paragraphs.

Consumer jury test

This is a type of pretest designed to determine the effectiveness of an advertisement before it is run, and is known as a form of copy testing, a general term used to describe tests designed to evaluate advertisements before they are run, or measure expected results from an advertisement. The consumer jury test obtains the preference of a sample of typical prospective consumers of the product for one advertisement or some one part of an advertisement out of several being considered by the advertiser. The prospective consumer, or juror, rates the advertisements, the headlines, or the theme, by direct comparison. Since the advertisement is designed to influence the prospective consumer of the product being advertised, it is believed that he is in a better position to determine what advertisement or message will influence him than is a member of the general public or the advertising expert.

In the case of advertisements designed to be run in print media, the test usually is conducted in the following manner. A small group, or sample, of people, considered to be typical prospective buyers or users of the product to be advertised, is selected to serve as the "jury." This jury should be representative of the consumers or prospective consumers for the product. A group of advertisements is prepared which are based on different themes, or in which the headline or some other part of the advertisement is varied. These advertisements are then shown to the individual jurors, and they are asked to express their preference for the different advertisements by answering such questions as the following:

1. Which of these advertisements would you notice first?
2. Which of these advertisements is most interesting to you?
3. Which of these advertisements is most convincing to you?
4. Which of these advertisements would be most likely to cause you to buy this brand?

The juror may be shown all the advertisements being tested in turn, and asked to rank them in order of relative value or merit. This method is known as the "order-of-merit" rating technique. The weakness of this technique is that it is quite difficult for any person to rank more than five or six advertisements consistently in the same order, although with less than this number jurors can rank rather accurately. The other technique for juror ranking is the "paired-comparison" method, in which the juror will be asked to rate or compare only two advertisements at a time. Every possible combination of advertisements is paired, so that an opinion is obtained from each juror regarding each pair of advertisements. Although this method produces more accurate and consistent rankings of advertisements, it poses a serious problem if there is a large number of advertisements to be tested, since the number of combinations then becomes very large.

It is desirable to control closely the circumstances or conditions in which the juror rates the advertisements, as in such matters as the length of time they are permitted to see the advertisements. If the juror is permitted too long a time to make his decision, it is believed he is apt to assume the role of a critic and try to determine what he thinks other people would think or like rather than to give his own first reaction.

There are several variations in the handling of juries and in the techniques used in this test. In most cases, the advertisements are shown to jurors as individuals. However, in some instances, researchers attempt to obtain suggestions and ideas regarding a group of advertisements by presenting the advertisements to be tested to groups of jurors, usually ranging from six to ten people. The group is permitted to discuss the advertisements and express their opinions and ideas regarding them, with the interaction and stimulation of discussion among the jurors supposedly providing better results than those obtained from the members acting purely as individuals.

Since the usual method of rating advertisements by jurors, the comparative ranking of the advertisements, gives no indication that any of the advertisements is really good or effective, or any indication of the relative superiority of the preferred advertisement, some researchers use attitude scales. This technique obtains the absolute score or opinion of the juror regarding the advertisement's effectiveness.

Although usually the consumer jury test is conducted by personal interview, it is sometimes conducted by mail. Some firms conducting this test include with the advertisements being tested one or two old advertisements which actually have been run before, and for which they have some measure of effectiveness, to serve as control advertisements and thus measure the relative quality of the advertisements selected by the jurors.

The consumer jury method is also used to pretest radio and television commercials. They can be shown to individuals or to groups (studio audiences) very much in the same manner as print advertisements. Frequently commercials are pretested simultaneously with the testing of programs, using the studio audience approach. The concept here is the same as with print media advertisements, the difference being in the methods required to run the actual testing procedure.

Problems in conducting consumer jury test. Among the problems connected with the use of the consumer jury method of testing advertisements are the following:

1. Selection of a valid sample of "prospective consumers" for the product being advertised.
2. Preparation of the advertisements so that only one element or concept is tested at one time.
3. Proper wording of the questions to be asked the jurors.
4. Handling the showing of advertisements, the time they are shown, and the instructions to the members of the jury, to maximize the probability of obtaining the personal reaction of the juror, rather than his idea of what he thinks his reaction should be.

Evaluation of consumer jury test. This method of testing can be done in a short period of time, usually requiring less than two weeks to complete. It can be done at relatively low cost, since it does not involve actually running the advertisements in some medium. The advertisements can often be prepared in rather rough form and still obtain desired results. It does not require a particularly large sample, the usual size ranging from 50 to 200 people. The test is fairly easy to conduct. It can be used to test a number of different features or aspects of advertisements. There are no "outside influences" to distort results, such as position of the advertisement in the medium. It is generally conceded to be of real value in separating the very strong from the very weak advertisements. It is believed valid for determining such things as whether the advertisement is interesting to the juror, whether the juror believes the claims made for the product, and whether the advertisement's copy stimulates his desire for the product.

There are several criticisms leveled at this method of testing. The chief one is that the entire test is somewhat unrealistic in nature. The juror cannot be a "normal" prospect, but tends to place himself in the position of a critic or expert. He is not viewing the advertisement as he would under normal real-life conditions. If he is asked, "Which advertisement would attract your attention first in a magazine," or "Which advertisement would most likely cause you to buy the product?" his answer is purely hypothetical Some critics of the consumer jury test believe jurors try to please the person conducting the test, vote for the advertisements they feel they should like rather than ones they actually like personally, prefer advertisements that resemble others they have seen before, and seldom vote a preference for advertisements based on a negative appeal or containing very hard-sell copy. Also, this method of testing gives no indication that the advertisement selected by the jury as best is really good or effective (unless control advertisements are included among those tested), and no indication of the relative superiority of the preferred advertisement over others (unless some scaling technique is used in the testing program).

The inquiry test

The inquiry test is another method of copy testing which may be used to check the relative effectiveness of several advertisements by running them on a limited basis, or to test the reaction to one of a series of advertisements on a comparative basis. The method used is to include in the advertisement an offer to send something to the reader if he will write for it—hence, the name inquiry test. The offer stimulating the inquiry may be made by including in the advertisement an actual coupon which can be cut out and mailed in, by giving the offer a prominent position in the headline or copy of the advertisement, or by a "hidden offer," that is, an offer included in the body of the copy with no unusual stress on it so the offer will not be noticed by a casual reader but only by a careful reader of the larger part of the copy. Frequently, in order to discourage so-called professional coupon clippers, children, and those only casually interested in the product, the offer may require sending in a nominal sum of money with the inquiry. By coding the coupons and advertisements in appropriate ways, the advertiser can determine which of the different advertisements obtained the responses.

If the test is being used to determine the relative effectiveness of one or more variations of a single element of an advertisement, such as the headline or illustration, the other elements must be the same in each of the advertisements.

Split-run tests. Since one of the main problems in conducting the inquiry test is that returns may be influenced by such factors as the position of the advertisement in the publication, the amount of competing advertising, the editorial content of the publication, the time of appearance of the publication, and other variables, some newspapers and magazines will divide their pressrun to enable the advertiser to use a different advertisement in each of the splits or portions of the printing. If the portions of the printing containing the different advertisements being tested are then distributed alternately among subscribers receiving the publication, all the above variable factors are eliminated, since the two advertisements being tested appear in the same position, with all other conditions being the same for each.

A relatively fast and inexpensive manner of conducting the inquiry test is by direct mail. Obviously, this method is best when used to test advertisements to be used in direct-mail advertising. However, it is sometimes employed when the advertisements are to be run in magazines and newspapers, even though obviously the conditions in which the advertisements are exposed to the reader are different than if they were run in the publication. In this direct-mail method of inquiry testing, the advertisements are prepared as though for publication, then mailed to comparable groups of people, preferably a sample of the readers of the publications in which the advertisement is to appear. Again, the advertisement eliciting the greatest number of responses is considered the best.

The inquiry test also, of course, can be used with radio and television. The above discussion of the inquiry test in published media would apply to these media, except that no actual coupon can be used, nor is it possible to use the split-run technique.

Evaluation of the inquiry test. The inquiry test is rather easy to execute, and the conditions in which the reader responds to the advertisement are comparable to those in which the reader normally will be exposed to the advertisement. However, it does involve the actual running of the advertisements in the media and, hence, may be somewhat costly and require a considerable amount of time. Unless the split-run method can be used, it is very difficult to control, or allow for, the variables that may influence the returns from the different advertisements being tested.

The chief criticism of this test is with regard to its basic validity. It is generally conceded the test is quite valid when testing advertisements that are intended to bring specific and immediate results, such as mail-order advertisements actually selling by means of the advertisement. However, when the purpose of the advertisement is indirect in nature, to achieve sales results over a period of time, or to stimulate primary demand for the product, or to build the prestige of the brand, there is considerable difference of opinion as to whether or not inquiries actually measure the effectiveness of the advertisement to achieve its purpose, or merely measure the ability of the advertisement to obtain inquiries.

The sales-area or sales-results test

The sales-area test can be used as another pretesting form which involves the experimental method of research. The basic concept involved in this test is to run an advertisement or campaign (or several different ones) on a small scale to determine effectiveness before running the campaign over the entire marketing area with its attendant large costs. The test can be used to evaluate different themes or various different copy techniques.

The procedure is to run the advertisements with different appeals (or copy or headlines) or the different campaigns in separate comparable markets, usually cities, for the determined desirable period of time. By comparing the actual sales to consumers taking place in the different markets through the retail stores, the more effective appeal (or copy or headline) or campaign is selected. The test is only valid for advertising designed to obtain immediate sales responses and for items that are bought frequently, where the influence of advertising can exert itself quite quickly.

In the actual conduct of the test, the advertiser, who, it is assumed, is interested in testing the effectiveness of a completely new appeal as compared with the one he is now using, would first select his test areas. Normally, these would be two groups of cities, as comparable as possible in all respects influencing sales of the product (and also representative of the whole market in which the advertising is to be run later). One of these groups of cities would constitute his "control" group of cities, and one his "test" group of cities. The control group will provide the data which will serve to measure the influence of the factors other than the advertising on sales, while the new appeal advertising will be run in the test group to provide the data which will serve to measure the influence of this new type advertising. Normally there should be at least three cities in each group, so that if some unusual event occurs in one city, the results of the test will not be spoiled. The usual advertising (and other selling efforts) would be continued in the control cities, while the advertising with the new appeal would be run in the test group of cities (where, again, all other selling efforts would be continued in the same manner as formerly). If two different appeals are being tested, usually three groups of cities would be used, one for control, two for testing. In this case, the advertising in the two test groups of cities would be run in the same media, the same size of advertisement, the same frequency of insertion, and so forth; that is, all conditions other than the appeal in the advertisements would be kept comparable. Sales in the control group of cities will indicate what sales are during the period in the usual conditions which exist during the period, while the sales in the test group (or groups) of cities will reflect the difference in sales resulting from the new or different advertising appeals.

Usually the test period is divided into three periods, with the first period being a pretest period. During this time, sales are checked in the several groups of cities to determine sales in normal conditions and to note any trends in sales. The test advertising campaigns are run during the second or actual test period. The third period is a posttest period, and sales are checked during this period to ascertain the carry-over effect of the advertising. The minimum length of time for each of the three test periods is 1 month; usually 2 months for each is preferable, and in some cases researchers advocate 3 to 6 months each, or 9 to 18 months for the whole test. Various factors influence the preferred length of time, although the rate of frequency of purchase of the item being advertised is probably the most important factor. The more frequent the normal purchase of the item, the shorter the test periods that can be used safely. Sales are measured for each of the three periods by checking the retailers' stocks and purchases at the beginning and end of each period. Every effort should be made to maintain "normal" conditions in all retail outlets in the various cities, since variations in display, promotion, and selling price can influence sales markedly. When interpreting the results of the test, it is important to check carefully for any outside factors that may have unduly influenced sales in any of the cities included in the study. If the factors appear to have been comparable in the various sets of cities, they can be ignored. If, however, some outside factor or factors appear to have unduly influenced sales in one or more cities, either a correction must be made for the effect of the outside factor, or if this does not appear feasible or if only one city is involved, the results from the unusual city should be discarded in making comparisons of sales.

Virtually all advertising people agree that the sales-area test provides authentic results when properly conducted, since it does measure actual sales under actual market conditions. However, it is a difficult test to conduct properly. The selection of cities to be included in the test, maintaining comparable conditions in the various groups or cities, and applying the proper corrective allowances when conditions do vary all pose very serious problems. It should also be noted that this test takes a long period of time (in addition to three to six months of actual testing time, considerable time also would be consumed by the other phases of the entire test, such as planning the project, selection of the cities, and tabulation of data and interpretation of results). It is also very costly. It can be used only for certain types of products, and can use only local media. Another serious problem is that competitors are alerted to the activities of the advertiser. They may then vary their promotional activities in order to create unusual or changed conditions in the test markets, hoping to cloud and confuse the test results. In some instances, they have been known to buy large quantities of the test item, both for analysis and to create confusing sales totals. This is especially significant if the test is being run in small markets, where such purchases can seriously distort the sales figures. A still more serious danger is that a competitor will copy the test product, or even improve on it, and still bring it to market ahead of the original testing company. Some of the largest companies have been known to send research teams into another firm's test markets, and conduct surveys to measure the results of the test, using such test results in aiding their decisions. Hence other methods usually are used if they will give results sufficiently accurate for the advertiser. Often other tests are used to screen appeals for campaigns or the concept to be tested, then the sales-area test is used as the final check on the advertising selected by means of the other tests.

The systematic rating list, or checklist

Another method of evaluating advertisements before they are run is the rating scale or checklist. Although this is not actually a method of testing advertisements, it is an evaluation method and should be mentioned here. The concept involved is to develop a list of qualities which the advertisement should contain, or a list of questions to be asked about each advertisement being evaluated, and then to check the advertisement against the list to ascertain whether or not it contains the features enumerated, or to rate the advertisement on each of the features listed. Usually, the lists include such factors as attention and interest value, although there are checklists designed to ascertain such features as the readability or understandability of the advertisements. The checklist method was given its greatest initial impetus by the Townsend Brothers, who developed a checklist of some 27 items, with a value assigned to each item. which was designed to enable one to determine the effectiveness of any advertisement in only a few minutes.

This method of testing has one real value. It does allow the one using it to be certain no important element has been omitted from the advertisement through oversight. In addition, this method is simple to carry out, takes very little time, and the cost is minimal. However, there are real problems involved in evaluating advertisements with this technique. What items or values should be included in the list? What relative weights should be assigned to each item or quality? In practice, different people usually score the same advertisement quite differently. A major criticism is that no one checklist can be appropriate for all types of advertisements, for different products, with different objectives.

Other methods of testing

There are several other tests quite widely used, normally to test advertising while it is being run, or campaigns after they have been completed. Among these are the recognition or readership test, the recall test in various forms, and attitude and opinion tests. In these tests, the objective is not to determine the selling effectiveness of the advertising directly but to measure whether the respondents have read the advertisement, what impression the advertising has made on them, or the attitude resulting from the advertising.

The recognition or readership test. This is a test conducted after the advertisement has been run to determine the number of readers of the publication who have seen and read the specific advertisements being tested. By analyzing various advertisements so tested over a period of time, the advertiser can determine to some degree what features of his advertisements result in increasing the number of readers who see and read his advertisements. He then can utilize such information to improve his future advertisements by incorporating the features that will obtain this higher seeing and reading.

The techniques used in this test can be illustrated by discussing how it would be applied in the testing of an advertisement appearing in a given magazine. Interviewers would call on a representative sample of the readers of the particular magazine at an appropriate period of time after the publication date and ask if the interviewee has read that particular issue of the magazine. If so, the interviewee is asked to go through the magazine page by page with the interviewer and to indicate which of the advertisements he has observed or seen and how much of the copy was read. Various influencing conditions, such as the order of going through the magazine, are controlled by the interviewer. This test of the number seeing and reading the advertisement is not so significant from the standpoint of the actual score made by the particular advertisement as it is from a comparative standpoint; that is, for comparing the figures for advertisements run in the magazine over a period of time, with the figures of other similar advertisements for the same category of product run in the same issue of the magazine.

Probably the best-known organization using the recognition test is Daniel Starch and Staff which conducts the Starch Advertisement Readership Service, covering all advertisements one-half page or larger in many national magazines and a number of newspapers. This service provides considerable information on recognition of the advertisement, including categories they term "noted," "seen-associated," and "read most," as well as for various component parts of the advertisements; and comparisons of these figures for various sizes of black-and-white and color advertisements, the readers per dollar for the advertisement, and the cost ratio for the various advertisements checked.

As a rule, the term "noted" includes all those respondents who tell the interviewer they remember seeing the advertisement in the particular issue of the magazine or copy of the newspaper involved. The "seen-associated" category includes all the respondents who have seen or read enough of the advertisement, such as the trademark or company name, to enable them to know the product or the advertiser involved. To be classified in the "read most" category, the respondents must say they have read 50 percent or more of the reading material in the advertisement.

Since one of the basic criticisms of the recognition test has been that although it might measure the attention value of the advertisement and the number of people who read it, this did not measure the value of the advertisement in selling the product, the Starch Service now attempts to measure the extent to which the readership of the advertisements has influenced the reader to buy the product. This is done by ascertaining the percentage of readers and nonreaders of an advertisement who have bought the product within a certain number of days prior to the interviewing. The difference between the percentages (when corrected for the greater readership of advertisements about a product by those who are interested in and loyal to it) measures the effectiveness of the advertisement in stimulating the purchase of the product by the reader.

Another weakness of the recognition test is the so-called confusion factor. That is, when a proposed advertisement that closely resembles an advertisement already run is being tested, many of the respondents may claim sincerely to have seen the advertisement in the particular magazine or newspaper being checked, when, in actuality, they had seen the very similar advertisement in this or another publication. Also, some respondents may claim to have seen advertisements they did not see.

Some research people using the recognition test attempt to correct for this confusion element by showing to a sample of interviewees several advertisements prior to their having appeared in any publication. The percentage that claims to "recognize" the unpublished advertisement is then applied as a reduction factor to the results obtained in the regular running of the test. No technique has been developed to correct for the understatement of recognition.

Considerable debate exists among researchers relative to the validity of readership tests in general. Some researchers have conducted tests attempting to duplicate the methods used by organizations such as Starch in obtaining their readership ratings. Some of these researchers feel that readership scores are influenced more by the respondent's imagination than by actual readership of the advertisements, some that the scores are unduly affected by the number of multimagazine readers included in the samples, while others believe that the readership scores are more a measure of reader interest in the product than of the ability of the ad to obtain readership and remembrance of the advertisement.

Recall tests. The recall type of test, like the recognition test, is based on the memory of the respondent, and is designed to measure the positive impression created by the advertisement on the person being interviewed. Probably the best known of the recall tests are the "impact" studies of magazine and television advertisements of Gallup-Robinson. The test can be probably best illustrated by describing the Gallup-

Robinson recall studies of magazine advertisements. The interviewer first ascertains that the respondent has seen the issue of the magazine being studied by showing him the cover of the magazine, but not opening it. He then asks the respondent to name all the advertisements he can recall having seen in the magazine. If the respondent has seen or can correctly identify at least one item in the magazine, he is handed a set of cards carrying the names of advertisers or brands appearing in the issue. He is asked how many of these he remembers having seen, and is then asked to tell the interviewer everything he can remember about each of the advertisements he can identify, including the appearance of the advertisement, what it said about the product, and the main message of the advertisement. This test measures the impression the advertisement made on the respondent and the meaning it had for him. What the respondents say they remember of the advertisement and its message enables the researcher to analyze the effectiveness of various parts of the advertisements and the ideas it contains. The number of respondents who can remember the advertisements under this test is normally lower than the number of readers under the Starch type of recognition test. It is believed the Starch type recognition test is more effective in obtaining quantitative data on readership, but that the recall methods will obtain more qualitative material from those few who can remember the advertisement.

The "triple-associates" test is another form of recall test. It was developed by Henry C. Link, and is used to test the effectiveness of a campaign rather than individual advertisements. In it, the interviewer asks the respondent what brand name or advertiser he associates with the product and theme or slogan which the interviewer names for him. For example, the interviewer will ask the respondent, "What brand of cigarette (product) is advertised as '_____ Tastes Good Like A Cigarette Should' " (slogan), or "What brand of cigarette is the cigarette that 'tastes good like a cigarette should?' " The correct answer to this would be Winston, of course.

Two organizations, Gallup and Robinson, and Young and Rubicam advertising agency, publish special testing magazines to pretest advertisements. The magazines contain editorial matter, advertisements to be tested, and a number of control ads (these have previously been tested in regular consumer magazines). Copies of the magazine are distributed to a sample of homes and the people are asked to read it as a regular magazine. The following day the interviewer conducts an aided recall test as with a regular magazine.

This method has the advantages of control of conditions surrounding the test, using an exposure method fairly near normal conditions, although its weakness is that the reading of the magazine and, hence, responses are somewhat forced.

Several organizations conduct either telephone or personal interviews with samples in certain major markets, to determine what television programs the respondent viewed, what products he saw advertised, and what he remembers of the commercials.

These recall tests thus measure not only that the respondent has seen or read some of the advertisements (which is measured by recognition tests, too) but also measure the lasting impression the advertisement has made on the reader, and to some extent the meaning the advertisement conveyed to the respondent.

However, the test does not indicate whether or not the respondent will buy the product because of his recalling the advertisement and its message, or even whether the respondent actually believes the advertiser's message, even though he may remember it.

Attitude and opinion testing

Many studies are made to measure the attitudes and opinions of customers or potential customers toward a firm's advertising, its branded products, and toward the company and its policies in general—or to measure the brand or company image. These studies are designed to measure the effectiveness of both the firm's product advertising and its institutional and public relations advertising.

The methods used in these studies include both opinion polls and surveys and consumer panels. Measurement may be made by using single spot surveys or by a series of periodic studies. The recurring study pattern has the real advantage of reflecting changes in the attitudes or opinions of consumers over time. The results of such attitude and opinion surveys enable the advertiser to plan his advertising program to offset any unfavorable attitudes and develop favorable ones. Additional follow-up studies enable him to ascertain the degree of success the changed advertising program is achieving.

Measuring scales. Direct questioning of people regarding their attitudes is not too effective, since many are not aware of their attitudes or have difficulty in formulating a statement of their attitude, which consists of a complex of many feelings. To date no standardized measuring scale or device has been developed to measure attitudes. The process of developing measuring devices that are used to measure attitudes is called scaling. These scales may be either ordinal or interval scales. The ordinal scale serves to rank correspondents according to some characteristic, such as liking or disliking a certain commercial, or to rank items, such as advertisements or brands, in order of preference. Such scales do not measure the degree of liking of the different rankings. Interval scales do measure the distance between such positions in equal units, in addition to separating the items by rank order.

A commonly used type of scale is one in which the respondent is asked to rank himself by checking the point most descriptive of his attitude on a scale running from one extreme of the attitude being measured to the other. For instance, if the researcher were determining attitudes toward a picture to be used in illustrating a certain advertisement, he could ask respondents to check the box most nearly expressing his feelings about the picture:

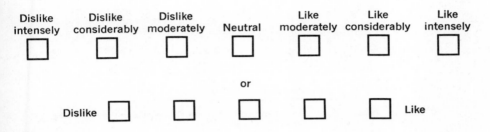

Graphic scales of this type can be constructed to fit the needs of the particular study and are relatively simple and easy to use.

Another of the attitude-scaling systems used is known as the "semantic differential." In this case, the researcher sets up a series of scales with extremes of positive and negative values which he obtains from his preliminary investigation of the subject. The respondents are asked to check on each scale a point that most nearly expresses their attitude or opinion of the subject under study. This method has been used mainly in company and brand image studies, since it enables the researcher to develop descriptive profiles to use in comparing his firm with competitors. An example of the application of this method is shown in Figures 15–1, 15–2, and 15–3 which show the profiles obtained in a study whose "purpose was

FIGURE 15–1. Specific product image

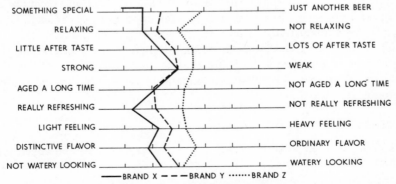

Source: William A. Mindak, "Fitting the Semantic Differential to the Marketing Problem," *Journal of Marketing*, Vol. 25 (April 1961), p. 31.

FIGURE 15–2. Company image

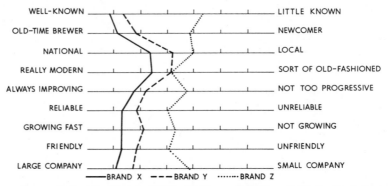

Source: William A. Mindak, "Fitting the Semantic Differential to the Marketing Problem," *Journal of Marketing*, Vol. 25 (April 1961), p. 31.

FIGURE 15–3. Advertising image

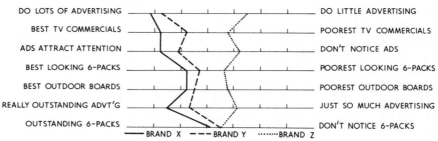

Source: William A. Mindak, "Fitting the Semantic Differential to the Marketing Problem," *Journal of Marketing*, Vol. 25 (April 1961), p. 31.

to determine beer drinkers' reactions to the personalities of three local brands of beer (and specifically Brand Y). . . ." "Various facets of this image were to be explored, such as specific characteristics of each brand, the attitudes toward advertising, the image of the company. . . ."[1]

The "semantic differential" is being adopted to a considerable extent because it is the simplest of the scaling methods and is believed to produce attitude measurements comparable with other more complex methods.

QUESTIONS

1. Why do some advertisers not use testing to determine the effectiveness of their advertisements?

---

[1] William A. Mindak, "Fitting the Semantic Differential to the Marketing Problem," *Journal of Marketing*, Vol. 25 (April 1961), pp. 28–33.

2. If you were an advertiser, would you insist that all of your advertising be tested? Why?

3. Do you think testing effectiveness will eventually replace the advertising man's reliance on experience and judgment?

4. Do you think the attitude toward testing advertising for effectiveness varies among advertisers, media owners, and advertising agency executives? Explain.

5. Why are direct measures of the sales effectiveness of advertisements seldom used?

6. Is it worthwhile to test ads for attention value, readership, effect on attitude, etc., when the usual objective of the advertisement is to sell the product? Discuss.

7. How would you proceed to determine whether or not the advertising effectiveness test itself is accurate and impartial?

8. Is it really important, in the use of the consumer jury test, to use in the sample only those people who have a distinct interest in the product? Why?

9. Evaluate the consumer jury test.

10. For what type of advertising is the inquiry test a valid measurement of effectiveness?

11. What is a split-run inquiry test? What variables that might influence results of the test are controlled by the use of the split run?

12. "Virtually all advertising people agree that the sales-area test provides authentic results when properly conducted, since it does measure actual sales under actual market conditions." If this is so, why are such tests used so infrequently?

13. For what types of products is the sales-area test of advertising effectiveness most suitable? Why?

14. Compare the recognition test with the aided-recall test with respect to information obtained and the usefulness to the advertiser.

15. Briefly describe how you would conduct an inquiry test to determine the relative effectiveness of two different magazines as media for your product ads.

16. Evaluate opinion and attitude tests.

CASE 1.   THE SUPREME RUBBER COMPANY
Testing advertising appeals

The Supreme Rubber Company, a large nationally known concern, had just developed a new synthetic type garden hose named "SUPREMO," which was in many respects far superior to currently available rubber, plastic, or synthetic garden hoses. Its outstanding features were extreme light weight, durability, ease of coiling, and resistance to sunlight which allowed the user to leave the hose out in the garden where it was to be used all summer long with no deleterious effects. The product had been thoroughly tested as to the quality of product, package, name, potential market, profitability, and so on. Before beginning his national introductory advertising campaign (which would use magazines and newspapers), the advertising manager decided to test several appeals suggested by the firm's advertising agency.

The three basic appeals suggested by the agency, and around one of which they wanted to build their campaign, were made up into three advertisements. Brief descriptions of the advertisements follow:

Ad. I   Headline: "So light—even your 10-year-old child can lift the SUPREMO with one hand!"

   Illustration: Picture of a cute little girl lifting a SUPREMO hose with her left hand.

Ad. II   Headline: "Stop worrying about replacements—SUPREMO is guaranteed for 10 years!"

   Illustration: Handsome young man, with frown on his face, inspecting a worn-out rubber garden hose.

Ad. III Headline: "No work, no bother—leave the SUPREMO out all summer with no harmful effects!"

   Illustration: Good-looking young couple, relaxing on patio of lovely home; a SUPREMO hose stretched out across the lawn, sprinkling flower bed on far side of yard.

Brief copy of each advertisement went on to tell the story of the new hose and to describe its many advantages and desirable features.

The advertising manager decided to test the advertising appeals by means of a consumer jury type test. For this purpose, he had the three advertisements made up exactly as they would appear in magazines, in four-color, on sheets the same size as a page of *Life* magazine. A panel of people who were prospects for the product was obtained as follows: a list of homeowners was purchased from a reputable list company, and from this list were taken the names of subscribers to the magazine *Better Homes & Gardens,* to insure an interest in gardening and care of the home. During August, interviewers (well trained and instructed) were sent out with the three advertisements to interview 3,000 people from the above list in the vicinity of Newark, New Jersey, location of one of the company's plants. The interviewers showed the three advertisements to each interviewee for a proper period of time, then asked them, "Which advertisement would you be most likely to notice first?" The advertisements were rotated in the order of showing to eliminate any possible bias resulting from sequence of showing. The results of the 3,000 interviews were as follows:

Ad. I
(Light weight appeal)   first choice of 1,425 people
Ad. II
(Durability-guarantee appeal)   first choice of   675 people
Ad. III
(Resistance to sunlight appeal)   first choice of   900 people

Although this test showed an overwhelming weight of evidence for Advertisement I, using the appeal of extreme light weight, the advertising manager decided to check on the accuracy of this test, in accordance with what he considered sound research procedure. He felt that the consumer jury test was rather artificial in some respects, and believed it wise to determine what results would be obtained when the advertisements actually were run in some medium and people were exposed to them in normal conditions of everyday living. So he decided to conduct a readership test to determine which of the advertising themes would achieve best results.

For this purpose he decided to use *Better Homes & Gardens,* which published nine zone editions of their magazine, as follows: New England, Metropolitan New York, Middle Atlantic (including Metro. New York), East Central, West Central, Central, Southeast, Southwest, and Pacific. Since the publisher would cooperate in setting up test programs, the advertising manager would be able to publish one of the advertisements in each of the three zone editions. Thus, most of the conditions surrounding the appearance of the three advertisements would be comparable and, in his opinion, would give him a much better testing situation than would be possible if he used different magazines or different months for running the test advertisements.

So the advertising manager arranged to have the three advertisements run in the October issue of *Better Homes & Gardens,* exactly the same as they had been prepared for the consumer jury test. Advertisement I, based on the theme of extreme lightness, was run in the edition of *Better Homes & Gardens* distributed to the Southwest zone. Advertisement II, stressing the durability and guarantee, was run in the edition going to the Southeast zone, and Advertisement III, stressing the resistance of the hose to sunlight, was run in the edition going to the New England zone.

He employed a well-known New York marketing research firm, which specialized in consumer surveys and opinion polling, to conduct the actual test for him. The research firm drew a random sample of names of *Better Homes & Gardens* subscribers and, one week after publication of the magazine, had their well-trained interviewers question these householders.

In conducting the interviews, the interviewer first ascertained that the respondent had read the October issue of *Better Homes & Gardens.* They then went through the magazine, opening it to five different full-page, four-color advertisements (this procedure was used to shorten the time of each interview, and also to minimize the fatigue factor which arises in the customary procedure of going through the entire magazine page by page), to determine to what extent the respondents had read each of the five advertisements in the magazine, but the sequence of showing the five advertisements to the respondents was varied periodically. The usual rating method of *noted, seen-associated,* and *read most* was used in measuring the readership of the advertisements. Approximately the same number of interviews was conducted in each area, the average number being 300 interviews. The results of the study were summarized by the research firm as follows:

	Percent of readers who:		
	Noted	Seen-associated	Read most
Ad. I: Light weight theme...............	67	32	5
Ad. II: Durability-guarantee theme.......	45	42	12
Ad. III: Resistance to sunlight theme.....	35	28	8

Since, in the opinion of the advertising manager, the high *noted* score which Advertisement I obtained in this second test clearly confirmed the results of the first test, he was certain that Advertisement I, using the theme of light weight, was the best appeal to stress in his advertising campaign for the new hose, "SUPREMO." He would, of course, include in the copy of all his advertisements the complete story of the many advantages and desirable features of the SUPREMO garden hose.

Case questions

1. Were the two tests used suitable as means of testing the effectiveness of the advertising appeals?
2. Was the consumer jury test well executed in this instance?
3. Was the readership test well conducted?
4. Was the advertising manager's interpretation of the results of the two tests sound?

CASE 2.   JACKSON PAPER COMPANY
Use of copy testing

Jackson is engaged in the manufacture of paper towels, tissues, household wax paper, and industrial cleaning tissue, and in the production of wood pulp. Finished paper products are distributed by Jackson throughout the United States and to a comparatively limited extent in the foreign market.

Of the net sales of Jackson, sales of tissues amounted to 41 percent. No other product accounted for as much as 18 percent of such sales.

Jackson's products are sold to more than 3,000 direct purchasers, primarily wholesale distributors, chain stores, department stores, and jobbers in the grocery, paper, drug, hardware, and janitor-supply trades.

The paper industry is highly competitive, and Jackson would be considered one of the four leading U.S. producers in tissues, paper towels, and household wax papers. Sales of the company average about $50 million per year.

Copy testing

The advertising director of the Jackson Company, although he used marketing research extensively, did not put much faith in copy testing. He stated:

There are so many variables involved in making a test of the copy that I do not believe the results warrant the cost involved. I have tested a number of our advertisements and have found that the correlation between what people say about the advertisement and how they will react at the store is relatively low. Therefore, I have been hesitant to ask our agency to make any such studies, although I do from time to time make some copy analysis.

Recently, the company shifted the appeal for its tissue advertising from an emphasis on color to one of softness. Jackson used a six-month-old baby as a pseudotrademark in the new series of advertisements. In the advertisements, the baby was pictured on a towel. The caption stated: "Your Baby Deserves the Best." The copy which followed compared the softness associated with a baby to the softness and purity of Jackson's tissues.

Copy testing study

Because the results of the campaign could not be measured satisfactorily, the director of research suggested that a "readership" test be made of the series.

The approach followed was to have the interviewer ask a number of persons selected at random which magazines they read. If the answer given included a magazine in which a Jackson advertisement had run, the interviewer then asked the person to check the magazine from cover to cover and indicate which advertisement had been read or noticed.

The results of the study showed that readership of the advertisements ranked high. The baby had won the public's heart. However, most of the people did not know what product was being advertised. Many stated that it was a towel advertisement. Some correctly said it was a tissue advertisement, but only a few related the baby with the Jackson Paper Company.

The advertising director indicated that, while the results of the study were somewhat different than he had expected, he believed that copy testing was too inexact to be used on a large scale by a manufacturer in the paper business.

The research director pointed out that the many methods of copy testing (consumer jury, split run, checklist, psychogalvanometer, and readership method, to name a few) are divided into two categories: those which are used to test the advertisement before it appears, and those which are used after the advertisement appears.

Recognizing the problem of convincing the advertising director of the value of copy testing, the research director suggested that the company use the inquiry method to make a study of two appeals that were being considered for the next campaign.

The inquiry technique, in his opinion, eliminated many of the variables that exist in other methods, because the results are based on actual returns received by people who have read the advertisements. He also felt that burying the free offer in the copy in the same place in the advertisements would discourage the "free-sample hounds" and children from writing for the samples.

Case questions

1. How important is it, in your opinion, for the Jackson company to test the copy in its advertisements?

2. Recognizing that the company is selling a product in which 65 percent of sales are made on impulse, if you were to use copy testing, would you put the emphasis on pretesting or posttesting?

3. Do you believe the research director was wise in recommending the inquiry test approach? Why or why not?

4. What method of pretesting copy could the company have used to determine "brand recognition" in the "Your Baby Deserves the Best" series?

CASE 3.   ROANOKE FOOD COMPANY

The Roanoke Food Company processes raw potatoes into a variety of convenient products for the retail, restaurant, and institutional markets. These products are precooked and are designed to simplify final preparation.

Sales in the past three years had begun to level off, and the vice president in charge of advertising was interested in ascertaining whether or not it would be advisable to subscribe to the National Food Survey at an annual cost of $50,000.

The National Food Survey would provide a bimonthly report of sales data pertaining to the competitive standing of the Roanoke brand. These data were developed from 2,500 selected retail stores located in 750 cities which were chosen from the census reports to provide an adequate cross section of the buying habits of the people in the United States.

The sample provided basic information about sales to consumers, purchases by retailers, retail inventories, stock turn, average order size, displays, retail gross profit, and total sales. These figures were then broken down into brands, store sizes, territories, size of packages, and cities.

Products

Frozen French fries were introduced in 1956 and the frozen potato line has since been expanded to include shredded potato patties (introduced in 1957), crinkle-cut French fries and hash brown potatoes (introduced in 1961), and cottage fried potatoes and small whole peeled potatoes (introduced in 1963).

The company also produces instant mashed potato flakes, which are prepared by adding milk and boiling water, and sells fresh potatoes in limited quantities.

The company seeks, through its product development program, to further expand its product line by the addition of other easy-to-prepare potato products. The company also has from time to time processed limited quantities of other vegetables, which include frozen whole kernel corn and corn on the cob.

During the last fiscal year the company's sales were divided approximately as follows:

> Frozen French fried potatoes................ 55%
> Crinkle-cut French fried potatoes............ 30
> Instant mashed potato flakes.............. 3
> Other potato products...................... 7
> Corn products.............................. 5

Sales

During the last year the company made food product sales to approximately 1,500 different customers, no one of which accounted for more than 5 percent of total sales. During the year sales for the retail market accounted for approximately 80 percent of frozen potato product sales, and restaurant and institutional sales accounted for the balance.

The company's food products are sold nationally through a food sales management company. This company supervises approximately 70 independent local food brokers who cover the major marketing areas in the United States. The Sales Management Company also advises Roanoke on its advertising program, provides sales projections, and performs other services related to sales.

Shipments are made from the company's cold storage warehouses or from inventories maintained in approximately 200 public warehouses throughout the country. Shipments from the company's plants to the public warehouses are made either by refrigerated trucks owned or leased by the company or by public or contract carriers.

During the last fiscal year the company marketed approximately 60 percent of its potato products under its own brand names and the balance was packaged for sale under buyers' labels.

The company competes with a number of other processors of frozen potato products and, in a general way, with processors or distributors of other food products. Among the company's competitors are potato-processing divisions of several substantially larger food processing companies.

Sources of supply

The company has in the past purchased substantially all of the potatoes required for processing operations from growers in the area of its plants. The company contracts in advance of the growing season with growers and growers' associations for a major portion of its potato purchases. Under such contracts, the company generally agrees to purchase at a basic price all of the potatoes meeting certain grading requirements grown on specified lands. The company works closely with growers to assist them in the application of modern planting, growing, and harvesting techniques, and sells to the smaller growers most of their seed potato requirements.

Potato planting normally is started in April, and the harvest period extends from August to mid-October, when raw potato inventories reach their peak. The company has been able to obtain short-term bank loans by pledging raw potatoes in storage and processed product inventories, and considers such banking arrangements adequate for carrying these inventories.

Statement of income

The statement of income for the last three years is given below:

| | Year ended December 31 (in thousands of dollars) | | |
	1965	1966	1967
Income:			
Net sales........................	$21,000	$21,100	$20,000
Other income..................	450	600	700
Total income..................	$21,450	$21,700	$20,700
Less:			
Cost of sales..................	$17,000	$17,500	$17,000
Selling & general expenses....	2,800	2,900	3,000
Interest.......................	300	350	360
Total expenses................	$20,100	$20,750	$20,360
Net income before provision for income taxes................	$ 1,350	$ 950	$ 340

Advertising

Approximately 2 percent of the planned sales was spent each year by the Roanoke Food Company on advertising. With this amount the vice president in charge of advertising directed the advertising primarily to the major urban areas, through national magazines, radio and television spots, point-of-purchase material, and newspapers.

The company had made a number of general market surveys about the consumers and their buying habits. It had relied on its sales figures to provide the necessary data for making marketing plans.

Because the advertising that the company had used was of a general nature which emphasized the appeals of the ease of preparing the Roanoke potatoes and the high quality of its brand, the vice president was of the opinion that it was not possible to test effectiveness of these appeals.

While the Roanoke line of frozen potatoes had been dominant in the market for the 10 prior years, the company believed that it was losing ground to the private labels. A number of the brokers and salesmen also reported that the retailers were not providing as much freezer space and these same retailers were using more and more of the space for their own private brands of frozen potatoes.

Case questions

1. Should the company subscribe to this $50,000 service? Why? Or why not?

2. What other methods might the company use to check the effectiveness of its advertising?

3. Is there other information that the company should attempt to secure about its market? Buying motives of consumers?

4. What precautions must Roanoke keep in mind about any research program that it might use?

PART **VI**————————

Integrating the
advertising
programs

chapter 16

THE ADVERTISING BUDGET

THE REASON for the prominence of basic financial and control devices in business today is because management realizes that business operations can be more effectively controlled by means of financial standards and measurements. It is also through these methods that one can establish a plan for accomplishing results and for checking up on the performance of those responsible for carrying it out.

One of the basic advertising, financial, and control devices is the budgeting process. This activity involves a planning and control system because it provides a continuing process throughout the year for checking on all phases of the advertising program. While some executives may look upon the very concept of a budget as a straitjacket type of control, it is important to keep in mind that budgeting is not synonymous with forecasting as such. Budgeting involves not only the planning activity, but also the controlling function, in order to maximize the chances of achieving the objectives.

General budget concepts

The process of setting the advertising budget involves four fundamental management requirements: anticipation, coordination, control, and payout evaluation. These requirements mean that advertisers are faced with the problem of anticipating customer requirements, product changes, and competitors' strategies. They must coordinate all phases of their advertising plan in order to have such details as the store displays and general promotion tie in with the advertising. At the same time all facets of the program need to be controlled, and, in the final analysis, payout evaluation will give management the information required to determine whether or not the objectives of the advertising have been attained.

The aim in setting the amount of money to be spent on advertising is to spend enough to attain the objectives of the advertising campaign but not to waste money by spending more than is necessary.

The determination of this optimum amount to spend on advertising is a problem that plagues virtually all advertisers. That is, although they may have decided on the amount of advertising which has obtained good results, from the overall marketing and profit standpoints, there still remains unanswered the question, "Would some other amount, either larger or smaller, have obtained even better results, or equally good results?"

This is true even of the major firms that plan their advertising very carefully and establish specific objectives to achieve with their expenditures. As an example, consider a national organization which sells its products on a national basis and distributes them through wholesalers to retailers to the consumers. This company uses national, regional, and local media as well as various forms of cooperative and point-of-purchase advertising. It also has a staff of missionary salesmen who advise the retail stores, besides a regular sales staff which handles the wholesale accounts. As a result of the variety of selling methods employed in moving the products, it is difficult to appraise the results of advertising.

On the other hand, a company which does all its business on a mail-order basis will find it easier to appraise the results of its advertising because it can correlate its sales to the advertising used. This can be done by observing the changes in sales where immediate increases in sales can be expected from advertising, or by counting the number of inquiries when the advertising was aimed at securing requests for information.

In other instances, however, the primary aim of advertising may be to develop favorable attitudes or to communicate an idea. One might expect that building acceptance in increasing awareness will be reflected in future sales. These results must be measured over long periods of time and are difficult to determine because there are factors other than advertising which may influence them.

This chapter will discuss some of the facets of setting the advertising budget, methods in common use for establishing this amount, and some aspects of allocation and control of advertising expenditures.

Forming the budget expenditure

A number of considerations are involved in the problem of determining the amount of the funds to be appropriated for advertising. These include: the sales forecast, the general marketing plan, customer density, customer size, product profitability, product popularity, channels of distribution, competitors' strategies, quantity sold, unit price, objectives, trading area, end use of product, and general economic conditions.

Time of establishing the appropriation

In actual practice, most firms that have been operating for a period of time establish the entire advertising appropriation for the coming year at one time, several months prior to the beginning of their budget year. This is done on the assumption that all marketing plans, both for old, established products and any new ones to be launched on the market during the coming year, are reasonably well known at the time. This, of course, also means that the executives must have developed their tentative advertising programs or campaigns for each of their products and for their institutional campaign (if any) by this same date and, hence, are able to recommend the desired amount for each of the advertising campaigns to form the basis for the entire advertising budget.

Other firms, which may be on a different budgeting period basis, such as semiannual or quarterly, would establish their advertising appropriations on a comparable time basis. It should be noted that such firms must, however, make plans for individual campaigns sufficiently far in advance to meet their particular needs and, hence, may find it necessary to set tentative advertising appropriations for such campaigns for longer periods of time than that noted. And many small firms do not have definitely established budgets for their operations or advertising and will establish the amount for each individual program or campaign as it is developed. Even for such firms, it is most important to devote care to the setting of the appropriation for a campaign early in its planning stage.

Flexibility of the budget

A firm that sets the amount one year in advance will do well to permit a certain amount of flexibility in its budgeting for advertising. Even when setting the appropriation for a shorter period, or for only one specific advertising campaign for an individual product, a certain amount of flexibility is necessary in order to meet changing and unforeseen conditions in the market. In the case of the firm establishing amounts a year in advance, a number of conditions may make it desirable to spend a smaller or larger sum than originally planned.

During the year, the general economic climate may change completely, and an unpredicted slump or rise in general economic activity may occur. A marked change of this type may call for a considerable change in overall marketing plans and strategy, with a resulting effect on the amount of money believed necessary for the advertising program. The objectives of the firm may well change due to such conditions, or it may become evident that more or less money will be required to achieve the desired objectives. For example, a manufacturing firm may have a maximum capacity of, say, 100,000 units of its one product. It has set up a marketing plan involving an advertising campaign designed to achieve sales of that 100,000 units in view of certain anticipated general economic conditions which it judges will enable the industry to generate total sales of that product of 1 million units, with its taking 10 percent of the market. If, fairly early in the year, general conditions change so that the rate of sale of the product is much greater than had been anticipated, and it becomes obvious that the firm will be able to sell its entire output with a considerably modified advertising and sales program, it would be questionable to continue with the original extensive program. In these conditions, the firm might revise its budget downward. Should the reverse have been the case, the firm probably would, and should, expand its advertising appropriation, if such is believed desirable to attempt to achieve its sales of 100,000 units.

In addition to general economic conditions, other changes may occur. The firm itself may decide to change general plans upon which the budget was based. It may decide that it should enter new markets, or due to some unforeseen developments, it may decide to expand its product line, or add new products to its line. Such changes would undoubtedly call for increases in advertising.

By the same token, decisions to drop lines or products or to retrench the market area might call for decreased sums for advertising. Advertising plans are usually predicated on certain assumptions regarding the competitive activity in the field. Should the competitive situation change markedly during the budget period, it may be decided that different sums will be necessary for advertising in order to achieve the desired objectives. It is also possible that changes will occur in the media situation, with regard to availability, rates, or desirability, which would indicate a need for varying expenditure. Conceivably, sudden changes might occur in the dealer picture that would call for increases or changes in the dealer phase of the advertising campaign.

Whatever the reason, it is clear that changes may occur indicating that either more funds will be needed to achieve the original or changed objectives of the firm or that the objectives can be achieved with a smaller expenditure than originally planned. Obviously, it is merely good business to change the planned budget to meet such changed conditions, assuming, of course, that the financial position of the firm makes it feasible. The budget may take care of normal, unexpected changes by including in the original allocation a certain amount for contingencies which is not budgeted for any specific purpose. If changes call for increased spending, such could be taken care of out of this contingency reserve. Other means for providing flexibility are to have a periodic and reasonably frequent review of the budget, to compare expenditures with original appropriations, and to check the results in relation to established objectives.

Some considerations influencing the size of the allocation

The most important factor influencing the amount of the appropriation is the general marketing mix of the company for the particular product involved, which in turn is determined by the type of product, the differentiating features involved, the appeals available, the volume and margin, company strategic considerations, company policy, and related factors. If the product is one for which a strong consumer demand can be stimulated, so that the pull strategy of marketing can be used effectively, the budget for advertising might constitute virtually the entire marketing cost and the firm show a profit even though advertising costs would run 40 percent of sales—as is true for some home-remedy type medicinal products with a wide margin of selling price over production costs. On the other hand, for some standardized basic products or materials, advertising may play a virtually negligible part in the marketing strategy, and it might be advisable to use other means.

Items to be charged to advertising

Obviously, the amount of money appropriated will be influenced also by the nature of the items to be charged to the budget. Policies and practices as to what items are properly to be charged to "advertising" vary considerably among companies. Some firms charge to this budget any sales promotion type expenditure or goodwill type expenditure which cannot easily be allocated to any other account presently set up in the budget. Some firms are also prone to charge to advertising such miscellaneous expenses as the cost of Christmas presents for employees, contributions to the community chest and other charitable organizations, tickets to the police ball, and costs of entertainment at sales conventions. Since there was no account to which such expenditures seemingly could logically be charged, the advertising account became a sort of catchall account for many charges that were not too closely related to advertising itself.

Printers' Ink has developed a recommended list of items that are unquestionably chargeable to advertising and a list of items that are borderline (their gray list) and should or should not be charged to advertising depending on the method used in carrying on the activity under question. The magazine also has what it terms a "black list" of items that should not be charged to advertising, even though in practice they often are. This list from *Printers' Ink* is shown in Figure 16–1.

The four major types of charges that are properly allocated to the advertising appropriation are the media costs, production costs of the advertising, advertising research, and administrative costs.

FIGURE 16–1. *Printers' Ink* guide to allocation of advertising appropriations (sometimes called the "white, black, and gray list")

White list (these charges belong in the advertising account)

Space.
(paid advertising in all recognized mediums, including:)
Newspapers
Magazines
Business papers
Farm papers
Class journals
Car cards
Theater programs
Outdoor
Point of purchase
Novelties
Booklets
Directories
Direct advertising
Cartons and labels (for advertising purposes, such as in window displays)
Catalogs
Package inserts (when used as advertising and not just as direction sheets)
House magazines to dealers or consumers
Motion pictures (including talking pictures) when used for advertising
Slides
Export advertising
Dealer helps
Reprints of advertisements used in mail or for display
Radio
Television
All other printed and lithographed material used directly for advertising purposes

Administration:
Salaries of advertising department executives and employees
Office supplies and fixtures used solely by advertising department
Commissions and fees to advertising agencies, special writers or advisers
Expenses incurred by salesmen when on work for advertising department
Traveling expenses of department employees engaged in departmental business
(Note: In some companies these go into special "Administration" account)

Mechanical:
Artwork
Typography
Engraving
Mats
Electros
Photographs
Radio & TV production
Package design (advertising aspects only)
Etc.

Miscellaneous:
Transportation of advertising material (to include postage and other carrying charges)
Fees to window display installation services
Other miscellaneous expenses connected with items on the white list

Black list (*these charges do not belong in the advertising account, although too frequently they are put there*)

- Free goods
- Picnic and bazaar programs
- Charitable, religious, and fraternal donations
- Other expenses for goodwill purposes
- Cartons
- Labels
- Instruction sheets
- Package manufacture
- Press agentry
- Stationery used outside advertising department
- Price lists
- Salesmen's calling cards
- Motion pictures for sales use only
- House magazines going to factory employees
- Bonuses to trade
- Special rebates
- Membership in trade associations
- Entertaining customers or prospects
- Annual reports
- Showrooms
- Demonstration stores
- Sales convention expenses
- Salesmen's samples (including photographs used in lieu of samples)
- Welfare activities among employees
- Such recreational activities as baseball teams, etc.
- Sales expenses at conventions
- Cost of salesmen's automobiles
- Special editions which approach advertisers on goodwill basis

Gray list (*these are borderline charges, sometimes belonging in the advertising accounts and sometimes in other accounts, depending on circumstances*)

- Samples
- Demonstrations
- Fairs
- Canvassing
- Rent
- Light
- Heat
- Depreciation of equipment used by advertising department
- Telephone and other overhead expenses, apportioned to advertising department
- House magazines going to salesmen
- Advertising automobiles
- Premiums
- Membership in associations or other organizations devoted to advertising
- Testing bureaus
- Advertising portfolios for salesmen
- Contributions to special advertising funds of trade associations
- Display signs on the factory or office building
- Salesmen's catalogs
- Research and market investigations
- Advertising allowances to trade for cooperative effort

This chart is based on the principle that there are three types of expenses that generally are charged against the advertising appropriation.

The first charge is made up of expenses that are always justifiable under any scheme of accounting practice. These have been included in the white list of charges that belong in the advertising account.

A second type consists of those charges which cannot and should not under any system of accounting be justified as advertising expenses. These have been placed on the black list.

There is a third type of expense which can sometimes be justified under advertising and sometimes not. Frequently the justification for the charge depends upon the method used in carrying on a certain activity. These charges have been placed in a borderline gray list.

The chart is the result of the collaboration of the editors of *Printers' Ink* and several hundred advertisers. It has been revised for a third time with the aid of advertising and accounting men. It may be considered, therefore, to represent sound, standard practice.

METHODS OF ESTABLISHING THE APPROPRIATION

Although various studies of methods for setting the advertising appropriation may list anywhere from 2 to 24 ways of setting the appropriation, there are three basic bases for establishing budgets. These are the percentage of sales method (and its variations), objective-task method, and the competitive parity method.

The percentage of sales method

This is generally considered the most widely used method of setting the appropriation, although its use has declined markedly in recent years. There are several variations in the actual application of this method. The percentage may be based on the past year's sales, on estimated sales for the coming year, or on some combination of these two. A variation of this method of setting the budget that basically involves the same philosophy is that of setting a certain per unit sum for advertising and multiplying that sum per unit by sales in units (past or estimated) to give the total advertising appropriation.

The wide use of this method can probably be explained on several bases. It is a relatively simple method to apply. Most companies relate the various items of cost in their operating statements by means of computing them as a percentage of sales, and have come to think of their advertising expenditures in terms of a certain percentage of sales. The overall operating budget is based on the sales volume, the margins available, and the profits to be realized. The advertising appropriation must fit into this budget which normally must show a profit for the firm. Also, usually in the overall marketing plan of the company the advertising is assigned a fairly fixed portion of the marketing task or marketing mix. If, on the basis of experience, a certain percentage of the marketing budget assigned to advertising has resulted in a profitable operation, it may be the best thing to do to continue assigning that part of the marketing budget to advertising. Then the question remaining is to decide how best to spend that amount of money to get the most from the advertising. When the method involved uses future sales, the method appears reasonably logical. If it normally takes a certain amount of advertising effort to move a number of units of merchandise or to achieve a certain dollar volume of sales, then appropriating that sum per unit or that percentage of sales for advertising for next year should result in achieving the projected volume of sales. In other words, a certain relationship exists between sales and the amount of advertising expenditures required to obtain such sales.

In practice, this method, when based on estimated future sales, may often actually work quite well. If virtually all conditions in the firm's market, including the general economic conditions and the competitive activity, remain rather constant, then it is quite possible that the same correlations will remain between the advertising and other sales and promotional activity expenditures and the resulting sales volume. Using future sales does overcome to a large extent the argument most frequently advanced against the use of a percentage of past sales, which is that such a method ignores the fact that advertising should precede and is an important factor in stimulating demand and obtaining sales, and is not something that follows sales. In other words, advertising should be considered the "cause" and not the "effect" of sales.

In actuality, of course, few firms ever face such a situation of "all other things remaining equal." The amount of advertising required to achieve a given level of sales in the coming period will be influenced by many factors which often change, such as the general level of income; changes in the firm's and competitors' products and prices; and changes in competitive marketing and selling, promotional, and advertising activity. Dynamic conditions change the relationship between the sums spent on advertising and the sales resulting therefrom. Hence, even the use of projected sales does not make this a truly sound method of establishing the appropriation.

Also, if a firm is using only a limited amount of consumer advertising primarily for the purpose of influencing the trade, the mere fact that consumer sales will be up next year does not mean that there is any real basis for increasing the number of advertisements being run to influence the trade. Or, if a good job has been done in the past on dealer advertising and promotion, it may not be necessary to increase this portion of the budget just because it is believed the consumer sales of the product will increase in the year ahead.

The objective-task method

The objective-task method is coming into wider use as it provides a more logical basis for establishing the advertising appropriation to meet the dynamic conditions facing marketing today. It directs attention to the objectives to be attained by the marketing program, the role that advertising is to play in attaining such objectives, and definitely recognizes the fact that advertising plays a vital part in stimulating demand and creating sales, and is not the result of a certain sales volume.

When the objective-task method is used, the first step is to set the objectives of the program for the coming year or budget period. There may be one or several objectives, such as obtaining a certain volume of sales, obtaining a larger share of the market, entering a new area, obtaining additional dealers, or launching a new product. Next, on the basis of experience or research findings, it is determined just what specific means will be necessary to achieve these objectives, or the task involved. Then it is necessary to determine how much and what kind of advertising will be required to accomplish the tasks established in the first two steps. At this point it may be advisable to take another step. The proposed appropriation for advertising is considered in light of the overall budget and financial position of the company. If the amount involved appears to be excessive, in view of the firm's financial position and overall budget situation, it may be necessary to reconsider both the objectives and the proposed advertising plans, and modify them so that they will fit into the overall situation of the company. In theory, this would appear to be the best method of setting the advertising appropriation. It does not rely on any specious fixed relationship between advertising and sales. It is not bound by historical precedent. In deciding how much and what kind of advertising will be necessary to achieve the objectives, full consideration can be given to the ever-changing conditions in the market as discussed earlier. It definitely relates the amount of money to be spent to the specific tasks required to achieve the established objectives.

In practice, there is one serious problem involved in the use of this method of setting the appropriation. That is, how does the advertiser determine just how much advertising and what type of advertising will be necessary to achieve the objectives as established? With the present available methods of measuring the effectiveness of advertising, it is difficult to say with any real certainty just how much and what kind of advertising is required to achieve a certain result. Although the experienced advertising man using the best research methods available can ascertain general answers to these questions, he still is not certain that he has selected the optimum expenditure. Until he has much better methods of determining the effectiveness of advertising, he will be faced with this problem of not knowing just what is the ideal amount of money needed to achieve certain tasks and objectives.

It is interesting to note that the various advertising objectives have been measured, in part at least, by some company or research organization. Among the objectives which have been measured as a result of advertising are:

1. Changes in sales
2. Changes in extent and nature of attitudes of the consumers
3. Changes in product usage
4. Increase in consumers' knowledge of the company or its product
5. Correlation of a purchase to the effectiveness of advertising
6. Impact of advertising on salesmen and outlets
7. Importance of advertising in the sale of a product
8. Development of a company or product image

The competitive parity method

Although few executives would indicate that this method is the one they use in setting their appropriation, it is generally believed that many do, in practice, actually follow this procedure. In essence, this method consists of setting the appropriation by relating it in some manner to the expenditures of the firm's major competitor or competitors. This may, in practice, be a matter of matching the actual expenditures of the major competitor, or attempting to maintain some set relationship between the expenditures of the firm and the competitor. In other instances, this method may involve using the average percentage of sales spent by the firms in the entire industry, and then applying that percentage to the firm's sales to establish the appropriation. The basis for the use of this method is probably that since advertising is a major competitive weapon, it is necessary for the firm to match its competitors' advertising if it is to hold its share of the market against such competitors.

Another rationale is that, since the firms in the industry are successful, the average of their expenditures is a figure that achieves relative success in sales and profits, and is an expenditure with which the firms can live and be successful. The average represents, in a sense, the combined thinking of all the advertising experts in the industry, and should normally be better than the thinking of any one man. And, since in many areas of business it is common to compare the firm's operations, as percentages of sales, with industry average figures to ascertain their relative efficiency of operations, it is easy to see how the advertising executive might come to think of the industry average as a sort of standard for that type of business and, hence, one that he should follow unless he can find a very good reason for varying from the standard.

However, there are weaknesses inherent in this method. The industry average or expenditures of major competitors need not have any relationship to the objectives or problems of this particular company. Not all companies use the same marketing methods, nor do they operate in exactly the same conditions from the standpoint of such things as brand reputation, entrenchment in the market, and cumulative effect of past advertising. Hence, no one figure is sound for all firms with their varying problems, varying marketing strategies and methods, and varying objectives and long-range goals. Also, there is not a valid basis for assuming that the competitors are setting their appropriations on a sound basis, or that they are attaining the same quality of advertising with their advertising dollar. From a practical standpoint, using this method generally means using historical figures or past advertising appropriations of the competitor or industry, since it is difficult to obtain such figures in advance.

In setting a budget under this method, however, it is important to

FIGURE 16–2. 125 leaders' advertising as percent of sales (covering total ad expenditures, including measured and unmeasured media)

Cars

AD RANK	COMPANY	ADVERTISING	SALES	ADV. AS % OF SALES
2	General Motors Corp.	$173,000,000	$20,733,982,000	0.8
4	Ford Motor Co.	116,500,000	11,537,789,264	1.0
9	Chrysler Corp.	80,000,000	5,299,934,803	1.5
59	American Motors Corp.	22,500,000	990,618,709	2.3
77	Volkswagen of America Inc.	17,000,000	500,000,000*	3.4

Food

AD RANK	COMPANY	ADVERTISING	SALES	ADV. AS % OF SALES
3	General Foods Corp.	120,000,000	1,381,049,000	8.7
17	National Dairy Products Corp.	56,927,000	1,815,489,000	3.1
22	General Mills Inc.	49,000,000	524,678,315	9.3
24	Kellogg Co.	46,000,000	366,000,000	12.6
25	Campbell Soup Co.	44,000,000	712,785,000	6.2
28	Standard Brands Inc.	40,500,000	727,801,679	5.6
32	National Biscuit Co.	38,300,000	627,300,000	6.1
41	Corn Products Co.	32,000,000	552,774,000	5.8
43	Borden Co.	31,000,000	1,385,518,426	2.2
45	Pillsbury Co.	27,000,000	470,046,502	5.7
47	Quaker Oats Co.	25,500,000	360,000,000*	7.1
49	Ralston Purina Co.	24,500,000	954,770,923	2.6
55	Carnation Co.	23,000,000	539,924,018	4.3
63	Pet Milk Co.	21,000,000	431,271,000	4.9
66	Armour & Co.	20,500,000	2,064,847,000	1.0
77	Swift & Co.	17,000,000	2,750,956,717	0.6
85	Nestle Co.	16,200,000	231,000,000*	7.0
90	Continental Baking Co.	15,275,000	524,936,394	2.9
95	Hunt Foods & Industries	13,500,000	445,649,000	3.0
102	H. J. Heinz Co.	12,500,000	620,262,649	2.0
121	California Packing Corp.	9,000,000	478,972,000	1.9
123	Morton International Inc.	8,000,000	123,018,781	6.5

Soaps, Cleaners (and Allied)

AD RANK	COMPANY	ADVERTISING	SALES	ADV. AS % OF SALES
1	Procter & Gamble	245,000,000	2,243,177,000	10.9
6	Colgate-Palmolive	95,000,000	400,130,000	23.7
7	Lever Bros. Co.	90,000,000	456,300,000	19.7
50	S. C. Johnson & Son	24,250,000	175,000,000	13.8
111	Purex Corp.	11,500,000	176,123,729	6.5

Tobacco

AD RANK	COMPANY	ADVERTISING	SALES	ADV. AS % OF SALES
12	American Tobacco Co.	71,000,000	1,231,628,708	5.8
13	R. J. Reynolds Tobacco Co.	70,000,000	1,639,148,320	4.1
27	Brown & Williamson Tobacco Corp.	40,612,000	634,575,000	6.4
31	Philip Morris Inc.	39,000,000	577,726,080*	6.8
33	Liggett & Myers Tobacco Co.	37,000,000	478,261,072	7.7
34	P. Lorillard Co.	36,460,000	479,046,310	7.6
113	Consolidated Cigar Corp.	11,000,000	165,204,868	6.7
123	General Cigar Co.	8,000,000	213,416,000	3.7

Drugs and Cosmetics

AD RANK	COMPANY	ADVERTISING	SALES	ADV. AS % OF SALES
5	Bristol-Myers Co.	108,000,000	391,433,053	27.6
10	American Home Products Corp.	75,000,000	627,579,550	12.0
15	Warner-Lambert Pharmaceutical Co.	64,500,000	383,837,000	16.8
35	Alberto-Culver Co.‡	36,000,000	88,855,898‡	40.5
36	Sterling Drug Co.	35,000,000	161,958,000	21.6
39	Miles Laboratories Inc.	33,000,000	137,557,638	24.0
44	Johnson & Johnson	25,500,000	431,009,367	6.4
48	Revlon Inc.	25,200,000	206,703,003*	12.2
58	Carter-Wallace Inc.	22,750,000	83,747,472	27.2
69	Smith Kline & French Laboratories	18,500,000	202,446,000	9.1
71	Chas. Pfizer & Co.	18,000,000	287,598,000*	6.3
74	Cheesebrough-Pond's Inc.	17,500,000	83,941,000	20.8
77	Richardson-Merrell Inc.	17,000,000	213,401,000	8.0
82	Shulton Inc.	16,591,000	63,157,500*	26.3
84	J. B. Williams Co.	16,350,000	50,000,000*	32.7
88	Plough Inc.	15,500,000	64,107,033	24.2
91	Block Drug Co.	15,000,000	36,000,000*	41.7
98	Avon Products	13,000,000	282,189,000	4.6
100	Mennen Co.	12,800,000	52,000,000	24.6
102	Lehn & Fink Products Corp.	12,500,000	66,702,978	18.7
110	Noxell Corp.	11,600,000	31,226,014	37.1
111	Norwich Pharmacal Co.	11,500,000	63,723,531	18.0
122	Beecham Products	8,280,000	215,670,000	3.8

Gum and Candy

AD RANK	COMPANY	ADVERTISING	SALES	ADV. AS % OF SALES
63	Beech-Nut Life Savers Inc.	21,000,000	201,000,000*	10.4
63	Wm. Wrigley Jr. Co.	21,000,000	128,555,210	16.3
116	Mars Inc.	10,500,000	125,000,000*	8.4

Tires

AD RANK	COMPANY	ADVERTISING	SALES	ADV. AS % OF SALES
29	Goodyear Tire & Rubber Co.	40,000,000	2,226,256,469	1.8
42	Firestone Tire & Rubber Co.	31,400,000	1,609,756,478	2.0
46	U. S. Rubber Co.	26,800,000	1,225,516,000	2.2
69	B. F. Goodrich Co.	18,500,000	980,122,000	1.9

Beer

AD RANK	COMPANY	ADVERTISING	SALES	ADV. AS % OF SALES
36	Jos. Schlitz Brewing Co.	35,000,000	324,043,086	10.8
38	Anheuser-Busch Inc.	34,200,000	553,509,809	6.2
73	Pabst Brewing Co.	17,750,000	253,585,672	7.0
83	Falstaff Brewing Corp.	16,500,000	228,150,782	7.2
92	Carling Brewing Co.	14,741,000	400,931,310*	3.7

Oil

AD RANK	COMPANY	ADVERTISING	SALES	ADV. AS % OF SALES
53	Standard Oil Co. (Ind.)	23,500,000	3,063,161,000	0.8
60	Standard Oil Co. (N. J.)	22,242,500	12,493,031,000	0.2
74	Shell Oil Corp.	17,500,000	3,104,918,000	0.6
101	Mobil Oil Corp.	12,708,000	5,517,426,000	0.2
106	Gulf Oil Corp.	12,000,000	4,185,253,000	0.3
113	Texaco Inc.	11,000,000	4,008,053,779	0.3

Soft Drinks

AD RANK	COMPANY	ADVERTISING	SALES	ADV. AS % OF SALES
16	Coca-Cola Co.	64,000,000	518,424,872*	12.3
30	PepsiCo Inc.	39,500,000	509,950,282	7.7
74	Canada Dry Corp.	17,500,000	170,856,000	10.2
81	Seven-Up Co.	16,908,000	40,000,000*	**
94	Royal Crown Cola Co.	14,125,000	53,422,325	26.4

Paper Products

AD RANK	COMPANY	ADVERTISING	SALES	ADV. AS % OF SALES
55	Scott Paper Co.	23,000,000	460,982,000	5.0
77	Kimberly-Clark Corp.	17,000,000	622,529,000	2.7

Liquor

AD RANK	COMPANY	ADVERTISING	SALES	ADV. AS % OF SALES
21	Distillers Corp.-Seagrams Ltd.	50,098,000	844,932,000	5.9
52	Heublein Inc.	23,609,000	328,000,000	7.2
54	Schenley Industries Inc.	23,252,000	460,762,963	5.0
62	National Distillers & Chemical Corp.	21,370,000	829,031,000	2.6
68	Hiram Walker-Gooderham & Worts	19,775,000	529,014,945	3.7

Appliances

AD RANK	COMPANY	ADVERTISING	SALES	ADV. AS % OF SALES
10	General Electric Co.	75,000,000	6,213,600,000	1.2
20	Radio Corp. of America	50,700,000	2,057,117,000	2.5
40	Westinghouse Electric Corp.	32,773,000	2,389,909,000	1.4
88	Sunbeam Corp.	15,500,000	306,758,854	5.1

Chemicals

AD RANK	COMPANY	ADVERTISING	SALES	ADV. AS % OF SALES
18	Du Pont	56,400,000	2,665,000,000	2.1
23	American Cyanamid Co.	46,785,000	708,528,000	6.6
51	Union Carbide Corp.	24,000,000	2,063,901,000	1.2
67	Monsanto Co.	20,000,000	1,468,147,000	1.4
87	Olin Mathieson Chemical Corp.	15,800,000	874,244,000	1.8

Metals

AD RANK	COMPANY	ADVERTISING	SALES	ADV. AS % OF SALES
99	Aluminum Co. of America	12,982,000	1,165,596,256	1.1
118	Reynolds Metals Co.	10,400,000	739,796,000	1.4

Airlines

AD RANK	COMPANY	ADVERTISING	SALES	ADV. AS % OF SALES
72	Pan American World Airways	17,800,000	669,000,000	2.7
93	United Air Lines	14,622,000	792,759,001	1.8
96	Eastern Air Lines	13,300,000	507,524,000	2.6
97	Trans World Airlines	13,200,000	672,787,000	2.0
113	American Airlines	11,000,000	612,435,000	1.8
125	Delta Air Lines	7,915,000	257,460,000	3.1

Photographic Equipment

AD RANK	COMPANY	ADVERTISING	SALES	ADV. AS % OF SALES
26	Eastman Kodak Co.	43,000,000	967,485,000	4.4
106	Polaroid Corp.	12,000,000	204,003,000	5.9

Others

AD RANK	COMPANY	ADVERTISING	SALES	ADV. AS % OF SALES
8	Sears, Roebuck & Co.†	86,000,000	6,390,000,312	1.3
14	American Telephone & Telegraph	69,900,000	11,323,000,000	0.6
19	Gillette Co.	52,000,000	339,064,000	15.3
55	Stanley Warner Corp.	23,000,000	190,817,000*	12.1
61	Columbia Broadcasting System	22,200,000	699,732,483	3.2
86	Armstrong Cork Co.	16,000,000	374,678,000	4.3
104	American Can Co.	12,345,000	1,265,062,000	1.0
105	General Telephone & Electronics	12,129,000	2,035,621,900	0.6
106	Philadelphia & Reading Corp.	12,000,000	288,366,000	4.2
109	3M Co.	11,650,000	1,000,261,000	1.2
116	Mattel Inc.	10,500,000	100,686,000	10.4
119	Evershap Inc.	10,000,000	53,424,708	18.7
120	International Telephone & Telegraph Corp.	9,095,000	449,800,000*	2.0

Note: All ad totals are domestic. Wherever possible, AA has reported the company's domestic sales figure in this table, although for some companies only a worldwide sales total was available.

*Domestic sales estimated by AA. **No % of sales figures is listed, because the ad total is for Seven-Up whereas the sales estimate is for sales of the basic extract only, which is all the company sells. ‡Percentage shown would be more than doubled if Sears' $131,-971,000 in local advertising were added to the $86,000,000 national ad total. ‡Sales for 10 months ended Sept. 30, 1965.

consider the amount of advertising which the leaders in the various industries are using. Figure 16–2 gives, by industry, the advertising as percent of sales for 125 leaders on the basis of their total advertising expenditures. One finds that the percent of the sales dollar devoted to advertising is the highest among the drugs and cosmetics industry where 15 of the 22 drug and cosmetic companies listed spent over 17 percent of their sales dollar for advertising.

FINALIZING THE ADVERTISING BUDGET

As noted through this chapter, there are a number of ways in which firms set their total advertising budgets. In deciding on this budget, however, it is important to consider the following points:

1. General business conditions
2. Capacity of the plant involved
3. Past sales of the article to be advertised and sold
4. Number of competitors in the field
5. Share of market for the company
6. Present distribution system
7. Importance of advertising in sale of product
8. Price of the product and profit margin
9. Amount of money which might be allocated for advertising
10. The stage of the product cycle for the article
11. Effectiveness of available appeals
12. Possibility of measuring advertising results

Checking the above list indicates that it is a complex problem to establish the advertising appropriation. As a result, most executives do not have a satisfactory basis for answering the question, "How much should we spend for advertising?" Although they may know, quite effectively, how to allocate the available advertising funds to various media and products, they are still seeking reliable techniques for determining accurately the overall effects of any campaign, or for measuring the effectiveness of their advertising in the total marketing mix of the firm.

Recommendation

Although the authors recognize the complexity of setting a satisfactory advertising budget, they have found the method listed below to be quite satisfactory for most organizations.

1. Analyze the sales of the prior comparable periods. The first step in planning advertising is to secure the sales figures of prior periods. A retail store might get an insight into the importance of the month's sales

potential to annual sales volume. A company selling air-conditioning units might get its information on a seasonal basis. A company selling industrial equipment might find it more advantageous to use a yearly basis. Break this information down for the periods in the following manner:

    a)   Actual sales in units
    b)   Average prices
    c)   Actual sales in dollars

2. Set the period's planned sales goal. Appraise the unit and dollar market potentials and set the justifiable unit and dollar volume at which to aim for the period.

3. Decide on the amount which is needed for advertising. This amount will vary widely depending on such factors as line of business, intensity of competition, broad goals, image of the company, and the like.

4. Set the period's total advertising media budget. Having established the period's planned sales goal and the amount to be spent for advertising, one is now ready to set the media budget. Put down the cost of television, radio, magazine, newspaper, direct mail, and all other advertising in an advertising budget as shown in Figure 16–3.

5. Allocate the amount among the company's products. Having decided on the total media budget, one must decide on the emphasis to place on the various commodity groups if the company sells a number of different products.

6. Decide how the media can be used most effectively throughout the period. The size of the media budget and the selling opportunities will be important factors in determining the timing of specific appeals and the general frequency pattern used.

7. Set up controls to show the actual record of use of advertising for the period in the media.

8. Provide some means of checking on the effectiveness of the advertising. This might include:

    a)   Observing changes in sales
    b)   Counting number of inquiries
    c)   Measuring changes in attitude of customers

While partial measurement of results is nearly always possible, one seldom is able to measure all of the effects of advertising. As an example, in a Fort Wayne, Indiana, study conducted by the Harvard Graduate School of Business it was pointed out that the consumer's image of a product is likely to be more influenced by actual usage than by any amount of advertising exposure. Yet, when advertising stops, awareness of a product decays. The study also indicated that "repetition of a message may heighten awareness of a new product without improving its image proportionately."

Progress being made in research would seem to indicate that within

FIGURE 16–3. Advertising budget (summary)

Summary page no._____of_____	Budget page no._____
Company_____	For year_____
Date_____	

Advertised products.	Market data—totals (*in company sales territory— for all industries*)		
		Last year	This year
	1. Potential units		
	2. Potential-dollars		
	3. Co. sales goal-units		
	4. Co. sales goal-dollars		
	5. %-adv. to sales goal		

Advertising program

Acct. No.	Activity units or media	Item totals		Activity totals	
		Last year	This year	Last year	This year
1–1	Newspapers				
2–1	Television				
3–1	Radio				
4–1	Magazines				
5–1	Customer service items				
6–1	Direct mail				
7–1	Paid space				
8–1	Services from outside agencies				
9–1	Exhibits				
10–1	Display material				
11–1	Art & engravings administration				
	Total				

the next decade it will be possible to predict to a greater degree the effect of advertising on profits, and that it will be possible to use such predictions to design efficient advertising programs.

CONCLUSIONS

1. The most important factor influencing the amount of the appropriation is the general marketing mix, which in turn is determined by the type of product, appeals available, the volume and margin, company policy, and related factors.

2. A good system of advertising budgeting is a two-sided affair that provides for a formal planning process which leads to an overall goal, with control procedures that enable management to assure that the objectives become results.

3. There is need for straighter, more businesslike thinking from minds

freed from tacit acceptance of certain stereotypes of long standing, about so-called methods of setting appropriations that are not real procedures but merely formalized labels used and reused. These include average industry ratios used as standards in spite of faulty averaging, and ratio data that are questionable and not comparable.

4. Decide on the source of advertising funds. Is it feasible—and really worthwhile—to separate costs of advertising into (a) what produces goodwill, and (b) what helps produce actual sales volume and profits? If these can be separated, should they be separately charged—the goodwill producing a capital charge, the sales producing an annual cost out of income?

5. It should be decided whether the advertising appropriation should be for a fiscal period or a continuing period.

6. Distribute between advertising costs and direct selling costs the items on the border line to be sure of having an overall schedule with no item missing and with each allocated to one or the other.

7. For this overall budgeting, and particularly for selling and advertising expense budgets, any business is likely to benefit from techniques not implicit in the appropriation way of operation. Correlation, mathematical or graphic, and estimating equations are two ways of approximating these optimum ratios; and learning these ratios may lead to even more far-reaching changes in advertising and selling.

8. Some of the new techniques in program evaluation and review techniques offer advertisers great promise for the budgeting and control of advertising.

QUESTIONS

1. One plan for setting the advertising appropriation includes the following steps:

   a) Determine the objectives for the period.
   b) Plan the sales goals.
   c) Determine the percentage of sales that will be invested in advertising.
   d) Set the total advertising budget.
   e) Divide the amount among the different items.
   f) Decide on how this is to be spread among the media.
   g) Set the time periods for the advertising to appear.

What recommendations would strengthen the above plan?

2. Many companies have a tendency to curtail advertising expenditures at the first sign of a depression or recession. Because of the reluctance of many firms to increase advertising appropriations at such times, it has been suggested that advertising reserves should be set aside in profitable years to be spent during such periods of depression. Comment.

3. Compare the objectives, control, and setting of a budget for a young married couple with that of the advertising budget for a corporation.

4. A local department store had used all its allocated budget for the period in question when the merchants' association of the city in which the store was located decided to hold some special sales days. What should the store do?

5. "In setting the appropriation, the firm should allow for a certain amount of flexibility." What is meant by this statement?

6. If you were requested by a client to let him know how much should be budgeted to introduce a new cereal on a national basis, what procedures would you adopt to give him an answer?

7. Why do you believe the drugs and cosmetics industries spend such a high percentage of the sales dollar for advertising?

8. At what time should the advertising appropriation be determined? Discuss.

9. The average selling cost (percent of sales) and percent of sales expended for advertising in a number of different lines of business are listed below:

Line of business	Average selling cost (percent of sales)	Percent of sales expanded for advertising
Automobile dealers	8.25	2
Burglar alarm services	5	2
Men's clothing	19	3.5
Electric heating appliances	9	3.5
Building materials	19	.25
Office appliances	30	2.2
Grocery specialties	15.5	4
Proprietary medicines	15	10
Shoes (women's)	11	.5
Shoe polish	25	10
Store fixtures	40	5

Indicate how the above percentage figures in the above lines of business would affect the setting of the budget.

10. An accounting executive made the following statement: "An advertising budget is best controlled through a job-costing procedure under which allowances, commitments, and actual costs are broken down and recorded by jobs or projects." Comment.

11. Under what conditions should an advertising budget be built for each unit of the company?

12. What advantages are gained by applying standard advertising budgets, which are developed by trade associations, to specific companies?

13. How does the organization structure of a company offset the placement of responsibility for the development of the advertising budget?

14. What administrative expenses would you recommend be included in the advertising budget?

15. Describe a procedure in determining an approximate break-even point

for an advertising budget, when data are not available to calculate it mathematically.

CASE 1.   HEURISTIC, INC.
Analysis of a budget

The Heuristic Department Store is located in a city of 250,000 people and is one of the five major stores. Heuristic carries the classes of merchandise usually handled by such stores, including men's, women's, and children's wearing apparel and accessories, home furnishings, housewares, and appliances.

Heuristic does business on both cash and credit bases, and in the prior fiscal year, of the $9.65 million sales, 28 percent were cash sales and 72 percent were sales on credit.

The general character of the business done by Heuristic had not changed in the past three years. However, the company had an average increase in sales each year of about 2 percent during this period.

While it was the policy of Mr. Frank Anthony, the advertising manager, to work closely with each department head in planning the advertising appeals for the various departments of the store, it was his opinion that he had to decide on the amount that was to be allowed each department.

EXHIBIT 1. Heuristic, Inc. sales (by merchandise lines, 19—)

Sales by merchandise lines	Actual sales last fiscal year
Upstairs departments	$ 500,000
Piece goods and household textiles	500,000
Small wares	1,000,000
Women's and misses' ready-to-wear	1,700,000
Accessories	1,800,000
Men's and boys' clothing and furnishings	1,000,000
Home furnishings	1,950,000
Miscellaneous (candy, books, etc.)	800,000
Basement store	900,000
	$9,650,000

Furthermore, he believed that he was best qualified to determine what media should be used.

Mr. Anthony followed the procedure of setting up the planned advertising budget for each department in the store about 45 days prior to the first business day of the month in which the advertising was to be placed. He then presented the recommended budget to the store manager for his general approval. After the budget was approved by the store manager, Mr. Anthony then consulted the department heads to determine what appeals they wished to use for their departments in the period under consideration.

In the middle of September, therefore, Mr. Anthony began to work out the planned advertising budget for the month of November. In Exhibit 1 the actual sales by merchandise lines, are given for the last fiscal year. In Exhibit 2 the expenses, by expense centers and by natural division, are given for the same year.

EXHIBIT 2. Heuristic, Inc. expenses (by expense centers and natural divisions)

Expenses by expense centers

Fixed and policy expense	$ 600,000
Control and accounting	100,000
Accounts receivable and credit	240,000
Sales promotion	395,000
Building operations	310,000
Personnel and employee benefits	265,000
Material handling	215,000
Direct and general selling	965,000
Merchandising	500,000
Total	$3,590,000

Expenses by natural divisions

Payroll	$1,820,000
Real estate costs	325,000
Advertising	270,000
All other	1,175,000
Total	$3,590,000

The store manager informed Mr. Anthony that he has set a goal for the current year to increase sales by 3 percent for the store and hopes to plan for 12 percent to be secured in November.

Case questions

1. Set up an advertising budget, by merchandise lines, for Heuristic for the month of November.

2. Divide this budget for each merchandise line into the following media:
   a) Newspapers
   b) Direct mail
   c) Television
   d) Radio
   e) Miscellaneous

3. What controls might Mr. Anthony adopt to see that the advertising budget for each merchandise line will be properly used?

4. How might the procedure which Mr. Anthony follows be improved?

CASE 2.   LONGCHAMP COMPANY
Deciding on advertising allocation

The Longchamp Company manufactures a superior line of beauty parlor products. The line includes three product divisions—hair-waving supplies, hair dyes and shampoos, and cosmetics. Principal sale of the hair-waving supplies is for professional use by beauty shops, and packaging is largely in bulk containers.

While the hair dyes and shampoos and the cosmetics are sold to beauty shops on a limited basis, 85 percent of the total sales of these two divisions are made to the ultimate consumer.

Distribution is national through a selective, nonexclusive jobber system. The country is divided into 16 sales regions. In common with trade practices, the company employs a force of skilled women demonstrators working under the salesmen, who combine missionary sales work and product demonstration.

The company makes some use of missionary salesmen in building up weak territories. However, due to the high cost and the management's feeling that product demonstration is a more primary function, it makes less use of them than do certain competitors. In practice, however, demonstrators' efforts have tended to expand to include more outright sales than missionary sales work.

Longchamp Company's prices on all its line are at a competitive level. However, the wave line price is higher than the competitors'. The president of the company sought to find a reliable method to evaluate the real importance of the several links in the distribution chain (advertising, salesmen, missionary salesmen, demonstration, jobbers, beauty parlor operators, ultimate consumer) so that the company might select the most effective promotional method.

Interpretation of sales results for the wave line is complicated because the trend for high-grade waves has been somewhat stationary, representing a loss relative to industry growth. Lower priced waves have shown a substantial increase, paralleling industry growth.

While sales of dyes and shampoos and cosmetics have increased, the company is concerned because certain competitors in each of its fields are known to have greatly outstripped the company. The president of the company believes that these gains were secured as a result of more extensive advertising.

The situation seems to be that the Longchamp Company, through early leadership and quality development, was able to secure higher prices. In the wave line, the policy continued to be successful. This success apparently influenced the company in maintaining a high price on this line. Other influencing factors were that management became preoccupied with the dye and shampoos and cosmetic lines, and failed to promote or meet the issues in the decline of the wave line. Competition was attracted and was able to undercut the company's position in the wave line market.

The lower price markets are, of course, the volume markets. In evaluating the current budget figures in Exhibit 1, the company is strong in the dye and shampoos and cosmetic lines. Although these are desirable markets from a profit standpoint, they are highly competitive.

On the other hand, the higher priced wave line beauty parlor business depends on a small field of better class shops which continues to prefer quality materials regardless of price, and a miscellaneous group carrying the product for very occasional sale to high-price trade.

The company is divided into three separate and autonomous divisions. Everything has been done to maintain the operating and financial

EXHIBIT 1. Longchamp Company (estimated income statement for year ended Dec. 31, 19—)

	Wave line	Dye and shampoo	Cosmetics	Total
Sales..	$1,000,000	$20,000,000	$30,000,000	$51,000,000
Variable cost of goods sold...................				
Material......................................	110,000	2,040,000	2,500,000	4,650,000
Labor..	150,000	2,390,000	5,000,000	7,540,000
Overhead....................................	210,000	3,500,000	4,300,000	8,010,000
Total....................................	$ 470,000	$ 7,930,000	$11,800,000	$20,200,000
Variable manufacturing margin[1]..............	$ 530,000	$12,070,000	$18,200,000	$30,800,000
Other variable expenses				
Advertising expense........................	$ 50,000	$ 1,000,000	$ 1,500,000	$ 2,550,000
Selling expense.............................	160,000	3,200,000	4,800,000	8,160,000
General and administrative expense........	90,000	1,800,000	2,700,000	4,590,000
Total....................................	$ 300,000	$ 6,000,000	$ 9,000,000	$15,300,000
Marginal income[2]............................	$ 230,000	$ 6,070,000	$ 9,200,000	$15,500,000
Direct fixed costs[3]				
Manufacturing expense.....................	$ 80,000	$ 1,600,000	$ 2,400,000	$ 4,080,000
Selling expense.............................	20,000	400,000	600,000	1,020,000
General and administrative expense........	100,000	2,000,000	3,000,000	5,100,000
Total....................................	$ 200,000	$ 4,000,000	$ 6,000,000	$10,200,000
Profit after direct costs[4].....................	$ 30,000	$ 2,070,000	$ 3,200,000	$ 5,300,000
Apportioned fixed costs[5]				
Manufacturing expense.....................	$ 70,000	$ 1,400,000	$ 2,100,000	$ 3,570,000
Selling expense.............................	8,000	160,000	240,000	408,000
General and administrative expense........	2,000	40,000	60,000	102,000
Total....................................	$ 80,000	$ 1,600,000	$ 2,400,000	$ 4,080,000
Net profit (loss)[6]............................	($ 50,000)	$ 470,000	$ 800,000	$ 1,220,000

[1] The "variable manufacturing margin" equals sales less variable cost of goods sold.
[2] The "marginal income" equals variable manufacturing margin less other variable expenses.
[3] The "direct fixed costs" are those direct costs which can be charged directly to one of the three product lines and which are fixed in nature.
[4] The "profit after direct costs" equals marginal income less direct fixed costs.
[5] The "apportioned fixed costs" are those fixed costs which cannot be charged directly to any one of the three product lines and, in this case, are apportioned among the product lines on the basis of sales.
[6] The "net profit (loss)" equals the profit after direct costs less the apportioned fixed costs.

independence of the three divisions. Each has separate management, and is individually responsible for financial results. Administrative offices of the manufacturing division are located in New York; the plant is in the Midwest. The sales division occupies separate offices in another part of New York. It duplicates, in some instances with even larger staffs, the offices of general manager, comptroller, purchasing agent (largely for packaging supplies purchases), and testing department. Coordination is chiefly through the president.

The separation tends to act as a barrier to overall economies, such as departmental consolidations, in the interior of the whole business. Thus at low operating levels, each division becomes a victim of its independence.

Budget

In the early part of August of each year, the president and his directors meet to review the current year's budget and to set the budget for the next fiscal year which begins on January 1. The budget for the current year is given in Exhibit 1.

The company had followed a policy of allocating 5 percent of the expected net sales of the current year as the amount the head of each division would be allowed. This amount was firmed before August 15 so the divisions would have sufficient time to make their commitments with the various media before January 1.

In the review of the budget, the manager of the wave line division indicated that he believed the $50,000 (or 5 percent of current projected sales) was inadequate. He emphasized the following points:

1. In order to increase sales, the wave line division had to develop brand awareness on the part of consumers, so that when a woman went to the beauty parlor, she would insist on Longchamp wave solution.
2. With more women working each year, there was every reason to believe that the sale of wave solutions to beauty parlors would increase.
3. The fact that more beauty parlors would use Longchamp solution and that more customers would ask for it would serve as one of the best appeals the other divisions could use in advertising their product.
4. Many women who go to beauty parlors rely on the recommendations the beauty shop operators give them on such products as dyes, shampoos, and cosmetics.
5. The wave line division cannot make a profit unless it increases its sales.
6. In order to get more beauty parlor operators to use Longchamp wave solution, the company must build such a strong brand preference that the operators will feature the solution and the customers will insist on it.

The manager of the wave line division requested that the president and his committee allow his division $250,000 for advertising during the next fiscal year. He believed it would require this amount to attain the sales he thought could be secured.

Case questions

1. What advertising budget policy should the Longchamp Company adopt?

2. What are some of the promotional problems which the company will face?

3. What are some of the reasons Longchamp has lost its position?

4. What approach should Longchamp adopt?

5. What amount should be allocated for advertising?

CASE 3.   LEO ELECTRIC COMPANY
Considering a detailed appropriation

The Leo Electric Company had followed the policy of allocating 1 percent of planned sales as the lump sum to be spent on advertising each year, and had given the advertising department the responsibility for allocating this amount to individual projects.

This budgeting policy had been followed for the past 10 years. However, about six months ago, John Gift was appointed treasurer of the company. Mr. Gift decided to adopt a new budget procedure and requested that the head of the advertising department submit a detailed appropriation prescribing the manner in which it would be expended.

Mr. Gift also asked the advertising head to indicate what percentage of the cost of the next year's advertising appropriation should be considered as a deferred expenditure. Mr. Gift believed that the next year's advertising and promotional campaign would benefit future periods and a part of these expenditures should, therefore, be charged against these periods. He wanted to correlate the advertising expenditures with the particular revenue secured from the advertising. "Otherwise," he said, "the advertising expenses for next year will be overstated, and the advertising expenses for future years will be understated."

Products

The Leo Company designs and manufactures both lighting fixtures which are directly connected to the permanent wiring system of a building, and lamps which serve the function of lighting fixtures but which can be plugged into existing outlets. The lamps manufactured by the company include desk, pinup, wall, pole, and tree lamps. The line of lamps consists of 150 designs and accounts for 52 percent of the company's sales. Most of the company's sales are concentrated in the medium-price field, although the line includes items which retail for prices ranging from $5 to $250.

Leo places great emphasis on styling and design, and emphasizes the development and use of interchangeable components which can be incorporated in many different styles of fixtures and lamps.

Marketing

The Leo Company sells most of its products in 15 eastern states. This is the company's principal market, and in the past fiscal year accounted for approximately 75 percent of sales.

The company has 15 full-time sales employees. Also serving the midwestern states which account for 20 percent of sales are 12 independent sales organizations employing 30 salesmen. All salesmen are paid a base salary plus commission. The independent sales organizations are compensated on a commission basis.

Leo's lamps are sold primarily through department stores, furniture stores, and lamp stores. The lighting fixtures are carried primarily by lighting fixture dealers and electrical jobbers. In the last fiscal year, the company made sales to over 4,000 customers, none of whom accounted for more than 2.5 percent of its sales. A substantial portion of Leo's lighting fixtures is used in new construction. The company plans to place greater emphasis on the replacement and redecorating market in order to protect itself from any general decline in new construction which would adversely affect its sales and earnings.

The statement of income for the three years ending June 20, 19—— is given below.

Statement of income (year ending June 30)

	(in thousands of dollars)		
	Year A	Year B	Year C
Sales..	$5,500	$6,500	$8,200
Cost of sales......................................	3,300	3,700	5,100
Gross profit......................................	$2,200	$2,800	$3,100
Selling and admin. expenses.......................	1,600	1,800	2,200
Income from operations........................	$ 600	$1,000	$ 900
General and other expenses......................	$ 100	$ 125	$ 125
Net income before federal income tax...........	$ 500	$ 875	$ 775

Competition

The lamp and lighting fixture industry is highly competitive. In the states where the company markets its products, it competes with a substantial number of larger manufacturers and numerous smaller companies.

As a result of this competition, the treasurer believed that a detailed appropriation for the advertising budget would help the company study and set its advertising objectives on a firmer basis. In order to accomplish these goals, he gave the advertising director the budget form in Exhibit 1, and asked him to complete it.

EXHIBIT 1. Advertising budget report (classification for six-month period Jan. 1, 19— to June 30, 19—)

	Lamp division	Lighting fixture division
1. Administrative expense		
a. Salaries		
b. Traveling expenses		
c. Telephone and telegraph		
d. Supplies		
e. Postage		
f. Association dues		
g. Miscellaneous		
2. Consumer contacts		
a. Newspapers		
b. Magazines		
c. Radio		
d. Television		
e. Direct mail		
f. Outdoor		
g. Car cards		
h. Other		
3. Dealer helps		
a. Store and window displays		
b. Dealer signs		
c. Stationery		
d. Imprinting		
e. Electros and mats		
f. Other		
4. Trade contacts		
a. Trade papers		
b. Dealer house organ		
c. Direct mail		
d. Postage		
e. Other		
5. Mechanical		
a. Artwork, photographs		
b. Typography		
c. Engraving		
d. Other		
6. Miscellaneous		
Totals		
7. Percent of appropriation to be charged against the expenses of the following years:		
1974		
1975		
1976		
1977		
1978		

The advertising director disagreed with the concept of developing such a detailed budget. He emphasized that the cost and effort required in the preparation of such a budget would be excessive for any benefit which the company might realize.

He was afraid that once the budget was set it would become too inflexible, and shifting one specific appropriation to another use would be too difficult. In discussing the matter with the treasurer, he said, "the competition in the industry is so intense that it just isn't realistic to firm in advance the exact percentage we are going to spend in each medium. Conditions change so rapidly in the industry and in specific markets that we are forced to place greater emphasis from time to time in an area to meet the competition. As an example, we had to give the retailers special cooperative advertising allowances last year in four Eastern cities because of special concessions our competitors had begun to offer."

The advertising director also disagreed with the treasurer's plan of deferring the cost of advertising. He stated, "there is no question that the current advertising will benefit future periods and should constitute an expense for these future years. However, I do not see how I can correlate a particular advertising expenditure with the revenue resulting therefrom. I believe the practical difficulties of setting a reasonable basis of amortization are too great to make it worthwhile for us to attempt this."

Case questions

1. Should the Leo Electric Company adopt the recommendations of the treasurer?

2. What are the objectives of advertising control?

3. Is a policy of allocating a percentage of planned sales to be spent on advertising realistic?

4. What method of accounting and appropriation should Leo company use for its advertising budget?

5. When is a policy of deferred advertising expense realistic?

CASE 4.   RULES, INC.
Planning a budget

Rules, Inc. is in the business of selling fashion wearing apparel and sportswear for adults by direct mail. For 55 years Rules has operated a specialty mail-order business. Rules serves selected customers, most of whom live in or near large metropolitan areas throughout the United

States, and has over seven million customers who have purchased merchandise from it in recent years. In the last fiscal year, Rules had a sales volume of $86.5 million.

Products

Rules confines its merchandise offerings to men's and women's apparel, and present sales volume is divided almost equally between the two. The women's items include several types of dresses, knit suits and pant suits, casual fashions, sports outfits, nylon stockings and panty hose, bonded slacks, nightgowns and pajamas, jackets, coats and raincoats. Men's garments include a diversity of slacks, dress and sport shirts, sweaters, sport coats, car coats, raincoats, ties, socks, underwear, and shoes. Rules endeavors to maintain its styles and colors in keeping with current fashions and to make available a broad range of sizes. It follows a policy of offering quality merchandise at attractive prices.

All merchandise is designed and manufactured to Rules' specifications by a number of independent suppliers located throughout the country. Rules does not have any long-term contracts with its suppliers and is not dependent upon any single supplier. Company stylists and merchandising staff collectively review fashion submissions from apparel manufacturers and, working closely with these suppliers, assist in the design of the offerings that eventually reach the customer. Selections and specifications are set and deliveries of finished garments are planned to coordinate closely with these suppliers and the arrival of customer orders.

Marketing and distribution

Over the years Rules has developed its own customer lists. These lists are maintained with source and experience data in its computer system. The locating, testing, and developing of lists of new customers is a continuing activity of Rules.

All selling is done by means of carefully prepared direct-mail letters, colorful folders, and individual order forms which offer Rules merchandise. Each mailing presents a limited number of items. Rules does not issue catalogs.

Rules also offers its customers a seven-day free trial of all merchandise ordered. Full payment for the merchandise is due at the end of the free trial period. If payment is not made, Rules initiates a series of payment request letters and eventually places unpaid accounts into collection.

While Rules has experienced increased collection activity in recent years, due to its expanded sales volume, such increase has not been material and Rules' collection experience has been satisfactory over the years.

Rules maintains its own in-house direct-mail advertising department which creates, designs, writes, and directs the preparation of all selling material. Photography, artwork and printing are produced by outside suppliers. All orders are received at, filled, and mailed from, Rules' central facility and warehouses. Mail preparation—addressing, collating, enclosing, sealing, tying into bundles, sacking, and transporting to postal trucks for nationwide distribution—occupies a large number of people even though mailing operations are highly mechanized. Rules maintains an extensive system of electronic data processing equipment for control functions in order processing, payroll, receivables, handling, inventory control, and other functions designed to reduce costs and provide improved customer service.

It has been Rules' practice to pay postage and handling costs on orders accompanied by full payment for the merchandise ordered, whereas such costs are borne by the purchaser if the merchandise is paid for after delivery. The Federal Trade Commission advised the company that it believes that, under these circumstances, the postage and handling costs constitute "finance charges" within the meaning of the Truth in Lending Act and the regulations thereunder, and Rules should make the disclosures required by those regulations and the Act.

Postage rates

Rules uses the U.S. mails extensively, and its postage costs exceed $10 million per year.

Competition

Rules business is highly competitive, as it competes with other direct-mail and catalog businesses, retail department and specialty stores, and discount stores, many of which have significantly greater financial resources than Rules.

Future plans

It was the opinion of the executives that Rules had reached its maximum sales potential with its current method of using direct mail as the major media. They also believed that the postal rates would continue to rise. As a result, they decided that they should consider setting up an advertising budget in which other media would be utilized.

The most difficult phase of the planning of the advertising budget was to determine the income from sales using the new media. This appeared to be quite complex to the executives because it involved unknown and imponderable factors. There was no past history of sales volume which could be used; yet, they did not want their estimates to be too conservative or too optimistic.

One of the executives recommended that they project the demand for their products which would result from the use of the new media over a five-year period. Another recommendation was to have each one of the executives prepare estimates of the volume which they believed might be received. While such a method is a composite guess, it was believed that these pooled estimates would be quite dependable.

It was the belief of another executive that the "batting average" of most forecasting is notoriously poor, and, as a result, he believed that they should simply allocate a given amount for the next year, and then try to determine from internal records what the results were.

Lastly, the controller recommended that Rules should set an objective of getting $5 million in sales from orders received from other media advertising and then arbitrarily allocate 10 percent of expected sales for general media advertising.

Case questions

1. How might Rules use economic and market forecasts in developing its media budget?

2. Who should be responsible for firming the marketing plan?

3. Should the advertising budget for the general media be fixed or variable? Give reasons.

4. For how long a period of time should the general media budget be set?

5. Establish a budget for Rules' general media and indicate what techniques you recommend to control it.

chapter 17

CAMPAIGN STRATEGY

A CAMPAIGN consists of the correlation of all advertising and related efforts on behalf of a product or service, directed toward the attainment of predetermined objectives. It should be viewed as a long-range overall plan consisting of a number of short-range plans and goals.

A campaign should also be considered as a cumulative sales effort and should be consistent throughout the time period in which it is used.

A campaign must be coordinated with the various parts of the marketing program if it is to be successful. That is, the various parts of the overall plan, such as the consumer advertising, the trade advertising, dealer cooperative advertising, and dealer point-of-purchase displays must be carefully meshed with all other types of sales effort to attain full effectiveness. This means that the campaign must be correlated with the personal selling activities of the sales force, those of the various distributors of the product and their salespeople's activities, and with the various other promotional efforts which may be a part of the marketing mix.

Thus, in the broad sense, planning the advertising campaign is but one phase or part of planning the total marketing plan. And, as any marketing plan must have definitely established goals and purposes, so also must the campaign be designed with certain definite goals or purposes in mind. The objectives of the campaign may be quite broad in scope, or may be quite specific. The purpose may be to stimulate primary demand for a product, or to build a brand preference. On the other hand, the program may be designed to educate customers to a new use of a product, to stimulate dealers, to teach consumers the correct pronunciation of a brand name, to elicit inquiries, or one of many other possible objectives that fits into the company's marketing strategy.

In Figure 17–1, South Central Bell as an example, uses the curiosity appeal for the purpose of encouraging direct dialing.

FIGURE 17–1. South Central Bell ad

One nice advantage of a Lovin' Phone Call is you don't have to lick the stamp.

Dialing a long distance Lovin' Phone Call direct is faster and easier than writing a letter—plus there's no bitter aftertaste.

First dial "1," then the area code (if different from your own), then the number.

And remember, rates begin to go down at 5 p.m. on weekdays. Check the front pages of your phone book for details, and weekend bargain rates. So why not address yourself to a Lovin' Phone Call tonight? What else that costs so little puts you in touch so fast?

Ⓐ **South Central Bell**

Continuing their successful "Lovin' Phone Call" theme, South Central Bell recently ran this cartoon newspaper advertisement containing the suggestion to dial direct plus instructions on how to do it.

FACTORS INFLUENCING THE PLANNING OF THE CAMPAIGN

Many factors influence the planning of the advertising campaign. While these are, of course, factors that are included in planning the over-all marketing program, they also influence the advertising strategy. The exact sequence in which these factors should be considered will vary depending on individual circumstances. Some will even be evaluated simultaneously, since they are so closely interrelated, and should not be handled as independent variables.

Among the most important of the factors are:

1. *The organization:* its reputation, position in the market, financial strength, etc.
2. *The product:* the type of product, whether it is new or already established on the market, its differentiating features, the package, the product line
3. *The market:* the number and types of potential customers, their location, the total potential volume
4. *The competition:* number and strength of competitors, their advertising and marketing strategy
5. *The price:* absolute price of product, relationship to competitive prices
6. *The channels of distribution:* the number and types of distributors, their location, degree of cooperation currently obtained from them
7. *The sales force:* brochures and kits to be supplied, their activity in merchandising the advertising to the trade
8. *The budget:* the amount of money needed, the amount of money available
9. *The advertising theme:* the various appeals that might be used, the one appeal that will best meet the needs of the objective, the campaign keynote theme or idea
10. *The media:* the various media that would reach the potential market, the most appropriate type of media to use for this particular product and purpose, the appropriation to be allocated to various major media, the specific publications and radio and television stations most appropriate
11. *The advertising schedule:* the timing of ads, the frequency and size of ads to be run
12. *The dealer program:* the cooperative advertising, the point-of-purchase display materials, merchandising tie-ins, reproductions of ads to be supplied to dealers
13. *Correlation* of all phases of the program so that materials will be in the hands of retailers before campaign breaks, etc.
14. *Coordination* of all phases of program so the dealer and consumer advertising is properly timed, the advertising materials will be pro-

vided salesmen and dealers when needed, and merchandise is in hands of retailers before campaign breaks

15. *Government regulations and controls*

PLANNING THE CAMPAIGN

The actual planning of the advertising campaign for major companies will be a joint effort of the advertiser and an advertising agency, since the agency usually works very closely with the marketing division of the client, through the client's advertising manager. This is particularly true if the product is a new one being introduced to the market or is a product to be advertised extensively by the client for the first time.

So the advertiser, working with the account executive and the various appropriate people in the agency (such as the merchandising director, the research director, the production manager, the media director, and the head of the creative department)—possibly organized into some sort of plans board to handle the particular account—will begin by collecting and organizing all available data about the product and the market.

In small-sized companies, the proprietors can often get help from the media and agencies which specialize in smaller accounts. They may also get advice from suppliers, trade associations, and the like. Regardless of the size of the firm, however, the general procedures in planning the campaign will be somewhat similar.

Much information about the firm, the product, the competition, and the channels of distribution can be supplied by the company, although it may be necessary to obtain some information from other sources. In any event, the data on the 15 factors listed above will be collected and organized in such a manner as to throw the maximum amount of light on the problem at hand.

The market

Before any real planning can take place, many questions about the market or potential market for the product must be considered. It will be necessary to determine who the potential users of the product are and how many there are. If a new product is involved, the advertiser will want to know who will buy the product, who will use the product, and who will influence the decision to buy the product. He will want to know just how the customer might use the product, and, hence, which features of the product are important to the customer. He will want to know if the potential customers are men, women, or children, or some combination thereof. He will also want to know if age is of significance, and whether marital status has any importance. Will the product be bought only by people in high income brackets, or in specific occupations, or in various social strata? And, finally, he will want to determine how often they may buy and whether they buy all during the year or only during one season of the year. If a product is already on the market, he will want to know the above information and, in addition, how his competitors' brands share in the market.

The objectives of a campaign

Although, as noted earlier, it is difficult to give an exact sequence in which the individual decisions regarding the various factors involved are made, because of the close interrelationships of all facets of the campaign, it is probable that as this stage the advertiser would decide the objectives or purpose of the particular campaign. That is, it would be decided just where the advertising was to fit into the overall marketing program and just what purpose the campaign was designed to accomplish. It is vital to determine quite early in the planning stage the specific objectives of the advertising program, since so many of the later decisions depend, to such a significant degree, on this factor.

It should also be noted that in setting the objectives there is, in many instances, an underlying assumption that the maximization of profits through increased sales is the major purpose of the advertising campaign. However, there may be other objectives of even greater importance for a specific campaign. Listed below are some objectives which a company might wish to consider for a campaign.

1. Stimulating demand for the product through:
   a) Appealing to the person who buys the product
   b) Appealing to the person who influences the person who buys the product
   c) Emphasizing new uses of the product
   d) Emphasizing more frequent use of the product
   e) Attracting a new class of consumers
   f) Providing better services
   g) Extending the territory in which the product is sold
   h) Offering combined sales with other products
   i) Developing new distribution techniques
   j) Giving easier credit terms
2. Building a "family" concept for the products which the company manufactures
3. Using the "hitchhiker" tactic for a new variety of a product debuting under an old, established brand name
4. Extending the brand image of the company
5. Meeting the strategies of competitors

6. Influencing the dealers to "push" the product more extensively
7. Changing the buying season for a product
8. Developing a new image for the company
9. Educating the public about the product use
10. Building a broad general public relations program
11. Informing the public what the *actual* product being sold is

While these are only a few of the various objectives which the advertiser might set for a campaign, they indicate a number of the types of goals which various companies have set.

There are, of course, parameters on such goals, set by company tradition, product mix, competitive position, and just plain consumer habit, which do place limitations on the possible scope of these. There is a fundamental marketing maxim in this sort of strategy of brand-image-sales management objectives: When consumer tastes are changing, the product itself must change with them, but the established image must be revamped in such a way that the changes appear to be only normal evolution.

It is generally more effective for the advertiser to limit his campaign to a specific purpose. By pinpointing his advertising efforts to one objective, he will be able to control his advertising and, at the same time, be able to measure the results of the approach that has been used.

Setting the budget

In general it is advisable when the study of the market has projected the scope of the task involved, and the purpose indicates just what is to be done by the advertising, to determine at that time how much money will be required to do an effective job and how much money may be available for the program. It should be kept in mind that the amount of money appropriated will be influenced by many of the other factors involved in planning the campaign, and at the same time will, in turn, influence many of the other decisions, such as the media to be used, the number, frequency, and size of advertisements, and other related factors. Thus again, the close interrelationships of the decisions on each phase of the campaign planning become evident; hence, the difficulty in setting up a specific sequence of steps to be taken in the planning of the campaign.

The appeal or theme

Once the objective and the budget have been determined, the advertiser should review the data collected on the various factors discussed up to this point. He would then consider, on the basis of all the known information about the product, the market, the customers, and the objectives, just what appeal or appeals would be the most effective in achieving the desired results. It is quite probable that a study would be made using motivation research, since this method is a satisfactory one to use in determining just why people buy certain products or brands and, hence, makes it possible to determine an effective appeal in stimulating sales.

It should be stressed that the research study will not actually produce the campaign theme or keynote idea. Research will produce the basic information regarding possible appeals or themes that could be effective in stimulating the consumer. But the actual selection of the theme, as well as putting it in its final form, is the work of the creative thinking of one or several people, often the copywriters, who devote much of their effort to creative thinking in order to evolve new and effective themes. For instance, one of the interesting copy themes which American Telephone and Telegraph Co. uses for its Yellow Pages is "Let Your Fingers Do The Walking." This keynote concept gets the message across in a challenging manner and has been used effectively in both print and broadcast media.

In a similar vein, it will be noted that a successful advertising campaign is built around one central idea, or theme, which is normally carried throughout all the advertising, whether printed or broadcast, all promotional materials, and usually is also the main theme of the salesmen's presentations.

In other words the "one sell" concept requires a single basic selling proposition that can be treated visually and audibly so as to enable it to be used in other marketing areas such as equipment, packaging, public relations, promotion, and sales. At the same time this basic idea should be of such a nature that it can be supported by subordinate concepts and presentations which will make it more motivating and more acceptable.

Listed below are examples of some keynote ideas which have been used in various campaigns:

1. A lifetime of writing pleasure
     Cross
2. You can't replace a $30,000 house with $20,000 worth of insurance.
     State Farm Insurance
3. This little bike could broaden your horizons.
     Honda
4. Come to where the flavor is.
     Marlboro
5. The simple machine
     Maverick
6. Last summer two million dogs wore Sentry collars instead of fleas.
     Sentry collar

7. Your breath stays fresh because your mouth is clean.
   Listerine
8. Fastest tan under the sun
   Coppertone
9. King of beers
   Anheuser-Busch Budweiser beer
10. The candy with the hole
    Life Savers
11. Let Hertz put you in the driver's seat.
    Hertz Rent-A-Car
12. Scovill is a gay blade around women.
    Scovill electric scissors
13. The most service-free automatics made
    Maytag
14. Only her hairdresser knows for sure.
    Clairol
15. A cup and a half of flavor
    Maxwell House instant coffee
16. Trust your car to the man who wears the star.
    Texaco
17. The best to you each morning
    Kellogg's Corn Flakes
18. Keeps you fresh all day
    Dial soap
19. Relief is just a swallow away.
    Miles Products-Alka Seltzer
20. Your children can be only a whisper away.
    Sonotone
21. For four generations we've been making medicines as if people's lives depended on them.
    Lilly
22. A diamond is forever.
    DeBeers Consolidated Mines
23. Things go better with Coke.
    Coca-Cola
24. Nothing protects wood more beautifully.
    Olympic stains
25. Ford has a better idea (we listen better).
    Ford Motor Co.

The media

On the basis of the knowledge obtained previously about the market to be covered, the people to be influenced, the funds available, and the appeal to be used, the advertiser should be able to determine what media will be best for this particular campaign. Since the relative advantages and disadvantages of the various media and the general principles governing the selection of media have already been discussed at some length in prior chapters, they need not be discussed further here. At this point, the types of media to be used will be determined, and the allocation of appropriated funds to each type of media will be decided. After the media have been selected, the specific media must be chosen. That is, if the major media are to be magazines and newspapers, the advertiser will determine which particular magazines and newspapers will best meet the needs of the particular campaign.

The schedule

When the media have been selected, the advertiser should then proceed to draw up a detailed schedule for each of the individual media involved to submit to the account executive for approval. In planning the schedule, a number of variables must be considered. Among these are such factors as coverage of the particular publication or station, size of the advertisement, frequency with which advertisements will be run, and timing.

These must be considered not only for each specific medium being used but also as related to the various other individual media that may be in use, and, of course, always with relation to the specific purpose of the particular campaign being planned.

One of the most difficult problems in scheduling the advertising for a specific medium, say a magazine, is that of the relation of the size of the advertisements and the frequency with which ads shall be run, or space size and frequency of insertion. The space size is significant from the standpoint of impact of reader impression; while frequency is important from the standpoint of the continuity of reader impressions. Although larger space usually obtains a stronger short-run visual impact, it often does not obtain an increase in attention proportional to the increased size. And, of course, the larger the space taken for the individual insertion, the less frequency of insertion that can be obtained with the amount of funds appropriated for the particular medium. The advertiser must, therefore, attempt to obtain the best compromise between size and frequency for his particular campaign.

In reaching this compromise, the advertiser must consider virtually every factor that enters into advertising, including object of the program, appropriation, nature of the medium, characteristics of the readers, kind of product, degree of acceptance of the product, competition, and planned duration of the campaign. For example, if the purpose of the campaign is the speedy introduction of a new product, it is probable that best results will be obtained by the use of large space at the beginning of the campaign in order to obtain strong initial impact. But if the purpose is to stimulate repeat purchases of a well-known convenience good bought very often, frequency of insertions might be more important than large space for impact.

The other main problem in scheduling is that of timing the advertising. Timing includes the selection of the months, weeks, or seasons of the year when the advertisements will be run; and the days of the week for the advertisements to be used in newspapers, radio, or television. Here again, many factors, such as the objective of the campaign and the buying habits of the customers for the particular product, will influence the strategy of timing the advertising.

If the product involved has definite seasonal peaks in sales, such as the graduation gift period and Christmas gift period in the case of watches, much of the advertising might be concentrated in the weeks ahead of these two periods, with the appearance of the advertisements so timed as to achieve maximum cumulative effect for these two heavy buying periods. And if the product has differing sales periods in different parts of the country, due to the influence of weather, the timing would involve running the advertisements at different times in the various parts of the country. Thus, if the campaign for a lightweight suit was being run in newspapers, the advertising might appear considerably earlier in the southern part of the country than in the Midwest or in the New England states. And the advertiser of a food specialty product would face the problem of whether to have his advertisements appear on the same day of the week as the heavy supermarket advertising appears, or to run them on the alternate days when his advertisements would not compete with so much price advertising.

The competitive situation may also influence the timing of a campaign, since if most competitors have developed a particular pattern of timing an advertiser may elect, for strategic reasons, to adopt a somewhat different timing pattern, such as starting his campaign earlier in the season, or allocating some of his funds to an off-season program of advertising.

It must be remembered that the buying periods of dealers are several months ahead of buying periods for consumers. Thus, the timing of the advertising directed to dealers should take this factor into consideration. The advertising directed at the dealer must appear sufficiently ahead of the consumer advertising to achieve its desired effect of having the dealer stock the item, or the entire consumer campaign may well be rendered ineffective.

When the above decisions regarding the scheduling of the advertising have been worked out, the advertiser will draw up a detailed media schedule. This would show in detail the names of the specific media to be used, the size of the advertisements to be run (or length of time periods for broadcast media, or duration of showing in the case of outdoor signs or car cards), the dates on which the advertisements are to appear, the costs, and any other pertinent information. After this detailed schedule has been approved, the actual insertion orders can be prepared and the work of preparation of individual advertisements can begin.

The dealer program and promotional activities

During the period the above decisions on media and allied problems have been under consideration, the advertiser should be making decisions regarding the details of the dealer portion of the campaign. Decisions should be made on whether or not dealer cooperative advertising will be a part of the campaign, what advertising will be directed at the dealers, what types of point-of-purchase display materials are to be provided for the dealers, whether reproductions of media advertisements will be utilized in dealer display materials, what brochures or kits of advertising materials are to be provided for the salesmen to use in their activities, what materials will be provided for dealers' salespeople, and whether any direct-action stimuli (such as sampling, premiums, introductory price offers, or contests) are to be used in the marketing campaign. For example, if the advertiser's salesmen are to use kits of advertising (including the detailed schedules of appearance of the advertisements and actual reproductions of the advertisements to appear in national magazines, as is often done), in their selling program to obtain stocking of the product by the dealers before the consumer advertising appears, it will be necessary to have the detailed advertisements created very early in the program. Thus, the time at which the artists and copywriters must finish their work and the production department of the agency must have advertisements actually produced will depend on the decisions regarding salesman activities and use of advertising reproductions.

SUMMARY

In summarizing some of the concepts involved in campaign strategy, the authors wish to emphasize that there are a number of important factors which must be considered.

As an example, Company X makes men's dress shirts and sport shirts along with pajamas, underwear, and sweaters. The company is one of the three largest sellers in the shirt field, uses national distribution, and concentrates its advertising on dress and sport shirts.

The consumers recognize that Company X offers good quality, style, and value. For many years, the officers believed that by adding more style, they could provide the glamorous image that would reflect product improvements. However, the growth of consumerism (in which the features tumbled dry, durable press, and others have become more important) has changed the situation so that the short-term and long-term objectives have become more divergent.

To set the campaign strategy Company X should evaluate the following factors:

1. Study the products and determine what characteristics or features to emphasize. (Should company emphasize contemporary styling, durable press, color combinations?)
2. Evaluate the market conditions and decide who the buyers of the product are and who influences the buyers. (To what extent do the wives influence their husbands in the purchase of shirts? How would this be decided if the emphasis is on color combinations?)
3. Look at how the product is being distributed and consider the best ways of utilizing the channels of distribution. (To what extent are the shirts presold? How effective can the salesmen in the retail store be in reaching the buyer?)
4. Determine what the plans of competition will be for the ensuing period, but do not allow this competition to dominate your planning. (Will the competition emphasize style and color?)
5. Ascertain in what stage of the product cycle the produce is at the current time. (The changes in style are still somewhat limited. Company X's products are in competitive stage.)
6. Review past advertising, sales figures, and market trends.
7. Correlate the planned campaign objectives with the long-term goals of the company.
8. Set the advertising budget on the basis of the objectives or purposes of the campaign.
9. Decide on the keynote appeal for the campaign.
10. Check on the media that can be used for the campaign.

QUESTIONS

1. In evaluating the strategy to use in an advertising campaign, one finds that few competing brands and products spend their advertising media allocations in the same proportions. Indicate how this should be considered.

2. A major advertising study concluded that the customers harbor resentment when they are subjected to information which carries no useful meaning for them. How might this conclusion affect the planning of a campaign?

3. What is the relationship of the advertising campaign to the marketing plan?

4. Contrast the planning of a campaign for a product with that of a political campaign.

5. How would the planning of a campaign for a local retailer differ from

planning a campaign for a manufacturer distributing a product on a national basis?

6. From a current issue of a general magazine find five advertisements which contain keynote ideas revealing strong creative insights which you believe are effective for a campaign.

7. An executive, in planning strategy for a campaign, recommended to the advertising department that it use a simulation method. It was his opinion that mathematical techniques could be applied to sift through the many different strategies which might be used. Comment.

8. Since the attitudes which people form toward products seem to be more dramatically influenced by actual usage and experience, it is difficult to develop a scientific approach to planning campaign strategy. Comment.

9. Develop a step-by-step procedure that you believe an advertising agency should follow in planning a campaign for a product.

10. How should a company decide whether or not it should vary the keynote theme in a campaign?

11. Assume that you are the account executive for a major advertising agency handling the following accounts:

  a) Polident (a preparation for cleaning dentures)
  b) Eversharp (new safety razor blades)
  c) A patent medicine
  d) A major piece of industrial equipment which is manufactured on order and will cost from $100,000 to $200,000 per unit.

Indicate what procedures you would recommend that the advertisers use to plan a campaign for each of these products including the selection of the keynote theme.

12. Although advertisers can use past experience, the way in which this can be correlated to the planning of current advertising strategy may be difficult to attain, because present problems are unique to the product, the company, and the competition. Comment.

CASE 1.   ARTHUR FOOD CO.
Planning a new special campaign

Arthur Food Co. and its domestic and foreign subsidiaries are engaged in the manufacture, packaging, and sale of an extensive line of food products. As a result of some test market studies the company has decided to offer a new line of prepared ready-to-serve foods.

The decision to offer prepared products of this type was based on the data of other firms in the field. The companies showed that they could provide better and more nourishing meals at lower costs to school districts, restaurants, hotels, airlines, and hospitals, than these organizations had been able to do.

Marketing

Arthur sells directly to chain, wholesale, cooperative, and independent grocery accounts, to distributors and to institutions, including hotels, restaurants, and certain government agencies, and sells indirectly through brokers and agents. In the United States, the Company has sales offices in most principal cities and distributes its products to approximately 10,000 customers. Arthur has a domestic sales force of approximately 750 employees who call on special customers and retail service stores.

Arthur uses advertising and sales promotional programs as important marketing tools. Almost all types of advertising media are used on both a national and local basis. During the last fiscal year consolidated expenditures for advertising and sales promotional activities were approximately 10 percent of consolidated sales.

Raw materials and supplies

Arthur manufactures its products from a wide variety of raw food products. Preseason contracts are made with farmers for a substantial portion of such raw materials as tomatoes, cucumbers, onions, potatoes, corn, and other vegetables. Such materials as fruits, dairy products, meat, sugar, and flour are purchased on the open market. Fish is obtained through direct negotiations with boat owners, at auctions, by posted offers, by periodically negotiated contracts, and by bid and ask transactions with suppliers. The cost of purchasing and processing seasonal materials necessitates borrowings which generally reach an annual peak in November.

Manufacturing processes

Substantially all the Arthur's products are manufactured and packaged ready to serve. Most products are prepared from recipes developed in the company's research laboratories and experimental kitchens. Ingredients are carefully selected, washed, trimmed, inspected, and passed on to modern factory kitchens where they are processed; after which the finished product is filled automatically into containers of glass, metal, plastic, paper, or fiberboard; which are then closed, sterilized (where appropriate), labeled, and cased for the market. Finished products are processed by sterilization, freezing, or pickling so that they will keep a reasonable length of time.

Tomato, potato, cucumber, and some other fruit and vegetable products are manufactured primarily on a seasonal basis. Many other products are produced throughout the year including baby foods, tuna and other fish products, beans, cooked spaghetti, soups, mustard, salad dressing, sauces, relishes, and vinegar.

Arthur has participated in the development of much of its food processing equipment, certain of which is patented.

Quality control and research

Arthur pioneered in the development of quality control in the processed food industry. Quality control staffs in the factories aid the manufacturing staff in obtaining the required degree of quality and uniformity of the finished product. Arthur also maintains an active research program, including research and development of mechanical harvesting methods and crop research, which has been successful in increasing the disease resistance, quality, and yields of tomatoes, cucumbers, pineapples, and other crops.

Agricultural specialists, working in association with personnel from universities and government, furnish contract growers for Arthur with new and improved tomato, cucumber, and potato and other plants and with advice about fertilizer technology and crop protection. Arthur also experiments with new methods of food processing and the development of new food products.

International operations

Arthur carries on extensive international operations. The major portion of Arthur's foreign sales is made in the United Kingdom, Canada, Italy, Australia, Mexico, Peru, Venezuela, the Netherlands, and Portugal, where processing facilities are located. Sales are also made in many other countries in Europe, South and Central America, Asia and Africa. Arthur's United Kingdom subsidiary accounted for 19 percent (no other foreign subsidiary accounted for as much as 10 percent) of the company's consolidated net sales. It is the intention of the Arthur Food Company to continue its policy of development of international markets. Financing needed to carry out this policy is generally sought in the countries concerned and from the cash resources of the company's subsidiaries involved.

Income from international operations is subject to fluctuation in currency values, export and import restrictions, and other factors. From time to time exchange restrictions imposed by various countries have restricted the transfer of funds between countries and between Arthur and its subsidiaries. The Arthur executives believed that because the other major competitors had set up subsidiaries to manage the food services on a professional basis, they would limit the market segment to working women and housewives for the prepared puddings, rices, fruit cups, and dinner items which they planned to offer.

Suggestions for advertising

The advertising agency account representative prepared the recommendations listed below:

Target audience to be reached. Working women (or housewives whose schedule doesn't leave time for preparation of meals) of middle-class (or higher) income status.

Advertising message. These products are part of an exclusive new line that—

a)   is fast, easy and convenient to prepare

b)   offers a variety of delicious dishes

c)   contains special, high quality, expensive ingredients not normally found in products of this type

d)   can be used to complement a special meal, enhance everyday meals, or be a complete meal

Media used and reasoning for same. Sunday supplements, women's service magazines (*Better Homes & Gardens, Sunset, McCall's, Ladies Home Journal, Woman's Day*), plus *TV Guide* and *Life*

1.   High quality reproduction will be necessary to bring across the message of quality, to show the ingredients in an appetite appealing way and to highlight usage.

2. Sunday supplements and women's magazines will be the most effective print media available to reach target consumers, in terms of readership and cost per reader. *Life* and *TV Guide* also will be included to gain immediacy of impact, especially in the introductory coupon ad. All other publications used will be monthlies, except for Sunday supplements.

3. A limited budget will not permit effective usage of broadcast media.

Sequence of advertisements.

The first ad should:

a)   illustrate that these products met a specific consumer need,

b)   make the consumer aware that these are exclusive products and part of a new line,

c)   emphasize the quality ingredients used which mandate a higher price.

d)   have considerable appetite appeal,

e)   entice the consumer to try the product.

(Since the products are more expensive than competitors', it is believed that a reduction in cost might stimulate initial trial. Therefore, a coupon will be added to the original ad. Although this coupon covers part of the list of ingredients, which were vital to the advertising message, it is considered to be important to initial usage, even though it detracted from the appetite–appeal objectives.)

Subsequent ads should:

a) emphasize individual products in the line,

b) introduce the consumer to various uses of the products

c) be appetite appealing,

d) include the fact that these products are part of a new product line and that other products of this nature are also now available for a variety of new, good-tasting, meal-enhancing dishes.

The vice president in charge of marketing believed that the campaign recommendations were satisfactory and indicated that Arthur Foods Co. should proceed. However, the president was not too satisfied with this approach. He stressed, "The approach is the same old sterotyped one that does not excite the housewife. I think it is essential for us to make a big splash in the announcement and the only way that this can be accomplished is with broadcast media with a dramatic appeal. If we follow the plan of the agency representative, we are not going to be able to get the consumer even to try the product. The industry is too competitive for us to enter what I know are the highest quality products in the market with this old establishment plan."

Case questions

1. Evaluate the suggested campaign as outlined by the advertising agency.

2. How important is it for Arthur to make a dramatic entry into this product field?

3. To what extent should information, argumentation, and motivation be used in appealing to the consumer for these products?

4. Do you believe the company should pinpoint the advertising to the female segment of the market? Why not put emphasis on men? On school children?

5. How will Arthur be able to get the stores to give adequate shelf space for the products?

CASE 2.   BROOKS, INC.
Deciding on the policy for an independent store

Brooks, Inc., a juvenile department store, is located on the outskirts of a major shopping area. The store was opened in 1960 and because of its location, it was able to secure a good selection of the national brands of merchandise. Each year the sales of the store continued to increase, so that by 1971 the sales volume was about two and one-half times greater than it had been in 1960.

The store handled only one make of shoes, the nationally advertised Buster Brown brand. However, for some time, Brooks had been receiving a great many requests from the customers for a cheaper shoe. Brooks checked the suppliers very carefully and found only one manufacturer who was turning out a lower-priced shoe of the quality it was willing to sell. This manufacturer did not do any advertising and sold primarily to large purchasers who sold under their own labels.

Unlike the large department store or chain outlet, the small independent retailer is much concerned with national brand merchandise. The chains and large stores are in a position to develop sufficient prestige of their own to secure public acceptance of the merchandise they sell. In fact, brand manufacturers will compete with each other to place their products with these stores.

The rapid growth of our suburban population, the substitution of the private automobile for public transportation, and the high cost rentals of central business districts have stimulated the spread of the type of retailer heretofore confined to Main Street into many outlying shopping districts. These retailers, in contrast to the exclusive specialty shop with its high-margin operation, are after high-volume, fast-moving, popular-priced, moderate-markup, and substantial-inventory merchandise. The successful operation of these stores depends in large measure on their ability to secure popular brands of merchandise.

When Brooks was opening its shoe department, the partners decided on handling Buster Brown shoes for the following reasons:

1. Potential volume. If more Buster Brown shoes are sold in the United States than any other brand, then Brooks should be able to sell more of this brand than any other brand that could be secured.

2. Popular or budget-priced. Brooks must be careful about handling low-priced merchandise. The chain stores, with their large purchasing power, can outbuy Brooks on low-priced goods. Neither can Brooks hope to build volume in a limited trading area of residents with moderate incomes if the store attempts to sell a high-priced shoe. The store must plan to sell a medium-priced shoe.

3. Quality and guarantee. The independent retailer must stand behind the goods he sells, the brand selected must prove its advertised worth, and its quality must warrant the building of customer loyalty.

4. Eye or style appeal. There are brands that have good customer acceptance but lack progressive designing. One of the other national brands offered excelled Buster Brown in styling but did not measure up in quality.

5. Protection against competition. There is really no advantage to building up consumer acceptance of a brand unless Brooks will be protected from unfair competition. The store must get an exclusive right to the brand in its trading area, and the price on the shoe should be set for all the merchants in the vicinity regardless of the volume they may sell. Not only in the shoe department, but in all the other departments, Brooks limited its merchandise to one brand. Only under the following circumstances did Brooks carry more than one brand:

   a)   Ample style selection could not be provided by one brand.
   b)   The brand selected was limited to a few special types of products within the line.

All products were in the moderate price range, except in a few cases where the top quality brand was only 15 percent to 20 percent more expensive. The difference in value to the customer in style and fit was so great as to make the price difference insignificant.

If Brooks decided to sell the cheaper shoes, it would be changing its basic merchandising policies. In adding this shoe to the shoe department, it would be in direct competition with the chain stores and large department stores. Furthermore, Brooks was worried that its regular customers might substitute the lower-priced shoes for Buster Brown products. Brooks realized, however, that it was losing a number of customers every day because it did not have a cheaper shoe to offer.

It was the opinion of Brook's general manager that the store should offer a cheaper shoe and it was not possible to maintain the current market position without adding this lower-priced product.

The president of the company, however, did not favor such a policy and stressed that it would be better to develop a more extensive promotional strategy for the Buster Brown shoes. He stated, "Brooks has the top shoe in the market. We have relied too much on national advertising and have failed to use local advertising to the degree that we should. Last year, we spent only $1,000 to advertise our shoe department. I am confident that if we double this amount in the current year, we will be able to increase our sales to a greater degree than trying to hold our volume through adding a cheaper shoe."

Case question (for cases 2–5)

Suppose you are an account executive in an advertising agency and have been assigned the job of developing the advertising strategy for these companies. Outline the strategy that you would adopt, taking into consideration:

1. Nature of the product
2. Consumer and market segment to be sought
3. Distribution policies
4. Buying motives and consumer behavior
5. Pricing policies
6. Marketing mix strategy

7. Advertising budget
8. Media selection
9. Competition
10. Economic effects

CASE 3. BUDGET, INC.

Budget, Inc. sells fabrics and sewing notions through 175 retail stores in 22 states. The company estimates that approximately 70 percent of its sales were fabrics and that the balance of such sales were sewing notions. Budget merchandise is in the medium price range and is sold primarily to housewives, schoolgirls, and working women for use principally in making women's and children's clothing. All stores are operated by Budget in leased premises located primarily in shopping centers and also in downtown business districts. Stores serve populations of at least 25,000. Budget does not franchise any of its operations.

Retail stores

Each store carries a large selection of fabrics, including cottons, rayons, silks, synthetics, woolens, and laces. These fabrics are first quality merchandise and do not include factory remnants, mill ends, or irregulars. Each store also sells notions, including threads, zippers, patterns, buttons, sewing accessories, and ornamentations. Approximately 75 percent of the yardage carried by each store is basic nonseasonal merchandise, and the remainder is for the spring and fall seasons. Seasonal fabrics are not carried over to the next season, but are reduced in price until sold.

A typical store consists of 4,500 square feet, of which approximately 90 percent is sales area. Most stores are air-conditioned, similar in physical layout, and contain fixtures made to Budget's specifications. Annual rent averages about $12,000 per store.

Each store has a manager, an assistant manager, and an average of four full-time sales clerks. Each store manager reports to a district manager, who is responsible for supervising a maximum of ten stores and who in turn reports to one of the area supervisors.

Suppliers and distribution

Budget has no long-term contracts for the purchase of merchandise and purchases no more than 10 percent of its merchandise from any one supplier. Budget has never experienced difficulty in obtaining satisfactory sources of supply.

Budget purchases substantially all of its merchandise directly from manufacturers. Most of the fabrics are delivered in bulk to Budget's distribution center and are unrolled, cut to 20 or 30-yard lengths and then double rolled on fabric boards labeled with its trademark. Merchandise is shipped from the center directly to its retail stores.

Up until two years ago, Budget's new stores were opened in major regional shopping centers. At that time, however, Budget began opening 50 percent of its new stores in neighborhood shopping centers, thereby broadening locations for expansion.

Budget plans to operate approximately 40 new stores in the current year. The average cost of opening a new store is $60,000, of which $45,000 is for merchandise inventory and the balance for fixtures. In recent years, a number of stores have been remodeled at a cost of approximately $15,000 each, and Budget plans to remodel approximately 20 additional stores within the next two years.

Budget is continuously seeking new store locations and reviews proposed sites for store locations recommended principally by shopping center developers and its own area supervisors and district managers.

Competition

The retail sale of fabrics and notions for home sewing is highly competitive. Budget's stores compete with large chain department stores, many of which have greater financial resources than Budget, and with independent and chain retail fabric stores. Budget believes that the variety of fabrics and notions it offers is greater than that generally offered by its competitors, and that its experience, volume purchasing, and specialization in the sale of fabrics and notions enable it to compete favorably with its rivals.

CASE 4.   HUBBARD COMPANY
Deciding on strategy for a technical product

The Hubbard Company manufactures dies, tools, and plastic molds. In addition, the products of these tools are carried through the manufacturing process to the production of finished pieces or completed instrument assemblies.

The work, composed of both industrial and consumer items, is largely on a job-order basis. The company employs from 100 to 125 and has been able to diversify its production quite satisfactorily.

Recently a designer, retained by the company on a consultant basis, designed a production tool that was accepted by the company on a royalty basis. The company decided to manufacture and sell this tool. The tooling and manufacturing problems were routine matters because of past experience in this work. However, the article to be made was the first product that the company planned to sell itself; therefore, it had to set up a marketing program. None of the company executives had had any marketing experience. This new tool, a unique electric soldering iron, was considered an advance in the soldering iron field. Because of the nature of the commodity, it was necessary to sell these irons through industrial outlets.

Twelve such outlets were obtained to cover all sections of the United States. Industrial trade papers and magazines carried full-page advertisements of the iron. The initial response was favorable and indicated that there was a potential demand from foreign, as well as domestic, markets.

At this time, a marketing research firm was engaged to analyze the sales possibilities of the iron. Although some attention had been given to marketing, it was easily apparent that it had been rather broad in nature and had extended mainly to plans on paper. The actual field work had not yet been undertaken.

As the field work was started, the advantages of the iron were studied:

1. The soldering iron's copper tip had a special plating which was good for approximately 400 hours of use. Because of this plating, it was not necessary to clean the tip.
2. The tip always maintained its original shape. This would offset at least $21 of the hidden costs in tip maintenance of ordinary irons.
3. A precise measurement of the amount of solder to be used was possible by adjusting a micrometer screw feed.
4. The plug-type tip was recessed so that the heater element was inserted into the tip. This was an important improvement because other irons on the market merely conducted heat from the element to the tip by a butt contact. Higher temperatures were possible with decreased wattage.

The research also revealed that:

1. The soldering iron was attractive to a wide market. Both skilled and unskilled persons expressed interest in the iron because of its simplicity of operation.
2. Factory personnel were difficult to train in new lines. Although the iron reduced the job of soldering to pulling a trigger, it would be difficult to train personnel to know what to solder and how to do it.

The research firm found that in a number of cases customers who had used the iron were not always pleased with the results. The follow-ups that were made showed that the difficulty came about primarily through improper use of the iron and ignorance of the principles of soldering. On the basis of its study, the research firm concluded that Hubbard Company must educate the trade in soldering techniques and in the adaptation of these techniques to its electric soldering iron.

To help solve this problem, the company began to send to all customers a monthly bulletin in which suggestions were included about the techniques the company desired its customers to use.

After the analysis, it was decided to use manufacturers' representatives, granting them the right to handle not more than three lines from three different companies. This policy was selected so that the representatives would have an adequate number of products to make their operations profitable; yet, at the same time, they would not spread their efforts among too many items. The representatives, in turn, selected distributors carrying both electrical and industrial items for the purpose of *demonstration selling only.*

CASE 5.   SUPERIOR, INC.

Superior, Inc. operates a chain of 40 supermarkets and one discount drugstore. In connection with its operations, Superior maintains centralized warehouse and distribution facilities. All of the supermarkets operate on a cash-and-carry basis under the name of "Superior."

Superior pursues a policy of selling its merchandise at relatively low gross-profit margins, which has resulted in a relatively high volume of sales per store. Superior's operations may be classified as "discount" rather than "conventional"—discount operations being differentiated from conventional by price-oriented merchandising, low gross-profit margins, and an absence of promotional items such as trading stamps, with the goal of obtaining high sales volume. Superior believes that its operations differ from the customary discount operation in that substantially all of its merchandise consists of nationally or locally known advertised brands instead of private labels.

Superior advertises through newspapers, radio, television, and handbills distributed to homes in the trading areas of its stores. Each store offers a wide selection of grocery products, meats, fresh fruits and vegetables, dairy and delicatessen products, frozen foods, beverages, beer and wine; and certain nonfood items such as housewares, hardware, dinnerware, glassware, health and beauty aids, and toys. Most departments are self-service.

Superior's gross sales in the last fiscal year consisted of: 65 percent groceries, 25 percent meat products, 5 percent produce, and 5 percent nonfood items. Superior has adopted an open dating policy pursuant to which many perishable food products are marked to indicate their age or the last date of their suggested use.

Superior also operates discount drugstores in four of its outlets. These stores offer a selection of nonfood products including health and beauty aids, nonprescription drugs, small appliances, toys, magazines, and sundries; and also sell certain food items such as candy, beer, and wine. The prescription drug departments are operated by a lessee. The drugstores are 3,700 square feet in size. Management is considering the conversion of certain of its smaller supermarkets to discount drugstores, and may open other drugstores.

Superior leases all of its stores. Nine of these stores were built to the company's specifications. The other were redesigned, remodeled, and expanded, or substantially refurbished, shortly after being leased to Superior stores. The supermarkets range from approximately 9,000 to 24,000 square feet.

Distribution

Superior operates a warehouse distribution system. Purchasing in large quantities for delivery to the warehouse distribution centers generally permits Superior to obtain better prices and maintain better inventory controls than could be obtained by purchasing for direct store delivery by each supplier. Substantially all of the items carried in the Superior stores, except for soft drinks, beer, wine, bakery products, and milk, are distributed from one of its distribution centers. The primary distribution center services all nonperishable products while perishable products are handled by the other center. The average distance from either distribution center to the stores is 11 miles.

To facilitate rapid inventory turnover, orders for merchandise are transmitted daily from the stores to Superior's data processing department which services the distribution centers. The order for each store is automatically keypunched and delivered to the appropriate distribution center. Store orders are processed through Superior's own computer, which is also used to control store and warehouse inventories and for other functions. The orders are then loaded on trailers for delivery to the individual stores. The merchandise ordered each day is delivered to the stores by the next morning, except for certain high-volume stores which also receive a night delivery.

Purchasing

Superior purchases its products from growers, manufacturers, processors, and brokers. New items are selected by a committee composed of

Superior's grocery merchandisers and the buyer specializing in that product. Because of the competition among Superior's suppliers Superior is not dependent on any individual supplier or suppliers for its products.

Competition

The supermarket business is highly competitive, particularly in the area in which Superior's stores are located. Superior competes with national and local chains and independent stores. A number of its competitors have larger financial resources. Although complete information is not available, Superior believes that it ranked fifth among the supermarket chains in its area in terms of sales.

CASE 6.   STERLING DRUG INC.
Responsibility in advertising

Sterling Drug Inc. was started on May 14, 1901, under the name The Neuralgyline Company. Its first employees were the two founders; now there are more than 15,000 men and women on the Sterling payroll. The first year's sales amounted to $10,000; sales today are in the vicinity of $300 million a year.

The founders were young men who pooled their talents, resources, enthusiasm, and hopes. W. E. Weiss, a pharmacist, and A. H. Diebold, his friend from high school days in Sistersville, West Virginia, started—appropriately as history was to prove—with a pain reliever called Neuralgine as their only product.

In the first year, Neuralgine was promoted by means of roadside signs nailed to fences and trees in the Wheeling area. In 1902, the management adopted an advertising budget of $10,000, an amount equal to the entire sales volume of 1901. Virtually the entire advertising appropriation was earmarked for expenditure in mass media in the form of two Pittsburgh newspapers. Sales increased, and the market was expanded from a local community affair into one of national dimensions and, decades later, of world scope.

The years went on and the business prospered. In 1917, the Neuralgyline Company name was dropped, and the business became known as Sterling Products Incorporated, the Sterling name, incidentally, coming from Sterling Remedy Company, one of the enterprises acquired in the early years.

When the United States entered World War I, the Alien Property Custodian seized the properties of enemy aliens. Among these properties were the shares of the Bayer Company of New York, Inc., which were owned at that time by aliens who had sought to establish a business in the American market.

A month after the 1918 Armistice, the government offered the Bayer stocks for sale at public auction to the highest American bidder. To the successful bidder would go a large plant, a relatively little known product called aspirin, a substantial number of physicians' drugs, and a line of dyestuffs.

Many American firms were interested in acquiring Bayer, including Sterling, which saw in Bayer Aspirin a product of genuine promise. Moreover, the Bayer business could provide the vehicle for diversification into the pharmaceutical field. The management asked itself: How much could Sterling afford to pay for Bayer? In their earlier years, the founders had had the courage to invest almost half their capital to acquire a business, now entirely forgotten, and to create an advertising budget equal to the previous year's entire sales. Now they decided to bid, if necessary, as much as their own business had earned in the almost 18 years of its existence up to that time.

More than 100 American firms participated in the bidding, which started at $1 million. When the auctioneer for the U.S. government finally banged his gavel as he said, "going, going, gone," Sterling had acquired the Bayer Company for $5.31 million, a figure which was only about $1 million less than the company had earned from 1901 through 1918.

Although the sales of aspirin were small, a separate Sterling subsidiary, also called The Bayer Company, was organized to market the product. An entirely new corporation, Winthrop Chemcial Co., Inc. (now Winthrop Laboratories), was formed to handle the pharmaceutical preparations, and the dye division was sold outright to another company.

That period, 1919–41, was an era in which the mission of the company —Sterling's business is everybody's health—began to be clearly defined. The business in Bayer Aspirin moved forward rapidly in response to the therapeutic magic of the product and the thrust of advertising in its behalf. In the United States, other products identified by honored names were added to Sterling's consumer lines—Phillips' Milk of Magnesia, Fletcher's Castoria, Haley's M-O, Dr. Lyon's Tooth Powder, Z.B.T. Baby Powder, Energine cleaner and lighter fluids, to mention a few. In addition, the business spread beyond U.S. boundaries—to Canada and Latin America in the western hemisphere, and overseas to the United Kingdom and as far away as the Philippine Islands. Today, the largest Sterling facility outside the United States is the manufacturing plant in the United Kingdom of Sterling-Winthrop Group, Ltd.

Year after year the advertising appropriations grew larger as sales increased. With the advent of radio, the management foresaw the extraordinary impact of this medium of communication and made the company a major radio advertiser. Such programs as the Bayer Album of Familiar Music and Manhatten Merry-Go-Round helped to raise the level of musical appreciation in the United States. The company also used the soap operas which morning and afternoon brought to the busy housewife stories that evoked gentle tears and happy endings.

Winthrop brought Sterling into the pharmaceutical field with a list of renowned preparations. One was Luminal, the original phenobarbital. Others were Salvarsan and Neo-Salvarsan, the first effective drugs in the treatment of syphilis. To bring these drugs into the widest possible use in the shortest time, the company collaborated with government agencies and with local clinics in giving to physicians demonstrations of the techniques of treatment with the famed "magic bullet" invented by Ehrlich.

The sulfa drugs represented still another advance in chemotherapy in the 1930s. Winthrop introduced Prontosil, first of the sulfas, to the American medical profession.

Winthrop made other significant contributions, notably in anesthesiology. Through Novocain and later Pontocaine, a new technique in anesthesia was unveiled.

Winthrop not only offered these anesthetics to the medical profession —it organized medical teams to work with anesthesiologists in clinics to perfect techniques in basal, intravenous, infiltration, and spinal anesthesia. Thereafter, Winthrop produced motion picture films demonstrating these specialized techniques, which were projected to tens of thousands of doctors and medical students.

Sterling products are available today in 123 countries. They can be found in the family medicine chest. Many are particularly useful in hospitals to save life, to relieve pain, to facilitate diagnosis, to build tissue, to control infection, to produce anesthesia, even to curb colds, clear stuffy noses, and eliminate sniffles. Also useful in their relation to health are other Sterling products such as animal vaccines and vitamins for food enrichment; disinfectants, insecticides, and rodenticides; even optical brighteners in laundry detergents. One more recent discovery is not a product but a process—the Zimmermann Process—which makes a significant advance in sanitary engineering through its efficiency in disposing of industrial and community stream-polluting wastes.

More than a thousand Sterling products—professional, consumer, and industrial—are identified by brand names and trademarks. Brand names enable the consumer to reward the producer by buying his product again when it gives satisfaction, or to punish him by not buying again if the product fails to deliver value. The goodwill which brand names symbolize is what makes tomorrow's business more than an accident. And perhaps most important of all, brand names encourage the pursuit of excellence in the marketplace.

Glenbrook Laboratories

Glenbrook Laboratories is a division of Sterling Drug Inc. engaged in the manufacture and distribution of medicinal preparations advertised to the public and available without prescription.

The executives of the Glenbrook Laboratories believe their expenditures for advertising represent investments to help insure the continuity of the company, not alone in the present but also into the future. This objective conditions all their business judgments, including those related to the selection of advertising media.

The products which Glenbrook advertises—such as Bayer Aspirin and flavored Bayer Aspirin for children, Phillips' Milk of Magnesia both regular and flavored—are in most of the medicine chests in America. As part of its total marketing concept, Glenbrook advertises in newspapers, magazines, radio, professional and trade publications, and television. (See Exhibits 1, 2, and 3.) As to television network shows, its advertising participation is directed to those shows which will give it maximum advertising impact and the kinds of audiences indicated for each of its advertised products.

Glenbrook is a participating advertiser on television shows and a participating advertiser on nighttime and daytime television network shows with other advertisers.

Generally speaking, the selection of network television shows into which Glenbrook buys reflects, in a major degree, the recommendations of Dancer-Fitzgerald-Sample, its advertising agency associated with it for three decades of Sterling's growth. Neither Glenbrook nor the agency chooses any show because it happens to fall into a particular category —i.e., mystery, situation comedy. Their selections are made solely on the basis of specific shows which, in their judgment, reach in each case the kind of audience appropriate to Glenbrook's products. The agency's recommendation is made on the basis of a pilot film of a specific show. This permits the agency to form a judgment as to the type of audience the show is likely to attract, how the audience fits into its overall marketing program, and, hopefully, the size of the audience.

The agency receives advance scripts of various shows. Primarily, the agency examines each script from the viewpoint of insuring that it reflects the character of the show that Glenbrook bought into, as that character was projected in the pilot film. Glenbrook makes no attempt at censorship. It has no list of "musts" or "must-nots."

Glenbrook believes that an American business enterprise has a responsibility to serve a social as well as economic function. It acknowledges a social responsibility to the television audience, which it exercises by associating Glenbrook only with those shows that, in its judgment, are fit to be seen in the American home.

EXHIBIT 1

HOW TO BE SURE
your youngsters take the laxative they need

Give them Mint-Flavored Phillips' Milk of Magnesia. They'll like the taste. And it's the kind of laxative doctors recommend.

Mint-Flavored Phillips' tastes so good, children and grownups alike take it happily. What's more, when the makers of Phillips' Milk of Magnesia asked thousands of doctors, "Do you ever recommend milk of magnesia?" the overwhelming majority said, "Yes."

Phillips' Milk of Magnesia brings really complete relief because it is both a laxative and antacid, so it relieves both constipation and the acid indigestion that so often accompanies it. Get Mint-Flavored Phillips' Milk of Magnesia for your family. Also still in regular form. Get Phillips' today.

Courtesy: Glenbrook Laboratories
Division of Sterling Drugs, Inc.

EXHIBIT 2

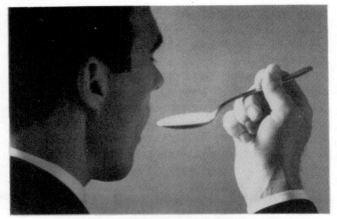

When you've got acid indigestion...

"Boy, what a difference Phillips' Milk of Magnesia makes!"

That's the feeling of Phillips' Milk of Magnesia! As soon as you take it, Phillips' liquid action goes right where the trouble is, to relieve upset stomach, heartburn, queasiness, and other discomforts of acid indigestion *in seconds!*

Many people like the feeling of Phillips' Milk of Magnesia even better in its refreshingly tangy mint-flavored form. Either way, Phillips' is one of the fastest and most effective stomach acid neutralizers known to medical science.

Next time you suffer from upset stomach, heartburn, or other discomforts of acid indigestion, take Phillips' Milk of Magnesia and feel better *in seconds!*

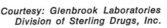

Courtesy: Glenbrook Laboratories
Division of Sterling Drugs, Inc.

EXHIBIT 3

The most important minutes of your summer day

When hot weather makes you feel tense, irritable, headachy, two Bayer Aspirin and a short rest can help you feel better fast!

It happens to most of us on a hot, humid summer day, when the pressures of daily living mount up. By mid-afternoon we feel so head-achy and edgy that we're in no mood to enjoy life or the company of others.

Here's how to turn that mood around: just take two Bayer Aspirin for your headache, sit down for a few minutes and re-lax. These few minutes can make a world of difference in the way you feel and act. You'll enjoy being with people, and they'll en-joy being with you.

When you get headachy and out of sorts on a hot afternoon, set aside a few minutes for Bayer Aspirin and a brief rest. These can be the most important min-utes of your day.

Courtesy: Glenbrook Laboratories
Division of Sterling Drugs, Inc.

Insofar as television advertising—and all other activities—are concerned, Glenbrook believes it has economic and socioeconomic responsibilities to sections of the American audience: to its shareholders, in providing a fair return on investment in the company; to employees, in assuring continuing job security at good pay and in working conditions that meet today's standards; to the 19 communities in 14 states in which Sterling's facilities are located, in contributing to job opportunities for local residents; to the retailers of America who have invested capital, time, skill, and energy in its products, in helping them to move Glenbrook's goods off the shelves into the medicine chests of America.

Beyond these responsibilities, Glenbrook is mindful that Sterling's business is everybody's health. It hopes, therefore, that the total operation, including advertising, prospers so well that it will be in the future, as it is today, in position continually to expand its research looking to the development of new and improved products that will contribute to the preservation of life and the protection of health.

Case questions

1. In your opinion, does Glenbrook plan its advertising programs effectively?

2. What changes would you suggest, if any?

3. Should advertising inform the public not only about the products but also about the principles, goals, and objectives of the Glenbrook company?

4. How can Glenbrook maintain or improve its image through advertising?

5. What other policies should Glenbrook consider in advertising is products?

CASE 7. FRUIT EXCHANGE
Reaching minority groups

The Fruit Exchange is a large agricultural cooperative with annual fruit and juice sales valued at more than $90 million. The company has recently received a letter from CORE, a group supporting racial equality. The letter stated that unless the faces of minority groups appeared on an equal basis in all of the future advertisements of the exchange that action would be taken against the exchange.

The Fruit Exchange. Individual growers band together in local associations, which in turn are members of a district exchange. Each district is a member of the parent Fruit Exchange. Membership is limited to actual producers.

Local packing units. Most of the local packing units are cooperative associations of growers, incorporated for business purposes. Others are large producers, individuals, and corporations who pack only the fruit from their orchards in their privately owned packing houses. Still others are commercial packing companies which grade and pack the fruit of individual growers at a fixed charge.

Local cooperative associations pack and market the fruit products of the members. Member growers own and control these local associations. Before he can have a voice in the management of his association, each member is required to sign a uniform contract. This contract binds the grower to deliver all fruits grown upon his property.

There is no charge for membership. To provide physical facilities and operating funds, almost all associations use "revolving funds," a revolving capital plan, whereby a specific retainer is deducted from sales proceeds due members for fruit handled.

District exchange.   Each local packing unit is represented on the board of directors of one of the 20 district exchanges. And the number of local packing units making up district exchanges ranges from 3 up to 20.

The district exchange is strategically placed between the local packing unit, whose members grow the fruit, and the central exchange, which coordinates all the activities of the entire exchange system. The main function of a district exchange is the shipping and distribution of packed fruit received from member packing units. Such involved marketing functions are impossible for the individual grower or shipper to operate efficiently.

Each member unit agrees to market all fruit products subject to its control through the district exchange with which it is affiliated. The district exchange, in turn, agrees to market all fruit products subject to its control through the central exchange. As in the case of the local packing associations, both district exchanges and the central exchange have authority to retain from sales proceeds sufficient sums to cover all charges and expenses, and to establish reasonable reserves.

Not more than one quarter of the district exchanges own physical facilities other than office furniture and fixtures. A few own their own office buildings, but generally little capital is required.

Central exchange.   Each of the 20 district exchanges elects a representative to serve on the board of directors of the central exchange. Exchange directors receive no salary for this service. The directors, who elect the officers and general manager of the central exchange, hold open meetings. The central exchange is divided into six main departments, each responsible for certain functions:

The sales and advertising department handles the sale and advertising of all products.

The traffic department handles all routing of shipments, inspections, claims, and freight and shipping cost problem.

The field service department provides the growers with scientific information on culture, harvesting, packing, and pest control. It is also responsible for enforcing the strict grading regulations. Field men make frequent inspections on the quality of fruit packing and on the grading done in the packing houses.

The research department studies and develops new products, processes, and methods. It is concerned with both fresh fruits and by-products. Its two laboratories study such problems as the storage, precooling, and respiration of various fruit products and the development of products from juices and peel constituents.

The functions of the *executive* and *treasury departments* are self-explanatory.

Advertising

The exchange advertises extensively in all national media and has placed more emphasis on the cumulative value appeals than on those which might produce immediate sales.

The advertising varies in summer and winter. In summer, emphasis is on the exchange's juice products. In winter, emphasis is on the distinctive qualities of the exchange's fruit products in order to hold and increase consumer demand and to maintain the premium price which the exchange has been able to secure.

Problem.   The above letter was a result of several factors. A few years ago, CORE achieved its first successful breakthrough in the area of integrated advertisements with Lever Brothers, the nation's sixth largest advertiser. This gave the organization a strong basis from which to launch its campaign to make advertising in general a "more realistic reflection of the composition of the American population."

A second factor was centered around a meeting called by CORE. This was a group approach in its drive and there was an attendance of 64 of the country's advertisers. The group listened to CORE's presentation and was asked to keep the committee informed of individual plans for the utilization of blacks in advertisements. Representatives of the exchange did not attend the meeting.

The letter sent to the exchange noted that a review of the exchange's advertising had shown there was no discernible progress toward the use of blacks in general media. It also said that the exchange appeared to have a general lack of understanding of and appreciation for the civil rights efforts to make advertising a more meaningful reflector of all segments of American life. It further stated that, while the exchange had stepped up its advertising in black media such as *Ebony* and *Amsterdam News,* the exchange had made no use of blacks in general ads, "even those including group scenes where it would have been quite possible to do so." It added pointedly that increased schedules in black publications "is not what we are after."

The letter then went on to state that if there was no answer from the exchange officials, and no signs of "good faith," the exchange might be singled out for selective patronage (boycotting) techniques.

Another part of the problem stems from the following:

An executive of the publishing company which puts out the prominent magazines *Ebony, Jet, Negro Digest,* and *Tan* stated that in order to achieve maximum impact within the black market, integrated advertisements must be placed in media which are orientated to the whole of black existence. Unless the advertisement is supported by an atmosphere geared or oriented to meet the needs of all consumers, it will not have the most efficient and effective selling power.

He also indicated that the basic problem found in using integrated advertising in general media is that this media is really a special media geared primarily to a special white audience. The editorial features in such white-orientated media are predominantly about people with whom blacks cannot identify in realistic, true-to-life experience. Many of the advertisements, especially those of a service or recreational nature, are obviously not for black participation.

While some of the "white-orientated media" run occasional stories on blacks, they do not give substantial attention to the black as a human being. It is impossible to expect maximum results from integrated advertisements in media which ignore these vital dimensions of the black consumers' lives.

The executive also pointed out that until there is a truly integrated society and until all media reflect the needs and desires of all consumers, it will not be possible to base an effective campaign on integrated advertising appeals alone. Until that day arrives, he recommended that a study of the black consumer be made in the various markets in which he lives.

Supplementing the above are the findings about the media study as related to the black market, in Exhibit 1.

EXHIBIT 1. Black viewers of top shows in prime time

Rank with blacks	Rank total audience	Show	Black hshlds. (000)	Total hshlds. (000)	Black percent of total
1	13	Jackie Gleason	2,685	14,767	18.2
2	3	Perry Mason	2,590	19,489	13.3
3	10	Gunsmoke	2,261	15,474	14.6
4	30	Defenders	2,190	11,658	18.8
5	17	Sat. Night Movies	2,049	13,566	15.1
6	6	Red Skelton	1,641	16,628	9.9
7	25	Route 66	1,526	12,107	12.6
8	9	The Nurses	1,517	15,689	9.7
9	5	Ed Sullivan	1,497	17,835	8.4
10	16	Rawhide	1,369	13,648	10.0

Analysis. The black represents a purchasing power in the United States of some $20 billion—approximately equal to that of Belgium, Sweden, Denmark, and Norway combined. Even more significant is the expected increase over the next decade and a half. The black population, which in 1962 was 19 million in the United States, is expected to number 33 million by 1980, when the black purchasing power will reach a level of $38 million.

Advertisers who talk to blacks never have to look hard for them. The Census Bureau reported nearly one third of the 19 million U.S. blacks live in the 25 largest cities, comprising 20 percent of the total population of these cities. In 78 of the largest cities, where 90 percent of wholesale sales and two thirds of all retail sales in the United States are made, the black makes up 25 percent of the population.

An attempt to appeal simultaneously to both the black and the white market is very complex. The dangers involved lie in extremes. On one extreme is the direct-appeal approach—selecting media and copy directly for blacks. On the other is the policy of using indirect appeals for the general market on the assumption that blacks will also be reached.

Using the direct appeal often assumes that the black market is more special than it is, and because of this assumption one misses the heaviest and most persistent purchasers—the more stable majority.

Case questions

1. Is there a significant difference in the appeals that should be used for the different minority groups?

2. What recommendation would you give to the Fruit Exchange to follow in answering the letter it received?

3. Plan a campaign for the Fruit Exchange that would attempt to reach the black and other special racial groups. To what extent could one general campaign be used for everyone?

chapter 18

CAMPAIGN EXECUTION

T<small>HE</small> <small>SUCCESSFUL</small> execution of an advertising campaign depends upon the alertness with which the advertiser senses the consumers' desires and his speed in satisfying them. This is because the market condition are dynamic and the nature of the buying process is subject to rapid variations. As a result, the proper timing of a campaign can be even more essential than the development of the keynote idea and the selection of the media.

As an example, studies have pinpointed that advertisers can speed up fashion movements, but they generally cannot profitably move styles as they wish. The consumer wants what she wants at the time when she wants it. When a high percentage of men decided to stop wearing hats, the industry advertised to convince them how they might profit by wearing hats. However, the advertising did not convince them to change their habit and the negative shift in the demand curve for hats continued.

For an advertising campaign to be successful, the advertiser must evaluate not only all the major campaign decisions which should be made in order that the details of the program will be carried out, but it is also critical to be sure that the timing of when it will be executed fits market conditions.

KINDS OF CAMPAIGNS

The following are a few of the principal bases of classification of campaigns usually used. Frequently, the basis will be the audience to be reached and influenced by the campaign, such as consumer, trade, or industrial campaigns. The media may be the basis, such as direct-mail, magazine, newspaper, outdoor, radio, or television campaigns. At times, the function or objective may be the basis, as in the case of primary demand or selective demand campaigns, institutional campaigns, or introductory or continuation campaigns. One of the more important bases of classification is geographical, or that of the territory involved, in which instance the usual division is that of local, zone or regional, and national campaigns. In the local and zone campaigns, the advertiser selects a restricted or limited geographical area and concentrates his advertising efforts in that particular area. The national campaign is broader in scope and is directed to consumers in several regions or throughout the nation. The chief differences lie in the size of the territories covered, the media used, and in the fact that for the local and regional campaigns such types of advertising as direct-action advertising may be used to a greater degree than in the national campaigns.

Local campaigns

Local campaigns are those that are confined to a single trading area. Most such campaigns are those of retail stores, although some wholesalers who limit their distribution primarily to one large trading area may use local campaigns. Also, some small manufacturers with a strictly local market use this type of campaign for promoting their products. In certain circumstances, large manufacturers who normally use national advertising may also use the local campaign. For example, they may use such a campaign in testing proposed advertising programs designed for later use on a national scale. However, since most local campaigns are retail campaigns, the discussion will be centered on such.

The retailer should plan his advertising program with the same care as was outlined above for the national advertiser's campaign. He should think in terms of what image he is trying to create for his store, his present and potential customers, the objectives or purposes of his coming period's advertising, the media available and best suited to his needs, the necessary budget, the coordination of all phases of his advertising and selling activities, and other necessary considerations.

He should plan the desired amount for institutional advertising, the regular merchandise advertising in terms of items and departments of his store, the holiday promotions pertinent to his line of merchandise, and the special promotions and sales that he plans for the year. He must also allocate funds to the various media.

Most retailers rely heavily on newspapers, shopping news type publications, and direct-mail media, although some may make fairly heavy use of local radio and television, and of transportation and outdoor advertising. For any seasonal or special promotion, there should be close coordination of the media advertising and the displays, and the salespeople should be trained to gear their selling efforts into the promotional activities.

The retailer can obtain aid in the planning of his advertising programs from materials and information provided by national trade associations, such as the National Retail Dry Goods Association, or by local media, such as local newspapers. They normally will provide a "Retail Planning Guide" which will list such dates as all-important national holidays, "weeks," as well as special local events, conventions, and activities that may provide the occasion for special promotions. Many national advertisers provide their retail outlets with advertisements in the form of mats, point-of-purchase materials, spot announcements, and proposed advertising schedules for the coming six months or year that are geared into their national advertising program. Thus, although the retailer may have many more short-term, special-event promotions than the national advertiser, which require, to a degree, a special advertising theme or program, he should still keep in mind that there must be an underlying basis or purpose for his entire advertising program.

The zone or regional campaign

The zone or regional campaign is one that is limited to a geographical region consisting of several trading areas. It might be a portion of one state, or include a whole area, such as the New England states. Distributors and wholesalers whose distribution is limited to such a region, retail chain organizations with outlets covering only a limited area, and manufacturers whose distribution is geared to a particular area use the zone type of campaign. National advertisers may also use the zone campaign in various circumstances. For example, a manufacturer of lightweight suits might regularly launch his advertising at different times in various regions of the country in order to take full advantage of the beginning of warm weather. He might also wish to vary his advertising by regions to meet area differences in buying habits and living conditions, to satisfy unusual trade conditions in the area, to meet the competition of a strong regional brand, or to bolster sales in regional zones in which he has traditionally been weak.

The regional campaign may be used by the national advertiser for testing purposes rather than restricting it to a local campaign. In this manner he can uncover faults, weaknesses, or omissions in his advertising and selling methods without the risks involved in a national campaign. Probably the most frequent use of the regional campaign is for the introduction of a new product. In the first instance, the regional method of introduction not only enables the firm to test its product before launching the program nationally, but also has advantages in facilitating the starting of regular plant production and the training and supervising of its sales force for the introductory program.

For example, a major soft drink bottler used the zone campaign approach to introduce its product. It faced strong competition from established brand names, such as Coca-Cola. These other soft drinks could be bought throughout the country, and had gained general acceptance on a national basis, and were advertised heavily on a national scale. In order to sell its product on a national scale, the company would have been required to spend millions of dollars in advertising to stimulate demand. To minimize its risk and to facilitate its operational efforts, the firm decided to follow the zone campaign method of marketing in introducing its product. Its first zone embraced only a small area of a few counties around Dallas, Texas. Intensive advertising and selling efforts resulted in intensive distribution, good sales, and a satisfactory profit from operations. Additional areas were added, until the firm attained national distribution and could use national advertising. In this manner, the firm was able to develop its national market with a relatively small amount of invested capital, and with a minimum of risk.

In most respects, the planning and execution of the zone campaign are similar to the strategy discussed earlier for a local campaign. Here again, the main difference arises in the media to be used. Zone campaigns can use newspapers, local radio and television, direct mail, and transit, outdoor, and point-of-sale materials. Today magazines can also be utilized effectively, as it is possible to buy space in the geographic and/or demographic editions of most national magazines that match the advertiser's distribution. Media must be selected carefully to obtain adequate coverage of the zone involved at a reasonable cost per thousand potential customers.

The national campaign

The national campaign is one embracing a number of zones or regions, or the entire country. It is used by the manufacturer who has become so well established that he has distribution of his product in a number of regions or nationally, and by the new manufacturer when he has obtained satisfactory distribution in a number of areas and wishes to use a single campaign to bolster his zone campaigns and cover gaps between the zones that may not be covered satisfactorily by the individual zone campaigns. Occasionally, a national campaign is used by a new manufacturer entering the market, as was true of the introduction of a number of the brands of cigarettes. Some of the large national firms introduce new products to the market with national campaigns. An example would be the introduction of new razor blades by the Gillette Company.

The introduction of a new product by means of a national advertising campaign and marketing plan calls for expenditure of a major sum of money and for considerable skill in coordinating all parts of the overall marketing plan. An example of the scope of a national campaign is the one used by the Westinghouse Electric Corporation. This was the largest advertising and promotion campaign in the company's history and was the first step in a program to achieve a billion dollars in annual sales of consumer products and to gain dominance in each of its product fields. The same program included intensified efforts in behalf of all the firm's industrial products, with dominance in each product field as the ultimate goal. The campaign was designed to embrace all media and "to tell and show all segments of the American public, everywhere and time after time, that Westinghouse is the company to watch." The campagin was spearheaded by the company's consumer products division, but cut broadly across all the varied Westinghouse product lines. The advertising campaign included six broad efforts:

1. A product presell campaign in newspapers in all the nation's market areas
2. A simultaneous and continuing campaign addressed to Westinghouse dealers in the leading dealer trade publications
3. An image-building campaign comprising multicolor, often multipage, institutional-type and product ads in major magazines
4. Messages on the Westinghouse television show keyed to "Watch Westinghouse" theme
5. The most extensive and effective dealer-aid program in Westinghouse history, comprising more and better displays, customer literature, demonstration devices, vastly enlarged cooperative advertising opportunities, and plans for training salesmen and increasing store traffic
6. Advertisements for the company's utilities, again keyed to the same theme, in leading trade and technical publications

Much of the advertising emphasized the full line of Westinghouse consumer products, attempting to capitalize on the inherent strength of Westinghouse and its importance to the company's distributors, dealers, and customers. The product presell campaign comprised four big one-a-week advertisements in newspapers in the major nation's markets, and a saturation campaign on radio stations in those markets that included as many as 100 messages a week, where time was available. This blended into a continuing product advertising program in the same markets, and both campaigns were augmented by dealer-company cooperative advertising in papers in many cities, hamlets, and rural areas. The objective of the product presell campaign was to stimulate the public appetite for familiar Westinghouse products. The image-building campaign was designed to build in the public mind a picture of Westinghouse as a company of people working to produce more and better products for the American home and industry.

The overall program was more than an advertising and promotion program. Stepped-up product development and better styling was also a vital and integral part of the program. All facets of the program were part of a long-range plan to put Westinghouse consumer products in a position of dominance.

Another example of a national campaign is the one of Douglas Fir. This firm decided to concentrate its advertising dollars in print media. In attempting to reach the five major markets for plywood—residential construction which accounts for 45 percent of plywood sales, commercial construction (20 percent), industrial (15 percent), and do-it-yourself and agricultural construction (each 10 percent)—Douglas used publicity and sales literature which it distributed through lumber dealers. It also used a small schedule in *Family Circle, Home Craftsman, Mechanix Illustrated, Popular Mechanics, Sunset* magazine, *Family Handyman,* and *Science and Mechanics.* The general business publications included were *Business Week* and *Fortune* to reach top management.

American Builder, NAHB, Journal House & Home, and *Practical Builder* were used to present case histories of use of plywood. *Building Standards Monthly* and *Southern Building* were included in order to reach building code officials. *Building Materials, Merchandiser, Plywood, Building Products, Building Supply News* and a number of regional publications were used to reach dealers. Publications which were added to reach architects included *Architectural & Engineering News, Progressive Architecture, AIA Journal,* and *Architectural Record.*

Advertising directed to engineers and contractors was placed in *Contractors & Engineers, Engineering News Record, Contractor News,* and *Construction* Methods. *The Farm Journal, Successful Farming, Pacific Poultryman, Broiler Business,* and *Poultry Tribune* were used for the promotion of plywood for farm buildings.

Campaign execution

The details of the execution of the campaign will vary depending upon whether the campaign is one for: a consumer product; an industrial product; a product which will be pushed or pulled through the channels of distribution; a product that is being introduced into the market for the first time; a shopping good; or a fashion good. The size of the budget, the length of the campaign, and the economic conditions that exist are also factors which must be taken into account.

The coordination of the execution of the campaign is generally the responsibility of the company's advertising manager. That is, the advertising manager must work closely with all parties involved to see that the preparation of the advertisements and the materials meets the scheduled planned programs for the salesmen, middlemen, retailers, and consumers.

When an advertising agency is used, the agency team for the account would normally take over the details of executing the direct facets of the campaign. That is, the account executive and his account group (usually including representatives of the copywriting group, research department, art department, and media department) take over the responsibility for seeing that the advertisements are produced and published or broadcast on schedule. This is true for all the advertisements to appear in media directed to the consumer, as well as for those directed to various levels of the trade, which include display materials, salesmen's aids, publicity releases, and any other materials to be used in merchandising the advertising.

In addition to the above, the advertising manager must control the advertising budget. He must handle the approval and payment of the invoices for the advertising materials and services involved in the campaign. He must be sure that all people involved use the budgeted advertising dollars economically. Periodically he should review the advertising expenditures to date, and analyze and evaluate the advertising done and the results obtained, in terms of such factors as sales volume, share of market, competitive marketing activity, status of general economic conditions, and profit. This evaluation should, in turn, be reviewed by the top marketing and financial executives of the firm, and consideration should be given to several questions, including:

1. Are the basic economic conditions on which the campaign planning was done still in existence?
2. Are we presently within our budget, and shall we stay within it?
3. Are our tests of advertising effectiveness indicating that our campaign is accomplishing the objectives we established? If not, why is it failing?
4. In view of the results achieved to date, is there any reason why we should decrease or increase our advertising effort? If so, what changes should be made?
5. Have any new and unexpected developments taken place, either internally or externally, that would call for changes in the planned campaign?

Other aspects of coordination

In the actual carrying out of the campaign, the advertising manager and the agency account executive must work together to see that all facets of the program are properly coordinated. Also, if the advertiser has a number of divisions or product lines with individual advertising programs, the advertising manager must check closely to see that all the individual campaigns are coordinated and compatible in terms of objectives, and that there is consistency in the appeals and copy of the advertisements.

It is also the responsibility of the advertising manager to insure that other departments of the company are notified in proper time of the advertising program, so that they can carry out their obligations. This is especially true of the production departments and the sales departments. If, for example, a special promotion and intensified advertising campaign is to be carried on for a certain period, the production department must be able to plan to have adequate stocks available in the proper areas, and the sales force must have notice so they will be sure all retailers and wholesalers have adequate stocks on hand prior to the anticipated sales increase.

The salesman should also be informed about the trade advertising which is being done to pave the way for his sales calls. Such trade advertising normally tells the dealer (or industrial user) how he will gain by stocking or purchasing the advertiser's product. The salesman can then coordinate his sales approach with the advertising message.

For these reasons the sales force should know the underlying basis for the campaign, the basic theme of the advertising (and the reason for its adoption), the type of ads to be used, the media to be used, and the schedule of advertising. This information can be given to them in various ways—through letters, sales meetings, films, brochures, closed-circuit television presentations, and so on. In many cases, firms also provide the salesmen with portfolios containing samples of national consumer ads to be run, media schedules, and samples of materials available to the retailer.

Since frequently display materials are distributed to dealers through the sales force, it is important that the advertising manager work closely with the sales managers to see that the salesemen give proper push and stress to obtaining wide use of these items. It usually takes aggressive and enthusiastic support from the sales force to achieve good distribution and use of such point-of-purchase materials. As noted elsewhere, there is such keen competition for shelf space in the retail store today that it takes unusually effective personal selling to achieve reasonably satisfactory use of an advertiser's point-of-purchase materials. In some instances, in order to obtain dealer support in the form of display and push of their advertised product, advertisers pay the retailer for preferential display or shelf space. Since this is a form of advertising allowance, the manner in which such allowances are made available is covered by the provision of the Robinson-Patman Act. In essence, this act states that such advertising allowances are discriminatory, and thus illegal, unless made available on proportionately equal terms to all competing customers.

As part of the overall program to achieve effective marketing of his product, the advertiser may wish to have the retailer promote his product through the use of dealer cooperative advertising (also known as manufacturer's cooperative advertising, or vertical cooperative advertising). This is the policy on the part of the advertiser to make an allowance to the retailer for a part of the cost of advertising his product on the part of the retailer. For example, the manufacturer might adopt a policy of paying one half of the space cost of any advertising of his product done by the retailer. The manufacturer may have a number of policies regarding the type and amount of advertising which will qualify for the allowance. He may specify that only certain media be used. He may insist that the advertisement itself meet certain specifications such as: it must be devoted to the manufacturer's products; it must be regular price advertising of the merchandise; it must contain certain copy appeals; and so forth. And he may place restrictions on the total dollar amount that will be paid, such as a certain percentage of total purchases of his product by the retailer.

Putting campaign to work

As an example, consider the problem of a major bus company which had centered its appeal on "cheapest way to get there." As a result of improvement in equipment and in types of travel service offered, it wished to change its image and attract customers who would appreciate the "fun" of traveling by bus. The company believed that it had much "happy travel" to offer. It was now able to preplan vacations; it had slumber-stop service, through-express schedules, and a fleet of long-distance coaches, all available at low cost.

Its preplanned vacations include transportation, hotels, and sightseeing tours. The vacations are entirely flexible and may be shortened or lengthened to fit the traveler. Slumber-stop service means that the traveler can travel by bus from New York to San Francisco with a hotel reserved automatically along the way every night. Through-express buses operate from principal cities. The scenicruiser and highway traveler buses include wide-view picture windows, air conditioning, roomy, adjustable seats, and an air-suspension system which consists of flexible rubber-nylon air bellows and take the place of conventional metal springs. In addition, the scenicruiser has a unique two-level seating arrangement for passengers. The upper deck, seats 36 passengers who ride "above the traffic." Complete washrooms are also a part of each bus.

The strategy that was selected in the campaign was to concentrate on the "happy travel" connotation that would be associated with the fun of traveling by bus.

In putting this campaign into action, it was necessary for the company to take this general appeal and correlate it to the media (radio and television spots, magazines, transit advertising, outdoor boards, and such point-of-sale material as folders, quarter cards, posters, and window banners) that were selected, as well as to get the message to the traveling public through club and school lectures, guest appearances, and radio and television interviews.

The company also recognized that it had to do a thorough training job with its sales personnel because it had found that agents and ticket clerks can convince the traveler to buy round trip tickets by asking, "Round trip?" instead of simply taking an order.

The company recognized in setting up the campaign that it not only had to do a broad promotional job with the general traveling public, but also had to get full participation from its employees if the campaign was to be successful.

Conclusion

An advertising campaign is a complex plan and must be kept fluid enough to meet the shifts in consumer demand and the intensification of competition. Decisions for the campaign must also be made in the light of both the long-run effects as well as the attainment of short-term objectives. How will a campaign emphasizing price affect a long-range guide to action of producing high-quality products for a small segment of the market? How will giving "free samples" of candy affect the sales of a high-quality candy manufacturer?

As a result, within the framework of the basic marketing strategy, the details of the campaign must be constructed and executed. The basic activities are listed below, although it must be kept in mind that they will vary depending upon such factors as objectives, budget, and schedules.

1. Review the long-range marketing strategy and objectives of the company.
2. Set reasonable and, whenever possible, measurable objectives for the campaign.
3. Evaluate the timing strategy that will be adopted.
4. Determine the budget that will be needed to attain the objectives which have been set.
5. Firm the pricing strategy.
6. Design the package and trademark when necessary.
7. Select the media and firm the time and space schedules.
8. Develop the copy, scripts, etc. for the advertisements.
9. Establish the controls so that all phases of the campaign will be completed on schedule.
10. Develop the dealer merchandising plan that will be used.

11. Keep other departments of the company informed of what advertising is to be done for what products, and of the implications thereof for the department.
12. Work with the sales department to insure proper correlation with the use of trade advertising, consumer advertising, and cooperative advertising.
13. Control the advertising budget.
14. Evaluate the results of advertising as rapidly as possible after it is run, and assess the implications of findings.
15. Modify plans as is indicated by unexpected results of advertising or changes in actual conditions from those conditions assumed when plan was designed.

QUESTIONS

1. Discuss what you consider to be the important differences in executing an advertising campaign for a retailer and a national advertiser.

2. What are the distinctive features of a regional campaign?

3. Under what circumstances might a manufacturer with national distribution and advertising of his products utilize a regional campaign?

4. Do you think a large manufacturer of food products with national distribution and advertising (such as General Foods or General Mills), would ever use a local campaign? If so, under what circumstances?

5. One advertising manager states: "Recent changes in media arrangements are such that the choice of media for use in a regional campaign do not differ materially from those available for a national campaign." Would this statement be accurate for the geographical region in which you are living? Explain.

6. What are the responsibilities of the company's advertising manager in connection with the execution of the advertising campaign?

7. Which aspects of campaign execution would normally be handled by the agency account executive?

8. What do you understand by the statement: "It is the advertising manager's responsibility to exercise financial control of the campaign."?

9. As the advertising manager, what should you cover when you make your periodic review and evaluation of your advertising campaign?

10. Why is it important for the advertising manager to work closely with other departments of the company in the execution of the advertising campaign?

11. Explain how the advertising manager should work with which other departments of the company to assure success of his advertising campaign.

12. Assume you are the advertising manager for a large food products manufacturer, with national distribution, a sales force of 240 men organized in 24 districts, running campaigns for 11 major product lines, with a total budget of approximately $50 million, some $500,000 of which is budgeted for

trade advertising, some $3 million for point-of-purchase materials and promotions, and about $2 million budgeted for dealer cooperative advertising:

   a)   To what extent do you think your department should work with the sales department?

   b)   Explain how you would go about working with the sales department to assure maximum effectiveness for your advertising campaigns.

13. As the advertising manager, how would you try to assure effective use of your dealer cooperative advertising budget?

14. Visit a local supermarket or department store and determine their use of, and attitude toward, dealer cooperative advertising. What do they think are the good features and the weaknesses of such programs? Evaluate their comments.

15. Discuss what you consider to be the key aspects of executing the advertising campaign.

CASE 1.   MELVILLE SHOE CORPORATION
Considering a promotional campaign

Melville Shoe Corporation, a leading manufacturer and merchandiser of footwear, apparel, cosmetic, and health products is faced with the problem of developing an advertising campaign.

The Melville Shoe Corporation became an official entity in 1916 and by the early 1920s was a recognized leader in the industry.

As a result of the combination of Frank Melville's desire to work out a new and different arrangement for marketing a good quality, low-priced, mass-produced shoe, and his son, Ward, urging him to consider further expansion, the two began working out plans for a new Melville chain. The idea—developed with leading New England shoe manufacturer J. Franklin McElwain—was to establish a new kind of relationship between a manufacturer and a retailer. It guaranteed the manufacturer a steady market for his output and enabled the retailer to rely on a steady supply of good quality shoes manufactured to his specifications at reduced costs that allowed a low selling price, giving better value. J. F. McElwain Co., as the manufacturer, shared in the Melville profits, while Melville shared in the manufacturing profits. This arrangement, which is said to have been sealed with a simple handshake, continued until J. F. McElwain Co. became part of Melville in 1939.

On the retailing end, the Melvilles envisioned a chain with a standard store format that would be recognizable across the country and a brand name that could be considered truly national. Ward Melville, who had long been interested in architecture, played a major role in the development of the familiar "white front" Thom McAn store with the name attached in large script to the storefront itself. It is believed that this was the first time in the history of retailing that the store sign had been made a part of the storefront.

Ward Melville was also responsible for the name of the new chain. He found the original name in a roster of Scottish golf pros, added the *h* to "Tom" and took an *n* and a *c* out of the "McCann" and capitalized the *a*. The net result was to give the name novelty and brevity as well as projecting an image of quality and thrift. Originally, there was a picture of Thom McAn used in the firm's advertising, but it is said that it was actually a sketch of a Bowery bum, who had agreed to pose for the artist.

Today, Thom McAn—"the best selling shoe in all America"—is sold through 900 Thom McAn stores located in 44 states and Puerto Rico. Mostly because of Thom McAn's domination of the low-priced shoe field —as the Model T dominated the low-priced automobile field—Melville kept on growing and making a profit during the depression years. The worse things got, the more men turned to the shoe into which Melville had packed so much quality. Customers got their $4 worth—and then some—when they bought Thom McAn shoes.

Through the 1930s and 1940s, until the end of World War II, the combination of good quality and low price attracted the buyers. But to the men coming back from the war, a "good bargain" wasn't enough. After years of wearing combat boots, the veterans wanted a little flash, a little style. They wanted barge toes and more bounce to the ounce.

Unfortunately, Melville, geared up as it was to the "You can have any color you want as long as it's black" philosophy went right on grinding out the shoes that, as events proved, nobody wanted. There was also another trend running that by-passed Melville. This was the flood tide of the residential flow from the cities to the suburbs.

The combined effect of Melville's failure to get with the style trends and its missing of the commuter train to the suburbs, cut heavily into the company's profits and put it in near jeopardy in the middle 1950s. Fortunately, there proved to be a way—in fact, three ways—out. The first was a mass shift of Thom McAn stores from downtown to the suburbs. In this crash program—under the able leadership of Robert C. Erb, who was President of Melville from 1956 to 1964—the company closed the old, unprofitable, downtown stores and opened new suburban ones as fast as it possibly could. In the ten years between 1955 and 1965, Melville closed 278 stores and opened 417. When it finished this re-structuring of its retailing operations they were located where the people were once again—at the very core of the population explosion with millions of shoe-buying young families at their door.

Secondly, Melville stopped thinking of itself as being in the shoe business, and started thinking of itself as being in the fashion business.

It stopped concentrating on selling what it made, and started concentrating on making what it could sell. It turned its whole operation around and looked at it from the marketing, rather than the manufacturing, end of things. It came to view its stores as profit centers and the factories as cost centers. The company came to realize that the way to make money was to appeal to customer wants, not by cutting prices, or leather, in a different way.

In the third place, there were strong currents of change running in the marketplace itself. The most important of these—besides the shift to the suburbs and the new demand for style and variety in footwear—was the steadily dropping median age of the population.

However, knowing there was an expanding youth market and getting the young people to buy Melville's product instead of those of its competitors were two entirely different propositions. How was the company going to bridge not only the generation gap, but the marketing gap? How was it to get the youngsters to come into Thom McAn stores?

As if often happens, the answer came almost by accident and from a highly unlikely source—in the person of a young singer named Chubby Checker. He set off what was probably the biggest rage of the 1950s—a dance called The Twist.

As most rages do, The Twist started with the teens and spread to the adults; and Melville was lucky enough to catch up with both the dance and Chubby Checker in the early stages. It signed Chubby Checker to promote Thom McAn shoes well before he hit his peak. By using his name and picture and calling just about every pair of shoes "Twisters" Melville began selling a lot of shoes to teenagers.

The company found that the best way to reach the youngsters was through their sense, or lack of sense, of hearing. The young people don't always listen to their parents, but they do listen to "sound radio" and its blasting of the airwaves with the "top 40" hits.

From practical experience, Melville became an expert in what in the early 1960s was the relatively new art of teenage marketing. It tied shoe styles into all kinds of teen fads and favorites—the Pontiac GTO car, surfing, rock bands, the Monkees, Indian music, motor bikes—and got its shoes associated with the teen way of life. At the same time, in appealing to the adult market, it advertised heavily on television. Some of the ads, such as the famed "Man in the Shoe" commercial, became classics. Moving into the latter half of the sixties Melville's combination of the accent on youth, shopping center concentration, and "excitement" selling resulted in the best growth record in the shoe business. It seemed that Melville's only remaining challenge was to expand its position as a leader in footwear.

Operating in the front lines of change, however, the modern retailer must be a man in constant motion, detecting and reacting to change not on a ten or twenty-five year basis, as used to be the case, but rather on a year-to-year, or even month-to-month time scale.

In Melville's case, as it moved to shoes, to footwear, to fashion, and into apparel, it became apparent that as well as it did in these areas no one of them actually defined its business. Rather, it was pretty obvious that merchandising was its business, and a very special kind of merchandising at that.

Determining what kind of business a company is in, with things changing as rapidly as they are today, is not nearly so easy as it sounds. Not only is it not easy, but the price of miscalculation in making this determination is inordinately high, often adding up to the difference between success and failure. There are a number of industries today that have found themselves in this dilemma. The railroads, for example, failed to realize that transportation was their business. Steel did not see that materials was its field. The oil companies were slow to recognize that they were in the energy business.

Melville acknowledged that merchandising was its game. But, again, given the incredible rate at which conditions in its operating environment change, it knew that it could not sit back and contemplate its accomplishments even at this level of the company's evolution. As a result, in further refining its role, the company now sees itself as a specialty merchandiser. In recent years, rather than responding to the pressures of a technologically oriented mass society by lining up like automatons, and thinking, dressing, acting, and buying with unvarying sameness, consumers have been "doing their own thing." Perhaps, because they want to feel different to emphasize their individuality, today's consumers like to shop in stores that cater to them in a special way. To a retailer, this means being small enough to treat the customer as someone important, yet, as the result of specialization, being able to carry a much more complete line within a given product area. This also means better, more personal service all around. Most importantly, it means more sales.

Specialty markets have developed out of increased education, sophistication, affluence, and leisure time. People today have an interest in more things, are active in more ways, have better developed and more specific tastes, have more time to spend doing more things, and, to top it off, have more money to spend in a discretionary way. All this adds up to a wider ranging, more demanding consumer, who is an "expert" purchaser and wants to deal with an "expert" seller who is interested in giving him complete "customer satisfaction."

As the result of these factors, people buy for different reasons than they used to buy. As professor Theodore Levitt of the Harvard Business School has put it, rather than buying a product itself, today's consumers buy "with an expectation of benefits." Their purchasing decision is not determined by the simple, straightforward reasoning that they need a pair of shoes to keep their feet warm and dry, but rather because the shoes are going to help them make a good social impression, or help them "feel better" in a number of ways.

The term, "product augmentation," has replaced the emphasis on product characteristics. This has grown to some extent out of the fact that almost any competent company in a given field can manufacture a product that is as good as his competitor's and can usually meet his competitor's price. The competition begins, and is decided, at the "value satisfaction" level. As Charles Revson, president of Revlon, has expressed it, "In the factory we make cosmetics. In the store we sell hope." In retailing, "product augmentation" means a good shopping environment, created by a conducive store format. It also means a high degree of personal involvement on the part of both buyer and seller. It means a complete in-depth coverage of a given product line.

In a way, the trend toward specialty merchandising represents a return to the small, intimate shops characteristic of Europe and of this country in its earlier days. How then can it be possible for a company the size of Melville, that has gotten where it is primarily through the mass merchandising of a single product line, to provide the kind of intimate, concentrated merchandising involved here?

Melville has answered this question by becoming a company made up of a number of retail chains in a variety of fields. Each chain specializes in its area, providing the kind of concept, store format, merchandise, and service that add up to specialty merchandising.

While such a course may seem an abrupt turning from Melville's past, it is actually, in many ways, a logical extension of many of the elements that have contributed to its progress in recent years. Thom McAn, with its emphasis on the teenage and young family market, has been a specialty merchandiser to some extent.

Miles has been developing into a specialty chain with its new small and intimate stores. Designed to appeal to the young woman, these new Miles shops feature soft lights, bright colors, and pleasant background music. Low pads have replaced the customary chairs and Miles advertising and promotion is keyed to what the young people are thinking about and talking about.

In March 1968, Melville made its first completely new move into specialty merchandising, when it opened the first store of Chess King teen-male apparel chain. Created for the 12 to 20-year-olds, Chess King exemplifies the "product augmentation" theory of specialty merchandising.

Chess King merchandise has special appeal for the market—bell bottoms, white jeans, necklaces, Marlene Dietrich hats, and incense. The store environment literally makes shopping a "happening" for the youngsters. On special occasions, rock bands blare forth from a permanent raised platform at the back of the store. Shopping at Chess King is so much fun for the kids that the stores now rival the drugstore as the favorite teen hangout in today's shopping centers.

The launching of Chess King marked Melville's first expansion outside the shoe field. In December 1968, Melville purchased Foxwood Casuals, the fast-growing young women's sports apparel chain. Foxwood fit perfectly into the specialty merchandising concept with a recognizable store format designed to appeal to the suburban young woman along with clothes consistent with her active, informal life-style. It is the girl's own Chess King.

In still a third move into specialty merchandising, this time completely outside both the footwear and apparel business, Melville acquired a health and beauty aid chain, New England-based Consumer Value Stores, specializing in a complete line of cosmetic and health products bought primarily by the young woman. The Consumer Value acquisition gave Melville a good foothold in a fast-growing field that will almost certainly grow bigger with each passing year.

More important, the Consumer Value acquisition gave Melville another unit to use in making its specialty merchandising concept a practical reality. Specialty merchandising is much more than a merchandising theory with Melville, it is a plan of physical action with the goal of establishing a half-dozen, or even more, Melville stores in as many shopping centers as possible.

This means that with a multiple chain approach, with each unit designed to fit into the shopping center mix on its own, Melville multiplies the number of shopping centers with each new chain it creates or acquires. With one brand name chain, the expansion of a retailing organization is limited by the number of new shopping centers constructed. With six or more chains, shopping center representation is increased six-fold. In implementing its specialty merchandising program, Melville expects to open about 1,000 new stores and leased departments within the next three years which would give the company a total of 2,400 outlets. Melville's sales are about $500 million. The company is the largest combined retailer and manufacturer of footwear which it sells through its Thom McAn and Miles stores and its Meldisco division which operates leased departments in discount stores.

In recent years Melville has, for the first time in its history, expanded beyond the footwear field. In March 1968, Melville started the Chess King chain of young men's apparel stores, and in December 1968, it acquired the Foxwood chain of young women's sportswear stores. It has 1,600 stores, 15 factories, 12,000 employees, and 18,000 stockholders.

EXHIBIT 1

EXHIBIT 2

"If you can't find anything wrong with our shoes within 30 days, they're yours."

"We make Thom McAn shoes for children and we honestly believe they're the best you can buy.

But we don't expect you to go along with that just because we say so.

We think you should have a chance to make us prove it. And that's just what you're going to get.

From now on, when you buy a pair of our boys or girls shoes, we're going to give you thirty days to put us to the test.

If, during that time, you are dissatisfied with our shoes for any reason whatsoever, bring them in and we'll buy them back from you.

Or give you a new pair, if that's what you prefer. And we'll do this with no questions asked, and no rigmarole to go through.

You just give us back our shoes and our sales slip and we'll give you back your money.

You may be wondering how we can afford to do something like this and still stay in business.

Well, we couldn't if we didn't make such good shoes. But we test and retest all the leathers and other quality materials we use at our Melville Testing Labs.

We test and retest the stitching and cementing that holds our shoes together.

And we test and retest everything else that goes into the making of a fine shoe.

So when you buy Thom McAn shoes for your son or daughter, we're pretty sure you'll be happy with them.

And we don't think very many of you will be back to complain or ask for your money back.

But we still feel obligated to give you that opportunity. Because we believe that any shoe company that isn't willing to buy their shoes back, shouldn't sell them to you in the first place."

Lawrence E. McGourty
Lawrence E. McGourty
President of the Thom McAn Shoe Company

Thom McAn Children's Shoes $5.99–$9.99

Infants' shoe sizes 2 to 8, Girls' 8½ to 4, Boys' 8½ to 6

Advertising expenditure

Melville spends somewhere between 2 percent and 3 percent of gross sales for advertising and 1 percent to 1.5 percent for window and store display material. The actual percent will depend on the autonomous decision of the president of each Melville division.

Advertising policy

Each division of Melville sets its own advertising strategy. This approach of autonomous decision is necessary and efficient when one considers that each Melville division presents entirely different product lines to entirely different customer groups. However, it is generally true that all Melville divisions have taken up the general direction set by Melville management of creating a feeling of *excitement and fun* in advertising and display.

In Exhibit 1, is an advertisement that was placed in such newspapers as the *Albany Times Union, Boston Globe, Hartford Times, Charleston News-Courier, Honolulu Star Bulletin, Kansas City Star, Seattle Times,* and *Washington Post.* Exhibit 2 is another advertisement in the Thom McAn promotion of its children's shoes.

Case question

1. Develop a campaign for Thom McAn children's shoes in which you will define the market, set the objectives, firm the budget, decide on the appeal, and select the specific media.

CASE 2.   BUKER ENGINEERING COMPANY
Planning a campaign

The Buker Company designs and manufactures vapor recovery systems, pressure relief valves, flame arresters, pressure and vacuum relief valves, explosion relief valves, automatic tank gauges, swing line equipment, tank winches and sheaves, sediment and drip traps, monometers, internal safety valves, water drawoff valves, and waste gas burners.

Buker sold its products to three major industries—the petroleum industry, the chemical industry, and the sewage treatment industry. Sales of venting, gauging, swing line, regulator, and relief valve equipment to the petroleum industry amounted to 60 percent of Buker's total sales. Chemical industry business accounted for 30 percent of the sales; while the sewage treatment industry sales were the source for the other 10 percent of the volume.

The company never had followed any formal advertising program, because the management believed that personal contact plus a thorough knowledge of the engineering problems involved in the installation and operation of Buker equipment was the best way to sell its products.

While Buker was an important company in the industry, its volume was surpassed by several other manufacturers. As a result, the executives of the company contacted an advertising agency and requested that the agency submit a suggested campaign which would help the company strengthen its position in the industry.

The agency first made a survey to determine how the Buker Engineering Company was accepted in the petroleum industry. Over 6,000 engineer, superintendent, and foreman readers of *Petroleum Processing* were surveyed to determine their recognition and preferences among manufacturers of specified refinery equipment. These were the men recommended by their management as the key equipment-buying personnel in refining and natural gasoline manufacturing plants, and among construction engineering firms serving this industry.

The men were asked to list, in order of preference, the manufacturer they would turn to first or whose product they would prefer if they were faced with the problem of buying each item of equipment for a new plant. The results of the survey are given in Exhibits 1 and 2, listed below.

As a result of the above study and an analysis of Buker's products, markets, competition, and position in the industry, the agency recommended:

1. That Buker's advertising in the trade journals be reallocated to achieve the greatest possible coverage within the budget.
2. That a systematic publicity campaign be started.
3. That an even closer relationship be set up between sales and advertising.
4. That all Buker catalogs be revised and revisions mailed as soon as possible.

EXHIBIT 1. Geographical breakdown of mailout and returns

Area	Number mailed out	Number returned	Percentage of returns
Middle Atlantic..........................	1,622	82	5.1
East North Central......................	1,150	78	6.8
West South Central.....................	1,657	87	5.3
Pacific..................................	822	69	8.4
Total of remaining five areas..........	805	53	6.6
Total.............................	6,056	369	6.1

EXHIBIT 2. Pressure relief valve manufacturer recognition and preference survey conducted by *Petroleum Processing*

	Number of mentions					
	First place	Second place	Third place	Fourth place	Fifth place	Total
Smith Steam Gage & Valve Company....	171	37	3	2	—	213
Welsh, Inc...............................	63	97	3	2	—	165
Viaduct..................................	18	11	10	2	—	41
Crandall Company.......................	15	9	2	1	1	28
Buker Company..........................	13	5	3	1	2	24
Yellowstone Company....................	6	10	2	2	—	20
Minnesota...............................	7	5	4	—	1	17
Fletcher.................................	1	—	10	3	1	15
Anderson Company......................	2	—	7	2	1	12
Hadley Company........................	3	2	1	—	—	6
Comet Company.........................	1	—	2	1	2	6
Forty additional companies received these total mentions.........................	15	19	19	10	5	68
Total.............................	315	195	66	26	13	615

On the basis of an approximate gross volume of $1 million, the agency believed a total trade publication budget of $13,189 should be spent. This represented 1.4 percent and permitted an additional 1.1 percent for catalogs and direct mail, which would bring the total advertising budget up to 2.5 percent of gross sales. This percentage is within the average for industrial manufacturers in the $1 million gross sales volume, as well as the percentage allowed by fabricated equipment manufacturers. The proposed advertising budget appears in Exhibits 3 and 4.

The agency justified its media recommendations on the following bases:

MEDIA RECOMMENDATIONS
MARKET NUMBER 1
The Petroleum Industry

1. *Oil and Gas Journal*—ABC—Because it is the Number One trade publication in the industry, we select it as the Number One book on our list. We propose to use 6 *full pages and 12 two-thirds pages* allowing an insertion once *every 3 weeks—minimum frequency* for a weekly publication.
2. *Petroleum Processing*—CCA—Because of the method of distribution (direct to the reader at his home address), the careful selection of readers by occupational titles and the *vertical refinery* editorial content, we propose to schedule 6 *two-thirds pages* on a bimonthly basis in this publication.
3. *Petroleum Refiner*—ABC—Because of its established acceptance and its showing in readership surveys, we propose to schedule 6 *two-thirds pages* on a bimonthly basis to run alternately with the schedule in *Petroleum Processing*.

We suggest the above split schedule to take full advantage of the potential readership in the refinery field. The duplicate circulation between the two magazines is quite large so as to give *the effect of 12-time frequency,* yet there is *enough variance* between both readerships to warrant the split.

The use of these publications will deliver approximately 95 percent readership in the refinery, storage, and natural gas fields.

MEDIA RECOMMENDATIONS
MARKET NUMBER 2
The Chemical Industry

1. *Chemical Engineering*—ABC—According to numerous readership surveys this publication is Number One in field. However, its dominance is *not sufficiently great* over the Number Two book to warrant a full schedule. Therefore, we recommend *6 two-thirds pages* on a bimonthly basis.
2. *Industrial & Engineering Chemistry*—ABC—The official organ of the Chemical Engineers Society, this publication has considerable duplicate circulation with that of *Chemical Engineering.* However, there is some variance, and the editorial approach is more academic. *A 6 two-thirds-page schedule* on alternate months with *Chemical Engineering* is recommended.

The use of these two magazines will deliver approximately 88 percent readership.

EXHIBIT 3. Buker Engineering Company publication (advertising budget)

		Percentage of business	Percentage of space budget
1.	The petroleum industry..................... $ 5,221.00	60	44.8
2.	The chemical industry....................... 3,420.00	30	29.3
3.	The sewage industry........................ 1,373.75	10	12.1
4.	General.................................... 1,575.00		13.7
5.	Estimated layout art and production costs.. 1,600.00		
	$13,189.75		

MEDIA RECOMMENDATIONS
MARKET NUMBER 3
Sewage Industry

Sewage Works Journal—(S R & D Sworn)—A careful analysis of the magazines in this field reveals they are practically equal in circulation figures, and the circulation breakdowns indicate so much duplication that obviously one publication will give complete coverage.

The Sewage Works Journal has enjoyed an 81 percent paid circulation increase since 1942, from 2,840 to 5,132. It is the *official* publication of the federation of sewage works associations and ranks high in readership prefer-

EXHIBIT 4. Buker Engineering Company advertising program

	No. of inserts	No. of full pages	No. of 2/3 pages	Total pages	Earned rate per page	Total space expenditures
1. Petroleum industry publications:						
Oil and Gas Journal	18	6	12	14	$230.00	$3,320.00
Petroleum Processing	6	—	6	4	260.00	1,040.00
Petroleum Refiner	6	—	6	4	195.00	780.00
Daily Oil News	3	—	10 in.	30 in.	1.69 in.	81.00 $ 5,221.00
2. Chemical industry publications:						
Chemical Engineering	6	—	6	4	425.00	$1,700.00
Industrial & Engineering Chemistry	6	—	6	4	430.00	1,720.00 3,420.00
3. Sewage industry publications:						
Sewage Works Journal	6	6	—	6	90.00	$ 540.00
Sewage Manual	1A	1	—	1	200.00	200.00
Sewage and Water Works Annual	1A	1	—	1	220.00	220.00
Municipal Index	1A	1	—	1	373.75	373.75
California Sewage Works Journal	1	1	—	1	40.00	40.00 1,373.75
4. General publications:						
National Fire Prevention Association	4	4	—	4	143.75	$ 575.00
Engineering and Industrial Catalogue (Canada)	1A	1	—	1	135.00	135.00
Pacific builders and engineering	1	—	2½	1	145.00	145.00 855.00
5. Miscellaneous publications						720.00
						$11,589.75
Estimated layout, art, and production costs............						$ 1,600.00
						$13,189.75

ence—as evidenced by a recent survey. It maintains an approximate ratio of 83 percent editorial to 17 percent advertising content. Because *Sewage Works Journal* is bimonthly and because the Buker budget permits only six insertions in the sewage field, a split schedule is impractical. Therefore, we recommend *six pages* in the *Sewage Works Journal* for the current year. To support this schedule, we further recommend the use of one page in each of the following annuals: *Sewerage Manual, Water and Sewage Works Annual, Municipal Index*.

The agency concluded its presentation by showing that its suggested advertising strategy included:

1. The use of page black-and-white advertisements in the petroleum field for dominance.
2. The use of two-thirds-page, black-and-white advertisements in the petroleum and chemical fields to insure next-to-reading position.
3. The use of page black-and-white advertisements in the sewage field.
4. The starting of a product-selling copy theme for the most part supported by a limited number of scare-copy advertisements.
5. Revision, reprinting, and mailing of new pages for the *Petroleum Chemical Sewage Catalogue*.

Case questions

1. Evaluate the campaign which was planned for the Buker Company. Are there any changes you would recommend?
2. How important is a marketing study as given in Exhibit 2 in helping to set the strategy in a campaign?
3. Is the selection of media satisfactory?

CASE 3. INTERNATIONAL DRUG COMPANY
Handling cooperative advertising allowances

The International Drug Company, faced with aggressive competition in a number of its key markets, decided to liberalize its cooperative advertising allowances to the retail outlets in these areas.

It, therefore, contracted with a number of the chains and retail drugstores last year and offered allowances for special services:

1. Paying money amounting up to 5 percent of purchases of International's products in consideration of these customers paying said money to its salesclerks in the form of "push money" to promote the sale of the products.
2. Paying 5 percent of net purchases in consideration of these customers maintaining a permanent daily counter and window display.

3. Making available a cooperative newspaper advertising agreement under which these customers were reimbursed for the cost of advertising International's product. These advertisements were run as a listing with the customers' own advertisements.
4. Paying to these customers certain allowances for radio, TV, and direct-mail advertising.
5. Encouraging both the large and small retailers to engage in joint price advertising. In some cases, special consideration would be given to the large retailers in the area.

For the first six months after the cooperative advertising allowances were given, International Drug's sales increased 7 percent in the market in which these were granted.

The executives were pleased with results and were planning to extend these allowances on a national basis when their attorney called to their attention the various interpretations the Federal Trade Commission had made in the use of cooperative advertising.

Joint advertising

The right of retailers to engage in joint price advertising is questionable. The Federal Trade Commission warned that joint ads involve antitrust violations. However, the antitrust division of the department declared that FTA has given retailers some bad advice.

The particular dispute rates as one that veteran observers find most difficult to comprehend. To help eliminate uncertainty, the FTC offered to give advance advisory opinions to businessmen concerned about the legality of their activities.

Among the first in line when FTC's advisory opinion service got under way were representatives of retail drug organizations. Some of these organizations had recently submitted to antitrust consent settlements which involve heavy penalties for future price-fixing activity. They wanted assurance that their plans for joint advertising activity would not lead to new antitrust trouble.

Some of the sponsors of specific plans had had indications from the Department of Justice and FTC that their particular plans were doubtful. FTC's staff seemed to be convinced that the co-op plans that were submitted would represent price fixing. But as a special service they took the proposals to the Department of Justice.

The commission claimed the ban on joint advertising was inescapable, and that the Department of Justice agreed. While the ruling indicated that plans had been submitted, it stated, "that no prices, terms, or conditions of sale of any kind should appear in the advertising."

It is interesting to note that in the testimony, it was stated, "the fact that prices are quoted in joint ads has not in the past, and is not now, regarded as conclusive proof of price fixing."

This testimony, however, did not appear to be fully adequate. A member of the FTC majority suggested that the differences are more than semantics. This member emphasized that the drug industry plans which were before the committee involved an arrangement whereby a committee of retail druggists selected the items to be featured and the prices to be listed. The mere existence of this mechanism to select items and designate a price represents the essential ingredients of illegal price-fixing arrangements.

To some, the existence of a mechanism to select items and designate price is per se an offense. But, to others, the existence of the mechanism is meaningless, unless the result is a binding arrangement which results in a restraint of trade.

On the other hand, a House committee reviewed the ruling and decided that it does not mean what it says. The House Small Business Committee said that it is legal for independent retailers to pool their funds and purchase joint advertising. It also asserted that the advertising could include prices of products shown. It was the opinion of the committee that the independent retailer generally is too small to take full advantage of these cooperative allowances unless joint advertising is allowed.

Cooperative advertising for apparel makers

The Federal Trade Commission listed 163 wearing apparel manufacturers who have promised not to give discriminatory allowances in the future, and 76 others who face complaints for failing to reach agreement with the commission.

The report involves the first public identification of the wearing apparel industry members whose cooperative advertising payments were challenged in the commission's industry-wide attack on cooperative advertising arrangements in the apparel industry. Earlier, the commission announced that about 250 companies had been given an opportunity to sign standard consent settlements to discontinue discriminatory payments which had been turned up in an investigation of apparel industry suppliers and retailers.

In its announcement, FTC warned that the companies which refused to accept the opportunity for a standard consent settlement will face "appropriate action" on "a priority basis." FTC said some large stores received "thousands of dollars," and it is also reported to be preparing cases against retailers who solicited discriminatory payments from the suppliers.

The investigation included sworn reports by mail from scores of leading department stores and apparel shops, which were required to list all the advertising allowances they received from suppliers. Later, the reports from the retailers were matched against similar reports obtained from several hundred suppliers.

An initial FTC effort to induce about 150 suppliers to accept a standard consent settlement bogged down when industry leaders protested that the commission was punishing some suppliers and failing to enforce similar restraints on their competitors. FTC subsequently enlarged its investigation and brought charges against 100 additional suppliers.

Case questions

1. Is International's cooperative plan a good one? Why, or why not?
2. How should the cooperative advertising plan be implemented?
3. What problems may the company encounter with its plan?
4. Do the terms of International Drug Company's cooperative advertising plan fall within the area of activity allowed by federal regulations?
5. How can International modify its cooperative advertising plan to comply with the existing regulations?
6. What procedure should International adopt when it extends its cooperative advertising on a national basis?

Case questions (cases 4–8)

1. For cases 4 through 8, follow the recommendations as outlined, and prepare campaigns for each of the companies. In preparing the campaign, you should consider:

   a)   *Definition of the market. Describe clearly the market you are going to try to influence with your advertising campaign.* What type of person is your best prospect—income, occupation, social status, etc? How many of him or her are there? Where do they live—national or regional; urban or rural? Where do they buy this type of product? When and how often? Do others influence buying decisions, and if so, are you going to address some of your copy to them? *What is your target?*

   b)   *Objectives.* An early step in planning the complete campaign for the next year should be the setting of an objective (or objectives). *State such an objective.* It need not be identical with, or similar to, the advertiser's objectives in recent years.

   c)   *Appropriation and budget.* You are now in a position to proceed with advertising plans for the next year. At some point, obviously, you must arrive at a figure representing your total advertising appropriation. For the present, *set a tentative figure.* While this seems to be contrary to the ideal "research-objective" method of determining the appropriation, it is neither an impractical nor an unwise way to start. In the light of the past experience of the company, and the objective of the next year, you can set a figure which seems reasonable.

    d)   *Appeal to be emphasized.* Now you must decide upon the appeal or appeals you are going to emphasize. *Present the appeal or appeals and the reasons for their selection.* If you feel a test is necessary to check the wisdom of your selection, *describe the test you would recommend.*

    e)   *Types of media.* Next, proceed to consider the types of media which seem likely to serve your purposes best. *List the types of media you plan to use.* State clearly why you include each type. Explain the exclusion from your list of any of the major media— newspapers, magazines, radio, direct mail, transportation, outdoor, and window display. Think in terms of "impressions per dollar" or some other useful standard.

    f)   *Advertising schedules.* With one eye on your advertising appropriation and the other on the buying motives, buying habits, reading and listening habits of your customers and potential customers, as well as on the advertising of competitors, you can now determine the size (or length) of your advertisements and the frequency of their appearance.

    g)   *Checking effectiveness of the advertising.* Most large advertisers, and many small ones, attempt to measure the effectiveness of their advertising efforts, within reasonable cost limits. *List and describe briefly the nature of the pre- and post-checks you would use in attempting to measure the effectiveness* of your recommended advertising.

    h)   *Differentiating ideas.* Not every advertising campaign succeeds in the competitive selling job for which its was planned and executed. It is not easy to reach and influence favorably potential customers. In this final section, point out and comment on the particular features of your campaign which endow it with adequate selling power.

CASE 4.   METRO OIL CO.

Metro Oil Company owns and operates three refineries with a total capacity of 500,000 barrels of crude oil per day. Practically all of the gasoline and other refined petroleum products sold by Metro Oil Co. are marketed on the Eastern Seaboard and in the midwest under the trademark of Metro. Metro Oil Co.'s domestic sales are made through 10,000 retail outlets.

About 6,000 of these outlets, accounting for approximately two thirds of Metro's total domestic gasoline sales are owned by Metro, or are under long-term lease to it, and are operated by individual dealers. The other outlets are owned or leased by independent dealers and distributors. All of the stations are somewhat similar in design. The identification sign hanging at the curb distinguishes independent stations from employee-operated stations.

Although the company's sales to the retail trade were increasing, Metro's percentage of the total retail market was declining. Therefore, the company executives decided that some corrective action should be taken. Public opinion polls were taken by private marketing research organizations. Dealers were contacted. District managers in the field were consulted. The problem was discussed with top-level management of Metro Oil Stations.

Some of the more important results of the analyses were the following:

1. A high percentage of motorists preferred to buy at independent dealers, *except when traveling*. A small percentage preferred to buy at company-operated stations. Market surveys indicated that of those motorists expressing a choice, 68 percent preferred to purchase at independent dealers in their home communities; whereas 81 percent expressed a preference for company-operated units when traveling.

2. When both dealer and company-operated stations were painted the same color, the public could not identify the type of operation. Surveys showed that 95.4 percent of all motorists believed the company's retail outlets were all company-operated—only 4.6 percent knew the company sold through independent dealers. Efforts to correct this impression through signs and other elements of station identification—without changing building colors—were unsuccessful.

Thus, the common color scheme, which had been considered an asset not only to the company but also to the independent dealers appeared to be the root of the problem. The first recommendation was that company-operated stations continue the use of their red and white colors and that yellow and white be used on the independent stations.

Reasons for changing brand name

It was also recommended that, as part of the program of segregation of Metro's retail outlets, the brand name of independent dealers be changed from "Metro" to "Ancon." This change was suggested for many of the same reasons as the change in color.

The director of research of Metro stated that anyone marketing convenience goods—cigarettes, food, and gasoline—is dealing with a mass market. Unlike durable goods—automobiles, appliances, and furniture—which require a considerable investment by the buyer, convenience goods are purchased on the impulse of the moment. Sales result more quickly from advertising or publicity (be it good or bad) that appeals to the buying habits of the masses and emphasizes *brand* rather than *manufacturer*. Thus, a considerable advantage accrues to marketers of this kind of product.

The most successful marketers of convenience goods stress brand rather than manufacturer (for example, Crest, Pepsodent, Pall Mall, Chesterfields, Camels, Arrow Shirts, Jello, and Wheaties).

The Ancon plan was pretested

After studying these recommendations, an extensive pretesting plan was developed. Ten units in the Midwest were converted simultaneously to yellow and white colors, and the dealer's name replaced the word "Metro" at the most prominent location on the canopy and over the pumps. The public was informed of the change through newspaper ads, dealer pass-outs, and direct mail—all of which emphasized the independent status of the units by prominently featuring the dealer's name.

Fifty-one additional dealers' stations—approximately four in each sales district, balanced between metropolitan, medium-size, and small communities—were painted with the new colors.

Initially, dealers included in the test lost some volume because of diversion of business to Metro Oil Stations. However, the public quickly became familiar with the yellow and white colors, and dealers were able to pick up enough new business to offset their initial losses.

The results of the tests were such that it appeared advantageous to make the change in identification on the 4,000 independent stations. Metro Oil Stations continued to use the Metro name, their red and white colors, and their well-known identification sign. The independent dealer stations took on an entirely new appearance. The dealer's name replaced the word "Metro"; the colors became yellow and white; and the word "Ancon" supplanted Metro as the gasoline brand name.

To convince the dealers of the advantages of the separate identification, an intensive public relations and advertising campaign was conducted. The emphasis was placed on the ability of the dealers to secure business not available to the Metro Oil Stations, Inc. As one executive stated:

Our company is unique in its ability to address itself specifically to two distinctly different markets, inasmuch as we are one of the few companies that has a substantial number of company-operated stations.

Here is a good illustration of the division of the market between those customers who prefer company-operated stations and those who prefer dealer operation. We had a Metro Station at one location for many years, which we must assume was securing the maximum volume in the area through this type of operation. When threatened with the loss of this location, we purchased a site across the street, previously owned by a competitor. His gasoline was displaced by our product and, without any changes in facilities or dealer, we converted the unit to an Ancon operation for our test study. From the time it opened this station has averaged an increase of 37 percent over the sales formerly enjoyed by the prior owner. The effect on the Metro Station across the street was a loss of only 46 gallons per month.

It was the hope of Metro executives that the Ancon plan would produce the following results:

1. Overcome Metro Oil Company's declining sales trend.
2. Preserve Metro Oil Stations, Inc. for customers preferring company-employee operation.
3. Open a new market for dealers handling Metro Oil Company's products.
4. Eliminate public confusion.
5. Increase the volume at both types of outlets.
6. Provide the basis for different types of national advertising campaigns.

CASE 5.   RYAN, INC.

Ryan, Inc. operates retail furniture showrooms. The executive offices are located in Chicago, Illinois. The company operates 12 of these retail furniture showrooms in Missouri and Illinois. They feature a selection of contemporary and transitional home furnishings and accessories, including living room, bedroom, dining room, and occasional furniture, carpeting, draperies, lamps, pictures, mirrors, and shelving. In the last fiscal year, sales of furniture represented 90 precent of total sales, and carpeting, draperies, and other accessories accounted for the balance. Ryan does not sell appliances.

Operating policies

Ryan's showrooms are architecturally standardized and are located on main thoroughfares close to neighborhood shopping areas on sites that provide ample parking. The typical showroom contains approximately 20,000 square feet, is carpeted, air-conditioned, and of modern, clear-span construction. Furniture is displayed in typical room groupings in keeping with a substantially standardized merchandising program. Inventory clearances at reduced prices may take place at the times of display changes and include primarily items previously used for display.

Substantially all of the furniture sold by the Ryan Co. is custom ordered from a wide selection of floor samples, with customers being given a choice of upholstery fabrics. Certain high-turnover wood furniture items are warehoused for delivery to the customer. The company's inventory investment is minimal, consisting primarily of such ware-housed items and showroom floor samples.

Ryan fosters a high degree of personal service in its dealings with customers. Sales personnel receive instruction in interior decorating and are prepared to assist customers with individual decorating and furnishing problems. Helpful and courteous service is stressed in all customer contacts, including those with delivery personnel. Ryan also provides its customers with the benefits of a liberal warranty and refund policy.

Ryan buys from over 250 suppliers. Last year the 10 largest suppliers accounted for approximately 33 percent of Ryan's purchases. Although some purchases are made from suppliers of nationally advertised brands, most suppliers are local manufacturers capable of meeting Ryan's rigid standards. It is the company's objective to be an important customer to its major suppliers in order to influence styles and assure good service.

Ryan's merchandising and advertising effort is focused primarily on the large middle-price-range market. By imposing high standards on its suppliers, by reason of efficient management concepts (including computerized accounting and sales analysis systems), and by minimizing inventory risk, Ryan is able consistently to price its merchandise on a basis that provides quality at competitive prices.

Installment sales

During the last fiscal year, approximately two thirds of the company's sales were for cash, with the remainder represented by installment purchases. Currently, the company sells all customer installment obligations to banks with limited recourse or to finance companies without recourse. In either case, customer installment obligations are sold for their full prinicipal amount, with Ryan receiving a portion of the customer service charge at the time the obligation is sold.

Competition

The retail furniture business is extremely competitive. Competitors include other furniture, department, and discount stores. Ryan believes it is the fifth largest distributor in its total market.

CASE 6. BY BOLT CO.

By Bolt Co.'s principal product is beer. Its brands are used on a nationwide basis, and, to a limited extent, in foreign markets. Breweries are located in five states in the United States. Company sales have averaged over 11 million barrels (31 gallons each) during the past five years.

Products

By Bolt's brands of beer are sold as packaged beer and keg draft beer; malta, a nonalcoholic malt beverage, is sold in packaged form. Over 98 percent of the company's total volume is sold in the domestic market. Packaged beer is sold domestically in both pasteurized and draft form. The packaged draft beer is processed through Millipore filters and need not be refrigerated. In the domestic market, the industry's sales over the past five years were approximately 80 percent packaged beer and 20 percent keg draft beer. Profits in packaged beer are higher per barrel than in keg draft beer. By Bolt sells packaged beer and keg draft beer in virtually all the types and sizes of containers customary in the industry.

Other products of By Bolt include spent grains, which are sold as high-protein cattle feed, either in wet or dried form, and brewers yeast. These products accounted for less than 1 percent of net sales.

Materials and supplies

By Bolt maintains strict quality controls on both raw materials and its production processes. The principal materials purchased for brewing operations are malt, rice, barley, hops, and corn grits. Approximately 40 percent of the malt requirements are produced in By Bolt's own malting facilities; the balance is purchased from commercial malsters. Barley, rice, corn grits, and hops are purchased from outside sources. Materials and supplies for packaging beer—including cans, bottles, cartons, kegs, crowns, and labels—are purchased directly from suppliers as required. The raw materials used in By Bolt's products and the necessary packaging materials are purchased from various suppliers.

Distribution

By Bolt's beer is sold to retailers throughout the United States, primarily through about 850 independent wholesalers who account for approximately 95 percent of the company's domestic beer sales. Sales are f.o.b. By Bolt's breweries. No one wholesaler accounted for more than 1.5 percent of the company's sales. By Bolt or its wholly owned subsidiaries employ division and district sales managers and merchandising specialists to advise and counsel wholesalers and their sales forces. Advertising, including point-of-sale advertising, and sales promotion programs are furnished by the company to help stimulate sales.

The remainder of the By Bolt's domestic sales is made through its branches in California, New York, Oregon, and Illinois. Branches operate as wholesalers in their respective areas.

Competition

In the United States the beer industry is highly competitive and the By Bolt company competes with national, regional, and local brewers and with imported beers. The company has a line of products competing in different price markets. By Bolt is a premium beer. Tasty, Old Chicago, and Quenchy are sold on a popularly priced basis; By Bolt Malt Liquor is sold as a premium specialty product. The company accounted for almost 10 percent of the total industry tax-paid sales in the United States.

Regulation

The Federal government has established regulations governing operations of brewers which deal with arrangement of plant facilities, trade practices, advertising, and related matters. A brewer pays a nominal federal occupational tax, and a similar tax is required at the wholesale and retail levels. Bonds must be filed with the federal and various state governments to insure payment of excise taxes. By Bolt is also required to obtain certificates of approval in certain states where beer is shipped. Most states have laws governing terms of sale, advertising, trade practices, and similar matters. By Bolt is subject to the Federal Drug and Cosmetic Act as to safety of product and labeling. The federal excise tax on beer is $9 per barrel. States also levy taxes ranging from 62 cents per barrel in Wyoming up to $13.95 per barrel in South Carolina. The federal excise tax and substantially all state taxes are levied at the time of sale, but they do not apply on beer which is exported to foreign markets.

Research and development

By Bolt is continually engaged in quality control, research, and development. The quality control group maintains supervision of the production of all beers sold under By Bolt's brands, in order to assure uniform quality. Company personnel are engaged in research in the brewing operations, concentrating on the improvement of existing products and the development of new brewing processes and methods. Research personnel of the company are also employed in the improvement of packaging methods and processes. By Bolt has spent approximately $700,000 in research and development in each of the last three years.

CASE 7.   FASHION HANDBAG COMPANY

The Fashion Handbag Company, located in New York City, is engaged in manufacturing ladies pocketbooks. The company's products are distributed nationally under the trade name "Fashion" and retailed through specialty shops, department stores, and shoe stores. The leathers and skins used in the bags made by Fashion are all genuine calf, snake, or lizard, and in the past five years a new group of synthetic materials has been emphasized. This use of genuine leather results in a large price spread for the same style bag made in different materials. The line retails from $25 to $200, depending upon the material and the style. Eighty percent of the total sales is in the $25 to $60 range.

Four salesmen travel from headquarters in New York and make two trips during the spring and fall seasons to the larger buying centers within their territories. This enables Fashion to reach those retailers who do not come to the New York market, or who come only once a year.

Fashion bags are accepted as "high-style" products. This reputation has been maintained by a dynamic styling policy. In the spring of each year, the designer makes a trip to the fashion centers in Europe and studies the latest style trends. As a result, the new line introduced in the fall season is always highly styled and up-to-date.

After completing their regular end-of-season trip in the spring, the company salesmen submitted comments as to the condition of the market, and the price and type of products that would go well in the fall season. The sales manager summarized these comments by stating that the Fashion line was overpriced when compared with competitive lines. He believed that this price advantage had resulted in a low volume of sales. The sales manager felt that Fashion bags were too heavily built internally, with unnecessarily elaborate waddings, muslins, and papers. The excessive construction elements used to give the "right feeling" to the bag brought about a price that was too high. He pointed out that, when selling handbags, the important factors are price and style. He said that women do not buy handbags to last forever, and the present type of internal buildup was unnecessary. Since women rarely look beyond the outside appearance of a bag, this executive suggested that it would be best to meet competition by using fewer internal materials, thereby making possible a lower schedule of prices.

The vice president in charge of manufacturing stated that it is very difficult to compare values in handbags because competitors in this price range never manufacture comparable styles. Although price seemed paramount at the moment, he felt that the workmanship in Fashion's line was more detailed and usually better than the workmanship offered in competitive lines. This executive felt that arguments about the proper internal buildup of a bag were futile because this was primarily a matter of personal opinion. He pointed out that savings in materials and labor through use of fewer internal parts would usually result in insignificant reductions in selling price. Essentially, the price of a handbag is determined by its size, which affects the amount of leather used, and by its styling, which affects the amount of labor required.

This vice president voiced the opinion that the sales force was not well enough versed in the quality selling points of each bag to be able to sell aggressively to retailers and to aid them in their merchandising programs. Considering that the product line was highly styled, he felt that more consumer advertising and particularly more trade advertising was necessary to establish the brand name as synonymous with high style and high quality. This executive recommended that the company maintain its high-style, high-quality, high-price line. He indicated that it would be better to meet price competition by introducing several simpler styles, and possibly by extending the company's retail price range to bags under $25.

CASE 8.   NUTRITIOUS SPECIAL CO.

Nutritious Special Co. is engaged in manufacturing donut mixes and selling them, together with paper products, soft drink mixes, and other products, to franchised operators of donut shops leased to them by Nutritious Donut House and fresh donuts and beverages are made on the premises and sold at retail to the public.

Flour, shortening, sugar, spices, and flavorings—the ingredients used to make the donut mixes—are used to prepare the mixes in accordance with special formulas developed and tested over the years by Nutritious Special Co.

Franchise outlets

The company's products are sold through 126 retail outlets which are operated under franchises from the company. The donut shops average approximately 1,200 square feet each and are equipped by Nutritious to prepare and serve fresh donuts and beverages. The shops are located on leased land which has either been improved by the company or leased with existing improvements. Such leases are separately negotiated and vary from short terms to leases for periods of up to 20 years. They generally provide for a fixed rental to be applied against a stated percentage of the gross sales of the donut shop located on the premises. Prospective sites for donut shops are carefully investigated by Nutritious and it maintains a separate real estate department to discover and obtain desirable locations for its shops. Many of the shops are located in or near shopping centers. The shop and equipment are subleased to a franchised operator. Except for one shop located in the Los Angeles area the existing donut shops are located primarily in the East.

The agreements between Nutritious and its franchised operators require each operator to purchase from the company all donut and beverage mixes, paper goods, containers, and other supplies used in the operation of the business. The company requires deposits up to $3,000 from each franchised operator as security for the performance of his obligations under the agreement with the company and for payment for supplies purchased from the company. To assure uniform standards of operation, including the quality and freshness of the donuts which are all prepared on the premises, each franchised operator is trained by Nutritious and pays up to $1,000 to the company to cover the cost of this training. A portion of the training fee is refunded by the company if the franchised operator remains with the company for 18 months.

The franchised operators pay a monthly rental based on gross sales of the donut houses. The franchised operators pay no fixed monthly rental other than the percentage rent; the percentage rental does not operate until the gross monthly sales of the franchised shop exceed $2,500. Nevertheless, Nutritious remains and is primarily liable for all rent payments to the lessors of the property.

The company also charges the franchised operators a monthly fee for accounting, advertising, and maintenance services. Each franchised operator is in an independent business for his own account. The franchised operators may employ such personnel as they deem necessary to properly operate their shops. Such employees are not employees of the Nutritious Company. Operators are required to keep their shops clean, attractive, and open for business for a prescribed minimum number of hours each day. Regular inspections of the preparation and merchandising of products and of the general appearance and cleanliness of the premises and equipment encourages compliance with these requirements. Each lease and license agreement with a franchised operator is terminable upon written notice from either party.

For the last fiscal year approximately 85 percent of Nutritious' combined gross income was derived from the sale of donut mixes, paper products, beverage mixes, sugar, and other items. Approximately 15 percent of the company's total gross income was derived from rent paid by the franchised operators for use of the donut houses and equipment.

Competition

Nutritious Special Co. is the largest of its type of operation in its area. However, it must compete with other donut shop chains which operate in the same areas, as well as a considerable number of individually owned shops. Nutritious is unable to estimate the number of such other donut shops. In addition, Nutritious must compete, to some extent, with donuts and similar products sold in groceries, markets, and bakeries and with most other establishments serving food and beverages in areas in which the company operates.

The president of Nutritious at the last stockholders' meeting informed those in attendance that he believed the company should begin to extend its franchises throughout the United States. He proposed that the company should develop an advertising campaign that would attract new operators.

chapter 19

ORGANIZATION FOR CONTROL

$\mathbf{T}$HE ORGANIZATION for advertising control has a variety of forms in different companies within even the same industry. Regardless of whether or not the functions of advertising control are under one organization, however, someone must perform these functions.

How the organization should be set up, to whom reports should be given, how extensive the system should be, and how thoroughly it should attempt to plan and control the advertising are matters to be decided for each business. There is no rigid rule which can be set to determine which is the best procedure. This is determined by such factors as the size of the company, the objectives of the company, the type of product, the nature and extent of the market, the marketing experience and expertise of the company executives, and the nature of the advertising job. As a result, in some companies the entire advertising job may be handled by one person. In other companies, it may require many people and a complex structure. Two companies of the same size may not handle advertising in the same manner. Even companies of similar size selling competitive products may use different organizational structures and different approaches to working with their agencies in controlling their advertising.

Regardless of what organization or method is used, the primary purpose of the advertising organization is to provide the means by which the advertising job will be done on an efficient, systematic, and economical basis.

Each advertising function or unit operation should be established on an organized procedure which involves the relationships between the company, the media, and the advertising agency, whenever an agency is used. The coordination of all of these operations into a complete process of advertising requires setting up a pattern of relationships between the various activities. In other words, the detailed organization for a company should be arranged according to the importance of controlling each advertising function. To facilitate the reader's understanding of the organization and the cooperation of the firm and the agency to control the advertising of the firm, the authors will first discuss the internal organization of the advertiser, and then the organization and functioning of the advertising agency.

Location of advertising department within the company

A study of a number of American companies conducted by the Association of National Advertisers indicated that there are a number of different places within the company organizational structure to locate the advertising department. Which location is best depends on a number of factors, including: the size of the company; the general task that will be assigned to advertising in the company's marketing program; the amount and type of advertising the company plans to use; the general type of market in which the firm competes; and the extent to which top management is involved in the planning and handling of the advertising function.

In most firms the advertising department is one of several functions reporting to the chief executive, the chief marketing executive, or the chief sales executive of the company.

For a multiple-division company, advertising can be a centralized operating department or it can be decentralized, operating at a division level.

Organization of the advertising department

The organization of the advertising department itself within the company is influenced also by several factors, such as the position of advertising within the company, the number and types of activities included in the advertising function, and the extent to which the various functions and responsibilities of advertising are performed in the advertising department, or are carried out by the advertising agency and other outside agencies.

The study conducted by the A.N.A. indicated that there are five basic ways of organizing an advertising department. These are:

1. By subfunction of advertising (sales promotion, production, copy, etc.)
2. By media (magazine advertising, direct mail, etc.)
3. By product
4. By end user (consumer, institutional users, farm market, etc.)
5. By geography (regional managers)

Size of the advertising department

The size of the department and the number of people in the department need bear no particular relationship to the size of the company or its advertising appropriation. The advertising departments of national advertisers may literally vary in size from one individual to departments employing over a thousand people.

The size of the department is related primarily to the extent to which the company relies on its advertising agency, or agencies, for the creation and production of its advertising. It is also influenced by such factors as the amount of advertising, the type of advertising, the number of products and brands advertised, the market and its nature, and the philosophy of the company management. For instance, in tobacco companies, which are large advertisers in terms of dollars and percentage of sales, the advertising departments tend to be quite small, because the companies rely on their agency, or agencies, for the creating and producing of their advertising. In contrast, many industrial products firms (which tend to spend relatively much smaller dollar sums and percentage of sales on advertising) create and produce much of their own advertising material, such as brochures, direct-mail pieces, and catalogs, and have large advertising departments. Eastman Kodak, which has complete photographic production facilities, employs more than 400 persons in its advertising department. General Electric has a central advertising department of 400 persons at Schenectady, N.Y., and each of its 15 apparatus divisions maintains its own advertising department. This type of large advertising department staff is the exception in American business firms. Most firms have relatively small numbers of people employed in their advertising departments.

WHY ADVERTISERS USE AGENCIES

Although, as noted above, national advertisers have advertising departments and advertising managers, virtually all national advertising is actually prepared and placed by advertising agencies, who make the contracts for space and time with the media. There are several reasons why the advertisers normally use agencies rather than relying upon their own facilities for all the work of planning, preparation, and placement of advertising. The two principal general reasons for the use of agencies are the belief that agencies will result in producing more effective advertising and the fact that the use of agencies, in a sense, does not cost the advertiser anything. Among the factors causing advertisers to believe agencies are more effective are: the greater objectivity and independence of an outside agency compared with an internal department; the fresh approach of an outside organization; the experience and advantages gained by the agency from its work on a number of accounts in various fields and industries, resulting in the cross-fertilization of ideas; the motivation of the agency to do a good job of planning and executing the advertising in order to hold the account; the ability of the agency to bring together a highly skilled group of specialists that only a very few of the largest advertisers could possibly afford to do for themselves in a department.

Under the present widely used method of compensation of the agency, many of the services which the agency performs for the client in essence cost the client nothing, since the agency's compensation is obtained in the form of commissions from the media used. However, if the company established a house agency it would be possible for this agency to receive the commission.

Another reason sometimes advanced favoring the use of agencies to handle the advertising is that it is much easier to change agencies if the company becomes dissatisfied with its advertising than it would be to eliminate its advertising department.

Selection of the agency

Making the right selection of an agency is a very important decision for the company, to insure obtaining good service. The general approach to the selection of the agency would be similar to that used in the selection of any other professional type service. First the company should determine the nature of the advertising "job" the agency is expected to do for the company. On the basis of this job description the firm should set up the criteria for selection. Then it should draw up a list of possible or prospective agencies. The criteria listed earlier should then be applied to this list of possible agencies, and the agency best qualified to provide the effective counsel and services as described by the standards set up should be selected.

The first step in this selection process should involve the preparation of a written statement covering in detail the exact type and extent of the services which the agency will be expected to perform, and which functions the advertising department of the firm will perform. Some companies want their agency to perform "full service" (which means everything, including marketing plans, research, copy, art, production, media selection and placement, publicity, sales promotion materials, and so forth), while others desire only a very limited number of services from their agency.

On the basis of this statement of agency services desired, and the company's general philosophy, criteria should be established for the selection of the agency. Some of the factors that are usually considered in establising the list of criteria are the following:

1. Advertising philosophy. Unless the general attitudes of the firm and the principals of the agency toward advertising and its place in the marketing program are similar, the probability of the relationship's being a happy one are remote.

2. Size. This is important from the standpoint of the advertiser in several possible ways. A large advertiser needs an agency of sufficient size to be in a position to handle all its work and services satisfactorily. A small advertiser wants an agency that will take a deep interest in it, and fears that if it is relatively too small an account, the large agency may not give it such interest. The thinking is: "It is better to be an important account to a small agency than just another account to a large agency."

3. Services rendered. The important question is whether or not the agency has facilities and manpower to render all the services the client will need. Special service requirements should be included here.

4. Experience. The advertiser is interested in the types of accounts the agency is handling, and what products it now handles that are comparable from a marketing and advertising standpoint to its own. Other questions raised under this topic would be how long the agency has had its accounts, its familiarity with the advertiser's industry, and its record of success with other accounts. Some firms would also include here questions relating to the agency's record with various types of media.

5. Personnel. The ability and background and experience of the agency principals, top creative men and account men, as well as the ability and records of the executives who would actually be assigned to the advertiser's account. If the firm has some special requirements relative to personnel for their account (for example, a woman copywriter), they should be considered here.

6. Method of compensation. Since there are differences in the manner in which agencies do handle charging for research and certain other services, it should be ascertained in advance just what services the agency would render for the normal commission, which services would be charged for (whether at cost or cost plus usual markup), or, if a smaller account, details of the fee system proposed. Details of method of compensation should be carefully agreed upon beforehand.

7. Location. Although this would not be significant for most large national advertisers, in some instances firms do insist that the agency have an office in the same city as their head office. And, many smaller firms using small agencies will desire to use an agency in a convenient geographical location.

In selecting the agency, the advertising manager (and other involved executives) should consider the above factors and any others that he deems pertinent in his particular situation. The list of agencies to which these considerations would be applied can be compiled in a number of ways, depending on circumstances. At times some one key criterion will be the basis for compiling the list; for example, if the company has made location a key criterion, then this could be determining, and all agencies with offices in its home city might be listed. Major criteria are then applied, eliminating agencies as they fail to meet the standards. Information for checking against criteria can be obtained through the use of mailed questionnaires, and is sometimes done by personal interview. After the list has been winnowed down to those who meet all criteria acceptably, the advertising manager would usually have at least one meeting with the executives of the agency and would probably also visit some of the clients of the agency. This final group of agencies may or may not be requested to make a "presentation" to the key executives of the firm.

Working with the agency

Below are a few rules that have been evolved by advertising managers and account executives to help maintain good relationships with the agency and enable the firm to get the best results from its advertising agency:

1. The company should have in writing clear marketing objectives and goals for the company and clear marketing plans for each major product line. This will enable the advertising agency to know what the advertising goals and objectives should be and how to plan the advertising to fit into the overall marketing plan.

2. The company should have a clear working arrangement with the agency, in writing, as to just what the responsibilities of the agency are, what the company expects of the agency, what the agency will do in the way of service for its 15 percent commission, and what the company will do. The channels of communication, the contact man, the method of approval, between firm and agency should be clearly spelled out.

3. There should be very close cooperation between the advertising manager and the account executive in planning and executing the work of the agency. The firm should give the agency full and complete information. For example, research findings of the firm should be made available to the agency to aid it, and not used to "trap" the agency.

4. There should be an attitude of mutual confidence and trust. The agency should be encouraged to participate fully in the planning and be expected to contribute ideas and make suggestions or recommendations, although on major areas such as the budget, major media, and a campaign theme, the company should have the final decision. However, normally the firm should then permit the agency to carry on with its creative work, and with details of media selection, with a minimum of

interference. The company should, of course, feel free to contribute creative ideas when it has them, and the agency should be happy to accept and consider such. The firm's executives should learn that creative people want to be "appreciated" and "respected." A little of this appreciation may help in getting much extra effort from the creative staff of the agency.

5. The firm should set up criteria for evaluating the agency and its work in light of the original objectives that were established in the plan.

If, in general, the company executives will work with the agency people as though they were partners in the marketing program, sharing information, ideas, trust, and confidence, they should get a maximum amount of effective advertising from their agency and have a happy working relationship.

Evaluation of agency performance

After the agency has been selected and the bases for a good working relationship evolved, as discussed in the preceding paragraphs, the advertiser has the task of carrying out the last of the rules for insuring effective advertising on the part of the agency, namely, the evaluation of the work of the agency. If there were some sound and reliable basis for obtaining accurate measures of the effectiveness of advertising, the problem of evaluating agency performance would be much easier than it now is. Since it is not possible to attain such accurate measurement for most types of advertising, the advertiser must use other criteria.

Although such performance standards can be quite easily developed for the advertiser's particular situation, it is still difficult to judge performance against these criteria. Some standards should attempt to evaluate the quality of the creative work performed by the agency, and the quality of the planning work of the agency. If any standards have established quantitative measures (such as increasing brand awareness in a new territory by x percent), these should be included in the quality evaluation. Some evaluation should also be included of such factors as the technical aspects of the advertising work of the agency, including art, layout, and production. Some firms also place some emphasis on the actual quantity of work performed by the agency, including the number of advertisements produced and the number of pieces of sales promotional material produced. However, most agree that major emphasis should be on the results of the advertising, to the extent this can be evaluated.

THE RETAIL ADVERTISER

Since as a rule the retail store does not handle its advertising through an advertising agency, a large percentage of all advertising (approximately one third) is done locally by retail organizations and is familiar to all; and, since virtually every retail store does advertising in some form, a few words should be devoted to the different aspects of the retail advertising picture.

Retail advertising organization

As a rule, the small retail store does use less advertising as a percentage of sales than the larger store. In many cases, the store owner or manager also acts as the advertising manager. He may have a small advertising department to assist in the planning and preparation of the advertising or no advertising department. In either event, he usually will obtain a great deal of assistance from several outside sources. The local media (newspapers, radio, and television stations) have people who will help him in all facets of his advertising, from the planning of his campaign and establishing his advertising budget to the actual preparation of his individual advertisements, including the selection of items to advertise, the layout, the writing of copy, and the supplying of illustrations. His suppliers (manufacturers of branded items he carries) will in many cases furnish him recommended guides for advertising schedules, mats for newspaper advertisements, film, and transcriptions for broadcast media, inserts for direct mail, as well as point-of-purchase display materials. He may also obtain assistance from his trade association, since most of these provide suggestions for advertising programs, scheduling of advertising, and ideas for the details of individual advertisements.

The large store will have a complete advertising department, with almost all the same specialists found in the advertising agency. In a large department store, the advertising is generally under the control of the advertising or the sales promotion manager, who usually reports either to the general manager or to the merchandising manager. The sales promotion manager will normally have his division divided into three departments: advertising, display, and publicity or promotion. The completeness of the work of the advertising department will be evident from the typical department store organization chart of the advertising department shown in Figure 19–1.

The department plans all advertising, in cooperation with the general merchandising manager, and has the task of the actual preparation and production of all advertising and display and the selection of media and placement of the advertising. They normally do not use an agency for their advertising (for the reasons discussed in the following section), although in some instances they will use an agency for certain special parts of their advertising, such as the production of television programs or advertising placed in national media. And, in the case of the large national chains, which now are doing a good deal of national advertising in magazines and television, they are handling this through advertising agencies.

Why retailers normally do not use agencies

Although virtually all general advertisers use advertising agencies, as discussed earlier in this chapter, very few retailers do. Large retailers typically plan and prepare all their own advertising in their own internal advertising departments, and small retailers usually utilize the assistance

FIGURE 19–1. Department Stores, Inc. organization chart: advertising division

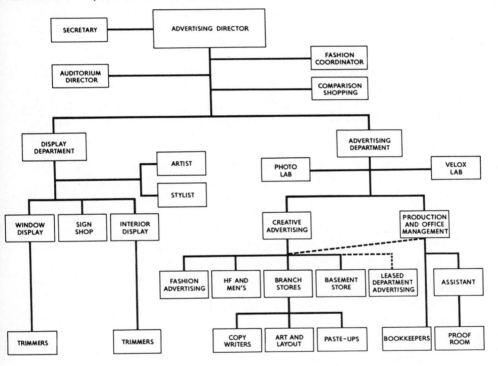

of media and the manufacturers who supply their merchandise. The following factors are most significant in the nonuse of advertising agencies in the planning and preparation of retail advertising.

1. By far the largest share of retail advertising is placed in newspapers at "local," or retail, rates. These are normally considerably lower than

national rates, and the newspaper does not grant a commission to an agency for placing such local advertising. Hence, if the store were to use an agency to handle its advertising, it would probably have to pay the agency a fee, since generally newspapers will not grant a commission to the agency. Hence, there is not the "no cost" for services of the agency feature which is an important factor in the wide use of agencies by general national advertisers.

2. The retail store normally works on a very close time schedule. That is, although the general program of the advertising and the strategy is planned well in advance, the actual individual advertisement is often written "against time" or "against a deadline." Frequently the final touches are put on the advertisement at the last minute. Factors in causing this delay in preparation include the desire to take advantage of weather conditions, competitors' activities, and consumer reactions. Most retailers feel that their internal department can handle these last-minute revisions better and more easily than an outside organization, regardless of its technical competence.

3. The average retail store handles a large number and wide variety of products, many more than the average national advertiser. In a large department store, several dozen of these items may be advertised on any single day and hundreds over a period of time. With the department right in the store, the creative people can work closely with buyers and merchandise managers to obtain information on the merchandise and customers necessary to create effective advertising. It would be quite difficult for the account executives of agencies and the agency creative people to know so many products and markets so well.

4. Many retailers obtain a great deal of free counseling and creative work from the media they use and from their merchandise suppliers. Closely related to this feature is the fact that much of the help from their sources of merchandise is in the form of mats (or transcriptions) furnished by the manufacturer to be used exactly as furnished if the retailer is to be elegible for the cooperative deal (in which the manufacturer usually pays for at least one half of the cost of the media space or time).

THE ADVERTISING AGENCY

The advertising agency is a unique type of business organization that has over the past century played a very significant part in the development and growth of advertising as a part of the American economy. The standard Directory of Advertising Agencies lists approximately 4,800 national advertising agencies. It is estimated that they prepare and place about 75 percent of the national and regional advertising.

Definition[1]

An advertising agency is—
1. an independent business organization
2. composed of creative and business people
3. who develop, prepare and place advertising in advertising media
4. for sellers seeking to find customers for their goods and services.

An agency may do things related to advertising and to help make the advertising succeed, but if the agency does not prepare and place advertising, it is not an advertising agency.

Note the key words in the definition:
1. Independent

   An advertising agency is an independent business organization—independently owned and not owned by advertisers or media or suppliers—

   a) independent so as to bring to the clients' problems an outside objective point of view made more valuable by experience with other clients' sales problems in other fields;

   b) independent of the clients so as to be always an advocate of advertising (seeking to apply advertising to help clients grow and prosper);

   c) independent of media or suppliers so as to be unbiased in serving its clients (the sellers of goods and services).

2. An advertising agency is composed of creative and business people. They are writers and artists, showmen and market analysts, media analysts and merchandising men and women. They are research people, sales people, advertising specialists of all sorts, but with all this, they are business people, running an independent business, financially responsible, applying their creative skills to the business of helping to make their clients' advertising succeed.

3. These people develop, prepare, and place advertising in advertising media.

   Adertising agencies seek in every way they can to apply advertising to advance their clients' businesses. Everything that goes before and everything that comes after the advertisement is preparation for the advertising or follow-up to help make it succeed. To prepare and place advertising—successful advertising for the advertiser—is the primary purpose of the advertising agency.

4. The agency does this, not for itself, but for sellers seeking to find customers for the sellers' goods and services.

Agency organization

A typical organization chart for an agency, showing the functions performed, is shown in Figure 19–2.

---

[1] Reprinted with permission of the American Association of Advertising Agencies, Inc., 420 Lexington Avenue, New York 17.

FIGURE 19–2

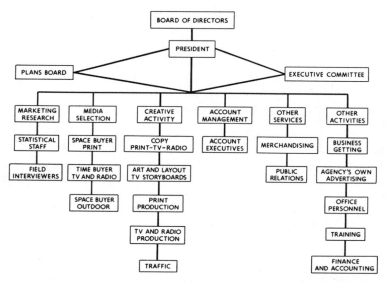

Source: "The World of Advertising," *Advertising Age*, Vol. 34, No. 3 (January 15, 1963), p. 38.

Types of agency organization

Agencies are organized in many ways—no two, perhaps, in exactly the same way. Management may elect to organize the larger agency in either of two major ways—as a group agency or as a departmentalized or concentric agency.

In a group agency (and these are usually larger firms), a group of people handles the contact, planning, and creative work for one or more clients or products. Similar groups handle other accounts. Each group does its contacting, works out the plans (subject to check by the agency's planning board or its chief officers), writes the copy, and makes the illustrations. Parallel to that group, another does the same for other accounts. Usually all groups use the centralized research, media, print production, and accounting departments. All have the benefit of a general planning board.

The second type of agency, the departmentalized or concentric, is completely departmentalized by the functions performed. Each department serves all clients. The account executive calls on the copy department for the copywriting for his accounts, the art department for the layouts and illustrations, and so on.

Some agencies are a mixture of the group and departmentalized types, incorporating certain features of each. There are many possible variations.

For a view of agency organization and work, it is usually best to consider the various nonadministrative jobs, treating each one as a separate function.

The account executive's job (which is usually a combination of contact, plans, and merchandising work) is one of the top positions in the field. As liaison between the advertising agency and the client whose product is being advertised, the account man must have a good general knowledge of all phases of advertising, merchandising, and general business practice. In many cases, he must also be a creative man, able to aid in building plans for a campaign and to suggest solutions to the client's special advertising problem.

Copywriting furnishes jobs for another large group of people in the agency business, and several thousands more for people in firms that produce at least part of their own advertising or help others to advertise. One point often overlooked is that the copywriter often does more than write headlines, copy, captions, and the rest. He frequently is called on to produce the entire idea for an advertisement, or a complete plan, and to have a hand in planning the layout and illustration for his written copy.

Art and layout men, working with the advertising manager, account executive, or copywriter establish the layout for advertising copy and see that proper artwork is prepared.

Research people provide the facts on which advertising can be built. They carry on the kinds of research discussed in chapter 14 and 15. Mechanical production men and women have the task of translating artwork and copy into the mechanical materials used in reproducing the finished advertisement. A wide knowlldege of engraving, lithography, typography, electrotyping, and many other technical processes is needed to see that the most effective work is done as economically as possible. Responsible for coordinating the flow of advertising materials to publications, mechanical production people often oversee the flow of work (traffic) through their agencies as well.

Radio and television production personnel put on the shows that go over the air. Working closely with the directors of the shows, they see to it that casts are hired, physical properties procured, and the other problems solved that lie behind even the simplest radio or television performance.

Media selection is the job of finding the best possible places for the advertiser to present his message. Hundreds of magazines, each with a different combination of characteristics; thousands of business publications serving different business fields; thousands of newspapers, daily and weekly, each serving its geographical area; the national television and radio networks and the hundreds of television stations and thousands of radio stations serving local areas; outdoor plants where traffic congregates; car cards in buses, subways, taxicabs, trains, and stations; all these and more—windows and store displays, direct mail, premiums, and sampling—all are included in what agencies need to know about the available media and means which can be used to carry their clients' messages to potential customers or trade factors.

Media also are changing constantly, and require continuing study by hundreds of agency specialists and researchers who do nothing else.

Elements of agency service

"Agency service," as defined by the American Association of Advertising Agencies, "consists of interpreting to the public, or to that part of it which it is desired to reach, the advantages of a product or service." This interpretation is based upon:

1. A study of the client's product or service to determine the advantages and disadvantages inherent in the product itself and in its relation to competition.
2. An analysis of the present and potential market for which the product or service is adapted:
    a) As to location.
    b) As to extent of possible sales.
    c) As to season.
    d) As to trade and economic conditions.
    e) As to nature and amount of competition.
3. A knowledge of the factors of distribution and sales and their methods of operation.
4. A knowledge of all the available media and means which can profitably be used to carry the interpretation of the product or service to consumer, wholesaler, dealer, contractor, or other factor.
    This knowledge covers:
    a) Character
    b) Influence
    c) Circulation
        Quantity
        Quality
        Location
    d) Physical requirements
    e) Costs
5. Formulation of a definite plan, and presentation of this plan to the client.
6. Execution of this plan:
    a) Writing, designing, illustrating advertisements, or other appropriate forms of the message.
    b) Contracting for the space or other means of advertising.
    c) The proper incorporation of the message in mechanical form

and forwarding it with proper instruction for fulfillment of the contract.

d) Checking and verifying insertions, display, or other means used.

e) The auditing, billing, and paying for the service, space, and preparation.

7. Cooperation with the client's sales work, to insure the greatest effect from advertising.

These are the elements of agency service, whether all the above functions are shared by a few persons, or each function is carried on separately by a specialized department. Into this pattern fit account executives who contact the client, art directors, copywriters, space and time buyers, research workers, mechanical production and radio production people, and so on.

Additional agency services

In addition to advertising service there is a willingness among many agencies today to assist the client with his other activities of distribution. They do special work for the manufacturer in such fields as package designing, sales research, sales training, preparation of sales and service literature, designing and production of merchandising displays, public relations, and publicity. The agency, however, must justify such work by doing it more satisfactorily than can either the manufacturer himself or a competing expert.

Sources of agency compensation

Nearly all major media—newspapers, magazines, television, radio, business publications, outdoor plant owners, and transit advertising companies—allow commissions to advertising agencies, which they recognize individually.

The commission is usually 15 percent of the medium's published rate, although outdoor plant operators pay 16.66 percent.

The medium will bill the agency for the gross cost of the space (or time). In this instance assume the space cost is $10,000. The medium will allow an agency commission of 15 percent, or $1,500, so the agency would owe the medium $8,500. Since most publishers (but not broadcasters) also grant a 2 percent cash discount for prompt payment, the actual amount the agency would pay the medium would be $8,500 less $170, or $8,330. The agency would in turn bill the advertiser for the full gross amount of the space bill, $10,000, less the $170 cash discount for prompt payment.

This medium commission normally covers the planning and creative work of the agency, and the selection and placement of advertising in media, but does not cover the production costs involved for many of the materials involved. Suppliers of artwork, typography, and plates for print media, and electrical transcriptions for television do not allow an agency commission. The agency will normally bill the client for such production costs, and, depending upon its agreement with the client, will usually add its own service charge of 15 percent or 17.65 percent (to equal 15 percent on the "selling price" of the service) to the amount of the bill for each expenditure made on behalf of the client for production.

In some cases, and for some services, the agency may work on a fee basis. This may be the case for a market research study, the preparation of direct-mail or dealer displays, or for retail or industrial accounts.

Larger advertising agencies receive, on the average, about 75 percent of their income in the form of commissions allowed by advertising media, 20 percent from the agency's own percentage charges on purchases (which they specify and/or supervise for their clients), and 5 percent in fees of various kinds for special services. Among medium-sized agencies, the corresponding figures are 70 percent, 20 percent, and 10 percent; and among smaller agencies 60 percent, 25 percent, and 15 percent.

Agency service charges and fees are arrived at individually by agreement between each agency and client.

Agency recognition

In order for an agency to qualify to receive media commissions, it must be "recognized" by the medium involved. The procedure generally followed is that no person or firm should be able to receive the commission until he (or it) has satisfied the medium that it is qualified to provide the services required to "earn" the "functional discount" the medium grants the agency. The services listed below are what media say agencies do for them:

1. The advertising agency develops new business.
2. The agency reduces the hazards of advertising, and thereby the mortality rate in the medium's business.
3. The agency advocates the idea of advertising.
4. The agency creates the advertising messages which are an essential element in the sale of the space or time which media wish to sell. This is the conversion of white space or blank time into advertising influence.
5. The agency develops and improves advertising techniques, and thereby increases the productivity of advertising.
6. The agency simplifies the medium's credit operations and reduces the costs of these operations.

7. The agency carries the cost of credit losses.
8. The agency simplifies and reduces the medium's cost in the mechanical preparation of advertising.
9. The agency reduces the medium's cost in following up advertising schedules to meet publication or broadcasting deadlines.

The requirements that an agency must meet to qualify for the commission are:

1. To be free from control by an advertiser, or from control by a medium owner.
2. To have sufficient personnel of ability and experience to serve properly general advertisers.
3. To have sufficient financial resources to meet obligations it might incur with media.

It should be noted that, prior to 1956 (the year a consent decree was entered into by the Justice Department, the American Association of Advertising Agencies, and the media associations, restraining these organizations from enforcing uniform standards for "recognition" and from withholding commissions from agencies not recognized by the associations), a requisite for recognition was that the agency not rebate any commissions to clients.

Since then, recognition is strictly a medium decision. However, in practice most media adhere to the old rules, and the procedure for obtaining recognition is essentially the same as prior to 1956. Media still grant the commission only to recognized agencies. However, in a few instances, so-called "house agencies," controlled by an advertiser, are recognized and granted commissions by media. But there has still been no major shift away from the usual commission method of agency operation.

The commission system

There has been criticism of the commission system of payment of advertising agencies for many years. For example, why should an agency still be paid by the medium instead of by the client? (in contrast to the early 1900s, when, in essence, agencies were sales organizations for the print media). Does this arrangement serve as an inducement for the agency to recommend more expensive media? Does it cause agencies to recommend larger budgets, to increase media expenditures? Is agency compensation correlated with services rendered? That is, it may not take a great deal more agency time and effort to produce the full-page advertisement to run in a consumer publication whose page rate is $60,000 per page than for the advertisement to run in an industrial trade magazine whose page rate is $300. But, the agency receives $9,000 commission in the first instance, and only $45 commission in the second.

Another argument advanced is that there is no established rule for what services are included in the 15 percent commission. Hence, either the advertiser may be paying for "free" services he does not want and would not order if he were controlling payment arrangements, or else he is paying fees for services that should be included in the commission.

Some of the main arguments *for* the commission system are: It is a simple system that the industry has learned to "live with" over the years and that has worked reasonably well; it eliminates the need to haggle over rates of compensation, and puts agency competition on nonprice factors, such as creativity and service; it is a fairly flexible system, in that agencies may give more "free" services to large and profitable accounts, and put the top people and more time on the advertisements of the major accounts.

Most agencies, media, and advertising managers still consider the commission system a satisfactory one, although approximately one third of the advertising managers are of the opinion that some fee system would be preferable.

The agency industry

In 1972 there were approximately 4,800 agencies in the United States, employing an estimated 75,000 people. Of these, 624 agencies included in a compilation by *Advertising Age* billed a total of $10.5 billion in 1971. And the top 66 agencies, each billing over $25 million, billed $8 billion of this, or four fifths of the total. The top ten agencies billed a total of $4.1 billion, or 39 percent of the total.

On the basis of total (world) billings for 1971, the 10 largest American agencies and their billings are given in Figure 19–3.

FIGURE 19–3. Ten leading agencies on basis of total billings, 1971*

Billing world	Rank U.S.		World billing	U.S. billing
1	1	J. Walter Thompson Co.	$774.0	$419.0
2	7	McCann-Erickson	593.9	232.9
3	2	Young & Rubicam	503.5	317.3
4	5	Ted Bates & Co.	424.8	244.8
5	3	Leo Burnett & Co.	422.7	296.8
6	4	Batten, Barton, Durstine & Osborn	331.5	296.1
7	10	Ogilvy & Mather International	296.5	176.5
8	6	Doyle Dane Bernbach	280.3	234.9
9	8	Grey Advertising	255.9	195.0
10	9	D'Arcy-MacManus-Intermarco	245.0	185.0

* *Advertising Age*, February 21, 1972, p. 30.

QUESTIONS

1. Discuss briefly the factors you think are most important in determining where the advertising department should be positioned in the company organization.

2. Do you think the location of the advertising department within the company really makes much difference in its functioning? Explain.

3. Why do advertising departments of companies, spending about the same amount of dollars on advertising, vary so in terms of size and number of employees?

4. Why do industrial product firms, which normally spend relatively far less on advertising than consumer product firms, often have larger advertising departments?

5. Do you agree with the reasons given for "why most large national advertisers use advertising agencies"? Explain.

6. If you were a large national advertiser whose present agency had just "resigned" your account,
   - *a)* How would you proceed to select a new advertising agency?
   - *b)* What criteria would you establish for selecting the agency?
   - *c)* Who in the company should make the final decision on the agency? Why?

7. As an advertising manager, how would you work with the agency to get maximum results?

8. If you were the advertising manager for a large national firm, how would you evaluate the work of your advertising agency?

9. Some large national advertisers with wide lines of products use four or five different advertising agencies, giving each certain products. Why do you think they do so? Do you think this is a good policy? Why?

10. Why do retailers seldom use advertising agencies? Do you think this explanation is valid? Why?

11. Explain the commission system of compensating agencies. Why has this system been questioned in recent years?

12. What method of compensating agencies do you think is best? What method do you think will predominate in the future? Why?

13. Do you think an agency should have to turn down an account because it already has a competitive account? Why?

14. Do you believe it is advisable for a company to have an advertising department and also hire an advertising agency? Give reasons.

15. A large manufacturer recently announced a change in its advertising agency. For a period of 15 years, Agency A had represented the company, and during that period of time the company had become one of the three leaders in its field. Sales had been increasing each year, and current-year figures indicate that sales should exceed last year's volume by 5 percent. The relationships between the company and the agency were of the best. However, the president of the company stated that it was for the best interest of both parties to make a change. Give your reasons as to why you believe

the company followed this policy. Check in a current issue of *Advertising Age* and find other cases in which an account has changed hands.

CASE 1.   NORTHERN ELECTRIC COMPANY
Location of advertising function

The Northern Electric Company has expanded its operations into new product lines to try to stabilize its sales, which have fluctuated widely during the past five years. As a result, the company is faced with the problem of developing a new organizational structure.

Northern began its operations by manufacturing audio recording-reproduction equipment which was used primarily for recording and reproducing music, voice, and other program material for radio and television stations, recording companies, and allied groups.

In the initial stages of the company's development, its products were handled by an exclusive distribution agency. The company's organization structure at that time appears in Exhibit 1.

EXHIBIT 1

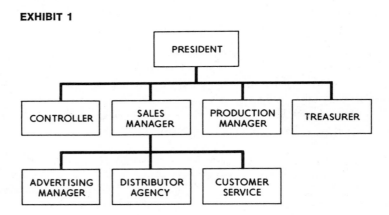

Later the company engaged other distributors, and then established distribution through nonexclusive local distributors. However, the organizational chart of the company was not changed, and the sales manager remained responsible for directing all the advertising of the company.

By modifying and extending the range of its audio receivers, the company was able to record measurement information and control information on tape. As a result, whole new markets of specific applications in the use of the equipment for telemetering, securing data on aircraft performance, shock and vibration control opened up for the company.

In order to handle the new markets, the company decided to change its method of distribution and set up its own sales staff, and, at the same time, changed the responsibility and authority of the sales manager. See Exhibit 2.

 EXHIBIT 2

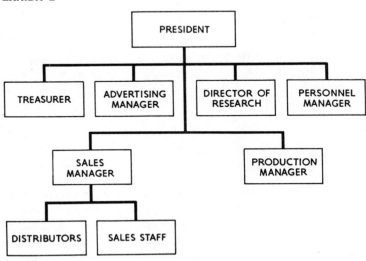

The sales manager argued against the new organizational structure. He emphasized that the objectives of the sales department were centered on providing the means to sell the goods. In the new structure, he no longer directed the advertising of the company. He also believed that there might be a tendency to place too much emphasis on general advertising and overlook the use of advertising as a selling tool.

The advertising manager did not agree with the sales manager and believed that the new organizational structure would provide a satisfactory supporting arrangement so that each function could work most effectively and in balance with the other functions. It was his opinion that the advertising function had to be considered in a context broader than that of a strictly selling function. He considered that advertising is both a line and staff operation. On the one hand, he stated that he advised, assisted, and counseled both the president and his staff on broad matters which would affect the long-term image of the company, and, on the other hand, he was directly concerned with carrying out the necessary creative work which the sales manager required for securing adequate sales.

In the organizational structure recommended in Exhibit 2, he believed that he had the authority and responsibility to handle the advertising function in the manner that this activity demanded.

The sales manager did not agree and contended that in the new structure he would not have control over the complete sales activity of the company.

Case questions

1. What organizational structure should Northern Electric adopt?

2. Where should the advertising function be placed in a company?

3. What effect will a change in organizational structure have on the individuals involved?

CASE 2. DAJ PAPER COMPANY
Recognizing the advertising function

The DAJ Paper Company manufactures and sells industrial and household paper products through the company's salesmen to wholesale distributors and jobbers in the industrial grocery, paper, drug, hardware, and janitor supply fields. The advertising has been handled on a decentralized basis, with the sales manager of each division being responsible for the advertising of the products which he was responsible for selling.

The company has expanded rapidly and only recently purchased a competitor, the CIV Industrial Paper Company, in order to be able to offer a more extensive line of industrial products. The advertising and sales organization has not been changed for a period of 20 years and, as a result, has developed a number of overlapping functions between the different sales divisions. See Exhibit 1.

The industry in which DAJ Paper Company is engaged is highly competitive. There are specialized firms as well as national concerns which compete in the market for each product that the company sells. Two of the national brands are backed with heavy national advertising and the local specialized firms have developed strong customer preference and loyalty over the years.

The company has five sales divisions: industrial, gummed and coated products, waxed papers, wrapping papers, and consumer products. The sales organization plan of the company resulted in the salesmen from the different divisions calling on the same distributors and customers in many instances. The salesmen and agents of the company were located in the cities as given in Exhibit 2. The agents operated on a 5 percent commission and originally had been used by the company to contact distributors prior to the period when the company extended its sales

XHIBIT 1

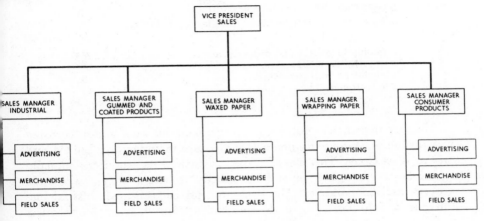

force. These agents had done a satisfactory job in building demand and had been allowed to continue to be credited for the business which they secured.

Shortly after the purchase of the CIV Industrial Paper Company, the vice president of sales retired and the sales manager of the Consumer Products Division was promoted to the vacated vice presidency. He wanted to reorganize the sales force and centralize the advertising function to eliminate as much duplication in sales promotion and sales coverage as possible and to make his salesmen more effective. He also wanted to eliminate 11 of the 14 industrial agents to whom the company paid a 5 percent commission, because cost of sales by the company's

EXHIBIT 2

	Industrial agents	Industrial salesmen	Gummed and coated products Pacific coast salesmen	Waxed papers salesmen	Wrapping papers salesmen	Consumer product salesmen	Total salesmen
Seattle.............	2	1	1		1	1	4
Portland...........	2				1		1
San Francisco......	3	2	1	1	2	1	7
Los Angeles........	3	2	1	1	2	1	7
Salt Lake City......	2				1		1
Denver.............	2	1			1	1	3
	14	6	3	2	8	4	23

salesmen was only 2 percent. These agents were competing with the company's salesmen for the same accounts.

Total sales of the company were divided as follows:

```
To wholesale grocers and cooperatives..................... 20%
To paper wholesalers......................................... 30
To wholesale drug companies............................... 5
To industrial users.......................................... 45
```

The vice president's problem in reorganizing his sales and advertising was further accentuated when a large eastern manufacturer built a mill on the West Coast. This manufacturer advertised its products nationally and followed a policy of selling directly to chain stores, wholesale grocers, and cooperatives. The company did not sell an industrial line but put its full efforts on resale outlets. As a result, both the products and brand names of this eastern manufacturer were well established in the consumer market. This company sold 60 percent of its volume to chain stores and 40 percent to wholesale grocers and cooperatives.

The vice president pointed out that he was planning to centralize the advertising function for the following reasons:

1. To consolidate the function so that one person would be responsible for the total advertising.
2. To have a unified advertising program.
3. To purchase advertising space more effectively.
4. To coordinate and guide all the activities.
5. To stimulate more aggressive selling.
6. To relieve the sales managers of the responsibility of placing advertising.
7. To make all the divisions more profit conscious.
8. To meet the sales challenge of the national firm that has invaded the market.
9. To improve the corporate identity.
10. To have the sales managers specialize in sales and general merchandising functions.

When the sales managers were told about the plan, a number of them objected and indicated that they would not be able to perform their jobs as effectively. Among the reasons which they emphasized were:

1. Under decentralization, the advertising decisions could be made more speedily.
2. The divisions of the company were unique and each division had specialized advertising problems.
3. Since they had the responsibility for making the quotas that were assigned, they should have the authority to decide what type of advertising should be used.
4. The sales managers had the background and experience to shoulder the responsibility of deciding on the advertising.

5. Each division of the company had been making satisfactory progress and during the last 10 years, sales of the company had increased faster than those of its competitors.
6. The sales managers were closer to the market and had a better insight as to the kind of advertising that should be used.
7. Decision-making power should be given as close to the place where the action takes place as is feasible.
8. There would be danger of too much image-building advertising which might clash with the assignment of responsibility and authority of the sales managers who need these funds for increasing sales of their divisions.
9. It would take away the initiative of the sales managers.

Case questions

1. Evaluate the reasons which the vice president and the sales managers gave for and against the centralization of the advertising function.

2. What are some of the major functions which the central advertising department might perform that are not being done on the present decentralized basis?

3. What other factors would determine whether or not the DAJ Company should centralize its advertising activities?

4. Do you believe it requires a different type of person to handle the advertising for each of the product divisions of the company?

5. What advertising organization plan would you recommend for the DAJ Company?

CASE 3. MYERS CANDY COMPANY
Importance of using an advertising agency

In June, Carl Myers, president of the Myers Candy Company, called his two sons into his office. He asked them to consider if it would be advisable to check with an advertising agency about handling the advertising for the company.

The Myers Candy Company was located in New York City and had built a premium business for its high-grade candy in the city. All its candy was manufactured and packaged on the second floor of the New York building which the company owned. The first floor of this building was used for the sale of candy and for restaurant purposes.

Myers' candy was considered to be one of the premium products in the area, and, as a result, the company charged a price which averaged about 50 percent above prices at which nationally advertised boxes of candies were sold.

With the continued growth of the suburbs and the development of large shopping areas, Myers had found that its candy sales had continued to decrease each year during the last five years. (See Exhibit 1.)

EXHIBIT 1. Myers Candy sales

Year A	$265,000
" B	232,000
" C	212,000
" D	195,000
" E	194,000

Sales operations

Until Year E, all the candy had been sold through the Myers store in the city of New York. In June of Year E, however, the company had leased space for a candy department in a department store in a major shopping center outside New York City. It had been selling candy in this new department for three months in Year E. While the sales in this outlet had not reached the level which was hoped, nevertheless, Myers was optimistic about the long-term potential of this department.

Curve of seasonal influence in the company's candy sales is approximately as follows: Peak sales occur at Christmas, Valentine's Day, Easter, and Mother's Day, with a declining trend during June to October and a rise thereafter to the peak period.

All candies are sold under Myers' trade name. The trademark of the company is registered.

Advertising

Two New York newspapers and one radio station had been used in advertising the company's candies. The advertising always had been written by Mr. Myers. He believed in a personalized type of message which he featured in each advertisement. As an example, he had a special portrait sketch made of himself, and this was used with the copy he wrote. He generally tried to emphasize the reasons why Myers' candy was the finest candy that could be purchased. He pointed out the great care he took in buying the ingredients. In other instances, he would include letters he received from some distinguished person who wrote to him and stated how much he had enjoyed Myers' candy.

General comment

After an analysis of the company's sales, the sons recommended that Myers go after selective distribution on a more extensive basis in the New York area. It was their opinion that Myers had adequate production facilities to increase its output by about 40 percent. However, they questioned the need for hiring an advertising agency because they believed that the advertising would have to be concentrated in the local newspapers and other media of this nature. They doubted that an advertising agency would be of much help in working with a company that sold only in a very limited market.

Case question

What advantage would it be for Myers to use an advertising agency?

CASE 4. R & J DRESS MANUFACTURER
Selecting an advertising agency

The R & J dress manufacturer is engaged in the design, production, and sales of a diversified line of misses' casual dresses which are sold in the budget departments by department stores and specialty shops.

R & J introduces four seasonal lines each year, with transitional lines added periodically. The dresses produced by the company are sold to about 2,000 department, specialty, and women's apparel stores through its own officers, salesmen, and sales representatives. It has a sales office and showroom in New York.

All advertising has been handled by its own staff because R & J has not attempted to build a national brand appeal, but has depended on its styling, price, and service to sell the stores.

The women's apparel industry is highly competitive, and no one company accounts for more than a small part of the national output. Sales of the company had increased to such a degree that the officers decided to try to create a demand for the R & J brand. As a result, the company asked several advertising agencies to present information about their experience. One of the agencies, the KD & A Agency, presented the following material:

Introduction

KD & A Advertising Agency is a flourishing and expanding one, and has been in the advertising business for more than 40 years. In this period, it has catered to the needs of advertising programs for various types of clients from all over the United States. However, more of the advertising business of this agency is concentrated on the East Coast. It is interesting to note that the ownership of this agency has remained with its employees.

In order to understand better the workings of an advertising agency, it is deemed important to discuss in brief the development and concepts of advertising in general.

What is advertising?

A great many marketing transactions involving both the transfer of ownership and physical movement of goods take place in this country daily. Most purchases of goods—whether by manufacturers for use in their factories and offices, by wholesalers and retailers either for equipment purposes or for resale, by consumers for household or personal use, and others—are the result of some sort of selling effort on the part of vendors. Advertising and personal selling play an indispensable role in our economy. Advertising has become an integral part of present economy.

Modern advertising is a recent development, its growth having come in less than a century—the period of the industrial development of this nation. At the close of the Civil War, the American economy was predominantly agricultural, characterized largely by small communities. Now the country has a highly advanced industrial economy in which large-scale producers of a great variety of products sell on a nationwide basis. Advertising has played a major role in this development into an industrial economy, the annual national expenditure on advertising rising to $12.5 billion in 1962.

Advertising must be viewed in perspective as constituting only a part of the whole selling process, and, as such, its effectiveness must be evaluated.

What is an advertising agency?

Advertising agencies play an important part in conducting the advertising of most manufacturers today. The advertising agency is a firm, specializing in advertising, which provides counsel relative to the advertising and allied operations of its clients, and actually prepares, buys space and time for, and places a large part of the advertising of its clients. In addition, it may perform other services, such as conducting market research, preparing sales promotional materials, counseling on public relations, preparing and distributing public relations messages, and so on.

Since the turn of the century, with the general agency plan crystallized and with agents more and more accepting responsibility for offering full plans and preparing as well as planning advertisements, the trend has become strong for agencies to offer more service and to become not just advertising counsels but also marketing counsels. The number of services offered and the competency in the services vary, of course, among agencies, and so do their internal organizations.

There are account executives who contact the clients, and there are art directors, copywriters, space and time buyers, research workers, mechanical production workers, and so on. The problem of effective organization of an agency, particularly a large agency, is not an easy one. An advertising agency is a collection of advertising and marketing specialists—specialists in planning, advertising, and selling, in copywriting, in layout and typography, in production of advertisements, in production of radio and television shows, in marketing research, in consumer research, and so on. To service a client well calls for the assignment of competent men to the account and good coordination of the work of the various types of specialists.

KD & A advertising agency

A. *Location.* The advertising agency's main office is located in New York, and it has offices in San Francisco, Chicago, and Washington. The company runs its business in this nation through its four offices, but a major portion of its business activity is located on the East Coast.

B. *Personnel.* This company has 84 employees running the various activities of the agency.

C. *Structure.* The stockholders of this company elect the board of directors, which in turn elects the chairman of the board and appoints the president, who is the executive head of the company. Four executive vice presidents and 15 other vice presidents are is charge of specific operations of the company in all its offices. Each of the offices is in charge of the manager, who is a vice president. The accounts function is carried out mainly at the New York office. Other important office bearers are production manager, who is in charge of the mechanics of advertising; media manager, who is concerned with buying space and time in the media; television and radio director; creative director; and research director.

D. *Clients.* KD & A has clients with various types of products such as apparel, groceries, building materials, home equipment, travel, and others such as insurance, department stores, and cosmetics. However, apparel and food products have been the important advertising clients. The agency enters into a contract with its clients to offer its services demanded by clients under the general contractual arrangements.

E. *Current Business.* KD & A reports billings of $8,645,000, of which $2,750,000 was in capitalized fees and $100,000 in billings outside the United States. Billing breakdown by percent was: newspapers, 22.1; magazines, 31.1; radio, 1.1; television, 15.1; outdoor, 19.1; business papers, 10.1; and point of purchase or sales, 2.1.

F. *Agency Services.* The agency envisages in its field of operations the services described below:

1. A study of the product or service in order to determine the advantages and disadvantages inherent in the product itself and in its relation to competition.
2. An analysis of the present potential market for which the product or service is adapted; as to location, the extent of possible sale, season, trade and economic conditions, nature and amount of competition.
3. A knowledge of the factors of distribution and sales and their methods of operation.
4. A knowledge of all the available media and means which can profitably be used to carry the interpretation of the product or service to consumer, wholesaler, dealer, contractor, or other factor.

This knowledge covers: character, influence, circulation (quantity, quality, location), physical requirements, costs. Acting on the study, analysis, and knowledge as explained in the preceding paragraphs, recommendations are made, and the following procedure ensues:

5. Formulation of a definite plan.
6. Execution of this plan:
    a) Writing, designing, illustrating of advertisements or other appropriate forms of the message;
    b) Contracting for the space or other means of advertising;
    c) The proper incorporation of the message in mechanical form, and forwarding it with proper instructions for the fulfillment of the contract;
    d) Checking and verifying of insertions, display, or other means used;
    e) Auditing, billing, and paying for the service, space, and preparation.
7. Cooperation with the sales work, to insure the greatest effect from advertising.

Conclusion

The President of R & J decided in favor of the RD & A Agency, and gave the following summary to his board:

1. KD & A is a relatively small agency and will have a personal interest in our account.
2. The agency has had experience in the apparel field.
3. The agency is in a sound financial position and has been in business for over 40 years.
4. The agency has offices in several states and will be able to make market studies for us in a number of areas.
5. The agency has handled a variety of products.

Case question

What additional information should R & J have considered before selecting an advertising agency to handle its account?

PART **VII**—————————

Legal aspects

LEGAL AND PUBLIC POLICY

THE INFLUENCE of government on business has evolved not only through the design of federal administration, but also through the demands of business itself. Step by step, business has grown to the point where it no longer can control its own destiny and has found that it needs help and guidance. As Thomas C. Cochran, in his book *The American Business System* (Harvard University Press, 1957) stated,

Loss of confidence in the theory of self-regulation was bound to lead to reassessment of business ideas and new conceptions of the place of business in American society. This painful struggle for readjustment must be seen in relation to another major change in society, the rise of bureaucracy . . . whether one looked at government as did most business leaders when they lamented the loss of concern for the individual, or at big business as did novelists and some small businessmen, the conclusion was inescapable that individualism, as traditionally conceived, was declining. Fewer men were left in impersonal relation to markets where their personal eccentricities did not count, and where individual cleverness might win immediate cash rewards. More men had to try to please their organizational associates by some degree of conformity. Businessmen were voluntarily surrendering individual freedom in order to get ahead in a bureaucratic society.

The point of greatest importance that stands out is that businessmen have sacrificed individualism in order to gain in size and power, and with this loss of individualism has come a decrease in idealism and a limitation of a sense of individual responsibility.

POWER OF GOVERNMENT

There was a time when the influence of government was largely limited to providing machinery whereby individuals could enforce agreements and be protected against fraud. Government sometimes sought to foster its own policies and its political life by operating and controlling business. Business, on the other hand, sometimes sought to manipulate the government and the economic life of the country by forming monopolies.

Under our constitution the federal government has: (1) the power to intervene directly and to operate businesses either as monopolies or in competition with private business (for example, the government operation of the railroads during World War I, the government ownership and operation of the T.V.A.); (2) the taxing power to regulate business indirectly (for example, the tax on sulphur matches and the federal gambling tax); (3) the power to act indirectly through monetary controls (such as regulation of the availability of money, foreign exchange, interest rates, credit limitations); (4) the power to regulate through government agencies (for example, the Interstate Commerce Commission, the Civil Aeronautics Board).

Government exercises its greatest impact on business today through regulation by government agencies. Any form of government regulation may bring about unwanted political influence and its accompanying political, economic, and business problems. This possibility must be weighed against the needs of society. The impact of government intervention must be considered from the standpoint both of its potential and its present activities. If the very existence of a business is dependent upon the grace of the government, it is generally agreed that such business will not achieve dynamic growth.

GOVERNMENT REGULATION

In dealing with protection of both the businessman and the consumer, legislative bodies have been sympathetic in passing a number of laws. We have acquired national and state laws which protect less efficient firms from the full impact of competition. We have laws which protect the rights of the consumers. We have laws which attempt to maintain fair and ethical competition.

Among these laws are the Sherman Antitrust Act of 1890, which attempted to maintain competition by forbidding conspiracies in restraint of trade and agreements to fix prices; the Robinson-Patman Act, an amendment to the Clayton Act, which also attempted to maintain price competition through limiting discounts to cost differentials and requiring promotional and other allowances to be offered on a proportional basis; the Federal Trade Commission Act of 1914, which attempted to provide protection against unfair practices that did not harm particular firms but might generally harm business; the 1938 Federal Food, Drug, and Cosmetic Act, which attempted among other things to protect the consumer against misbranding as well as controlling the qualities and ingredients of such products; the 1938 Wheeler-Lea Act (an amendment of the Federal Trade Commission Act), which attempted to extend the jurisdiction of the Federal Trade Commission to include unfair acts in commerce in addition to unfair methods of competition (this act also attempted to grant more power to the Commission in issuing cease and desist orders and to grant the Commission jurisdiction over false advertising in cosmetics, drugs, food, etc.); the 1941 Products Labeling Act and the 1951 Fur Products Labeling Act which attempted to protect both consumers and producers from the unrevealed presence of substitutes by requiring that labels must show their true compositions. The various state unfair and fair trade practice acts also fall in this category of attempting to maintain fair competition.

All these acts (and various others) have as a basic objective the maintenance of fair competition. It is apparent, however, all segments of society do not look on the definition of "fair competition" in the same manner. On the one hand, as an example, legislators may interpret fair competition to mean it is necessary to keep in business as many companies as possible, while on the other hand, the businessman's interpretation may be that it means he has the right to attempt to obtain more business at the expense of his less efficient competitors.

It must also be kept in mind, however, that regardless of what government regulations are adopted in a free society, competition cannot be completely avoided. If we limit price competition, we encourage the use of nonprice competition. If we limit the use of advertising, we encourage the use of other methods of stimulating demand. If we restrict the development of one type of economic control, we encourage business firms to adopt some other method.

We should also, when we evaluate the use of legislation for the control of advertising, question if such legislation is actually needed for the preservation of fair competition and not primarily for the purpose of keeping incompetent firms in operation. This question cannot easily be answered, because it is difficult for us to judge when a firm is competent or incompetent. Some industries require a certain degree of bigness to gain the required efficiencies in production and distribution. In other industries, the small firm can operate with a higher degree of efficiency than the large firm.

Consider a Federal Trade Commission report on "Economic Inquiry to Food Marketing." In this study of the frozen fruit, juice, and vegetable industry, the commission indicated that there existed complex marketing patterns, with 270 freezers pitted in sharp competition in the institutional and retail markets, and with branded products competing against private brands.

The Commission pointed out that large advertising and selling expenditures constituted a major barrier to the entrance or survival of newcomers in the packer-label portion of the frozen food industry.

It went on to state General Foods and Minute Maid had set such a major marketing pace that it is improbable that Libby, Seabrook, and Stokely would be able to increase their share of the market.

Reports from 235 packers indicated that selling expenses were about 7 percent of sales. However, the $9.8 million advertising expenditures of General Foods and Minute Maid represented 46.2 percent of the entire industry total. These two leaders accounted for about 40 percent of the packer-label frozen food products sold.

It would appear from this report that even relatively large firms would find it difficult to make advertising product differentiation pay for itself, and since there was an inverse relationship between the relative burden of advertising and the size of firms, it seemed that advertising requirements alone could provide an effective barrier to new entry into the packer-label section of the industry.

In the soap and detergent industry, three companies (Procter & Gamble, Lever Bros., and Colgate) dominate the field. However, there is marked disparity in size and the share of the market they have. Advertising expenditures again play such an important part in merchandising these products that it is difficult for even Lever Brothers and Colgate to increase their market share. At the same time, these advertising requirements are such that they may preclude small companies from entering the industry.

In some way or another, however, we must come to a consistent policy with regard to how business shall be regulated. And, within this regulatory framework, it is important to reevaluate how advertising shall be regulated. Under our present public policy, there is still too much inconsistency in the interpretations of the acts. Consider some of the problems arising out of the following list of situations:

1. "Consumer protection" high on Congress' list.
2. Better Business Bureaus keep watchful eye on advertisers.
3. Antimerger policy tougher in future.
4. Identical bidding on government contracts not as frequent as thought.
5. FTC hits false prices.
6. Don't let clients waste money on ill-conceived promotions.
7. Counter a rising tide of criticism of drug advertising.
8. House unit hits FTC as ineffectual, apathetic.
9. Antitrust still perils publishers.
10. Decision time is at hand for pay TV.
11. Direct mail will benefit as controls get tougher.
12. British ad group hits newspapers' tie-in ad deals.
13. One-cent sale is questioned.
14. Business rivals spur some attacks on network TV.

15. Post Office drops effort to ban magazine.
16. Kick out the kickbacks.
17. FTC criticizes magazine dealers' payoffs; deplorable but vital.
18. We fail to communicate the worth of ad business.
19. FTC isn't Gestapo.
20. Newspaper groups object to odd-shaped ads as "space stealing" and "self-defeating."
21. Some consequences of advertising psychology.
22. Should we blame advertising?
23. Advertisers give conflicting views in FTC probe of list prices, "free" offers.
24. FCC and FTC probe use of ratings by broadcasters.
25. Appeals Court rejects FTC plea to enjoin Bayer.
26. House sets probe of FTC ban on joint retailer ads.
27. FCC asks commercial limits, station fees.
28. "Truth in packaging" bill stalled.

What action should be taken in each of these situations? Should the action be by the federal government? by the state government? by the local government? by the industry? by private agencies?

What effect will the regulations have on the economy? Will self-regulation be effective? Will the regulations stifle our economic growth?

There are no easy solutions to these questions. While the objective of government regulation of advertising and business should be to provide the best possible conditions for the economy to grow in a natural and balanced manner, it is difficult to predict the effects of any imposed regulation.

It is of interest, therefore, to look at some of the decisions which have been given by the government in order to have a better understanding of what to expect.

DOCUMENTATION OF ADVERTISING CLAIMS[1]

In one of its new approaches designed to "assist consumers to make rational choices, the Federal Trade Commissions is requiring the documentation of advertising claims. The new procedure, outlined in a resolution adopted by the Commission, requires that advertisers submit on demand by the Commission such tests, studies, or other data that purport to substantiate advertised claim regarding a product's safety, performance, efficacy, quality, or comparative price.

In discussing the significance of this resolution, the chairman stated that public access to all documentation will mean that consumer groups and competitors, as well as Commission staff, can screen all available data to determine the "adequacy" to support claims. In addition, publication of data will enhance

---
[1] Excerpts from *Journal of Marketing*, Vol. 34, no. 4, October 1971, pp. 67–79.

the role of competition as an effective regulator of advertising practices. The thrust of this approach is not a pre-clearance requirement for advertising, since the Commission will merely ask for documentation supporting past and current advertisements after they are run. Moreover, it is not a rule requiring adequate substantiation, but merely discloses such substantiation as exists. Nor is it intended to cast doubt upon the continued propriety of "puffing" in advertising. Thus if someone says "tastes great," no documentation will be required; however, if someone says "stops three times as fast," the Commission will ask to see proof.

Following this resolution the Commission has ordered seven domestic and foreign automobile manufacturers to submit documentation to support advertising claims regarding the safety, performance, quality, and comparative price of advertised products. The orders identify specific advertisements and the claims made, and require the submission of all documentation and other substantiation for each identified claim. Examples of these specified claims are "low on insurance rates, low on service cost," and "a car with . . . an energy-absorbing steering column."

Regulation of competition

The Federal Trade Commission has put into effect one of its latest remedies for the "residual effects" of deceptive advertising—"corrective advertisements." Although the agency has announced in a number of recent cases that the proposed orders will include "corrective advertisements," the first order to contain such requirements emerged from a consent order agreement between the ITT Continental Baking Company and the Commission. The agency has charged that the company's Profile bread was not lower in calories than ordinary bread and would not help the purchasers to lose weight, contrary to representations. The consent order provides that for one year after it becomes final, at least 25 percent of the expenditures (excluding production costs) for advertising for each media in each market be devoted to FTC-approved advertisements that the product is not effective for weight reduction, contrary to possible interpretations of prior advertising. Charges involving nutritional claims for Wonder bread and Hostess snack cakes remain pending against the company and its advertising agency.

Consumer advocates have protested the acceptance of the consent order on the grounds that the "corrective advertisements" should have been available for inspection prior to such acceptance. The company has declared that such a requirement would subject them to an unfair exposure of trade secrets since competitors may then see these advertisements before their commercial appearance.

Ecology emphasis

As a result of greater emphasis on ecology, more advertisers have begun to stress their products' antipollution qualities and ecological benefits. The Federal Trade Commission has indicated that it will not allow anyone to take advantage of the consumers' environmental concerns by falsely suggesting that products have "antipollution" qualities.

In one such case the Commission has announced a proposed complaint against a petroleum corporation which states that the firm has falsely advertised that Crown gasolines with CA-101 produce generally pollution-free exhaust. The additive, the complaint says, has no effect upon industrial pollution nor does it significantly reduce air pollution by motor vehicles. In reality, the exhaust contains unburned hydrocarbons, carbon monoxide, nitrogen oxides, and particulates all of which are pollutants.

The proposed order would halt the alleged misrepresentations and forbid any claim concerning a product's characteristic, capacity, or result unless it has been fully and completely substantiated through tests.

Free encyclopedias

The Federal Trade Commission recently charged Crowell-Collier Publishing Co. and a wholly owned subsidiary, P. F. Collier and Son Corp., with making false claims through their door-to-door salesmen and in promotional material.

Some people have been misled by the salesman who tells them that they have been selected as a leading citizen of the community to receive a set of encyclopedia free merely for allowing his company to use their testimonials in making future calls.

This is a rather common "gimmick" used by some salesmen, who state that there is no charge for the set of books, but who insist that the customer contract for the supplemental service for keeping the set up to date. In every instance, the cost for the "supplemental service" equals or exceeds the actual cost of the encyclopedia.

Control of advertising

In the above examples, the companies involved were trying to crystallize the demand of the consumers for products by using arguments which in some cases were derived from depth psychology. Should they be allowed to continue these approaches? Some critics would say that these approaches are unfair. On the other hand, some advertisers would indicate that these sellers simply overestimated the value of the understatement.

One general need of the consumer is to get information that will help him reach decisions about specific products. To the extent that advertising does help consumers in specifying need and justifying choice, it must be regarded as a consumer service. Yet we must recognize that the line between the control of advertising and false advertising should be sharp.

The merits of free enterprise, individual initiative, inventiveness, and endeavor underlie the economic and democratic development of the United States. As with all systems, there are abuses, and consequently, there has evolved regulation of some phases of advertising and business activity. In recent years this government regulation has come increasingly under question. Does it contradict the founding fathers' precept that "that government is best which governs least"? Has it, in certain aspects at least, gone too far? It is difficult to deal conclusively with this elusive topic, but the authors believe that the analysis of the Federal Trade Commission given below will indicate the activities of this agency.

Federal Trade Commission analysis

The Federal Trade Commission has control over the advertisement of commodities. The Supreme Court has held that: "Advertising is merely identification and description, apprising of quality and place. It has no other object than to draw attention to the article to be sold. . . ."[2] However, more recently, the Supreme Court reversed its decision, stating:

Appellee contends that the circulars constituted advertising and, therefore, did not constitute labeling within the meaning of the Act. The contention assumes that printed matter (such as a circular) cannot constitute both advertising and labeling. The assumption is unwarranted. Most, if not all, labeling is advertising. The term, "labeling," is defined in the Act as including all printed matter accompanying any article. Congress did not, and we cannot, exclude from the definition printed matter which constitutes advertising.[3]

General provisions of the Federal Trade Commission Act, Sections (5) and (12) through (18), dealing with the powers and jurisdiction over false advertisement of commodities are quoted in the following paragraphs.

Sec. 5. (a) (1) Unfair methods of competition in commerce, and unfair or deceptive acts or practices in commerce, are hereby declared unlawful.

Sec. 12. (a) It shall be unlawful for any person, partnership, or corporation to disseminate, or cause to be disseminated, any false advertisement—

(1)   By United States mails, or in commerce by any means, for the purpose of inducing, or which is likely to induce, directly or indirectly the purchase of commodities; or

(2)   By any means, for the purpose of inducing, or which is likely to induce, directly or indirectly, the purchase in commerce of commodities.

Sec. 12. (b) The dissemination or the causing to be disseminated of any false advertisement within the provisions of subsection (a) of this section shall be an unfair or deceptive act or practice in commerce within the meaning of Section 5.

Sec. 13. (a) Whenever the Commission has reason to believe—

---

[2] *Rost* v. *Van Demon and Lewis Company,* 240 U.S. 342.

[3] *U.S.* v. *Lee,* 131 F. 2d 461.

(1)   that any person, partnership, or corporation is engaged in, or is about to engage in, the dissemination or the causing of the dissemination of any advertisement in violation of Section 12, and

(2)   that the enjoining thereof pending the issuance of a complaint by the Commission under Section 5, and until such complaint is dismissed by the Commission or set aside by the court of review, or the order of the Commission to cease and desist made thereon has become final within the meaning of Section 5, would be to the interest of the public.

the Commission by any of its attorneys designated by it for such purpose may bring suit in a district court of the United States or in the United States court of any Territory to enjoin the dissemination or the causing of the dissemination of such advertisement.

Sec. 14. (a) Any person, partnership, or corporation who violates any provision of Section 12(a) shall, if the use of the commodity advertised may be injurious to health because of results from such use under the conditions prescribed in the advertisement thereof, or under such conditions as are customary or usual, or if such violation is with intent to defraud or mislead, be guilty of a misdemeanor, and upon conviction shall be punished by a fine or not more than $5,000, or by imprisonment for not more than six months, or by both such fine or imprisonment. . . .

Sec. 15. For the purposes of Sections 12, 13 and 14(a) The term "false advertisement" means an advertisement, other than labeling, which is misleading in a material respect; and in determining whether any advertisement is misleading, there shall be taken into account (among other things) not only representations made or suggested by statement, word, design, device, sound, or any combination thereof; but also the extent to which the advertisement fails to reveal facts material in the light of such representation or material with respect to consequences which may result from the use of the commodity to which the advertisement relates under the conditions prescribed in said advertisement, or under such conditions as are customary or usual. No advertisement of a commodity shall be deemed to be false if it is disseminated only to members of a profession, contains no false representation of material fact, and includes, or is accompanied in each instance by truthful disclosure of, the formula showing quantitatively each ingredient of such product.

Sec. 16. Whenever the Federal Trade Commission has reason to believe that any person, partnership, or corporation is liable to a penalty under Section 14 or under subsection (1) of Section 5, it shall certify the facts to the Attorney General, whose duty it shall be to cause appropriate proceedings to be brought for the enforcement of the provisions of such section or subsection.

Food advertising is not exempt from the rules which apply to misleading advertising in general, regardless of whether or not the food complies with standards set forth by the Food, Drug, and Cosmetic Act. We assume that these standards are met so that now we are primarily interested in the claims made by the manufacturer concerning source, quality content, strength, effect on health, flavor, and purity.

Oftentimes, it is quite misleading as to the product source. Take the term "Swiss" applied to cheese; many consumers may think that this cheese is made in Switzerland. The same applies when a manufacturer refers to a maple syrup which is not 100 percent pure, "New England" or "maple goodness."

A manufacturer may not claim his food product is "pure," or made from "pure fruit," unless his product truly is made from fruit and nothing else.

A manufacturer may not claim his product to be of exceptional quality enriched with important elements like vitamins, unless the food product meets such standards. However, the product may be honestly advertised if the food does not exceed the norm set up by objective as well as accepted standards.

Some manufacturers state that their food has special or particular therapeutic effects. The states have, as has the FTC, stopped such untrue claims as: "furnishing more energy" or being "more nourishing" while with a lower caloric content; being more "nutritious," "promoting growth and benefiting the nervous system."[4]

Due to the great strides made over the last few decades in processing and marketing, we have a more concentrated and reconstituted food product. Food must be clearly labeled to this effect when so processed. If any artificial material is added, then this fact must also be known. The courts have consistently backed up the FTC with reference to the ruling that fruit without indication of artificial flavor will be banned. It has been stipulated in many cases that "imitation" or "artificially colored" must be stated.[5]

UNFAIR TRADE PRACTICES

In this particular instance, the government holds an extremely tight grip. It insists that advertising "talk straight," and at such time as this ceases we have false and deceptive advertising or what the FTC calls "unfair practice."

In deception cases, the most important function of the FTC, perhaps, is to determine whether an advertisement is materially misleading. The test of falsity must be made, however, in the atmosphere and under the circumstances in which the advertisement is intended to do its job. Therefore, FTC bases its test upon the more or less casual reaction of the so-called ordinary consumer to the advertising language and to the overall impression which it makes upon this average reader, listener, or viewer.

Impressions and understandings derived from an advertisement are

---

[4] FTC Stip. 3704.
[5] *FTC* v. *Good-Grape Company*, F. (2) 70 (C.C.A. 6, 1930).

acquired under vastly different circumstances from those gained from a contract. So, language which would not be considered legally deceptive in a contract will be so regarded in an advertisement. Likewise an advertisement may be technically truthful, but still be deceptive. Thus, "copy" must not only tell the truth but it must tell it in a truthful way.

Since the principal check on advertising is the policing activity of the FTC, that agency's own catalog of methods and practices against which they have moved is of particular interest to the advertiser.

The use of false or misleading advertising concerning, and the misbranding of, commodities, respecting the materials or ingredients of which they are composed, their quality, purity, origin, source, attributes, or properties, or nature of manufacture and selling them under such name and circumstances as to deceive the public. An important part of these includes misrepresentation of the therapeutic and corrective properties of medicinal preparations and devices, and cosmetics, and the false representation, expressly or by failure to disclose their potential harmfulness, that such preparations may be safely used.

Describing various symptoms and falsely representing that they indicate the presence of diseases and abnormal conditions which the product advertised will cure or alleviate.

Representing products to have been made in the United States when the mechanism or movements, in whole or in important part, are of foreign origin.

Making false and disparaging statements respecting competitors' products and business, in some cases under the guise of ostensibly disinterested and specially informed sources or through purported scientific, but in fact misleading, demonstrations or tests.

Passing off goods for products of competitors through appropriation or simulation of such competitors' trade names, labels, dress of goods, or counter-display catalogs.

Making use of false and misleading representations, schemes, and practices to obtain representatives and make contracts such as pretended puzzle–prize contests purportedly offering opportunities to win handsome prizes, but which are in fact mere "come-on" schemes and devices in which the seller's true identity and interest are initially concealed. . . .

Using merchandising schemes based on lotteries or on a pretended contest of skill.

Aiding, assisting, or abetting unfair practice, misrepresentation, and deception, and furnishing means or instrumentalites therefore; and combining and conspiring to offer to sell products by chance or by deceptive methods, through such practices as supplying dealers with lottery devices, or selling to dealers and assisting them in conducting contest schemes as a part of which pretended credit slips or certificates are issued to contestants, when in fact the price of the goods has been marked up to absorb the face value of the credit slip; and the supplying of emblems or devices to conceal marks of country or origin of goods, or otherwise to misbrand goods as to country of origin.

Sales plans in which the seller's usual price is falsely represented as a special reduced price for a limited class, or false claim of special terms, equipment, or other privileges or advantages.

False or misleading use of the word "Free" in advertising.

Use of misleading trade names calculated to create the impression that a dealer is a producer or importer selling directly to the consumer, with resultant savings.

Offering of false "bargains" by pretended writing of a fictitious "regular" price.

Use of false representations that an article offered has been rejected as nonstandard and is offered at an exceptionally favorable price, or that the number thereof that may be purchased is limited.

Falsely representing that goods are not being offered as sales in ordinary course, but are specially priced and offered as a part of a special advertising campaign to obtain customers, or for some purpose other than the customary profit.

Misrepresenting, or causing dealers to misrepresent, the interest rate of carrying charge on deferred payments. . . .

Misrepresenting seller's alleged advantages of location or size, or the branches, domestic or foreign, or the dealer outlets he has. . . .

Alleged connection of a concern, organization, association, or institute with, or endorsement of it or its product or service by, the Government or nationally known organization, or representation that the use of such product or services is required by the Government, or that failure to comply with such requirement is subject to penalty.

False claim by a vendor of being an importer, or a technician, or a diagnostician, or a manufacturer, grower, or nurseryman, or a distiller, or of being a wholesaler, selling to the consumer at wholesale prices, or by a manufacturer of being also the manufacturer of the raw material entering into the product or by an assembler of being a manufacturer.

Falsely representing that the seller owns a laboratory in which the product offered is analyzed and tested.

Representing that an ordinary private commercial seller and business is an association, or national association, or connected therewith, or sponsored thereby or is otherwise connected with noncommercial or professional organizations or associations or constitutes an institute, or, in effect, that it is altruistic in purpose giving work to the unemployed.

Falsely claiming that a business is bonded, or misrepresenting its age or history, or the demand established for its products, or the selection afforded, or the quality or comparative value of its goods, or the personnel or staff of personages presently or theretofore associated with such business or the products thereof.

Claiming falsely or misleading by patent, trademark, or other special and exclusive rights.

Granting seals of approval by a magazine to products advertised therein and misrepresenting thereby that such products have been adequately tested, and misrepresenting by other means the quality, performance, and characteristics of such products. . . .

Misrepresenting that seller fills order promptly, ships kind of merchandise described, and assigns exclusively territorial rights within definite trade areas to purchasers or prospective purchasers.

Obtaining orders on the basis of samples displayed for customer's selection and failing or refusing to respect such selection thereafter in the filling of orders, or promising results impossible of fulfillment, or falsely making promises or holding out guaranties, or the right of return, or results, or refunds, replacements, or reimbursements, or special or additional advantages to the prospective purchasers such as extra credit, or furnishing of supplies or advisory assistance; or falsely assuring the purchaser or prospective purchaser that certain special or exclusively personal favors or advantages are being granted him.

Concealing from prospective purchaser unusual features involved in purchaser's commitment, the result of which will be to require of purchaser further expenditure in order to obtain benefit of commitment and expenditure already made, such as failure to reveal peculiar or non-standard shape of portrait or photographic enlargement, so as to make securing of frame therefore from sources other than seller difficult and impracticable, if not impossible.

Advertising a price for a product as illustrated or described and not including in such price all charges for equipment or accessories illustrated or described or necessary for use of the product or customarily included as standard equipment, and failing to include all charges not specified as extra.

Giving products misleading names so as to give them a value to the purchasing public which they would not otherwise possess, such as names implying falsely that—

The products were made for the government or in accordance with its specifications and of corresponding quality, or that the advertiser is connected with the government in some way, or in some way the products have been passed upon, inspected, underwritten, or endorsed by it; or

They are composed in whole or in part of ingredients or materials which in fact are present only to an extent or not at all, or that they have qualities or properties which they do not have; or

They were made in or came from some locality famous for the quality of such products, or are of national reputation; or

They have been inspected, passed, or approved after meeting the tests of some official organization charged with the duty of making such tests expertly and disinterestedly or giving such approval; or

They were made under conditions or circumstances considered of importance by a substantial part of the general purchasing public; or . . .

They are of greater value, durability, and desirability than is the fact, as labeling rabbit fur as "Beaver"; or

They are designed, sponsored, produced, or approved by the medical profession, health and welfare associations, hospitals, celebrities, educational institutions and authorities, such as the use of the letters "M.D." and the words "Red Cross" and its insignia and the words "Boy Scout . . . ."

Misrepresenting, through salesmen or otherwise, products' composition, nature, qualities, results accomplished, safety, value, and earnings or profits to be had therefrom.

Falsely claiming unique status or advantages, or special merit therefore, on the basis of misleading and ill-founded demonstrations or scientific tests, or of pretended widespread tests, or of pretended widespread and critical professional acceptance and use.

Misrepresenting the history or circumstances involved in the making and offer of the products or the source of origin thereof (foreign or domestic), or of the ingredients entering therein, or parts thereof, or the opportunities brought to the buyer through purchase of the offering, or otherwise misrepresenting scientific or other facts bearing on the value thereof to the purchaser.

Falsely representing products as legitimate, or prepared in accordance with government or official standards or specifications.

Falsely claiming government or official or other acceptance, use, and endorsement of product, and misrepresenting success and standing thereof through use of false or misleading endorsements or false and misleading claims with respect thereto, or otherwise.

Making use of misleading trade name and representing by other means that the nature of a business is different than is the fact. . . .

Misrepresenting fabrics or garments as to fiber content; and, in the case of wool products, failing to attach tags thereto indicating the wool, re-used wool, reprocessed wool, or other fibers contained therein, and the identity of the manufacturer or qualified reseller, as required by the Wool Products Labeling Act, or removing or mutilating tags required to be affixed to the product when they are offered for sale to the public.[6]

BUSINESS ETHICS

When we face competition, in which the survival of business enterprises and even the continued economic welfare of individuals are at stake, compliance with ethical codes becomes institutionally and individually difficult.

Is business, then, a jungle? Certainly not. Commercial behavior is guided by a slowly accumulated set of guides which have been found to be necessary for the continuous conduct of commercial relationships. A historical instance will indicate the type of guide that has developed. Before the mechanization of the textile industry, all textiles exported were called "cloathes" and were of varying size and quality. Each one had to be inspected with care and could be priced only after such an examination. As long as these textiles were produced in small quantity, this inspection amounted only to an inconvenience. But with the mechanization of the textile industry, textiles were manufactured in much larger quantities. Individual examination and pricing would have slowed trade in textiles to the point that much of the benefit of mechanization would have been lost. Only when traders in other countries came to have confidence that the goods would be as labeled was it possible for the volume of trade in textiles to be increased beyond the amount that could be handled as individual transactions.

Ultimately, with the standardization possible through mechanization,

---

[6] Annual Reports of the Federal Trade Commission, 1954–64.

it became possible to export textiles satisfactorily by specification alone. In this way, with no attempt at codifying virtue, a code of ethical concepts came to be necessary, and then generally expected, in British and European trade. In the same way, craft and merchant guild regulations grew up, standardizing conditions of handicraft manufacture and quality, covering sales territories, conditions of employment, pricing, and other variable aspects of business. In the guild halls, and in the "piepoudre" courts in markets, there grew up *a lex mercantorium* which enforced these many understandings, attitudes, and arrangements. In Europe and later in the 13 colonies and then in the United States of America, canons of commercial conduct came to be recognized. There came to be acceptable conduct for businessmen—fabricators, factors, and retail merchants.

This kind of acceptable conduct, or this code of commercial ethics, is not universally followed because there will always be some who are knaves and some who are weak. In the early 19th century businessmen were controlled by guild regulations and by the action of the piepoudre courts—which were actually juries of merchants called together wherever there was a complaint to hear, and to enforce conformity to a growing code of commercial ethics. As business has become more massive and complex, many of these items of business ethics have evolved into statute law. Fair weight, truthful labeling, the fulfillment of contracts, fairness (or what seems to be fairness) in pricing, relations between employer and employee—these and similar aspects of business are regulated by statute in the United States. Departures from the code of commercial ethics can be checked, though it is to be doubted that the small businessman will ever be free from suspicion of sharp dealing when his business existence is threatened by competition.

Businessmen are guided by a code of commercial conduct, or ethics, which has been worked out over hundreds of years, and which provides for adherence to the truth, for fair weight, honest measure, enforcement of contracts, the payment of debts, and the fair treatment of employees. It must be remembered that such a code of ethics will not satisfy everyone. Those who believe that it should have only a religious basis may be disappointed. Those who believe that it should point to artistic or aesthetic achievement and appreciation may find it wanting. Those who believe that business for profit is bad may find no solace in it. It is not the expression or realization of anyone's system of value judgments. It is the set of guides worked out by trial and error over hundreds of years for dealing with the friction points of business.

ETHICS OF ADVERTISING

We can now consider advertising from the point of view of commercial ethics. Advertising is by its nature so complex that its ethical problems should be considered from various points of view. In the first place, it is conducted by both small and large companies, by advertising agencies, by advertising departments, by media of all kinds, by individuals, and with a hierarchy of sales organizations acting in complicated commercial relationships. These firms have office staffs, executives, contractual relations with other groups, and responsibilities toward these as well as toward the owners and the stockholders of the firms themselves. They will be faced with the ethical problems of employer-employee relations, of civic responsibility, of compliance with tax and labor laws, of contractual compliance, and, finally, of the extremely subtle problems of mass communication and of sales promotion.

Waste in advertising

When people speak of waste in advertising, they do not generally refer to the plush offices of advertising agencies or the assignment to manufacturers' advertising departments of executives and clerical workers who possibly might be more productive assigned to other duties. When people speak of waste in advertising, they usually mean that more money is spent for advertising than they think is appropriate. This argument is advanced in spite of the fact that the percentage of gross national product devoted to advertising has varied little over the years, during good times and bad. Sometimes an advertiser may invest more in advertising than might be necessary. Sometimes an expensive commercial picture is ordered when a photograph costing but a fraction of the artist's bill might have sufficed. Sometimes a manufacturer may allocate funds for advertising a product for which there is no ready market because suitable marketing research was not done. While the above examples indicate some waste, one can find some superfluous expenditures in almost all business activities.

Social waste is a difficult subject to interpret. The expenditure of a million dollars for advertisements in the newspapers of a particular trading area, as an example, may be quite conspicuous. But if the stores in the area can save a greater amount in payments to retail sales personnel, it is difficult to determine that there is wastefulness without research to substantiate it.

General criticisms

When we consider the problem of ethics, we are even more in the area of value judgments. On what do the critics base their allegations of the unethical nature of advertising?

1. They say that advertising makes false statements, which confuse and mislead consumers, and that often these statements are made by implication.

2. They say that advertising forces customers to want goods and services they really do not need.
3. They say that advertising promotes the use of products which are inherently harmful.
4. They say that advertising, as it is exposed to the consumer, lacks aesthetic attributes.
5. They say that advertising (particularly the television commercials) is forced on the consumer.

The truth or falsity of a statement is difficult to ascertain. Automobile tires are sold with the help of advertising. In general each manufacturer will emphasize certain features of his tires. At first glance, it might seem that one tire must be best, another second best, and another third best. But actually, testing laboratories find difficulty in making such clear-cut demarcations. One tire will give a "softer" ride; another will last longer; a third will "corner" better. Each manufacturer attempts to emphasize the characteristics that he believes interests the most people. The advertising appeals will state, "This tire will last longer on rough roads," or "This tire will make your old car ride like a new car." Even the U.S. Bureau of Standards, which spends millions of dollars each year attempting to help the federal government select the "best" buys, has a hard time making its selections.

Let us consider another situation. A manufacturer of cosmetics uses the appeal that his cosmetics will make a young woman more lovable and will attract young men to her. Certainly, in her fantasy life, the young woman will probably want to be lovable and to attract a young man. And certainly she will be more attractive in real life if she is well groomed than if she is not. We learn, from advertising, that a particular brand of carpet will make a living room more attractive, that this new lighting fixture will make a hallway brighter. These, and many other similar statements, are true. They do not, however, say that they will accomplish the impossible.

People want to look better, eat better, live in better houses, drive better cars—in fact, to improve all aspects of their standard of living. Merchandise which may satisfy, entirely or partially, the wants of the consumer may be sold more easily through persuading the prospect with the right appeal. One finds that not only in the advertising for dentrifices but also in sermons from the pulpit, in lectures from the rostrum, and in directives from the government similar tactics of persuasion are used.

Let us consider the next criticism, that advertising forces consumers to want merchandise that they cannot afford. The ubiquity of advertising does not give it compulsive force. Indeed, advertising cannot move people in directions contrary to social trends. One of the reasons companies use marketing research is to find out how to advertise goods and services to coincide with the demand of the consumers. At a time when women used leg makeup rather than hosiery, manufacturers of hosiery advertised heavily to get women to wear stockings instead of leg makeup. But no movement contrary to the social trend was started. When men decided that they did not need to wear hats, the hat industry tried to reverse this trend without satisfactory results. When men decided they did not want vests with the suits they bought, the association of waistcoat manufacurers advertised extensively without shifting the declining trend.

When electric ranges were first developed, they were advertised heavily by leading manufacturers of electric appliances. Women, according to various marketing research studies, were afraid that the change from gas cooking to electric cooking would impair their cooking skill. Although extensive advertising was done, it required 20 years to get women to start using electric ranges. Then, as more and more women used electric ranges, advertising helped to speed the acceptance trend.

On authority in the field of advertising has said that advertising never brings about anything that would not occur without advertising, but that it does hasten product adoption and use. The number of instances which can be advanced to show that advertising has not been able to get consumers to buy products with a declining trend or that advertising was not able to get consumers to adopt a product in advance of the time it seemed propitious, is great enough to dispel the belief that advertising has the ability to do more than advance effective suggestions.

Does advertising promote the sale of products which are harmful? There is a variety of legislation which is supposed to prevent the promotion of the sale of baneful products. There are many marginal questions here. Does one of the conventional shortenings build up the cholesterol content of the blood sufficiently to make it harmful to many people? We don't know. And in our confusion, we can find evidence suggesting that our conventional shortenings are entirely satisfactory. Are cigarettes harmful? Again, the evidence is not conclusive. So far as we can tell, smog is more harmful than cigarette smoke. And the studies attempting to show that cigarette smoking is harmful are not regarded as convincing by all statisticians. Are alcoholic beverages dangerous and immoral? Intemperately used, they are dangerous. Yet our one attempt to abolish them seemed to advance their use rather than restrict it. Again, the evidence is not in.

Probably no product sold to the public causes more death and injury than the automobile. Yet few believe that it is immoral or that it should not be sold to the American public although federal laws now are requiring more safety features.

On the other hand, items whose disrepute is due to the adverse opinions of people who object to the American standard of living, or to the price system, should not, for those reasons, be banned!

Is advertising lacking in good taste? Laxatives, depilatories, liniments for aching muscles, and cemetery lots are all a part of the American scene. If the advertiser is not to advertise the goods and services that the American public openly buys, by what standard should he select what he is to advertise? Many radio and television commercials are obtrusive and irritating. If the public is offended by the appeals used, the advertiser may soon find out about their disapproval through his decrease in sales.

The first obligation of advertising is to communicate with the American public. Magazines, newspapers, television programs, and radio programs are molded to the public taste. Some people are more aesthetic and more sensitive than the general run of advertising readers, listeners, or viewers. If so, they may find some consumer advertising distasteful. That fact does not mean that the advertising now done is not gauged carefully to the level of most Americans. If it were not, it would indeed be wasteful.

Finally, we are told that advertising, particularly television advertising, forces its way into the American living room. Under our system of advertising, television comes to us without charge, at all times, and with a great variety of programs. Advertisers pay the costs of maintaining this service—evidently a service that the American public values—in order to advertise their products. The television viewer who is affronted by the television commercials is not obliged to keep listening to the commercials. If he wants to watch the programs, he may either submit to the commercials or he may turn the set off during the commercials. He is under no obligation to view the commercials or the television programs.

If he believes that the television service should be provided without the interference of commercials, then he must be willing to recommend that television programs be prepared at public expense and the taxpayer be assessed additional taxes to pay for this entertainment.

SUMMARY

The current regulation of advertising as outlined above has limitations because controls may prevent, through holding back natural growth, the development of a proper balance in the economy. In a free economy, where the essential basic worth of the individual is stressed, businessmen like the acceptance that comes with observance of the rules of fair play.

It is the belief of the authors, however, that as society has grown more complex, government controls have had to play an even greater role, direct and indirect, in the checks on what might otherwise become abuses in advertising. Furthermore, we believe that advertisers should not attempt to resist all kinds of government control. The problem is to try to see that government provides the right kind of control over advertising and that it avoids those methods that are economically harmful.

The authors recommend:

1. The preventive role and educational acts of the Federal Trade Commission should be emphasized.
2. Both government and business should make every effort to meet their mutual obligation to "satisfy the public."
3. The distinction between the control of advertising itself and false advertising should be kept sharp. Advertisers should consider extending a program of voluntary grade labeling for established and common consumer goods, to help reduce socially wasteful advertising costs.
4. Government agencies, in enforcing controls, should differentiate between *cause* and *effect*. (The amount of the advertising budget may not be the reason a company has gained market control.)
5. Advertising should not have the kind of barriers placed against it that would limit its functions of communication and stimulating demand in our fast-changing dynamic economy.
6. The various agencies should penalize false advertising, but not advertising per se.
7. Government agencies should attempt to regulate more on a case-per-case basis instead of an industrywide approach because of the variations in conditions which exist in the different markets.
8. Since technology and automation are here to stay and will continue to increase, it would appear to be more realistic to use the best possible tools at our command to satisfy the consumer. This would include the use of advertising as a tool of education and communication.
9. There is no way to eliminate all competition and maintain free competition.
10. It should be kept in mind that much of the criticism of advertising comes from persons who favor control of production and consumption. Since such control attempts to regulate consumption, the importance of advertising under such controls would tend to decrease.
11. Advertising cultivates the tastes of consumers; it does not create them.
12. It is not unethical for an advertiser to stress the advantages of his product without pointing out the disadvantages. It is unethical, however, for an advertiser to communicate what he knows to be untrue.
13. Ethics of advertising are complex and must be considered from various points of view.

14.   It is essential to place intellectual honesty as the important element of management-consumer relationships.

QUESTIONS

1. How can the government regulate advertising without restricting the natural role of the economy?

2. Why has our policy in control of advertising appeared to be inconsistent?

3. To what degree should advertisers be given the privilege of following a program of self-regulation?

4. Advertisements are sometimes criticized on the basis that they do not give all the facts. Evaluate this statement from the ethical point of view. In what way have the religions of the world played a part in the development of ethical concepts?

5. How have mass production and mass distribution been dependent upon a system of commercial ethics?

6. Does a seller have the right to tell all the weaknesses about the products of competitors? Is there any restraint from the ethical point of view that is required? What steps can be taken to integrate advertising into our industrial system? Is this primarily an economic and social problem, or is it one of an ethical nature as well?

7. For many years, critics have voiced criticisms about television commercials. To what extent should the FTC adopt a program of controlling these commercials?

8. In a recent speech, a public official stated the following: "We should place a greater control upon advertising because advertisers are now paying a major share of the cost of producing the various television programs, magazines, newspapers, and other media that, in my opinion, the freedom of the press no longer exists." Evaluate this statement.

9. Give the advantages and disadvantages of the government not placing any control over advertising.

10. What are the obligations of the advertiser in advertising his product?

11. It has been stated, "Because of the unwillingness to change and of the inclination of advertisers to behave in a socially irresponsible way, the government has found it necessary to institute regulations and controls—not because these are necessary in all cases, but by default." Comment.

12. Assume that you go to a drugstore and you ask for a brand of aspirin. The clerk hands you another brand and tells you that his brand is exactly the same as the brand you requested but, because it is not advertised, he can sell it to you at a lower price. Is this ethical? Would your answer be the same if the salesperson in a clothing store made the same comment about a suit you were planning to purchase?

13. What is meant by truth in advertising?

14. "Advertising is found to be right when judged by right reason." How is it possible to draw a conclusion from such a statement?

CASE 1.   HEALTH CARE, INC.
Considering use of advertising

Health Care, Inc.'s primary business is the ownership and operation of eighteen acute-care hospitals in the United States. In addition, Health Care operates a central medical laboratory, provides inhalation therapy equipment, services, and personnel training, and other ancillary services to hospitals.

As a result of the decrease in the rate of occupancy in eight of its hospitals, to an average rate of 65 percent or lower, the directors were considering whether or not they should adopt a "professional" type of advertising program in the areas where their hospitals were located.

It has been the policy of Health Care's management to expand the scope of the services it offers for health care in the communities it serves, through increased services, expansion of existing facilities, and acquisition of additional acute care hospitals.

Hospitals

Health Care's hospitals are classified as investor-owned hospitals, as distinguished from "nonprofit" hospitals operated by tax-exempt organizations or governmental agencies. All of its hospitals are acute-care facilities and, except to a minor degree, do not provide for extended care. During the last fiscal year, it derived more than 95 percent of its revenues and income (before incomes taxes) from hospital operations.

All of Health Care's hospitals are accredited by the Joint Commission of Hospital Accreditation of the American Medical and American Hospital Associations.

Rate of occupancy

On the basis of figures contained in the guide issue of *Hospitals*, the journal of the American Hospital Association, the average rate of oc-

EXHIBIT 1

City	Percent of Occupancy	City	Percent of Occupancy
A	75	J	63
B	84	K	76
C	66	L	65
D	62	M	60
E	82	N	79
F	78	O	81
G	64	P	63
H	73	Q	83
I	87	R	64

cupancy of proprietary hospitals during the latest year for which such figures are available, was 74.6 percent nationally. The average occupancy rates of the company's hospitals were as given in Exhibit 1.

It was the opinion of the directors that the services in all of its hospitals were comparable and that their administrators were competent in handling the details.

Medical staff

Approximately 3,400 licensed physicians and surgeons are members of the medical staffs of Health Care's hospitals. Many of these physicians and surgeons are also on the staffs of other hospitals. Patients are admitted only upon request of the members of the medical staff. The physicians and surgeons are not employees of Health Care and any of them may terminate his connection with the hospital at any time. Rules and regulations concerning the medical phase of each hospital's operations are adopted and enforced by its medical staff. Such rules and regulations provide that the members of the staff elect officers, who, together with additional doctors selected by them, constitute the medical executive committee of the hospital which, subject to general control of the hospital's board of directors, supervises all medical and surgical procedures and services through various subcommittees.

Medical laboratories

Health Care's hospitals operate the medical laboratory through its laboratory division. In addition to its hospital laboratories, it operates a central medical laboratory which provides specialized services for the company's hospital laboratories in the area, and, to a limited extent, performs specialized laboratory analyses for clinics and physicians not having qualified personnel or specialized equipment available. The central medical laboratory is divided into biochemistry, toxicology, microbiology, serology, and hematology departments and is equipped for automated biochemical analysis.

Inhalation therapy services

Inhalation Therapy Services, Inc., a wholly owned subsidiary of the company, provides inhalation therapy equipment, services, and personnel training. Inhalation therapy involves the use of intermittent positive-pressure breathing machines and other devices to aid in the treatment of pulmonary emphysema and related respiratory conditions.

Competition

In the areas in which Health Care operates, there are other acute care hospitals which provide services comparable to those offered by Health Care. Some of these hospitals are owned by governmental agencies and others by tax-exempt entities supported by endowments and charitable contributions, which support is not available to Health Care's hospitals. A number of the larger hospitals employ interns and resident physicians who are available to assist in the treatment of a patient. Such services are not provided by Health Care's hospitals.

The occupancy rate of a hospital depends upon the utilization of the facility by doctors on its staff. Any doctor may terminate his connection with the hospital at any time. Health Care endeavors to merit the continued support of the doctors on the staff of a hospital and to attract other qualified doctors by a program which includes the improvement and modernization of its facilities and equipment and, in addition, the enforcement of high ethical and professional standards.

Government regulation

The operation of hospitals and medical laboratories is subject to compliance with various federal, state, and local statutes and regulations. The regulatory agencies administering such statutes and regulations have the power to fix standards of care and service and to determine the adequacy of facilities and the qualification of management. Health Care's hospitals must also comply with the requirements of municipal building codes and local fire departments. Health Care's present facilities hold all required state and local licenses and permits. Expansion of hospitals generally requires the approval of local hospital planning councils.

Medicare, Medicaid and other insurance

Health Care receives payments for services rendered to patients from private insurers, the federal government under the Medicare program of assistance to indigent patients. Under the Medicare and Medicaid programs Health Care is reimbursed for the reasonable direct and indirect costs (as defined by the program) of the services furnished, plus a return on equity. However, Medicaid reimbursement is limited to retail billings. Claims for payment under Medicare, Medicaid, and Blue Cross are subject to audit by agencies administering the program, and portions of the amounts claimed are withheld pending such audit and final settlement. Health Care computes the amount to which it will be entitled from these sources, and, for accounting purposes, establishes a reserve equal to the difference between the charges billed to these programs and such computations.

Employees

Health Care employs approximately 4,750 persons of whom approximately 50 percent are nurses or other licensed technical personnel engaged in hospital and laboratory work. Labor relations have been satisfactory. Approximately 90 percent of such persons are full-time employees.

Its hospitals, like others, experience a relatively high rate of turnover of employees and difficulty in employing and retaining an adequate number of nurses, technicians, and other employees.

Advertising policy

One of the directors at the annual meeting of the board stated as follows:

I recognize that the operation of a hospital is a professional endeavor and that any advertising to get business is frowned upon by the Joint Commission of Hospital Accreditation of the American Medical and American Hospital Associations. Yet, when I see our census (occupancy rate) in eight of our hospitals below the "break-even point" I am convinced that we should be allowed to let the people know that our services are superior to those offered by some of our competitors.

I made a point to visit the competition in three of these cities and I found that their occupancy rates were above 75 percent in each case, yet, the services which were offered to the patients, I believe, were inferior to what we offered. The rates were all comparable, and, as a result, I concluded that if we could let the people know about some of our innovations, we could increase our census above the break-even point.

It is also my opinion that we could really bring down this astronomical cost of hospital care for the patient if we would take the leadership in promoting our hospitals and get our census up close to the 90 percent level.

Case questions

1. Why do you believe it has been the policy of professional groups (lawyers, accountants, and doctors) to refrain from advertising?

2. Do you believe this general policy should be changed? Give reasons.

3. To what degree should hospitals be competitive in seeking patients?

4. As a media representative would you accept advertising from Health Care, Inc. which indicates how its services are better than those of the other hospitals in the area? Why or why not?

CASE 2.   ADOIT TOBACCO, INC.
Evaluating advertising policy

Adoit Tobacco, Inc. is engaged in the tobacco business through the manufacture and sale of cigars, the growing of wrapper tobacco for use on its own cigars and for others, and as a distributor of cigars, cigarettes, health and beauty aids, candy, and other items. As a part of its tobacco business, Adoit licenses the manufacture of, or sells to others, tobacco binder and tobacco wrapper. It also licenses brand names, and certain of the machinery it has developed. In the face of changing conditions in the tobacco industry, the directors of Adoit were considering what they would do about the cigar advertising.

Tobacco business—production and sale

Adoit is engaged in the manufacture and sale of cigars which sell in all major price categories. These cigars are sold primarily under brand names—all of which are registered trademarks of the company. The market for cigars is highly competitive. In order to maintain its position in the industry, Adoit advertises extensively and carries on a variety of promotional activities. The resources of some other producers of cigar products are greater than those of Adoit.

Adoit's cigars are produced with three tobacco components: filler, binder, and wrapper. The tobacco used for filler and binder is purchased from a large number of growers and suppliers in the United States, Puerto Rico, and Far East, Latin America, and elsewhere. The binder, except in certain of the highest-priced cigars, is a homogenized tobacco binder. Most of the natural leaf wrapper tobacco used for the company's cigars is grown by Adoit on its farms. The remainder of its requirements for natural leaf wrapper tobacco is purchased from a number of growers and suppliers in Florida, Latin America, and elsewhere. To an increasing extent, Adoit is relying upon homogenized tobacco wrapper.

Adoit maintains inventories of wrapper and filler tobaccos sufficient to meet its estimated requirements for more than one year, as well as ample supplies of tobacco for the production of tobacco binder and tobacco wrapper. This practice conforms to that of the industry. In certain types and grades such inventories, at current production rates, are sufficient for a period substantially longer than one year. Most of its inventories are stored in warehouses in the United States and Puerto Rico.

Adoit's cigar sales, as well as those of the cigar industry as a whole, increased substantially following the release of the Report to the Surgeon General on Smoking and Health in 1964. From 1966 through 1972 the dollar volume of its large-size cigar sales declined by 26 percent and the dollar volume of its small-size cigar sales increased by 45 percent.

The dollar sales of small-size cigars have increased in every year since 1966. Dollar sales of cigars as a whole have been substantially unchanged over this period. Adoit believes that small-size cigars currently represent approximately one third of the unit volume of industry cigar sales and that this proportion is increasing.

Adoit is currently producing most of its small-tipped cigars, which use homogenized tobacco binder and wrapper, with machinery producing at rates up to 1,000 cigars per minute. Using conventional automated machinery, it can produce only approximately 16 cigars per minute, and using natural leaf wrapper tobacco, on nonautomated conventional machinery, it produces only 9 to 16 cigars per minute.

Adoit cannot use its new high-speed cigar manufacturing machinery for shaped cigars, but conventional automated cigar manufacturing machinery can produce such shaped cigars with homogenized tobacco wrapper. Adoit cannot predict the extent to which the cigar-consuming public will accept homogenized tobacco wrapper on its nontipped cigars. Finally, it is unable to predict the effect, if any, of publicity which may arise from existing or additional studies which link the use of tobacco with human diseases, or of regulations on advertising and labeling, should any be enacted. The restriction on the advertising of cigarettes on radio and television does not apply to cigars.

Tobacco business—distribution

Adoit's cigars are distributed in the United States to 14 sales branches, approximately 1,000 wholesale distributors, and about 60 direct retail accounts.

In addition to distributing Adoit's cigars, the sales branches distribute other products. These outlets operate general distribution businesses for cigars, cigarettes, tobacco, pipes, health and beauty aids, candy, and other products.

Advertising policy

Adoit, in its advertising since 1964, had been very careful not to emphasize any appeal which might bring adverse reaction from the Surgeon General's office. It had used general appeals that were centered on such points as flavor, satisfaction, pleasure, and a psychological lift.

However, Adoit's research studies showed that these appeals were not attracting more young men and women into smoking cigars. (The average age of the cigar smoker was over 30 years.) The antagonism of women, though not as prevalent as ten years ago, still existed.

Adoit's marketing director, in commenting to other members of the board about its advertising, made the following statement:

As to cigars, thus far they are not included in the cigarette indictment. I do not believe they ever will be, because there are significant differences in smoking cigars and cigarettes. As you know, one does not have to inhale to enjoy a cigar. I believe I am safe in saying that not 5 percent of cigar smokers actually inhale.

With all due regard for the fact that I may be slightly prejudiced, I claim that no article of popular consumption offers more to the consumer than his cigar, nor does any article of popular consumption have such area of affectionate usage.

In closing, I would say that we should make a major effort to attract the young men and women to smoke cigars!

Case questions

1. To what extent should or should not the federal government restrict the advertising of cigars?

2. Only a negligible number of women smoke cigars. Should there be any public policy regarding the industry's attempt to gain sympathetic appreciation of cigars by women?

3. A critic of cigar advertising commented recently, "Cigar advertising makes people want what they don't need, and, at the same time, it gets them to prefer something that is superficial."

4. Recognizing some of the general controls which might be enacted regarding advertising in the cigar industry, what policy would you recommend for Adoit to follow?

CASE 3.   POPULAR RECORDS, INC.
Misleading advertising

The Federal Trade Commission issued the following complaint against Popular Records, Inc.

The respondent, Popular Records, Inc., is a corporation which, for some time, has been engaged in the advertising, offering for sale, sale, and distribution of phonograph records and record-vending racks. The respondent has maintained a substantial course of trade in interstate commerce, as "commerce" is defined in the Federal Trade Commission Act. Furthermore, Popular Records, Inc. has been in substantial competition with corporations, firms, and individuals, in the sale of phonograph records and vending racks of the same general kind and nature as those sold by Popular.

In the course and conduct of its business, Popular Records, Inc. has made various statements and representations concerning its products and methods of conducting business, for the purpose of inducing the sale of its phonograph records and vending racks, which have been false or misleading. These statements have been made by means of advertisements published in the *Wall Street Journal,* a number of local newspapers in areas where the respondent does business, and by means of letters, brochures, and other promotional material mailed to prospective purchasers.

Among some of the typical statements and representations made are the following:

(1) By newspaper advertisements:

DISTRIBUTOR

MALE OR FEMALE

FULL OR PART-TIME

Earn extra money in your own business. No experience or personal selling necessary. Requires only few hours a week spare time to service CHOICE BRAND RECORD DISPLAYS, located by us in food markets, drugstores, etc. Cheap record racks are rapidly being replaced by SENSATIONAL CHOICE BRAND SELF-SERVICE RECORD DISPLAYS. Store makes money, so do you. Excellent profit . . . but his is NOT A GET RICH QUICK SCHEME, as we are a highly respected record company rated in Dun & Bradstreet. Must have car and minimum of $975 for record inventory, displays, store accounts, and advertising material. Write for local appointment, include phone number.

CHOICE RECORD DIV.

POPULAR RECORDS, INC.

(2) By letter:

. . . this is an ideal opportunity for you to own . . . a full-time, high-profit, volume business. . . .

. . . Choice Brand Record Displays, located by us in high traffic retail stores. . . .

. . . keep your racks filled with fast moving record selections.

(3) By promotional brochure:

HERE'S THAT ONCE-IN-A-LIFETIME OPPORTUNITY FOR Unlimited Success on A Limited Budget.

Make more money in less time than you thought possible.

YOU CAN SERVICE 5 RACKS IN ONLY 5 TO 6 HOURS A WEEK and Pocket Tremendous Profits.

5 to 6 hours a week servicing your locations can bring you clear profit you never dreamed of making in so little time with so little effort. . . .

It won't take long to learn this money-making business and once you do— the sky's the limit.

CHOICE UP-TO-DATE RECORDS SOLD AT YOUR LOCATIONS. . . . Customers will quickly discover that the newest hits from stage, screen, etc. . . . are always available at *your* Choice racks.

Popular Records can bring these superb recordings to music lovers everywhere at prices far below those being charged for records of comparative value.

If you cannot service "Fast-turnover" "High-profit" locations—DO NOT APPLY.

Q. HOW DO I KNOW THAT YOUR COMPANY IS RELIABLE?

A. We are listed by Dun & Bradstreet. . . .

. . . we give the public a truly fine $4.98 Hi-Fi value for the really sensible price of $1.98.

In response to inquiries induced by such advertisements, letters, and literature, the respondent or its employees, agents, or representatives call upon members of the public initiating such inquiries; and then make oral representations repetitive or elaborative of and in addition to those contained in the aforementioned printed materials.

Through the use of such statements and representations, the respondent has represented, directly or by implication, that: (1) the respondent's newspaper advertisements constituted offers of employment, (2) a highly profitable business could be obtained for an investment of $975, (3) all money invested by a purchaser of records and racks was secured by the stock purchased and that a full refund of the investment would be made by the respondent upon the return of the stock, (4) weekly net profits of $50 to $100 and more could be easily obtained by the purchaser for his investment of $975, (5) the respondent implied that he has negotiated contracts with The Great Atlantic & Pacific Tea Company, The Kroger Company, Safeway Stores, Inc., Sears, Roebuck & Company, Peoples Drug Stores, Inc., and other large and reputable food, drug, and general merchandise companies and stores, by which it was agreed that the respondent's distributor in a given area would install vending racks with phonograph records in such companies' "high-traffic" retail stores located in the area, (6) the purchaser would be the sole distributor of the records in a defined geographical area, (7) a portion of all the records sold by the respondent to a purchaser were "hit" tunes currently being sold throughout the nation, (8) the records sold by the respondent had a retail value of $3.98 or more each, (9) the purchaser's opportunity for expansion, with concomitant earnings of incredible amount, was limited only by the industry of the purchaser and the size of the trading area wherein he would be the distributor, and (10) the respondent's integrity was avouched by the fact that they were listed in *Dun & Bradstreet Reference Book*.

These statements are false, misleading, and deceptive because in truth:

1. The respondent did not offer employment to persons answering the advertisements. The purpose of the advertising has been to obtain leads to persons of established finances in order that a concentrated effort might be made, through personal solicitation, to induce them to enter into contracts for the purchase of phonograph records and vending racks.
2. Seldom, if ever, has an investment of $975 in the respondent's phonograph

records, vending racks, and plan of merchandising resulted in the establishment of a highly profitable business.

3.   Money invested in phonograph records and vending racks was not secured by stocks. The maximum amount returnable to an investor who wishes to terminate his contract is limited by contract to $360 for each unit investment of $975.

4.   Seldom, if ever, have net profits of $50 or more weekly been realized by purchasers of Popular Records, Inc.'s phonograph records and vending racks costing $975. Net profits at certain rates cannot be expected by the purchaser from the beginning of operations or at any other time.

5.   Popular Records, Inc., the respondent, does not have contracts with the Great Atlantic & Pacific Tea Company, The Kroger Company, Safeway Stores, Inc., Sears, Roebuck & Company, Peoples Drug Stores, Inc., or other large food, drug, or general merchandise companies or stores, whereby agreements had been reached which would permit purchasers of the respondent's products to place vending racks and records on store premises. Invariably, store locations were not determined until after contracts for the sale of records and racks by the respondent had been negotiated, and then the purchasers learned that locations were available only in independently owned restaurants, drugstores and variety stores not having the high-traffic and sales potentials promised by the respondent.

6.   The respondent breached promises made to purchasers of their products to preserve sales territories for the sole and exclusive distributorship of purchasers.

7.   Few, if any, records available from respondents at the time of the initial sale thereof to purchasers, or later, contained what the consuming public considered to be current "hit" tunes.

8.   Most of the records sold by respondents could be obtained from retailers selling records in competition with the respondent's customers in the same trading area for $1.98.

9.   Seldom, if ever, has the purchaser of Popular Records, Inc.'s products for the $975 investment found that his return therefrom warranted any effort to expand his operations.

10.   The respondent's listing in *Dun & Bradstreet Reference Book* signified nothing more than it had a certain credit rating and a certain estimated financial worth.

The use of these false, misleading and deceptive statements by the respondent has had the tendency to mislead members of the purchasing public into the erroneous and mistaken belief that these statements were true and into the purchase of substantial quantities of its phonograph records and vending racks. As a consequence thereof, substantial trade in commerce has been unfairly diverted to the respondent from its competitors. These acts and practices of the Popular Records were and are to the prejudice and injury of the public and of the respondent's competitors, and constitutes unfair and deceptive acts and practices and unfair methods of competition, in commerce, within the intent and meaning of the Federal Trade Commission Act.

Popular Records, Inc.'s reply

1. We deny the charge that our newspaper advertisements constituted offers of employment as alleged in the complaint. In all our advertisements we used such phrases as: "your racks," "your investment," and "your own business." Such statements clearly indicate that the individuals who would apply are not to be employees of the company but are entering into a business of their own.

2. We believe that a highly profitable business can be obtained for the investment of $975. The two tables given below show that according to generally accepted standards of "highly profitable business" individuals have established very profitable businesses. As is shown by the first chart, 70 percent of those who have invested $975 in the business, for the purchase of our records and record racks, are making a return of 21.7 percent on their investment. Over half of the people are making a return of 53.5 percent. Because of this, we believe that a highly profitable business can be and usually is established by those who invest $975 in this business.

Return in investment on Popular Records Inc.'s $975 investment package

Percentage of individuals who make the stated net profit or more	Average net profit earned per week	Average net profit earned per year	Less labor expense of $520 per year*	Percentage return on invested capital—annual net profit less expense divided by $975
100	$ 1	$ 52	loss	0.0
95	5	260	loss	0.0
85	10	520	$ 0	0.0
70	15	780	260	21.7
50	20	1040	520	53.5
30	25	1300	780	80.0
20	30	1560	1040	107.0
15	35	1820	1300	133.3
10	40	2080	1560	160.0
5	45	2340	1820	187.0
2	50	2600	2080	222.0

Percentage of individuals who make the stated net profit or more	Average net profit earned per week	Average net profit earned per year	Less interest expense of $60 per year*	Earnings per hour of work—net profit less interest expense divided by 260 hours**
100	$ 1	$ 52	loss	$0.00
95	5	260	$ 200	0.77
85	10	520	460	1.77
70	15	780	720	2.77
50	20	1040	980	3.77
30	25	1300	1240	4.77
20	30	1560	1500	5.77
15	35	1820	1760	6.77
10	40	2080	2020	7.77
5	45	2340	2280	8.77
2	50	2600	2540	9.77

* Interest expense of $60 is based on 6 percent interest on $975 for a period of one year. $975 x .06 = $58.50 plus $1.50 = $60.00
** The 260 hours is based on the average number of hours worked by each person per week times the number of weeks in a year, 52.

3. To the complaint that the investment was not completely secured by stocks and that the maximum amount which the individual could get for the return of all the stock was $560, we reply: (a) that the most he can hope to recover is $560. (b) In the newspaper advertisements and other promotional material, the purchasers are told that the $975 investment covers not only the stock of records and vending racks but also displays, store accounts, and advertising material. We do not allow any allowance for the return of these. (c) There is an expense for closing the accounts when an individual returns the stock which he purchased from us, and the individual helps to cover this expense by receiving a slight reduction in the amount of money which we will allow him for the return of his stock. (d) There is a loss of good-will when one of our distributors withdraws his racks from a store. In order to insure that the individual will not enter the business unless he fully realizes what he is getting into, we assess him for a small penalty fee as compensation for the loss of good-will which he has caused us. We have found that it is extremely difficult to get the racks reinstalled in stores from which they have been removed. (e) Because the racks are usually damaged in use, we seldom allow more than $30 per rack, while the cost of each of the five racks to the purchaser is $50.

4. We grant that no one has earned $100 per week on an investment of $975 and only about 2 percent of the people make more than $50 a week. However, as can be seen from the preceding charts in section two, very good profits can and are obtained by individuals who have made the $975 investment.

5. Although it is true that no prior contracts with large and reputable food, drug, and general merchandise companies and stores have been made by which it was agreed that Popular Records' distributors in a given area would install vending racks in such companies' "high-traffic" retail stores, we do not believe that such a representation was never made. We did make contracts with these and other stores after negotiations on the contract with the distributors had begun. We could not make the contract with the stores until service could also be promised because, among other things, if we could not service the stores, they would want to commit the floor space our distributor needed for other uses. Because the best locations in a trading area were often in local, fairly small establishments, we often chose to get contracts with these smaller companies. The teenagers make up a large percentage of those who buy our records, and because they usually shop at these smaller stores, these locations are often the choicest spots available. It is also important to keep in mind that we did not claim any specific sales potential, and most of the locations which our distributors set up have a turnover which is fast enough to make a good return for them. Furthermore, the turnover at these locations is at least up to the average record turnover in the surrounding area.

6. When a purchaser was not the sole distributor in some defined geographical area, it was usually due to changing conditions in that area. For example, population increases, inadequate saturation of the sales potential within the market area, etc. allow us to expand with other distributors at no detriment to the old distributor. In any such case, before we accept another distributor to service the same area (using different stores), we give the old distributor a

chance to expand or improve his service so that the new distributor would not be necessary. Finally, it should be kept in mind that since most of the customers of our records (a) do not go shopping specifically for the records and (b) the customers of one store where the Popular Records racks are installed do not generally shop at the other stores where they are installed, sales of the original distributor were not affected.

7. Although it is true that there are similar records being sold by retailers for $1.98 or less, it is our opinion that these records are inferior to the ones which we are offering for sale. Our records are technically superior to most $1.98 records. The quality of the records which we sell is usually associated with $4.98 hi-fi records. Also, the talent which is on our records is superior to the talent which is on most $1.98 records.

8. Some of the reasons why only a very small percentage of people have made an investment of a second or third $975 are (a) many individuals do not have another $975 which they have free to invest; (b) most of our purchasers handle their own racks and they are satisfied with the present results which they are getting; and (c) most of our purchasers use this investment only as a source of marginal income and, therefore, do not want to spend more than a few hours a week in this type of work.

Case questions

1. What legislation empowers the Federal Trade Commission to make a decision in a "misleading" advertisement?

2. How would you define "false" and "deceptive" advertising?

3. Has Popular Records been deceptive in its advertising?

4. To what degree should controls be set for protecting the consumer in advertising of this nature?

CASE 4.   AMERICAN TELEPHONE & TELEGRAPH CO.
Considering telephone hour

In 1967, Walter Straley, an A.T.&T. vice president, made a speech, in accepting an award of the American Symphony Orchestra League—an honor resulting from sponsorship of the "Telephone Hour," which presents musical documentaries.

Mr. Straley said what he had to say better than anyone could interpret it. Moreover, he said it with grace and rare style. His statements follow, in excerpted form:

I could offer the not unusual public relations rationale that being aware, as we are, of the significance of the cultural community and its influence upon our corporate well-being, that we seek through this medium your goodwill, and this, of course, would be nonsense. We are glad to have it, if we have it, of course, but we will continue to merit your goodwill only by keeping your telephone working for a fair charge and fixing them promptly when they do not. . . .

To level with you, the "Telephone Hour" is mostly a corporate whim, and as a more or less responsible Bell System organization man, I am grateful beyond words that we allow ourselves the indulgence in it. The "Telephone Hour" as a part of our advertising program is difficult—nay, impossible—to justify. It costs a good deal and is clearly a Nielsen rating failure.

The present youth of our country will, I suppose, ultimately control our corporate destiny. Yet, our audience is heavily weighted with people past 50. A reputable public relations analyst showed me irrefutably recently that we could reach the same opinion-forming group and millions more of it with National League football and "I Spy," and I am sure he is right. . . .

Excepting the shows themselves, there really isn't very much about the "Telephone Hour" which seems really reasonable, and this, I think, makes it unreasonable, and I am very glad of that, for too much reason is not sweet, and corporate life is filled with reason.

Obviously, we cannot permit ourselves much of this cultural frivolity, and I hasten to assure our stockholders among you that we take in dead earnestness through other means, of course, our marketing responsibility to use sex, success, and other love in appropriate advertising lures to secure longer long-distance calling and passionate accommodations to our rainbow-hued array of extension telephones. I am grateful that you honor this single idiosyncrasy, and I am hopeful that your recognition will not, however, cause the whole thing to seem logical, for I am delighted with the illogic of it. . . .

Other advertising

Secretary of State Edmund Brown, Jr. said a ban on advertising by state-regulated public utilities would save Californians $200,000 a day in reduced rates. Spokesmen for the major utilities disputed Brown's figures.

Brown said public utilities spent more than $73 million on public relations and advertising, although none faced direct competition. He cited Pacific Telephone as an example, claiming it spent $30 million a year on advertising and sales. "Where else can you go to obtain telephone service other than to Pacific Telephone," Brown said.

A vice president of PT&T in Southern California said Brown was giving out "bad information." "We only advertise in three categories. The first is to inform the public about our services, the second is to promote the use of those services, and the third is to recruit workers." He said Pacific Telephone spent $8 million specifically on advertising last year with the balance of the $30 million going to tell customers how they could get maximum service at minimum cost.

"Utility rates are actually lower because of advertising," the vice president claimed. He said a "direct distance dialing" campaign saved the company $1 million a year for each 1 percent of the population that used it.

Case questions

1. Point out the economic advantages and disadvantages of not controlling the amount of the expenditures for advertising which is done by public utilities.

2. To what extent should public utilities have their advertising controlled?

CASE 5.   CIGARETTE ADVERTISING
Control of advertising

Cigarette sales rose again during 1971, despite the ban on television and radio commercials.

At the first anniversary of the ban, consumption had risen in 1971 by 1.5 percent to 535 billion cigarettes. Sales grew by the same amount in 1970, after two years in which consumption declined.

Cigarette sales were $11 billion for 1971, up 22 percent from $9 billion in 1970. Price increases prior to the wage-price freeze accounted for much of the rise in dollar sales.

Industry analysts estimated that R. J. Reynolds, the industry leader and maker of Winstons and Camels, sold 169.9 billion cigarettes in 1971, compared with 165.7 billion in 1970. Philip Morris sales reached 96.3 billion, up from 87.5 billion, while Brown & Williamson, maker of Viceroy, sold 91.2 billion against 88.2 billion in 1970.

Of the top six companies, only American Tobacco, maker of Pall Mall, and Liggett & Myers reported lower sales. American's sales dropped to 93.5 billion from 100.5 billion in 1970, and L & M slipped to 32.5 billion from 34 billion in 1970.

"One of the things that had been holding sales down in the past was very effective antismoking ads on television," said Irwin Kellner, an industry specialist with Manufacturers Hanover Trust Co. "Since the ban, these commercials rarely appear."

Before the ban took effect January 2, 1971, television stations had to run one antismoking commercial for every three cigarette commercials aired. Since the ban, airing antismoking commercials has been voluntary for station managers.

John C. Maxwell, a tobacco analyst for Oppenheimer & Co., a brokerage firm, also attributed the renewed growth in cigarette consumption partly to the increased number of people in the 20 to 40 age group where smoking is heaviest.

During 1971 the industry stepped up advertising expenditures in print and outdoor media sharply, but outlays fell short of the level that existed when television was used.

Cigarette companies spent about $220 million on television ads in 1970, according to *Advertising Age*, the advertising industry publication. It estimated, however, that spending on other media in 1971 rose by only about $120 million. The magazine estimated cigarette advertising expenditures in magazines doubled in 1971 to $112 million; outlays in newspapers doubled to about $60 million; billboard advertising rose 1,000 times to $36 million to $40 million; and advertising on buses, trains, and subways doubled to $5 million.

Manufacturers also boosted their spending for point-of-sale advertising, promotional allowances, premium offers, and sponsorship of sports events. But industry observers said expenditures were still very modest compared with those made for television ads.

R. J. Reynolds spent 30 percent less in 1971 for cigarette advertising than in 1970, when expenditures totaled about $76 million. However, the company went into a new promotional area, donating some $400,000 in prizes for sports events this year.

The continued growth of cigarette sales despite a cutback in advertising was no surprise, producers said. "We didn't expect a turndown because of our experiences in the world market," said a spokesman for Philip Morris, which sells half its production abroad. "Sales of our Marlboro brand in Italy, where no cigarette advertising whatsoever is allowed, have been growing at a rate of 4 or 5 percent a year." He added that television advertising "never was designed to create new smokers; its main purpose was to switch people from one brand to another." The company, which spent $55 million for cigarette advertising in 1970, spent 10 to 15 percent less in 1971. Even so, Philip Morris, which moved up to the No. 2 spot in the industry, as sales increased 11 percent over 1970. An exception to the industry trend was Liggett & Myers. That company, citing costs involved with the introduction of new brands, had an ad budget for 1971 exceeding the 1970 level.

Some analysts had predicted that money once spent for television would simply go into the profit column. But Kellner said that situation didn't materialize because producers used the savings from TV ads for such purposes as more print advertising, product research and development, and diversification.

Case questions

1. Evaluate the comments above and indicate the importance of advertising in the cigarette industry.

2. To what degree should government place controls on cigarette advertising?

3. To what degree do you believe advertising (either *anti* or *pro*) plays a significant role in causing the consumer to make a decision in regard to smoking cigarettes?

4. Do you believe the cigarette industry should be allowed to adopt a program of self-regulation? Give reasons.

5. If you were associated with an advertising agency, would you recommend that the agency accept the account of a cigarette company? Why or why not?

Supplementary
Information

SOURCES OF SUPPLEMENTARY INFORMATION

PERIODICALS

Since advertising is a field of rapid change and development, students will find it interesting and worthwhile to follow current happenings by reading the periodicals, which cover the field quite well. The following list includes the leading magazines in the major areas of advertising believed to be of most value to students.

General advertising periodicals

Advertising Age, 740 Rush Street, Chicago, Illinois 60611
Advertising & Sales Promotion, Crane Communications, Inc., 740 Rush St., Chicago, Illinois 60611
Industrial Marketing, 740 Rush Street, Chicago, Illinois 60611
Journal of Advertising Research, Advertising Research Foundation, Inc., 3 East 54th Street, New York, N.Y. 10022
Journal of Marketing, 230 N. Michigan Avenue, Chicago, Ill. 60601
Journal of Marketing Research, American Marketing Association, 414 David Kinley Hall, Urbana, Ill. 61801
Marketing Communications (formerly Printers' Ink), 501 Madison Avenue, New York, N.Y. 10022
Sales Management, 630 Third Avenue, New York, N.Y. 10017
Southern Advertising and Publishing, 75 Third Street, N.W., Atlanta, Ga. 30308

Specialized advertising periodicals

Art Direction, 19 W. 44th Street, New York N.Y. 10036
Broadcasting, Broadcasting Publications, Inc. 1735 DeSales Street, N.W., Washington, D.C. 20036

Food & Drug Packaging, 777 Third Avenue, New York, N.Y. 10017
Incentive Magazine, 111 Fourth Avenue, New York, N.Y. 10036
Industrial Design, 18 East 50th Street, New York, N.Y. 10022
International Advertiser, Hotel Roosevelt, New York, N.Y. 10017
Media Decisions, Decisions Publications, Inc., 342 Madison Ave., New York, N.Y. 10017
Packaging Design, 527 Madison Ave., New York, N.Y. 10022
Premium Merchandising, 41 E. 42nd Street, New York, N.Y. 10017
Printing Production, Penton Bldg., Cleveland, Ohio 44113
Reporter of Direct Mail Advertising, 647 Franklin Ave., Garden City, N.Y. 11530
Sign & Display Industry, 2828 Euclid Avenue, Cleveland, Ohio 44115
Signs of the Times, 407 Gilbert Avenue, Cincinnati, Ohio 45202
Sponsor, 25 W. 45th Street, New York, N.Y. 10036
Spot, 6 W. 57th Street, New York, N.Y. 10019
Television, 1735 DeSales Street, N.W., Washington, D.C. 20036
Television Age, 1270 6th Avenue, New York, N.Y. 10020

SPECIAL REFERENCE SERVICES

The special references listed below are also of importance in securing specific information.

Advertising Checking Bureau, Inc. (ACB), 353 Park Avenue South, New York, N.Y. 10010.
Ayer, N. W., & Son's Directory of Newspapers and Periodicals (Annual), N. W. Ayer & Son, Inc., West Washington Square, Philadelphia, Penna. 19106.
Brad Vern's Reports, Inc., Woolford, Maryland 21677.
Broadcast Advertisers Reports, Inc. (BAR), 750 Third Avenue, New York, N.Y. 10017.
Broadcasting Publications, Inc., 1735 DeSales Street, N.W., Washington, D.C. 20036.
Broadcasting Yearbook, Broadcasting Publications, Inc., 1735 DeSales Street, N.W., Washington, D.C. 20036
Leading National Advertisers, Inc. (PIB), 347 Madison Ave., New York, N.Y. 10017.
Lloyd Hall Reports (Magazine Editorial Reports), Lloyd H. Hall Co., 261 Madison Avenue, New York, N.Y. 10016.
Media Records, Inc., 63 Vesey Street, New York, N.Y. 10007.
National Directory of Weekly Newspapers (Annual), American Newspaper Representatives, Inc., 404 Fifth Avenue, New York, N.Y. 10018.
Newspaper Circulation Analysis (Annual), Standard Rate & Data Service, Inc., 5201 Old Orchard Road, Skokie, Ill. 60076
Printers' Ink Executives' Guide to Marketing, Decker Communications Incorporated, 501 Madison Avenue, New York, N.Y. 10022.
Product Advertising Records (PAR), 750 Third Avenue, New York, N.Y. 10017.

Standard Directory of Advertisers, National Register Publishing Co., Incorporated, 5201 Old Orchard Road, Skokie, Ill. 60076.

Standard Rate and Data Service, Inc., 5201 Old Orchard Road, Skokie, Ill. 60076.

Survey of Buying Power (Sales Management), Sales Management, Inc., 630 Third Avenue, New York, N.Y. 10017.

Television Factbook, Television Digest, Inc., 2025 Eye Street, N.W., Washington, D.C. 20006.

Advertising associations

Some of the more important advertising associations that are good sources of information about advertising are listed below.

The Advertising Council, 825 Third Avenue, New York, N.Y. 10022

Advertising Research Foundation (ARF), 3 East 54th Street, New York, N.Y. 10022

The American Advertising Federation, 1225 Connecticut Ave., N.W., Washington, D.C. 20036; and 337 World Trade Center, San Francisco, California 94111

American Association of Advertising Agencies (AAAA—the 4 A's), 200 Park Avenue, New York, N.Y. 10017

American Marketing Association (AMA), 230 North Michigan Avenue, Chicago, Ill. 60601

Association of Canadian Advertisers (ACA), 159 Bay Street, Toronto 1, Canada

Association of Industrial Advertisers (AIA), 41 East 42nd St., New York, N.Y. 10017

Association of National Advertisers (ANA), 155 East 44th Street, New York, N.Y. 10017

Audit Bureau of Circulations (ABC), 123 North Wacker Drive, Chicago, Ill. 60606

Bureau of Advertising of the American Newspaper Publishers Association, Inc. (B of A, ANPA), 485 Lexington Avenue, New York, N.Y. 10017

Business Publications Audit of Circulation, (BPA), 360 Park Ave., South, New York, N.Y. 10010

Canadian Association of Advertising Agencies (CAAA), 2 Carlton Street, Toronto 2, Canada

Council of Better Business Bureaus (CBBB), 845 Third Ave., New York, N.Y. 10022

Direct Mail Advertising Association, Inc. (DMAA), 230 Park Avenue, New York, N.Y. 10017

Federation of Canadian Advertising and Sales Clubs, Suite 369, Queen Elizabeth Hotel, 900 Dorchester West, Montreal, Canada

Institute of Outdoor Advertising (IOA), 625 Madison Avenue, New York, N.Y. 10022

International Advertising Association (IAA), 475 Fifth Ave., New York, N.Y. 10017

Magazine Publishers Association (MPA) (Marketing Division, and Publishers Information Bureau), 575 Lexington Ave., New York, N.Y. 10022

Marketing Communications Research Center (MCRC), 15 Chambers St., Princeton, N.J. 08540

National Retail Merchants Association (NRMA), 100 West 31st Street, New York, N.Y. 10001

Outdoor Advertising Association of America (OAAA), 625 Madison Ave., New York, N.Y. 10022

The Point-of-Purchase Advertising Institute (POPAI), 521 Fifth Avenue, New York, N.Y. 10017

Premium Advertising Association of America, Inc. (PAAA), 366 Madison Ave., New York, N.Y. 10017

Radio Advertising Bureau, Inc. (RAB), 555 Madison Ave., New York, N.Y. 10022

Sales Promotion Executives Association (SPEA), 2130 Delancey Place, Philadelphia, Pa. 19103

Specialty Advertising Association, International (SAAI), 740 North Rush Street, Chicago, Ill. 60611

Television Bureau of Advertising, Inc. (TvB), 1 Rockefeller Center, New York, N.Y. 10020

Traffic Audit Bureau, Inc. (TAB), 708 Third Avenue, New York, N.Y. 10017

Transit Advertising Association (TAA), 500 Fifth Avenue, New York, N.Y. 10036

Western States Advertising Agencies Association (WSAAA), 435 So. La Cienga Boulevard, Los Angeles, California 90048

INDEX OF CASES

INDEX

Douglas Fir campaign, 531
Drives
    emulation, 136
    happiness, 134
    necessities, 134
    recognition, 135–36
    security, 135
    sex, 134
Dun and Bradstreet, Inc., as data source,
    415

E

Eastman Kodak, 169, 206, 567
Ecology emphasis, 602–3
Economic, advertising function, 74–76
Economic and social concepts, 59–91
Economic aspects, 66
Electronics, 9
Electrotypes, 255
Emotional motives, 138–39
Encyclopedias, free, 603
Engravings
    electrotypes, 255
    line, 255
    relief printing plates, 254–55
    zinc etchings, 255
Ethical codes, 610–15
Ethics
    of advertising, 611–15
    business, 610–15
Evaluation of agency performance, 571
Envisioning, 241–43
    setting, 246
Executive gifts, 388–89
Exhibits, 386–87
Expenditures
    advertising, 12
    budget, 462
    company, 16
    media, 14
    national income, 16
    national leaders, 15
    U.S. advertising, 13
Experience (agency), as factor in agency
    selecting, 569
Experimental method of collecting data,
    417
Export advertising, 12

F

F.W. Dodge Corporation, as data source,
    415
Faces of type, 253–54
Factors
    influencing campaign, 492–93
    in selection of agency, 528–70
"Fair competition," 598–601

Farm magazines, 311
Federal Antitrust Agency, 44
Federal Communications Commission,
    335
Federal Fair Credit Reporting Act, 41,
    42
Federal government, as source of data,
    414
Federal Trade Commission, 38, 40, 41,
    42, 44, 45, 599–610
Federal Trade Commission Act of 1914,
    598
Federal Trade Commission Analysis,
    604–6
Federal Trade Practices Agency, 44, 45
Flexibility, budget, 463–64
Food and Drug Administration, 38, 42,
    45
Food, Drug, and Cosmetic Act, 599–605
Ford, Henry, 162
Ford Motor Co., 68
Form letters, 371–72
Foster and Kleiser, 379
Free encyclopedias, 603
Functions, layout, 221
Fur Products Labeling Act, 599

G

Gallup Robinson, 445
    as data source, 415
General criticism of advertising, 612–15
General Electric Co., 70, 100, 567
General Motors, 68
Generic term, 160
Getting best results from agency, 570–71
GMAC Corp., 125
Good Housekeeping, 273, 277
Gosset, William, 44
Government
    power of, 597–98
    regulation, 598–601
Greyhound, 159
Greyser, Stephen A., 17
Gross National Product, 12, 59, 60

H

Habits
    dynamic qualities, 132, 133
    nature of, 131, 132
Haire, Mason, 131
Halftone, 255
Harvard Business Review, 17
Hayden Stone, Inc., 128
Headline
    aptness, 203
    brevity, 203
    clarity, 203
    classification, 200–203